W9-DGR-011

# THE CRITICAL TEMPER

# THE

*A Survey of Modern Criticism*
*from the Beginnings*

*In Three Volumes*

# FROM MILTON TO

# CRITICAL TEMPER

*on English and American Literature*
*to the Twentieth Century*

MARTIN TUCKER
*General Editor*

## Volume II

## ROMANTIC LITERATURE

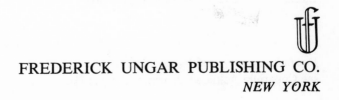

FREDERICK UNGAR PUBLISHING CO.
*NEW YORK*

Copyright © 1969 by
Frederick Ungar Publishing Co., Inc.

*Printed in the United States of America*

Library of Congress Catalog Card Number: 68-8116


For material reprinted by permission
see Copyright Acknowledgments, Volume III.

# CONTRIBUTING EDITORS

*General Editor,* Martin Tucker

OLD ENGLISH LITERATURE

Martin Tucker
*Long Island University*

MEDIEVAL LITERATURE

Robert Raymo
*New York University*

ELIZABETHAN AND JACOBEAN LITERATURE

Irving Ribner
*State University of New York
at Stony Brook*

SHAKESPEARE

Paul N. Siegel
*Long Island University*

MILTON, AND NEOCLASSICAL LITERATURE

John T. Shawcross
*University of Wisconsin*

ROMANTIC LITERATURE

Frances K. Barasch
*Bernard Baruch College
of The City University of New York*

VICTORIAN LITERATURE

Wendell Stacy Johnson
*Hunter College
of The City University of New York*

AMERICAN LITERATURE

Ray C. Longtin
*Long Island University*

# CONTENTS

*VOLUME II*

FROM MILTON TO ROMANTIC LITERATURE

| | |
|---|---|
| *Bibliographical Note* | xi |
| *Periodicals Used* | xiii |

MILTON, AND NEOCLASSICAL LITERATURE      1
*John T. Shawcross, editor*

| | |
|---|---|
| Joseph Addison, 1672–1719 | 3 |
| James Boswell, 1740–1795 | 6 |
| John Bunyan, 1628–1688 | 9 |
| Robert Burns, 1759–1796 | 15 |
| Samuel Butler, 1612–1680 | 18 |
| Thomas Chatterton, 1752–1770 | 21 |
| Charles Churchill, 1731–1764 | 23 |
| Colley Cibber, 1671–1757 | 26 |
| William Collins, 1721–1759 | 29 |
| William Congreve, 1670–1729 | 32 |
| Abraham Cowley, 1618–1667 | 37 |
| William Cowper, 1731–1800 | 41 |
| Daniel Defoe, 1660?–1731 | 45 |
| John Dryden, 1631–1700 | 52 |
| George Etherege, 1634?–1691? | 63 |
| George Farquhar, 1678–1707 | 68 |
| Henry Fielding, 1707–1754 | 70 |
| David Garrick, 1717–1779 | 80 |
| John Gay, 1685–1732 | 83 |
| Oliver Goldsmith, 1730–1774 | 86 |
| Thomas Gray, 1716–1771 | 91 |

Thomas Hobbes, 1588–1679 — 97
Samuel Johnson, 1709–1784 — 101
Nathaniel Lee, 1649?–1692 — 109
John Milton, 1608–1674 — 111
Thomas Otway, 1652–1685 — 147
Samuel Pepys, 1633–1703 — 150
Alexander Pope, 1688–1744 — 152
Matthew Prior, 1664–1721 — 166
Samuel Richardson, 1689–1761 — 169
John Wilmot, Earl of Rochester, 1647–1680 — 177
Nicholas Rowe, 1674–1718 — 181
Thomas Shadwell, 1642?–1692 — 184
Richard Sheridan, 1751–1816 — 187
Christopher Smart, 1722–1771 — 190
Tobias Smollett, 1721–1771 — 193
Sir Richard Steele, 1672–1729 — 200
Laurence Sterne, 1713–1768 — 204
Jonathan Swift, 1667–1745 — 212
James Thomson, 1700–1748 — 224
John Vanbrugh, 1664–1726 — 228
Horace Walpole, 1717–1797 — 232
Isaak Walton, 1593–1683 — 235
William Wycherley, 1641–1716 — 237
Edward Young, 1683–1765 — 243

## ROMANTIC LITERATURE

247

*Frances K. Barasch, editor*

Jane Austen, 1775–1817 — 249
Thomas Lovell Beddoes, 1803–1849 — 266
William Blake, 1757–1827 — 271
George Noel Gordon, Lord Byron, 1788–1824 — 295
Thomas Campbell, 1777–1844 — 321
Samuel Taylor Coleridge, 1772–1834 — 324
George Crabbe, 1754–1832 — 350
Thomas De Quincey, 1785–1859 — 356
Maria Edgeworth, 1767–1849 — 360

William Hazlitt, 1778–1830                          363

Thomas Hood, 1799–1845                            370

[James Henry] Leigh Hunt, 1784–1859              376

Francis, Lord Jeffrey, 1773–1850                  381

John Keats, 1795–1821                             384

Charles Lamb, 1775–1834                           411

Walter Savage Landor, 1775–1864                   417

Matthew Gregory Lewis, 1775–1818                  424

Thomas Moore, 1779–1852                           427

Thomas Love Peacock, 1785–1866                    433

Mrs. Ann Ward Radcliffe, 1764–1823                438

Samuel Rogers, 1762–1855                          442

Sir Walter Scott, 1771–1832                       446

Percy Bysshe Shelley, 1792–1822                   462

Robert Southey, 1774–1843                         493

William Wordsworth, 1770–1850                     500

# BIBLIOGRAPHIC NOTE

Below the introductory paragraph for each writer included in these volumes, the reader will find bibliographic entries of standard editions and biographic studies published through 1967. The scheme of these entries is as follows:

The standard edition (or editions) of the writer's work is placed first; in certain selected cases a study of a single work, as distinct from the collected edition of an author's work, will be found in the bibliographic listings; occasionally there is no listing when no standard work exists. Following the list of editions is the standard biographic study. In cases where scholarly biography has been particularly active, or literary issues remain in the realm of disputation and/or doubt, several biographical sources may be noted.

Abbreviations used in the entries are: *repr.* for reprint; *rev.* for revision; *ed. for* "edited by"; *tr.* for "translated by"; *n. d.* for no date of publication listed; *n. p.* for no place of publication listed.

The abbreviation BC/Longmans, Green means: published for the British Council by Longmans, Green of London The abbreviation *CHEL* means: The Cambridge History of English Literature.

In citation of books throughout the text, the place of publication is always given, with the exception of Oxford University Press and Cambridge University Press, where the places of publication are readily identifiable. Places of publication for The Clarendon Press at Oxford, as well as the New York offices of Oxford University Press and Cambridge University Press, are notated.

# PERIODICALS USED

*Listed below are titles, their abbreviations, if any,
and place of publication.*

| | |
|---|---|
| | The Academy (later The Academy and Literature), London |
| Adel | The Adelphi, London |
| ABR | American Benedictine Review, Latrobe, Pennsylvania |
| | American Imago, Boston |
| AL | American Literature, Duke University Press, Durham, North Carolina |
| AM | The American Mercury, New York |
| | The Proceedings of the American Philosophical Society, Philadelphia |
| AQ | American Quarterly, University of Pennsylvania, Philadelphia |
| AmR | The American Review, New York |
| AmS | The American Scholar, Washington, D.C. |
| | Anglia, Tübingen, Germany |
| At | The Atlantic Monthly (later The Atlantic), Boston |
| Boston Univ. Stud. in Eng. | Boston University Studies in English, Boston |
| | The Proceedings of the British Academy, London |
| BR | The Bucknell Review, Lewisburg, Pennsylvania |
| BJRL | The Bulletin of the John Rylands Library, Manchester, England |
| CambJ | The Cambridge Journal, Cambridge, England |

| | |
|---|---|
| CR | The Centennial Review of Arts and Science, Michigan State University, East Lansing, Michigan |
| CE | College English, Champaign, Illinois |
| | Commentary, New York |
| | The Commonweal, New York |
| CL | Comparative Literature, University of Oregon, Eugene, Oregon |
| Criterion | The Criterion, London |
| CQ | The Critical Quarterly, London |
| | Criticism, Wayne State University, Detroit, Michigan |
| | Delaware Notes, University of Delaware, Newark, Delaware |
| | The Dial, Chicago, then New York |
| | Discourse, Moorhead, Minnesota |
| DR | The Dublin Review, Dublin (since 1961 The Wiseman Review, London) |
| | Encounter, London |
| Eng | English, The Magazine of the English Association, London |
| | English Institute Essays, New York |
| ELH | English Literary History, Johns Hopkins University, Baltimore, Maryland |
| EM | English Miscellany, Rome, published for The British Council, London |
| ES | English Studies, Amsterdam, the Netherlands; *also* Englische Studien |
| | English Studies Today, Oxford (International Conference of University Professors of English, 1950) |
| Essays and Studies | Essays and Studies by members of the English Association, Oxford |
| EIC | Essays in Criticism, Oxford |
| Glasgow Univ. Publications | Glasgow University Publications, Glasgow, Scotland |

| | |
|---|---|
| Harpers | Harper's Magazine, New York |
| HJ | The Hibbert Journal, London |
| | History, London |
| HdR | The Hudson Review, New York |
| HLQ | The Huntington Library Quarterly, San Marino, California |
| | The Proceedings of the Second Congress of the International Comparative Literature Association, Chapel Hill, North Carolina |
| IER | Irish Ecclesiastical Record, Dublin |
| Irish Monthly | The Irish Monthly Magazine, Dublin |
| JAAC | The Journal of Aesthetics and Art Criticism, Cleveland, Ohio |
| JEGP | The Journal of English and Germanic Philology, University of Illinois, Urbana, Illinois |
| JHI | Journal of the History of Ideas, Princeton, New Jersey |
| JR | The Journal of Religion, Chicago |
| K-SJ | Keats-Shelley Journal, New York |
| KR | The Kenyon Review, Kenyon College, Gambier, Ohio |
| Library | The Library, London |
| LL | Life and Letters (later Life and Letters Today), London |
| List | The Listener (now The Listener and BBC Television Review), London |
| L&P | Literature and Psychology, University of Massachusetts, Amherst, Massachusetts |
| | Mediaeval Studies, University of Toronto, Toronto, Canada |
| | Papers, Michigan Academy of Science, Arts and Letters, Ann Arbor, Michigan |
| | Modern Language Association, see PMLA |
| MLN | Modern Language Notes, Baltimore, Maryland |

| | |
|---|---|
| MLQ | The Modern Language Quarterly, University of Washington, Seattle, Washington |
| MLR | The Modern Language Review, Cambridge, England |
| MP | Modern Philology, Chicago |
| Month | The Month, London |
| NR | The National Review, London |
| NEQ | The New England Quarterly, Boston |
| | News, A Review of World Events, London |
| | The New York Review of Books, New York |
| | Nineteenth-Century Fiction, Berkeley, California |
| NAR | The North American Review, Boston, then New York |
| NQ | Notes and Queries, London |
| | The Open Court, Chicago |
| PQ | Philological Quarterly, University of Iowa, Iowa City, Iowa |
| | Poetry, Chicago |
| Poetry R | The Poetry Review, London |
| PMLA | Publications of the Modern Language Association of America, New York |
| QJS | The Quarterly Journal of Speech, New York |
| QQ | Queen's Quarterly, Queen's University, Kingston, Ontario, Canada |
| QR | The Quarterly Review, London |
| | Research Studies, Washington State University, Pullman, Washington |
| RES | The Review of English Studies, London |
| PTRSC | The Proceedings and Transactions of the Royal Society of Canada, Ottawa, Canada |
| | The Transactions of the Royal Society of Literature of the United Kingdom, London |
| Sat | The Saturday Review of Literature (now The Saturday Review), New York |

|  | Scrutiny, London |
| --- | --- |
| SwR | The Sewanee Review, University of the South, Sewanee, Tennessee |
| SQ | The Shakespeare Quarterly, New York |
| SS | Shakespeare Survey, Cambridge, England |
|  | The South Atlantic Quarterly, Duke University, Durham, North Carolina |
| Spec | The Spectator, London |
| Sp | Speculum, Cambridge, Massachusetts |
|  | Stanford University Publications in Language and Literature, Palo Alto, California |
| SN | Studia neophilologica, Uppsala, Sweden |
|  | Studies in English, University of Texas, Austin, Texas |
| SEL | Studies in English Literature, 1500–1900, Tulane University, New Orleans |
| SP | Studies in Philology, Chapel Hill, North Carolina |
|  | Studies in the Renaissance, New York |
| Texas Studies in Lang. and Lit. | Texas Studies in Language and Literature, University of Texas, Austin, Texas |
| TLS | The Times Literary Supplement, London |
| TDR | Tulane Drama Review (now TDR, The Drama Review), New York University, New York |
| Tulane Studies in Eng. | Tulane Studies in English, Tulane University, New Orleans |
| Univ. of California. Publications in Eng. | University of California Publications in English, Berkeley, California |
| UKCR | The University of Kansas City Review, Kansas City, Missouri |
| UTQ | The University of Toronto Quarterly, Toronto, Canada |

Univ. of Wisconsin
Studies in Lang. and Lit.   University of Wisconsin Studies in Language and Literature, Madison, Wisconsin

Victorian Newsletter, New York University, New York

Victorian Poetry, West Virginia University, Morgantown, West Virginia

Victorian Studies, Indiana University, Bloomington, Indiana

West Virginia Univ. Studies   West Virginia University Studies, Morgantown, West Virginia

The Transactions of the Wisconsin Academy of Sciences, Arts and Letters, Madison, Wisconsin

YR    The Yale Review, Yale University, New Haven, Connecticut

# MILTON, AND NEOCLASSICAL LITERATURE

*John T. Shawcross, editor*

# JOSEPH ADDISON
1672-1719

A classical scholar from Queen's and Magdalen Colleges, Oxford, Addison was undersecretary of state in 1706-1711, a member of parliament from 1708 until his death, and secretary of state in 1717-1718. A member of the Kit-Cat Club, he was a friend of Swift and Steele, to whose *Tatler* he contributed a number of papers and whom he joined in the *Spectator*. *Cato* was produced in 1713, and *The Drummer* in 1715. He married the Countess of Warwick in 1716. He was buried in Westminster Abbey.

A. C. Guthkelch, ed., *The Works of Joseph Addison* (1914), 2 vols.; excludes prose essays, to be found in Rae Blanchard, ed., *The Tatler, The Spectator, and The Guardian* (1955)
Paul Smithers, *The Life of Joseph Addison* (1954)

It is, of course, easy enough to destroy *Cato*, and Dennis did so pretty thoroughly in his *Remarks* upon that play. . . . He claimed that Addison fell into three sorts of absurdities: those due to observing the unities too closely; those due to not observing the unities closely enough; and those which could not be attributed to either cause. Chief among these last is the character of Cato himself, who was framed by Addison to symbolize a new kind of object for admiration—a sage who was also a selfless statesman. It was moral valour, not pragmatic valour, he meant to hold up for praise. But in fact Cato is an intolerable prig. . . . It is on most counts a thoroughly bad play; but it deserved to be something better.

For Addison was definitely trying, apart from political delicacies, to do something really worth while. He was trying to restore to tragedy an element which had gone out of it, not only with Rowe, but with the rise of the idea of heroic tragedy. He wanted to rid it of sentimentality and to excite our pity, not by unfortunate love . . . but by the death of an admirable hero, of a hero whose death meant the destruction of a fine idea.

Bonamy Dobrée
*Restoration Tragedy, 1660-1720* (Oxford Univ.
Pr., 1929), pp. 174-75

Thus we find in Locke and Descartes and, to a lesser extent, in Hobbes, the components that enter into the psychology upon which Addison built

3

his conception of the imagination as perceptive response. All three had considered in one way or another the problem of pleasure and pain; all three had more or less pointedly related pleasure and pain to the passions; all had ascribed the capacity to experience these emotions to a sort of sixth sense, or to internal sense or sensation. Locke particularly had invited investigation, through the introspective method, of the true nature of this complex phenomenon. Descartes had furnished most clearly the conception of the imagination as an intermediary between sense and understanding, though this is also implicit in Hobbes; and it was Descartes, too, who had gone so far as to link the imagination with internal sensations of pleasure and pain, extending this function, somewhat tentatively and obscurely, to be sure, to the enjoyment of literature.

Yet, though the psychological basis is here, the complete conception is not. Addison's theory is eclectic. It cannot be facilely traced too exclusively to Hobbes, to Descartes, or to Locke. From these philosophers Addison unquestionably derived much. . . . There remains, still, to account for the basic idea of imagination as the organ of taste. . . .

Addison's contribution is not so much in the discovery of new elements of aesthetic thought as in the combination he makes of the old. It lies as much in method he adopts as in theory. A Lockian and an empiricist, the method he adopts is patently the introspective method of the new philosophy. He proposes to look into the mind to find there what objects please, how they please, and why. He will analyze both the causes and the effects of the pleasures in question, and from this analysis will attempt to deduce new principles by which to judge art, in place of the then prevailing Rules of neoclassic criticism.

Clarence D. Thorpe
*Papers Michigan Academy of Science, Arts, and Letters,*
(1935), pp. 529-30

The third series of critical papers [in *The Spectator*] dealt with the nature of wit. Here Addison's missionary purpose was especially pronounced. He consistently sought by criticism and example to prune from contemporary humour all "Gothic" excrescences. Under this epithet he included quaint conceits and artificial turns, puns, rebuses, and other forms of wit not founded in reason, observing that a pun can be neither translated nor engraved. He likewise excluded from true wit all ill nature, and any immoderate quality conducive to laughter as opposed to mirth. When stripped of such defects, the central structure of wit was that proposed by Locke, founded in the similarity of ideas. He tried to relate the concept of wit thus simplified to that of "truth," in a genealogical parallel. . . . But his expansion of critical theory lay in the realm of demonstration rather than of exposition. His own works were the most effective criticism of the faults of others. . . .

Peter Smithers
*The Life of Joseph Addison* (Oxford Univ. Pr., 1954), pp. 216-17

Addison's criticism is the thematic, not the chronological, end of English neoclassicism and, though he did not know it, the beginning of a new critical theme and idiom which was to be expanded upon only many decades later. The death of Samuel Johnson seventy years after the publication of the last issue of the *Spectator* should serve as a reminder that the most notable figures in the history of English criticism have been her practical critics rather than her theoreticians. Johnson's view of poetry as moral discourse is closer to the Greek and Latin conceptions of poetry . . . than it is to Addison's discussion of natural genius in terms of a highly endowed imagination which functions creatively just as a gentleman of taste's imagination functions critically. As much as Addison's view of the poetic imagination owes to Plato's *Ion* and Longinus's *On the Sublime*, his papers on *The Pleasures of the Imagination* present a new interest in the workings of the imagination which is independent of its function implicit in the classical conception of a craft in which the maker creates with a pre-established end in view.

Addison's respect for natural genius, especially Shakespeare's, led him not only to hold "Mechanical Rules" in contempt, but, also, to waive the rule of reason and order where such genius was in evidence. Nor is Addison entirely content with supernatural and physiological explanations of this phenomenon of the imagination. Although both Dryden and Pope shared Addison's low regard for abjectly applied rules and his high opinion of the inventive powers of natural genius, neither of these critics examined the operations of the imagination in terms of the philosophical psychology of Hobbes and Locke. Addison did not pursue his affective argument to its logical conclusion, the rejection of genre criticism for the extensive analysis of subjective responses to works of art, because contemporary psychology provided no explanations for aesthetic responses to beauty, greatness, and novelty which were significantly different from those inherited from Aristotle and the Renaissance neoclassicists.

. . . In one sense, issues underlying Addison's discussion of both the sublime and pastoral poetry are intrinsic to the more radical changes which literary criticism experienced in his papers on *The Pleasures of the Imagination*. The interest in empirical nature and the psychology of effects which appears in Addison's papers on poetic justice is re-enforced by the belief that physical nature is one of the glories of God. The universe is not a colorless and lifeless mass, but a true reflection of the greatness of its creator. This appreciation of physical nature tended to encourage an examination of empirical nature and its effects upon the human mind in a manner which was foreign to those who supported the doctrine of poetic justice or the "Tory" theory of pastoral poetry. The conception of nature as a Platonic Idea is especially congenial to those who believe that the world of matter is a reminder of man's imperfection, rather than God's perfection. Addison's view of nature is not only more optimistic; it is also more scientific in its interest in the operations of the natural world and the relation to the mind of man.

Lee Andrew Elioseff
*The Cultural Milieu of Addison's Literary Criticism* (Austin, Tex.: Univ. Texas Pr., 1963), pp. 191-92, 194

## JAMES BOSWELL

1740-1795

> As Lord Auchinleck and lawyer from Edinburgh and Glasgow, Boswell met Samuel Johnson in 1763 while on a trip to London. His poetry and pamphlets, indeed all his writing except that connected with Johnson, have fallen into general disregard; it is thus through his journals of trips and conversations with Johnson that Boswell lives. After 1766 he lived primarily in Scotland, marrying in 1769, until the end of 1788. His *Life of Samuel Johnson* was published in 1791.
>
> R. W. Chapman, ed., *The Life of Samuel Johnson* (1953)
> F. A. Pottle, gen. ed., *The Private Papers of James Boswell* (1950-1955), 5 vols.
> Chauncey B. Tinker, *Young Boswell* (1922)

How did Boswell make his note-books? In general, he wrote up his records in the first convenient interval after the conversation had taken place, depending on his memory for the general scope and order of the remarks. *In certain exceptional cases,* he appears to have jotted down notes on the spot. . . .

These two are the chief passages on which a comparison of Boswell to a stenographer can be based; and we are to remember that it is a kind of evidence which people are likely to exaggerate, in their desire to find proof of a notion which has already been formed in their mind. It would certainly be a most serious error to think of Boswell as recording any large amount of his conversational material "at the moment." The bulk of it unquestionably was written down in private, as he himself has told us was his habit. The note-book which we have been examining supports this view, as I have tried to show; and so does the well-known anecdote in the "Life," in which, during a particularly brilliant conversation of Johnson's, Boswell remarked to Mrs. Thrale, "O for shorthand to take this down" and she replied, "You'll carry it all in your head. A long head is as good as short hand."

If the fact that he did most of his writing after the event tends to make anyone doubt the accuracy of his record, it is because he has failed to reckon with the fidelity of the man's memory. It is to be recalled that Boswell began keeping a journal before he was eighteen years old, and, so far as we know, never interrupted the practice. He was constantly engaged in recording conversations that he had heard, and the resultant training of his literal memory we are not likely to exaggerate. Most of us have no memory of conversation, for two very simple reasons. In the first place, we have no great desire to preserve it; and, secondly, we have never tried writing it down. It is probable that a training of two weeks in such a practice would enable a man to make a fairly faithful record of conversation. In Boswell's case that training was extended over the whole of his maturity, called forth all the power that was in him, and was regarded by himself as his most precious faculty. . . .

In view of this meticulous carefulness, it is not surprising that he boasted of the "scrupulous fidelity" of his journal. He knew the value of what he was doing. He knew that his journals were, even in their undeveloped form, very near to the level of literature. . . .

He had found his vein of genius. It ran in the direction of personal reminiscence, not in the direction of history. He had records of all his experiences on the Continent, and had planned some time or other to publish them, including the conversations which he had held there with the Great.

Chauncey Brewster Tinker
*Young Boswell* (Boston: Atlantic Monthly Pr., 1922), pp. 201-6

Boswell's habit in keeping his journals was to make an abbreviated memorandum of the events of the day, either before going to bed or next morning; and to follow this at leisure by a fuller account in regular diary form. Enough of the original memoranda have survived to reveal an interesting fact. In them, Boswell habitually addresses himself in the second person. Probably most people do this when making notes of things yet to be done. But surely few practice the form except in the imperative, and fewer still when referring to the past. Boswell constantly writes to himself in this style. "[You] received a letter from Mr. Johnson treating you with esteem and kindness," he will record: "[you were] nobly elated by it, and resolved to maintain the dignity of yourself."

Now this use of the second person is a highly indicative trait in Boswell. It calls attention to his double consciousness of himself. This state of mind in him deserves our observation. With the keenest awareness of immediate sensations, he displays at the same time an even stronger impulse toward the objective view. The divided vision is constant to him. Frequently the cleavage is so wide that the two roles seem independent of each other, simultaneously activated by different intelligences. . . .

Such, then, are the elements that compose for Boswell the most intense and valuable experience: a vivid realization of the color and quality of the moment, an awareness made acute by comparison and contrast, an occasion that is in its own right rich in its revelation of human nature, and one that he himself consciously helped to bring about.

Bertrand H. Bronson
*Johnson and Boswell,* in *Univ. of California Publications in Eng.*
(1944), pp. 405-6, 418

The great difference that the new Boswell material does make is to render untenable any simple formula for handling him. Most of the Macaulayan adjectives are properly applicable, but one must be very careful to tie them up to the right portions of the evidence. He was one of the most complex literary characters on record, combining in uneasy equilibrium a host of contradictory traits. The easy way out is to say that he thought he was, or pretended to be, this and was really that. Nothing is farther from the truth. He was a well-instructed and sincerely religious man with an unusual capacity for worship, and he was also a notable fornicator. He savored as few others have the delights of intellectual conversation, and he was a sensualist. He was weak of will, and he sat up all night through four nights in one week to record Johnson's conversation. He loved Scotland deeply, and he preferred to live in England. He was inordinately proud of his ancestry and his status as a gentleman, and he associated with the lowest of low people. He was an affectionate husband, painfully dependent on his wife, and he was unfaithful to her and kept her sitting up for him when he knew she was mortally ill. He was a thoughtful and indulgent father who found it difficult to endure his children's company. He was dissipated and restless, and he carried on an extensive legal practice. He was often gloomy to the point of suicide, and Mrs. Thrale gave him a perfect score in good humor. (Johnson got zero.) He was stately and Spaniard-like in his bearing, and he played the clown with or without provocation. He was proud and he deferred to Johnson. He was independent and he licked Lonsdale's boots. He did and said many foolish things but he was not a fool.

Frederick A. Pottle
*YR* (Spring, 1946), p. 455

# JOHN BUNYAN
1628-1688

Born of humble parentage in Elstow, Bedfordshire, and without formal education, Bunyan owes his literary and religious life to his own wide reading and conversion after a dissolute youth, including service in the parliamentary army from age sixteen to nineteen. His life was probably not so dissolute as he alleges in his autobiography *Grace Abounding to the Chief of Sinners,* written during the 1660's. He married at age twenty-one, and became a Baptist minister. His wife died in 1656 after having borne four children. He remarried in 1659. Around this time he began writing controversial and devotional books, forty-eight of which were completed at the time of his death. After the Restoration he was imprisoned for preaching without a license. The original three-month sentence stretched to twelve years because of his refusal to stop preaching. During this period *Grace Abounding* was composed. Released in 1672, he again preached and was again imprisoned in 1675. During his six-month prison term he began the work by which he is remembered, *The Pilgrim's Progress.* Part one was published in 1678; part two, in 1684. He died in 1688 of a fever supposedly contracted on a journey taken to reconcile a father and son who had become estranged.

Roger Sharrock, ed., *Grace Abounding to the Chief of Sinners* (1962)

Louis L. Martz, ed., *The Pilgrim's Progress* (1949)

J. Brown, ed., *The Life and Death of Mr. Badman* and *The Holy War* (1905)

J. Brown, *John Bunyan: His Life, Times and Work,* rev. ed. F. M. Harrison (1928); Henri Talon, *John Bunyan: The Man and His Works* (1951); Ola E. Winslow, *John Bunyan* (1961)

## *The Pilgrim's Progress*

In both parts of *The Pilgrim's Progress* there is much that can be related in general terms to the emblem convention. It was part of Bunyan's design to make use of emblems in the course of the story and he introduces them in groups from time to time. The various scenes, for example, which Christian and, afterwards, Christiana witness in the house of the Interpreter are nothing less than a series of emblems; in fact, the Interpreter in expounding one of them calls it "an emblem, very apt to set forth some Professors by." Another set of a similar nature occurs when the Shepherds reveal to the pilgrims a number of visions from the top of the Delectable Mountains. Among others they show Christiana and Mercy "one *Fool* and one *Want-wit* washing of an *Ethiopian* with the intention to make him white, but the more they washed him, the blacker he was," and explain their meaning as follows:

> Thus shall it be with the vile Person; all means used to get such
> an one a good Name, shall in conclusion tend but to make him
> more abominable. Thus it was with the *Pharisees*, and so shall it
> be with all Hypocrites.

The scenes described on such occasions as these belong quite explicitly to the genre to which Bunyan was later to make his own contribution, and they can be treated entirely independently of the main story. The development of the action is held up while the moral lessons are expounded, and the attention of the pilgrims and the reader is focused wholly upon them.

For the content of these emblems Bunyan owes little to his predecessors. As is to be expected from his fertile power of image-making, the majority of them are original, though there may be behind others a memory of emblematic pictures he had seen. . . .

The feature of *The Pilgrim's Progress* which makes it so unusual, and so successful, as an allegory is its realism. The story concerns a number of figures who are designated as types, and the typical, although by definition it cannot be entirely individual, is not necessarily unreal or lifeless. Bunyan has various means by which his type figures move and act credibly in a setting which is naturalistic in comparison with that of *The Faerie Queene*.

Rosemary Freeman
*English Emblem Books* (London: Chatto
and Windus, 1948), pp. 216, 223

How could a progress the end of which was fore-ordained keep the interest of a novel? For *The Pilgrim's Progress* considered as a secular work of art gives an impression of unified power beyond the attractions of romance. Nor do the vigor and purity of the English comprise the whole of its appeal. As well as romantic variety of incident, giants and hobgoblins, and racy common speech, there is something which breeds a continuous interest in what the main characters are doing. We do not come away with the feeling that we have witnessed a merely inevitable progress of the chosen believers to the Kingdom of Heaven, although the Calvinist framework might seem to entail that. This is because the dramatic excitement of the struggle with evil is transferred to the inner life of Christian; the spectres of doubt and spiritual terror which still raise themselves in the confirmed professor provide the interest, because they are seen from his side. We look through his eyes and share his own uncertainty about the outcome, though actually on the longer view of the divine purpose there is no uncertainty. . . . This is the form taken by many a Puritan spiritual autobiography: conversion, calling, and ministry are recounted, with a wealth of detail expended on the second division. Once again the psychological method of the preachers explains why this should be. The two great sins of Puritanism . . . were excess of confidence leading to hypocrisy, and, at the other extremity, diffidence leading to despair in vocation.

Roger Sharrock
*RES* (April, 1948), pp. 106-7

What differentiates this book [*The Pilgrim's Progress*] from the conversion stories of worthy Quakers and other sectarians of the seventeenth century is Bunyan's superior power of conveying the momentousness of his experiences. All these converts claim to have endured paroxysms of remorse, doubt and despair and to have received personal assurance of salvation. Nor is there any reason to accuse them of hypocrisy. The religious climate of the time was full of electric storms and encouraged the display of individual disturbances. Besides, as William James wisely and charitably observed, "A small man's salvation will always be a great salvation and the greatest of all facts *for him*." But Bunyan's imaginative powers and his command of the English language set him far above the rank and file. He could re-live in imagination the turmoils of his youth and could also find terms to describe them which, by their sheer nervous strength and intensity, convince us of the authenticity of his experiences. . . .

Bunyan's adherence to truth was not literal-minded or all-inclusive. The very sincerity of his wish to encourage the faithful made him over-dramatise his own emotional conflicts, and his desire to glorify God made him minimise the importance of human agents in his conversion and leave unsaid very much that would appear vitally important to a more mundane kind of biographer. He does not, for instance, mention the names of his father or mother—the Bedford congregation might be assumed to know them, as they would certainly know that Elstow was his birthplace, though he does not name or describe the village in his narrative. But Bunyan would have echoed St. Augustine's dictum that life does not begin with father and mother but with God and Sin.

Margaret Bottrall
*Every Man a Phoenix* (London: John Murray, 1958), pp. 88-89

*The Pilgrim's Progress* immediately touched some universal chord in men's understanding. Its success was phenomenal and not only in England; it was translated into several languages even before the author's death and since then into over a hundred. John Bunyan, pursuing and elaborating the substance of his dreams, had written a universal parable. It was such a thing as only a very simple mind could have achieved so late in time.

The language is sometimes that of the Bible; more often, and more touchingly, that of the simple folk among whom Bunyan lived. . . . But the language alone cannot be studied with advantage, for there is nothing to be learned from it. No educated and conscious writer could safely copy Bunyan. His unforced words are the apt instruments of inspired ideas. The symbols which Bunyan chose in his simplicity to convey his meaning have fixed his conceptions as irrevocably as the Biblical parables themselves. It is more than a little absurd to try to place *The Pilgrim's Progress* as literature. It stands outside literature, one of the innocent, inspired creations of man's mind, of which the author and the date seem—and indeed are—insignificant, compared to the message conveyed.

C. V. Wedgwood
*Seventeenth-Century English Literature* (New York:
Oxford Univ. Pr., 1961), pp. 170-71

Bunyan's first sentence projects the reader into a world where anything can happen. The familiar is made immediately strange. The man has no name. The place has no geography. It is in a "certain place," no more definite than "the wilderness of this world." The teller of the story is sleeping "in a denne." In two sentences Bunyan has created a setting in which whatever happens will be accepted without challenge. The picture comes with the words, the man in rags, the scene outside his own house, the book in his hand, the burden on his back. Joseph Conrad said that he did not begin a story with an idea but with an image, and so it would seem Bunyan does likewise. He thought in pictures; he wrote in pictures. Christian opened his book. He read. He wept. He trembled, and then he asked the question, "What shall I do?" The whole book is the answer. In some of the long disquisitions to follow, a multitude of words drown the memory, but not here.

Ola Elizabeth Winslow
*John Bunyan* (New York: Macmillan, 1961), pp. 152-53

GENERAL

Concerning the holy war "made by Shaddai upon Diabolus for the regaining of the metropolis of the world": its object was millenarian, its scene the Holy City, which in 1665 had achieved its insubstantial destiny in the vehemence of Bunyan's applause. *The Holy War* is an allegory of conversion, but to indulge the more sedentary Baptists, whose displeasure with the Fourth equaled their delight in the Fifth Monarchy, Bunyan followed the progress of rebirth in the imagery of the millennium. By this pleasing device he expressed at once his opinions of state and soul, flattered the grateful understandings of his audience, elevated the new life to the dignity of his allegorical vehicle, and added splendor to the designs of the church by the analogy of individual salvation. The blameless character of his theme gave him security and freedom to reveal, by the arts of metaphor and illusion, the truth about the empires of Jesus and the Beast.

. . . Bunyan intended this allegory to provide a convenient history of the successive victories and defeats of good and evil in the soul during conversion, but *The Holy War,* like other more illustrious allegories, has several layers of meaning. Though its main allegorical subject is conversion, that mysterious and, in the light of foreknowledge and election, perhaps unnecessary struggle between God and Satan for the individual soul, this ambitious work admits of several other interpretations both allegorical and literal: the ecclesiastical, the political, and the millenarian.

William York Tindall
*John Bunyan, Mechanick Preacher* (New York:
Columbia Univ. Pr., 1934), pp. 144, 147

The truth is that Bunyan was possessed of the spirit and natural disposition of the mystic, but these could not expand because his religious convictions stultified their growth. Protestantism, by harnessing faith to the Scriptures, usually puts a check on the introversive movement of the soul and deflects religious feeling into other channels. The individual, aware that he has no rôle of his own in justification but that the drama is played out quite outside him, lays the main emphasis on the sacred texts whence he draws his convictions; he inclines his flight towards external ends.

Bunyan had his hours of mute contemplation but, on the whole, his life became one impassioned dialogue between his soul and a God whose voice came from without. This God, now father, now judge, now affectionate, now severe, enjoyed being petitioned and importuned. He smiled at His creature's wilfulness, answered him, encouraged him and, affectionately imperious, urged him on to further labours. And so Bunyan's road went from obstacle to obstacle, and on each, as he passed, he left one of the doubts and difficulties that at first had laid him low. The pilgrim's way was a way of health and joy. Christian quitted the city where he could not breathe and set out towards ever vaster and brighter horizons. His pilgrimage was his growth.

But the allegory is a diptych in which each panel is necessary for the understanding of the other. Christian gives place to Great-heart, or rather let us boldly say that Christian becomes Great-heart. When characters are incarnations of their author's spirit we should see, not a substitution, but a metamorphosis.

Thus the man who set out alone and fought solitary battles finished his journey in numerous company; the man who strayed in the slough of despond ended up by leading others. The man in rags, plaintive and vulnerable, became successively the ferocious adversary of Apollyon and the Knight in invisible armour.

Henri Talon
*John Bunyan: The Man and His Works*, tr. Barbara Wall
(Cambridge, Mass.: Harvard Univ. Pr., 1951), pp. 306-7

In Bunyan's spiritual sickness the extreme Protestant idea of the Bible as the Word of God was always present to him. Like the majority of Puritan Englishmen of his day, he believed that each verse of the Bible, taken out of its context, still held a message of truth. The fanatics of the sectarian left wing believed that a single text, met at a certain point in time, might have a special message for an individual. The sermon habit, and the tendency to draw providential lessons from the scriptures commented on in a sermon, encouraged this belief. Bunyan's treatment of the Bible reflects the extreme viewpoint; he shows his kinship with the Quakers, who were his bitter rivals as popular evangelists, by interpreting all his texts as if they applied to the condition of the individual soul. When his fear of having committed the unforgiveable sin of betrayal reduces him to a state of physical suffering ("a clogging and heat at my stomach . . . as if my breast-bone would have split asunder"), he thinks of the death of Judas as recorded in the Acts as being directly applicable to him: "Judas, who, by his falling headlong, burst asunder, and all his bowels gushed out." Here we see the remarkable way in which the tradition of bibliolatry harmonized with the psychological temperament of Bunyan, so abnormal in its subjection to verbal automatisms. In the grasp of his powerfully concrete imagination, the quotations from Scripture are, even within the limits of autobiography, on the way to becoming personified. There are no abstract ideas in *Grace Abounding*; his notions about justification always take on a sensuous life; his theological doubts are expressed as a battle between friendly and hostile texts, and the battlefield is not his mind or his emotions, but his flesh and bones, quaking, sweating and burning by the agency of anxieties which have developed into physical illness. . . .

One literary consequence of Bunyan's theology is that there is no possibility of a treatment of the full life of man like that in Catholic allegory, or even in Spenser. The power of final perseverance granted to the pilgrims in election limits the range of human experience Bunyan can deal with. Thus the Hill Lucre episode does not treat avarice with anything like the fullness of Spenser's picture of the Cave of Mammon: Guyon is led aside from the way; he falls to rise again. A few words shouted from the roadside are all that Christian needs to settle with Demas: there is no question of a choice of two ways of life presented and a decision to be made. Christian has "heard of this place before now"; it is By-Ends and his companions who go over "at the first beck," and perish in the pit. Likewise Faithful's encounter with Wanton is the merest flirtation with the sins of the flesh. It is only in Part Two that we get something of the rich bustle of the life of believers in society. But that was written years later in the time of Bunyan's fame and prosperity: its atmosphere is altogether more mellow. In Part One the humorous passages are mostly about backsliders and heretics. Yet Bunyan's world, so conscientiously symbolic in each detail, everywhere retains the savour of common life. It is in these character sketches that his genius for realistic observation is exercised in a manner which prevents the conversion allegory from becoming too inward and obsessed. The source from which Bunyan drew for his main characters—Christian, Faithful and Hopeful— was his own introspective imagination. However, in his pictures of the reprobate and in his account of the ups and downs of the way we see his sharp eye for behaviour and his sardonic humour. There is no real division in his imagination between this gift of observation and his intro- spective faculty; both are strongly visual: it is the same quality of mind which conveys types of character by fixing on small traits of gesture, and which reduces Scripture texts to concrete, touchable presences.

Roger Sharrock
*John Bunyan* (London: Hutchinson's Univ. Library,
1954), pp. 64-65, 89-90

# ROBERT BURNS

1759-1796

Born in Ayrshire, Burns pursued various labors in the impoverished area, and became known for his promiscuity which resulted in the births, among others, of twins in 1786 and 1788 (by Jean Armour, whom he married in the later year). His beloved Mary Campbell ("Highland Mary") died in childbirth, apparently, in 1786. His *Poems, Chiefly in the Scottish Dialect* appeared in 1786, being reprinted in Edinburgh the next year, where he had gone to seek his fortune. Later that year he returned to marry Jean and settle near Dumfries as a farmer. In 1791 he moved to Dumfries, becoming an officer in the excise.

A. Gray, ed., *Poems and Songs* (Edinburgh, 1945)
Franklin B. Snyder, *The Life of Robert Burns* (1932)

One observation suggests itself instantly: Burn's metrical skill was almost uncanny. Blank verse, the ten-syllabled couplet, and the sonnet, he rarely attempted; the Spenserian stanza he used with little success. But in the many forms which had come down to him through Fergusson and Ramsay, and in the countless varieties of song-patterns which his work for Johnson and Thomson required him to use, in all these he moved with consummate ease. Some of these verse-forms were as simple as an English quatrain well can be; others were bafflingly elaborate. But it made little difference to Burns what the metrical patterns might be; he was the assured master of virtually everything that he attempted.

The exigencies of an elaborate rime-scheme never perplexed him. So large and flexible was his vocabulary, and so sure his skill in selecting words, that he became actually playful in his versifying. Internal rimes, double and even triple rimes, lend their touches of whimsical effectiveness to his verses, and never are they used merely to display his metrical virtuosity. In different mood, when playfulness would have been inappropriate, Burns could be grimly laconic, and could round off a stanza with the sharp crack of a single monosyllable.

. . . He had, moreover, unusual skill and good taste in selecting a verse-form appropriate to the thought he wished to express. Granted that for many of his lyrics the form was virtually dictated by the tune to which he was fitting words, the fact remains that for the rest of his work he had no such guide, and that never did he compose a Scots poem which is ineffective because of incongruity between the metre and the idea or mood. Indeed, test Burns as one will, on this score the verdict is always the same: he was one of the relatively few unquestioned masters of English metrics.

Franklyn B. Snyder
*The Life of Robert Burns* (New York:
Macmillan, 1932), pp. 468-70

Burns himself began the mystery [of Mary Campbell] by his curiously veiled allusions to the affair, but the real work of obfuscation was done by biographers who erected upon exiguous foundations of fact an ornate superstructure of legend.

The exact date at which Burns composed the "Jolly Beggars" is uncertain—if it was really written after a slumming frolic with John Richmond it must have been in 1785—but the closing episode is either autobiography or prophecy. The Bard, whose sentiments in the closing chorus are definitely Burns's own, is depicted with a doxy upon either arm. After the stormy spring and summer of 1786 Burns confessed to Robert Aiken that he had plunged into all sorts of riot, Mason meetings, and dissipation, to distract his mind from the humiliation of the Armour affair. What form his dissipation took may reasonably be guessed not only from Burns's own temperament but from human nature in general. Yet nothing about his relation with Mary Campbell is free of doubt. All that can definitely be proved is that there was a servant-lass of that name to whom Burns apparently addressed certain lyrics and to whom he certainly gave a pair of Bibles bearing peculiar inscriptions. It is useless to rehearse the endless controversy between the romantics to whom Mary Campbell was a Lily Maid of Astolat and the realists to whom she was just another girl who couldn't say no. But a few facts must be underscored. The critical analysis of the legend made with caustic humour by Henley in 1896 and subsequently elaborated by Professor Snyder has never been rebutted nor even answered. The scripture texts Burns wrote on the fly-leaves of that Bible are such as would have been chosen by a man to whom a frightened girl was appealing for protection and who was impulsively promising it on his word of honour as a man and a Mason. That he also sang Mary's praises as "Highland Lassie" and in another lyric asked—for poetic effect at least—if she would go to the Indies with him means little, if anything. The enthusiasts prefer to forget that during the same summer Burns said farewell to Eliza Miller in a lyric quite as fervid as any of those addressed to Mary.

Out of the mass of legend and conjecture the only solid facts which emerge are that during this spring of 1786 Burns was having some sort of love affair with Mary; that she left Ayrshire in May, and that she died in the early autumn. Burns may have turned to her for consolation after the breach with Jean; the affairs may have been simultaneous.

DeLancey Ferguson
*Pride and Passion* (New York: Oxford
Univ. Pr., 1939), pp. 144-46

Among the many qualities of "Tam o' Shanter" which show Burns's technical skill in handling this kind of verse narrative—the effective use of the octosyllabic couplet, the variations in tempo, the use of the verse paragraph, and the placing of the pauses—perhaps the most remarkable is his handling of the *tone* of the poem. The tone is at once comic and full of suspense, shrewd yet irresponsible, mocking yet sympathetic; there is a fine balance here between mere supernatural anecdote and the precisely etched realistic picture, and it is maintained throughout the poem. "Tam o' Shanter" is the work of a virtuoso. Yet it is the only verse narrative of its kind that Burns wrote, the product (if tradition is to be trusted) of one day's truancy from the work and worries of his farm and his excise duties during one of his most troubled periods. Clearly, with a little leisure and a little relief from the "carking cares" that continually pressed on him, many other aspects of his poetic genius might have been as profitably explored. It is easy to see why Burns, wiser than his Edinburgh advisers, continually longed for a government job which would leave him with some time of his own.

David Daiches
*Robert Burns* (New York: Rinehart, 1950), p. 292

Placed individually under the lens of criticism, it is easy to detect minor flaws and blemishes in many of the poems in the Kilmarnock volume. It is equally easy to see clearly the astonishing technical accomplishment of the best poems, though much less easy to analyse and describe that accomplishment in exact critical terms. In the end, however, the poems in the Kilmarnock volume cannot only be regarded as individual pieces— superb though many of them are in their own right—but as a *corpus*; the great centre-piece of Burns's whole remarkable output. For they also make a collective impact, and have a collective significance. . . .

Taken all in all, the Kilmarnock poems preserve, with extraordinary vigour and clarity of detail, the life and manners of rural Scotland just before the ever-pressing influences of Industrialism and Englishry disrupted the ancient traditional pattern. Lord Cockburn considered the 18th century to be the last truly *Scottish* century. Burns caught and fixed that Scottishness before its cracking fragments disintegrated.

Maurice Lindsay
*Robert Burns* (London: MacGibbon and Kee, 1954), p. 127

# SAMUEL BUTLER
1612-1680

> Born in Worcestershire, Butler may have attended Cambridge briefly, later serving the Countess of Kent and then Sir Samuel Luke, a Presbyterian justice of the peace who is thought to be the model for Sir Hudibras. Butler's important political satire was published in three parts, in 1663, 1664, and 1678. His prose characters were not collected and published until the eighteenth century.
>
> A. R. Waller, ed., *Hudibras* (1905)
> J. Veldkamp, *Samuel Butler, The Author of Hudibras* (1923)

## Hudibras

Much of Samuel Butler's satire, in *Hudibras* and his other works, is not directed at specific social institutions, but at society at large. Butler has been viewed too exclusively, perhaps, as an arch-opponent of seventeenth-century Puritanism. This, certainly, he was. His chief work, *Hudibras*, almost the only one of his works published in his lifetime, is a vitriolic attack on the rebels, and through it his reputation was gained, and has continued. However, a study of his posthumously published writings shows that the point of view implicit in *Hudibras* also received a rather different illustration and application from his hand. In other words, Butler was not a bigoted Royalist, nor merely a partisan. It is true, he presented the world with a ridiculous picture of Puritanism that has lived almost to our own time—but he waited until the Restoration to present it.

... Even a cursory examination of *Hudibras* reveals a scepticism of man's uprightness. Though most of the satire is aimed at the Puritans, Butler does not stop with them, for many of the allusions are general and are unsparing of mankind as a whole. Sir Hudibras, by his confidences, clearly expresses the poet's scorn of Puritan integrity. The very title assumed by Puritans, that of "Saints," seemed to imply, to Butler, a self-righteous freedom from ordinary bonds of honour. For, by such a title, and by the "dispensation" which accompanied it, the sectaries claimed a privilege of holding their oaths lightly and of forswearing them without compunction. Ironically Butler asserts that it was the peculiar distinction of the Puritans that those acts which were sinful in other men were pious in them, so that really by that fact were they distinguished from the wicked. This charge of antinomianism is repeatedly made in the poem; but the attack is not confined to Puritans. Sir Hudibras becomes involved in a situation whereby he is bound under oath to suffer self-inflicted punishment. As a result of his mental debate, he casts aspersions on the morals of all men. Discussing the punishment with his squire, the knight asserts that the oath is not binding; for oaths are but words and are not obligatory, because they are made only by those that impose them, not by those who swear to them.

Dan Gibson, Jr.
*Seventeenth-Century Studies,* ed. Robert Shafer (Princeton, N. J.:
Princeton Univ. Pr., 1933), pp. 279, 280

But if *Hudibras* is a romance, it is many things besides. For one thing it is travesty; for another, it is satire; for a third, it is burlesque.... The author's literary originality lies not so much in the sustained use of the verse form, excellently as he adapted that to his purpose, as it does in the balance which he keeps between the real and the fantastic, or burlesque, elements in his design; between the identification of historical social forces that he was satirizing and the never-never land traversed by his characters.

Edward A. Richards
*Hudibras in the Burlesque Tradition* (New York:
Columbia Univ. Pr., 1937), p. 25

The aptness of Butler's allegory in its broad outlines is as striking as its characters. Hudibras (the Long Parliament) and Ralpho (its army) set out—hypocritically—to break up a bear-baiting, i.e., the baiting of the kingship (Bruin), which they are defending "the clean contrary way." This action precipitates a battle, i.e., a civil war, outside the bear garden

(London). The bearbaiting sounds like the attacks on the Presbyterian bear (synods) by Independent dogs in 1643 or 1644.... Butler uses "bear" rather loosely, however, to denote any kind of intolerant church rule as well as for the king in whom such rule had culminated before 1641.

... The impressive fact about analyzing Part I of *Hudibras* as an allegory of forces rather than of persons or qualities is that it makes excellent sense. The order in which the name characters are presented in the procession is very much the order in which the corresponding forces emerged with decisive effects historically; and the correspondences between the characters thus interpreted and their actions in the story are surprisingly close. Such an interpretation of *Hudibras* gives rather convincing evidence that allegory was intended, for it makes even the actions in the bear garden quite intelligible allegorically.

Ward S. Miller
*HLQ* (August, 1958), pp. 338, 343

## GENERAL

Central to all of Butler's thought is the opposition between truth and opinion. In terms of this opposition he took up the problem of human intellectual endeavour, commented on the world's moral behavior, and analysed the religious troubles assailing Europe since the beginning of Christianity. With this opposition in mind he formulated his theory of knowledge.... There is only one truth; there are many false counterfeits.

... His theory of knowledge and the metaphysical views attaching to it were called forth by this truth-error dichotomy. In a descending scale we have God, nature, and man: God the divine wisdom, the first cause of all things, by whom the order of nature has been contrived; nature, ever faithful to the religion of causes, moving towards ends pre-determined by the first cause; man, who alone of mortal creatures is able to read the book of nature. Human knowledge begins in sense perception and is completed by reason.... Truth results from a right performance of reason, error from a false performance, the sphere of wit ... falling between these two.

Ricardo Quintana
*ELH* (March, 1951), pp. 13, 14

Since, as Quintana makes clear, the object of mockery in the satire was to be the misuse of the mind, all the extravagances of unreason, Butler chose the strongest illustration available to him in the religious bickerings of the mid-century. In the quarrels of the Saints he saw illustrated the human faults that most repelled him: argumentativeness and a manipulation of reason for the rationalization of false arguments, together with a setting aside of reason to trust individual, irrational manifestations of so-called truth. Combined with and accentuating these defects of intellect were those of spirit: avarice as a motive, self-righteous arrogance, hypocrisy about virtue of behavior, and dishonor regarding oaths. Such was Butler's view of the Puritans as it is directly set forth in one biting portrait after another in his *Characters.*

. . . Butler's artistic point of view is perfectly consistent. It is an angle of vision that creates steady distortion and persistently reveals the perverted human mind that he scorns. But it is exactly his unmitigated scorn which prevents the final success of his point of view. . . . What is important is not so much whether the Presbyterians had each particular folly displayed by Hudibras, but whether he is a satisfying symbol of human extravagance of mind. His not quite being so is what keeps him from supreme artistic fitness.

Ellen D. Leyburn
*HLQ* (February, 1953), pp. 144, 154-55

# THOMAS CHATTERTON

1752-1770

Chatterton, the creator of Thomas Rowley, a fictional priest of the fifteenth century and alleged poet, began writing poetry at eleven. He sent Horace Walpole a poem purportedly written in 1469, which Walpole at first praised and then, suspecting something amiss, rejected. Chatterton, destitute and discouraged, soon after destroyed his remaining manuscripts and committed suicide alone in his attic room by taking arsenic.

E. H. W. Meyerstein, *A Life of Thomas Chatterton* (1930)

The poet's four methods of forming words . . . were:
1. To copy exactly what he found in Kersey, &c. e.g. *cherisaunei.*
2. To take a groundwork, but alter the termination, e.g. *adrames* (*adraming*, Kersey).
3. To alter spelling capriciously, e.g. *anere*, for *another.*
4. To coin words at pleasure (a) from some intelligible root, e.g. *hopelen* for *hopelessness.* (b) from imagination, e.g. *bayre* for *brow.*

His rhyming is careless; in the same stanza *run* rhymes with *gone*, and *ryne* (for *run*) with *twyne; night* he spells *nete, twain, twaie; banèd* is found in the first line of a stanza and *bante* in the last, and *words* close to *wordès.* Sometimes singular rhymes with plural, e.g. *Thys Celmonde menes* with *bewreene*; and no grammarian would have written *glare* in the *Songe to Ælla.* But it is hopeless to criticize him on these lines.

His was an eager, impressionistic, unscholarly mind, alive to sound and colour; Kersey was his paint-box, and he mixed the tints he found there with others of his own fancy. No proceeding could be more opposed to eighteenth century formality.

E. H. W. Meyerstein
*A Life of Thomas Chatterton* (London:
Ingpen and Grant, 1930), pp. 174-75

Too brilliantly gifted for his environment but not strong enough to triumph over it, Chatterton tried to escape through the portals of imagination. He toyed a little with the familiar conventions of sensibility, but they were of small use to a boy who had created a medieval city of his own. Rowley, however, was not his only mask. In many of his modern-English poems he pretended to be a man like Churchill—a witty, satirical libertine, a devil with the ladies, a thorn in the side of the respectable. This creation of his fancy, however, had other concerns than a wench and a bottle. He was a foe of priestcraft and tyranny; a champion of reason, nature, and the chainless conscience. Unfortunately this ideal figure, unlike Rowley, could be imitated in real life as well as in poetry. There is a reason to fear that Chatterton's precocious efforts to dramatize himself as a sentimental libertine were only too realistic. I would merely suggest that even here he was trying to escape, though by means of an aesthetic figment which was not sufficiently detached from actuality. This is the disguise which he usually wore among the apprentices of Bristol and which he took with him to London. He was wearing it when he died.

Hoxie Neale Fairchild
*Religious Trends in English Poetry,* vol. II (New York:
Columbia Univ. Pr., 1942), p. 352

The Rowley Poems are something more than a collection of pseudo-archaic verse. Behind them is a deliberate and painstaking effort to reconstruct the manners, the customs, and the civic ecclesiastical spirit of the fifteenth century in England. Apparently unwilling to let the poems speak for themselves, Chatterton invents copious explanatory notes, an imaginary correspondence between Rowley and Canynges, and to *The Storie of William Canynge* appends a biographical narrative in Rowleian prose which was intended to give unity and verisimilitude to what was, for so young a mind, a truly epic conception.

John C. Nevill
*Thomas Chatterton* (London: Frederick Muller, 1948), p. 111

Chatterton's genius may be explained in part by his powers of concentration that made him a solitary even in the crowded dormitory of Colston School. He was "driven" not so much by his natural genius as by the circumstances of his life. He was an indulged child who grew up without direction, stimulated by his surroundings—the light and color of the cathedral windows, the darkness and terror of its stairways, the peace and happiness in carved faces in the close proximity demanded by a child's stature, and the organ music that poured over all these wonders. At home he was enthralled by the colors and textures of the fabrics his mother handled; he was made conscious of his own strangeness by the admiring cluckings of too many women. When, at five, he was sent home from the charity school as a dunce, there had been nothing to stimulate his imagination and much to arouse passive resistance. People did not yet exist for him as persons; they were only a part of the picture of life. His sister noticed that he thought a picture real and treated the small boys in the neighborhood as if they were actors in a play—part of the drama that went on in his own brain. That desire to use people for his own purposes persisted nearly all his life; he wanted to be not only the chief actor, but the director, in the story of his life. He wanted also to design the scenery and set the stage. This, indeed, he did successfully in his Rowley poems.

Mary Graham Lund
*UKCR* (Spring, 1959), p. 216

# CHARLES CHURCHILL
1731-1764

Intending a clerical career, Churchill was blocked from entering Cambridge when it was discovered that he had married at eighteen, but he was ordained in 1756, nonetheless. He became curate of St. John's, Westminster, upon his father's death. His verse satire, the *Rosciad* (1761), brought fame. His association with John Wilkes, the political reformer, moved him into political satire against the Tories; some of these satires appeared in the newsheet, *The North Briton*.

Douglas Grant, ed., *Poetical Works* (1956)
Wallace C. Brown, *Churchill: Poet, Rake and Rebel* (1953)

*The Prophecy of Famine*, with its 562 lines, may be divided roughly into four parts: (1) lines 1-92, an attack on the taste of contemporary poets; (2) lines 93-272, ironical praise of Scotland as a place where the poet takes refuge from modern taste; (3) lines 273-402, a dialogue between Sawney and Jockey, two Scotch lads; (4) lines 403-562, Famine and her prophecy.

... A satire so virulent, so abusive, naturally makes one wonder whether it was in any way justifiable—whether it was an outburst of righteous indignation or whether it was merely the outpouring of political spite. Lord Bute's policy toward Prussia, England's ally, and toward France her enemy, was treacherous and weak. He had given many important posts in his government to Scotchmen, who were usually shrewd and able managers. In the English people there had been toward the Scotch from time immemorial, a deep-rooted enmity which was inflamed anew both by the conduct of the minister and by the influx of Scotchmen to London.

The Prophecy of Famine was a product of the same spirit of enmity—its wild and general condemnation of the Scots, its caricature of the true conditions, were characteristics that would appeal to the masses—who were the only group that could be influenced by such appeals. We must not forget that Churchill was from the common people himself, and that his was a nature capable of working itself up to a high pitch of excitement at the words of a demagogue. That demagogue was Wilkes. . . . Churchill hated the Scotch, but his hatred would not have been so virulent had he not been under the spell of the greatest demagogue of his time.

Joseph M. Beatty, Jr.
SP (July, 1919), pp. 313, 316

Churchill's best work reveals him as a master craftsman and a poet who, within the neo-classic tradition, altered it by certain technical achievements in the couplet form that were new or that were used in new ways by him. These achievements, however, did not flower until past the midpoint of his short career. Churchill's early poems ably continue the established tradition of heroic satire. The Rosciad is a series of biting portraits of contemporary actors and actresses, but there is nothing in it that Dryden had not done more brilliantly in Absalom and Achitophel. The Apology is also largely traditional, comparable in structure to the Epistle to Dr. Arbuthnot. The only notable change from The Rosciad is the increased use of irony—later to become the staple of Churchillian satire. The irony appears chiefly in lines 148-85, as part of the attack on critics and pastoral poets; but it lacks finish and subtlety. In Night, Churchill's third heroic satire, there is nothing new: on the whole it is an inferior performance.

More than a year later, however, appeared The Prophecy of Famine, in which Churchill struck the notes that were to characterize his mature work and his own contributions to heroic satire. In this poem irony, as a method of satire, becomes dominant, and lyrical overtones, based on the device of ironic eulogy, develop. The heroic couplet becomes freer and less limited to the epigrammatic norm. The sentence structure lengthens and becomes more involved, a change in syntax that vitally affects the versification. These developments are often crudely managed, but in extent and emphasis they are fresh and original achievements.

Wallace C. Brown
The Triumph of Form (Chapel Hill, N. C.:
Univ. North Carolina Pr., 1948), pp. 102-3

The success of *The Rosciad* was due not to the novelty of the poem, but to the sharp, biting, brilliant personal satire it contained. Indeed the idea behind the poem was an old and familiar one in 1761. It had been used . . . with considerable success the year before by Lloyd in *The Actor*. As a matter of fact, both *The Actor* and *The Rosciad* derive from a long line of poems and essays on actors and acting, which for twenty years had been popular in London. Two aspects of the subject particularly appealed to mid-eighteenth-century readers. One was the lively controversy over the relative merits of "ancient" and "modern" drama; the other was the conflict between the older more formal style of acting and the newer more natural method introduced by Garrick at his Drury-Lane Theatre.

. . . Even a casual reading of *The Rosciad*, particularly in its first edition, reveals that the poem is not and was never intended to be an *indiscriminate* attack on the actors. Churchill, that is, was not merely slinging mud, as his enemies accused him of doing. *The Rosciad* is an essay in criticism, intended, on the whole, to be fair and just. It is, of course, extremely outspoken; but it is outspoken in praise as well as criticism. . . .

One of the last poems that Churchill wrote (he left it unfinished) probably contains, all things considered, his best poetry. It is the *Fragment of a Dedication to Dr. W. Warburton, Bishop of Gloucester*. The device of a formal dedication was perfectly suited to Churchill's talent for "profound and bitter innuendo." He had employed ironic eulogy before, especially in *The Prophecy of Famine* and *The Candidate*; but the formula of a dedication is the medium for eulogy *par excellence*. When it is used as the vehicle for subtle and sustained irony, the effect is comparable to that of the mock-heroic at its best.

Although it is unfinished, the *Dedication* forms a complete structural unit which may be divided into three parts. The first seventy-two lines introduce the subject and give the reasons why the poet admires Warburton. . . . The next forty lines describe the assistance that Churchill had hoped to get from him . . . and the last sixty-eight lines deal with the futility of that hope, because Warburton had more important things to do than "waste his precious time, On which so much depended, for a rhyme."

. . . Lyrical qualities are more marked than ever in the *Dedication*. They arise chiefly out of four characteristics of the poem: syntactic repetition with the effect of a refrain, the constant intrusion of the personal note, the rhetorical device of exclamations, and the Churchillian non-epigrammatic norm for the heroic couplet, which creates larger rhythms and a more lyrical swing.

Wallace C. Brown
*Charles Churchill* (Lawrence, Kans.: Univ. Kansas Pr., 1953), pp. 39-40, 139-41

# COLLEY CIBBER
## 1671-1757

An actor, Cibber's first play, *Love's Last Shift*, appeared in 1696, setting a vogue for sentimentalism. *Love Makes a Man* (1700), *The Careless Husband* (1705), and *The Provok'd Husband* (1728), his completion of Vanbrugh's *A Journey to London*, indicate the staple of his work. He was made poet laureate in 1730, which evoked invective from many, including Pope, who made him the hero of the *Dunciad* in its final edition. His autobiography, *Apology for the Life of Mr. Colley Cibber, Comedian* (1740), gives an informative picture of the theater of his day.

R. H. Barker, *Mr. Cibber of Drury Lane* (1939)

Confidence in the goodness of average human nature is the mainspring of sentimentalism. That confidence became in the eighteenth century the cardinal point of a new gospel, and the underlying ethical principle of a new school of literature. It was the fundamental assumption of the dramatists of sensibility.

. . . The drama of sensibility, which includes sentimental comedy and domestic tragedy, was from its birth a protest against the orthodox view of life, and against those literary conventions which had served that view. It implied that human nature, when not, as in some cases, already perfect, was perfectible by an appeal to the emotions. It refused to assume that virtuous persons must be sought in a romantic realm apart from the everyday world. It wished to show that beings who were good at heart were found in the ordinary walks of life. It so represented their conduct as to arouse admiration for their virtues and pity for their sufferings. In sentimental comedy, it showed them contending against distresses but finally rewarded by morally deserved happiness. In domestic tragedy, it showed them overwhelmed by catastrophes for which they were morally not responsible. A new ethics had arisen, and new forms of literature were thereby demanded.

Ernest Bernbaum
*The Drama of Sensibility* (Cambridge, Mass.:
Harvard Univ. Pr., 1925), pp. 2, 10

Cibber paid for . . . [his] unpopularity in several ways. His acting, particularly in tragedy parts, was often hissed, his plays were howled down, his benefit nights were neglected, and his character was abused in every coffee-house and newspaper in London. On one occasion at least, the first performance of his comedy *The Provok'd Husband*, his life was even in some danger. . . .

What is the explanation of the animosity Cibber provoked on almost every side? It was principally . . . due to that quality in him which his enemies called his insolence, his brazenness, his unabashedness, his impenetrability, but which a more democratic age will call independence. At a time when an actor was expected to kowtow to the aristocracy and to flatter the public, Cibber did neither. There are many anecdotes, often recorded by his enemies, which show that he refused to be overawed by mere rank or mere authority. . . . Cibber's character was certainly far from perfect: he was a reckless gamester (a trait inherited from his luckless and talented father), he was selfish and conceited, he was often too free with his sarcasm; but he deserves the credit of the moral courage which this quality of independence implied and necessitated.

> F. W. Bateson
> *English Comic Drama, 1700-1750* (Oxford Univ.
> Pr., 1929), pp. 16-17

*Love's Last Shift* is a play which belongs to two traditions—the tradition of the comedy of manners, which culminated in the work of Etherege and Congreve, and the sentimental tradition, which flourished during the Elizabethan period in the bourgeois drama of Heywood and reappeared during the Restoration in the work of such writers as Shadwell, D'Urfey, and Mrs. Behn. The sentimental aspect of the play has been emphasized— possibly overemphasized—by Croissant, who calls Cibber a deliberate reformer, and by Bernbaum, who credits him with the first significant expression of confidence in the goodness of human nature. But . . . it is indeed a landmark in the history of English comedy. It came out at a time when taste was changing—when wit and cynicism were becoming less acceptable, when priggish characters, emotional scenes, and obtrusive morality were beginning to appear. It was more sentimental than any earlier Restoration play; it was a brilliant success on the stage; it probably influenced Steele, Vanbrugh, and Farquhar as well as Cibber himself in later years. Hence in our time it has not unnaturally come to be regarded as the first sentimental comedy. . . .

Cibber and Pope first clashed in the year 1717. Cibber, then forty-five years old, was at the height of his reputation. . . . Pope was seventeen years younger, but he too was already famous. . . . Their battle of 1717 arose from the fact that Pope had just assisted his two friends Arbuthnot and Gay in writing the farce of *Three Hours after Marriage* [in which Cibber is represented as the actor Plotwell]. . . .

Ten years passed, Pope turned his attention almost exclusively to satire, and again Cibber found himself the object of the poet's ridicule. In March, 1728, he appears in the *Art of Sinking in Poetry*, and in the first edition of the *Dunciad*, published in May of the same year, he is mentioned five times—once as a plagarist, once as the Lord Chancellor of Plays, once as the father of an infamous son, and once as the manager who had countenanced—and acted in—the pantomimes. In 1730 he figures in two epigrams and an article—all published in the *Grub Street Journal*—on the subject of the contest for the laureateship, and in 1733 his odes are contemptuously mentioned in the *First Satire of the Second Book of Horace*. But the most unkind of all Pope's references to Cibber occur in the *Epistle to Arbuthnot* (1735).

. . . Cibber had sworn to have the last word in the controversy, and shortly after the appearance of the new *Dunciad* [1743] he published still another [the third] open letter to Pope. . . . He again examines Pope's insane irritability and modestly contrasts it with his own Olympian indifference.

Richard H. Barker
*Mr. Cibber of Drury Lane* (New York: Columbia
Univ. Pr., 1939), pp. 21-22, 204, 206-7, 219

Cibber . . . need not detain us long. His comedies have, it is true, vestiges of ideas. His main theme throughout was the marriage, basically sound enough, broken by the "affected' humour of the typical Restoration hero or heroine healed by experience on the one hand, and devotion on the other. All the time, in effect, he is vulgarizing Dryden's *Marriage-à-la-Mode*, adding for irrelevant relief, the egregious fop, here vulgarizing Etherege's Sir Fopling Flutter, his first re-creation, Sir Novelty Fashion, being his best. But he had a sense of the stage, and had he been less pleased with himself might have penetrated deeper. The attraction of most of his comedies must have been the blatantly fleshly treatment of sex combined with a briskness of movement that masks the improbability of the action. His first play, *Love's Last Shift* (1696), was an attempt to inculcate a good-goody moral, and his reformed rake proved an easy butt for Vanbrugh. Lewdness for four acts was an unconvincing preparation for a virtuous fifth, but the attempt chimed with the mood to which Collier so vociferously gave expression; and since, in Congreve's well-known phrase, the play contained a great many things which were like wit but were not really wit at all—so making no demands on the brains of the audience—the play took. . . . For all its intrinsic weakness, Cibber's work cannot be denied a brittle vivacity, such as will in some part account for its contemporary success.

Bonamy Dobrée
*English Literature in the Early Eighteenth Century*
(New York: Oxford Univ. Pr., 1959), pp. 229-30

The usual objections to *Love's Last Shift*—the inconsistency of the character-drawing, and the lack of integrity—make the author seem a crude opportunist, clumsily trying to pique the public fancy by the grossest means. . . . He is on the contrary the most suave and devious of literary entrepreneurs, striving continually and successfully to please two antipathetic audience groups, always seeming to commit himself to one viewpoint, while never antagonizing the other. Cibber's equivocation extends through the areas of class, morality, and character traits; there is hardly a character who appeals, throughout the play, to the same audience group for the same reasons. His ingenuity in keeping a moral balance, which is at the same time something of a class balance (tipped slightly, perhaps, in favor of the aristocracy), is one of the most remarkable factors in his performance. Sentimentality, the best-publicized aspect of the play, should evidently be seen as only one of the ingredients, a very conspicuous one to be sure, but not one to which the author is irrevocably committed. In fact his businesslike impartiality requires him to avoid any commitment. He knows, just as any other entrepreneur does, that a passionately defended viewpoint causes disagreement, and possibly hurts sales; and Cibber is primarily dedicated to the pursuit of success. He does not hesitate to carry his equivocation so far that it calls into question his integrity, and compromises his characterization. This ruthlessly clear knowledge of his purpose may be said to put him nearer the Restoration than the eighteenth century, but his sensitiveness to middle-class demands brings him closer to the drama of sensibility. Actually, the play resists conventional classification. Perhaps the best solution . . . is to invent a new term, "the comedy of equivocation," for this work that looks both ways and hedges its conclusions so carefully.

Paul E. Parnell
*SP* (October, 1960), pp. 533-34

# WILLIAM COLLINS
1721-1759

Educated at Magdalen College, Oxford, Collins published the "Persian Eclogues" as an undergraduate in 1742, continuing to write a small quantity of lyrics, particularly odes. The twelve *Odes* of 1747 included the well-known "Ode to Evening." However, he became insane in the last years of his life.

W. T. Williams and G. H. Vallins, eds., *Gray, Collins and Their Circle* (1937)
Edward G. Ainsworth, Jr., *Poor Collins* (1937)

. . . the grandeur of wildness and the novelty of extravagance were always desired by him, but were not always attained.

The last sentence goes far toward canceling what the eighteenth century said about Collins's ungovernable imagination. It may be hard to recognize in the fantastic Gothic poet of Johnson's description the Collins whom we know, but the central truth about him is reached in this criticism, for his inclinations did indeed outreach his genius, and he aspired to a grandeur and extravagance which he achieved not more than once or twice. The way in which he sought his romantic goal is not described by Johnson, whose account refers primarily to his reading rather than to his poetry. What Collins did in his own verse was to take seriously the neoclassical commonplaces about verse and inspiration, and to try to achieve poetic ecstasy within the narrow limits set for him by the current conventional imagery. He earnestly sought "rapture" and "enthusiasm" where many a third-rate writer of Pindarics told him he might find them. It was an enterprise which was doomed to failure, and indeed no one could be more deeply conscious of his failure than he was himself—no one felt more keenly the impotence of British poetry in the middle of the eighteenth century.

Alan D. McKillop
*SP* (January, 1923), pp. 6-7

The *Persian Eclogues*, modeled so closely after the prevailing taste in pastoral, are naturally somewhat conventional or bookish in the descriptions of nature. He employs much of the generalized scenery so characteristic of Pope. "Limpid springs," "verdant vales," "flow'ry valleys," "sylvan scenes," "shady groves," "wanton gales," "breezy mountains" are among the stock descriptive phrases. Some of the less conventional pictures, drawn from his reading in Salmon's *Modern History*, are calculated to furnish the exotic atmosphere one would expect in poems purporting in Collins's fiction to be the work of "one Abdallah, a native of Tauris." These pictures are invested with something of the delicate perceptiveness of the poet, and, appropriately enough for an oriental study, appeal to the sense of smell as well as to the world of eye and ear. . . .

The descriptions of nature in the odes are less conventional than those in the *Persian Eclogues*, and over all of them there is "a glamour of the imagination." They represent nature viewed at the twilight hour, when to the mind of the visionary she is most shadowy and most enchanting; or she is viewed from a distance so that her realistic aspects are softened. Or some wholly fanciful and visionary scene is clothed with "the light that never was on land or sea." If nature is represented in her harsher moods, as in the description of storms and of the sea, a kind of imaginative terror aroused by the scene takes it from the real. Collins did not see nature so sharply as did some of his contemporaries like John Dyer, or even Gray, but certain aspects of her beauty or her grandeur appealed to him, and to these few images he returned again and again with a growing sense of their charm.

Associated with Collins's concept of Fancy and his idea of the subject-matter of poetry is his treatment of "allegory," or more directly, his use of personification, surely part of "invention and imagination" which Collins, with Joseph Warton, felt to be "the chief faculties of a poet." Collins's treatment of his personifications is one of the most characteristic qualities of his poetry, at once one of his merits and one of his faults, and especially indicative, too, of the poetical traditions which he followed. . . .

In most of the odes the major personified figure is shadowy, and, instead of being directly described, is suggested more by its influence. There is relatively little in Collins of the sharp, colorful, and picturesque delineation of a virtue or vice so characteristic of Spenser. Instead, Collins employs a few descriptive epithets appropriate to the figure described and subordinates these to the effect which the personified quality produces on the poet or the reader. And since Pity, Fear, Fancy, Peace, Mercy, and Simplicity are part of that visionary world to which Evening belongs, the descriptions are, appropriately enough, shadowy and vague, the presence of these god-like figures being more often felt than fully seen.

Edward G. Ainsworth, Jr.
*Poor Collins* (Ithaca, N. Y.: Cornell Univ. Pr., 1937), pp. 45-47, 107

In so far as the characteristics of Collins' technique as a whole are concerned, much could be said. First, there is a marked tendency towards stanzaic regularity. The best odes in the book are written in stanzas of four or six lines. The Pindaric poems, similar in this respect to "Lycidas," tend to conclude with passages in even meter. Thus "The Passions" closes with a section in iambic tetrameter, and the Epodes in "To Liberty" are in the same measure. The "Ode on the Poetical Character" deviates only occasionally from regularity. Comparing Collins with Dryden, one sees clearly that the poetic practice of fifty years had led gradually and naturally from irregularity at any price to irregularity as counterpoint. Second, Collins seldom appears to have any clear impression of his poems as wholes. Each does, to be sure, have a theme, but this is developed by arranging comment on it in stanzaic parallels. The "Ode to Liberty" might almost be three separate poems; and even the "Ode to Evening" could stop at the end of stanza five. Third, the element of parallelism within the stanzas often suggests that the unifying force is not any kind of logic but rather only a zest for expression.

George N. Shuster
*The English Ode from Milton to Keats* (New York:
Columbia Univ. Pr., 1940), pp. 194-95

Collins's admitted peculiarities, then, by no means completely separate him from those literary trends which are usually associated with the cult of feeling. He is a lover of patriotism, of liberty, and of nature. The *Ode to Evening* is a beautiful variant of the contemplative-retirement type. *The Ode on the Popular Superstitions of the Highlands of Scotland* suggests that his imagination, granted a longer period of sane development, would have moved from a sentimental Neo-Hellenism to a sentimental blend of naturalism and medievalism. His closest friends were such men as Thomson, Mallet, Cooper, John Langhorne, and the Wartons. His dread of didacticism and his personal reserve do not always prevent him from showing his intellectual kinship with these men of feeling.

Hoxie Neale Fairchild
*Religious Trends in English Poetry,* vol. II (New York:
Columbia Univ. Pr., 1942), pp. 355-56

# WILLIAM CONGREVE
1670-1729

A graduate of Trinity College, Dublin, and student at the Middle Temple, Congreve turned to literature in 1692 with a novel, *Incognito,* and a comedy, *The Old Bachelor,* in 1693. Other important comedies are *The Double Dealer* (1694), *Love for Love* (1695), and *The Way of the World* (1700); his only tragedy is *The Mourning Bride* (1697). Attacked by Jeremy Collier for immorality in the theater, he replied in 1698, but gave up writing for the theater in 1700. He was buried in Westminster Abbey.

Bonamy Dobrée, ed., *William Congreve* (1925-1928), 2 vols.
John C. Hodges, *William Congreve the Man* (1941)

## THE PLAYS

*Love for Love* is essentially an acting play with an intelligible plot and the wit subordinate to it. *The Way of the World,* Congreve's literary masterpiece, was a failure on the stage and deserved to be. An audience cannot be expected to sit with any pleasure through five acts of drama (particularly an abstruse fifth one), if there be no coherent plot to hold one's interest and, in fact, no attraction but enchanting dialogue. . . . Congreve's last and most characteristic play is not a play at all, but a so-called "closet drama," written in well-nigh perfect dialogue, which must be read and reread to be appreciated.

Henry T. E. Perry
*The Comic Spirit in Restoration Drama* (New Haven:
Yale Univ. Pr., 1925), pp. 77-78

Congreve's art transformed the humour and type [of his characters] into the individual possessed of distinctive personality. To fuse this realism of the characters with the essential unreality of pure comedy was a wellnigh impossible achievement, but Congreve came as near to reconciling these opposing factors as was humanly possible. The balance inclines toward realism in *Love for Love* and toward pure comedy in *The Way of the World*. Because his genius found its most complete expression in pure comedy his last play is generally acknowledged to be his masterpiece.

*Love for Love* is a great improvement over the first two comedies. Its buoyant tone and broadly humorous characters are reminiscent of *The Old Batchelor*, while his satire, less cynical and personal in its application than in *The Double Dealer*, is not less forceful. The wit is finer than in either comedy, more subtle, pointed, deft, and graceful. Although each character is endowed with far more than his share of cleverness, not one speaks out of his part for the speeches of each are perfectly adapted to him. . . . The Aristophanic frankness of this comedy verges upon the obscene more frequently than is the custom of Congreve; but it must have gratified the public taste, for every element of the play was devised to win popularity, as he explains in the prologue. When one considers that some of these elements were not particularly congenial to him his performance becomes all the more amazing. His usual saturnine wit relaxed into genial merriment, and he brought more clear air and sunlight into this one comedy than in all his others put together. He proved that a dramatist of genius can make a great play popular.

D. Crane Taylor
*William Congreve* (Oxford Univ. Pr., 1931), 75-76

Congreve declared frankly that artistic values meant more to him than popular applause. He had catered to the favor of the audience in *The Old Bachelor*. But as he looked back over that play his aesthetic conscience rebuked him because he had treated his audience "cheaply" then, and he scorned it for applauding. Even *Love for Love,* much superior to the first comedy, did not satisfy Congreve, and he called the play but "Homely Fare." For *The Way of the World* he made no such apology. In that play, he knew that he had "gain'd a Turn of Stile, or Expression more Correct, or at least more Corrigible." He believed that he had come nearer to his ideal than in any other play, and he might well question whether he could hope to write anything superior. If the audience would not accept it, he could only conclude that it would be impossible for him to satisfy both his audience and himself. Should he now drop down from the level he had reached and prostitute his muse to the lower taste of the town? His decision not to do so remained firm throughout the remainder of his life. He

had outgrown the technique of *The Old Bachelor,* and the London audience would not accept the type of high comedy that now satisfied his
artistic sense. At the age of thirty, therefore, he decided, as a matter of
principle, to write no more for the popular stage.

John C. Hodges
*William Congreve the Man* (New York: Modern
Language Assn., 1941), pp. 69-70

In the spring of 1776, when Garrick retired in a grand finale of his best
parts, there was no Congreve role among them. Congreve's plays had
clearly lost their former high place in the repertories. Not one of them had
had more than five performances in a single season since 1764-65, when
*Love for Love* and *The Way of the World* had had their last really genuine
shares in the repertory. *The Old Batchelor* and *The Double Dealer* had
been so nearly neglected that any Londoner who wished to see either one
would have had to scan the playbills closely to catch their infrequent
performances.

. . . At the same time that the older plays were disappearing, there was
a movement to restore them in altered form if need be. If it was not
feasible or wise to revive them in all their original glory, a compromise
could be achieved. Perhaps a new sparkle could be given tarnished plays
by a rewriting which would remove the blemishes and heighten their
dramatic virtues. . . . The revisions of Congreve's plays followed a relatively consistent pattern: the expunging of "exceptionable passages" without really significant change in the plot or characterization. This process
usually involved the removal of words, phrases, sometimes whole speeches,
but it rarely—except in some portions of *The Mourning Bride*—included
the elimination of a sequence of speeches or an entire scene. It was a
purifying by the cutting of detail rather than by genuine rewriting.

Emmet L. Avery
*Congreve's Plays on the Eighteenth-Century Stage* (New York:
Modern Language Assn., 1951), pp. 122-23

## The Double Dealer

Congreve's second play, *The Double-Dealer* (1694), has many characteristics of the comedy of wit, but it is a poor example of this type. In writing
it, he apparently had a moral purpose in mind, if we are to believe the
statement in his dedicatory epistle that he designed the moral first. Its
ill-success Dryden attributed to the fact that Congreve had exposed the
"Bitchery" of women too much, as well as the folly of men. But the lack
of success might also be due to the fact that the standards in the play are

inconsistent; for not only is there the usual interest in true and false wit, but there is also a great deal of concern with barefaced villainy.

Thomas H. Fujimura
*The Restoration Comedy of Wit* (Princeton, N. J.:
Princeton Univ. Pr., 1952), pp. 170-71

## The Way of the World

Congreve's muse is the full-blooded jade of Etherege and Wycherley come to discretion. . . . Congreve's theme is often but simple wickedness, empty of pleasure or lust. There is an equable finality about the morality of *The Way of the World*—a dead level of conscience against which is vividly thrown a brilliant variety of manners and habits. It is a final assertion of that noble laziness of the mind which began with Etherege, in accepting and enjoying the vicissitudes of fortune, and ended, with Congreve, in despising them. Congreve seems ever to be passing his creatures in review with faint, expressive smiles of disdain.

John Palmer
*The Comedy of Manners* (London: G. Bell, 1913), p. 192

To establish our point of view we begin with a number of assumptions diametrically opposed to those now generally accepted: (1) that the plot is primarily a legacy conflict centering in Lady Wishfort and the four adulterers; (2) that the theme is the danger of losing "fame and fortune" through the exposure of adultery; (3) that the title is an oblique thrust at evils inherent in the contemporary marriage of convenience; (4) that the stock characters (the rake, the cast [off] mistress, the adultress, the cuckold, and the irresponsible guardian) hitherto usually regarded as embodiments of folly, are deliberately modified to reveal how unchecked folly degenerates into vice; (5) and finally, that the epigrammatic, antithetical form of wit formerly associated with the ridicule of folly is taxed with a dual function, sometimes to ridicule folly, other times to expose vice. . . .

The surface brilliance of the dialogue in [the proviso] scene . . . marks the culmination of Congreve's wit. But there is far more than surface brilliance; here, Congreve combines a surface of sparkling wit with an undercurrent of penetrating insight, and so harmonious is the combination that neither the surface of sallies nor the undercurrent of sense has been sacrificed. . . . Ever present beneath the scintillating wit is the conviction that unchecked indulgence in folly often ends in vice; that unrestrained affection may degenerate into immorality. . . .

It is misleading to assume that all satire on vice is reserved for the grave scenes, or conversely, that all satire on folly is relegated to the gay scenes—Congreve is too astute a dramatist to draw so rigid a contrast. What he . . . does stress is that folly may deviate into vice; the fool may turn knave; or conversely vice may revert to folly, the knave may turn fool. . . . Knave and fool alike retain enough intelligence to be potentially corrigible, consequently after each has been shown the error of his ways, he may either mend them or go his perverse way. In comedy, as in life, knave or fool can be shown the way but he himself must choose whether to follow it.

Paul and Miriam Mueschke
*A New View of Congreve's Way of the World* (Ann Arbor, Mich.:
Univ. Michigan Pr., 1958), pp. 10, 32, 62

The ways of the world, then, are cyclic. The play assumes two kinds of reality, public appearance (typified by family relations) and an inner personal nature (typified by emotions). One "way" is that there is an organic flux of both inward and outward natures. Passions are quickly born, grow, and die. From them grow more slowly the outer, social relations of people (marriages and "breeding"), which in turn define and limit future passions. The other "way" is that there is and ought to be a difference (with Congreve, not necessarily a contradiction) between these two kinds of reality; one must retain a decorum and balance between them (as exemplified by the match between Mirabell and Millamant). Too much of a difference (Mrs. Fainall's marriage or her husband's blackmail) results in a situation where the social fact exerts undue restraint on the emotional. Too little difference leads to the absurdities of Sir Wilfull's behavior.

Norman N. Holland
*The First Modern Comedies* (Cambridge, Mass.:
Harvard Univ. Pr., 1959), pp. 194-95

## GENERAL

. . . Congreve's metaphorical structure creates an impression of that most characteristic of seventeenth-century inventions—the co-ordinate system. We have seen how the individuals in the play present themselves as in tension—between conversion up and conversion down, between consuming and being consumed in love, and between reason and passion in the forward progress through time. . . . The "journey of life" idea presents itself as forward and backward; the relation to ideals as up or down; the love-relationship as from side to side. At the same time that the individual stands in the center of these tensions, he stands outside them as a spectator of himself. . . . We could say that Congreve's three-dimensional conception is mannerist in having unresolved tensions and a shifting point of view (spectator's and actor's), but baroque in that these tensions are seen along orthogonal, clearly defined directions.

Norman N. Holland<br>
The First Modern Comedies (Cambridge, Mass.:<br>
Harvard Univ. Pr., 1959), pp. 144-45, 146-47

# ABRAHAM   COWLEY
1618-1667

The precocious Cowley, born in London, the son of a stationer and book-seller, published *Poetical Blossoms* when a fifteen-year-old student at Westminster School. At Trinity College, Cambridge, which he entered in 1636, he wrote three plays, remaining in 1640 as a Fellow. A Royalist, he fled to Oxford first and then to Paris where he became cipher secretary to Queen Henrietta Maria. He was imprisoned in 1655, upon his return, as an alleged spy. Upon release he studied medicine, receiving a medical degree in 1657, and this study and writing occupied his time upon retirement in 1663. He was one of the first members of the Royal Society, his *Proposition for the Advancement of Experimental Philosophy* (1661) proposing a "Philosophical College" similar to Bacon's "Solomon's House."

A. R. Waller, ed., *English Writings* (1905-1906), 2 vols.

John Sparrow, ed., *The Mistress and Other Select Poems* (1926)

Arthur H. Nethercot, *Abraham Cowley, The Muse's Hannibal* (1931)

## THE POEMS

The word-for-word, literal type of translation, Cowley held, was actually the least literal of all. For the lapse of time between different ages changes the colours of poetry as much as of painting; and the "no less difference betwixt the religions and customs of our countries, and a thousand partic-ularities of places, persons, and manners" merely confuse the eye without aiding the understanding.

. . . Having thus shown himself to be one of the first of English critics to grope toward the historical point of view in critics, Cowley then pro-ceeded to illustrate his own principles by imitating, or paraphrasing, or naturalizing Pindar's second Olympic and first Nemean odes, and by fur-nishing them with an imposing array of notes and comments, as he had done before with the *Davideis*. But again he proved himself to be a better explorer, a better Columbus, than a practitioner. . . . On the whole, all that he succeeded in catching in his work was the superficialities, the tricks, of the Greek poet. . . . Digressions, addresses to the Muse, allusions to myth and history, omitted transitions, discussions of art versus nature

(with the preference always given nature) in the poem itself—all these
are present as in Pindar, and yet the poems fail to stir the reader deeply.
Short passages strike and impress him, but the odes as a whole leave him
cold.

Arthur H. Nethercot<br>
Abraham Cowley, The Muse's Hannibal (Oxford<br>
Univ. Pr., 1931), pp. 137-38

At any rate, Cowley's numerous poems in this form [the ode]—or lack of
form, if one prefers—produce in the main three effects. First, they give
free rein to the poet's "wit," which then rears and paws about in a fashion
which sometimes only too completely justifies his own poetic injunction
in the "Resurrection". . . . Still at their best these poems do have a rich
eloquence which may not always be poetry as we have come to understand
the word, but which normally remains far above the level, say, of the
verse in Saintsbury's *Caroline Poets*. Second, they permit of prosodic experimentation which must not be judged by the use it makes of "emotion
recollected in tranquillity" but which as a medium for the coruscating intelligence is highly impressive and successful. Cowley is merely baroque to
a point bound to exasperate even those who do not dislike the baroque
under any and all circumstances.

If one studies the poems from the structural point of view, it will be
found that on the whole they are more regular—i.e., more nearly mono-
strophic—than their reputation would have it. The translations from Pindar
are, for example, written predominatingly in various arrangements of four
and five stress lines. "Life and Fame" is also comparatively even, and the
first two stanzas of "Life" differ little from each other. "Destinie," on the
other hand, contains a large number of three-stress lines and ends with a
queer seven-footer. Yet here, too, the device is not juxtaposition of highly
variegated stanzas, but rather a varying arrangement of long and short
lines. Sometimes, as in the "Resurrection," special effects are obtained—at
least in the poet's intention—by the verbal and metrical patterns adopted.
The music of language becomes a matter of minor import. Cowley was,
if his verse is any criterion, singularly deaf to the melody of language as
the Elizabethans or the Romantics have understood that. And he was not
a poet of the senses. Only the sea appears to have awakened him to the
presence of sheer natural beauty.

George N. Shuster<br>
The English Ode from Milton to Keats (New York:<br>
Columbia Univ. Pr., 1940), pp. 111-12

The poems in *The Mistress* are witty and ingenious, a brilliant display of
poetic inventiveness, but not insincere. They are light in tone, but they have

genuine and serious things to say. Their distance between the imagined and the real is precisely the distance of artistic detachment. Until effectively articulated, a state of mind, however firmly based on a real event, has little reality for the participant and none for anyone else. An effective articulation of a state of mind based on a pretended event may be psychologically accurate, and hence true. Good lyric poems, no matter how concrete the incident underlying them, must use the incident only as pretext. The poem itself is reverie and reflection upon the pretext, a daydream or an association raised to the level of art. *The Mistress* is made up of such lyrics.

These lyrics do not say everything to be said about love. No love poem or collection of love poems does. But what they do say is perceptive and sound. Although their initial appeal is intellectual and artistic, their very intellectuality and artistic finish finally convey emotional intensity and conviction. Although the heart they reveal is too sophisticated to be naked, it is a thinking heart, and a candid one. Through exploration of the real world and honest thought about the relationship of love to that world, Cowley achieves novelty without being fantastic. He has seemed fantastic to those who have not recognized his fidelity to the world of his day, but to his contemporaries his original and independent creation with data accepted as true gave an illusion of passion. Not ingenious artifice based upon reality but hollow clichés were considered emotionally sterile. . . .

By "wit" Cowley means the exalted poetic power defined in his ode "Of Wit," which strikingly reveals Hobbesian aesthetic theory. "Of Wit" discusses complex and elevated poetic creation, not just elegance or happiness of language or a limited concept of decorum. In fact, Cowley's Hobbesian definition of wit remarkably parallels the definition of the sublime by Longinus. . . . In "Of Wit" Cowley argues that native wit can be and must be developed; Longinus insists that the sublime, though akin to genius and inspiration, is an art that can be learned. Cowley's Hobbesian-Aristotelian theory of the relationship between art and nature is similar to Longinus' view that "art is perfect when it seems to be nature, and nature hits the mark when she contains art hidden within her." The close resemblance between the ideas of Hobbes and those of Longinus indicates that in becoming a disciple of Hobbes Cowley did not capitulate to antipoetic materialism. . . . Cowley identifies wit with both the sublime and decorum because Hobbes demands both sublimity and judgment of successful poets. Hobbes calls fancy the sublimity of the poet, but he does not separate the poet's chief attribute from serious purpose. Cowley makes "wit" a synonym for "fancy," both source and product of the artist's success.

Robert B. Hinman
*Abraham Cowley's World of Order* (Cambridge, Mass.:
Harvard Univ. Pr., 1960), pp. 52, 123-24

GENERAL

It was in this poem ["The Motto"] that Cowley confessed his ambition to become "the Muse's Hannibal." Knowing too well that he had neither birth nor wealth to help him, he realized that his fortune must be struck from himself alone. . . . Yes, he would be the Muse's Hannibal, and conquer the Alps of verse which had never before been scaled. For the sake of the Muse and the elegy Fame might write, he promised to renounce honours, wealth, estate, love, and all that might prevent him from taking a place among Aristotle, Cicero, and Virgil, the greatest writers of the past. Nor could a faithful Achates such as [his friend William] Hervey have failed to applaud the grandeur of the resolution and to encourage the youthful votary. . . .

The attitude of the Neo-Classicists toward such a writer as Cowley is easy to understand. At first admiring him for his moral and intellectual qualities, they soon began to grow disturbed by the lack of simplicity in the expression of his ideas and in the seeming lack of polish in some of his verse. "This age of taste" demanded that its literature be clear, elegant, and urbane; that it shun the extravagant and the *outré;* that it fix on the natural and the normal instead of the individual and the striking. Reason made a stronger appeal than emotion. The fact that Cowley had written several pieces with these Neo-Classical requirements served to keep him read by a limited group while greater poets such as Donne were stuffed away on the highest and dustiest shelf. Cowley's simple and frivolous little ballad, "The Chronicle," was, like the Anacreontics, always admired.

Arthur H. Nethercot
*Abraham Cowley, The Muse's Hannibal* (Oxford
Univ. Pr., 1931), pp. 47-48, 287

Whether he writes in Latin or in English, the earth and the universe to which it belongs are not alien to Cowley. He uses his numerous poetic gifts to assert man's position in a harmonious order. In vigorous words he announces that men have only begun to discover life's possibilities, that human efforts can realize a poet's dream. His imagination reconstructs and expands the world in poetry of faith and praise. The facts and attitudes of modern science contribute vitally to his conviction that human life can have dignity and beauty. The pull between order and chaos frequently gives his work strength and imaginative brilliance. He sweeps from high heaven to earth and back again like the life-giving light that irradiates many of his images, a light now pure and ineffable, now dancing in sunbeams, now glowing in the colors of flowers, now enclosed in heavy clouds from which it will burst accompanied by thunder. Cowley attempts to follow that light, through all phenomena, back to God. He speaks in noble language to men standing somewhat tentatively, even a little apprehensively, at the portals of a brave new world. He speaks reassuringly of God's goodness and glory, of the scientific evidence that no gap need divide the realm of physical fact from the realm of spirit. His work explores all the varieties of experience through which men enter those realms: sacred and profane love; religious and natural philosophy; moral and political conduct.

Robert B. Hinman<br>
*Abraham Cowley's World of Order* (Cambridge, Mass.:<br>
Harvard Univ. Pr., 1960), p. 297

# WILLIAM   COWPER
1731-1800

> Having studied law at the Middle Temple, Cowper was called to the bar in 1754. He was forbidden to marry his cousin Theodora ("Delia") in 1756 primarily because he had already suffered a mental lapse. With the pressure of a law examination in 1763, his sanity again lapsed and he attempted suicide. Later, recovered, he lived with the Reverend Morley Unwin and his daughter Mary, until the father's death in 1767; he and Mary then moved to Olney. In 1773 another period of insanity was followed by periods of melancholia, seriously in 1787 and 1794. Cowper lasted four years after the death of his Mary.
>
> H. S. Milford, ed., *Poetical Works* (1934)
> David Cecil, *The Stricken Deer* (1930)

## The Task

. . . *The Task* . . . *is* unified. Most conspicuously, it presents a central theme to which everything is connected and upon which everything reflects—the theme of seeking the ideal of stability, harmony, order. In "The Sofa" this theme is delicately explored in various ways, with the sofa itself acting as a symbol of the edge of excess, with rural nature seen as the best earthly balance between wildness and savagery on the one hand and the city's profligacy on the other. In "The Time-Piece," the latter is developed, in both its causes and its consequences, and is balanced by the manifestations of the former in natural disturbances which are reflections of God's wrath. "The Garden" shows the precariousness of this natural balance on earth—to achieve an ordered life, the retreater must occupy himself with minute discriminations . . . in a small, enclosed domestic group; he derives from the garden only a diluted, corrupted remnant of man's lost paradisal innocence and must work hard to retain it. "The Garden" ends with an awareness of London, an earthly hell existing in opposition to any earthly version of paradise. In "The Winter Evening" the fallibility of this earthly retreat is first suggested and then demonstrated. . . . God's storms and man's corruption disturb, each in its way, the unstable simulacrum of stability that man can build up in the country. Book V, in the sharp clarity of the morning, shows primarily the awareness of how delusive appearances of earthly stability may be, using as example what is presumably the highest power available on earth, that of absolute monarchs. It argues that their authority is based on futile and barren excess which causes distortion in both the kings and their subjects. The only escape from the chaos of arbitrary human activities is conversion, through which comes an internal order ("freedom") for one with grace. In the last book, which appropriately begins with a recollection of innocent childhood and a stern but kindly father, we see a vision in Judgment Day of primal innocence and the primal Father. . . . In the Judgment Day scene, all the narrative and thematic "rays of information," as Cowper called them in another context, meet—God, both stern and kind, destroys and creates, in a vision of ultimate harmony and balance. . . .

Similarly, *The Task* fulfills the final test for unity—break it where we will, its contents are discoverably arranged in their characteristic triple form: brutalism-balance-decadence (which, in view of Cowper's mental preoccupations, could also be written: God's power—harmonious and static balance—man's intolerable chaos). From the stool, elbow-chair, sofa triad at the very beginning to the heaven, Judgment Day, earth triad in the end, everywhere Cowper's theme appears, whether in major symbolic structures such as the quiet country between the wilderness and the city or in lesser ones such as the decent, virtuous poor between the brutalized wagon-driver and the drunken thief. . . .

Morris Golden
*In Search of Stability* (New York: Bookman
Assoc., 1960), pp. 151-52, 154-55

The plan of *The Task* exquisitely reveals the peculiar quality of the poet. It is a minor masterpiece in the art of digression. But digression here is not the art of wandering from the subject to conceal want of matter, as Swift accounted it. Nor is it the kind of digression that makes *Tristram Shandy* the most wonderfully erratic of English novels. "Great wits jump," wrote Sterne. And they jump, as he plainly advertises, to the tune of Locke's theory of the association of ideas. In *Tristram Shandy* . . . attention is like a monkey swinging from limb to limb in the forest of the mind. The forest—the "contiguity of shade"—is in *The Task,* but hardly the monkey. Cowper's own explanation is simple enough: "the reflections are naturally suggested by the preceding paragraph." This is plainly the flow of easy conversation, with a natural passage from subject to subject sometimes so artless that one is hardly conscious of a change.

No less individual than the structure, and more of a break with the neo-classical tradition, is the blank verse. In this no one would maintain that Cowper was a trail-blazer. Thomson had used blank verse in the same sort of peotry and, like Cowper, his great model was John Milton. But Cowper imitated neither. If Thomson wrote much good blank verse, Cowper at his best could do better. Avoiding Thomson's frequent end-stopped lines that give the impression of unrhymed couplets, Cowper achieves greater flexilibity and length of phrasing. Although he misses the vigor and sweep of Thomson, he has more ease and variety. And if he does not have the "organ" quality that he admired in Milton, he does develop a well-tuned stringed instrument that is both effective and distinctive.

Interestingly enough, Cowper becomes less plainly a neo-classical poet when he abandons the couplet, but he also reveals how close to the main stream of classicism he is.

Lodwick C. Hartley
*William Cowper: The Continuing Revaluation* (Chapel Hill, N. C.: Univ. North Carolina Pr., 1960), pp. 62-63

## GENERAL

From henceforward the story is clouded by the smoke, distorted by the lurid light of madness. Horrible hints reach us as to the nature of the fears that tormented him. In the hurricane that was sweeping over him the depths of his personality were stirred up and obscene monsters that had slept there for years came to the surface. He believed, it is said, that his enemies had discovered his secret deformity and were threatening to expose it. It is an unlikely story. How could it help them? Why should such a deformity prevent a man being made Clerk of the House of Lords? On the other hand, there may well have been a more intimate reason for such a catastrophe as overtook him than the mere fear of making an exhibition of himself. And if it is true he was deformed it is possible that, already suffering from some kind of persecution mania, he now associated it with the shameful secret which had done so much to infect him with his fundamental distrust of life.

In his despair he cut himself off from his friends. Aloud in his solitary chambers he cursed the hour of his birth. If he was weak, he was no worse than many other men. He had tried to be good. What had he done to deserve this frightful crucifixion? To ease his pain he began taking drugs. But they only numbed, they did not remove it. And such comfort as they gave was neutralized by the awful awakening, when he looked out wretchedly into the dawn, livid over the Temple roofs, and realized that the relief of the night before had been an illusion.

David Cecil
*The Stricken Deer* (Oxford Univ. Pr., 1930), p. 61

The "stricken deer" reference, . . . while itself sane enough, is less typical than is often supposed. Cowper's major poems are, on the whole, remarkably objective for the work of one prone to introspection. His mind was basically critical, and the writing of verse diverted his thoughts from the preoccupation with self which his morbid taint induced in idle hours. Even when he was mad, he did not, in his own words, lose his senses—only the use of them. He was sane when he wrote most of his poetry: sane, by contemporary standards, even in his Calvinism. It is the standards themselves which have changed. The contradictions in Cowper's poetry are the contradictions of his age, which only a great creative artist could have surmounted.

Cowper was temperamentally not a creator, but a commentator. . . . Cowper . . . had *some* creative ability. Certain of his shorter poems, like *The Shrubbery,* have a pure lyrical note. . . . But . . . though he did not entirely lack creativeness, the *determining* motive was critical. His true "lyrics" are few in number. And though the genuine spirit of poetry animates the best portions of the satires and *The Task,* such passages are incidental and are seldom long sustained.

Gilbert Thomas
*William Cowper and the Eighteenth Century* (London:
George Allen and Unwin, 1948), pp. 263-64

Though there is no one poem or piece of prose that is in itself unusually important, the early works of Cowper nevertheless contain passages which adumbrate almost everything he did later. His genius developed late, yet in his first writings the variety of his individual abilities is shown, and small fragments of each type of mood and verse in which he was later to excel are clearly created. The humour characteristic of "John Gilpin" is there, and the mock-heroic of *The Task.* So is his tenderness, his particular description of nature, his mild but firm rebellion against the Augustan mode. There is at times the terror of "The Castaway." The poetry is largely impromptu, and lacking the real occasion for poetry it remains polite but undistinguished armchair verse. It follows in the Cowper family tradition, and seems many times to be no better than that which any well-tutored, moderately sensitive gentleman could write. And then, suddenly, there comes a line which is a foretaste of his very best poetry of twenty or thirty years later.

Charles Ryskamp
*William Cowper of the Inner Temple* (Cambridge
Univ. Pr., 1959), p. 102

In *Table Talk,* the initial poem of the 1782 volume, Cowper sets up his poetic ideal, the Miltonic ideal of poet-prophet. His modesty causes him to disclaim immediately any similarity; but anyone who has attempted to follow his serious thought will be convinced that he aimed at the qualifications of his true poet: a sensibility to human woe, the fire of indignation and the lash of scorn for ignoble deeds and ideals, and a "terrible sagacity" informing the poet's heart. Although he promises different methods and a different emphasis, he plainly sets out to scourge folly in the succession of the century's great satirists. It is true that his aspirations are toward religious poetry—religious poetry, of course, far different from that of Donne, Crashaw, and Herbert. But if he did not feel worthy of being considered a poet-prophet in any sense, he was at least eager for a "monitor's praise." Though this may not be a lofty poetic ideal, we at least owe Cowper the compliment of taking him at his own word.

Lodwick C. Hartley
*William Cowper, Humanitarian* (Chapel Hill, N. C.:
Univ. North Carolina Pr., 1938), pp. 247-48

# DANIEL DEFOE
1660?-1731

The son of James Foe of London, Defoe changed his name ca. 1703. His political persuasions toward the Duke of Monmouth and then William III were reflected in his satirical *The True-Born Englishman* (1701). *The Shortest Way With the Dissenters* (1702) caused his imprisonment, and this and financial difficulties seem to have led him to insincerity and mercenary activities. He was a not entirely trustworthy agent of Harley and Godolphin in Scotland, and an anti-Jacobite pamphleteer, who nonetheless was imprisoned by the Whig government for treasonable writing. Though convicted in 1715 of libel, he was not imprisoned through the aid of the secretary of state, for whom he operated as secret agent. His newspaper *The Review* was begun in 1704 and replaced by *The Mercator* in 1713; *The True Relation of the Apparition of One Mrs. Veal* appeared in 1706, *The Life and Strange Surprising Adventures of Robinson Crusoe, of York, Mariner*, in 1719, *The Fortunes and Misfortunes of the Famous Moll Flanders* and *A Journal of the Plague Year*, both in 1722, and his guidebook *A Tour Thro' the Whole Island of Great Britain*, in three volumes in 1724, 1725, and 1727. In all, Defoe wrote over 400 items.

G. H. Maynadier, ed., *Works* (1903-1904), 16 vols.

W. L. Payne, *Mr. Review* (1947)

## Moll Flanders

Strip *Moll Flanders* of its bland loquacity, its comic excess, its excitement, and we have the revelation of a savage life, a life that is motivated solely by economic need, and a life that is measured at last by those creature comforts that, if we gain them, allow us one final breath in which to praise the Lord. Yet this essence is not the book as we have it, as Defoe wrote it, any more than the acquisitive impulse is the whole of middle-class value. For there is also the secondary interest of the book, which is to reveal to us the condition of women, . . . the small choice that Moll could have made between disreputable and reputable enjoyment. The infant Moll, born in Newgate, becomes a public charge; education is an impossibility; independent work is likewise an impossibility; and as young men are by nature wolves, so the world at large is wolfish. Women, like men, are forced into the realm of trade, they offer such goods as they have for such prices as they can command.

This secondary interest suggests the softer side of Daniel Defoe, his will to create a less savage world than the world he knew. The paradox of the middle class has always been its hope to create, through its values of mere measurement, values that did not have to measure in its way. And the social pathos of *our* lives is largely to be traced to our illusion that we have done so. This is also the final pathos of Moll Flanders' life, whether Defoe was aware of it or not.

Mark Schorer
*Thought* (June, 1950), pp. 285-86

But in the novel which stands second only to *Crusoe, The Fortunes and Misfortunes of Moll Flanders,* Defoe used his method not to make the incredible credible but to reveal the absorbing interest of the ordinary, the completely unromantic. Moll Flanders is anything but an admirable woman; she has been many times married, not by any means always legally, she is a thief and a pickpocket. But she is still one of the most vibrantly living characters in fiction, and, even more than Crusoe himself, she is Defoe's greatest triumph of impersonation. In a sense, *Moll Flanders* is what today we would call a sociological novel: Moll has never had a chance; circumstances have made her what she is—as Defoe himself might have said that circumstances over which he could have no control had made him what he was. And she is certainly like her creator in one vital respect, which lifts her right above the sordid details of her life and gives her perennial attractiveness: no matter how much circumstances are against her, she can't be kept down; she bobs up again with no self-pity, with a perky cheerfulness and a resolve to behave better in the future. She is indomitable. And, like Crusoe, she is a universal figure; we must all, if we are honest, recognize ourselves in her, not so much in what she does as in the reasons she produces for her behaviour, the dishonest, self-comforting reasons the psychologists call rationalizations.

Walter Allen
*Six Great Novelists* (London: Hamish Hamilton, 1955), p. 35

The great innovation in Defoe's first social novel was not in his vivid portrayal of the expert pickpocket and the accomplished prostitute, remarkable as this is in its way. It was not even in his account of the new life that beckoned in a new land—although no other writer of the age gave so encouraging and yet so realistic an account of the advantages a transported felon might have if he thought of himself as a colonist who might acquire a stake in the land of his enforced adoption. So far this would be the Crusoe story in another guise, with transportation serving instead of shipwreck, and with a thinly settled colony replacing the desert island.

Defoe's originality appeared more clearly in his going back to the beautiful little girl long before she acquired the notorious name of Moll Flanders—the innocent but sensuous Betty, born in Newgate to a mother who escaped hanging only because of the expected birth of her child. The crime for which Betty's mother was convicted, and which shaped little Betty's future life, was the stealing of three pieces of holland from a mercer in Cheapside—"a petty theft, scarce worth naming."

John Robert Moore<br>
Daniel Defoe (Chicago: Univ. Chicago Pr., 1958), p. 243

## Robinson Crusoe

Due in part no doubt to Defoe's dependence upon authentic narratives, whether of history or of travel, are the structural defects of his plots; that is to say, those features which appear to be defects in the light of more recent development of plot construction. He writes in imitation of true records. If the narratives of the military careers of the Cavalier and of Carleton are to pass as authentic, they must resemble history; if "Robinson Crusoe" and "Captain Singleton" are to receive credence they must resemble the genuine accounts of travellers and adventurers. Obviously these genuine records, whether of military activity or of travel, have little to offer as models of well designed plot. . . .

The fact that Defoe is attempting to have his stories pass as authentic relations means that he must give the larger features of history and of geography with fidelity. . . . When he fabricates the journal of an imaginary saddler who endured the rigors of the great plague, or describes fictitious exploits of Carleton in the wars of Flanders, Defoe incorporates in the narrative a large proportion of authentic happenings; not to do so would lay him open to immediate detection as a writer of fiction. Where does he get those facts? He borrows them from histories and newspapers. In the invention of action the writer of historical fiction is always limited more or less to matters in which he will not seriously conflict with the statements of history.

It is evident that Defoe had no conscious intention of constructing what we now mean by plot. For the account of Crusoe's journey through Tartary and Muscovy, he consulted but one source, taking therefrom fact after fact without any great effort to transform them; the narrative, consequently, suffers a distinct loss of interest.

Arthur W. Secord
*Studies in the Narrative Method of Defoe* (Urbana, Ill.:
Univ. Illinois Pr., 1924), pp. 232-33

The Key to the Allegory is very simple. The whole of Defoe's life is given us in the Crusoe story. *He merely antedates every event in his own life 29 years, and represents it by some adventure of Crusoe's at that time.* Thus Defoe was born in 1661, Crusoe in 1632. Defoe left college and went out into the world in 1680, Crusoe goes out in 1651. Defoe's first political publication . . . was in 1687, on the eve of the Revolution. This beginning of his isolation corresponds with Crusoe's shipwreck . . . in 1658. . . . Why he chose 29 as the key number is not easy to say.

To return to the details of the correspondence. Both Defoe and Crusoe went out into the world at the same age after offending their fathers. Defoe's parents wished him to enter the ministry at the end of his course at Newington College, 1651/1680, but his advice and persuasions were useless, and Defoe like Crusoe chose a path for himself which was thorny enough. In the seven years before their final isolation and shipwreck both got into difficulties . . . Defoe's chief quarrel with his friends, when he made a final shipwreck of his character and commenced his political career, began with the royal Declaration of Indulgence, 1658/1687. . . . Crusoe began his lonely life on his 26th birthday, 1658/1687, and he had to work hard for his living, for most of his goods and all his friends were lost. His first year of solitude pictures the stirring times of the Revolution. The earthquake in April and the hurricane which broke up the old ship point to the second Declaration, the revolt, and the flight of the King. . . . Crusoe's tame goats are his publications, and the dates of these agree with what is known from other sources. The first was the attack on the Declaration, 1658/1687. The second, "A New Discovery of an old Intrigue," came out in 1661/1690, when Crusoe got his second goat in his third year on the island. In 1697 he published three more books, and from that time every year saw a crop of pamphlets, newspapers, histories and essays. Crusoe accordingly says that in his eleventh year, 1668/1697, he captured three more, which multiplied so fast that he soon had some scores of them. . . .

Crusoe gets away from the island at last just as Defoe escapes from isolation now that the Protestant Succession is established, for which he had quarrelled with friend and foe for 28 years.

George Parker
*History* (April, 1925), pp. 17-19, 22, 23

Although Defoe claimed in the *Serious Reflections* that *Robinson Crusoe* was in part an allegory of his own life, attempts to connect details in the book with specific experiences in the life of Defoe have not been found convincing. Complicated as the connection is between Defoe's life and his works, I believe that the claim may yet be found valid if we look at the book as a symbolic account of a spiritual experience rather than a kind of cipher of its author's life.

. . . *Robinson Crusoe* is far more than the account of a practical man's adjustment to life on a deserted island. Side by side with Crusoe's physical conquest of nature is his struggle to conquer himself and to find God. It is really a conversion story . . . with the classic symptoms of supernatural guidance (in this case in a dream), penitential tears, and Biblical text. Despite repeated signs and warnings, Crusoe only gradually awakens to the necessity for salvation; and it is not until in his illness he stumbles to the tobacco box and comes upon the Bible that he crosses the hump. The final stage is his realization that his deliverance from the island is unimportant in comparison with his deliverance from sin through the mercy of God. . . . From this point on, his mind is essentially at peace, and the remainder of his autobiography is in the nature of an account of the due rewards and powers of the man who has been saved.

Edwin B. Benjamin
*PQ* (April, 1951), pp. 206, 207

One of the reasons for the canonization of *Robinson Crusoe* is certainly its consonance with the modern view that labour is both the most valuable form of human activity in itself, and at the same time the only reliable way of developing one's spiritual biceps. Defoe's version of this attitude is at times overtly religious in tone. Crusoe's successful improvisations, his perfectly controlled economy, foreshadow his ultimate standing in the divine design. Defoe has taken the idea from his own dissenting milieu, and from its conduct books, . . . and given it a fascinating narrative form.

Ian Watt
*EIC* (April, 1951), p. 105

## GENERAL

Defoe is not among the great creators of character. So far as any of his figures come to life, it is through their being chips of himself. His two Quakers are perhaps an exception, and they probably originated in other heads. The subtleties of personal disposition, the arcana of temperament, the inner world of the feelings, were to him a sealed book. All his men and women are extremely simple and strikingly bare of idiosyncrasy. He certainly did not exhibit any remarkable intuition of feminine character in

Moll Flanders or Roxana, both admirably commonplace women. The art of life-like and expressive dialogue he never mastered. It cannot be mastered without a finer psychology than he knew. The conversations in his *Journal of the Plague Year* are more natural than his average, perhaps because the theme had gripped him; but, as a rule, he failed to get out of the old rut, and remained stiff and conventional. It is, above all else, in his superlative excellence as a story-teller that his power consists; it is in the shape of narrative that he presents his view of the world. Nothing holds the imagination like straightforward narrative. Defoe gave us human histories, not galleries of human characters. He put the interest not in personal traits, but in what the people of the story do and undergo, and what effect it has upon their lives. And since he always seems to be speaking the unvarnished truth, his people, what they do and what befalls them, and the world in which they move, seem as actual as the world of our own sensations.

Ernest A. Baker
*The History of the English Novel* (London:
H. F. and G. Witherby, 1929), vol. III, p. 229

Of all his impersonations, or creations, the one who comes closest to Daniel Defoe is perhaps the saddler in his *Journal of the Plague Year*. Here he is attempting less disguise; the saddler belongs to the same class, the same sex, and the same moral order as Defoe himself. But one suspects, too, that there was a good deal of him in Moll Flanders. She has the jolly facetious air that Defoe so often assumed in the most vigorous years of his *Review;* she keeps her spirits up, she never stands upon her dignity, she is thoroughly human. She can tell us undoubtedly a great deal about the man who created her, and what she tells us is almost all to his credit. The writer of *The Family Instructor* and of *Religious Courtship* might be merely a prig or a hypocrite; but the author of *Moll Flanders* has proved his humanity. He has shown beyond all possible doubt the kindliness and tolerance that lay behind the stiff front of his nonconformity. And he has shown that not all his queer dealings with Robert Harley and the prevarications forced upon him by circumstances have been able to destroy his intellectual honesty. He can still look facts in the face. There is nothing that he better likes doing.

It is here, indeed, that his claims to being an artist, so grudgingly admitted by some of his biographers, become most apparent. He took a quite un-puritanical delight in experience for its own sake. He enjoyed the mere variety of human life, the bustle of active people, the shopkeeper scratching his head with his pen, the fine lady cheapening a piece of silk, the beggar limping by on his crutches, the stir and commotion of market-day in a small town, the forest of shipping on the river at Gravesend. For all his

Puritanism—and even when he is writing in his most practical and improving manner—those things keep breaking in.

James Sutherland
*Defoe* (Philadelphia: J. B. Lippincott, 1938), pp. 244-45

Defoe's reputation as a writer and a man (and the two are hard to
separate) has had a curious and fluctuating history; but the extreme estimate of his unreliability is now much out of date. If the literary convention
that demanded the appearance of truth is recognized, the skill and energy
with which Defoe satisfied it can be praised. His art as a novelist, it is
often said, was to make fiction as real as fact. Looked at another way, it
was to translate fact into fiction. Investigation tends more and more to
uncover the solid material, in something experienced or something read,
with which he built and ornamented his narratives. In a busy and varied
career he can have wasted little. A detail recaptured is as bright as new,
and it sparkles still for us. For that very reason, perhaps, we judge his
occasional lapses from historical or autobiographical truth more severely.
The inaccuracies and inventions in the *Journal of the Plague Year* may
affront our ideas of historical method. But consider that remarkable work
—one of several in which Defoe treated of the supernatural—the *True
Relation of the Apparition of Mrs. Veal*. This was celebrated by Sir Walter
Scott and other[s] as a work of fiction put out as fact, a brilliant device to
serve as a puff for a fellow-writer. It has since been proved to have been
indeed a true relation of evidence, a straightforward piece of reporting on
a matter of topical and popular interest.

Francis Watson
*Daniel Defoe* (London: Longmans, Green, 1952), p. 29

What places Defoe in the picaresque tradition is his anti-romantic, anti-
feudal realism, his concern with the feel and texture of the life he conveys
and his lack of pattern. It is not true to say that there is no pattern in
any of Defoe's novels, but certainly there is not the kind of concern which
infuses and shapes the moral fable. Defoe's novels are not illustrations.
He is careful to point out the moral, insistent in his claim to be instructing
the reader, but in fact the insistence is quite bogus. There is no "moral
discovery" to be made in *Moll Flanders* for all the moral talk. . . . There
is a tentative sort of pattern, the pattern of a man's or woman's life. The
shape of these books is the shape of their heroes' existence. We follow
them from birth to old age and even the most immense section, like
Crusoe's time on the island, has the status of an episode. This is something
rather different from the early "rogue" novels in which there is no attempt
thus to see a man's life whole, and this biographical element in Defoe has
its importance. It corresponds to the bourgeois—as opposed to the feudal

—way of looking at the world, this sense of life's being what a man makes it, this essentially individualistic attitude to existence.

Arnold Kettle
*An Introduction to the English Novel* (New York:
Harper and Row, 1960), pp. 55-56

# JOHN DRYDEN
1631-1700

Born of a Puritan family, Dryden was educated at Westminster School and Trinity College, Cambridge, from which he was graduated in 1654. He was in London three years later, producing *Heroic Stanzas* to the memory of Oliver Cromwell and the following year *Astraea Redux* for the restoration of Charles II. He turned primarily to plays (with attendant excursions into literary criticism) during 1666 through 1681, when the political satire *Absalom and Achitophel* heralded a new strain of poetic form. Dryden had been appointed poet laureate in 1668, and the issue of the early 1680's—the Popish Plot and the conspiracy of Monmouth to exclude the Duke of York from succession—offered immediate satiric subjects, in defense of Tory government. *Religio Laici* (1682) defended the Anglican Church, but perhaps through the accession of James II he turned to defend Roman Catholicism in *The Hind and the Panther* (1687). Replaced by Shadwell as poet laureate with the Glorious Revolution of 1688, he shifted his literary activity to translation of Ovid, Vergil, and Horace, among others.

E. N. Hooker and H. T. Swedenberg, Jr., eds., *Works* (1956-    )
James Kinsley, ed., *The Poems of John Dryden* (1958), 4 vols.
Charles E. Ward, *The Life of John Dryden* (1961)

## Essay of Dramatic Poesy

A great merit of Dryden as a critic and as a critical influence is that he never transgresses the line beyond which the criticisms of poetry become something else. In that happy age it did not occur to him to enquire what poetry was *for,* how it affected the nerves of listeners, how it sublimated the wishes of the poet, whom it should satisfy, and all the other questions which really have nothing to do with poetry as poetry; and the poet was not expected to be either a sibyl or a prophet. The purpose of poetry and drama was to *amuse;* but it was to amuse properly; and the larger forms of poetry should have a moral significance; by exhibiting the thoughts and passions of man through lively image and melodious verse, to edify and to refine the reader and auditor.

T. S. Eliot
*John Dryden* (New York: Terence and
Elsa Holliday, 1932), pp. 64-65

In the same year that Dryden published *The Rival Ladies* [1664], with its prefatory defence of rhyme in serious plays, Samuel Sorbière published his *Voyage to England* and raised a storm of indignation, which was embarrassing to the Royal Society because he had been "admitted a member". . . . The issues raised here concern the rejection of the unities and decorum as well as the use of rhyme. Rhyme is rejected by the English because it is neither natural nor pleasing. The English . . . are open to attack because they are nonconformists to European dramatic standards. . . .

If Sorbière may be said to have initiated the occasion for the *Essay,* and the *Essay* itself may be allowed to reveal an appropriate orientation, the question may then be asked why Dryden delayed its publication from 1665-6, the apparent date of composition, until 1668. The most obvious answer is supplied by the Plague and Fire. Actually the *Essay* was entered in the Stationers' Register, 7th August 1667, and thus was probably intended for publication in the same year as the *Annus Mirabilis*. . . . No doubt Dryden wrote the *Essay* chiefly to explore and define his own theories of dramatic art—not without regard to the taste of the Court, to which he owed so much—and his recent success with *The Indian Empress* encouraged him to undertake it.

George Williamson
*Seventeenth Century Contexts* (London: Faber and Faber, 1960), pp. 273, 276, 285-87

## POEMS

Dryden's lyrics have been praised, and justly, for the variety of their harmony. Dryden and his fellows among Restoration song-writers are the last of a long tradition. And yet . . . he is also the first writer of operatic songs, glittering rhetoric for musical elaboration. *Alexander's Feast* is a brilliant *tour de force,* the finest piece of noise in English poetry till we come to Mr. Vachel Lindsay, and there is more of true poetry in the *Chinese Nightingale* than in all Dryden's Odes, which are surely not great odes in the same sense as *Intimations of Immortality, Dejection,* or *The West Wind,* or the *Nightingale.*

Satire is admittedly Dryden's vogue, and one may allow that Dryden was quite sincere in his defence of authority and contempt for the mob. Yet even as a satirist one feels that Dryden's art is greater than the temper that informs it. . . . With Dryden it is all business, admirable in execution. . . . Thus Dryden's most serious and ambitious effort [*The Hind and the Panther*], a poem full of just sentiments and eloquent writing, abounding in art of a kind, is yet a poem written to order, wanting in conviction. Dryden would have better served his cause, in great measure a just cause, by less wit and adroitness, less of politics, and more of religious conviction.

No English poet of anything like the same genius and talent has suffered so obviously from . . . spiritual emptiness, . . . [meaning] not . . . that he did not write specifically religious poetry, but that he had no sense of the ideal, the poetical aspect of any subject on which he wrote—nature, character, politics, or religion.

Herbert J. C. Grierson
*Cross-Currents in 17th Century English Literature* (London: Chatto and Windus, 1929), pp. 325, 327-28

The Pyrrhonistic defense of faith supports the whole logical structure, and inspires the loftiest poetical flights, of both of Dryden's poems on religion. It prompts the slow and solemn rhythms of the opening lines of *Religio Laici*. . . . In *The Hind and the Panther* the argument is extended, in defense of transubstantiation, to a questioning of sense as well as of reason. . . . The identity of thought in the two poems is so close that the second, almost unavoidably, repeats some of the first. . . . The fact that Dryden's polemics in the second poem are directed at the church to which he adhered when he wrote the first, should not be permitted to obscure the consistency of the purely philosophical content of both. In *Religio Laici* he was defending Christian revelation against Deism. The greatest pagan philosophers, he said, have not been able to find the true source of human happiness; the Deist is presumptuous in asserting that there is a universal religion of prayer and praise discoverable by the reason of man. . . . But in *The Hind and the Panther* the polemic is Roman Catholic, and directed against the rationalistic principle inherent in Protestantism. It is true that the long discourse on reason is, in appearance, aimed at Socianism; but Dryden, like the other Catholic controversialists of his time, believed that Protestantism inevitably tended toward this heresy. . . . The second poem is imbued with the same anti-rationalism as the earlier; though Dryden had changed his church allegiance, he had not changed his fundamental philosophical convictions. His criticism of Protestant principles in 1687 is only a more extended application of his animadversions against Deism in 1682.

Louis I. Bredvold
*The Intellectual Milieu of John Dryden* (Ann Arbor, Mich.: Univ. Michigan Pr., 1934), pp. 122-25

Whether Dryden brought English poetry back to the main stream of tradition is an academic question, but an interesting one. It has to be considered in the light of  actual accomplishment, which determines tradition much more than abstract critical principles. From the point of view of the latter it is all too easy to say that Dryden checked the extravagance of the metaphysicals and brought poetry back into line with the greatest poetry of the past, such poetry as Drummond had in mind when he objected to metaphysical quiddities. Yet Donne's greatness stares us in the face. The most sensible course is to recognize that tradition itself is nothing more or less than great poetry. Whatever poetry has the truth and beauty to live beyond its own time establishes a place for itself in the line of tradition. Donne, Milton, and Dryden are the three great poets of the seventeenth century. In what way is one of them more a part of tradition than another?

. . . What had poetry lost by discarding the metaphysical style? It had lost its subtlety, its indirection, its hidden layers of reference; it had lost its consciousness of the other world, with its finespun intangibilities; it had lost its sensibility, the amazing range of its feelings and moods, from the heavy and gross to the almost imperceptibly light and transient; it had also lost its subjectivity, its psychological intricacies, its puzzling individual patterns of logic. And in losing these qualities it had shed its obscurity, harshness, and extravagance.

And what had poetry gained? It had gained a certain detached point of view. More aloof than the metaphysicals, and consequently calmer and more reasonable, the neoclassicists looked on life from a vantage ground; they had a norm, a standard to judge things by, to judge even individuals by, as they were judged themselves. The fixing of a norm sharpened their sense of the ridiculous, it made satire possible, it added a new kind of awareness to life to replace what was lost, even while its main function was to make people conform to a pattern. Poetry gained in clarity of meaning and precision; the thing uttered had one meaning, clear and unambiguous. Poetry also gained a greater sense of form through its respect for regularity and well-marked boundaries. . . . Most important of all, poetry had gained a sense of social responsibility.

Robert L. Sharp
*From Donne to Dryden* (Chapel Hill, N. C.:
Univ. North Carolina Pr., 1940), pp. 210-11

It is perhaps easier to bury Dryden than to praise him: so much depends on the tradition we choose to place him in and on the standards by which we measure poetic success. If we follow Dr. Johnson and set Dryden in the succession of Waller and Denham, we arrive at a pious tribute to the "reformer of our numbers." If we follow Dr. Leavis and trace "the line of wit," we bring out Dryden's undeniable limitations as compared with Donne or Marvell. . . . But if we are to make a positive estimate of Dryden's achievement, we should include in his ancestry English poets of the earlier and later Renaissance and their ancient predecessors, and we need to maintain a keen sense of what Dryden accomplished for his contemporaries. So viewed, Dryden marks the reaffirmation of "Europe" in English poetry and culture after an experiment in insularity and at a time of artificial essays in continental "Classicism."

. . . Why may we reasonably describe this success as "European"? Not simply because Dryden's satiric mode was widely and often precisely allusive to European writers and styles and to English writers who were most consciously European in their styles and critical standards. Nor simply because he satisfied a Continental standard of literary craft, although this is significant. But rather because he brought the larger light of European literature and a European past into verse of local public debate. He invited his readers, including Nonconformists, to take a less parochial attitude toward the persons and events of contemporary history.

Reuben A. Brower<br>
ELH (March, 1952), pp. 38, 46-47

Dryden makes it clear from his prefatory account of *Annus mirabilis* that he attempted to follow classical example. The same desire underlay his satires, and we are therefore justified in inquiring to what extent these poems embody the main features of classical pictorialism. We should also observe that in drawing the analogy between painting and satire, Dryden followed the example of Marvell and other seventeenth-century satirists, who had used this parallel frequently enough to make it a convention.

The motto of *Absalom and Achitophel* is inadvertently significant. The sentence "Si propius stes, / Te capiat magis" immediately follows the famous words *ut pictura poesis* in the *Ars poetica* and begins Horace's famous comparison of painting and poetry. The motto also suggests strongly that one is to view this poem as one views a picture in a gallery. . . .

What does the analogy imply? Principally, what the motto suggests: that the poem, taken as a whole, should be viewed as a painting. We have already seen that the pictorialist tradition contained implications for poetic form and that in antiquity there was created and in the seventeenth century there was further developed what we have called the picture-gallery type of structure, in which we move from scene to scene, tableau to tableau. . . . "Absalom and Achitophel" stands in precisely that tradition. Neither a narrative sequence of Aristotelian complication, development, and resolution nor an argument moving deductively from general thesis to exemplum or inductively from premise to conclusion, the poem is a *display* of personages whose mental and physical measure is being taken and who reveal their character in what they are seen to be and heard to say.

The massing of particulars on this crowded canvas is more dramatically conceived than the comments have so far revealed. It is not only that the eye and mind move from one individual to another. Opposing groups that include the individual figures are arrayed against each other and are portrayed in separate and contradictory motion: the downward motion of conspiracy, which could bring destruction to the whole fabric of society, and the ennobling and socially redemptive motion of loyal men looking upward to their divinely appointed ruler. Dryden has given us a "Last Judgment," or at least a "Judgment." He distributes reward and punishment. In Achitophel we see Satan and in David, Christ; and Christ stands over the people forgiving when he can, condemning when he must. Unlike Milton's epic, which he everywhere echoes, Dryden's is not a narrative with supporting visual particulars; it is a pageant with interpretive comment.

Jean H. Hagstrum
*The Sister Arts* (Chicago: Univ. Chicago Pr., 1958), pp. 180-81

Appreciation of the devastating satire of *MacFlecknoe* should not be allowed to blind us to its sheer comedy. It is one of the few poems that Dryden wrote for his own satisfaction, and there is no doubt that he enjoyed himself. His delight is evident everywhere, in the brilliant imagery lavished on Shadwell . . . or in the hilarious couplet of advice which Flecknoe bestows on his successor. . . . Throughout the poem there is an element of imaginative fantasy surpassed in *The Rape of the Lock* but lacking in many parts of the *Dunciad*. Shadwell is a *creation* in a sense in which Cibber is not. *MacFlecknoe* is not only a satire: it is also a comedy. Mere scorn withers. It is the ironic sympathy in Dryden's poem, the mischievous joy in contemplation, that gives life to a creature of the comic imagination. Shadwell takes his place as a member of the same company as Sir John Falstaff himself.

Ian Jack
*Augustan Satire* (Oxford Univ. Pr., 1952), pp. 51-52

## Ode to Mrs. Anne Killigrew

The music of Dryden's ode, like its invention and its imagery, is true to neo-classical principles of formal design. Its beauty is inherent in the pure metrical pattern of the ode itself, objectively conceived, in the varied cadences of the lines within the stanza. It is conceived and managed with perfect artifice. To my ear, despite its fine numerousness, it never, like his lines on Oldham, takes emotion from its theme.

The ode on Mrs. Killigrew is at once illustrative of the grandeur of Dryden's analysis and reconstitution of the great formal genres of literature, and of the thin spiritual air he often had to breathe in his perennial struggle between the fading mediaeval world and the rising world of science and social enlightenment, in the midst of the disillusion of the first Stuart courts. Sometimes he failed to find a soul to inform what he designed, leaving it as yet only a bodily essence. But he maintained in England the tradition of high poetry. And it was by no trivial ideal of expression but by a profound sense of the forms of great poems that, even where he could not succeed himself he had left so much ready to the imaginations of those who followed.

Ruth Wallerstein
*SP* (July, 1947), pp. 527-28

[*Ode on Anne Killegrew*] is built on the two themes of earth and heaven, which themselves are linked by the commonplace that earthly poetry partakes of the divine; and it evolves as follows. The first stanza gives the three main themes: poetry, for Anne Killigrew is even now singing; heaven and earth, for she sings in some heavenly region, while her earthly songs served as prelude and probation for the heavenly music. The second stanza has the same mixture of theme but with the emphasis on earth and her prenatal poetical antecedents. By immediate heredity she comes of poetical stock, by reincarnation from Sappho. The stanza ends with heaven. Anne Killigrew's is too pure a soul to suffer further incarnation: when she has ceased listening to the poem now addressed to her she must return to the quire of heavenly singers. The third stanza again contains all three themes but with emphasis on heaven, which celebrated her birth with joy. This pure heavenly rejoicing suggests its contrary in stanza four, the general impurity of contemporary poetry; and the pessimistic satirical and urgent tone contrasts finely with the serene static tone of the first three stanzas. It comes to rest on Anne Killigrew and the thought that she was both an exception and an atonement. In so doing it introduces the body of the ode, stanzas five to eight, which deal with the lady's attainments on earth. Heaven is kept in the background, and we hear of her successes in poetry and in painting and of her untimely death. Death leads to mourning, and in stanza nine her brother's sorrow when he learns the news is conjectured. But he is at sea and has no news. Only, if sailorlike he scans the stars, he might notice a new bright member of the Pleiades—the star which is his sister's soul. This mention of the stars is the return of the theme of heaven; and it leads to the last stanza, where poetry, heaven, and earth are brought together in the description of the opening graves and the Last Judgment with Anne Killigrew leading the poets, the first souls to join their resurrected bodies, to their heavenly mansion.

E. M. W. Tillyard
*Five Poems* (London: Chatto and Windus, 1948), pp. 50-51

## Religio Laici

This [*Religio Laici*] is not, when analysed, convincing theological argument —Dryden was no theologian—but it is first-rate oratorical persuasion; and

Dryden was the first man to raise oratory to the dignity of poetry, and to descend with poetry to teach the arts of oratory; and to do any one thing with verse better than anyone else has done it, at the same time that one is the first to attempt it, is no small achievement. But it is not only by biting passages like this that a poem of Dryden's succeeds, but by a perfect lifting and lowering of his flight, in a varied unity without monotony. . . .

The main point, which I wish to drive home about Dryden is this: that it was Dryden who for the first time, and so far as we are concerned, for all time, established a *normal* English speech, a speech valid for both verse and prose, and imposing its laws which greater poetry than Dryden's might violate, but which no poetry since has overthrown. The English language as left by Shakespeare, and within much narrower limits, by Milton, was a language like the club of Hercules, which no lesser strength could wield; so I believe that the language after Shakespeare and Milton could only have deteriorated until some genius appeared as great as they—or indeed, greater than they: for the language would have been quickly in a far worse case than that in which Shakespeare found it. It was Dryden, more than any other individual, who formed a language possible for the mediocrity, and yet possible for later great writers to do great things with.

T. S. Eliot
*John Dryden* (New York: Terence and
Elsa Holliday, 1932), pp. 17-18, 21-22

In *Religio Laici* we find four modes of thinking specified in which, Dryden is convinced, human reason has failed. First of all, the great philosophic systems, constructed with the utmost of human ingenuity, fall short of religion in accounting for the origin of the world and of the life in it; the best of the philosophers merely guessed, and his guess was no better than that of Epicurus, whose world consisted of an infinity of atoms whirling, bumping in infinite space until some of them, by merest chance, leap into a common rhythm and an intelligible form. Philosophic systems, again, have failed in defining the way to happiness, for they have all attempted to comprehend the *summun bonum* in the formula for adjustment, instead of recognizing that, except on a purely bovine level, men are incapable of happiness unless their imagination and faith are touched and informed.

The second abuse of human reason is represented by the Deists, to whose position Dryden devotes much of the first half of the poem. The summary of the Deists' tenets is given in terms which make it clear that the poet is thinking of Lord Herbert of Cherbury's five common notions. He has no objections to the beliefs of Deism; he merely intimates that unaided reason is given rather too much credit. The error of the Deist is the belief that nothing of unique value is embedded in tradition or history, that it is possible to wipe the slate clean (as Descartes did) and start all over again, and by the pure exercise of reason to discover "all ye know, and all ye need to know."

The third abuse of reason involves an excessive reliance on tradition, combined with the assumption that under certain circumstances reason may determine infallibly which elements in tradition are valid. The error consists in dogmatic certainty in an area in which certainty is inadmissible.

The fourth abuse of reason occurs in what Dryden describes as the operations of "the private spirit." The error grows, first, out of the assumption that the conclusions of individual reason, even when it is exercised without training and without knowledge, are precious discoveries; and, secondly, out of the belief that in areas where mathematical certainty is not to be expected, there is no real knowledge and that, therefore, one man's conviction is bound to be as valid as anyone else's.

Edward N. Hooker<br>
ELH (September, 1957), pp. 183-84

## PLAYS

*The Wild Gallant* is the last comedy in the *précieuse* manner before the date of Etherege's first play. The testimony of these comedies readily convinces us of the strength of social sympathies between court society just before the civil war and court society just after the Restoration. Various interregnum writers had made the transition an easy one. Loveby and Isabelle in *The Wild Gallant* still quote Suckling, with a pleasant familiarity which suggests that Dryden's audience continued to cherish the memory of the greatest of cavalier wits. In the same play Dryden renews and amplifies with animation and charm the best features of earlier *précieuse* comedy and in so doing defines, to a considerable degree, the comic program of Etherege and of Congreve.

Kathleen M. Lynch<br>
The Social Mode of Restoration Comedy (New York:<br>
Macmillan, 1926), pp. 135-36

The blank verse of *All for Love* is not the heroic couplet gone flabby for want of rhyme, nor is it an uncontrolled instrument for rant and gaudy rhetoric. It is remarkable, in view of the similarities in plot with the heroic play, that there should be so few traces of those brisk paradoxes and tight antitheses which seemed so inseparable a complement of the situation in the language. Occasionally in such a phrase as Ventidius' "You speak a hero, and you move a god," traces of the couplet style appear, and something of the antithetical pointing up of a dilemma occasionally survives in a speech like that of Dollabella when he considers betraying his friend. . . . To appreciate further the transformation in style which this play represents, it should be noted that this speech occurs in the only interview between Octavia and Cleopatra, one of those contentions between rival interests which customarily called forth the fullest display of rhetorical brilliance in the heroic play. This verse has the clarity which training in the couplet might have produced, and the discipline; but it has ease and suppleness as well. It is a fine medium capable of absorbing the strain that any dramatic necessity can place upon it.

Moody E. Prior
*The Language of Tragedy* (New York: Columbia
Univ. Pr., 1947), pp. 196-97

The next several years saw no gay couples, save for two feeble examples in tragicomedies. And then came *Marriage A-la-Mode,* December 1671. Here are no actions leading to an agreement to marry, but in the comic scenes of this play Dryden constructs a situation which anatomizes the code of the period more deeply than in any other of his comedies.

As has been made clear, it was a fundamental of that code to doubt "true love," and to rail at marriage. Of course the gallants were fond of crying it down . . . but such arguments . . . could be discounted as a species of special pleading, not to be taken too seriously. There were, however, valid arguments against the institution. Some were those set forth by Wildish and Olivia in *The Mulberry-Garden.* Compared to that free state in which, not having committed oneself, one was still free to do so, marriage could scarcely seem desirable. And there was the frequency—patent to all observers—with which marriages failed. The fashionable theory is thus that if a man carries, under the stress of—say—what Celadon felt for Florimel [in Dryden's *Secret Love*], the very compulsion of the bond will kill the love of the couple for each other: they will cease to care for each other, merely because they can have none but each other.

Rhodophil in *Marriage A-la-Mode* is a devout believer in this doctrine, for, after a half-year of marriage to Doralice, it has apparently come true in his case. He and Doralice have gone the way of all flesh, as the world of fashion held it to be—at least they are on the point of doing so. For, although excessively polite to each other in company, in private they have come to treat each other with nagging or studied indifference. Rodophil has already commenced a flirtation with Melantha, an affected piece who has beauty but cannot compare with his wife in wit, sense, and charm; and Doralice, neglected, and conscious of not deserving to be, is already looking for someone to turn up. All of this is because Rhodophil is a slave to the mode. He confesses that he knows no fault in Doralice except that she is his wife. . . .

John H. Smith
*The Gay Couple in Restoration Comedy* (Cambridge, Mass.:
Harvard Univ. Pr., 1948), pp. 69-70

GENERAL

The reputation of Dryden as a poet is scarcely international. Where English is not spoken his name may be respected, but his poetry is seldom read. It is only a few poets who can be or need be translated. Dryden, in whom style was paramount, and whose manner proved generally incommunicable even to native successors, can hardly have expected to prevail in other tongues.

> Mark Van Doren
> *John Dryden, A Study of His Poetry* (New York:
> Henry Holt, 1920), p. 233

Dryden is undoubtedly the purest artist of all the Restoration writers of tragedy, besides being the most accomplished craftsman. It may be wondered why he, who stated expressly that plot was not merely a peg to hang fine things on, should so often have been contented with poor ones, until we remember that for him plot did not mean fable: it was definitely the arrangement of emotions that he meant. Although his work is pretty, it is strong and solid as well, as it had to be to make the grace bearable. He was an artist because his eye and his mind were always on the object made; the general moral of his work might be allowed to take care of itself, to filter in unconsciously through his general temper, which, if anything, was one of tolerant scepticism. . . . The great statement of tragedy, whether as drama or as novel, "This is what happens to man," hardly concerned him, and it is really this failure which keeps him out of the company of the very greatest. In truth, he was more eager to note, "This is what people are like or would wish to be like," which is the observation of a writer of comedy.

> Bonamy Dobrée
> *Restoration Tragedy, 1660-1720* (Oxford Univ.
> Pr., 1929), pp. 108-9

Too much can still be made, I think, of Dryden's debt to Waller and Denham, and to his contemporary Oldham. Oldham, certainly, is very near to him; Oldham is rough and unpolished, but occasionally in his "rugged line" there breaks out a vigour not unlike Dryden's. His satires are still readable. But to Waller and Denham, as practitioners of the heroic couplet, his debt can be exaggerated. As Pope says, "Waller was smooth," indeed, but his smoothness is feebleness, compared to anything accomplished by Dryden or Pope himself: the smoothness of an ambling pad-pony compared to that of a fiery horse with an expert rider. Waller mostly, and Denham except in one passage, send us to sleep; and Dryden never allows us to do that. I think that Dryden owes more to his reaction against the artifices of the late metaphysical verse, than to any sedulous study of Waller. For the content of his couplet, the sensibility which informs it, is as different from that of Waller as well could be.

T. S. Eliot
*John Dryden* (New York: Terence and
Elsa Holliday, 1932), pp. 10-11

# GEORGE ETHEREGE

1634?-1691?

> Little of a definite nature is known about Etherege's life. He was knighted and served the government as an envoy late in life. His comedies, with sections in rhymed heroic verse, set the mode for Restoration and eighteenth-century plays. *The Comical Revenge, or Love in a Tub* was produced in 1664. In 1668 appeared *She Would if She Could*, and eight years later his influential masterpiece *The Man of Mode*. The long periods between the plays indicate his casual, though significant, contribution to the theater.
>
> H. F. B. Brett-Smith, ed., *Works* (1927), 2 vols.

## PLAYS

Perhaps in grace and ease of diction *She Would if She Could* reveals the influence of Molière's drama. In spirit the play is more akin to Dryden's earlier plays. Indeed, the *beau monde* of *She Would if She Could* is distinctly the *beau monde* of *The Wild Gallant* and *Secret Love*, depicted, at last, with perfect clarity, and released, in the main, from superfluous and confusing farcical entanglements. Etherege's people of fashion enact with unswerving devotion a social rôle which is amply commended by its artificial elegance. So supreme has the new social mode become that it energizes the entire action of the play.

Kathleen M. Lynch
*The Social Mode of Restoration Comedy*
(New York: Macmillan, 1926), p. 149

With this comedy, Etherege reached his climax; regrettably it was also his last literary effort. *The Man of Mode* is the brightest, gayest, wittiest comedy produced in the Restoration proper. In its brittle, polished way, it is great. Less satiric than the best of Wycherley, less humorous than the best of Shadwell, less witty than the best of Congreve, it is nevertheless nearly perfect as an example of brisk, clever, comedy of manners.

There has been much useless breaking of brains over the questions whether Dorimant, the leading rake of the play, was designed to represent

Rochester, Dorset, or Etherege himself; Medley to represent Sir Charles Sedley, Fleetwood Shepherd, or Etherege himself; and Sir Fopling to stand for Sir George ("Beau") Hewitt, a pattern of Restoration foppery, or Etherege himself. The important fact is that Etherege, the complete courtier, had studied the Wits and their ladies so well that his idealized portraits are recognizable as the patterns of mannered, aristocratic society. Here is no question of realism; Etherege seized upon and embodied in his play not the real, day by day life of Whitehall, but the life which Whitehall was pleased to imagine it led. Individual items may be factual, but the total picture is a comic illusion.

J. Harold Wilson
*The Court Wits of the Restoration*
(Princeton, N.J.: Princeton Univ. Pr., 1948), pp. 163-64

In his three wit comedies, Etherege shows a progressive development in his art. *The Comical Revenge,* his first attempt at the comedy of wit, shows an uncertain mastery: the heroic-moral world is not properly subordinated, Wheadle and Dufoy are not perfect Witwouds, and Sir Nicholas is not a very amusing Witless. The Truewits are also deficient. . . . In the second comedy, *She Would if She Could,* Etherege successfully poked witty fun at the conventional notion of honor, in the person of Lady Cockwood, and he brought together a quartet of spirited Truewits. The wit in the play, however, seldom reaches a very high level: the repartees are characterized more by high spirits than by an original exchange of ideas; there is a preponderance of wit play over comic wit. . . .

The last play, *The Man of Mode,* is superior in every respect. Not only does it have a fine Witwoud in Sir Fopling Flutter, but it has three notable Truewits, in Dorimant, Harriet, and Medley, who are carefully distinguished by Etherege in terms of their wit: Dorimant is characterized by malice and judgment, Medley by fanciful and skeptical wit, and Harriet by natural, spontaneous wit.

Thomas H. Fujimura
*The Restoration Comedy of Wit*
(Princeton, N.J.: Princeton Univ. Pr., 1952), p. 115

. . . [*The Comical Revenge*] seems neither overpoweringly funny, nor startlingly new. It uses a number of Restoration devices developed before 1664: the witty lovers, the concentration upon the upper class, and the cynical, competent rake-hero. In many ways, moreover, it stands closer to Tudor-Stuart dramatic techniques than to those of the Restoration, particularly in the religious imagery of the high plot and the extended use of parallelism and analogy. Nevertheless, the play did, for those who first saw it, define a new comedy. Although the dominant humor of this new comedy was to be antiheroic, its techniques grow from the same sense of schism that shows in the rigid patterns of love and honor in heroic drama and the antithetical structure of heroic verse. Its cynicism is that of a disappointed idealist. Things are either perfect or awful: the hero, if he cannot be a heroic Cavalier, becomes a rake.

This antiheroic comedy found three characteristic devices of language and action. First, love is shown with a strong component of hostility or reluctance (a comic and truer version of the artificial love-honor conflicts of heroic drama). The lovers engage in a verbal duel, pretending indifference and comparing themselves to adversaries. Second, abstractions and ideals are converted downward into physical realities: love into sex, reputation into a possession, and so on. Finally, the outer appearance of a thing or person and its inner nature are shown as separate, indeed, inconsistent, and this division is seen as usually true, not an aberration that the action of the play corrects. The cuckold is not given justice as he would be in an Elizabethan play; rather Cully must set out to pass Frollick's ex-mistress off as an honest lady to his country neighbors.

Norman N. Holland
*The First Modern Comedies*
(Cambridge, Mass.: Harvard Univ. Pr., 1959), pp. 26-27

## GENERAL

. . . He is as little of the kindred of Moliere, whom he so clearly admired, as of Jonson, whom he so clearly displaced. There is nowhere the corrective laugh of the intellectual satirist. . . . There is nowhere the grave purpose and intentness of mind, which we find in comedies of the pattern of Moliere. The comedies of Etherege are the natural product of an age for which life was an accepted pageant, incuriously observed, uncritically accepted, stuff for a finished epigram. . . . He intercepted without effort for his immediate purpose the things that came to him, and gracefully encountered the one problem which his generation acutely recognised. . . . There was form; and there was bad form. The whole duty of man was to find the one, and to eschew the other. Etherege found a form for the spirit of his age; wherein . . . lies his unquestionable merit.

John Palmer
*The Comedy of Manners*
(London: G. Bell and Sons, 1913), pp. 90-91

Etherege . . . is a minor writer, in his exuberance nearer Mrs. Behn than to Congreve with his depth. But from another point of view he is far above all the other playwrights of his period, for he did something very rare in our literature. He presented life treated purely as an appearance: there was no more meaning in it apart from its immediate reactions than there is in a children's game. . . . This sort of comedy, while it is realistic in semblance, and faithfully copies the outward aspects of the time, creates an illusion of life that is far removed from reality. Here is no sense of grappling with circumstance, for man is unencumbered by thoughts or passions. . . . Nor is it life seen at a distance, but the forms of those known and liked seen intimately from a shady arbour in an old, sunny garden.

Bonamy Dobrée
*Restoration Comedy, 1660-1720*
(Oxford Univ. Pr., 1924), pp. 76-77

For it is always the woman who first falls in love, who tantalizes her victim until he becomes interested in her, who finally gets a declaration from him, and who melts not too easily into his arms at the last. This is Etherege's comic formula. . . . it is Etherege's distinction to have used it so persistently that we identify it with his notion of comedy.

He might begin with a practical joke, a thwarted intrigue, or a satire on contemporary manners; he always ended with a duel of sex. It is not sex treated in the heavy-handed emotional manner of the "problem play," but sex in its lighter and more impersonal aspect. He takes a man and a woman in love with one another, with no bars and impediments to their marriage except those set up by their own self-consciousness and pride—a much more common human situation than that developed by a serious triangular plot. These two lovers must have minds of a fine enough calibre to realize that people can, as in the higher levels of society they often do, wrap their true feelings in a cloak of words. The characters themselves need not appreciate the humour of such emotional evasions, but the author of their being must do so.

Henry T. E. Perry
*The Comic Spirit in Restoration Drama*
(New Haven: Yale Univ. Pr., 1925), pp. 31-32

Sir George Etherege, a typical gentleman of his time, turned to the writing of plays not as a serious pursuit, as had Jonson, but as a pastime and as a means of becoming known as a wit. . . . His plays were reactions to what he saw around him, but they must not be considered as propaganda for morals. It must be remembered that Etherege had no ethical principles to urge him to produce any satire for the correction of morals. Any contemporary satire in his plays is accidental. His purpose, in so far as he had a serious purpose, was to picture things in such a way that they would be amusing. The result is that his plays are works of art, designed only, to borrow Dryden's words, "to give delight." Thus they become the spontaneous productions of a man who was, as we have said, "too lazy and too careless to be ambitious."

F. S. McCamic [Tinker]
*Sir George Etherege, A Study in Restoration Comedy (1660-1680)*
(Cedar Rapids, Iowa: Torch Press, 1931), p. 55

This is . . . what constitutes the salient features of Etherege's comic writing: witty dialogue, especially between the gallant and his mistress in raillery and "proviso" scenes, a naturalistic view of man (and a consequent disregard of conventional morality), and realistic technique. These are the points in which Etherege excelled as a writer, though not every critic approved, as one gathers from . . . censure of Etherege for being too photographic in his realism. . . . What we should look for in Etherege's comedies, then, is not interest in "manners," but such features of wit comedy as witty dialogue, naturalistic content, and realistic technique. We should also expect malicious laughter at fools, and the expression of a skeptical and libertine philosophy in witty form.

Thomas H. Fujimura
*The Restoration Comedy of Wit*
(Princeton, N.J.: Princeton Univ. Pr., 1952), pp. 86-87

Etheregean comedy proposes its own order—its own set of realities and values. But as with all thoughtful comedy, the order emerges from the comic fact and form of man's inveterate disorder. The disorder is surely not confined to that of a specialized society. On the contrary, the wit by which that society most clearly announces its own special character becomes the principal vehicle for universalizing the comic ritual which the plays project. For the comedy, finally, is one in which not merely libertine but Christian, classical, "heroic," courtly, and honest-man postulates concerning the nature of man are brought to the test of human experience. And from this point of multiple vision, the comic ritual of the plays is primarily one in which man in the pride and assertiveness of his wit progressively reveals its and his own general insufficiency and confusion.

Dale Underwood
*Etherege and the Seventeenth-Century Comedy of Manners*
(New Haven: Yale Univ. Pr., 1957), pp. 109-10

# GEORGE FARQUHAR
1678-1707

A student at Trinity College, Dublin, an army officer, an actor, Farquhar became a dramatist with *Love and a Bottle* in 1699, followed by *The Constant Couple* (1699), *Sir Harry Wildair* (1701), *The Inconsant* (1702), *The Twin Rivals* (1702), *The Stage Coach* (1704), written with Peter Motteux, *The Recruiting Officer* (1706), and *The Beaux' Stratagem* (1707). He died in poverty shortly after his last play was produced.

Charles Stonehill, ed., *The Works of George Farquhar* (1930), 2 vols.

Willard Connely, *Young George Farquhar: the Restoration Drama at Twilight* (1949)

That Farquhar was the last of the comic dramatists, that he really succeeded Etherege and Wycherley, is one of those too obvious facts which invariably escape. Between the lines of most criticisms of the plays of Farquhar, more especially those which were written in the late nineteenth century—we detect an indulgence, a determination to make the most of his good, and the least of his bad qualities, which contrasts remarkably with the treatment usually bestowed upon his predecessors. The explanation of this is that Farquhar is invariably approached as a late nineteenth-century author, who, from youth, inexperience, hot blood, and high spirits, did not quite come off either morally or artistically. His heart is felt to be in the right place. He introduced, it is said, fresh air into the theatre. He took a serious interest in moral problems. The nauseous comedy of Wycherley; the heartless comedy of Congreve, is abandoned. Farquhar, in fact, has been treated as a reformer of the old theatre; and as the possible founder of a better type of play.

This is history inverted. When we come to consider his plays in detail we shall find in Farquhar precisely that acceptance of an outgrown convention which mars the comedy of Vanbrugh. Where the critics find in Farquhar humanity and fresh air we shall detect an emotional and romantic treatment of sex stifling the parent stem of a comedy whose appeal depended upon an entirely different system of moral and imaginative values. Farquhar's comedies are the direct result of an author, whose temperament and environment were not much unlike those of his nineteenth-century critics, trying to write comedies like Congreve. The consequent inconsistencies, often resulting in serious moral and artistic offence, are more patent than in Vanbrugh's case; for Farquhar was more careless a writer than his predecessor, and never really discovered in his art a neutral territory where the values he borrowed were reconciled with the values he contributed.

John Palmer
*The Comedy of Manners*
(London: G. Bell and Sons, 1913), pp. 242-44

It was in [1698] . . . that the *Short View of the Profaneness and Immoral-ity of the English Stage* [by Jeremy Collier] struck terror into the hearts of such essentially comic dramatists as Congreve and Vanbrugh; almost immediately a new ally for them appeared on the London boards in the person of Farquhar, whose *Love and a Bottle* was acted late in 1698 or early in 1699. . . . [After five more pieces] in 1706 he again made an important contribution to English dramatic literature. In fact, Farquhar's chief claim to fame rests upon his last two plays, *The Recruiting Officer*, produced in 1706, and *The Beaux-Stratagem*, acted in 1707. This last, his comic masterpiece, he composed while in a "settled sickness," which resulted in his death a few weeks after the première. His premature end has caused much idle speculation as to what he might have later accomplished, had his life been spared.

Henry T. E. Perry
*The Comic Spirit in Restoration Drama*
(New Haven: Yale Univ. Pr., 1925), pp. 107-8

So ended this extraordinarily *busy* play, busy as its author's own life at the moment of writing, a play percipient of the ways of human nature. Farquhar in spite of himself had nearly given way to the unity of time, compressing his whole sixteen scenes into a day or two. Its unity of place, in and about Shrewsbury, was also conspicuous. It was a comedy skilfully balanced in its components, though woven into a tapestry elaborate enough. Written in obvious high spirits, within a few weeks in the early winter of 1705-6, *The Recruiting Officer* expressed a joy of life not seen in Farquhar's work since his earliest effort, *Love and a Bottle,* and a freshness, an originality, a spontaneity, which only an absorbing knowledge of his material could have given him. Possibly the breezy rural surroundings of the Wrekin, instead of the congested rivalries of Covent Garden, lent him the impetus of novelty, as in his first play the novelty of writing at all had furnished his pen with a certain sparkle. Yet the germ of *The Recruiting Officer* lay definitely in *The Stage-Coach.* That playlet had unlocked the countryside to the genius of Farquhar, who has then only to hit upon a theme that was timely. When he had the luck to be sent away from London, he found his theme in his daily and hourly life. . . .

Otherwise the [*Beaux'*] *Stratagem* as written played on in its conquering course. Not the least of its strong points, still another hint, perhaps, taken by Farquhar from *The Stage-Coach,* was that it nowhere brought on a character in disguise. It was the first full-length comedy by this author so to be distinguished. . . . To do away with that facile but unconvincing device, bothersome to the audience and not too helpful to the actor involved, was itself a leap forward.

But it was the boldness of the moral in the *Stratagem* that broadly

pleased the town. This play, to the astonishment of everyone bred on
Wycherley and Congreve, had made morality actually an engaging theme.
. . . Beginning with *The Twin Rivals*, and to an increasing degree as he
produced his later comedies, he had almost broken away from the taint of
the age of Charles II. . . . Farquhar was discussing a deeper thing, the
question of right and wrong, and he did it not thumpingly, not in the rant-
ing manner, but in a way to make his new play chime in with the thoughts
of many a Londoner matrimonially askew.

Willard Connely
*Young George Farquhar*
(London: Cassell, 1949), pp. 247, 299

# HENRY FIELDING
## 1707-1754

> Born into an aristocratic family, Fielding studied law in Leyden, married
> in 1734 (his wife being the model for Sophia and Amelia), and became
> manager and chief playwright of the Haymarket after his legacy ran out.
> The licensing act of 1737 ended his theatrical career, and he returned to
> law at the Middle Temple, being called to the bar in 1740. He then edited
> a number of news magazines, wrote *Joseph Andrews* and *Jonathan Wild*,
> became a justice of the peace, and in 1749 produced *Tom Jones* and
> finally *Amelia*. His first wife dying in 1744, he remarried three years later.
> Because of illness he resigned his legal office in 1753, moving to Portugal
> where he died.
>
> Wesleyan Edition in progress, *The Works* (Vol. I, *Joseph Andrews*, ed.
> Martin C. Battestin, 1966)
>
> F. H. Dudden, *Fielding: His Life, Works and Times* (1952), 2 vols.

### Joseph Andrews

The characters and plot of *Joseph Andrews* mutually function to illustrate
the dominant thematic motifs of the novel, namely, the exposure of vanity
and hypocrisy in society, and the recommendation of their antithetical virtues—charity, chastity, and the classical ideal of life. The journey in *Joseph
Andrews* is not a mere picaresque rambling, a device solely for the introduction of new adventures such as we find in the *Roman comique, Gil Blas,*
or *Don Quixote*. The wayfaring of Fielding's heroes is purposeful, a moral
pilgrimage from the vanity and corruption of the Great City to the *relative*
naturalness and simplicity of the country. . . .

   The two heroes of *Joseph Andrews,* furthermore, are more than merely
a prudish young footman and a naive parson. They embody the essential
virtues of the good man—chastity and good nature. In accord with the

preference for Christian heroes found both in the tradition of the biblical epic and in the homilies . . . , the careers of Joseph Andrews and Abraham Adams comprise brilliantly comic analogues to those of their Scriptural namesakes, likewise patterns, according to the divines, of the good man's basic virtues. Joseph chastely resists the charms of his mistress and is at last reunited with the father from whom he had been kidnapped as a child. Brandishing his crabstick like a pilgrim's staff, Adams, the good patriarch and priest, travels homeward through strange and idolatrous countries, and is "tempted" by the near drowning of his son. The use of biblical analogues here, like the adaptation of the *Aeneid* in *Amelia,* is surprisingly subtle, contributing to the mock-heroic character of the novel while at the same time reminding readers of the function of Joseph and Adams as exemplars. Finally, Adams as the true Christian minister has a more specific role in Fielding's efforts to correct a growing popular contempt of the clergy.

Martin C. Battestin
*The Moral Basis of Fielding's Art*
(Middletown, Conn.: Wesleyan Univ. Pr., 1959), pp. 88-89

## Tom Jones

*Tom Jones* fully exemplifies Fielding's theory of the novel. To *Tom Jones* the "comic romance" theory applies as well as to *Joseph Andrews.* In addition, the rules introduced in *Tom Jones* are put in practice. Like the earlier novel it contains all the elements of the epic except numbers and differs from comedy as the serious epic differs from tragedy. The action covers the youth of its hero, from his birth until he is about twenty-one years of age, dealing with dozens of significant episodes during that period, comprehending everything of importance to the portrayal of Tom's character. This comedy could not do. Forty-four characters, at least twenty of whom are important to the story, appear in *Tom Jones,* in even greater variety than in *Joseph Andrews.* The fable and action are "light and ridiculous" in lesser degree than in *Joseph Andrews,* containing more of the "grave and solemn." The prevailing tone is still comic, however, and there is much ridicule of affectation. More instruction is to be found here than in *Joseph Andrews.*

Frederick O. Bissell, Jr.
*Fielding's Theory of the Novel*
(Ithaca, N.Y.: Cornell Univ. Pr., 1933), pp. 74-75

*Tom Jones* . . . is a classical example of a perfectly coherent story, most carefully planned from the very beginning, progressing slowly but surely through a succession of strictly relevant characters and events, and terminating in a logically appropriate catastrophe. No doubt it was mainly on account of his superb constructive art that Scott bestowed on Fielding the honourable title of "Father of the English Novel."

The unity of *Tom Jones* is not secured by mere limitation of the subject-matter. The book is a large, full, complex book, abounding in incidents and characters. There is certainly nothing meagre or contracted about it. The unity of the whole is achieved solely by means of a secure subordination of all the multitudinous details to the central plan. In the long and elaborate history hardly anything is found which does not in some way or other contribute to carry forward the main action to its conclusion.

F. Homer Dudden
*Henry Fielding: His Life, Works, and Times*
(Oxford: Clarendon Pr., 1952), vol. II, p. 616

We can thus indicate, in some degree, the aesthetic necessity of elaborate plot in Fielding's novel: the episodes must cumulate functionally toward a final, representative revelation of character; but, because the significance of this revelation is for all men in a given society, the episodes must illustrate subtle varieties of character and interaction, at the same time representing the complexities of human nature and contributing toward the final revelation which will be, although narrowed down to hero and villain, symbolic of all those complexities. The book must, therefore, have both variety of episode and "unity of action." But we must now describe the plot as it signifies a "theme" or "meaning." In *Tom Jones,* life is conceived specifically as a conflict between natural, instinctive feeling, and those appearances with which people disguise, deny, or inhibit natural feeling—intellectual theories, rigid moral dogmas, economic conveniences, doctrines of *chic* or of social "respectability." This is the broad thematic contrast in *Tom Jones.* Form and feeling ("form" as mere outward appearance, formalism, or dogma, and "feeling" as the inner reality) engage in constant eruptive combat, and the battlefield is strewn with a debris of ripped masks, while exposed human nature—shocked to find itself uncovered and naked—runs on shivering shanks and with bloody pate, like the villagers fleeing from Molly Seagrim in the famous churchyard battle.

Dorothy Van Ghent
*The English Novel: Form and Function*
(New York: Harper, 1953), pp. 67-68

Yet fine as *Joseph Andrews* and *Jonathan Wild* are, they scarcely prepare us for so great an achievement as *The History of Tom Jones,* which, after two centuries, remains among the handful of supreme novels. The new element in *Tom Jones* is Fielding's architectonic quality; no plot has ever been carried through with more consummate skill, and the skill can be truly appreciated only after the book has been closed. In reading, one is delighted with the swiftness of the narration, the economy, the nimble and inexhaustible invention. Fielding had learned much from his experience in the theater, especially how to break up the narrative, set his scene in a minimum of words, and carry on the action in short, swift passages of dialogue. But it is only after reading that we realize how every detail has its place in the action, is a preparation for what is to come, the full significance of which cannot be apparent until the novel has reached its end; then, what seemed at first glance a happy stroke of invention reveals itself as part of the essential structure of the book, without which the whole could not exist. Fielding was as superb a craftsman in his own way as Henry James. There is only one blot on the novel judged as a formal whole: the introduction of the extraneous story of the Man of the Hill, and even that can plausibly, if not convincingly, be justified.

Fielding was an innovator not only technically. Tom Jones was a new kind of hero, one might say the unheroic hero. He is handsome, brave, generous, and well meaning, it is true . . . but though his heart is in the right place, his instincts are not always in his control. He is a depiction of ordinary, weak man *l'homme moyen sensual.*

Walter Allen<br>
*The English Novel*<br>
(New York: E. P. Dutton, 1954), pp. 53-54

There is, then, an absolute connection in *Tom Jones* between the treatment of plot and of character. Plot has priority, and it is therefore plot which must contain the elements of complication and development. Fielding achieves this by superimposing on a central action that is, in essentials as simple as that in *Clarissa,* a very complex series of relatively autonomous subplots and episodes which are in the nature of dramatic variations on the main theme. These relatively independent narrative units are combined in a concatenation whose elaboration and symmetry is suggested in the most obvious outward aspect of the book's formal order: unlike the novels of Defoe and Richardson, *Tom Jones* is carefully divided into compositional units of different sizes—some two hundred chapters which are themselves grouped into eighteen books disposed into three groups of six, dealing respectively with the early lives, the journeys to London, and the activities on arrival, of the main characters. . . .

This is typical of the narrative mode of *Tom Jones:* the author's commentary makes no secret of the fact that his aim is not to immerse us wholly in his fictional world, but rather to show the ingenuity of his own inventive resources by contriving an amusing counterpoint of scenes and characters; quick changes are the essence of Fielding's comic manner, and a new chapter will always bring a new situation for the characters, or present different characters in a similar scene for ironical contrast. In addition, by a great variety of devices, of which the chapter headings are usually significant pointers, our attention is continually drawn to the fact that the ultimate cohesive force of the book resides not in the characters and their relationships, but in an intellectual and literary structure which has a considerable degree of autonomy.

Ian Watt
*The Rise of the Novel*
(Berkeley, Calif.: Univ. California Pr., 1957), pp. 276-77

Superficially *Tom Jones* resembled Fielding's earlier novel in many ways. There is a mystery about Tom's parentage, as about Joseph's; both heroes make long journeys across England, encountering odd characters and dangerous mishaps; Benjamin Partridge accompanies Tom as faithfully as Parson Adams accompanied Joseph. Basically, however, the two books are totally unlike. One feels that the author chose to rework the same material in order to prove how much better he could do it. Instead of having the one-line structure inherited from picaresque fiction, *Tom Jones* offers a complex pattern of interaction among persons who are kept in conflict with steady tension. Even the minor characters contribute directly to the unfolding of the plot. Therefore, when the carefully preserved secret of Tom's parentage is finally revealed, it has none of the implausibility of an afterthought concocted by the author to bring the story to a spectacular end. Instead, it seems as inevitable as the "discovery" at the climax of a classical Greek tragedy, which Aristotle prescribed as an essential element of plot. Aristophanes, Shakespeare, and Molière are among the authors whom Fielding extols in his frequent critical digressions; and his handling of the story has the tight construction of a well-made play. . . .

The main power of the book, of course, is in characterization. The central character is not the conventionally perfect hero of romance. A weakness of *Joseph Andrews* had been the author's inability to depart from his initial concept of Joseph as an absurd paragon of moral purity. Tom Jones, on the contrary, is a normal young man, good-natured, generous, and brave, but impulsive and sensual. Though he sincerely loves Sophia Western, he indulges in casual affairs with three other women. If Fielding had been writing a tragedy in the vein of Euripides or Shakespeare, this would be termed Tom's "tragic flaw." He is cured of his incontinence only after the shocking experience of believing for a while that one of the women with whom he has had sexual relations may prove to be his mother.

Lionel Stevenson
*The English Novel*
(Boston: Houghton Mifflin, 1960), pp. 103-4

## Amelia

As a novelist Fielding was subject to two opposite influences which were to leave their mark on the English novel for a hundred years and to ensure that it had little resemblance to the French and Russian novels: he was trained in the rogue's tale which introduced untidiness and irresponsibility into the English novel; and . . . he was trained in the theater, which gave our novel its long obsession with elaborate plot. *Amelia* is a compromise. By the time he came to write this novel, Fielding seems to have lost the heat of the theater's inspiration. The first chapter describing the prison is in the old manner, but presently the narrative digresses and dawdles. The didactic intention comes out frankly and, alas, unadorned. There is white-faced indignation where before there was irony, and indignation is the weaker strain, for it interrupts, where irony undermines. . . . In *Amelia,* there is more psychological complexity than there was in *Tom Jones;* it is the book of an older man who has grown tired. If we contrast Tom Jones with Mr. Booth of *Amelia,* we see that Tom commits his sins, repents in a moment and ingeniously forgets them. Mr. Booth is far more complicated. He is a married man to start with; he sins with caution, is transfixed by remorse and then settles down to brood with growing misanthropy. The wages of sin is not death, but worry—middle-class worry. . . . Fielding's rising interest in psychology marks a break with his interest in moral types. It is a signal of the coming age. And if *Amelia* indicates a decline from the brilliant fusing of gifts that went to make his earlier books, it points the way the English novel would go when a new genius, the genius of Dickens, seized it.

V. S. Pritchett
*The Living Novel*
(New York: Reynal and Hitchcock, 1947), pp. 22-23

In two respects, however, the portrayals in *Amelia* are noteworthy. First, in this book we find Fielding's most delicate, subtle, and sympathetic delineations of female character. Amelia herself, regarded simply as a creation of literary art, is unequalled even by the exquisite Sophia. In the opinion of most critics Amelia is Fielding's feminine masterpiece. But the other women also in the book are drawn with a keenness of insight and sureness of touch rather superior to that displayed in the representations of female characters in the earlier novels. Secondly, *Amelia* particularly illustrates Fielding's power of understanding and picturing ordinary, normal, everyday people. In his earlier fiction many of the characters are to some extent singular and out-of-the-way. In *Amelia,* however, with the exception of Colonel Bath, there are no eccentrics. . . . In short, in this

book Fielding succeeded, in a higher degree than ever before, in displaying
the more familiar and commonplace realities of human nature.

F. Homer Dudden
*Henry Fielding: His Life, Works, and Times*
(Oxford: Clarendon Pr., 1952), vol. II, p. 837

## Jonathan Wild

We have seen that Fielding wrote *Jonathan Wild* with his eye steadily on
the Great Man of the age [Robert Walpole]; that he wrote in the tale
many passages of comment and application with the end of satire against
Walpole and the politics of the day; that he even went out of his way,
to the detriment of the unity of the story, to drag in at prominent places
many of these comments and applications, even proceeding to the length
of introducing three whole chapters and a number of large sections of
chapters, the matter and form of which are not in accord with the plot,
the personages, the setting, or the form of the surface-story itself, and the
omission of which would cause no noticeable gap in the tale.

Possibly . . . there is under all the book, or was under all of it before
it was altered, an elaborate and consistent political allegory. But we can be
safe only in holding that the attacks on satesmen and on Walpole and on
politics of the day in the story, *do not constitute a consistent whole and
probably never did;* that the story was not written with the chief purpose
of affording a *consistent* and *unified* political satire; and that the satire
against politicians and against Walpole was *introduced merely as the story
in its development offered from page to page opportunity for introduction
of such satire.*

John Edwin Wells
*PMLA* (March, 1913), p. 54

Jonathan Wild stands for something more fundamental and universal than
an arbitrary and corrupt statesman. He is a personification not merely of
political but of general evil.

Thus symbolized, Jonathan Wild takes his place in the ethical conflict
which provides the motivation of the whole work—the conflict between
greatness and goodness. . . .

It is impossible to label the form into which the biographical, political,
and ethical substance of *Jonathan Wild* is cast. Although it follows a prose
narrative pattern, it is plainly not a novel. It contains elements of the
sensationalized criminal biography popular in the early part of the eighteenth century. Likewise it shares certain characteristics with other low-
life writings of that period and with the classic picaresque tale. A somewhat
better explanation of the form of *Jonathan Wild* follows from the compari-

son of this work with Fielding's conception of the comic epic poem in prose. In most matters of technique and spirit *Jonathan Wild* nicely satisfies Fielding's requirements for the comic prose epic; in certain respects, however, it fails to fulfill them.

It is likely that Fielding, being far less concerned with form than with substance, was content, perhaps unconsciously, to mix without fusing elements from previously existing literary modes and from his own form, the comic prose epic. In general, *Jonathan Wild* incorporates these elements into a biographical narrative pattern, a form which because of its very looseness is best adapted to a digressive, moralizing, allegorical tale.

William Robert Irwin
*The Making of Jonathan Wild*
(New York: Columbia Univ. Pr., 1941), pp. 107-8

Human indignation is Fielding's weapon . . . in *Jonathan Wild* which is sometimes referred to as a picaresque novel because the chief character happens to be a rogue, but which is in fact a moral fable. For there is no doubt about Fielding's moral intention or the moral pattern which shapes the book: indeed it may well be argued that this moral pattern is too insistent; certainly the story cannot be said to have that haphazard quality which we have seen to be typical of the picaresque tradition. It is all most carefully planned and controlled.

The theme of *Jonathan Wild* is the antithesis between greatness and goodness. . . . It is this abstract antithesis that informs the whole novel and makes it into the kind [of] thing it is, and unless the reader quickly realizes the kind of book he is dealing with his reactions to it are likely to be always a shade off-centre, his criticisms a trifle irrelevant. *Jonathan Wild* is not a psychological study nor even an exposure of criminality. The characters are all relevant to the basic pattern of the book, the antithesis already mentioned. It is not Wild himself, in glorious isolation, that interests Fielding, not simply Wild the super-criminal who lives by exploiting other criminals, but Wild as a representative symbol. The chief protagonists of the contending camps, the great and the good, are Wild and Heartfree, the innocent jeweller; but the novel is not *about* Wild and Heartfree, it is about eighteenth-century society. The great are the successes of that society, not just the Wilds but the Robert Walpoles, the politicians, the rulers, the exploiters; the good are not just the Heartfrees but all those who put human values, the values of the heart, above such success. . . .

Almost every aspect of bourgeois society is satirized in *Jonathan Wild*. Whigs and Tories, the party system itself, the corruption of office, all are transported to Newgate jail where, in the fantastic world of conscious criminals and unfortunate debtors, everything is seen with a new and piercing clarity. . . .

The basic weakness of *Jonathan Wild* . . . is that no one on the "good" side actually fights for human values. . . . This is why as far as the success and vitality of the book go, the rogues have all the life. And the weakness is not an abstractable "aesthetic" weakness. It is a weakness which springs directly from the limitations of Fielding's social vision.

Arnold Kettle
*An Introduction to the English Novel*
(New York: Harper and Row, 1960), pp. 45-51

GENERAL

Lying behind Parsons Adams and most characters in "Joseph Andrews" is a definite theory of humour, which Fielding, as may be seen from several of his articles in "The Champion," had been working out for himself from the examples of his great predecessors and from various disquisitions that had got into literature on the source and the nature of the ridiculous. . . .

In the process, Fielding quite naturally considered what qualities, characteristics, and actions are legitimate objects of ridicule. . . . Fielding would ordinarily, though not always, exclude from ridicule misfortunes, poverty, ugliness, and all physical deformities, inasmuch as they should call forth our pity.

As soon as he thus clearly saw that the border line between the serious and the ridiculous is neither fixed nor straight, he was face to face with an unsolved problem. Thereupon his reflections turned to the practice, sometimes conscious, sometimes unconscious, of English comedy since Ben Jonson; wherein the characters are strongly marked by some "humour," as it was called—that is, by some trait, notion, idiosyncrasy, or mere affectation which by the consent of everybody exposes them to ridicule. By Fielding's time, opinion had become settled that affectations were the source of ridicule, that humour consisted in portraying them.

Wilbur L. Cross
*The History of Henry Fielding*
(New Haven: Yale Univ. Pr., 1918), Vol. I, pp. 331-34

The fantasist [using the devices of "parody" and "adaptation"] here adopts for his mythology some earlier work and uses it as a framework or quarry for his own purposes. There is an aborted example of this in *Joseph Andrews*. Fielding set out to use *Pamela* as a comic mythology. He thought it would be fun to invent a brother to Pamela, a pure-minded footman, who should repulse Lady Booby's attentions just as Pamela had repulsed Mr. B.'s, and he made Lady Booby Mr. B.'s aunt. Thus he would be able to laugh at Richardson, and incidentally express his own views of life. Fielding's view of life however was of the sort that only rests content with the creation of solid round characters, and with the growth of Parson Adams and Mrs. Slipslop the fantasy ceases, and we get an independent work. *Joseph Andrews* . . . is interesting to us as an example of a false start. Its author begins by playing the fool in a Richardsonian world, and ends by being serious in a world of his own—the world of Tom Jones and Amelia.

E. M. Forster
*Aspects of the Novel*
(New York: Harcourt, Brace and World, 1927), pp. 119-20

During his apprentice years from 1729 to about 1740, Henry Fielding developed the aesthetic and techniques upon which his great works were written. Particularly important were: (1) his impatience with the restrictions of comedy and his consequent developing of farce as a satiric and moral medium for a criticism of life, (2) his adapting of the commonplace "humour" as a basis for the study and analysis of the springs of human action, (3) his developing of words as symbols, which in context often carry allegorical meaning, (4) his developing of a genuinely comprehensive and inclusive allegorical method of interpreting life, in which farce, "humour," and other word symbols, played an integral part.

Winfield H. Rogers
*SP* (October, 1943), p. 529

Fielding satirized in books and literary men the same inclusive folly which he regarded as the source of the ridiculous in all human action. That folly is affectation. Likewise, his chief method—simple exposure of words and actions—remained pretty much constant. In revealing literary aberration Fielding could not dissociate the republic of letters from human society as a whole. The latter contains the former. The same laws govern both and the same privileges and obligations obtain in both. The author, like any other private citizen, is expected to conform to a code of common decency and good sense. "Genius" does not excuse violations. Consequently, Fielding generally punishes literary affectation in the same spirit and by the same methods which he uses against general human folly. In each case, Fielding is more intent on exposure of the offense than on amendment of the offender. He did not hope to change the ways of Colley Cibber; he probably did not anticipate that a Lady Booby would remake herself after reading *Joseph Andrews*. But more tender sinners might laugh themselves out of follies not yet pernicious. Others, still innocent, ought to be warned against pretenders and shown their characteristic guises. Still others, although sophisticated, might nonetheless be pleasurably and profitably reminded that masquerade is only masquerade. Essentially a serious man, Fielding wrote comedy for the serious reader.

W. R. Irwin
*ELH* (September, 1946), p. 170

Henry Fielding's comedies, farces, burlesques, and ballad operas, in their forms and in their themes, provide an epitome of the dramatic activity from 1728 to 1737. With a facility rarely surpassed in England, he produced twenty-odd plays in the nine-year span, some of them brief and inconsiderable farces obviously turned out in the short pauses of an active career, but others memorable dramatic expressions of the age. He was intensely in touch with his times: the contemporaneity of his plays is at once their merit and their limitation, the source of their vigor and their value as records of London life in the age of Walpole, Pope, and Hogarth, but the source also of the barrier to intelligibility that now limits the number of their readers to special students of the age. Fielding followed contemporary theatrical fashions and at the same time modified them: he wrote, but with a difference, comedies of fashionable life in the manner of Congreve; political and theatrical burlesques, some of them in the ballad opera form popularized by Gay; and farces, some in the native tradition and some in the French. Like nearly every other important writer of the 1730's he was caught up in the political debates; and like most of his fellow dramatists he wrote plays with political overtones. Finally, of course, his dramatic forays into politics terminated his career in the theater. He is the single most important figure in the theater of the 1730's, but rather because of his cumulative achievement than because of high achievement in particular plays.

John Loftis
*Comedy and Society from Congreve to Fielding*
(Stanford, Calif.: Stanford Univ. Pr., 1959), pp. 114-15

# DAVID  GARRICK
## 1717-1779

Primarily known for his acting ability, Garrick had first tried dramatic writing, and in 1747, when he purchased part of the patent for the Drury Lane, he became a successful stage manager. He was instrumental in creating a Shakespeare revival, often through revision of the plays. His playwriting often produced short pieces and farces in which he starred, and his most significant collaborative piece was George Colman's *The Clandestine Marriage* (1766). After this date he acted seldom, but continued with his writing and managerial duties, returning to the stage in 1776 for a gala of his favorite characters.

Elizabeth P. Stein, *David Garrick, Dramatist* (1938)

He seems, first, to have believed in the ethical or moral purpose of the theatre; to have thought that the critics had a function above fault-finding, though I have not discovered what he thought this function was; he had no objection to borrowing material, even, despite his patriotic speeches, to borrowing liberally from the French. He vigorously opposed opera, spectacle, and pantomime in theory; but he produced them throughout his career as manager. He objected to the rise of sentimental comedy, but he approved of individual examples of the species, especially encouraging Kelly and Cumberland. Finally in passing judgment upon plays submitted to him for performance at Drury Lane, he seems to have accepted or rejected solely on the basis of the actability of the play at his theatre. This is probably the correct attitude for a manager to take. Beyond this he did not choose to go, or he was incapable of going.

Dougald MacMillan
*SP* (January, 1934), p. 82

Despite the fact that *The Clandestine Marriage* is so magnificently welded together, a Garrick scene or even a Garrick bit is almost always fairly distinguishable from the work of his collaborator, and what gives his work this prominence is the manner of its presentation. In the case of Colman, for instance, we discover that he writes in a much slower tempo than does Garrick. It is his use of the long and carefully pondered-over sentence that makes his portions of the play less animated and more slow-moving than Garrick's. Colman's is a studied, a polished, and, hence, a somewhat formal style of writing. His humor, too, is not of the effervescent and spontaneous kind. Like his writing, it is deliberate. On the other hand, Garrick's is a rapid and nervous type of writing. His sentences at times give the impression of having been struck off in white heat and under great stress. In texture his prose is lighter than Colman's, and his manner is less deliberate. He achieves his effects of speed and animation through the use of short sentences and a rapid give and take in the dialogue. He does not very frequently permit long unbroken passages to creep into his scenes. More usually he allows one character to break into the conversation of the other. Stage business, too, which plays so important a part in his scenes, adds greatly to their vivacity. His spontaneous and over-bubbling humor is a characteristic of those scenes in which his workmanship is discernible. His dialogue carries with it a sprightliness that is wholly lacking in the Colman portions. The geniality, buoyancy, and freshness that pervade his scenes, the briskness and bustle of action, the rollicking good fun, and the ingenuity of his situations—these are the elements that make a scene peculiarly Garrick's and, moreover, cause them to stand out from those of his collaborator.

Elizabeth P. Stein
*David Garrick, Dramatist*
(New York: Modern Language Assn., 1938), p. 227

It is evident that Garrick's fame and continued success were due not so much to his originality as to his showmanship and his ability to make novelty popular. Of course, he had more than that; but, copier of nature rather than imaginative creator, he was also a follower in adopting the technique, theatrical innovations, and current, progressive fashions that were sure of public favor. He was supersensitive of censure and, consequently, rather timid and hesitant about either introducing or continuing anything which was not approved by the spectators. Nevertheless, he was sufficiently progressive to keep pace with the leaders and innovators in the new movements. This was evident in his choice of plays, interpretations of character, costuming, lighting, staging, and removing spectators from the stage. His observation was constantly alert, and his appraisal of ways and means of gaining profit in the theatre was exceptionally keen. Of course, he was not infallible and his hesitance at times did not place him in the best light (especially when his behavior included timidity and duplicity).

He was not a leader in the extent to which he produced Shakespeare. Other managers and actors had preceded him in this and had already developed in the public an appetite for Shakespeare's plays. It is to his credit, however, that his performance of Shakespeare made his audiences still more avid for those plays.

William Angus
*QJS* (February, 1939), pp. 36-37

Garrick had a care, then, for Shakespeare which was the guiding force in his whole career. It prompted him to talk and write about the dramatist from his earliest letters to the end of his life. Shakespeare dominated his theorizing and acting. Shakespeare dominated his sense of dramatic values. He was accustomed to evaluate new plays submitted to him as manager by the measure of Shakespeare's plays. Fully cognizant of the changing taste of his age he strove with remarkable consistency to mold dramatic taste more and more towards Shakespeare—authentic Shakespeare. He used the dramatist to  quicken national pride, especially where the French were concerned.

Garrick's statements on drama and acting show Shakespeare's influence. His practices relative to Shakespearian drama show how he relied upon the Elizabethan as the backbone of his theatre. During his twenty-nine-year term of management it was customary to present about 175 performances yearly at Drury Lane. During the whole period he presented twenty-eight different Shakespeare plays with texts that approached authenticity more closely than those of any previous manager since the closing of the theatres. He himself assumed eighteen different Shakespearian rôles, each of which stamped indelibly upon the minds of his audiences a living, moving Shakespeare character. This fact gave credibility to the increasing contention of late eighteenth-century critics that dramatic greatness centered not, as Aristotle had suggested, about the pole of plot structure, but about the pole of character delineation.

George Winchester Stone, Jr.
*Joseph Quincy Adams Memorial Studies*
(Washington, D.C.: Folger Shakespeare Library,
1948), pp. 127-28

Garrick's health did not allow him to act very often now (he appeared 29 times during the season of 1772-1773 as compared with 101 times ten years earlier), but when he made the effort to act at all he wanted to occupy the centre of the stage throughout the entire play. If a speech delivered by any other character received much applause, it would somehow be incorporated into his own part before the next performance of that play; for no dramatist, living or dead, was safe from Garrick's pen when one of his star rôles needed strengthening. It was because the part of Hamlet as a vehicle for his genius fell short of perfection that he started tinkering with the play in the winter of 1772. Hamlet had always been one of his favourite parts and, with all its drawbacks, had provided many opportunities for the display of his particular gifts. . . .

Margaret Barton
*Garrick*
(New York: Macmillan, 1949), pp. 221-22

# JOHN GAY

1685-1732

Gay's first important work was *Shepherd's Week,* a mock series of six pastorals published in 1714, his first play, *What d'ye Call It,* appearing the next year. He joined Pope and Arbuthnot for *Three Hours after Marriage,* a comedy from 1717. His popular *Fables* were published in 1727 with a second series posthumously in 1738. But his most popular work, *The Beggar's Opera,* and its sequal *Polly,* 1728, gained both fame and notoriety for him. He wrote the libretti for Handel's *Acis and Galatea* (1732) and *Achilles* (1733). He was buried in Westminster Abbey.

G. C. Faber, ed., *The Poetical Works of John Gay, Including "Polly," "The Beggar's Opera," and Selections from the other Dramatic Work* (1926) Lewis Melville, *Life and Letters of John Gay* (1921)

As a poet Gay seems to us in this late day to have followed the conventional patterns of his own time; he created several of them, and occasionally even a greater artist like Pope followed his lead. He never indulged the larger epical ambitions of the poet, nor undertook any task monumental to perpetuate his fame. Perhaps the spectre of Sir Richard Blackmore was too much for him, or more likely—since Milton had come and gone—his modesty or his frivolity turned him rather to burlesque. There was gaiety in his nature as in his name, and, I think, an incapacity for the sustained effort necessary for the larger projects. His genius was for minute description in verse and for lighthearted song. The strain of melancholy is only occasional, and the pathos is usually mocking. Though one notices a growing scorn for the set design in verse and the merely imitative, Gay usually did his best writing when some model was firmly fixed in his mind. He could vary the scrolls and surprise with new motives, but he needed the support of a preconceived "scheme," to use his own word for his poetic practice. The genres of poetry, as such, seemed unimportant to him; he was constantly irreverent in his treatment of them, and yet he owed many of his best conceptions to them, stale as many of them were by the beginning of the eighteenth century, and his refurbishing of their faded glories is to some extent the measure of his genius. We love him most of all, however, for his Hogarthian exactitudes, and we love him for his songs.

William Henry Irving
*John Gay*
(Durham, N.C.: Duke Univ. Pr., 1940), pp. 313-14

What has neither been forgotten nor ignored is the poet's ability to devise excellent lyrics for his tunes. In approaching this aspect of the play, we move at once from the ephemeral causes of its popularity to grounds which have permanent validity. Gay's easy grace, his power of being witty whilst remaining fluent and singable, have never been touched unless by poets who have written with a tune in mind. Even Burns—who did so write—though his emotional range was much wider and deeper, seldom hit the level of Gay's succinct wit in song, but generally resorted to ampler forms for his most pungent expression. In mere singing quality, few English lyric poets have surpassed Gay at any time since Elizabethan days, and probably none save Burns since his own day. Everyone has his own favorites in *The*

*Beggar's Opera,* and it is almost an impertinence to single out for quotation things so familiar and beloved. But Gay's special flavor, his ironic wit, his perfect sense of how to match a tune with words, are brilliantly displayed in Macheath's sardonic meditation upon experience. . . .

Bertrand H. Bronson
*Studies in the Comic*
(Berkeley, Calif.: Univ. California Pr., 1941), pp. 217-18

In his use of the heroic couplet, Gay is best at narrative, description, and satire; and of these his most distinctive and original achievements are in satire. For the most part the narrative poems are translations, and as such and as narrative they are not exceptional, particularly when compared to the best of Dryden. Gay's descriptive poems are his best-known work in heroic couplets, and "Trivia" perhaps deserves its reputation. But *in toto* these poems tend to be weakly unified and mechanical in structure, although in passages the couplets are often technically excellent.

It is, however, as a satirist that Gay excels, despite the seemingly formidable competition with Pope and Dryden. But the nature and effects of Gay's satire, due in no small measure to his handling of the couplet, are distinctive enough to set him apart from even his strongest competitors in poetry. Gay's satire is mild and non-malicious; it gently rebukes rather than stingingly attacks; and its object is usually the type rather than the individual.

Wallace Cable Brown
*PMLA* (March, 1946), p. 121

From [an] outline of the plot of *The Beggar's Opera* it is evident that even when stripped of its musical setting the piece has its own interest. It is a keenly observed presentation of the rogues' gallery of its day. And the struggle between the two girls for the love and the hand of the fascinating highwayman appeals to the emotions. The only feature that seems out of key is Lucy's attempt to poison Polly. One source of attraction to the contemporary audience has passed. Among hits at the Whig government by the Tory Gay was the quarrel scene between Peachum and Lockit, here standing for Walpole and Townshend. Sir Robert, who was among the very distinguished first-night audience, had the tact to applaud it.

But what turned the scale, for a time doubtful, in the opera's favour were the airs, which, with the exception of a march from Handel's *Rinaldo,* were set to traditional English and Scottish tunes. . . . The final result was a triumph. The piece had an unprecedented run of sixty-three days and was revived year after year in different theatres. It made its way to the chief

English provincial towns, to Wales, Scotland, and Ireland, and even to Minorca. Seven editions were published by 1745.

Frederick S. Boas
*An Introduction to Eighteenth-Century Drama*
(Oxford Univ. Pr., 1953), pp. 183-84

. . . Gay makes it clear that it is the insufferable pride and egotism of man that debases his human dignity and makes him blind to the evil aspects of his nature. The relativity of such a vain viewpoint (a time-honored satiric device) is asserted by the remonstrance of the flea [in *Fable* I, xlix, 39-46]. . . .

Gay, in accord with his friends, was seeking a truth beyond this relativity of viewpoint, a genuine universal truth. But these truths are often most difficult to find; Gay as usual can discover approximate certainties in nothing but the truths of human nature gained through self-analysis, "Be humble, learn thyself to scan." The morals of all the *Fables* are predicated so that we may learn to know ourselves, which is much more important than knowing the external world. He devotes an entire Fable (II: vii) to this task; it is dedicated *"To* Myself," and in it Gay examines his motives and desires in the vein of Pope's *Epistle to Arbuthnot.* The introductory essay sums up in a direct manner his appraisal of himself and what he has discovered about "right conduct."

Sven M. Armens
*John Gay, Social Critic*
(New York: King's Crown Pr., 1954), pp. 218-19

# OLIVER GOLDSMITH

1730-1774

Born in Ireland, Goldsmith attended Trinity College, Dublin, graduating in 1749. He was rejected for ordination in 1751, studied medicine, perhaps receiving a degree from a continental university, and returned to England in 1756 where he worked as a physician and hack writer. Not qualifying for a medical post in India, he continued publication through pamphlets and monthly magazines (including the "Chinese Letters" or "Citizen of the World"). He was an original member of "The Club," having met Samuel Johnson in 1761, who sold *Vicar of Wakefield* for him in 1762 (published 1766). Further attempts at a medical career were followed by more hack work, dramatic presentations (*She Stoops to Conquer* being played successfully at Covent Garden in 1773), and poetry (including "The Deserted Village" in 1770).

Richard Garnett, ed., *Selected Works* (1950)
Ralph Wardle, *Oliver Goldsmith* (1957)

## The Deserted Village

Thus *The Deserted Village* succeeds on two levels that are scarcely touched in *The Traveller:* the appeal to the emotions and the appeal to the eye. It is more than a clear, harmonious expression of its thesis: it blends the characteristics of eighteenth century poetry with those of Romantic poetry, and in doing so it achieves virtual universality. Sophisticated readers today may find it ingenuous and sentimental, but the common reader from Goldsmith's time to the present has found it pleasing—and often moving.

. . . Although Goldsmith probably had in mind the classical ideal of cultivated retirement—Horace's Sabine farm—the great popular success of *The Deserted Village* sprang largely from the fact that its ideas were related to the Romantic primitivism which was already gaining ground. The poet's praise of rural life, his appreciation of nature, his humanitarianism, and his subjectivity all found sympathetic readers in his own time and, even more, in the generations which followed. Whether he wished to or not, Goldsmith virtually anticipated the Romantic Revival in all but his adherence to neo-classical diction. . . . His poem was addressed to all men, not the cultivated few, and he revised it carefully both before and after publication in order to heighten its clarity and simplicity. He wanted to speak to all kinds of readers, to stimulate their thoughts and to touch their hearts; and he succeeded. And although today the poem is perhaps more quoted than read, it has not lost its elemental appeal. Nor is it likely to do so.

Ralph M. Wardle
*Oliver Goldsmith*
(Lawrence, Kans.: Univ. Kansas Pr., 1957), pp. 203-4

The method Goldsmith selected to present his ideas in *The Deserted Village* is a series of contrasts. He alternates passages showing the rural ideal—England blessed by a happy and "a bold peasantry"—with passages decrying the loss of that ideal state through the corrosion of luxury and its attendant ills. His economic Toryism is most evident in these latter passages that develop a fourfold theme out of related economic and social tendencies regarded as evils—mercantilism, concentration and display of wealth ("luxury"), enclosures or aggrandizement of small holdings, and depopulation. These four evils are as difficult to separate in the poem as in Tory theory, but one may say that for poetic purposes Goldsmith seems to treat them as a causal chain: mercantilism causes luxury; the few wealthy buy up or enclose the little villages; and this aggrandizement necessitates emigration to the cities or to the terrors of America. Rural England suffers under the weight of every link in this chain.

Earl Miner
*HLQ* (February, 1959), pp. 131-32

Seen from this viewpoint—that the poem is a symbolic picture of the disintegration of the author's dream world of childhood innocence—the exaggerations and inconsistencies, of which Goldsmith's dedication indicates his uneasy awareness, are explainable. Commerce, industrialization, which Goldsmith generally and consciously admired, here are so violently castigated because they are fairy-tale ogres which make a nightmare of a dream of childhood; the rich, selfish merchant is a grotesque monster because his very existence implies a more complicated set of values than a child can cope with. And the much discussed problem of Goldsmith's view of luxury becomes more soluble. He is here describing the process of civilization in much the same terms as in his other writings, but in language oppositely charged. That is, Goldsmith everywhere analyzes the history of societies as a development from rude agricultural barbarism to graceful though perhaps effeminate sophistication; his considered opinion, in the abstract, is that the process is good and, what is more to the point, an inevitable one. But here, again, it is the very inevitability that is most distressing. It seems to me that he is so violent against luxury precisely because it is a function of time—as a society evolves, it must become luxurious: the child and his world *must* be destroyed in order that the adult world, with all its demands, may exist. The unadorned female must grow older and discover paint. The village girl must in time experience sex. Oliver Goldsmith must become an adult, and face evil.

In view of the symbolic structure of *The Deserted Village* and the actual nature of its poetic impulse, it seems not only worthwhile but necessary to reconsider the poem in our time. It is, undoubtedly, an essay on England's threatened decay of luxury, enclosures, depopulation, and the emigration of the best English stock; it is also a fine sympathetic picture of the sorrows of the sufferers from enclosure, of the English farming village as an idyllic place, and of Goldsmith's happy childhood years. But I believe its essence is something far more meaningful in our modern conception of poetry—the author's anguished discovery, spurred by events in his own family, that every child must grow up, that the adult world necessarily carries with it an admixture of evil, that none can be pure except the dead.

This theme is worked out symbolically (very probably unconsciously) and not, as the others are, through prose discussion. The childhood world is shown directly as harmless, gregarious, asexual, trusting, innocently unaware of ventitious (though sometimes eloquent) political and sociological cover, is pretty much what Eliot, Hemingway, and Faulkner have accustomed us to: disintegration, loneliness, sex, the necessary contamination with evil, the obligation to judge and the attendant oppression by guilt.

Morris Golden
*L & P* (Summer and Fall, 1959), p. 44

## The Vicar of Wakefield

Goldsmith not only questioned the wisdom of the sentimentalist, he doubted his sincerity. The compassion of Zelis in her flight from London was "sentimental only as it served to protract the immediate enjoyment" of a situation. The sentimentalist, in general, is seeking a glib palliation for an indulgent Epicureanism of life.

Though it must be granted that Goldsmith was instinctively sensitive, and, in the non-technical sense of the word, sentimental, he was able to keep from being entangled in the doctrinaire sentimental movement of Shaftesbury, Richardson, and Rousseau. He was continually checking the rush of the heart with the reins of common sense, in literature with considerable success, though in life with perhaps too little. He is aware that the sentimentalist is an idealist viewing life through the false glasses of romance, and not seldom an unconscious hypocrite seeking an escape from a realism he found unpleasant and a morality he found severe. Goldsmith the writer must be identified not with the Vicar, though one phase of the man is mirrored there, but with the far more sensible and prudent Sir William Thornhill. It is even possible that *The Vicar of Wakefield* should be regarded not as an idyll of simple life in rural England, but as a satire on idealism comparable to *The Good-Natured Man*—a satire broken in the end by an indulgence of the novelist to his own heart and to the hearts of a sentimental reading public.

W. F. Gallaway, Jr.
*PMLA* (December, 1933), pp. 1180-81

But therein lies, in part, the greatness of the novel: it is capable of varying interpretations. It was something new and something old—a penetrating study of human character and a melodramatic romance. It can be read as idyllic or ironic, it can be regarded as representative of the sentimental novel or of the trend away from such fiction; it has meant many things to many readers, and future generations may regard it in varying or in wholly different lights. In effect it is an anomaly like its author and is therefore, in one respect, his most typical work. Like him it shows traces of genius and traces of absurdity; it has obvious weaknesses and yet irresistible charm. And anyone who would truly appreciate it should not try to criticize or analyze it, but should read and enjoy it as people have been doing ever since it was published. For despite its palpable faults, despite innumerable attempts to determine the sources of its plot, the prototype of the Vicar, or the locale of the action, it is an original and delightful novel which is likely to remain . . . "the best-read from that day to now, all the world over, of the books of the Fielding epoch."

Ralph M. Wardle
*Oliver Goldsmith*
(Lawrence, Kans.: Univ. Kansas Pr., 1957), p. 171

Into these patterns of disguise, truth and appearance, blindness and sight which give the main part of the *Vicar of Wakefield* its strong thematic unity fit with astonishing exactness those parts of the novel that have often been called extraneous. Since even the seeming digressions relate directly to the central theme of disguise, the book is a consistent and coherent whole. In addition, the fact that through the theme of disguise the apparently extraneous parts can be closely fitted into the whole structure of the *Vicar* helps support the thesis that disguise-and-reality is the book's central theme. . . .

Thus the *Vicar of Wakefield* in its constantly shifting patterns of truth and disguise is in a real sense a well constructed masque. Though realistically improbable, its conclusion is a wholly consistent "unmasking" cleverly and indeed wittily tightening the thematic screw one more turn. To object, as Baker and others do, to the reversal of fortune at the end as inconsistent and unmotivated is to miss the lightness and dexterity with which Goldsmith in his frankly unrealistic and almost allegorical fable amusingly yet ironically rings practically every possible change on his theme. The novel is not in the tradition of the Book of Job or of *Pilgrim's Progress* but of eighteenth-century dramatic comedy or, if one insists on a great progenitor, of *Don Quixote* or *Tom Jones*. The improbabilities far from being faults, are the dramatic conventions that give the novel its life. Freed from the restraints of reality, Goldsmith can wittily design shifting patterns of disguise that express his keen insight into reality.

Curtis Dahl
*ELH* (June, 1958), pp. 96, 99

GENERAL

The best authority that I can consult tells me that the humors of *She Stoops to Conquer* are hard to "put across" nowadays. Modern actors do not easily feel them and enter into them. That is not surprising. Nothing, not even a dead novel, is quite so dead as a dead comedy. The surprising thing is that the play should be alive at all. Out of that whole century of wit, only this play and Sheridan's survive without the help of music, which did so much for "The Beggars' Opera"; and even that has had only a sudden and occasional revival. But Goldsmith and Sheridan have been played without ceasing over a century and a half. The same authority holds that the screen scene from *The School for Scandal* has something in it which keeps it immune from decay: that no such difficulty exists there as with *She Stoops to Conquer*. . . . But in the plays you have Sheridan at full stretch of his amazing wit; all you get from *She Stoops to Conquer* is Goldsmith's fun. It is fun of the simplest and most primitive kind; bucolic comedy, if it can be called comedy at all; and the country changes less quickly than the town. That, I think, is why it has been able to survive; that and the extraordinary force of Goldsmith's hilariousness.

Stephen Gwynn
*Oliver Goldsmith*
(New York: Henry Holt, 1935), p. 285

Goldsmith's most pervasive and characteristic theme is the contrast between the family circle and the wandering son who leaves it. It is of major importance in a number of his essays, in his novel, and in his two best known poems, and it affects his thinking on such apparently unrelated matters as literary criticism and political theory. . . .

Goldsmith's most obvious attitude toward the family and the wanderer is that which might be gathered from a casual reading of *The Vicar of Wakefield, The Traveller,* and *The Deserted Village*—that one is the promised land and the other a forlorn exile. But there was more than nostalgia and yearning in Goldsmith, though the sincerity of these is unquestionable. It is true that he saw himself often as a lonely, unfriended wanderer, obsessed with the delights of a home to which, for some mysterious reason, he could not return; but he was, or rather he became in time, an adult, and saw the relationship in a more complex way. Why, after all, should the son continue to be an exile? Or, put another way, why should he not go home again to Lissoy, or to Auburn? Why had he left in the first place?

The theme of the lonely wanderer is of course closely connected with Goldsmith's own life; the autobiographical nature of parts of the novel and the two poems has long been noticed and sometimes injuriously overemphasized.

Morris Golden
*ELH* (September, 1958), p. 181


# THOMAS GRAY

## 1716-1771

Gray met his close friends Horace Walpole, Richard West, and Thomas Ashton at Eton. He joined the first, after leaving Peterhouse, Cambridge, without a degree, on a trip through France and Italy. He was back in England without Walpole in 1741 as a result of a quarrel, the friendship not picking up again for four years. His return to Peterhouse and then to Pembroke resulted in his being appointed Professor of Modern History at Cambridge in 1768. He was well known as a scholar and antiquary.

H. W. Starr and J. R. Hendrickson, eds., *Complete Poems of Thomas Gray: English, Latin and Greek* (1966)

R. W. Ketton-Cremer, *Thomas Gray* (1955)

*Elegy Written in a Country Church-Yard*

In its essence, the poem combines the assertion of the right to individual tastes and feelings—to the choice of a way of life different from the prevailing one—with the benevolent atttitude of Shaftesbury's school of philosophy. The upshot of its argument is that life may be well lived by a man of quiet tastes, "to fortune and to fame unknown," who has given to the poor only sympathy, and has confined his social activities to a very narrow circle. But all the first part of the poem up to the stanza where the grayhaired villager begins to describe the character of the young observer, is given up to the expression of "benevolent" sentiments. The poet thinks gently and pityingly of the humble, simple lives of the peasants buried in the country churchyard. If their experience has not been very wide, they have nevertheless been preserved from great crimes and great miseries. To be well spoken of after their death, is not an inadequate reward, for the most conspicuous life, like the most obscure, ends at last in an epitaph. And this is well because the excellence of life lies not in the outward deed, but in the character. Both the actual ideas of the poet and his attitude towards his fellowmen are "humane," as that word was understood by his time. He has, furthermore, by representing his own life and character as obscure but not therefore despicable, identified himself with average humanity, after the manner of truly great poets.

Amy L. Reed
*The Background of Gray's Elegy*
(New York: Columbia Univ. Pr., 1924), p. 247

The rural graveyard in its simplicity calls up for the speaker memories of another kind of burial-place, one in which heraldry visibly makes its boast, and one filled with "storied urn" and "animated bust." "Honour," at least, it must be granted, is treated as one of the personifications on an allegorical monument . . . .

But whether we treat the personifications as sculptures, or as terms used in the grandiloquent epitaphs, or merely as the poet's own projections of the pomp implied by the ornate burial-place—in any case, they are used ironically. That is to say, they are contrasted with the humble graves of the country church-yard, and they are meant, in contrast, to seem empty, flat, and lifeless. For "Honour" to possess more vitality as a metaphor would run counter to the intention of the poem. We can put the matter in this way: the more richly and dramatically realized Honour becomes, the more plausible it would be to feel that "Honour" could "provoke the silent dust." Conversely, the more fully dead, the more flatly abstract Flatt'ry is, the more absurdly ironical becomes its attempt to "sooth the dull cold ear of Death." . . .

Once we see that the purpose of the poem demands that the personifications be used ironically, one is allowed to see some of the supporting ironical devices.

Cleanth Brooks
*The Well Wrought Urn*
(London: Dennis Dobson, 1949), p. 101

In a sense, the interpretation of the poem revolves around placing the emphasis in a single line. It lies in the difference between saying, "The paths of *glory* lead but to the grave," and saying, "The paths of glory lead but to the *grave*." The first is like saying, "Although the paths of glory lead to the grave, the paths of virtue lead elsewhere." The second is like saying, "The paths of glory, and all other paths, lead but to the grave." The first is either a consolation prize held out to the cheated underprivileged, or it is a sop to the chafed consciences of the "enlightened" rich. The second is a reminder to all men that, whatever their achievements, they face a common doom. The first makes Gray out to be a double-talking hypocrite, for who would claim that the man who took such pride in being a gentleman and such pains in being a poet had no consideration for differences in rank and ability? The second makes him out to be an honest man, who recognized the essential paradox of human life—that its deepest core is death, "the skull beneath the skin."

The chief difficulty in interpreting the *Elegy* lies in the fact that the two subjects (1. the poor and obscure are essentially as favored as the wealthy and famous, and 2. death is the common destiny of all men) are overlapping so that it is easy to make the mistake of thinking that they are synonymous. The difference between them is in fact considerable. The first is chiefly political and social in its implication, the second chiefly religious and philosophical.

Lyle Glazier
*UKCR* (Spring, 1952), p. 174

The original impulse of the *Elegy*, as of so much more of Gray's earlier poetry, must surely have been the death of West; and a quatrain in one of West's own poems . . . may conceivably have suggested its stanza, its diction and even something of its mood. It is possible also that Gray's impulse to bring the poem to a close, after so many years of hesitation, was connected with the death of his aunt Mary Antrobus in the previous autumn. Her loss affected him deeply; he could never forget how much he owed in the past to her devotion and self-sacrifice. . . . But whatever part these two bereavements may have played in the inspiration of the *Elegy*, the poem transcends the private sorrows of its writer. . . . By some miraculous chance this most retiring of men had built out of his lonely meditations, the musings of his obscure and secluded life, a poem which should reach the hearts of all mankind.

R. W. Ketton-Cremer
*Thomas Gray*
(Cambridge Univ. Pr., 1955), pp. 98-99

Some readers have been eager to find a subject other than the narrator for the epitaph because the tone of the poem seems unpleasant if it is read as applying to Gray himself. However . . . the epitaph can properly be read as referring to a fictional narrator, and—if we think the "Elegy" as the meditation of this narrator—"these lines" can be read as referring to the poem as a whole. There is one possible difficulty with this interpretation: it is in the apparent shift in point of view from the "me" of the first stanza to the "thee" of line 93. Professor Cleanth Brooks seems to accept the case for a fictional narrator and explains the shift as dramatic in nature. If read in this way, the shift reveals that the speaker is viewing himself objectively, that he has started to think of himself with the same sorts of feeling that he has previously expressed about the inhabitants of the graveyard. Thus the shift may be construed as an appropriate introduction to the speech of the "hoary-headed swain" and to the epitaph itself.

The character of the narrator can be drawn, in general terms, from the poem: he posed as "Il Penseroso" (ll. 98-108); he dreamed of dying young and ever making a name for himself (ll.93 ff.); he was well educated (l.119), charitable (l.121), and sentimental (*passim*). Certainly Professor Shepard was right in feeling that this narrator may have had personal origins involving West as well as Gray himself. However, these origins merely furnished raw material from which an impersonal figure was evolved. In the final poetic structure Gray most certainly did not wish the narrator to resemble any specific person. All that can be said is that the narrator and the subject of the epitaph are the same person and that that person is described as an educated young gentleman, not as an unlettered village stonecutter.

John H. Sutherland
*MP* (January, 1957), pp. 12-13

The prevailing impression we have on considering Gray's *Elegy* in retrospect is of its distinctive "atmosphere," contemplative and Horatian. There is the stoic reflection on the transcience of earthly glory that we associate with this tradition, the same apparent preference for a Sabine Farm, "far from the madding crowd's ignoble strife." The gentle melancholy of the mood, as well as the syntax of stanzas 24 and 25, points to Gray himself as the subject of the Epitaph. It expresses a wish which, in this particular mood, he has for his whole future: to be "marked out" by melancholy for her own, to live and die in peaceful rustic security.

But this is by no means all that the *Elegy* says, and it ignores some powerful emotional undercurrents. For Gray is seeing the "rude Forefathers"
of the hamlet in two roles simultaneously, both as the happiest of men, and
as victims. The plowman in stanza I is "weary," the slumbering dead are
rude and unlettered. The tombs "with uncouth rhimes and shapeless sculptures deck'd" implore the passing tribute of a sigh as much for their un-
couthness as for the death of their inmates. The obscurity of country life
has restrained and killed the innate potentialities of the rustics, for good as
well as for evil. Not only is the possible Cromwell comparatively guiltless,
but the possible Milton is mute and inglorious, both forbidden by their lot
any spectacular fulfilment. The obscurity, therefore, in which their happiness is supposed to consist is felt in terms of waste. The words "mute" and
"inglorious" acquire an ambiguity from their context. They are words of
deprivation and defeat, but they are here levelled up by juxtaposition with
the "guiltless" Cromwells almost to the status of happiness.

A. E. Dyson<br>
*EIC* (July, 1957), p.257

## GENERAL

We must not forget that, first and last, Gray was essentially a poet. Under
the warming influence of his love for West he composed plentifully, and
then on the death of his friend in 1742 he lost the urge. But even with his
retirement to scholarly pursuits, his fondness for poetry and beauty never
became entirely submerged in erudition. His love of Vergil and other great
classical poets led him to the study of Greek civilization and history. His
love of travel and the romance of distant lands ended naturally in a thorough knowledge of Oriental history. His interest in poetry, especially in the
work of Chaucer, Spenser, Shakespeare, and Milton, found rich pasture in
the study of early English poetry and of its roots reaching back into the
French, Italian, Welsh, and Scandinavian prosodies. His love of Gothic
architecture was a part of the background of his research in English history.
His lifelong interest in the beauties of nature led him to a passionate and
scientific study of natural history. The poet in him was always alive, even
when dimmed by the varied tastes of the eighteenth-century gentleman.
Guided by the appeal of beauty, he was willing to dig deeply into a subject
until his knowledge assumed scholarly proportions. The very pursuit thus
instigated by his poetic nature left him, however, little time or energy for
creative work.

... Thus his poetry borrowed from his learning, even as his love of poetry
had led him in the beginning towards learning. He might have more evenly
mingled scholarship and creative work but for his inertia, born of ill-health,
and his contempt for professional writing, born of his desire to be a gentleman. Milton before him had done it, guided by a fixed purpose; Johnson

in his own day was driven to it by necessity; and Goethe in the generation after him was able to become both scholar and poet through his abundant energy. Gray had the mind for it, but he failed, and the failure has interested thousands who have felt his power in the *Elegy*.

William Powell Jones<br>
*Thomas Gray, Scholar*<br>
(Cambridge, Mass.: Harvard Univ. Press, 1937), pp. 142-43, 145

Gray's mode of expression is as typical of him as is his choice of themes. His style is pre-eminently an academic style, studied, traditional, highly finished. His standard of finish, indeed, was so high as sometimes to be frustrating. He could take years to complete a brief poem. During the process he sent round fragments to his friends for their advice. Like Mr. James Joyce, though not so publicly, Gray was given to issuing his work while "in progress." Sometimes it remained for ever in this unreposeful condition. He never managed to get the *Ode on Vicissitude* finished at all. His choice of forms, too, is a scholar's choice. Sedulously he goes to the best authors for models. He writes the Pindaric Ode—making a more careful attempt than his predecessors had, exactly to follow Pindar—the Horatian Ode, the classical sonnet, and the orthodox elegy, leading up to its final formal epitaph. His diction is a consciously poetic affair; an artificial diction, deliberately created to be an appropriate vehicle for lofty poetry. "The language of the age," he stated as an axiom, "is never the language of poetry." Certainly his own language was not that of his age—or of any other, for that matter. It is an elaborate compound of the language of those authors whom he most admired: Horace and Virgil, Pope and Dryden, above all, Milton—the youthful Milton who wrote *L'Allegro* and *Lycidas*. For Milton, as the greatest English Master of the artificial style, appealed peculiarly to Gray. Sometimes the influence of one of these poets predominates, sometimes of another, according to which Gray thinks is the best in the kind of verse he is attempting. He follows Pope in satire, Dryden in declamation, Milton in elegiac and picturesque passages. . . . Gray curiously reminds us of a modern author. This device of imbedding other people's phrases in his verse anticipates Mr. T. S. Eliot. Gray's purpose, however, is very different. The quoted phrase is not there to point an ironical contrast as with Mr. Eliot; rather it is inserted to stir the reader's imagination by the literary associations which it evokes. Conscious, as Gray is, of poetry developing in historic process, he wishes to enhance the effect of his own lines by setting astir in the mind memories of those great poets of whom he feels himself the heir.

Lord David Cecil<br>
*The Poetry of Thomas Gray*<br>
(London: Geoffrey Cumberlege, 1945), pp. 12-13

There is little that is either remarkable or new in Gray's poetry. There is little that is remarkable except its comparative excellence in an age of mediocrity, and that excellence is Augustan in its proportion, economy and unity. Where these things are lacking, as they are in *The Progress of Poesy* (though even here *the attitude towards poetry* which Gray displays is Augustan) their absence cannot be excused on the grounds that they have given place to other excellencies of a new age of poetry. There is little that is new, since Gray succeeds in that part of his work where he is writing not in the new Romantic way but in the old Augustan way against which the Romantics revolted. Where Gray himself is in revolt against the tradition of his age (though revolt is perhaps too strong a word to apply to him) his poetry suffers from the uncertainty of his position. If Milton feared that he would fail as an epic poet through being born in "an age too late," Gray fails as a would-be Romantic through being born in an age too soon.

D. S. Bland
*CambJ* (December, 1948), p. 180

# THOMAS HOBBES
1588-1679

Educated at Magdalen Hall, Oxford, Hobbes was in the service of the Cavendish family and during the 1620's was a kind of secretary to Francis Bacon. He travelled in Europe and lived in Paris with other Royalists for eleven years during the Civil War period. He was basically a materialist philosopher, concerned with utilitarian and sensational knowledge. His *Leviathan* (1651) was greeted with general disfavor since both the Parliament and the Royalists could find argument for their respective points of view in it. *The Elements of Law, Natural and Politic* was published in 1650 as *Human Nature* and *De Corpore Politico; Behemoth, or the Long Parliament,* finished ca. 1668, was suppressed until 1679.

Sir William Molesworth, ed., *The Works* (1839-1845), 16 vols.
Leslie Stephen, *The Life of Thomas Hobbes* (1904)

. . . the final importance of Hobbes's political philosophy is found in its attempt to make the subject secular and scientific. Not merely in external matters was he motivated by the conflict of civil and ecclesiastical power, but even more in intellectual aim and method. We fail to get the full force of Hobbes's conception of sovereignty until we see that to Hobbes the logical alternative is setting up the private opinions of individuals and groups of individuals as the rule of public acts—a method whose logical inconsistency has division and war for its practical counterpart.

There exists, indeed, a paradox in Hobbes. On one hand, we have the doctrine of the sovereign's arbitrary institution of duties, and rights and wrongs. On the other, we have his doctrine of the strictly scientific character of morals and politics.

John Dewey
*Studies in the History of Ideas*
(New York: Columbia Univ. Pr., 1918), Vol. I, p. 107

Hobbes's strictly empirical psychology thus establishes imagination on a sufficiently high level: a result of sensation, it provides man with a natural, unerring test of the validity of notions; names which stand for ideas "unknowable" to it must be taken merely on faith—they do not represent a higher department of knowledge to which imagination cannot aspire.

Furthermore, Hobbes's psychology, in abandoning the old distinction between a rational and a sensitive soul, does not regard the imagination as a mistress of error, a dangerous guide to behavior, who may incite a lower soul to revolt against a higher, rational soul. Hobbes's whole psychology of the passions makes such a dichotomy pointless. The desire for satisfaction which the organism feels is not regarded as a rebellion against reason, but as something entirely natural and good. . . . Far from being disparaged, the imagination is looked upon as an important useful faculty in man's makeup, not primarily an inner sense in a lower, nonrational soul.

Of even greater importance for literary criticism is Hobbes's interest in the combinatory powers of the imagination—not merely so much its ability to form compound images . . . but to function freely in what was later to be called the association of ideas.

Donald F. Bond
*ELH* (December, 1937), pp. 257-58

Wit also means judgment, however, when it dissociates and discerns differences or "dissimilitude in things" apparently alike. It is exactly the opposite faculty from that of the fancy, which associates by means of resemblances. . . . Because fancy is not commended for itself, it must be constantly watched and checked by judgment. . . . And so, he who has the ability to use his fancy can adorn his discourse with "apt metaphors" and rare inventions. A danger constantly present, however, is that the exuberant fancy will approach madness and run amok with countless resemblances and digressions. Thus Hobbes must needs use the judgment in order to see that only the proper images are associated by the fancy. Judgment and fancy are therefore equally necessary for art: the one checks on the unity and propriety of the other's resemblances or figures. . . .

In the course of his examination of natural wit, Hobbes emphasizes the importance of speed in making and arranging associations. Wit is judged by the rapidity in which associations are made. Natural wit consists in "celerity of imagining" and "steady direction to some approved end," while dullness or stupidity signifies "slowness of motion," or "a slow imagination."

Martin Kallich
*ELH* (December, 1945), pp. 297-98

Judgement, [Hobbes] has said, observes differences, fancy similitudes; also judgement constructs a poem, fancy supplies the ornaments in the form of simile. But strictly, where the mind creates "fictions" it does so . . . through the power of fancy where "fancy" is identical with "imagination"; "Fictions of the mind" . . . are "compounded imaginations." Here the fancy is constructive, however inconsistent Hobbes may be in saying so. He also sees the fancy as the power which discerns similitudes and gives rise to metaphor and simile. These two powers of the fancy are intrinsically wild and unrestrained and require the check of the judgement; and when he says, as in the *Answer to the Preface of Gondibert*, that "judgement begets the strength and structure . . . of a poem," we must take him to mean not that judgement by its restraining and ordering power gives shape and unity to what otherwise would be confused and wild. But Hobbes wavers and is unclear about all this. For in *Leviathan* fancy creates fictions, in the *Answer* the judgement *begets* the structure and fancy begets the *ornaments;* and it is plausible to believe that Hobbes is trying to maintain a sharp dichotomy between fancy and judgement analogous to that he upholds between sense and reason, and will not be drawn into recognizing that, in fact, fancy and judgement *co-operate* in designing the structure of a poem.

D. G. James
*The Life of Reason*
(London: Longmans, Green, 1949), p. 38

Most of the ideas of the *Leviathan* can be found already expressed in pithy and concentrated form in this small volume [*The Elements of Law*], so clearly and trenchantly arranged, written ten years earlier, though actually printed only a year before the appearance of his greater work.

Here are already the following propositions: (i) the state of nature is a state of war; every man has a right to all things by natural right, an assumption which cuts across the whole orthodox tradition of natural law and a benevolent cosmic order; (ii) the surrender of natural right by mutual covenant; (iii) the setting up of a sovereign power on a purely utilitarian basis; (iv) subordination of ecclesiastical to civil power; (v) the right of the subject to transfer allegiance if the sovereign fails in his primary task, the maintenance of security.

John Bowle
*Hobbes and His Critics*
(Oxford Univ. Pr., 1952), pp. 49-50

The genesis of Hobbes's political philosophy is characterized by the following processes: (1) the movement away from the idea of monarchy as the most natural form of State to the idea of monarchy as the most perfect artificial State; (2) the movement away from the recognition of natural obligation as the basis of morality, law, and the State to the deduction of morality, law, and the State from a natural claim (and thus to the denial of every natural obligation); (3) the movement away from the recognition of a superhuman authority—whether of revelation based on Divine will or a natural order based on Divine reason—to a recognition of the exclusively human authority of the State; (4) the movement away from the study of past (and present) States to the free construction of the future State; (5) the movement away from honour as principle, to fear of violent death as principle.

Leo Strauss
*The Political Philosophy of Hobbes*
(Chicago: Univ. Chicago Pr., 1952), p. 129

Neither Hobbes' man nor the society that man seemed to demand was acceptable to them [the Cambridge Platonists]: Hobbes envisaged his man as completely dominated by fear, whose society therefore must protect him against the dangers that fear implied. Armed with God's right reason and using it both as an intellectual and a social weapon, the Cambridge Platonists like Milton wielded a two-handed engine for the creation of a better world; clad like his lady in complete steel, they recognized fear for what it was, an emotion merely temporary and a trap of the devil. In the interests of civil quiet, Hobbes' Leviathan-state crushed sectarianism as sedition and breeder of anarchy—and Hobbes, like More, resorted to the familiar argument of seventeenth-century political theorists, this time with a different purpose behind the utterance: whatever the State's spiritual restrictions, a man's private conscience was his own and remained inviolable by civil insistence. Leviathan ordered religious conformity; in so far as the church exercised power, it exercised it as an arm of the State. Small wonder that the tolerant Platonists and Arminians, wise in the ways of the persecuted, reacted so bitterly against Hobbes. He seemed to them to employ a cynicism in religious matters that no sweet words, no Biblical quotation, could conceal; and that cynicism, in their view, was the inevitable result of mechanist philosophy.

Rosalie L. Colie
*Light and Enlightenment*
(Cambridge Univ. Pr., 1957), pp. 61-62

# SAMUEL JOHNSON
1709-1784

Son of a bookseller of Lichfield, Johnson attended Pembroke College, Oxford. He began writing periodical essays, as he did often later, after his father's death left the family in poverty. Married to Elizabeth Porter, who died in 1752, he next began an unsuccessful private school. Accompanied by a student, David Garrick, he went to London in 1737, joining the firm of Edward Cave, founder of *The Gentleman's Magazine*. In 1749 he wrote "The Vanity of Human Wishes" and Garrick produced *Irene*, written during his teaching days. *The Rambler*, begun in 1750, ran almost two years; his famous *Dictionary* appeared in 1755; and *Rasselas, Prince of Abyssinia* came forth in 1759. In 1763 Johnson met James Boswell and started "The Club," whose members included many illustrious figures. His edition of Shakespeare was published in 1765. He met the Thrales in 1764, touring Wales with them in 1774, after a trip with Boswell to the Highlands and the Hebrides. At the request of a number of booksellers, he undertook *Lives of the Poets*, published 1779-81. The death of Thrale and a quarrel with Mrs. Thrale saddened his last years; he was buried in Westminster Abbey.

E. L. MacAdam, *et al., The Yale Edition of the Works of Samuel Johnson* (1958-1965), 6 vols.

James L. Clifford, *Young Sam Johnson* (1955)

## WORKS

But in 1748 Tetty was still very much alive and Johnson was involved in many vexing problems. Everything seemed to increase the "gloomy irritability of his existence." Unhappily he looked about him, only to find much to be endured and little to be enjoyed. In his sober, depressed mood he wrote his finest poem, *The Vanity of Human Wishes*.

. . . Though fashioned in the classic mode, *The Vanity of Human Wishes* was not a mere imitation. Even more than in *London*, Johnson allowed himself every liberty. He took what he wanted from Juvenal and infused it with his own personality. The tone was changed and there were constant shifts of emphasis. As one recent critic has commented, Juvenal's "mordant mockery" was transmuted into "abstract gloom." In many ways the resulting poem was just as much Johnson's as if he had had no model.

Many of the details came directly out of Johnson's own experience. He had been a sensitive observer; he had seen only too well the struggles of those about him for happiness. He was not fooled by the mirth and jollity of the merrymakers. Underneath, he suspected, there was universal disappointment. The pleasures of this world were only drugs to keep the mind occupied. . . .

As he composed his sonorous lines, Johnson must have been haunted by the inevitable question of what all this meant to him. Had he found anything the philosophers of the past had missed? Had he, Sam Johnson, anything of consequence to look forward to? Great wealth, power, beauty—these were obviously beyond him. Love and passion, domestic bliss? He thought of what had happened to his own marriage. He remembered the quarrels of his own parents. A tranquil old age? The years would bring only more physical infirmity. Fame as a scholar and author?

James L. Clifford
*Young Sam Johnson* (New York: McGraw-Hill,
1955), pp. 317, 319, 320

For Johnson's contemporaries *Irene* was a noble poem, whatever its defects as a tragedy. It was based on the old story in which Mahomet II fell in love with a beautiful Christian captive after the fall of Constantinople. The work had been hammered out painfully and slowly, and as Johnson himself observed in another context: "success in works of invention is not always proportionate to labour." He had little notion of constructing a play or writing blank verse dialogue. The plot of *Irene* is ill-balanced and quite without dramatic tensions; and while there are a few good lines, there is scarcely a speech of any length that strikes home to the modern reader. One must be careful of course in judging an eighteenth century tragedy to allow for what has been called "the shift in sensibility," and one must remember that Addison's *Cato,* so frigid to our taste, was applauded by excellent judges for more than a generation; but whereas there is still a flicker of life in *Cato* as a distinguished period piece, *Irene* is now barely readable. Johnson himself seems to have thought well of his play when it was written, but later he was disillusioned.

Michael Joyce
*Samuel Johnson* (London: Longmans, Green, 1955), p. 47

If Johnson's recognized supremacy over other English dictionaries extended his influence in lexicography throughout western Europe for so many years, it must be expected that within England his influence on histories of the language, on glossaries, grammars, synonymies, dictionaries, and theories concerning them, was all-pervasive. So indeed that influence was; but it was not easy to state with concise clarity, for a good deal of the statement must deal with compilers who undertook tasks which Johnson had refused or neglected. Though his book is not easily comparable with theirs, his influence may be suggested in the very fact that they assumed his work as done. Further complications arise from Johnson's debts to his own predecessors, from his failure to state any systematic theory of language, and from the relative inferiority of his history and grammar to the body of the

*Dictionary*: the maintenance of a common tradition must not be mistaken for the individual influence of Johnson, and to some extent the separate parts of his work demand to be treated separately, with statements concerning his theories sometimes drawn largely from his practice.

James H. Sledd and Gwin J. Kolb
*Dr. Johnson's Dictionary* (Chicago: Univ. Chicago Pr.,
1955), pp. 163-64

A single respect remains in which Johnson must be credited with a large measure of originality. He was the first English dictionary-maker to collect and insert substantial illustrations of his meanings—authorities or testimonies from the wealth of documents in which the English language had been achieved and preserved. With respect to the use of authorities, simply considered, it is true, however, that certain anticipations of Johnson's method may be pointed out. These appear on the Continent, in Italian, French, Spanish, and Portuguese dictionaries, and especially in the revised *Vocabolario* of the Italian Accademia della Crusca issued in 1729. And once again we have our warning from the recent scholars. It would be "hardly wise" to view Johnson's Dictionary as the first English dictionary of its kind, a conspicuous transcendence of all earlier English dictionaries in the feature of its quoted authorities, the fulfilment of a demand which Englishmen had been voicing for nearly two hundred years. We are only "wise" if we try to see Johnson's Dictionary in an international perspective and to assimilate it as far as possible to Italian and French models.

W. K. Wimsatt, Jr.
*New Light on Dr. Johnson* (New Haven:
Yale Univ. Pr., 1959), p. 67

CRITICISM

Today quotations from *The Rambler* are relatively infrequent even in the writings of professed Johnsonians who, for obvious reasons, prefer to cite from either Boswell's record of Johnson's conversation or from one or the other later works. Yet a surprising number of his favorite themes, interests, opinions and prejudices appear in these essays for the first time. Here, for example, and choosing almost at random, one may find his love of London and his strong sense of the difference between personal liberty, which he loved, and political liberty, which he distrusted; his contempt for parental authority and his admiration for realistic writing of the sort that was just giving birth to the novel; his distrust of "the rules" in literature and his assumption that public favor is the final test of literary excellence. His later criticism of Milton is foreshadowed in a paper on *Samson Agonistes* and his criticism of the "metaphysical poets" already implicit in a paper on wit.

Indeed, if nothing of him survived except *The Rambler* it would still be possible to form a pretty accurate idea of his opinions on moral, intellectual and artistic questions. Yet we do not commonly so form our idea partly because of the relatively unattractive style in which the opinions are presented, even more because Johnson seems not yet to have learned the art of distilling his own essence. The characteristic opinions are lost among the more numerous commonplaces. One does not feel, as one so constantly does in later writing, the flavor of a personality which gives special significance to even the eccentricities and the perversities. This means, among other things, that if Johnson were known only by *The Rambler* we should never think of him as a "character." But it means more than that. We should also not think of him as a man whose opinions, even when conventional or even reactionary, were defended with an arresting originality and force. . . .

Joseph Wood Krutch
*Samuel Johnson* (New York: Henry Holt, 1944), pp. 110-11

Samuel Johnson practiced most of the forms of literary criticism known to his day. He amended corrupt passages and explained obscure and difficult ones. He traced the development of an author's genius—that "chymical process," in the words of a contemporary review of his criticism, by which the earliest yield is "transmuted into a substance of a more valuable kind" while "still preserving some analogy of its pristine form." He occasionally studied "the gradual progress and improvement of our taste," and he comprehended "as it were in one view the whole circle of the arts and sciences, to see their mutual connections and dependencies." But above all he sat on the judicial bench of criticism, inquiring into the beauties and faults of literary works and pronouncing "with great accuracy on the merits of literary productions.". . .

Johnson persistently demanded a scientific and dialectical criticism, which would reduce the flux and change of literature to principles upon which sound judgment could be based. And yet he found unsatisfactory the tradition of codified rules which he had inherited, which within limits he drew upon, but which never brought him the certainty and success that he was seeking. He was too much aware that literature, produced in part by that "licentious and vagrant faculty," the imagination, was material too intractable for the codified rules of the rationalists. . . . If investigation of literary art and its genres and of the work itself as an embodiment of literary type proved nugatory, there still remained other areas: the outside truth and reality which the work attempted to represent and by which it could be tested, the mind of the author that produced it, and the emotions that it evoked. And in each case Johnson was able to subsume such data under those empirical-rational realities about which he felt the highest degree of certainty. . . .

His whole critical career is as notable for what it attacked as for what it attempted to establish. From its beginning to its end—both in the earlier topical essays on such matters as the pastorals, versification, exordial verses, romances, and letter-writing and in the later considerations of specific literary works one by one as they had appeared chronologically in the production of an author's lifetime—he waged relentless war upon authority, prescription, imitation, and outworn tradition. He attempted to cut away the overlaying and obscuring growth of pseudo-statement and to substitute only such determinations as were capable of verification by firsthand experience. Johnson's reader is never asked to believe that a general law has been operative from Homer to Blackmore or from Vergil to Pomfret. He is asked instead only to accept whatever general principle seems to arise from an inductive and empirical process of specific examination, sometimes line by line and stanza by stanza, and sometimes work by work through the entire career of an author.

Jean H. Hagstrum
*Samuel Johnson's Literary Criticism* (Minneapolis, Minn.:
Univ. Minnesota Pr., 1952, repr., with new preface,
Univ. Chicago Pr., 1967), pp. 21, 36, 37, 177-78

In 1778, Johnson, now aproaching seventy, began writing the *Lives of the English Poets* (1779-1781). A group of forty booksellers joined together to publish a large collection of the *Works of the English Poets* spanning the century from about 1660 to 1760, excluding whatever poets were still alive. The publishers appointed a committee to ask Johnson to write what finally amounted to fifty-two biographical prefaces, one for each poet, indicating that he could name his own terms. Johnson agreed, gave much more than was expected, and took virtually nothing. For it is understatement to say that most of the *Lives* turned out to be far from mere biographical prefaces. . . . Drawing on his own copious memory, often dealing with writers at whom he had hardly glanced for many years, these volumes are not only a landmark in the history of criticism. They are also the finest example of one of the great English prose-styles.

Characteristically Johnson took no initiative in his last great work. He had no particular "theory" of literary biography in mind. He simply wrote the requested prefaces in so superior a way that, in the process of doing so, he "gave to the British nation" as the editor of the 1825 edition said, "a new style of biography"—of biography, that is, extensively filled with specifically literary criticism of the man's works and general attainment. . . .

Certainly most of Johnson's strictures on poetic style are really reactions against the use of what we now call stock devices—the use of allusions, phrasing, and images that have no active and functional value, but simply make up the "pomp of machinery" of which he speaks in writing of Thomas Gray's formal odes, where Gray acquires a "strutting dignity and is tall by walking on tiptoe." Hence Johnson's antagonism to the "ready and puerile expedient" of sprinkling a poem with allusions to classical mythology. . . . So with Johnson's dislike of the "easy" use of archaic language, common at that time, in order to give atmosphere. His grumblings about blank-verse usually have to do with the monotonous blank-verse imitations, ostensibly imitations of Milton's special style, that were current in the eighteenth century. The reaction is against one more stock mannerism. . . . So on other problems of style, as they relate to language, metaphor, or imagery, Johnson's premises are not couched in the form of a manifesto, or a categorical thesis. They are once again the by-products of his practical criticism.

Walter Jackson Bate
*The Achievement of Samuel Johnson* (New York:
Oxford Univ. Pr., 1955), pp. 54-56, 210-211

GENERAL

Johnson's talk was remembered and recorded by many of those who had to do with him. His lightest sayings had a quality about them, an appositeness and a sincerity, which often stamped them even upon the laziest imagination. If they sometimes seem more wonderful to the recorder than they seem to a later and less excited audience, that is because they had all the force of a massive character behind them when they were spoken, and not less because they were always opportune, and took a great part of their meaning from circumstances which we cannot perfectly recreate. Boswell is fuller and more accurate in his accounts than any other of the chroniclers. But the work that he did was not peculiar to him, and if he had never written, Johnson's conversation would still be known to us for a live and luminous thing. . . .

To get rid of the affectations, conventions, and extravagances of literature; to make it speak to the heart on themes of universal human interest; to wed poetry with life—these were Johnson's aims. It is a little bewildering to the student of literary history to find that Pope, Johnson, and Wordsworth, each and all regarded themselves as the champions of a Return to Nature. Johnson, like Pope, confined nature somewhat too rigorously to human nature, and over-estimated the power of direct moral teaching. He speaks slightingly of the innovators who "seem to think that we are placed here to watch the growth of plants, or the motions of the stars. Socrates was rather of opinion that what we had to learn was, how to do good and avoid evil." Yet in criticizing the works of other men he does not apply this doctrine in any narrow or unintelligent fashion. He praised Shakespeare; he praised Boccaccio; and he would doubtless have praised the great poets of the nineteenth century, whose work conforms very little to his own stricter code.

Walter Raleigh
*Six Essays on Johnson* (Oxford: Clarendon
Pr., 1910), pp. 45, 156

Johnson was a realist only in the larger sense that he clung to truth, which was to him not only the ultimate value, but the one thing in life to be faced, however unpleasant, in hopes of salvation. Truth as he conceived it, may have been overaustere; in its name he made serious mistakes, about himself as well as other people; he was rude, savage, outrageous; but, however faulty at times his means, it was by this adherence to what he regarded as truth that he maintained his admirable integrity of mind and personality. He spared himself even less than others, as his torturing sense of his own personal insufficiency shows. When we are lost in the complexities of this problem, the attempt at a solution of which makes us contemporaries of the Renaissance, when we are inclined to look upon this particular apostle of truth as narrow, limited, we should try to recall any man who has laid a firmer foundation stone for an intellectual life than "Clear your mind of cant," Johnson's constant advice to himself and to all men. . . .

It was shortly after he met the Thrales that Johnson suffered his most severe attack of melancholia; they were shocked to discover him one day on his knees in the presence of a comparative stranger, confessing the stain on his soul and beseeching God to spare his understanding. They carried him off to Streatham and nursed him back to health; but during that period he would remain for whole days shut up in his own room, writing, as a prisoner to his jailer, strange notes in French to Mrs. Thrale, holding on to sanity and stifling imagination by spending hours in elaborate mathematical calculations, his favorite safeguard in such a crisis.

The results of this lifelong struggle are plain in his works, even when they do not emerge obviously. It is this power of emotion and imagination, so severely disciplined, which gives depth and meaning to what at times on the surface seems platitudinous, and which explains why his most commonplace remarks frequently are strangely moving. Their roots are all deep in his own experience, even apparently serene pronouncements springing from suffering and despair. We should remember, too, that Johnson is silent on some things simply because he could not bear to talk of them, as he could not bear to talk of death. The body of his imaginative, interpretative criticism would undoubtedly have been greater if he had not been forced to cling in self-distrust and self-preservation to reason. But he has left us a heritage of triumphant sanity, all the finer for being maintained with such difficulty, and of a profound and moving, if sometimes limited, undertsanding of the human soul.

W. B. C. Watkins
*Perilous Balance* (Princeton, N. J.: Princeton
Univ. Pr., 1939), pp. 90-92

Outwardly Johnson's attitude toward freedom of the press has a curiously disinterested cast. But that is not because he felt it to be an unimportant matter. Rather, as his frequent allusions indicate, he considered it an indissoluble part of his entire philosophy of human liberties. His suspicion of popular government is not to be dissociated from his lack of faith in popular expression. He therefore felt implicitly that the British press was as free as it should be for the good of the citizenry.

Edward A. Bloom
*Samuel Johnson in Grub Street* (Providence, R. I.:
Brown Univ. Pr., 1957), p. 245

These pieces, *London, Marmor Norfolciense,* and the *Compleat Vindication* (together with the "State of Affairs in Lilliput"), have always been a difficult problem for those who wish to store Johnson's political philosophy away in a neat pigeon-hole marked "Tory reactionary." Too much of what Johnson condemns in them, especially in the *Vindication,* sounds like a malicious travesty of the later Johnson as Boswell has taught us to see him. Perhaps it is all insincere. So Joseph Wood Krutch seems to think. . . . Conceivably so. Yet it is hard to read through the *Vindication* and not catch some warmth from the white heat in which Johnson forges his shafts against the "petty Tyrants" of vested bureaucracy, types of anti-intellectualism of all ages and places. "Incendiary" and "sulphurous" are the adjectives one student uses to describe the *Marmor* and the *Vindication,* and they are well chosen.

It is easy enough to find "explanations" of Johnson's political extremism during these two years, 1738 and 1739—for instance, the suggestion made above that, embittered at his failures in the Midlands and still unsure of himself in Grub Street, he was easily persuaded by the irresponsible and attractive Savage, perhaps with help from Harry Hervey and Guthrie, to find an outlet for his emotional violence in the opposition cause. Certainly, greater experience and maturity modified this violence. It is wrong, however, to view this episode, as Krutch and others have done, as an aberration from Johnson's "real" political attitudes. For one thing, we do not know that Johnson, up until this time, had formulated any very definite opinions about politics at the national level. Second, and more important, there is no reason for believing that the political principles underlying these early pamphlets are in fact essentially different from those underlying his later political writings. There is no evidence, in his later works, that he ever retracted his affirmation, implicit in the *Marmor* and the *Vindication,* that the only satisfactory basis for a political system must be the enlightened minds of free and responsible individuals.

Donald J. Greene
*The Politics of Samuel Johnson* (New Haven:
Yale Univ. Pr., 1960), pp. 105-6

# NATHANIEL LEE
1649?-1692

> Educated at Westminster School and Trinity College, Cambridge, Lee pursued acting in London, unsuccessfully, became an important tragic dramatist, and through extreme intemperance was confined in Bedlam from 1684 to 1689. He died four years later in poverty. Among his important works are *Sophonisba,* 1675; *The Rival Queens,* 1677; *Mithridates,* 1678; *Lucius Junius Brutus,* 1680; and *The Duke of Guise,* 1682 (with Dryden).
>
> Roswell G. Ham, *Otway and Lee* (1931)

Yet he brought every one of his imaginary figures with him; they all spoke in the same cracked voice, so the atmosphere is maintained, even though it be a riven atmosphere. If by saying that Lee had good "thoughts" for tragedy Addison meant that he had an eye for a situation, and a knowledge of what ought to go to compose one, he was right. Although the verbiage seems to be the thought, it is just possible that had the words been toned down the emotions might have seemed congruous with the facts. There is stuff in Lee, and he took great stories to build on, though he did not hesitate to alter the foundations if it suited him to do so. . . . His mistake was, rather, to make his people act and speak all the while "in character," so that they seem possessed by one absorbing idea, with the result that we seem to be moving in a world of tragic "humours," where the "excess," instead of being exposed to cure by laughter, is held up to admiration, or used to promote revulsion.

Bonamy Dobrée
*Restoration Tragedy, 1660-1720* (Oxford Univ. Pr.,
1929), p. 122

In *Lucius Junius Brutus* he ventured farther. In the title rôle he created a character with no vestige of the soft sentiment, and that despite the fact that his original, in the *Clélie* of Mlle de Scudéry, was possessed by an intemperate love for Lucrece. Brutus as a "whining slave" reaches the nadir of romance. Lee displayed a new common sense in developing a conflict between parental affection and an all-absorbing patriotism. A father sacrifices his son's life as an example to the state. The larger issues of 1680 in English politics had directed the poet into new channels. To Nat. Lee love had hitherto been conventional, for so far as we may discover he had been schooled by no actual experience in that passion. But now the danger threatening England lent actuality to his life. The sole love interest in the play was thwarted by the central problem of its hero Brutus, and throughout it suffered self-effacement before the larger motives of honor and patriotism.

Roswell G. Ham
*Otway and Lee* (New Haven: Yale Univ. Pr., 1931), pp. 151-52

It is evident . . . that from the beginning certain questions of political theory were teasing Lee. The continual recurrence of criticism of a ruler by wise or admirable characters and the frequent discussion of political questions are far more insistent than is dramatically appropriate. It is possible that Lee accepted hereditary kinship as an institution, but from the unnecessarily emphatic treatment of the question of legitimacy in *Gloriana,* it would seem that Lee did not consider legitimacy essential and that he preferred a virtuous illegitimate ruler to a legitimate tyrant. . . .

Nathaniel Lee is consistently anti-divine-right and anti-Tory. Even at the time when the heroic play was the accepted vehicle for the glorification and popularization of divine right, he dared to portray the dangers of such a political doctrine. The impulse was, perhaps, instinctive rather than conscious, but at any rate it led to the production of plays which did not entirely conform to the pattern of the heroic play.

Frances Barbour
*Studies in English* (Austin, Tex.: Univ. Texas, 1940), Vol. XX, pp. 111, 116

It seems then . . . that *Constantine* must be considered essentially a political play, one reflecting the Popish Plot and its sequels (the triumph of the Tories and the Rye House Plot). It has in it more than casual reference to the political conditions of the time. . . . Indeed it would seem to reflect the political conditions, the intrigues and plots and characters especially, more accurately and adequately than such plays as *Venice Preserved.* It appears to have been written, perhaps hurriedly, in the summer of 1683 in order to make use of the newest developments in the political situation. Lee evidently saw a rough parallel between the political-religious events of a part of Constantine's reign and those of a part of Charles's reign, and he carefully, if cautiously, pointed these out to his audience, shaping his material into a compliment to his King and the Tory party. Dryden, in order to give the play the proper send-off, wrote for it an epilogue full of up-to-date political allusion. Far from being an old play brought out by Dryden and Otway for production after Lee was *non compos mentis,* as Ham suggests, it seems to have been written in the political heat of the times. It can well be considered as one voice in the paean of triumph raised by the Tories upon the flight of Shaftesbury, the execution of the Rye House Conspirators, and the victorious reassertion of the Royal Power in the fall of 1683.

A. L. Cooke and Thomas B. Stroup
*JEGP* (October, 1950), pp. 514-15

# JOHN MILTON
1608-1674

Educated at St. Paul's School, London, and Christ's College, Cambridge, Milton began writing verse while in school and published his collected poetry in 1645. This volume contained *The Nativity Ode* (1629), *L'Allegro* and *Il Penseroso* (1631?), *Comus* (1634), and *Lycidas* (1637). After a continental sojourn in 1637-1638, he returned to study and tutoring before joining the pamphleteering war in 1641 with an anti-prelatical tract, *Of Reformation.* Other similar pamphlets were followed by works urging approval of divorce, denouncing censorship (*Areopagitica,* 1644), and expounding his theory of education (1644). After the parliamentarian victory in the Civil Wars and the execution of Charles I, Milton joined the Cromwellian government in 1649 as Secretary for Foreign Tongues, a post held until the Restoration. Further prose, largely governmentally directed, appeared during this period. His sight had begun to fail during the 1640's, and he was totally blind by February 1652. His three major poems in three varying genres were published during his general retirement from public life: *Paradise Lost* (1667, 1674), *Paradise Regain'd* and *Samson Agonistes* (1671). A second edition of his minor poems in 1673 presents almost all that are known.

Frank Patterson, gen. ed., *The Works of John Milton* (1931-1938), 18 vols. in 21

David Masson, *The Life of John Milton* (1881-1894), 7 vols.

PERSONAL

There is no evidence supporting the theories of albinism and of congenital syphilis. There is medical authority for the theory of a streptococcic infection which could also cause arthritis. . . . There is considerable medical evidence in favor of the glaucoma theory and in favor of the theory of myopia and detachment of the retina. . . . Yet in view of the limited information . . . the cause of Milton's blindness remains, and must remain, unsolved.

Eleanor Brown
*Milton's Blindness* (New York: Columbia Univ. Pr., 1934), p. 48

His life had been lived and—by 1660—was apparently concluded.

But Milton would have none of that; he chose the moment to complete the very large thing which gave him not only much the most of his renown, but that element of solidity and permanence in fame which seems to adhere to achievements not only in proportion to their quality but to their bulk. And having done this, and spread out for the gaze of his fellow-countrymen that mountain range called the *Paradise Lost,* he was not content until he had set up one more isolated monument, that tall and single peak the *Samson.*

Then indeed the work was done and the character accomplished. Milton under the name of Samson had triumphed over his enemies, but not until Milton under the name of God Almighty had triumphed over the rebel Angels, nor until, under the name of Satan, he had made a fine and lordly thing of his throne in Hell—and all the while Milton as Adam was in imagination managing a wife for some few years without catastrophe, and moving in high company, giving good food to Archangels.

Hilaire Belloc
*Milton* (Philadelphia: J. B. Lippincott, 1935), p. 47

Milton had never been a democrat in the modern sense of the word. He did not believe that one man's opinion was as good as another's. But, both as humanist and as puritan, he had believed passionately in the collective wisdom, inspiration, and effectual power of the best men, whether Platonic philosopher-kings or puritan "Saints." There is little of that faith left in his later works. Samson, God's chosen hero, is now "Eyeless in Gaza at the mill with slaves." Milton tries to find a basis for hope in the scroll of future history revealed to Adam, but Adam hears no such story of national courage and triumph as Aeneas heard from Anchises. . . . Milton's hope of a new reformation, then, will be realized only at the day of judgment, when the evil world is cleansed by fire, and that is small comfort here and now. But if his old faith in men has proved vain, something can still be done by individual man; he can at least rule himself. So when Adam has learned the rational and Christian virtues, he has no need of an earthly paradise, he has a paradise within him, happier far. So Christ, man's perfect model, maintains his integrity against the allurements of the world. So Samson, resisting selfish and sensual temptations, achieves an inner regeneration which makes his outward fate of no account.

Douglas Bush
*The Renaissance and English Humanism* (Toronto:
Univ. Toronto Pr., 1939), pp. 123-24

## Paradise Lost

In a previous article [*SP,* XIV (1917), 196 ff.] I have sought to give meaning to Milton's praise of Spenser as "a better teacher than Aquinas" and thus to explain, in part, what he meant by telling Dryden that Spenser was his "original." This definition of Spenser's influence dealt with two topics. The first of these traced the influence on Milton of Spenser's philosophy, drawn ultimately from Plato and Aristotle, modified by Renaissance theories of beauty and virtue, and further modified by Milton by the fusion with it of the theological tradition of the Middle Ages as inherited and re-defined by religious thinkers of the sixteenth and seventeenth centuries. This evolution, characteristic of the Renaissance since the time of Ficino and the Florentine Academy, finds its last and perhaps greatest synthesis in Milton. The union of mysticism and the practical virtues, of the contemplative with the active life, present in Greek philosophy, is at once characteristic of the Renaissance as an epoch in history and of the great English interpreters of the ideal, Spenser and Milton.

In the second place, I sought to show that this relationship between the two poets was not, as might be argued had we no further basis than philosophical agreement, a mere consanguinity of the spirit. That Milton used *Spenser's* interpretation of classical and Renaissance idealism is, as I pointed out, proved by the debt of Milton's greatest poetry, and most of all *Paradise Lost,* to the second book of the *Faerie Queene,* a debt abundantly proved not only by certain correspondences in structure but also by specific incidents. This parallelism of incident affects *Paradise Lost* more than other works of Milton; it shows indebtedness not only to the Book of Guyon but also to the Book of Redcross, and, in the latter, suggests both debt for incident and debt for the fundamental thesis of the justification of the ways of God to man and the promise of the "greater Man" through whom redemption was to come.

Edwin Greenlaw
*SP* (July, 1920), p. 320

Milton's general moral teaching in *Paradise Lost,* then, is this: Reason, which is God's law in the cosmos and in the mind of man, must be observed. To observe it is to live in harmony with God; to trample it under foot is to separate ourselves from God and to break the cosmic unity.

Martin A. Larson
*The Modernity of Milton* (Chicago:
Univ. Chicago Pr., 1927), p. 232

The glory of *Paradise Lost* is that it resumes the essential medieval theme and combines it with Renaissance culture and exuberance and with neo-classic compression of form. *Paradise Lost* is a mental pilgrimage: the loss of one paradise and the finding, on this earth, of "a Paradise within thee, happier farr." That this paradise should have affinities with Stoicism and the Renaissance rather than with Dante does not prevent the poem's concerning the essentially medieval subject of the soul's pilgrimage. In still another way the theme of Milton's poem is medieval. Heywood's *Troia Britannica* shows that the old medieval subject of universal history (exemplified in *Cursor Mundi*) was not dead in the seventeenth century. *Paradise Lost,* for all its compression, deals with universal history from the creation of the angels to the final doom.

E. M. W. Tillyard
*The Miltonic Setting* (Cambridge Univ. Pr., 1938), p. 167

The most important question to decide is whether or not Milton was anti-Trinitarian when he composed *Paradise Lost.* The view I shall put forward is that Milton was Trinitarian when the early books were composed, but that his Trinitarianism is yielding to the pressure of other opinion in the later books. . . . When Milton wrote *Paradise Lost,* he seems to have accepted a Trinity of Manifestation. The Father is the Creator; the Son is the Mediator, King and Redeemer; the Holy Spirit works in the hearts of men. . . . I suggest, therefore, that Milton's view of the Trinity when he commenced to write the poem was one of three persons, each of whom manifested in their relations with man and with the universe of man something of the nature of Deity—Justice, Love, and Wisdom. I suggest, too, that the influence of this view persists through the later books of the poem.

Arthur Sewell
*A Study in Milton's Christian Doctrine* (Oxford
Univ. Pr., 1939), pp. 85, 93, 105-6

Necessarily conjectural are my conclusions regarding the order in which Milton composed the first three-fifths of the epic. Evidence chiefly internal, but supported by *Adam Unparadised* and the abandoned tragedy, suggests strongly that Books I-III, the third quarter of Book IV, and the first two-thirds of Book V were written later than the remaining parts of Books IV-V, Book VI, and apparently sections of Book VIII. On the basis of Milton's activities and his letter to Henry Oldenburgh, the two provisional periods were set as 1652-53 and 1655-58. Further evidence from probable sources corroborates the data to the extent of setting composition of the epic catalog almost certainly after 1652, and apparently after 1655. As a probability which merits careful consideration, and only as such, I suggest that Milton began composition with sections of Book IV, and that he wrote perhaps four-fifths of *Paradise Lost* during the three periods of 1652-53, 1655-58, and 1660-63.

Grant McColley
*Paradise Lost* (Chicago: Packard, 1940), p. 325

The *De doctrina* is the presentation of this body of belief in the manner of a systematic theology, and the principles that directed this logical presentation are those detailed in Milton's *Artis Logicae. Paradise Lost,* on the other hand, is the presentation of this same body of belief in the manner of a blank verse epic, and the principles that governed this poetic presentation are those of the great epic tradition as they were modified by Milton's aesthetic judgment. As a result, there are essential differences between the two works, both in nature and aim as well as in the relative importance of form and content. . . . In the treatise, content is the primary determinant of form: orthodox theologians, for example, usually devote only a single chapter to the Father, Son, and Spirit; whereas Milton's anti-Trinitarianism leads him to give a separate chapter to each of the three. In the poem, however, form is the primary determinant of content: the epic tradition necessitates that *Paradise Lost* contain a certain type of plot, narrative technique, and characters, and the fact that the work is poetry not only requires that it be concrete, but also permits its author a judicious exercise of his imaginative and inventive powers. Thus at the behest of form or artistic need, Milton may include in his epic allegories, debates, and interviews that find no mention in the *De doctrina,* but rather are figments of his imagination or borrowings from antiquity. . . . In the poem, moreover, Milton may emphasize certain sins in the fall, to which he accords only passing mention in his systematic theology; or some of the sins explicitly enumerated in the treatise may be present only by implication in the poem. Yet this mingling of theological fact with poetical fiction in no way disproves Milton's basic belief in the dogma; nor does this preciseness and emphasis necessarily indicate that between the composition of the two works Milton experienced a modification in religious belief.

Maurice Kelley
*This Great Argument* (Princeton, N. J.:
Princeton Univ. Pr., 1941), pp. 195-96

What we see in Satan is the horrible co-existence of a subtle and incessant intellectual activity with an incapacity to understand anything. This doom he has brought upon himself; in order to avoid seeing one thing he has, almost voluntarily, incapacitated himself from seeing at all. And thus, throughout the poem, all his torments come, in a sense, at his own bidding, and the Divine judgment might have been expressed in the words *"thy* will be done.". . . From hero to general, from general to politician, from politician to secret service agent, and thence to a thing that peers in at bedroom or bathroom windows, and thence to a toad, and finally to a snake—such is the progress of Satan. This progress, misunderstood, has given rise to the belief that Milton began by making Satan more glorious than he intended and then, too late, attempted to rectify the error. But such an unerring picture of the "sense of injured merit" in its actual operations upon character cannot have come about by blundering and accident.

We need not doubt that it was the poet's intention to be fair to evil, to give it a run for its money—to show it *first* at the height, with all its rants and melodrama and "Godlike imitated state" about it, and *then* to trace what actually becomes of such self-intoxication when it encounters reality.

C. S. Lewis
*A Preface to Paradise Lost* (Oxford
Univ. Pr., 1942), pp. 96-97

In *Paradise Lost,* setting fundamental motives in the clear relief of an ancient author, Milton showed the will to power, public and private, intellectual presumption, egoistic desire, seeking their ends through force and fraud and overthrowing the divine and natural order in the world and in the soul. He surveyed a world going through pride to destruction and issued a serious call to a devout holy life. . . . That is one prime reason for reading Milton. We need the shock of encountering a poet to whom good and evil are distinct realities, a poet who has a much-tried but invincible belief in a divine order and in man's divine heritage and responsibility, who sees in human life an eternal contest between irreligious pride and religious humility.

Douglas Bush
*Paradise Lost in Our Time* (Ithaca, N. Y.:
Cornell Univ. Pr., 1945), pp. 56-57

And finally, the paradise within him "happier far" that Adam is to achieve even in this life is not happier far than the happiness of innocence, but happier than the merely physical paradise that he is loathe to leave.

For all that, good has come from evil. Satan has won no partial victory. We began the present discussion by saying that the paradox was real. We return to that. Lovejoy suggests that Milton chose to keep two themes separate, the fall and the redemption, so that in the first part of the poem he could show the fall as the deplorable thing it must seem and in the latter could introduce the idea that it was after all a *felix culpa.* . . . This does not quite recognize how deeply rooted in Milton's story (and hence in his thought) the paradox really is. Judging from the care with which Milton, several times suggesting it, always refrains from saying that it was a *felix culpa,* from the care with which he presents the two prognostications of man's future—one before and one after the fall—in the same terms, we must conclude that he was unwilling to choose between the horns of the dilemma.

John S. Diekhoff
*Milton's Paradise Lost* (New York:
Columbia Univ. Pr., 1946) pp. 131-32

Here and there Milton's execution may falter. But if we look at his picture through seventeenth century eyes, if we try not to impose upon it the
deceptions of our own historic and personal perspectives, its implications
should be plain and unmistakable. The failure lies not in the depiction of
Satan but in that of the heavenly values which should subdue him. Those
values are only imperfectly realized. So, though one half of the picture may
be painted convincingly, the other half is sketched rather than painted.
Milton's God is what his Satan never is, a collection of abstract properties,
or, in his greatest moments, a treatise on free-will. The Son moves us more
deeply, particularly in the quiet, firm monosyllables in which he announces
his sacrifice. But the spare precision of the language Milton gives him is
lit only seldom by the ardour which should inform it. Clothed in the language of Ezekiel's vision his triumph over Satan must have its moments
of majesty, but it remains a moral rather than a poetic victory.

B. Rajan
*Paradise Lost and The Seventeenth Century Reader* (New York:
Barnes and Noble, 1947), pp. 106-7

The process of growth that has been described—growth from the first draft
for *Paradise Lost,* or even from the ambitions mentioned in *At a Vacation
Exercise*—is to be considered in relation to what may be thought the disjointed effect produced by the attempt to date the various parts of the epic.
To some extent the poem is the result of shifting matter and inserting it.
Some disadvantageous effects of that process remain, though the total
result of every shift and insertion was greater excellence. Yet the metamorphosis was under the control of a central purpose, clear at the outset, growing clearer as time went on, but gaining complete clarity only when the
*Paradise Lost* we know was complete. The fourth draft represents a full-
wrought unit. Yet it was inadequate to satisfy its author's growing vision
of his end. Though abandoned for the epic plan, it still furnished the center around which later work was to be grouped. It yielded, moreover, to
a long-considered epic scheme. Transformation or shifting of its parts—
large or small—was always controlled by design. Additional parts demanded by the epic form were also subordinated to the ruling intention, and
after they were thought out might be restricted, shifted, or rejected for
more adequate successors. The last additions also, as they fulfilled intentions
latent from the beginning but emergent only as the process drew to its close,
took the places demanded by the nature of work. The patchy effect of the
details when viewed one by one disappears when they are seen as components of the grand design.

Allan H. Gilbert
*On the Composition of Paradise Lost* (Chapel Hill, N. C.:
Univ. North Carolina Pr., 1947), pp. 160-61

It is possible, I think, to overrate very much Milton's *awareness* of the peculiar difficulties of his theme. The difficulties are of the kind that fairly leap to our eyes. . . . It is not absurd to mention the novel in connection with *Paradise Lost,* for the problems of such a poem and the characteristic problems of the novel have much in common. . . . We have only to look at the material that he was bent on disposing in his epic to see that some of the problems he faced were virtually insoluble. A glance at the story of the Fall as it is given in Genesis shows that it is lined with difficulties of the gravest order. God, to begin with, does not show to advantage in that particular story: the story is a bad one for God. Within that set of events to make God attractive to our common human sensibilities (and it is not to be forgotten that the *raison d'être* of the whole poem lies in its appeal to common human sensibilities) will be hard. Again, it will be necessary to mark the transition from innocence to guilt; somehow sinlessness has to give place to sin; and in a large narrative such a transition may not be easy to make plausible. There is, once more, the disproportion . . . between the offence and the punishment—bringing us back again to God. . . . Could any writer with an instinct for narrative, we ask ourselves, have failed to see what problems those first three chapters of Genesis held, and to shrink back deterred?

A. J. A. Waldock
*Paradise Lost and Its Critics* (Cambridge
Univ. Pr., 1947), pp. 17-19

. . . The Paradox of the Fortunate Fall . . . had nevertheless a recognized and natural place in the treatment of the topic in Christian theology—that of the culmination of the redemptive process in human history—which was also for Milton the culmination theme in his poem. Yet it undeniably placed the story of the Fall, which was the subject of the poem announced at the outset, in a somewhat ambiguous light; when it was borne in mind, man's first disobedience could not seem the deplorable thing which, for the purposes of the poet—and of the theologian—it was important to make it appear. The only solution was to keep the two themes separate. In the part of the narrative dealing primarily with the Fall, the thought that it was after all a *felix culpa* must not be permitted explicitly to intrude; that was to be reserved for the conclusion, where it could heighten the happy final consummation by making the earlier and unhappy episodes in the story appear as instrumental to that consummation, and, indeed, as its necessary conditions.

Arthur O. Lovejoy
*Essays in the History of Ideas* (Baltimore:
Johns Hopkins Pr., 1948), pp. 294-95

*Paradise Lost* . . . is to be regarded as no mausoleum of decayed classicism. It is rather to be read as a metaphor of spiritual evolution. Its structural pattern is neither rigidly fixed nor shifted; it is shifting. The firmness with which Milton defines his structural blocks serves chiefly to sustain the Christian paradox on which the metaphor is hinged. It would seem that in the redivision of 1674 Milton underlines the direction of the shifting. Whatever the cause . . . he remained intent on the perfect adaptation of the pattern to the end.

Arthur E. Barker
*PQ* (January, 1949), p. 30

God is in the story as a kind of theory; Christ is the foil of Satan and the instrument of his defeat. The angels, good and bad, are minor vehicles of Miltonic personality and idea. The obvious judgment that Satan is the true "hero" of *Paradise Lost* was first expressed by Dryden. Blake went further in defining Milton's attitude when he asked the question why Milton wrote with freedom when he talked of Hell and the rebel angels, in chains when he talked of God and Heaven—and answered, "Because he was a true poet and of the devil's party without knowing it." But the deeper truth is that Milton is of all parties and none. Satan is the representative of every power in him which battled against restriction. He is Milton defying the authority both of external circumstance and of his own reason. Christ *is* that reason—hateful, cold, relentless. There is no truce between the two and no real victory. Satan is triumphant but accurst; Christ, except in the passion of his obedience, is triumphant but joyless. The two represent the conflicts of a frustrated personality. They are essentially unmoral and unhuman, the upper and the nether millstones between which humanity is ground to dust.

James Holly Hanford
*John Milton, Englishman* (New York:
Crown, 1949), p. 182

This, then, [his intolerable melodious noise] and not any incapacity to be interested in myth, is why we find Milton unexhilarating. The myth of *Paradise Lost,* indeed, suffers from deficiencies related to those of the verse. "Milton's celestial and infernal regions are large but insufficiently furnished apartments filled by heavy conversation," remarks Mr. Eliot, and suggests that the divorce from Rome, following the earlier breach with the Teutonic past, may have something to do with this mythological thinness. But it is enough to point to the limitations in range and depth of Milton's interests, their patent inadequacy to inform a "sense of myth, of fable, of ordered wholes in experience." His strength is of the kind that we indicate when, distinguishing between intelligence and character, we lay the stress on the latter; it is a strength, that is, involving sad disabilities. He has "character," moral grandeur, moral force; but he is, for the purposes of his undertaking, disastrously single-minded and simple-minded. He reveals everywhere a dominating sense of righteousness and a complete incapacity to question or explore its significance and conditions. This defect of intelligence is a defect of imagination. He offers as ultimate for our worship mere brute assertive will, though he condemns it unwittingly by his argument and by glimpses of his own finer human standard. His volume of moral passion owes its strength too much to innocence—a guileless unawareness of the subtleties of egotism—to be an apt agent for projecting an "ordered whole of experience." It involves, too, a great poverty of interest. After the first two books, magnificent in their simple force (party politics in the Grand Style Milton can compass), *Paradise Lost,* though there are intervals of relief, becomes dull and empty: "all," as Raleigh says, "is power, vagueness and grandeur." Milton's inadequacy to myth, in fact, is so inescapable, and so much is conceded in sanctioned comment, that the routine eulogy of his "architectonic" power is plainly a matter of mere inert convention.

F. R. Leavis
*Revaluation* (London: Chatto and Windus, 1949), pp. 58-59

We come now to the question of how the plot fares when we compare not, as on the old plan, the action leading to Eve's Fall, but the behaviour of Adam and Eve after it, with Satan's behaviour after his revolt.

Now the acts of Satan, as set forth in the poem, are divided into two. The immediate consequences of his revolt, his seducing a third of the angels, the war in Heaven, the fall into Hell, are narrated halfway through by Raphael, while only the acts after this fall are presented directly. Further, it is God himself and the good angels that Satan's early acts concern. The result is that though the battle in Heaven and Satan's fall do correspond to the ruin Adam and Eve bring on themselves and on nature by eating the fruit, we simply do not, in reading, make the comparison. The virtue of the human action is not drawn on to counterpoise the Satanic action, the necessary counterpoise being supplied by the hosts of Heaven. It is far otherwise with Satan's action at the opening of the poem. Heaven is then remote; Satan's feelings are human feelings; the infernal council is a humanly political debate: and inevitably we compare the infernal action in and beyond Hell with the human action in Paradise.

E. M. W. Tillyard
*Studies in Milton* (New York: Macmillan, 1951), pp. 48-49

It is such an Adam and it is such an Eve who come to their fatal moment of trial beneath the forbidden Tree of the knowledge of Good and Evil. There, it is not the onset of sin we witness, so much as it is the beginning of self-discovery by creatures essentially human, which is to say, imperfect in a hundred ways, moved by the complex springs of impulse listed in the *De Doctrina Christiana*. And it seems to be Milton's thought that only by becoming conscious of these qualities does Man have hope of attaining that inner harmony and the unity with the cosmic purpose which is his true Paradise.

Millicent Bell
*PMLA* (September, 1953), p. 875

One of the most forceful dramatizations of the upward as well as of the downward swing of the pattern occurs in Book Ten. After Adam and Eve realize the effects of their sin, first he and then she journeys down into a longing for death as escape. . . . From the period of withdrawal, of symbolic death, the new attitude which emerges—an attitude of humility, repentance, and love of God—is featured by his conviction of guilt and his powerful desire that the wrath of God's justice might be directed upon his head only, instead of diffusing through all mankind to come. . . . His words, "on mee, mee onely," echo those of the Son when He offered Himself in place of Man to bear the burden of Man's guilt and God's justice. Adam wishes unwittingly—since he cannot foresee Christ's future sacrifice—to place himself in the role which the God-man is to fulfill; and his motives are also those of the Son. In so desiring, Adam has already implicitly, without the conscious understanding he achieves later, found the way to atonement with God. But Adam knows that he is not the man capable of supporting that burden. In like manner, Eve would bear all, for Adam's sake rather than for the sake of all mankind, which is consonant with her place. . . . Fittingly, it is immediately after both have expressed the wish to assume the role of the compassionate sacrifice that their discord is resolved.

As the pattern of fall and rise receives individual dramatic focus in Book Ten through the death in Adam and Eve of their sinful selves and the rebirth from that death of their new attitude of humility and love, intimating in its echo of the Son's offer that they have found the "upward way"; so in Book Eleven the pattern is reviewed within a universal circumference through the visions afforded Adam by Michael.

Robert Durr
*JAAC* (June, 1955), p. 525

Six years ago Dr. E. M. W. Tillyard's "The Crisis of *Paradise Lost*" appeared, and more recently Mrs. Millicent Bell's "The Fallacy of the Fall

in *Paradise Lost"* has followed. Both offer an interpretation of the poem
based on the fact that Adam and Eve are not "perfect" before the Fall.
From this premise Dr. Tillyard and Mrs. Bell develop theories about the
structure of the poem which are not, I think, tenable, in spite of some valuable insights which their essays contain. Stated broadly, their thesis is that
Adam and Eve are really "fallen" before the Fall, that consequently the
Fall itself is not the crisis of the poem, but that instead the regeneration
of Adam and Eve in Book X is the culminating event around which the
poem is organized. . . . [But] Adam and Eve, though not perfect before the
Fall, are by no means already "fallen,". . . the Fall is the central theological
event in the poem, and . . . it is likewise the climax of the narrative.

H. V. S. Ogden
*PQ* (January, 1957), p. 1

One doesn't need to go to the argumentative speeches of God the Father in
order to make the point that such an undertaking was one for which Milton
had no qualifications. Those speeches do indeed exhibit him as (considering his offer) ludicrously unqualified to make even a plausible show of
metaphysical capacity. But it is in the "versification" everywhere that the
essential inaptitude appears: the man who uses words in this way has (as
Mr. Eliot virtually says) no "grasp of ideas," and, whatever he may suppose, is not really interested in the achievement of precise thought of any
kind; he certainly hasn't the kind of energy of mind needed for sustained
analytic and discursive thinking. That is why the ardours and ingenuities
of the scholars who interpret *Paradise Lost* in terms of a supposed consistency of theological intention are so absurd, and why it is so deplorable
that literary students should be required to take that kind of thing seriously,
believe that it has anything to do with intelligent literary criticism, and
devote any large part of their time to the solemn study of Milton's
"thought."

F. R. Leavis
*The Common Pursuit* (London: Chatto and Windus, 1958), p. 23

The structure of *Paradise Lost,* if we look down on all this world at once,
is a great inverted V; or, seen in three dimensions, a mountain with its roots
in Hell and its crown in Heaven. We begin at the lowest point; we end at
a point not quite so low, but far below the heights to which we have soared
in the middle. Within this basic structure are a number of smaller patterns
where lesser ascents and descents are followed. The whole is a great vision
of rising and falling action; and in *Paradise Lost* the rise and fall are not
only emotional, moral, or social, as in tragedy, but literal and topographical as well. Image and meaning are one. . . .

A severely structured universe is essential to Milton's mythical vision, where clear outlines and pure, complete beings are part of the landscape. The definite, morally significant "places" of *Paradise Lost,* the solidity of the poem's outlines in space, its imitations of mortality and history within those outlines, and the interlocked intricacy of its verbal and imagistic patterns, are part of a world-view that we can know only through the hearsay of myth. The world of *Paradise Lost,* when we first see it, is a complete world; it ends by being a ruined one. But before it can be broken, the great structure must be built. It must stand before us, solid, finished, composed of contending stresses in perfect balance; and in the gigantic pyramid of his poem, Milton has given us this distant world, held for an instant within the sweep of a single vision.

Isabel Gamble MacCaffrey
*Paradise Lost as "Myth"* (Cambridge, Mass.:
Harvard Univ. Pr., 1959), pp. 56, 91

When the anti-Miltonists demand an "answer" to their charges, they are undoubtedly expecting an answer couched in the language in which these charges were made: otherwise they would not be able to recognize it as an answer at all. Leavis or Peter might be satisfied by an opponent who tries to show that Milton's Grand Style *did* possess the qualities of sensitivity and subtlety and expressive closeness to the movement of actual sensory experience that Leavis has so convincingly denied to it; but not otherwise. And it is most unlikely that anyone would be found to make the attempt. Leavis has certainly established that these qualities are *not* present in Milton's verse in the way that they are in much of Shakespeare's, and even such a convinced Miltonist as Professor Lewis has paid tribute to the accuracy of Leavis's account of Milton's verse. Within the limits of his particular critical language Leavis's attack is irrefutable. Similarly with Waldock's criticisms. A successful answer to Waldock would have to show that narrative structure of *Paradise Lost does* possess the kind of coherence and psychological plausibility that we have come to expect from the novel. Again, there can be no doubt that it does not.

But the anti-Miltonic arguments, though unanswerable, are also wrong. Wrong because, to speak for myself, they do not correspond with the facts of my literary experience; nor, I imagine with those of many other readers.

Bernard Bergonzi
*The Living Milton* (London: Routledge and
Kegan Paul, 1960), p. 174

The most serious result is failure to motivate Satan evilly. Satan's immediate motive for sin, the "begetting" of the Son, is ambiguous, vague (like the motives of Achilles) and confused by the ceremony after the war in

time but before it in the poem when the Son assumes the office of Redeemer. God himself is confused. . . . [The rebels] have refused the Son
as "Right reason" and as king; but it is not until after the creation of Man
that the Son assumes the messianic office of anointed liberator, and reigns
by merit of his self-sacrifice. Satan's conspiracy and the invention of explosive, which take up most space, are indecorous. We are witnessing the
birth of evil and all we see is Achaian warriors whispering in each other's
ears and letting off cannon. . . . Milton makes Satan "allure" the other
rebels and gives us the orthodoxy of the last sentence. But he does not give
us any vision of the germinal defection of Satan himself, such as the birth
of Sin provides in Book II and such as we have for Eve.

J. B. Broadbent
*Some Graver Subject* (London: Chatto
and Windus, 1960), pp. 223-24

Milton's difficulties in presenting God are sometimes represented as insur-
mountable, but most of them could have been avoided if he had used the
angels more effectively. As has been noted, the chief tension within the God
of *Paradise Lost* exists between his majesty, which should be inaccessible
and mysterious, and other less ineffable qualities: his anger, or the geniality
seen in his colloquy with Adam in Book Eight. Properly handled, the angels
might have removed this tension: they could have taken over God's practical functions and left his majesty unqualified and intact. If it is necessary
to explain Free Will at length, as indeed it is, the explanation is best left
to Raphael. If it is advisable to show God's friendliness to Adam before the
Fall, as again perhaps it is, an angel, Heaven's delegate, is a better instrument for the purpose than God himself, reduced and circumscribed, can
ever be. . . .

It is not only the angels' function that is mishandled. The poet's whole
concept of them seems inappropriate and refractory. At the root of this
refractoriness lies Milton's doctrine of the materiality of all Creation, a
doctrine quite acceptably set forth by Raphael and at this date sufficiently
familiar to students of the poem. Unlike the Gnostics, who held that matter was essentially evil, Milton believed that matter and spirit differed only
in degree, not kind, and that each contained the potentiality for goodness,
though in their different degrees. . . . But doctrines acceptable in theory
are easy to abuse in practice, and when this belief is applied directly to the
angels the abuse is blatant. For poet and reader alike it is again chiefly a
matter of indecision, of not knowing on what plane the poem's characters
exist.

John Peter
*A Critique of Paradise Lost* (New York:
Columbia Univ. Pr., 1960), pp. 21-22

## Paradise Regain'd

The true word for Milton's *Paradise Regained* is "Bad." It is a thoroughly bad exercise. It contains no quite first-rate line, hardly a couple of dozen good ones—and that is not enough to float nearly two thousand mean and flat.

It is an awful proof of the power which association in ideas has to confuse thought, that because John Milton's name is attached to the stuff— and perhaps because the subject is sacred and solemn—it should be treated with any respect at all.

Hilaire Belloc
*Milton* (Philadelphia: J. B. Lippincott, 1935), p. 263

. . . By overcoming gluttony, vain glory, and avarice, Christ might be said to have overcome all temptation, because all are mere variants of the three basic seductions typified by gluttony, vain glory, and avarice: concupiscence of the flesh, concupiscence of the eye, and the pride of life: the flesh, the world, and the devil. The three are arranged on a sort of ascending scale of potency, beginning with the lowest and most venial, and ending with the highest and most deadly.

The addition of this second set of parallels to the first one results in a sort of triple equation between the temptations of Adam, the temptations of Christ, and all the temptations of this world. As summarized above, it is postulated on the basis of the order of temptations given by Matthew. But it was also possible to postulate it on the basis of the order given by Luke. This entailed more than simply transposing the second and third factors of the equation, since it was desirable to keep the three sins in the proper succession: flesh, world, devil: bad, worse, worst. "Avarice" and "vain glory," however, are rather anomalous sins: it was quite possible to call the temptation of the kingdoms, the temptation of the world (*concupiscentia oculorum*), and the temptation of the tower, the temptation of the devil (*superbia vitae*). The Luke equation, in fact, actually made better sense than the Matthew: the *regna omnia mundi* is a more obvious and suitable temptation of the world than the *mitte te deorsum*, while the *mitte te deorsum* conforms to Satan's original offence—desire for vain glory, presumption in aspiring to be as God—much more closely than the *regna omnia mundi*.

Elizabeth Marie Pope
*Paradise Regained: The Tradition and the Poem*
(Baltimore: Johns Hopkins Pr., 1947), pp. 53-54

In arranging lures [in *Paradise Regain'd*] the poet ascended an ethical ladder, and thus Satan comes last to the highest—learning, or more exactly clergy-learning, the fairest and most plausible bait known to Antichrist. Against Satan's plea for ministerial learning, and countering it point by point, Christ maintains two theses. First, human philosophy cannot teach what it does not know. It cannot be indispensable to God's revealed truth, since at its Hellenic best it falls short of wisdom precisely where a minister needs wisdom. The philosophers could know nothing of creation, original sin, or man's impotence without grace. How could they teach truly of God and the soul? Their books are not therefore sinful, but in the Preacher's meaning "wearisome" perhaps, dangerous "trifles" if taken for "choice matters" by men shallow in themselves (IV.285-330). Second, the oratory, the political thought, and especially the bawdy poetry of Greece will not civilize, will not delight leisure hours better than Hebrew song and story. They will not "form a King" so well or so plainly as holy scripture (331-364).

Howard Schultz
*Milton and Forbidden Knowledge* (New York:
Modern Language Assn., 1955), p. 226

In *Paradise Regained*, as to some extent in *Comus*, the dramatic and the dialectical aspects of the conflict are opposed and in a paradoxical relation to one another. Comus and Satan get our dramatic attention because they show such energy and resourcefulness; the tempted figures are either motionless or unmoved and have only the ungracious dramatic function of saying No. Yet, of course, the real relation is the opposite of the apparent one: the real source of life and freedom and energy is in the frigid figure at the center. . . .

The temptation of the pinnacle corresponds to the point in *Samson Agonistes* at which Samson, after beating off Manoah, Delilah, and Harapha, refuses to go to the Philistine festival. He is right in refusing but has come to the end of his own will. At that point he appears to change his mind, but what has happened is that God has accepted his efforts, taken over his will, and changed his mind for him. In *Samson Agonistes*, which is a tragedy, this point is the "peripety": Samson is now certain to die, though also certain of redemption. Jesus has also made it impossible for himself to avoid death, as his prototypes Elijah and perhaps Moses did; but *Paradise Regained* is less a tragedy than an episode in a divine comedy, and we need another term for the crucial point of the action. . . . The Father recognizes Jesus as the Son at the baptism: Satan recognizes him on the pinnacle in a different, yet closely related, sense. That is, the action of *Paradise Regained* begins with the baptism, an epiphany which Satan sees but does not understand, and ends with an epiphany to Satan alone, the nature of which he can hardly fail to understand. Behind this is the still larger scheme in which *Paradise Regained* is the sequel of *Paradise*

*Lost.* The epiphany of Christ to the angels, which caused the original revolt of Satan, was chronologically the first event in *Paradise Lost*, and, with the climax of *Paradise Regained*, the great wheel of the quest of Christ comes full circle, as far as Milton's treatment of it is concerned.

Northrop Frye
*MP* (April, 1956), pp. 234, 238

My underlying assumption . . . is that *Paradise Regained* is a dramatic definition of "heroic knowledge," not of heroic rejection; and that the contest is a preparation for *acting transcendence in the world*, by uniting intuitive knowledge with proved intellectual and moral discipline. . . .

In *Paradise Regained* Milton is morally, poetically, dramatically right. Christ's kingdom is not of this world; his kingdom is the church, which governs the inner man; his role is that of symbolic illumination for the mind of man. The practical reason of prudence is united with the other virtues to serve a pure vision of wisdom which serves God. Knowledge of the fountain of knowledge is obedience, within and without, a "way of death" as positive moral example. Within the world of self this dying is true living. In the poem the symbolic role of illumination is radical and exacting, but it is also rich and dynamic. Milton intends no literal allegory which could be translated as meaning that every man should do precisely thus. The hero and the circumstances *are* unique, metaphorically relevant to every man, but who could presume a literal identification? This is part of the sustained tension of the poem, the dynamic degree of the reader's relationship to the hero's dramatic demonstration, intellectual, moral, and religious.

Arnold Stein
*Heroic Knowledge* (Minneapolis, Minn.:
Univ. Minnesota Pr., 1957), pp. 17, 74-75

With consummate architectonic skill, Milton has epitomized in the literal temptation story the "rudiments" of Christ's mediatorial office as Prophet, King, and Priest, and has shown his progress from a condition of human uncertainty to a full realization of each of these functions and of his divine nature and power. Satan by contrast . . . has displayed the literal mind of evil, unable to understand revelation and metaphor, and has experienced a foreshadowing of the destruction of all his powers—as Father of Lies, as Prince of This World, as Prince of Darkness, as Prince of the Air—as well as the final defeat of his cohorts, Sin and Death. This theme is enriched by means by several counterpoints. . . . Book I is wholly concerned with temptations to the Prophetic role, but Book II elaborates the motif of intemperance, either as related to bodily enjoyments or to external possessions and honors; Book III displays the motifs of "time" and "force," as related to personal glory and to the public, Mediatorial Kingdom, and Book IV sets forth a series of climaxes, each outdoing the last in scope and effect—there is Rome, then Athens, then the storm scene as a low point leading to the ultimate victory and full revelation on the Tower.

Barbara K. Lewalski
*SP* (April, 1960), p. 220

## Samson Agonistes

In considering the application of this principle to *Samson Agonistes* we must observe, first of all, that, by representing a clearly marked triumph of the human will over its own weakness, and by the substitution of Providence for blind fate as the power which overrules the action, the play provides material for a different understanding of catharsis from that contemplated by Aristotle, an understanding which falls in with the first part of Milton's description—that tragedy is the gravest, moralest, and most profitable of poetic forms—rather than with the last—that it transforms painful emotions into pleasurable. On a superficial view we might, indeed, be tempted to regard the purgation, as Milton actually worked it out, as a purely ethical and religious process, the result of a consciously didactic purpose by which our faith is strengthened and our sympathy with Samson's pain swallowed up in our exultation in his triumph.

James Holly Hanford
*Studies in Shakespeare, Milton and Donne* (New York:
Macmillan, 1925), pp. 181-82

We have seen that the "spirit" of Greek tragedy is of two kinds—artistic and (for want of a better word) intellectual. Moreover, in defining these distinct yet closely related categories, we have spoken of certain tones which *result from* various principles or ideas expressed by the Greek tragedians. The "spirit," in other words, is the tone or temper *resulting from* idea—it is not the idea itself. . . . The "indefinable something" which, according to Verity, makes *Samson Agonistes* truly Greek, I should want to call Milton's fine understanding of the tone, of the end, which the Attic dramatists attained by the expression of their various principles and beliefs. Milton was too great an artist to confuse means and end. He would not identify "rules" with "spirit." And no more, I think, would he feel it necessary to identify the spiritual tone, the "intellectual" impression left by Greek tragedy, with the specific ideas which, in their day, produced that impression. . . .

The theme of *Samson Agonistes,* then, is the hero's recovery and its result. In other words, it is regeneration and reward. . . . Regeneration, with Samson, involves at least four things: first, he must achieve patience; second, he must achieve faith; third, he must conquer the weakness which had led to his fall; and finally, he must recognize and obey the call to further service. Each of these steps is clear, with the exception, perhaps, of the second.

William Riley Parker
*Milton's Debt to Greek Tragedy in Samson Agonistes*
(Baltimore: Johns Hopkins Pr., 1937), pp. 196-97, 237-38

In Milton's poem Samson is visited by three principal agents, each of whom can be regarded as exemplifying one of the three temptations. . . . Manoa, the first of these agents, tempts Samson to forsake his vocation as *agonistes* by offering him liberty, ease, and peace in retirement. . . . This is the *concupiscentia carnis,* "the flesh," the temptation by necessity. And the temptation is directed against Samson's faith in his God. . . . Manoa's temptation fails only because Samson is convinced that his ills are not such as home and the kindly ministry of his father can cure. . . .

It is in this utter hopelessness that Samson is confronted next by Dalila, the "specious monster," the fraudulent one. It is she, more than either Manoa or Harapha, who uses arguments, who tries to *persuade* Samson. She, like Manoa, has a conception of the good life which is essentially different from Samson's. She, too, thinks in human terms alone. . . . Like Manoa, she tempts Samson to forsake his faith, but she does so by means of fraud and persuasion. . . . Her trial of his faith by the temptation of fraudulent persuasion has not succeeded, but Samson has not yet found any resolution of his own conviction of failure in a sacred vocation.

Harapha finds Samson at this depth of despair, and he plagues Samson finally with the temptation of "the Devil.". . . Harapha represents the temptation by violence and fear. . . . This temptation . . . is designed to call up the fear that he has been abandoned by his God. This is the utmost temptation of "the Devil," the most potent weapon the powers of darkness have at their disposal. But Samson somehow finds his faith still proof against temptation.

F. Michael Krouse
*Milton's Samson and the Christian Tradition* (Princeton, N. J.:
Princeton Univ. Pr., 1949), pp. 125-30

One explanation of such peculiarities as I have mentioned [inconsistencies with the Argument, comic elements, repetitions, etc.] is that *Samson Agonistes* did not receive Milton's final revision. If so, why not? My own impression . . . is that the tragedy is essentially an early work, following soon after the making of the notes in the Cambridge Manuscript. . . . The manuscript perhaps lay with him until he had *Paradise Regained* ready for printing. The publisher of that short epic . . . "hop'd to have procured some other suitable Piece of the same Author's to have joyn'd with it." When he applied to Milton, the poet thought of his old tragedy, had it found, and turned it over to the bookseller. I incline to think that he did no further work on it, feeling perhaps that the choice was between much labor and none; he must either revise to the standard of *Paradise Regained,* or leave the drama as it stood.

Allan H. Gilbert
*PQ* (January, 1949), pp. 105-6

I propose to show, first, that the traditional date is open to very serious doubt; second, that the usual autobiographical inferences are highly questionable; and third, that there are some reasons for dating the inception of *Samson Agonistes* as early as 1646-1648. . . .

When, exactly, was the play written? Unless additional external evidence comes to light, I do not think it possible to give a final answer to this question. My own guess, after more than a decade of studying the problem, is that *Samson Agonistes* was begun in 1646 or 1647, near the time of the *Ode to Rouse*, and that composition was discontinued in April of 1648, when Milton turned to the translating of psalms. My further guesses are that the drama was taken up again for its possible *katharsis* in 1652, or 1653, that Milton had some thought of including it in a revised edition of his *Poems* in 1653, that the projected edition was abandoned . . . , and that composition of the tragedy was again discontinued in August of 1653, when Milton turned again to translating psalms. Whatever the exact facts, both the style and the characterization of *Samson Agonistes* in its present form persuade me that its composition was several times interrupted.

William R. Parker
*PQ* (January, 1949), pp. 146, 158-59

The Officer, like a good angel, descends twice, and now proposes a "temptation" that is completely physical, the threat of violence, the machines that will drag Samson to the feast. As theme it echoes and varies Manoa on self-preservation and the physical trials offered by Dalila and Harapha. But now, for a moment at least, the offer has an attraction unlike theirs; it comes almost like another and rival inspiration, through human agency. Here is a chance to suffer something unexperienced, but as a champion again; a chance to fulfill the motion frustrated by Harapha; to burst through the patience of not moving by the release of a positive action; to win, at the worst, the release of death, for which he has longed. One sees and feels him respond to the flicker of possibility, as this new inspiration, the terms very definite, challenges the undefined "rouzing motions.". . . But he refuses the rival inspiration, and in doing so takes a firm step beyond the "hope" for death.

Arnold Stein
*Heroic Knowledge* (Minneapolis, Minn.:
Univ. Minnesota Pr., 1957), pp. 188-89

The effect of the final comments is at once to magnify Samson and to reconcile us to his fate: and this raises a problem. A common feature in all tragedies is a sense of disaster. A feature of very many is, at the end, some mitigation of this sense of disaster, some reconciling of the audience to the experience which they have witnessed and shared. This is true of many tragedies, but certainly not of all. . . . This reconciliation, this mitigating of the sense of disaster, is restricted to the human level, the level on which tragedy commonly moves (for the reference to God is in relation less to the outcome than to Samson's personal experience and feelings, and the image of the phoenix, which so often in Christian symbolism represents immortality, is carefully confined to the immortality of Samson's fame); and these considerations lead on to a first formulation of the tragic *katharsis* as Milton conceives it.

Only when this is accomplished is the Chorus allowed to raise its eyes to God's providential purpose and the place of Samson's sacrifice therein, and to correct, though not to deny, the doubts which have assailed it and Manoa and Samson himself. And since God's ways are just but also mysterious, acceptable by faith but often baffling to reason, the effect of the larger view is less to cancel than to confirm and complete the narrower, or so at least Milton's treatment would seem to say. . . .

A. S. P. Woodhouse
*UTQ* (April, 1959), pp. 214-15

## MINOR POEMS

What, then, shall we say of *Lycidas* as a work of art? Is it the less a perfect whole because it is composite? Does the fact that it is conventional make it any the less original in the highest sense? If we know *Lycidas* well and read it in a fitting mood, we find ourselves forgetting that its pastoral imagery is inherently absurd. The conventions which at first seem so incongruous with the subject, gradually become a matter of course. And when once we have ceased to regard these conventions as anything more than symbols, we find them no longer detracting from the beauty of the poem, but forming an essential element of its classic charm. For the supreme beauty of *Lycidas* lies partly in the very fact of its conventionality. Its grief is not of the kind that cries aloud; it soothes and rests us like calm music. For a moment, indeed, we are aroused by an outburst of terrible indignation, but the dread voice is soon past and we sink back again into the tranquil enjoyment which comes from the contemplation of pure beauty, unmarred by any newness of idea, unclouded by overmastering emotion.

James Holly Hanford
*PMLA* (September, 1910), pp. 446-47

Milton almost alone cultivated the sonnet in the middle of the seventeenth century; but he cultivated it with a difference. In his lines the old dialect of the sonnet is not to be found; its sentiments, conceits, and familiar images have vanished completely away. It is only in his Italian poems that we can still trace the ancient language—another sign that they were composed in his very early youth. Two striking differences become apparent when Milton's sonnets are compared with those of his English predecessors —a much greater variety of subjects, and a new poetic manner. The sonnet was now being composed by a poet whose standards were classical; precision of utterance, careful selection of words, the simple and clear expression of definite ideas, had superseded the old abundance and vague luxuriance. Such a change was passing over English poetry in his time, and Milton was one of the heralds of the coming age.

In the form of the sonnet he also appears as a reformer, his significance in this respect being such as only a later period recognised. He departed from the prosody most familiar to his English predecessors, and aimed at a more pure and regular method, according to Italian precedent.

John S. Smart
*The Sonnets of Milton* (Glasgow: Maclehose,
Jackson, 1921), pp. 12-13

In this uncertainty he is a modern poet. In the irregular stanzas and the rhymeless lines is registered the ravage of his modernity; it has bit into him as it never did into Spenser. And we imagine him thinking to himself, precisely like some modern poets we know, that he could no longer endure the look of perfect regimentation which sat upon the poor ideas objectified before him upon the page of poetry, as if that carried with it a reflection upon their sincerity. I will go further. It is not merely easy for a technician to write in smooth metres; it is perhaps easier than to write in rough ones, after he has once started; but when he has written smoothly, and contemplates his work, he is capable actually, if he is a modern poet, of going over it laboriously and roughening it. I venture to think that just such a practice, speaking very broadly, obtained in the composition of *Lycidas*; that it was written smooth and rewritten rough; which was treason.

John Crowe Ransom
*AmR* (February, 1933), p. 189

One thing in the end is certain, the "greatness" of *Lycidas* is determined by an intimate marriage of form and matter, expression and substance. He who would read the poem worthily must see this, and must be equally sensitive to the delicacy of its art and to the sublimity of its ideas. This does not mean that he will forget or slur the disagreeable traits of the poet's character or the repulsiveness of his ecclesiastical and political theories. But for our good fortune what repels us in the man and roused Johnson to a fury of protest is reserved for his prose and is excluded from his poetry—not completely indeed, for, not to mention the more outrageous sonnets, occasionally the bitterness of his disappointed soul breaks out in his later works, yet to such an extent that it is not impossible to keep the poet and the controversialist apart as two almost separate powers. That divorce has its unhappy aspect; for one thing it debars England. But it leaves to him the high credit of having raised in *Paradise Lost*, to the honor of his native land, the one monumentally successful product of that humanistic culture of the Renaissance in which originality of genius and faithfulness to the classical tradition are combined in perfect union. And for *Lycidas* there is this further apology, that the elegy was composed before Milton's splendid spirit of liberty was exacerbated by opposition into petulant license, when his personal pride flamed with a yet undiverted zeal to make of his own life a true poem and so to train himself for creating such a work of art as would lift his people from the ugly slough of faction and greed, where they were grovelling, into the finer atmosphere where pure religion and the love of beauty might flourish together.

Paul Elmer More
*AmR* (May, 1936), pp. 157-58

*Lycidas*, short as it is, presents many more problems than we can properly discuss here. Milton's early work plays on a conflict of the pagan-sexual with the Christian-ethical. *Lycidas* is therefore interesting in its attempt at friendly association of the two pastoral traditions, ecclesiastical and literary, in one poem. There is a clear personal cry questioning the wisdom of losing amorous joys with Amaryllis and Neaera through the high seriousness of a poetic temperament that may be allowed to illuminate the problems raised by *Comus* and *Paradise Lost*. Exquisite Spenserian melodies and flowery description do not cohabit very happily with the thunderous St. Peter. Learned references are perhaps too thickly clustered without context enough to create the interest they demand. Personification of the Cam is of doubtful success, but the use, as in *Comus*, of a river-symbol is interesting with reference both to Spenser and later English poetry; and, indeed, the main theme of "death by water" has numerous fascinating analogies. Exquisite in parts and most valuable as a whole, *Lycidas* reads rather as an effort to bind and clamp together a universe trying to fly off into separate bits; it is an accumulation of magnificent fragments. The elegiac interest itself has some pregnant moments in the association of human immortality with the natural process of sunrise; of Heaven with "nuptial song"; and, especially, in hint of some creative purpose within human disaster.

G. Wilson Knight
*The Burning Oracle* (Oxford Univ. Pr., 1939), p. 70

The common assumption, correct so far as it goes, is that the argument of *Comus* has for its theme chastity. But more careful examination reveals that coupled with the doctrine of chastity . . . are two others: a doctrine of temperament and continence . . . and a doctrine of virginity. . . . When these facts are brought into relation with the intellectual frame of reference, we observe that temperance and continence are virtues on the natural level; that chastity, the central virtue of the poem, moves in an area common to nature and grace; and that the doctrine of virginity belongs exclusively to the order of grace, which in the poem it is used to illustrate and even symbolize. Or, if one may resort to a simple visual formulation, what we have is this:

(1) The *doctrine of temperance*, which, in the circumstances presented in the poem, is necessarily:

(2) A *doctrine of continence*, which, to render it secure, and to translate it from a negative to a positive conception, requires to be completed by:

⎫ Nature

(3) The *doctrine of chastity*, which is thus grounded in nature. This is, moreover, elaborated, still on the level of nature, in terms of the Platonic philosophy, to the point where it can be taken over by Christianity, which sanctions the natural virtues and, by the addition of grace, carries them on to a new plane. Of this new plane

⎫ Nature and Grace

(4) The *doctrine of virginity* becomes in the poem the illustration and symbol (but not the complete synonym).

⎫ Grace

A. S. P. Woodhouse
*UTQ* (October, 1941), pp. 49-50


The Lady thinks herself cast for the part of Belphoebe or Parthenia; Comus would like to turn her into a Hellenore, a wanton. That is what he means when he says to her after praising her beauty,

There was another meaning in these gifts,

and that is what she understands him to mean, and what Milton in his first version meant him to mean and her to understand him to mean. But later Milton saw that both the Lady and Comus were wrong: that there *was* another meaning in these gifts, but that it was not Comus's. The meaning was marriage. The Lady was not really cast for Belphoebe but for Amoret, not for Parthenia but for Agnia. And he conveys his correction —too obliquely for some tastes—by the Attendant Spirit's references to the Garden of Adonis where Belphoebe and Parthenia were out of place.

E. M. W. Tillyard
*Studies in Milton* (New York: Macmillan, 1951), p. 94

In the "Hymn" there are two central contentions: the minor dissonance between the two aspects of Nature, and the major dissonance between the two kinds of harmony. These contentions are emphasized by the fact that the "Hymn" falls naturally into three sections: stanzas I-VII, VIII-XVIII, and XIX-XXVIII. The symbolic narrative of the sun (embodying the pun familiar to Donne and Herbert) controls the movement of the first section and binds it to the time theme of the induction. . . . The conflict between Christian and pagan harmony that governs the second and third sections makes the "Hymm" an artistic wonder.

> Don C. Allen
> *The Harmonious Vision* (Baltimore:
> Johns Hopkins Pr., 1954), pp. 26-27

The failure of this part of *Comus* to come off according to promise is further complicated by Milton's unsuccessful attempt to establish a true intellectual conflict in the debate between Comus and the Lady. . . . Its effectiveness as a dramatic episode is destroyed by a double flaw. Though it starts out with a certain amount of dramatic excitement, the scene quickly degenerates into a philosophic dialogue as electric as one of the dialogues of Cicero, and the initial excitement is immediately quieted by the fact that we know almost at once that there is not the remotest danger of the Lady's accepting the offer of Comus. The ethical premises of the debate are, in the second place, so mixed that the intellectual colors run together and are never well marked. Comus adopts a modified Neo-Epicurean argument that is reminiscent of all humanistic debates on this matter. For this we are hardly prepared. . . .

> Don C. Allen
> *The Harmonious Vision* (Baltimore:
> Johns Hopkins Pr., 1954), pp. 36-37

According to its position in the 1673 edition of the minor poems and its supposed position in the original manuscript quarto sheets, . . . Sonnet 19 should have been written by Milton after Sonnet 18 (c. June 1655) and before 20 (October-November 1655). The only argument against this date has been the interpretation of the half-line "E're half my days," for Milton would have been forty-six in 1655. To imply a life-expectancy of more than ninety-two years is patently absurd. It has been thought more reasonable to date the poem in 1652, just after Milton's total blindness, for at that date he would have been forty-three. Yet a positive life-expectancy of more than eighty-six years is equally as preposterous.

I believe that Milton is not talking of real life-expectancy but instead that he is making another Biblical reference . . . here to Isaiah lxv.20. . . . Clearly one's life on earth is said to be a hundred years and specifically that each man . . . shall fill *his days*. Milton's age of forty-six in 1655 is, Biblically speaking, ere he has filled half his days in this dark and wide world.

John T. Shawcross
*NQ* (October, 1957), pp. 442-43

*Lycidas* is the most poignant and controlled statement in English poetry of the acceptance of that in the human condition which seems to man unacceptable. I do not of course refer simply to the calm ending of the elegy, but to its whole poem-long attempt to relate understandably to human life the immutable fact of death—the pain of loss, the tragedy of early death, the arraignment of the entire natural world that did not avert this unnatural concluding of what was unfulfilled, the passionate indictment of an order that sets a fatal stop upon even man's Orphean task and the good report that would crown it, the depositions one after another of those who carry out the higher commands in orderly fashion, the accusers who still press for an answer, and finally the center and heart of the matter: the questioning of a justice that would take the young and leave the ripe, take the devoted and leave the self-indulgent, so too would take the shepherd and leave the destroyer. What answer? What order? to what end a human life, struck down and ended by an immutable will even as it consecrates itself to God's own uses on an earth sick and famished under the hand of His enemy? Disorder, no answer, death is our answer; the slit life, the ravaged commonwealth.

Rosemond Tuve
*Images and Themes in Five Poems by Milton* (Cambridge, Mass.: Harvard Univ. Pr., 1957), pp. 73-74

The action as well as the argument of *Comus* is designed to support the Christian view that nature (which includes the so-called natural virtues) is insufficient without grace, though good in itself. The Elder Brother's doctrine of chastity, which culminates in the Platonic fancy that the body may be transmuted into the soul's essence, symbolizes the highest reach of pagan thought (nature) unenlightened by Christian revelation (grace). The inadequacy of "nature" is translated into the action of the poem when it is revealed that the Brothers are powerless to release the Lady. The Lady herself represents the Christian soul on its journey to its heavenly home. On the moral level her virginity represents Christian purity of mind and body; on the spiritual level it represents the penetration of the natural order by grace, exemplified in the action of the poem by the intervention of the martyred virgin Sabrina, now transformed into a river-goddess. The role of the Attendant Spirit is somewhat difficult of interpretetation. His part in the action, where he is able to guide the Brothers and even the

Lady but is not able to free her from hellish charm, would suggest that he represents not supernatural grace but the higher potentialities of human nature, as Comus represents the lower; specifically perhaps the human soul. He represents the interpenetration of nature and grace from the point of view of nature; Sabrina from the point of view of grace. He symbolizes the knowledge of right and wrong conferred by reason; she the power of doing right conferred by grace.

William G. Madsen
*Three Studies in the Renaissance* (New Haven:
Yale Univ. Pr., 1958), pp. 215-16

The body of the poem is arranged in the form ABACA, a main theme repeated twice with two intervening episodes, as in the musical rondo. The main theme is the drowning of Lycidas in the prime of his life; the two episodes, presided over by the figures of Orpheus and Peter, deal with the theme of premature death as it relates to poetry and to the priesthood respectively. In both the same type of image appears: the mechanical instrument of execution that brings about a sudden death, represented by the "abhorred shears" in the meditation on fame and the "grim two-handed engine" in the meditation on the corruption of the Church. The most difficult part of the construction is the managing of the transitions from these episodes back to the main theme. The poet does this by alluding to his great forerunners in the pastoral convention, Theocritus of Sicily, Virgil of Mantua, and the legendary Arcadians who preceded both. . . . The allusion has the effect of reminding the reader that this is, after all, a pastoral. But Milton also alludes to the myth of Arethusa and Alpheus, the Arcadian water-spirits who plunged underground and reappeared in Sicily, and this myth not only outlines the history of the pastoral convention, but unites the water imagery with the theme of disappearance and revival.

Northrop Frye
*Proceedings of the Second Congress of the Internationanl
Comparative Literature Assn.* (Chapel Hill, N. C.:
Univ. North Carolina Pr., 1959), pp. 46-47

Milton divides the narrative action of the masque into three scenes corresponding to the three motions of the soul, descending, stopped, and ascending. We first see the soul moving away from God in the physical world subject to the demands of the flesh. Second we see the soul halt its downward (or outward) motion using reason and philosophy to reach the point of no motion, the "hinge" of its career; third we see it with the help of the *mens* begin its upward (or inward) motion away from the flesh and back toward God. The human soul is represented in the poem not merely by the Lady, but jointly by the Lady and Sabrina; the Lady represents the Reason, and Sabrina represents the *mens*.

Sears Jayne
*PMLA* (December, 1959), pp. 538-39

The foregoing allows the possibility of 1637 as the date of writing of the letter to an unknown friend. On the acceptance of this, all objection to dating the whole Trinity MS from that date forward is nullified. Under these circumstances the following conclusions may be suggested: (1) *On Time* and *Upon the Circumcision* were written before *Arcades* was transcribed (January-September 1637?); (2) *Arcades* was transcribed in the manuscript in (June-October?) 1637; (3) *At a Solemn Music* was composed; (4) later the letter was written; (5) probably next (September-October?) *On Time, Upon the Circumcision,* and *At a Solemn Music* were transcribed; (6) *Comus* was copied (September-October?) and revised (September-January?); and (7) *Lycidas* was written (November).

John T. Shawcross
*MLN* (January, 1960), pp. 16-17

For almost three hundred years editors and critics had assumed that Milton's last sonnet obviously referred to his second wife, Katherine Woodcock. Since William Riley Parker's article, "Milton's Last Sonnet," a considerable controversy has arisen concerning the identity of the "late espoused Saint." Parker's chief contention is that the reference to "Purification in the old Law" applies only to Mary Powell, who died three days after the birth of Deborah. . . .

Attempting to refute Parker's argument, Fitzroy Pyle points out that the "once more" is meant to contrast with the dream vision: that in Heaven Milton will see Katherine "without restraint." Pyle interprets "embrace" to mean "kiss" and supposes that the dream ended because, as the veiled figure began to put aside the veil to kiss Milton, he was unable to visualize the face about to be revealed. Following another line of argument, Charles Dahlberg notes that the sonnet is in the hand of Jeremy Picard, an amanuensis whose earliest work cannot be dated before January 14, 1657/8. Parker, in rebuttal, denies that "embrace" means "kiss," and asserts that for several reasons the fact that Picard transcribed the poem is irrelevant to the whole argument. Edward LeComte concludes that the emphasis on purity and purification indicates that Katherine is the subject, since her name is derived from the Greek "katharos," meaning "pure.". . . Only Leo Spitzer proposes that the "late espoused Saint" is not a real person at all but an ideal figure like Dante's *donna angelicata*. Spitzer's hypothesis has one advantage: it obviates the rather sterile argument over which wife

Milton is referring to. And it puts the problem of interpretation in the proper perspective. That is, it seeks to interpret the poem not on the basis of historical fact, as if it were an obituary notice, but in the light of what we know of Milton's mind. . . . He is writing primarily about loss—the almost insufferable loss of a beloved woman. It seems unlikely that Mary Powell, from whom he sought a divorce, could be the subject of his longing. And if he meant Katherine Woodcock, then he was wrong about "purification in the old Law," a possibility which one ought to keep in mind. But even if Milton did refer to Katherine and did make a mistake in referring to the Mosaic law, the figure presented in the poem is clearly idealized.

Thomas Wheeler
*SP* (July, 1961), pp. 510-15

## PROSE

Milton's main beliefs at the time of *Areopagitica* may be outlined as follows. Man is born with the seeds of good and evil in him: mere environment cannot determine his character: in the most favourable environment evil might come out. But man has the power of choice, and knowing both good and evil it is possible for him to choose good. The present world may not ever be perfect, but it may be very much better. It is reasonable to have very high hopes; and it still seems likely that, in spite of set-backs, some great good is to happen to England in the immediate future. There is therefore every incentive for the noblest and most strenuous action.

E. M. W. Tillyard
*Milton* (London: Chatto and Windus, 1930), p. 161

In 1642 Milton declared that, while writing prose, he had the use, "as I may account it, but of my left hand." His statement has become so well known that it has obscured the truth, for he quickly learned to forge "this manner of writing" into a two-handed engine. Not enough study has been given his prose style, as style. The most pointed and significant criticism is to be found in *The Censure of the Rota* (1660), which students, regarding as ephemeral satire, have more or less ignored. The analysis there is, of course, limited, but it can help us to understand the contemporary reputation of Milton's pamphlets. For example, although Milton often addressed himself to "the elegant and learned reader" and often expressed his disdain of the "common sort," his opponents sometimes considered him a rabble-rouser. This wide divergence in point of view must be explained, and the explanation is to be found in the quality of Milton's prose. He wrote prose like a poet. In saying this I do not mean merely that his prose is often rhythmical and is frequently adorned with figures of speech, although both of these things are true. I mean also that he writes with a constant awareness of the emotional values of words, that he appeals to the idealism of his readers more often than he appeals to logic, that he translates practical problems of the moment into universals, that he dresses reason in robes of eloquence, that the mood of prophecy is often upon him. He speaks, in an early pamphlet, of "the cool element of prose," but his own style is sensuous and passionate.

William Riley Parker
*Milton's Contemporary Reputation* (Columbus, Ohio:
Ohio State Univ. Pr., 1940), pp. 55-56

The balance between liberty and justice as it appeared in his political writings was a modification of the precarious balance between Christian liberty and reformation according to divine prescript. The natural right which he would make the foundation of civil society was the earthly expression of that condition of goodness and enlightenment whose other-worldly expression was the spiritual liberty of the Gospel. The natural justice he thought the basis of all civil law was the earthly expression of the right reason which was the spiritual law of God's own being. But as that law was perceived only imperfectly by man in his degenerate state, so men in that state were capable of exercising only a natural right limited by laws imposed from without. The full privileges of human dignity could be claimed only by those whose nature had been restored to its primitive perfection through the divine grace which renewed the original and inward law and added to the natural the privileges of Christian liberty. . . .

Though he revised his theory of the one right discipline prescribed by God, Milton never abandoned his belief in the need for discipline according to absolute divine truth, nor his conviction that this alone begot admirable and heavenly privileges. Throughout the revolution he was closing up truth to truth as he found it revealed in experience and clarified by that intellectual ray and the voice of reason. Because experience seemed to show that the only trustworthy discipline must come from within, he became increasingly certain of the intimate connection between Christian and human liberty. He was confirmed in his belief that the end and good of a people free by nature could not be achieved otherwise than through the real and substantial liberty fully to be enjoyed in a commonwealth modelled on that only just and rightful kingdom. These convictions were sharpened by the far surpassing light which accompanied his blindness, so that Christian liberty became for him the main end of government.

Arthur Barker
*Milton and the Puritan Dilemma* (Toronto:
Univ. Toronto Pr., 1942), pp. 213, 332

Milton is entitled to a place as a democratic reformer because in the course of history the liberties for which he stood have gradually become identified with those reforms demanded and achieved by an increasingly large number of voters. The elements of Milton's political philosophy which gave rise to his conception of liberty and which were inherent in the reform movement are his Christian individualism and his sense of abstract justice as embodied in the law of nature. His weakness as a democratic reformer lies in his inability to perceive the written law to be a necessary foundation for the building of a more ideal England. And this weakness, we should note, this too great dependence on the law of nature, made for his immediate failure as a reformer; whereas his political ideals so far removed from contemporary realization ultimately gave him an important place as a reform agitator.

Don M. Wolfe
*Milton in the Puritan Revolution* (Camden, N. J.:
Thomas Nelson, 1941), p. 336

In *Of Reformation,* which appeared in late May or early June, Milton made his first attempt at systematic prose, the work, as he afterward said, "but of my left hand." A gifted critic of his own talents, Milton was never more accurate than in this statement. His prose is like a hard pine log full of knots and unexpected twirls, rarely straight and smooth and easy to follow. Milton almost never strikes off a simple declarative sentence. Though his diction, as we might expect, is remarkable for its variety of stinging thrusts, his sentences are often long and unwieldy, encompassing at times the qualifying ideas of a modern paragraph. If Milton's diction has a tough, muscular quality communicating consistently the burning images of his many-faceted mind, his sentences, with exceptions of memorable beauty, are so bulky, cumbersome, and complex as to require often many readings for full comprehension. An even greater barrier to the modern reader is Milton's topical arrangement of ideas, which is often so disorganized as to defy logical organization and thematic unity of his verse paragraphs.

Don M. Wolfe
*Complete Prose Works of John Milton* (New Haven:
Yale Univ. Pr., 1953), Vol. I, pp. 108-9

Structure in prose, like structure in verse, is not mere external arrangement; nor is the poetry of this tract a matter of occasional purple passages. *The Doctrine and Discipline of Divorce* is in two books, in thirty-six chapters, divided logically according to the branchings of subject. The introduction and most of the content follow well-known rules of rhetoric. But there is the other kind of structure, too, the inner form created by motifs in scientific imagery that make the argument as well as support or embellish it. And the preliminary allegory gives us our warrant for this sort of study if we need it. To the encyclopedists, natural science had as one of its purposes the discovery of nature's truth as the physical manifestation of moral truth; and Milton's use of this material is consistent with their objectives. His systematic exploitation of scientific lore as a unifying and formative force in *The Doctrine and Discipline of Divorce* suggests that his prose has an even stronger claim to attention than has been thought. Perhaps, if this demonstration has been persuasive, one will say with an intent quite different from Eliot's in his belated and ungracious palinode, that Milton's prose is really close to half-formed poetry.

Kester Svendsen
*Milton and Science* (Cambridge, Mass.:
Harvard Univ. Pr., 1956), pp. 223-24

Of [his prose] works two or three stand among the great possessions of the race, two or more are at least required reading, and the rest, except for scholars, are mostly dead. Writing in the heat of the moment, and with his own views in process of change, Milton too seldom rose to philosophic principles of enduring wisdom; but that is not to say that his breathless exhortations do not contain much judicious and liberal thought on the problems of his time. They contain also, along with inevitable wrangling and an equally inevitable excess of citation, spontaneous jets both of the prophetic sublimity that we expect and of satirical wit that we may not expect. Though his tracts are built on rhetorical canons, and develop systematic arguments, the loosely Ciceronian prose of the most disciplined of poets seems remarkably undisciplined. . . . It is clear that, like other bookish idealists (and Church Fathers), he was moved by the enemies of a sacred cause to a kind of fury which left him honestly amazed and indignant when they returned the attack.

Douglas Bush
*English Literature in the Earlier Seventeenth Century*
(Oxford Univ. Pr., 1962), p. 390

GENERAL

Milton's chief ideas may be grouped under five heads:

I. The idea of God as the un-manifested Infinite, in whom is the Son (Creator and Creation), in whom is Christ (the elect);

II. The idea of free will, liberated by the retraction of God, and the union of the idea of reason to the idea of liberty, which is an original proof of free will (intelligence is impossible without free will);

III. The idea of Matter as good, imperishable and divine, a part of God himself from which all things issue spontaneously; so that there is no soul, and all beings are parts of God, arranged on an evolutionary scheme;

IV. The idea of the duality of man: reason and passion; the necessity of the triumph of reason; the fall as the triumph of passion;

V. The idea of liberty, based on the goodness of the normal being of divine matter and on the presence in the elect of the Divine Intelligence.

Denis Saurat
*Milton: Man and Thinker* (New York: Dial Pr., 1925), p. 198

The word *Miltonic* is almost synonymous with sublimity. As defined by Burke, the "sublime" is that which inspires awe bordering on fear by means either of greatness (the extensive sublime) or of power (the dynamic sublime). Milton is a master of both. Unabashed, he explores the abyss, the horrors of hell, and the magnificence of heaven; he relates how the rising world of waters waste and wild were formed into a firm terraqueous globe; he portrays the wars of heaven, which surpass anything elsewhere imagined by a mortal; and he is no less sublime in his portrayal of Satan's moral world—that second universe which, upon contemplation, as Kant said, fills the mind with awe and wonder. "The poet blind yet bold" leaves no portion of the physical or moral world unexplored. And the language of *Paradise Lost,* which we find prefigured in "Lycidas," is always congruent with the conceptions it reveals and conveys. One cannot read Milton's poetry without experiencing an emotion which is partly admiration, partly awe, partly aspiration, and closely akin to a thrill of terror. And this is sublimity.

Martin A. Larson
*The Modernity of Milton* (Chicago: Univ. Chicago Pr., 1927), p. 266

While it must be admitted that Milton is a very great poet indeed, it is something of a puzzle to decide in what his greatness consists. On analysis, the marks against him appear both more numerous and more significant than the marks to his credit. As a man, he is antipathetic. Either from the moralist's point of view, or from the theologian's point of view, or from the psychologist's point of view, or from that of the political philosopher, or judging by the ordinary standards of likeableness in human beings, Milton is unsatisfactory. The doubts which I have to express about him are more serious than these. His greatness as a poet has been sufficiently celebrated, though I think largely for the wrong reasons, and without the proper reservations. . . . What seems to me necessary is to assert at the same time his greatness—in that what he could do well he did better than any one else has ever done it—and the serious charges to be made against him, in respect of the deterioration—the peculiar kind of deterioration—to which he subjected the language.

T. S. Eliot
*Essays and Studies, XXI* (Oxford: Clarendon Pr., 1936), p. 32

With Mr. Pound a loathing of Milton had early become almost an obsession; and in an essay written, I believe, in 1918, but reprinted in a volume entitled *Make it New* (1934), he speaks of the personal active hatred of Milton, which he had already expressed in year-long diatribes, his disgust with all that he has to say, "his asinine bigotry, his beastly hebraism, the coarseness of his mentality."

Mr. Eliot is far too urbane to express his disapproval in such Miltonic terms; but he often hints at it in his quiet way—his "deft, inconspicuous sniping" as one of his admirers calls it. In his first volume of criticism, *The Sacred Wood,* when speaking, for instance, of the degeneration of blank verse from Shakespeare to Milton, he says that after the erection of the "Chinese wall of Milton," blank verse has suffered not only arrest but retrogression. . . . In addition to Mr. Eliot's deadly sniping . . . , what terrified the professors most was, I think, a theory he put forward (dark and difficult to understand) that in Milton there occurred a kind of disassociation of sensibility, a splitting up of the personality, which interrupted the progress of English poetry for a hundred years. This notion appears not infrequently in the pronouncements of almost all the Miltonoclasts. I confess frankly that I have never been able to grasp its meaning. But I have not been taught to think "in periods," nor do I find much evidence of the progress of art through this or that century.

Logan Pearsall Smith
*Milton and His Modern Critics* (Boston:
Little, Brown, 1941), pp. 20-22

My thesis is that *Paradise Lost,* with its rejection of science, of nationalism, of hope for man within the limits of history and society, expresses not only the collapse of the Puritan Revolution, but also marks the end of a great tradition of life and literature—the Elizabethan tradition. This comes out most clearly in the conflict between symbol and idea in *Paradise Lost,* and in Milton's awareness of the conflict. . . . The disappearance of the royalist symbol in its traditional connotation from *Paradise Regained* and *Samson Agonistes* is not merely a "literary" phenomenon, a detached problem in craftsmanship—it reflects a change in the social order.

Malcolm Mackenzie Ross
*Milton's Royalism* (Ithaca, N. Y.: Cornell Univ. Pr., 1943), p. 139

It may be said that such examples of Milton's allusiveness and complexity
—a few which must represent the general texture of *Paradise Lost*—only
confirm the notion that he is not for every reader and everyday reading.
On the other hand, for the complex sensibilities of the anti-Miltonists, he
is much too simple. As a matter of logic or probability, neither position
can be quite right. For many people, certainly, there does hang about Milton
a forbidding austerity not only of Puritanism but of learning. It is a fact that
for centuries before him, and for perhaps two centuries after him, a poet
could assume in his readers, as Milton assumed, a fair amount of classical
—and biblical knowledge. If that is no longer true, we can hardly claim
a large and peculiar fault in Milton's or a large and peculiar merit in ourselves. But the decline of classical education, and the metaphysical revival,
have brought about an odd result in a number of critical minds. Scholas-
ticism replaced the classics as the really respectable source of images and
ideas for the older poets—with this very important difference, that whereas "the classics" generally meant classical literature and thought, schol-
asticism has hardly ever meant scholastic philosophy but only a dialectical
texture and isolated scraps of curious learning. The anti-Miltonists, however, have little interest in the ideas of Milton, they merely express abhorrence and pass on to his craftsmanship. And on that level, when Milton
employs an image or idea or idiom not immediately intelligible, it is characteristic Miltonic pedantry; when Dante or Donne or Mr. Eliot does so,
it is characteristic metaphysical subtlety.

Douglas Bush
*Paradise Lost in Our Time* (Ithaca, N. Y.:
Cornell Univ. Pr., 1945), pp. 107-8

We may note first that his style, despite his employment of a verse form
identical with the Elizabethan dramatists, stands at an opposite pole from
that of Shakespeare and his colleagues. Milton's language, unlike theirs,
has little relish of the speech of men. Where their anomalies are colloquial
and idiomatic, his are the product of a preference for the unusual and
recondite, in vocabulary and construction, which leads him to archaism
on the one hand, and to the substitution of foreign idiom, particularly
Latin, for native on the other. Sometimes not even classical or earlier
English example can be alleged. Milton is simply carving for himself, re-
moulding and creating with fine disregard for precedent. In general, Milton's style may be described as almost uniquely literary and intellectual.
Freighted with learning and bookish phrase, elaborate in construction, often
alien in vocabulary, it achieves a uniform effect of dignity and aloofness
and becomes a perfect medium for the restrained and elevated yet intensely
passionate personality of its author.

James Holly Hanford
*A Milton Handbook* (New York: F. S. Crofts, 1946), pp. 293-94

This criticism seems to me substantially true: indeed, unless we accept it, I do not think we are in the way to appreciate the peculiar greatness of Milton. His style is not a *classic* style, in that it is not the elevation of a *common* style, by the final touch of genius, to greatness. It is, from the foundation, and in every particular, a personal style, not based upon common speech, or common prose, or direct communication of meaning. Of some great poetry one has difficulty in pronouncing just what it is, what infinitesimal touch, that has made all the difference from a plain statement which anyone could make; the slight transformation which, while it leaves a plain statement a plain statement, has always the maximal, never the minimal, alteration of ordinary language. Every distortion of construction, the foreign idiom, the use of a word in a foreign way or with the meaning of the foreign word from which it is derived rather than the accepted meaning in English, every idiosyncrasy is a particular act of violence which Milton has been the first to commit. There is no cliché, no poetic diction in the derogatory sense, but a perpetual sequence of original acts of lawlessness. . . . Milton's poetry is poetry at the farthest possible remove from prose; his prose seems to me too near to half-formed poetry to be good prose.

T. S. Eliot
*Milton* (Proceedings of the British Academy, 1947), p. 9

I find it difficult to avoid the conclusion that there can hardly be anything very wrong with the traditional chronology of Milton's major poems or their parts. The continuity in the statistical sequences is too striking, and the emerging patterns occur too persistently and seem too natural to be accidental. Certain features in particular, such as the treatment of feminine endings, of syllabized -ed endings, and of terminal pyrrhics, show a compelling logic in their development with which no order of composition very different from the traditionally accepted one seems at all compatible. The frequency with which major changes in trends of development begin in the middle PL, especially in Book VII, agrees remarkably with Professor J. H. Hanford's view that the composition of the poem was probably interrupted midway by the fall of the Commonwealth; especially the handling of -ed endings lends strong support to the theory that Book VII was the first part of the epic to be composed after the Restoration. The second half of PL is linked in so many ways with PR, and PR, in its turn, with SA, that the chronological sequence PL VII-XII: PR: SA seems inescapable.

This does not mean that smaller portions of these works may not have been composed somewhat out of sequence. However, in spite of a good deal of stastistical experimentation, I have failed to discover any convincing evidence of such chronological dislocation.

Ants Oras
*SAMLA Studies in Milton* (Gainesville, Fla.:
Univ. Florida Pr., 1953), p. 191

# THOMAS OTWAY
1652-1685

After Oxford, Otway found his way to London and unsuccessful acting, but under the patronage of the Earl of Rochester, he began his writing career. After a short stint in the army (1678), he returned to London and some stage success, but much dissipation and continued poverty. Among his main tragedies are *Don Carlos,* 1676; *The Orphan,* 1680; and *Venice Preserv'd,* 1682. His heroic dramas were well known for their rhymed verse.

Roswell G. Ham, *Otway and Lee* (1931)

In summary, then, it seems to me (1) that the unexampled prominence given to the act of swearing faith [in *Venice Preserved*] has in part a satirical reference to the professed revelations of the Popish Plot under solemn oath. (2) The character of Renault, both in the Prologue and in the Play itself, is almost certainly meant for Shaftesbury, and is in some ways a more fierce attack on him than his portrayal as Antonio. (3) In the character of Antonio the minor and more contemptible qualities attributed to Shaftesbury are ridiculed, as the major ones are in Renault; and some glancing allusion, at least, is possibly intended regarding the entanglement with Mrs. Cellier with which his enemies charged him. (4) The allusions to a plot . . . are . . . of a satirical nature; and nearly all of them are put in the mouth of Antonio. (5) The plot against Venice, although not itself ridiculed, is reduced in magnitude; and from an affair of international scope it has become . . . something like . . . "the attempt by a gang of foreigners to wreck a great historic state."

(6) A more general phase of the play is the continual and ferocious attack on the Venetian senate and the senators.

John R. Moore
*PMLA* (March, 1928), p. 180

If the fable of *The Orphan* is more fit to bear the treatment Otway was able to give a tragedy, *Venice Preserv'd,* grandiose and sombre in design, is continually marred by his preoccupation with his personal troubles. The theme of unfortunate love bulks far too large in it, and though Belvidera supplies a necessary element, one cannot always refrain from wishing her away. Being familiar with the atmosphere of fell designs, the Popish Plot still occupying the minds of men, Otway raises against the smoky background of sinister plotters, suspicious friends, and would-be Romans, a stark tragedy of personal friendship, betrayal, and consequent remorse and expiation.

Bonamy Dobrée
*Restoration Tragedy, 1660-1720*
(Oxford Univ. Pr., 1929), p. 144

Now that the Tory tide had risen, the air was full of counterplot. The play tells of a subterranean conspiracy of the Spaniards against the state of Venice, and of a vast projected massacre. It was in part a reflection of the old "Popish Plot" and in part a new interest added by a Whiggish plot, as yet unjustified by the event. In some manner, still undisclosed, an association of Whigs menaced the state. The seizure of Shaftesbury's papers had revealed two lists: one of men worthy of promotion, another of those intended for less dignified elevation. Later in the year 1682 a plot of assassination actually did come to light, though the connivance of Shaftesbury was never quite proved. All this was to be subject matter for *The Duke of Guise.* Everywhere the surface of England was felt to be mined, and he who trod abroad had need to look to his health.

Aside from this general attack upon the Whigs, the most hazardous adventure in *Venice Preserved* was that involved in the famous Nicky Nacky scenes. In the eighteenth century, when they had lost political point, they were banned from the stage as being abhorrent to all decency, and today they are repulsive to any but the avowed specialist in the literature of masochism. But the less squeamish Restoration was in raptures. . . . Upon the unfortunate Shaftesbury was debouched all the cloacal garbage of these obscene years: charges with some modicum of truth, charges with none at all. One must be unduly credulous to accept even half the filthy libel that circulated indiscriminate of party or person.

Roswell G. Ham<br>
*Otway and Lee* (New Haven: Yale Univ. Pr., 1931), p. 188

Although an analysis of the precise relationship which the main plot of *Venice Preserv'd* may bear to the national crisis of 1678-1682 is beset with almost insuperable difficulties, a glance at the rapidly veering political sentiment of the years 1679 and 1680 suggests that in such an atmosphere of uncertainty, Otway's delicately balanced main plot would have carried a significance which would have been impossible in the atmosphere of the royal triumph of 1681. . . . During the conflict between King and Parliament, which raged from the convening of the third Whig parliament on March 6, 1679, to the dissolution of the fourth on January 18, 1681, Whig sentiment was dominant in the nation, and so long as old Cavalier and old Parliamentarian stood united by a common terror of Rome, the King stood practically alone, surrounded only by a small band of unpopular councillors.

. . . It is not necessary to maintain that the main plot of *Venice Preserv'd* is a covert allegory of the Popish Plot against the King's life and the Protestant religion in order to maintain that it does reflect the mood of political imbroglio of 1679-1680 rather than that of the royal triumph of 1681 and the subsequent Whig rebellion. Belief in the Popish Plot was not suddenly exorcised in March 1681. . . . For a dramatist whose purpose was not to write occasional verse or political allegory, but simply to capitalize on public sentiment and woo official favor, "To make his Plot, or make his Play succeed," the safest course lay in ambiguity. The main plot of *Venice Preserv'd*, with its delicate counterbalance of sympathies, would seem to have a far greater rapport with the spirit of these unquiet years, than with the clearly defined Tory triumph of 1681.

Indeed, when it is read from the point of view of the Tory triumph of 1681, the main plot of *Venice Preserv'd* presents political implications, and suggests topical parallels, of the most perplexing ambivalence. Otway's conspirator-heroes are motivated not by political ideals, but by the ideals of conduct prescribed by the gentleman's code of honor. And though Venice is preserved from the conspirators, she owes her preservation not to anyone's political loyalty, but to the treachery of Renault, the filial devotion of Belvidera to her senator father, and Jaffier's devotion to Belvidera.

Aline MacKenzie
*Tulane Studies in Eng.* (1949), pp. 87-88, 90-91

*Venice Preserv'd*, then, takes place in a world of ambivalence where good and evil are inextricably mingled and where the human mind is not always capable of distinguishing between them. In this respect Otway has radically departed from the heroic world view in which the strong will can control its destiny by ordering the passions. Dryden's Indamora can rely on her inner order to meet all emergencies. . . . But Belvidera, no less "honorable," is driven mad by circumstances beyond her control. Yet a complex cosmology does not assure complex art; the other objection to the play, that it lacks sufficient poetic strength and that the language is ordered in the interests of passion rather than drama, is the more formidable. While no amount of discussion can alter the diffuseness of much of the verse, it is possible to view Otway's poetic organization as perhaps more profound than has heretofore been allowed, to see an integration of theme and form.

David R. Hauser
*SP* (July, 1958), pp. 488-89

This background against which Otway's hero and heroine move may be divided into political and domestic levels, the Spanish conspiracy and the foreclosure, which threaten and eventually destroy their personal happiness. A close examination of this dual background shows that both are essentially comic and linked by a dominant poetic image, that they are somber but hardly "grandiose . . . in design," as Dobrée has stated. On the political level, the dramatist presents an unrelieved picture of corruption, which is equaled in English tragedy only by the Italianate settings of certain Jacobean plays. The most obvious contributions to this atmosphere of political decadence are the Nicky-Nacky prose interludes which Dr. Johnson condemned as "vile scenes of despicable comedy."

. . . According to the title, the political action is comic rather than tragic. A dangerous plot against the Venetian state is discovered, the conspirators are apprehended and executed, and Venice is saved. Despite the "happy ending," in the course of the action every political value is confused or debased. The conspirators are unquestionably what they appeared to Belvidera—"hired Slaves, Bravoes, and Common stabbers, / Nose-slitters, Ally-lurking Villains" (III.ii.162-63). Nominally headed by the demonstrative Spaniard Bedamar, their real leaders are Renault, a sadistic lecher, and Pierre, a soldier of fortune who is basically motivated by anger at the loss of a prostitute's favors.

William H. McBurney
*JEGP* (July, 1959), pp. 386-87

# SAMUEL PEPYS
1633-1703

> With degrees from Magdalene College, Cambridge, Pepys became an important civil servant after the restoration of Charles II. He was Clerk of the Privy Seal and Secretary of the Admiralty, reorganizing the British navy economically. He joined the Royal Society, serving as president in 1684, and was a member of parliament in 1679. But with the removal of James II in 1688 his governmental work was ended; he was even imprisoned for a short while in 1690. He is remembered in literary circles for his diary kept in code from 1660 to 1669, and deciphered in 1819-1822. His descriptions of London during the period of the Restoration, the plague, and Great Fire, and his candid opinions of the cultural life around him make his document both important for information and highly amusing.

> Henry B. Wheatley, ed., *The Diary of Samuel Pepys* (1893-1899), 10 vols.
> Arthur Bryant, *Samuel Pepys* (1933-1939), 3 vols.

In short, it cannot be said that Pepys was either a professed literary critic or a typical Restoration playgoer. Beyond the average man, he was open-minded and sincere in his appreciation of various types of plays, and many-sided and indefatigable in his interest in the theatre. Yet while he was too individual to subscribe in every matter to the stage conventions of the period, his power of observing closely others as well as himself, enabled him to body forth with peculiar realism the attitude of his age.

Helen McAfee
*Pepys on the Restoration Stage* (New Haven:
Yale Univ. Pr., 1916), p. 27

Pepy's *Diary* contains some 1,300,000 words, covers over 3000 quarto pages and is contained in six volumes of slightly varying size. During his lifetime Pepys had these bound in leather, stamped in gold, with his arms, crest and motto, and placed on the shelves of his library, although, unlike his other books, they were not arranged in strict order of size but were kept together.

The *Diary* is written in Thomas Shelton's system of shorthand. Proper names and occasional words are written in longhand, and certain "roguish" passages in a curious intermixture of French, Spanish, Latin, Greek and English dialect words. These naturally add to the difficulty of transcription from the shorthand, which otherwise presents no great problem. As Shelton's shorthand was known to many of Pepy's contemporaries, and was not a secret cipher—as is sometimes erroneously supposed—it has of late years been argued that Pepys' sole motive in using it was to save time. But others . . . challenge this view on the grounds that the distinction between code and shorthand was for many years very slender, the same word "characterie" being used for both, and that English travellers of the period frequently carried MS shorthand bibles when visiting Catholic countries abroad in order to escape the attentions of the Inquisition. It seems probable that, although the facility it afforded of writing quickly was a primary motive for the use of shorthand, Pepys was not uninfluenced by the knowledge that it would not be understood by those whom he had most reason to wish not to read it. The final sentences of the *Diary* lend support to this view.

Arthur Bryant
*Samuel Pepys* (Cambridge Univ. Pr., 1934), Vol. I, p. 392

Pepys, therefore, was not disposed towards a literal transcription of the shorthand which he wrote, even when he was transliterating the report of his King. We may feel confident that, had he transcribed his own diary, he would have made much more drastic alterations. He would probably have made the style more periodic, and would certainly have regularised those sudden changes of tense that abound in the diary as we now have it. Such changes would certainly not have been improvements.

Quite apart from the question of improvements, it is indisputable that, owing to certain characteristics of Shelton's Tachygraphy, some few features of the diary are partly due to the impossibility of making an absolutely accurate transcription of the diary. . . . The style of Samuel Pepys when he writes in longhand is prosy, adopting long, periodic sentences and a rather pedantic vocabulary, while the style of his diaries, written in shorthand, is by contrast colloquial, with loose sentences and a racy, often homely, vocabulary. In some minor ways, the latter style is undoubtedly due to the use of shorthand instead of longhand, whether by reason of mistakes in transcription or in the shorthand, or of the limitations imposed by the system of shorthand used. This system was unfitted to facile use in any but a colloquial style; its speed in such a style naturally lent itself to the rapid outpouring of ideas and impressions, with some consequent neglect of the fashion in which they were set down; and the traditional shorthand device of abbreviation may have lent its force to the same end.

W. Matthews<br>
MLR (October, 1934), pp. 403-4

Now the first thing that strikes any sensitive and reasonably experienced male reader of the Diary is the likeness of Pepys to himself. Here, amid the pleasures of recognition, lies one of the main causes of this book's appeal. Who has read Pepys without noticing scores of little confessions, conscious or unconscious, but mostly designed, which fit like an old glove? How numerous are these points of sympathetic contact probably depends less on the reader's perspicacity than on his honesty. And unless intellectual integrity is implemented by a disciplined application of the historical method, it is possible to continue reading the Diary, after that first start of perception, with an increasing conviction of ethical superiority. Pepys is so frank; the guard is so utterly down. We can easily fall into the blunder of comparing the diarist's naked face with, not perhaps the elaborate mask with which we front the world, but that delicate vizard beneath it which we would fain preserve against our own gaze inward.

Hazelton Spencer<br>
ELH (September, 1940), pp. 165-66

# ALEXANDER POPE
## 1688-1744

Significant in the career of Pope was his Roman Catholic background, a severe illness when he was twelve that left him deformed and in poor health, and his lack of a university education. His entree to London life was through Wycherley, and to Addison's circle, his *Essay on Criticism* (1711). *The Rape of the Lock* appeared in 1712, being enlarged two years later, and Windsor Forest, where he had lived with his parents, furnished the background for a topographical poem of that name in 1713.

In 1714 he became a member of the Scriblerus Club, which included Swift, Gay, and Arbuthnot. *Miscellanies* of 1727 combined their efforts, and first printed Pope's *Martinus Scriblerus Peri Bathous, or the Art of Sinking in Poetry*, ridiculing Ambrose Philips, John Dennis, and Theobald. He translated the *Iliad* (1715-1720) and the *Odyssey* (1725-1726), which were financially successful enough to allow him to lease a house at Twickenham in 1719, where he remained until his death. His edition of

Shakespeare in 1725 brought scholarly criticism from Lewis Theobald, who thus made himself the "hero" of the *Dunciad*, the first three books of which appeared anonymously in 1728. It was enlarged the next year, another book was added in 1742, and the final four books came out in 1743, but with Colley Cibber replacing Theobald.

*An Essay on Man* (1733-1734) shows the influence of Henry St. John, Lord Bolingbroke, and the miscellaneous satires began to appear in 1733. Among those attacked were Lady Mary Wortley Montagu, formerly a very good friend, and Addison, who is Atticus in *Epistle to Dr. Arbuthnot* (1735).

He never married although his strong attachment for Martha Blount continued from 1717 throughout his life. He was buried in Twickenham Church.

John Butt, gen. ed., *The Works of Alexander Pope*, The Twickenham Edition (1940-1961), 6 vols.

George Sherburn, *The Early Career of Alexander Pope* (1934)

## POEMS

If we assume Pope to be a rhetorician, the *Epistle* [in addition to others] . . . is of extraordinary rhetorical importance: these works attempt to re-establish Pope, after such attacks as the *Lines to an imitator of Horace* and the *Epistle to a Doctor of Divinity*, as a man of good moral character. To a rhetorician the appearance of having a good moral character is a first concern. . . . Thus didactic and satire would have been vitiated alike, had such charges against Pope remained unanswered. The *Epistle to Dr. Arbuthnot* is, therefore, a piece of forensic in which Pope answers the accusations of his enemies; his audience consists of judges, not spectators, and they are judges of what has been done, rather than of what may be done, and because the end of the discourse is the "proof" of the justice of Pope's actions, i.e., the rehabilitation of his character. One thing must be remarked at once: such questions as whether Pope's indignation is sincere, or whether Pope was actually a man of good character—questions about which his critics have troubled so much—are entirely irrelevant here. . . .

Two rhetorical devices of extreme importance may be noted at the outset. First, the casting of the defense into the form of a dialogue was a stroke of rhetorical genius. By the portrayal of himself as closeted with a very close friend, Pope permits himself the most congenial and most disarming setting: the circumstance is one in which sincerity and frankness can be expected. . . . Secondly, there is much rhetorical force in that the answer to Pope's enemies should have been drawn up, not as the response of a defendant, but as Pope himself says, as a "sort of bill of complaint."

Elder Olson
*MP* (January, 1939), pp. 21-22

The burlesque of the *Rape* provides, then, an elaborate stratification of attitudes and effects: amusement at trifles taken seriously; delight at elegance; recollections of earlier literature (Homer and Spenser) in counterpoint against the current literary mode; juxtaposition of corresponding worlds (Achilles' shield, the great petticoat); reminders of the economic and political structures which make possible this leisure-class comedy, of the moral and religious structures which make possible a society at all.

In the *Dunciad,* the mock-heroic frame is intermittent. There are frequent local parodies of passages from Homer, Virgil, and Milton; there are classical devices like the Homeric games, the descent into the lower world, the preview of future history from the mount of vision; but there is no plot, no "fable." The loose organization is expressively loose. The poem tenders some recent episodes in a long contest between stupidity and intelligence, anarchy and culture, barbarism and civilization. In this long contest, stupidity and its allies win out, not because of their superior plans, designs, or purposes—for there is no real war of opposed strategies —but because of their sheer multitudinous mass, their dead weight. The poem, a kind of anti-masque, is a series of ritual tableaux and pageants and processions, chiefly sluggish of movement and visually dusky.

Austin Warren
*Rage for Order* (Chicago: Univ. Chicago Pr., 1948), pp. 48-49

If the reader objects that . . . [I have suggested for *The Rape of the Lock*] a too obviously sexual interpretation of the card game, one must hasten to point out that a pervasive sexual symbolism informs, not only the description of the card game, but almost everything else in the poem, though here, again, our tradition of either-or may cause us to miss what Pope is doing. We are not forced to take the poem as either sly bawdy *or* as delightful fantasy. But if we are to see what Pope actually makes of his problem, we shall have to be alive to the sexual implications which are in the poem.

They are perfectly evident—even in the title itself; and the poem begins with an address to the Muse in which the sexual implications are underscored. . . . True, we can take *assault* and *reject* in their more general meanings, not in their specific Latin sense, but the specific meanings are there just beneath the surface. Indeed, it is hard to believe, on the evidence of the poem as a whole, that Pope would have been in the least surprised by Sir James Frazer's later commentaries on the ubiquity of hair as a fertility symbol. In the same way, one finds it hard to believe, after some of the material in the "Cave of Spleen" section . . . , that Pope would have been too much startled by the theories of Sigmund Freud.

Cleanth Brooks
*The Well Wrought Urn* (London: Dennis Dobson, 1949), pp. 85-86

. . . [Other] patterns that are more pervasive . . . help supply the kind of unity in Pope's poems which he is popularly not supposed to have. Actually, there is a wide variety of such patterns. There are the characteristics of the dramatic speaker of every poem, who shifts his style, manner, and quality of feeling considerably from poem to poem, as anyone will see who will compare carefully the *Essay on Criticism* with the *Essay on Man,* or the *Epistle to Dr. Arbuthnot* with that to Augustus. There is the character of the interlocutor in the poems that have dialogue, by no means a man of straw. There is the implicit theme, usually announced in a word or phrase toward the outset of the poem, and while seldom developed in recurrent imagery, as in Shakespeare, almost always developed in recurrent references and situations. There is also, often, a kind of pattern of words that reticulates through a poem, enmeshing a larger and larger field of associations—for instance, words meaning light in the *Essay on Criticism,* or the word "head" (and, of course, all terms for darkness) in the *Dunciad.* And there are a great many more such unifying agents.

Maynard Mack<br>
Pope and His Contemporaries, ed. James L. Clifford and<br>
Louis A. Landa (Oxford Univ. Pr., 1949), p. 33

Pope's method of composing the *Essay* [*on Man*], so far as we can establish it, supports the view that we are concerned with philosophy versified. He seems often to have prepared prose statements of arguments later to be turned into verse; and even though there is no longer any very good reason to take seriously the legend that in writing the *Essay* Pope simply cast into verse a prose argument supplied by Bolingbroke, it may be that the argument of the greater part of the *Essay* was first set down in prose. This does not mean that the structure of the *Essay* or of any one Epistle is a prose structure the sequence of which is determined by the development of a continuous argument. The units of which the poem is composed are . . . verse paragraphs, and it is arguable that the order of these paragraphs is up to a point arbitrary.

J. M. Cameron<br>
DR (Second Quarter, 1951), p. 56

*The Rape of the Lock,* written at a time when Pope was often in the company of Wycherley and Congreve, is related directly to their plays through its theme, characters, and language. It is as though the high spirits of Restoration comedy, which the Collier controversy chased off the stage, were harbored in Pope's spoof of contemporary fashions and morals. The most obvious of the points of similarity between Pope's piece and the plays of his friends is the fact that the poem, like the comedies, has its *raison*

*d'etre* in the war between the sexes. In Pope's retelling of the dispute between the Fermor and Petre families, the Baron, like Horner in *The
Country Wife* and Dorimant in *The Man of Mode,* is concerned with conquest. In *The Rape of the Lock* the cutting of the lock is symbolic of a
greater victory, and its meaning is enforced by the outrage of a maiden
no less furious than her namesake, Etherege's Bellinda. Like her, Pope's
Belinda is a coquette. She belongs in the gallery of comic heroines whose
flirtatiousness is so predominant a trait of personality that it is the governing factor of their lives. . . . Borrowing a psychological principle of
the playwrights, Pope endowed her with the kind of personality that can
achieve fulfillment only through a teasing hostility toward men. In Restoration comedy this is seen most clearly in Millamant and the London
matrons who pursue Horner. In *The Rape of the Lock* the sex-antagonism
takes the form of the game of ombre, and the loss of the lock represents
the deprivation of virtue which the coquettes of comedy experience.

Malcolm Goldstein
*Pope and the Augustan Stage* (Stanford, Calif.:
Stanford Univ. Pr., 1953), pp. 68-69

*An Epistle to Dr. Abuthnot* offers striking illustration of this conception:
analysis reveals patterns of images running throughout, each one discrete
yet all so related as to give to the whole a metaphoric value which helps
to tie the poem together. . . .

Five main images emerge, all connected in a kind of evolution: animal-
filth-disease-persecution-virtuous man. The animal image yields the filth,
the noxious element out of which disease arises, disease turns into persecution, and persecution reveals the virtuous man.

The animal image comprises all references to animals, worms, and
insects in the poem, that is, to any sentient being below man. The basis
of this image seems to lie in the association of the poetasters with "low
Grubstreet.". . . It is by stressing this proud aloofness . . . that Pope can
make the transition to his final picture of himself as *vir bonus,* full of
love, nursing his aged mother and asking Heaven's blessing for his friend.
This is the culminating image of this *apologia* for his life and art in that
it represents the furthest remove from the popular conception of the
satirist as a malevolent man.

Elias F. Mengel, Jr.
*PMLA* (March, 1954), pp. 189-90

The argument of the second, third and fourth epistles [of *Essay on Man*],
then, depends to a great extent on the principles Pope sets up in the first
epistle. . . . The first epistle is a rhetorical persuasion drawn up along

the lines of the classical oration; for here is the *exordium*, preparing the minds of the audience to favor orator and oration, ll. 1-16; *narratio*, statement of the problem in brief, ll. 17-42; *probatio*, the bulk of the argument, setting up the terms, advancing the proofs, ll. 43-112; *refutatio*, objecions to the argument and answers to those objections, ll. 113-280; *peroratio*, summation of the argument, ll. 281-294. Pope allows himself no variation on this scheme; it seems to be a conscious use of the rhetorical form.

R. E. Hughes
*MLN* (March, 1955), p. 179

. . . in *An Essay on Criticism* the minor terms of Pope's images were fetched from common life, and so, the subject being reading and criticism, not fetched from far. In the love poems the same principle holds: unlike the metaphysicals, Pope agreed with most poets, ancient and modern, in feeling that remote and startling images were not in keeping, that tenderness made a display of wit-fancy look cheap and insulting. When writing poems other than love poems, however, where feeling did not run so high and he was intent on accuracy of thought, he found in similes a means of sharpening the accuracy: but for this end, he had to be free to choose whatever minor term, near or remote, was most suitable.

The main reason why Pope favoured drawing the minor term of a simile from things near at hand was that a minor term could add to the sum of thought as well as make part of it clearer. . . . This drawing close together of theme and "decoration" is according to a principle that Pope constantly followed, the principle of making the most of what lay nearest, of encouraging congenial things to cohere, of being jealous of anything centrifugal. He occasionally writes a poem which is self-proclaimed as all simile—the simile poem was a fashionable small "kind." But usually he drew on similes only for minor services: they seldom contribute to the structure of a poem, as they may in a poem by a metaphysical poet. The big exception to this is when Pope is writing satire, when similes become a part of the very method of attack. The minor term here needed to carry as much insult as possible.

Geoffrey Tillotson
*Pope and Human Nature* (Oxford: Clarendon Pr., 1958), pp. 80-82

The *Essay on Criticism* and the *Essay on Man* are classic examples of the need for distinguishing between what a poem *says* and what it *expresses*. Both say so much in the form of statement or argument that many readers, including some of Pope's contemporaries, have doubted or forgotten that they were poems of any sort whatever. Writers who have attacked or defended the *Essay on Man* have tended to treat it either as a philosophical treatise dictated by Bolingbroke or a defence of Deism or as a metaphysical and ethical discourse in the Neoplatonic-Christian tradition. Critics and editors in the nineteenth century and the early part of this century usually (with the notable exceptions of Haziitt and Courthope) regarded the *Essay on Criticism* as a versification of commonplaces gleaned from Greek, Latin, and French sources. Eighteenth-century readers were probably better prepared to take both works as poetic expressions rather than bodies of doctrine because they saw at once that both were collections of

What oft was thought, but ne'er so well expressed. . . .

Being thoroughly familiar with what was being said, they could relax and enjoy Pope's marvellous "feat of words" as he led them through familiar intellectual scenes. Their preparation for reading the two poems "with the same spirit that its author writ" was not doctrinal, not a matter of knowing the right things, but literary and poetic.

Reuben A. Brower
*Alexander Pope* (Oxford: Clarendon Pr., 1959), pp. 188-89

Loosely, the *Epistle to Bathurst* is of the rhetorical order of the Horatian epistolary satire. . . . We are to imagine the speaker and his friend engaged in easy, intimate conversation or some warmly familiar occasion. With impressive rhetorical skill the speaker persuades his companion to some ethical position, the satire of vices being one of the more significant means to that end. And the epistolary satire gains its final end not only by the reader's identifying himself with the speaker's friendly antagonist and being carried along by the current of suasion, but also by his observing impartially the dramatic interchange of views and being impressed that so worthy an antagonist has capitulated. To this extent Pope's poem is a highly artful adaptation of an established and effective rhetorical mode. Its distinctiveness, however, lies in the source from which its ethics derives its sanctions and by means of which the Horatian *sermo* is assimilated into a more inclusive rhetorical mode.

Earl R. Wasserman
*Pope's Epistle to Bathurst* (Baltimore:
Johns Hopkins Pr., 1960), p. 12

## Windsor Forest

Although he claimed to have composed the first part of *Windsor Forest* as early as 1704, Pope did not publish his poem until 1713 when he had turned it into an apology for the Tory peace policy which culminated in the Peace of Utrecht. Regarded as a topographical poem, its chief points of difference from *Cooper's Hill* [by John Denham] are in the lack of a hill-station and in the introduction of an Ovidian tale and a long prophetic address by "old father Thames" in a manner suggesting Virgil's personification of the Tiber. Pope shows no little independence of the earlier poem, moreover, in adopting familiar motifs from various sources. Thus he commences with a statement of his subject and an invocation to the "Sylvan Maids," an adulatory reference to a patron, a combination of the local pride and modesty devices in the allusion to the "groves of Eden" and Milton's account of them, a vague descriptive passage with emphasis on contrast, Claudian "order in variety," and a company of pagan deities and abstractions in apparent defiance of Blackmore's and Addison's disapproval of the practice. Then come historical recollections (partly to contrast with the satisfactory present), a ruin bit, rural sports, a catalogue of fish, the story of Lodona, the Ausonian water-mirror, an address to the Thames with retirement theme suggesting *Cooper's Hill* and indeed leading to a tribute to it in a "bear me" passage, an elegiac touch, more history, and finally the Father Thames episode with its possible reminiscence of the Elizabethan pageant of rivers and with prophecy of future prosperity, followed by a modest conclusion. *Windsor Forest* . . . is compounded of "description, incident, and history." One of its excellences is skill in passing from topic to topic, the difficulty of which had so impressed [William] Goldwin in the previous year and indeed racked the ingenuity of all topographical versifiers.

Robert A. Aubin
*Topographical Poetry in XVIII-Century England* (New York:
Modern Language Assn., 1936), pp. 122-23

. . . It was in *Windsor Forest* (1713) that Pope's predilection for colour was first allowed to have its way. Since writing the *Pastorals,* he had . . . been making some efforts to paint. Now, on the completion of *Windsor Forest,* he resolves to take up his residence with Jervas and study art seriously as a pupil.

However that may be, it would seem that Pope's conscious references to colour in *Windsor Forest* are carried to a pitch never before attained by any poet, in which the direct colour-words average as many as one to every seven lines—not counting numerous phrases in which this or that colour is suggested though not actually mentioned. With such a continuous naming and placing of hue and tint, Pope's colour-words may reasonably be said to take on something of the function of a painter's pigments. But that is not all. Whenever the earlier poets had occasion to use a colour-word it was an epithet that merely specified one of the qualities of the object mentioned. It never, or only rarely, had anything to do with other colour words occurring in the same poem, except in such obvious couples as the "red and white" of a woman's face. Normally, before Pope's experiments, colour-words in a poem were separate and distinct.

Now, in *Windsor Forest*, in addition to its unprecedentedly rich colour content, Pope is definitely beginning to see colours in relation to each other, and deliberately to group or compose them, like a painter, within the frame of his picture.

Norman Ault
*New Light on Pope* (London: Methuen, 1949), pp. 87-88

Even apart from the direct commentary of the Peace of Utrecht at the end of the poem [*Windsor Forest*], a number of factors at the beginning impel the description of the Forest in terms of *concordia discors* to yield an especially political interpretation: (1) the opening address to Granville, Jacobite sympathizer, opponent of the Whigs' general, Marlborough, and one of the twelve recently elevated to the peerage to give the Tories control over the House of Lords and so to make the peace possible; (2) the fact that the place chosen to be described as the ideal microcosm is the royal Forest and the monarch's home, and so stands for England at large; and (3) the pointed statement that the peace and plenty of the Forest proclaim that a *Stuart*—not the Whigs' Nassau or the Whigs' Hanoverians—is on the throne. But much more subtly indicative that the political theme is at the heart of the poem is another, more complex reference to the Stuart line; for it is clear that Bolingbroke and many of his Tory associates had strong Jacobite sympathies, whereas the Whigs were necessarily committed to the terms of the Revolution settlement. In the process of describing the Forest, Pope praises its trees. . . . The passage is, of course, strongly nationalistic; has special reference to England's pride in her control over maritime commerce, which is carried in her ships of oak; and helps make the oak forests of Windsor a synecdoche for England. But in addition, by causing the last line of *Windsor Forest* to echo the first line of his *Pastorals* —just as the last line of Virgil's *Georgics* echoes the first of his *Eclogues* —Pope intended that they be recognized as companion pieces. Now, the first of the *Pastorals* had concluded with a Virgilian pair of riddles, both political in meaning. . . . Pope, rather gratuitously, annotated the passage with the information that this alludes "to the Royal Oak, in which Charles II had been hid from the pursuit after the battle of Worcester." The precisely corresponding passage in Pope's georgic, then, is intentionally ambiguous, and the "precious Loads" borne by English oaks . . . are both her commerce and her Stuart monarchs. Indeed, this is considerably more than a pun, since the ability of the figure simultaneously to make a surface statement about commerce and covertly to allude to the Stuarts indicates that a Stuart reign is so exclusively a condition for prosperity that a single linguistic expression conveys both the economic and the political senses.

Earl R. Wasserman
*The Subtler Language* (Baltimore: Johns Hopkins
Pr., 1959), pp. 108-10

## Dunciad

The irritating proponderance of forgotten names is, as one of the notes all but suggests, itself part of the design: the persons seeming the more boring and therefore fatuous for our ignorance. Moreover, the darkness of poetic atmosphere is thereby increased. You are forced to wade through a stifling, clinging, muddy, bog-like substance of intractable references. The poem has actual bogs, mud, even "mud-nymphs" (II. 332). It is couched in Pope's more sensuous, rich-throated, slow manner and most precisely loaded with naturalistic and biological reference. Pope's work never shows the Miltonic emphasis on the hard or metallic. "Brazen brightness" and "polished hardness" are terms of critical opprobrium here (I. 219-20) while his impressions are naturalistic. . . . The cramming of jerky monosyllables into one line is a usual trick in Pope where absurdity is to be indicated. The awkward motion implied may recall his own expressly athletic grace, sense of vital movement, and consummate ease: correspondingly he sees his opponents as dull, and heavy in motion. Mechanic imagery is a precise association for the dull and inorganic: so bad poetry makes the muses "scream like the winding of ten thousand jacks" (III. 160). . . . *The Dunciad* is the condemnation, by as vital a poet as any in our literature, of the insidiously academic writer, the poet of outward form lacking spiritual energy—in short, the charlatan; one who, because he is out of contact with the springs of life, is necessarily dull.

G. Wilson Knight
*The Burning Oracle* (Oxford Univ. Pr., 1939, repr. in *The Poetry
of Pope,* [London: Routledge and Kegan Paul, 1965]),
pp. 175-77

Naturally perhaps, Pope's most significant application of his millennial thinking to poetry is negative—is the millennium transversed. Throughout his *Dunciad* the cosmic background is the warfare between God and Nature, on the one side, and Chaos and Old Night on the other. Nature is Order, and Dulness is the queen of Chaos. This idea, emphatic in Book IV of the poem, is not first found there. Pope had expressed it earlier in the *Dunciad* of 1728, where at the very start Dulness is "Daughter of Chaos and eternal Night." This parentage (I, 12) is echoed in the second

line of Book IV (thus tying together the poem?) and in various other lines
of Book IV, until the final passage (ll. 627-56) presents the awful triumph
"Of Night primaeval and of Chaos old!" Here instead of the millennium
that had so comforted Pope we find the scientific decay of nature blacken-
ing out the stars one by one; neglect of the Final Cause debasing philosophy, and, in general, conjectural theory leading to chaotic confusion.
Nature had begun with the fiat, Let there be Light! Here the opposite
takes place. . . . The great shew of Nature is over, and it proved a tragedy.

George Sherburn
*The Seventeenth Century*: Festschrift for R. F. Jones (Stanford,
Calif.: Stanford Univ. Pr., 1951), pp. 313-14

It is primarily at such key-points in *The Dunciad* as the openings of the
Books, the introductions of speeches, and the formal descriptions that the
idiom is unmistakably mock-heroic. In other parts of the poem Pope frequently makes use of mock-heroic touches; but he has also many passages
which are much closer to the lower and more direct species of satire, and
a number of sublimer passages. It was this mixture of styles that [Joseph]
Warton was censuring when he called *The Dunciad* "one of the most
motley compositions . . . in the works of so exact a writer."

Ian Jack
*Augustan Satire* (Oxford Univ. Pr., 1952), p. 133

Pope carries out his greatest project of inversion in the *Dunciad*, for there
he constructs a negative image of Christian theology, fashioning an inverse
paradigm of creation with a deity in it who parodies antithetically the
Christian Deity. Opposed to the ordered "nature" and light of a divinely
sustained creation the poem offers the disnature and darkness of a "new
world" ever verging on chaos; and opposed to God it offers the goddess
Dulness. The Christian positives—nature, Christ, Wisdom—are faced in
the *Dunciad* with their negative inversions—disnature, anti-Christ, Dulness
—as Pope seeks to convey the anti-religious values of duncery and to
realize imaginatively the negativism of evil and duncery.

    . . . In one sense the critical uncertainty about Dulness is understandable,
for unlike most poetic deities she is not conceived anthropomorphically.
Pope has modelled her, instead, on the Christian Supreme Being, has made
her an imitation of pure being, a condition the human imagination comprehends vaguely at best. And as the human effort to realize the nature
of pure being usually settles on qualities of mind, so does it, ironically, in
the case of Dulness. It is her divine "mind," a pure unthinking substance,
rather than any physical shape, which oozes in grey immanence throughout the poem's world. This accounts for the vagueness of her being. . . .
Dulness is essentially all "mind" in the poem, but as these examples make

clear it is the inversion of what is ordinarily thought of as the pure being of God, for whom to be is, as St. Augustine says, to be wise. For the creator of a world of duncery, to be is to be empty. The only real image we receive of Dulness in the poem is, furthermore, that of a being concealed, as the Christian God typically is, in darkness.

Aubrey L. Williams
*Pope's Dunciad* (London: Methuen, 1955), pp. 143, 144-45

The organizing image of light thus expresses Pope's sense of a positive moral order that stands behind and criticizes the "darkness" of human folly. Light is of course only one of a number of metaphors for this order that appear in the *Dunciad*—rising and falling, waking and sleeping, organic growth and decay are others that will be touched on in this section—but they all reveal Pope's grasp of a moral and natural order which he assumes his readers understand and share with him. The creation of beauty and coherence out of ugliness and confusion is one of the great Augustan achievements, and the *Dunciad* is probably the last great poem in English to have such a shared vision of order as its main structural principle.

Thomas R. Edwards, Jr.
*PQ* (October, 1960), pp. 457-58

GENERAL

Though in Pope's poetic theory clear primacy is given to the faculty which he calls Wit or Invention, the following of Nature demands that Wit be always accompanied by reflective Judgment. There will be quiet restraint rather than rapture and rhapsody. Pope's Muse will lead no mad Bacchanals; she is too civilized, too urbane, to play the Maenad. Poetic emotion will go hand in hand with poetic thought. Mere emotionalism, mere sensation without intellectual discipline and direction, will seem too cheap and easy an appeal to the mob spirit. To the invitation of unthinking sensation there is too ready a response. Pope and the Augustans sought to win not only the heart but the head. To read his close-knit couplets there must be alertness of mind as well as of imaginative sensation. A reader must have his "wits" about him.

Robert K. Root
*The Poetical Career of Alexander Pope* (Princeton, N. J.:
Princeton Univ. Pr., 1938), p. 30

The value of correctness in or out of the heroic couplet lies first of all in the effect it has on the reader's attitude. When a reader finds that his poet considers himself responsible for every syllable not simply in this or that poem but in every poem of his entire works, then his alertness is intensified, his curiosity aroused, his trust increased. Here, he sees, is a poet who will set him in a motion which will only change as a dance changes, not as a walk on ice changes. Correctness elicits and does not abuse the reader's confidence. The reader will, however, soon tire if nothing happens to show how strong his confidence is. Once he can trust his poet, he looks to have the steadfastness of his trust proved and deepened by variety of experience. Pope satisfies this expectation in a thousand ways. Pope's practice is to provide expectation rather than surprise. But the expectation is expectation *of* surprise. The reader of Pope anticipates perfect responsibility syllable by syllable, and awaits the changes which will show that the responsibility is being put to advantage. The thousand surprises come and they enchant all the more because, as certainly as rime in a known stanza, they have been subconsciously anticipated.

Geoffrey Tillotson
*On the Poetry of Pope* (Oxford: Clarendon Pr., 1938), pp. 115-16

After 1717 Pope preferred to subdue his powers of imagination. Looking back upon this early poetry in later years, he regarded it with indulgent condescension as a youthful excess. He liked to think that he had not wandered long in Fancy's maze (the distinction between Fancy and Imagination was not yet recognized), but had soon stooped like a falcon upon Truth and moralized his song. The association of description and fancy implied, and the dissociation of description and truth, are worth remarking. Pope's method in description never was to keep his eye on the object and to describe that object so accurately either by realistic or impressionistic means that the description corresponded with what other men might see. He preferred to describe something laid up in his imagination, something more splendid than could be seen by anyone else. What he describes are such scenes as I have already indicated, scenes bedizened with gold and silver—something quite unnatural, as unnatural as the decoration of Lycid's hearse; for neither Milton nor Pope wished to limit themselves to the comparatively mean resources of nature. Truth of description, like all other aspects of truth, Pope reserved to strengthen his moral purpose. The fineness of the spider's touch is part of his argument that "throughout the whole visible world, an universal order and gradation in the sensual and mental faculties is observed, which causes a subordination of creature to creature, and of all creatures to Man.". . . To appreciate Pope's imaginative description, therefore, we must be prepared to forget for the moment our breeding in naturalistic poetry. So much co-operation is essential to avoid misunderstanding.

John Butt
*Essays on the Eighteenth Century* (Oxford Univ. Pr., 1945), pp. 67-68

When the contemporaries of Pope thought of Nature they did not necessarily see it as a blessed escape from the ugliness and the distracting roar
and bustle of the town. Their towns were, generally speaking, not ugly,
and for the upper classes the life lived in them had a formal gaiety and
variety that have now largely disappeared. In such small cities as Norwich
and Bristol there were bad slums, and there were shocking slums in London; but there were also wide areas of pleasant streets, dignified terraces,
and spacious squares. Critics sometimes write as if the men and women of
the early eighteenth century had no interest in the country-side at all.
"When Pope was writing," we are told, "the love of Nature for itself had
quite decayed." But this is wildly wrong. The Restoration affectation that
all beyond Hyde Park was a desert had soon passed, though country
cousins continued to be laughed at, very naturally, in contemporary comedy. Pope, the poet of the Town, passed most of his life, from choice, in
the country; in the summer, when the roads were dry, he frequently rode
off into the country on visits to his noble friends.

James Sutherland
*A Preface to Eighteenth Century Poetry*
(London: Oxford Univ. Pr., 1948), p. 114

In the course of exposing false wit, Pope suggests two criteria by which
true wit may be determined. First, it belongs not to the part but to the
whole. It is the master idea which informs every portion of the body and
gives life and energy; it is the joint force of all components, and not the
beauty, regularity, or brilliance of any one feature. It unites the parts, and
prevents undue attention from falling on any one; and no part has goodness or badness in itself except in its relation to the whole. And if the
whole is properly informed with wit, it gives a generous pleasure, warming
the mind with rapture so that we are delighted though we know not why,
so delighted that we cannot be disturbed by trivial faults in the execution.

The second test is, that it must take its course from nature, that is, from
truth. But not necessarily from the worn or commonplace; enough that we
recognize, when we encounter it in art, its essential agreement with the
frame of our minds, with universal human experience. So far from being
commonplace, the whole piece gives the effect of boldness, not because of
style or artifice but because new life, energy, and insight have been added.
It comes with the graces of expression, which tend to heighten the outlines
of truth rather than to distinguish or conceal them. The expression, in
fact, should be as modestly plain as the subject and form permit; and
sprightly wit is so far from adhering to it that the expression may rather
be said to set off the wit. Nature alone is not true wit until it becomes
animated and is drawn into a unity by the shaping spirit.

Edward N. Hooker
*The Seventeenth Century*: Festschrift for R. F. Jones
(Stanford, Calif.: Stanford Univ. Pr., 1951), p. 235

Pope's death in 1744 ended the career of one who had thoroughly demonstrated his mastery of the art of verse satire. His achievement is especially notable, for he did not concentrate upon satire until relatively late in his life, and he did not produce a great quantity of satires. Nevertheless, he had convincingly demonstrated gifts that assured his pre-eminence in the genre. His work is distinguished by verbal smartness and variety as well as by acuteness of observation. If there is little of the natural ebullience or good-humored playfulness that has lent charm to the writings of some great satirists, there is the finish that comes from conscious artistry and that gives the aesthetic pleasure always to be derived from a work in which the writer exercises perfect control over himself and his materials.

Although the range of concern in the satires is largely limited to the moral corruptions that may assail persons of importance, the writings taken together represent a distinguished protest against depravity; and, in spite of all his enemies have said about him, there is no real evidence that his satire was consciously motivated by anything other than "the strong antipathy of good to bad." He may sometimes have confused personal animosities with the bad, and the intellectual assumptions of his day may have imposed limitations upon his perceptiveness. Nevertheless, the writing proceeded from what were essentially honest intentions.

Robert W. Rogers
*The Major Satires of Alexander Pope* (Urbana, Ill.:
Univ. Illinois Pr., 1955), pp. 113-14

# MATTHEW PRIOR

1664-1721

> Prior was engaged in various governmental activities at The Hague, at the Treaty of Ryswick, and at the Treaty of Utrecht (known as "Matt's Peace"). A Tory, he was imprisoned for two years upon Queen Anne's death. Known for his epigrammatic and satiric verse, he wrote *The Hind and the Panther Transvers'd to the Story of the Country and City Mouse* (1687) with Charles Montagu, *Alma or the Progress of the Mind, Carmen Saeculare* (1700), and *Solomon on the Vanity of the World* (1718). He was buried in Westminster Abbey.

> H. Bunker Wright and Monroe K. Spears, eds., *The Literary Works* (1959), 2 vols.
> Charles K. Eves, *Matthew Prior, Poet and Diplomatist* (1939)

"The Merchant, to secure his Treasure" begins a series of poems about Cloe—dainty pieces which Austin Dobson calls "wax-flowers to verse." In one of the series, Cloe goes ahunting only to lose her way and be mistaken by Apollo for Cynthia, much to the delight of an impudent Cupid, who laughs to see the god in error. In another, Cupid himself, misled by a likeness, shoots Venus, whom he mistakes for Cloe. Again there is the *motif* of mistaken identity, when Venus upon seeing Howard's portrait of Cloe bathing, takes it for her own image and is vexed with the painter for his daring. Still other poems follow Cloe through numerous playful adventures with Cupid, whom she finally disarms completely. These are Prior's contributions to the graceful, conventional, unimpassioned love verse then in fashion. The mythological fictions, considered despicable by Dr. Johnson, are pure decoration—a mere vehicle for Prior's whimsies about his mistress.

In a second group of poems centering on Cloe, the scene is shifted from imaginary woodlands of an unpredicated time to substantial London of Queen Anne's day. Instead of mythological characters, there are real persons engaging in brilliant repartee. To Cloe, to her fickle lover, and to Lisetta, a rival, the poet propounds riddles and questions provocative of witty answers on the perennial themes of love and beauty. . . .

Tiring of prose, Prior turned to poetry, only to produce another fragmentary work—"Alma: or, the Progress of the Mind." The poem is a purported dialogue in facile Hudibrastics between the poet and his friend Dick Sheldon upon the location of the soul. The subject might presuppose a serious interest, but Matt in his prison chose to laugh at philosophers. In place of the systems of Aristotle and Descartes as taught in the Universities, which after all were "only form'd to disagree," Prior proposed "a healing scheme" based, he said, on an absurd Spanish conceit to the effect that "as we are born our Mind comes in at our Toes, so goes upward to our Leggs to our Middle, thence to our heart and breast, Lodges at last in our head and from thence flies away." But Prior had forgotten his source or was deliberately hoaxing his reader. . . . The major conceit of the poem came directly from Montaigne, from whom Prior also took suggestions for some of his best passages. The poet rambled on, ridiculing all philosophical systems. All systems, he claimed, have unsound foundations: if one questions the premises of any philosopher's theory, then one is rendered helpless; deny to Descartes his subtle matter, and he has nothing left; refuse to accept the elastic force of matter, and Sir Isaac Newton would be discredited; disprove the existence of the philosopher's stone, and our "chymic friends" would be undone.

Charles K. Eves
*Matthew Prior* (New York: Columbia Univ. Pr., 1939),
pp. 212-13, 360

The subject of *Alma* is the problem of the mind's relation to, and situation within, the body—a problem given a new urgency by the dualism implied by scientific method and formulated philosophically by Descartes. . . . While the representation of the soul as a separate entity rushing about in the body is obviously alien to Aristotle, Prior's description implies the Aristotelian tenet most important for his purposes: that the soul is intimately united to the whole body. . . . The particular doctrine that Prior's burlesques, however, is not characteristic of Aristotle himself, but rather of such scholastic interpreters as St. Thomas Aquinas, who said, "The soul is wholly in the whole body and at the same time wholly in each part of the body." Evidently this conception had become a part of the contemporary teaching of Aristotle in the universities. . . . The "system" which Prior proposes . . . neatly reconciles the opposing theories in that it supposes the mind to be in the whole body, and wholly in each part of the body (though at different times), and yet confines it in the brain during one period. . . . The "system" provides, on the surface level, a coherent plan for the poem. *Alma* is in form a mock-philosophical dialogue, in which Matthew, after describing the controversy over the location of the soul to Richard, expounds his own system as the final word. . . . The first canto describes the mind's progress from the feet to the waist; the second deals with the stages of life in which the mind is in the waist and heart, or ranges about according to the dominant passion; the third, concerned with the final stage when the mind is in the head, naturally deals with the results of reason: the absurdities of philosophers.

Monroe K. Spears
*ELH* (December, 1946), pp. 271-72, 278, 282

Prior's conviction of man's inevitable woe is evident throughout his poetry. The passions are, as the second book of *Solomon* shows, a cause of suffering; in the third book Prior proceeds to give a systematic and eloquent survey of all the evils, natural and moral, that afflict man. . . . In that book, as well as in the first, Solomon exhibits the torments of thought: he considers the problems of determininism, and fears that "all is destin'd, which We fancy free"; he is unable to arrive at any conclusion about the nature of the soul, or whether it is immoral, or whether anything but matter exists; the nature of God and the origin of evil are insoluble problems. Reason perplexes him with these questions, but is unable to provide any satisfactory answers. The impotence of reason, then, is one of the chief causes of man's misery. And when reason is turned upon man himself, it shows him his true condition: a prey to passions which always bring sorrow. The worst of man's woes, reason and passion, are therefore in himself. . . .

Monroe K. Spears
*SP* (October, 1948), pp. 619-20

No one would claim for Prior a high place among poets; but because he has this quality of his own he is not of the flat-footed ruck, and has always been looked upon as the master artificer of the occasional poem; Praed, it is said (as though this were the highest possible praise), did not improve upon him. Undoubtedly the stanzaic poems addressed to Cloe, Nanette, Lisette, or whoever it might be, delightfully do what they set out to do; they may not be better or more valuable than what Congreve, say, was doing at the same time, or even Dorset before him; but they have the quality of extreme lightness combined with strength . . . , which is more in the French tradition than the English. Such a thing as "The Merchant, to secure his Treasure," is, of its kind, perfect. Yet it may well be held that where he is at his best, at once at his freest and most concise, is where he approaches nearest to Swift in the handling of the octosyllabic verse which Prior at any rate took over from Butler and made more easily readable.

Bonamy Dobrée
*English Literature in the Early Eighteenth Century*
(Oxford Univ. Pr., 1959), p. 166

# SAMUEL RICHARDSON
1689-1761

A well-known printer, Richardson counted among his clients the House of Commons. It would seem that the epistolary novel *Pamela*, appearing in 1740 and 1741, grew from the endeavor of producing a volume of letters as models and as didactic advice on the "common Concerns of Human Life." The father of the novel produced two further long works *Clarissa Harlowe* (1747-1748) and *Sir Charles Grandison* (1753-1754), the former masterpiece gaining much continental fame for its author.

W. M. Sale, *Samuel Richardson: Master Printer* (1950)

## Pamela

As a novelist, then, Richardson is capable of considerable objectivity; but it is clear that as a conscious moralist he is completely on the side of Pamela, and it is here that the most serious objections to his novel arise. His sub-title, "Virtue Rewarded," draws attention to the immitigable vulgarity of the book's moral texture; it is surely evident that Pamela is in any case chaste only in a very technical sense which is of scant interest to the morally perceptive, and that Fielding hit upon the major moral defect of the story when he made Shamela remark: "I thought once of making a little fortune by my person. I now intend to make a great one by my vartue." As to Mr. B's vaunted reformation it is difficult to see that it amounts to any more than a promise, in Mandeville's words, "never to be a deer-stealer, upon condition that he shall have venison of his own.". . .

Only by some such hypothesis can we explain the later course of the novel, or the remarkable paradox that Richardson, a leader in the crusade for sexual reform, and an avowed enemy of love both in its romantic and fleshly aspects, should have signalised his entry into the history of literature by a work which gave a more detailed account of a single amorous intrigue than had ever been produced before. It would seem that the opposite qualities in Richardson's outlook, his Puritanism and his prurience, are the result of the same forces, and this no doubt explains why their effects are so intricately connected. The complexities of the forces juxtaposed are largely responsible for the unique literary qualities which *Pamela* brought into fiction: they make possible a detailed presentation of a personal relationship enriched by a series of developing contrasts between the ideal and the real, the apparent and the actual, the spiritual and the physical, the conscious and the unconscious. But if the latent ambiguities of the sexual code helped Richardson to produce the first true novel, they at the same time conspired to create something that was new and prophetic in quite another sense: a work that could be praised from the pulpit and yet attacked as pornography, a work that gratified the reading public with the combined attractions of a sermon and a striptease.

Ian Watt
*The Rise of the Novel* (Berkeley, Calif.:
Univ. California Pr., 1957), pp. 171-73

We see from these dramatic *Pamelas* that the salacious element is an essential part of the novel. It is presented in terms which may amuse us today, but it is understandable that in Richardson's time it gave offense to many. That a swarm of unwarranted, captious, and misdirected criticisms obscured the objections on moral grounds does not negate the fact that these objections had a legitimate basis. The salacious element did indeed exist, even though one may feel that some critics' overweening dismay at its presence (their overreaction, we might say now) was quite as much a comment on the nature of their own inner thoughts as it was a condemnation of Richardson's fictionalized improprieties.

The other major moral defects in *Pamela* which the various dramas make more apparent—the class standards of virtue and the virtue-on-a-paying-basis type of morality—would go unnoticed by many who objected to the salacity simply because they, like Richardson, were infected with these very same faults. The dramas also disclosed defects in characterization—the weakness of B. and Williams—and the improbability of the denouement. But overriding all the negative considerations, what emerges from a reading of the plays is our mounting respect for Richardson's handling of a story which adapters and imitators were able only to weaken or corrupt.

Bernard Kreissman
*Pamela-Shamela* (Lincoln, Neb.: Univ.
Nebraska Pr., 1960), p. 60

## Clarissa Harlowe

Though *Clarissa* is about five times as long as *Pamela*, it has far more organic unity. Long-winded as some of the letters may seem at first sight, and redundant in their details, they will almost invariably be found necessary to that minute revelation of character by almost infinitesimal touches which is distinctive of Richardson's art. The truth of this statement will be discovered by any reader who, dismayed by the gigantic proportions of the work, seeks to evade his full responsibilities by "skipping." Views or observations thrown off apparently lightly by one of the correspondents, and perhaps scarcely noticed at the time, are taken up later by another character, and seen to be far more significant than appeared at first. There is thus a constant interlacing of phrases and of ideas throughout the work which reminds us of the repetition of the theme in a fugue. The author himself in an elaborate series of footnotes, like the critical apparatus to a classical text, frequently expounds the relations of one passage or letter to another and to the general scheme of the work. It is in its combination of infinitely detailed analysis with a structural unity sedulously kept in view that the peculiar impressiveness of *Clarissa* partly lies. In *Pamela* the interest is almost entirely focussed on the heroine, and the letters, with few and unimportant exceptions, are written by her. In *Clarissa* there are not only four principal correspondents, the heroine and her bosom friend Miss Anna Howe, Lovelace and his intimate and confidant John Belford, but a variety of other letter-writers of different social classes. Even the subordinate personages are clearly individualized, and each of them has a distinctive epistolary style. There is nowhere in the later work the shy and tremulous grace of Pamela's maiden pen, but in range and variety Richardson's powers of expression have immeasurably increased.

F. S. Boas
*Essays and Studies*, II (1911), pp. 49-50

Lovelace is Richardson's extravagant triumph. How did such a burning and tormented human being come out of that tedious little printer's mind? In the English novel Lovelace is one of the few men of intellect who display an intellect which is their own and not patently an abstract of their author's intellectual interests. He is half-villain, half-god, a male drawn to the full, and he dominates English fiction. He is all the more male for the feminine strains in his character: his hatred of women, his love of intrigue, his personal vanity, his captiousness and lack of real humility. A very masculine novelist like Fielding is too much a moralist, and too confidently a man, to catch a strain like that. And how Lovelace can write! When Clarissa's letters drag, like sighing Sunday hymns, or nag at us in their blameless prose, like the Collect for the day, the letters of Lovelace crackle and blaze with both the fire and the inconsequence of life. His words fly back and forth, throwing out anecdotes and the characters of his friends, with wonderful transitions of mood.

V. S. Pritchett
*The Living Novel* (New York: Reynal and Hitchcock, 1947), p. 28

These characters are presented with wonderful skill. Richardson's powers of characterization, besides his skill as a psychologist, place him in the very highest rank of novelists. Each one of his correspondents has a distinct style, appropriate to his or her personality. We can tell Clarissa's letters from Miss Howe's or Harriet Byron's, and Lovelace's from Belford's. Nor did Richardson always need two or three hundred thousand words to achieve his results. He was most at ease, doubtless, when he had unlimited space; but he can create a character for us in few lines, and many of his minor personages are amongst his best. Clarissa's mother, Lord M., Mrs. Hodges, Elias Brand, Lord W.: some of these creatures only appear once or twice, yet all are distinct and alive. Richardson owes much to the letter form, which enables his people to speak out with an immediacy impossible to a more objective technique. Yet his virtuosity is such that he can play infinite variations on the method. His characters not only reveal themselves, they also reveal one another. We see Lovelace through Clarissa's and Miss Howe's eyes as well as through his own, and each glimpse adds to the vitality of his portrait. The same may be said of Clarissa herself. Nor are these Richardson's only resources. He is also an incomparable master of scene-painting. Many of his finest passages describe situations which, were the pronoun "I" removed, would read quite objectively. . . . All these display great penetration of human behaviour, mixed often with a good deal of humour. For Richardson, all opinions to the contrary notwithstanding, was far from destitute of this quality. His method is not always analytic; he can use picturesque detail with wonderful effect.

A. E. Carter
*UTQ* (July, 1948), p. 395

*Clarissa Harlowe* (1747-48) was to be another *Pamela* but with all the imperfections removed. Clarissa is still a version of Griselda but much more completely realized and more finely observed and motivated. Because the author had resolved never again to let the rake marry the heroine, from its inception the novel was to be a tragedy, and as Clarissa's tribulations become more and more trying, one can catch glimpses of possible doors of escape being quietly closed. She was a doomed victim thrust by her pitiless family into the hands of a half-mad libertine. It must be admitted that the case is an extreme one. Clarissa's character, however, is convincing—certainly much more so than Lovelace's. Often Lovelace is simply incredible. This warped egoist with his cruelty and his miserable pretense of having a system of libertinage, as he is observed from the outside and from the feminine point of view, is totally lacking in good humor and the *joie de vivre* which are commonly traits of the rake in real life. Lovelace's ruling passion is pride, and his only motive for ruining the lives of his dupes is to get revenge on womankind because once upon a time a "quality jilt" had cast him off. . . .

Clarissa's fine sensibilities, her capacity for deep feeling, and her delicacy make her more sentimental than Pamela. In the melodramatic atmosphere of Mrs. Sinclair's house of ill fame, Clarissa runs the gamut from torpor to frenetic excitement. Her final days as she writes her letters on her "last house" are a deliberate orgy of tears, of heartbreak distilled drop by drop, of the kind of emotionalism dear to the disciples of feeling. However, the Hogarthian realism of Mrs. Sinclair's fall and death, and the stories of Sally Martin and Polly Horton were a little too coarse and low to suit certain sentimental palates.

James R. Foster
*History of the Pre-Romantic Novel in England* (New York:
Modern Language Assn., 1949), pp. 110-11

In understanding the Clarissa-symbol, we should add to its associations the effect of the optical framing. Naturally, given the point of view that Richardson has adopted, we must always see Clarissa through someone else's eyes or else as she sees herself in a mirror. This would seem merely an exigency of the letter form of the book; but when we consider, along with this natural optical tactic, the fact that special devices (such as mirror or keyhole) are so often employed to emphasize the *seeing* of Clarissa by someone, and usually under conditions where she must be unconscious of being looked at, we begin to feel that the optical tactic must be "working" in a somewhat complex strategic way. The most extreme case in point is, of course, the episode of the rape itself, when the door of the room is left open and "female figures flit" across it, watching. One effect of this strategy is to make of the reader a Peeping Tom, to make him share in the dubious delights of voyeurism. Also, as strategy, it is consistent with that of the letter vehicle: as the letters "tell all" and the letter writer exposes all, turning himself inside out to his confidant, so the handling of the images offers all—not particularly to be experienced (in imagination) at first hand —but to be *seen*. Paradoxically enough, though the material of the novel is so largely subjective, "inner," yet a definitive quality of the *Clarissa* world is its publicity: no one is alone, can ever be alone, in *Clarissa*, not even in the most private performances of prayer, sex, and death. *Clarissa* is not a world of the individual soul, but, in the most extensive sense, a social world, a public world. We shall perhaps see, in a later consideration of this novel as myth, how the publicity tactics of *Clarissa* are technically coherent with its mythical significance, its significance as a projection of a social dream.

Dorothy Van Ghent
*The English Novel: Form and Function* (New York:
Harper, 1953), pp. 49-50

It is not, then, an adequate view to consider Clarissa primarily as an example of deflowered virginity, of the death-wish with which sexual desire is associated, as a signal instance of Christian martyrdom and the workings of divine grace, or as the embodiment of an ideal produced by a certain society ("Puritan" and "bourgeois," of course). Such considerations bear on components of the work, particularly on the imagery, but the tragedy of personality does not yield its ultimate secret to such catalytic treatment. The use of the term "myth" for such a story solves no problems: "Myth," we may say, presents plot and characters in the light of ultimate moral and religious sanctions, but an explicit emphasis on such sanctions leads us back to the old didactic point of view; or if we choose not to tie up myth with formal systems and say that it inheres in some mysterious internal force operating through personality, what more are we saying than that the integral force of personality under stress is significant, mysterious, and ultimate? Similarly, much is lost if we consider Lovelace exclusively in terms of male sexual aggression or aristocratic libertinism; labels will not take us all the way, whether we call him sadist, rake, or Prince of Devils. This is not to deny that the novelist and the reader are confronted with the problem of evil. The reconciliation of sexual self-realization with transcendental or absolute values may well be the ultimate challenge to humanity, and calls for an imaginative reading of life which was beyond Richardson's power. There had long been a conflict between "troubadour love of women" and "Christian love of God," and recantation of sexual love had become part of the tradition.

Alan D. McKillop
*The Early Masters of English Fiction* (Lawrence, Kans.:
Univ. Kansas Pr., 1956), p. 75

What is remarkable about *Clarissa* is its power. There is an intensity here, an intimate involvement of the reader which is quite outside anything previously achieved in the English novel or, for that matter, achieved again before Jane Austen. . . . We are involved in a way in which we are seldom involved in the lives of others in actual life. As Clarissa's position is revealed and the intolerable situation closes in on her there is recorded on our own consciousness with a quite horrible intensity the sense of being trapped, of being unable to break through the web of misunderstanding and hatred and jealousy and sheer insensibility that are going to destroy her. . . .

The conflict of *Clarissa*—the individual heart versus the conventional standards of the property-owning class—is one of the essential, recurring conflicts of the modern novel, as of all literature of class society. It is the conflict of love . . . versus money . . . which lies at the heart of almost all the novels of Fielding, Jane Austen, the Brontes, Thackeray, unalike as they are in almost every other respect. And it is no chance or subsidiary theme. When we are moved by a novel it is because our human sympathies are aroused. Such sympathies are not awoken by nothing or by imaginary issues and conflicts which have no relevance to actual facts. We are moved by problems and situations which we know throughout experience of life to be the real and vital problems. What engages our interest and holds it in *Clarissa* is not some abstract quality of sentiment or analysis, but the presentation and examination of a real and concrete human problem.

Arnold Kettle
*An Introduction to the English Novel* (New York:
Harper and Row, 1960), pp. 65-67

The book's power does not depend upon its pathos or its puritan morals or its picture of contemporary manners. It takes on a more than life-sized magnitude not so much for its length as for the symbolic aura that accumulated around the protagonists. If Moll Flanders is to be called the quintessence of worldliness, Clarissa is the quintessence of emotional idealism. Her rebellion against a wealthy marriage and her death from shame would have seemed sheer insanity by Moll's standards. Clarissa is the archetype of inviolable spiritual purity, and Lovelace is a very incarnation of the devil, the arch-tempter whose power is challenged by the existence of an utterly virtuous woman. He wins the contest in terms of the flesh, but she triumphs in the spirit. In this view, *Clarissa* becomes as much an allegory of eternal principles as was *The Pilgrim's Progress*.

Lionel Stevenson
*The English Novel* (Boston: Houghton Mifflin, 1960), p. 97

GENERAL

First, he put forward as the criterion by which the true Christian gentleman might be tested his attitude towards women and his treatment of them, and it does not require any great ingenuity to find concrete exemplifications in all the three novels: Lovelace is put to the test and fails; Mr. B——— redeems himself after a long period of trial; Grandison always stands superior to the suggestion of any such test. Richardson advocated an abrogation of the old dual morality, with one code of sexual ethics for men and another, stricter one for women; he demands that men should behave in their relations to persons of the other sex as they require women to do. The second part of his reforms concerned women more directly; they were to be "levelled up" like the men, though elsewhere, he virtually claimed that they should behave and be as they conventionally expected men to be: not silly, wanton, frivolous pets, with the vices of captivity, but self-reliant, useful members of a Christian community. . . . Certain female emancipators of the time did not altogether approve of Richardson's pioneering, holding that he did not go far enough; but perhaps they failed to realize that certain qualities, which he still advocated for women and which they considered to have been unduly impressed upon them in the past—self-effacement, domestic devotion and the like, were by him advocated for men also.

Brian W. Downs<br>
Richardson (London: George Routledge, 1928), pp. 169-70

That Richardson is pioneer and innovator, beyond all this, in these novels, needs only the pointing of the fact that he gave to the literature of his day the establishment of a new form, the novel in letters. Further than this, that Richardson used the analytical, sentimental novel of his day, then so popular, to express the new form, shows his canniness, and his understanding of his public. But that the work remained enormously popular after his death is to be later shown. That Richardson had the courage not to have the greatest of his novels end happily speaks eloquently of his devotion to art for art's sake and of his realization of the fact that it was not fitting to end a novel happily wherein such an ending would destroy the great meaning of its pages that one soul may not destroy the individuality of another soul without some fearful disaster ensuing.

Godfrey Frank Singer<br>
The Epistolary Novel (Philadelphia:<br>
Univ. Pennsylvania Pr., 1933), pp. 97-98

Literary history has confirmed the claims of Fielding and Richardson to be considered the founders of a "new species of writing," and sweeping statements about the influence of both men can be made with some show of justification. But it is uncritical to treat later eighteenth century fiction as merely the lengthened shadows of the two great novelists, to credit all the humor and critical realism to Fielding, all the sentimentalism and feminine touches to Richardson. . . . Although reputation and influence are of course connected, there is a wider gap between them than is always realized. . . . In the case of Richardson, the highly individual, even abnormal quality of his work contrasts curiously with his wide-spread popular appeal. Despite the persistence of currents which could be called Richardsonian, he remained, perhaps fortunately, the dinosaur of English novelists.

Alan D. McKillop
*Samuel Richardson* (Chapel Hill, N. C.:
Univ. North Carolina Pr., 1936), p. 226

Richardson's is a dramatic technique; the letters the characters write to one another are the equivalent of dramatic speeches; and while we read *Clarissa* or *Sir Charles Grandison* we exist, as we do when watching a play or a film, in a continuous present, always at the cutting edge of the character's suffering, analyzing, experiencing mind. And we not only have the character as he sees and presents himself; through the letters of the other characters we see him as others see him. The result is a much greater immediacy and intensity in the rendering of character in itself than we find in almost any English fiction until we approach the present age. Yet though his novels could have been written by no other man, though they are impregnated with his values, though all things and modes of being shape themselves anew in him, Richardson himself, while telling his story, is quite outside the action; he never intervenes, he never speaks in his own voice. The most subjective of writers in that the world he created was an acutely personal one, specialized to himself, no man could have been more objective in his presentation of it.

Walter Allen
*The English Novel* (New York: E. P. Dutton, 1954), p. 37

# JOHN WILMOT, EARL OF ROCHESTER
1647-1680

Born in April 1647, Rochester, as he is most frequently called, succeeded to the earldom upon his father's death on February 9, 1658. He was educated at Wadham College, Oxford, travelling extensively after receiving the Master's Degree in 1661. His attempted elopement with Elizabeth Malet was thwarted by her guardians, but after distinguished service in the Dutch Wars, he married her on January 29, 1667. Although close to the king, he was frequently banished from Court for his scandalous exploits and satiric writings. He took Elizabeth Barry as his mistress and aided in her becoming an important Restoration actress. His dissolute life seems to have continued until his death-bed conversion by Bishop Burnet. He died on July 26, 1680, at High Lodge, Woodstock Park. Most of his works were published posthumously.

John Hayward, ed., *Collected Works of John Wilmot, Earl of Rochester* (1926)
Vivian de Sola Pinto, ed., *Poems* (1953)
Vivian de Sola Pinto, *Enthusiast in Wit: A Portrait of John Wilmot, Earl of Rochester, 1647-1680* (1962)

## A Satire Against Mankind

His greatest poem, *A Satyr against Mankind*, is something far more significant. It is a reasoned statement of the causes of . . . misery and an announcement of the discovery that reason divorced from morality was the chief cause. This poem was first printed as a broadside in June, 1679, but it was composed before March 23rd, 1675/76. Like *Timon*, it is suggested by a satire of Boileau, but like *Timon*, too, it is a thoroughly original poem. Boileau's eighth satire is a somewhat longwinded discussion with an imaginary divine concerning the alleged inferiority of man to the beasts. Rochester's poem is much shorter, much more concentrated and informed throughout by a passionate vehemence which makes the elegant and carefully meditated art of Boileau's satire seem frigid. Boileau discusses the matter as a pure affair of speculation. Rochester discusses it as though his life depended upon it. . . .

The *Satyr against Mankind* opens with the most memorable lines that Rochester ever wrote. They are an attack on Man, but still more an attack on Reason, the idol of Hobbes and the freethinkers of the Age. Hence they are in some measure a recantation, a turning-back of Rochester on himself. "Reason," naked rationality, has led Man only to misery, and Rochester sees the process in a moment of vision as the picture of a wanderer misled by a will-o'-the-wisp, through all kinds of difficulties to a miserable death.

Vivian de Sola Pinto
*Rochester* (London: John Lane, 1935), pp. 174-75

Rochester's "Satire against Mankind," a poem of passionate disillusionment, is a terrific indictment of human reason. Briefly stated the leading ideas which it contains are as follows: (1) If the author had his choice, he would be any animal but man, who foolishly prefers reason to instinct; (2) the follower of reason pursues a will-o'-the-wisp; (3) he prostitutes his mental powers to be a wit. (4) The interlocutor concurs in this condemnation of wit but defends reason. (5) According to the author man is presumptuous to reason about himself in terms of the Infinite; (6) reason concerns itself with nonsense and impossibilities; (7) the only value of thought is utilitarian; (8) rules of conduct should be derived from the senses; (9) beasts are mentally and morally superior to man; (10) man's best passions have their basis in fear; (11) his egoism makes him tyrannize over his fellows; (12) even magistrates are corrupt and unjust; (13) even churchmen are liars and reprobates, and bishops are bigger fools than young fops; (14) those few who are godlike differ more from other men than the rest of mankind from beasts.

S. F. Crocker
*West Virginia Univ. Studies* (1937), pp. 57-58

In Rochester's satire . . . the commonwealth of men has not achieved the peace and security that Hobbes depicts. Despite the existence of a human society, the state of war is maintained, though now through subterfuge; instead of open acts of aggression, men hypocritically undermine and destroy other men, through "smiles, embraces, Friendship, praise." Man has created a wretched society where *"Men* must be *Knaves,* 'tis in their own defence" (160). In place of Hobbes's more complex analysis of human motivation, Rochester offers just one dominant motive, the baseness of man, who, instead of using right reason to achieve happiness within the proper *"Sphere* of Action," has perverted even right reason to the base motive of fear. Every deed stems from fear of one's kind, and there is no hope of escaping the maze of hypocrisy and treachery. . . . Truth does exist, but it is weak; the only refuge is knavery, for no one is strong or courageous enough to withstand the knaves who dominate society.

The sharp contempt of Rochester cuts deeper than Swift's itself. The ridicule of mankind for his folly, his irrationality, and his baseness in *Gulliver's Travels* is here concentrated into one, fierce indictment of man's pusillanimity. Base coward, Rochester cries in his fury; man is a coward so base that he is trapped by his own cowardice. . . . The poet himself is a bitter, disillusioned observer of man's baseness. Hence, there is no hope, no escape from a wretched society at war with itself, where men must keep their hearts and doors locked for fear of their neighbors, every man must betray in order to survive, and most men stumble about in a bog of illusion.

The tone of the satire, in its bitterness, also differs sharply from Hobbes's calm, common-sensical approach. For Hobbes, honor and fame are distinct values, and so is power; for these contribute in some ways to the satisfaction of man's basic passions and the attainment of pragmatic ends. For Rochester, man's "boasted Honor, and his dear bought Fame" are hollow mockeries, and merely additional evidence of man's baseness.

Further, in Rochester's satire is implicit a moral standard of some sort.

Hypocrisy, treachery, cowardice, and living contrary to nature are condemned. By implication, honesty and truth are absolute values, and desirable, though unattainable in our corrupt society. By contrast, in Hobbes's
philosophy, virtues are merely relative. . . .

Thomas H. Fujimura
*SP* (October, 1958), pp. 586-88

## GENERAL

Rochester's name, even to-day, is almost a synonym for bawdry, an error
that is hardly justified even after his work has been removed from that
background of history without which it cannot be completely understood.
Rochester is not a great poet, although at times there is a charm in his
poetry so peculiar to him that it deserves recording; it is peculiar, also,
to the age in which he lived, and admirably characteristic thereof. The
pleasure to be derived from it is proportionate to our knowledge of the life
at Court in Charles II's reign. The reader must picture to himself the gaiety
and emptiness of that life, the men and women who shared its frivolity and
fatigue, and, above all, he must refer constantly to the character who gave
to it so much vitality and criticized it so bitterly.

John Hayward
*Collected Works of John Wilmot, Earl of Rochester*
(London: Nonesuch Pr., 1926), pp. xlvi-xlvii

"My lord Rochester, a very profane wit." Very profane, surely, but as surely a wit—and a wit not merely as wits went in London of the 1670's but
in the sense which passes current whenever men praise intellect. To be
sure, he veiled his quality from all but those who knew him best. Those
Englishmen who heard of him at all, during his short life, were most apt
to hear of him simply as a creature of vice. Even in London, outside the
limits of the court, there can have been few who thought of him except as
the perfect pattern of well-bred debauchery. . . . There, too, he proved
his wit. The foibles of his fellow poets and playwrights, the inanities and
viciousness of the court, Charles II's mistresses, and even royal Charles
himself, were targets for his satires. Most of them reek of spite, and any
nobler motive is usually far to seek. He seems to have found in London
little to elevate his thoughts, little that inspired his Muse to anything but
savagely coarse abuse, or lyrics in which lewdness is adorned with melody
and grace of phrase. But there was no hiding his intelligence, and even
those who smarted under his lashing couplets had grudgingly to admire
his skilful brain.

Kenneth B. Murdock
*The Sun at Noon* (New York: Macmillan, 1939), pp. 271-72

In the general collapse of moral values, Rochester falls back on the intellectual and aesthetic. What his satires lack is a clearly articulated system of values, an ethos. Having said this, however, one is obliged to admit that all satire involves a set of values, stated or implicit, in relation to which the object satirized is measured and found wanting. So, while Rochester persistently voices the tenets of a cynical materialism, his denial of the abstract virtues has a kind of desperate bravado. . . .

Perhaps it is this which, in the last analysis, accounts for the extraordinary quality of Rochester. He sliced like a knife through everything; at the same time he was outside, looking on. He lived in a precious, elegant, and reckless court, and he was the greatest rake of them all. But he never for a moment lost his overwhelming vision of deceit and knavery, of a world of "Spies, Beggars and Rebels," where hypocrisy was the vice in decay, since few men dissembled their knavery, and no women disowned their whoredom.

Fredelle Bruser
*UTQ* (July, 1946), pp. 394-96

The anti-woman theme was carried to its bitterest extreme by the Earl of Rochester, who was by turns the Restoration's most famous amorist and its most cynical misogynist. It must have been in a mood of savage disgust with all women that he wrote the scabrous "Against the Charms our Passions have," which exists in two versions, one bowdlerized and one frankly scatological. Similarly bitter moods must have produced such songs as "I Wench as well as others do," in which Phyllis is called a downright whore; " 'Tis not that I am weary grown," in which Phyllis is advised to fulfill her destiny—to be the mistress of all mankind; and "How now, brave Swain, why art thou thus cast down?" with its contention that all women are creatures "so mean, so senseless, and so common; That Nature blusht when first she made the Sex.". . . As far as Rochester was concerned, chivalric love was dead. He buried it, and sang his bawdy songs at its funeral.

J. Harold Wilson
*The Court Wits of the Restoration* (Princeton, N. J.:
Princeton Univ. Pr., 1948), pp. 104-5

# NICHOLAS ROWE

1674-1718

Although a lawyer from the Middle Temple, Rowe became a playwright with *The Ambitious Step-mother* (1700), *Tamerlane* (1702), and *The Fair Penitent* (1703), all produced at Lincoln's Inn Fields. *Jane Shore* and *Lady Jane Grey* (1714, 1715), two further well-known tragedies, were given at Drury Lane. Poet laureate from 1715, he was buried in

Westminster Abbey. He also translated Lucan and edited Shakespeare, dividing the plays into acts and scenes, supplying directions, and improving the text.

James R. Sutherland, ed., *Three Plays* (1929)
Oskar Intze, *Nicholas Rowe* (1910)

Nevertheless it would be absurd to credit Rowe with any real tragic sense. He was somewhat confused in his mind as to what tragedy was expected to do, as is proper to a man who was incurably gay, much to Addison's displeasure, and spent his days in bed and his nights out of it. There is, of course, no reason why a light heart and tragedy should not go together, as much as a heavy one with comedy, but the heart must hanker after solitude rather than after the Kit-Cat. Such a heart as Rowe's could feel pity, but could not face the terror of tragedy. His poetic justice . . . is too easy; the "principal contrivers of evil" are punished with death. . . . It is no shame to enjoy the plays of Rowe, so long as one does not confuse that pleasure with the quite different emotions of tragedy. His works are, as Smollett remarked, solid, florid, declamatory: solidity is no mean achievement.

Bonamy Dobrée<br>
Restoration Tragedy, 1660-1720 (Oxford Univ. Pr.,<br>
1929), pp. 150-51

[*Royal Convert*], generally considered superior to *Ulysses,* has no claims to greatness. A typical drama of the eighteenth century, it shows, like the *Ambitious Stepmother,* a mixture of diverse forces. The characters are noble, and small in number. They declaim in inflated language on the usual themes of Love and Honour, or Love and Liberty. Possessing the passions of ordinary mortals, they express their thoughts in rant and fustian.

. . . Rowe's professed imitation of Shakespeare [in *Jane Shore*] has been treated with scorn by some critics, and, as far as plot is concerned, the play bears little resemblance to *Richard III.* Apart from the character of Gloster and the short scene of Hastings' impeachment which follows Shakespeare closely there is no connection between the two dramas. . . . Rowe's tragedy, indeed, is more akin to Heywood's *Edward IV* than to *Richard III* although they, too, differ widely in detail. . . .

Although the restriction of characters and the absence of comedy betray French precept, the tragedy of *Jane Shore* shows indisputable marks of Shakespearian influence. Rowe's earlier methods are modified in accordance with Shakespeare's procedure. The romantic, oriental setting, prominent in his earlier dramas is rejected in favour of real history. The unities of time and place are definitely broken. The noble characters, essential to the pseudo-classicel creed, although still present, take second place to a figure of humble life. Rhetorical effusions, it is true, still abound, but they are less declamatory and have a ring of Elizabethan grandeur, especially in the soliloquies. The dialogue, stilted in the *Royal Convert,* is animated and less histrionic, the speeches following the natural development of the characters.

Alfred Jackson
*Anglia* (1930), pp. 309, 314-15, 316-17

When weighed with Massinger, Rowe [in *The Fair Penitent*] is found wanting in his representation of human nature and in his ability to perceive underlying moral principles, but possibly it was precisely these things which assured success. The tragic sense had changed. Rowe was not plagiarizing Massinger; he was adapting him to the taste of the early eighteenth-century theatergoer. The structural changes in the play show the new preference for neoclassic simplicity; the unruffled, flowing blank verse reflects the placidity and refinement of the era; the modification of characterization reveals the influence of Otwavian pathos and that of the new feminine element in the audience, which together produce English dramatic literature's first "she-tragedy," and the veneer of impeccable moral sentiment is evidence of the rise of a bourgeois morality which will shackle tragedy for more than a century to follow.

Donald B. Clark
*MLQ* (September, 1952), p. 252

Rowe occupies the foremost place as a writer of tragedy in the first part of our period; as closest inheritor of the form he worked in, he is the best of the tragic playwrights of the whole century, which is to make no extravagant claim. To write plays was, it may be imagined, not more than the favourite serious pastime of this apparently not very profound man, whose frivolity scandalized Addison. Nevertheless, his plays are not slapdash; they are well constructed, owing a good deal of their power and readability, and no doubt their stage success, to the arrangement of the acts, and the movement of the emotions within the acts. It is tempting to think that born into an age offering better material to handle, he would have been more important in the history of the drama than he actually is; yet the sentimentality of his diction, his frequent "Oh!"'s, the constantly recurring "never more" refrain, seem to fit in so pat with the sentiments he dealt with, that it is impossible not to concede that the man superbly fitted the occasion.

Bonamy Dobrée
*English Literature in the Early Eighteenth Century*
(Oxford Univ. Pr., 1959), pp. 245-46

# THOMAS SHADWELL
## 1642?-1692

Today primarily remembered as Dryden's MacFlecknoe, Shadwell was a prolific and well known dramatist immediately following the Restoration heyday. At the Revolution of 1688, Shadwell as a Whig succeeded Dryden as poet laureate and historiographer royal. His successful, if not important, plays include *The Sullen Lovers*, 1668; *Epsom Wells*, 1672; *Psyche*, 1675; *The Virtuoso*, 1676; *The Squire of Alsatia*, 1688; and *Bury Fair*, 1689. Not witty but coarse, not of the romantic comedy school but of the comedy of manners, Shadwell typifies the mediocrity of the late Restoration period.

Montague Summers, ed., *Complete Works* (1927), 5 vols.

Albert S. Borgman, *Thomas Shadwell* (1928)

### PLAYS

Shadwell's fourth comedy, *Epsom Wells* (1672), bears [a very close] resemblance to *She Would if She Could*. The young gallants, Raines and Bevil, "men of wit and pleasure," correspond to Etherege's Freeman and Courtal; Lucia and Carolina, the sprightly girls whom they woo, are very like Gatty and Ariana; Bevil's intrigue with amorous Mrs. Woodly is conducted in practically the same fashion as that of Courtal with Lady Cockwood; and the marital hostilities between the Woodlys are patterned after the domestic quarrels of the Cockwoods. The parallelism extends to the letter forgery, the subsequent railing scenes between the girls and their suitors, the polite defense by her lover of the angry mistress' honor, and the same lady's provocation of the quarrel of her husband and lover, followed by her attempt at a new amour with the latter's friend. The spirit of Etherege's comedy is amply reënforced.

Kathleen M. Lynch
*The Social Mode of Restoration Comedy* (New York:
Macmillan, 1926), pp. 163-64

. . . The case for Shadwell's authorship of the operatic *Tempest* is no case at all. Yet someone was responsible for the revised *Tempest*. . . . The likely person . . . was . . . Thomas Betterton. . . . If the *Tempest* . . . was being prepared as early as August 1673, it seems clear that Betterton must have been the person engaged in making it into an operatic entertainment; he was the most likely person to have had the legal right to Davenant's *Tempest*, the interest, the knowledge, and the skill to make it an opera.

Charles E. Ward
*ELH* (June, 1946), pp. 125, 128

. . . Let us return again to the first piece of evidence [for Shadwell's authorship of the operatic *Tempest*] that [W. J.] Lawrence considered, the statement of [John] Downes [in *Roscius Anglicanus*]. As prompter, Downes would have been familiar with the personnel and inner workings of the Duke's company and would not have connected Shadwell's name with the operatic version, had the latter not contributed to the production. Though it would be fatuous to claim that Shadwell "wrote" (meaning "invented") the *Tempest* of 1674, it is equally impossible, on the basis of available evidence, to claim that he had nothing to do with its revision and presentation. And though there is no real evidence that Betterton did any of the rewriting, it is inconceivable that he, as co-manager of the theatre, should not have taken a major part in the production.

William M. Milton
*ELH* (June, 1947), p. 217


Opposition to the strictly nonexemplary mood which dominated comedy in the early Restoration was first voiced by Shadwell; and at the time he was in a minority of one. The great comic theme of the first decade of Charles's reign was the love-game, in which a gay hero and heroine, both of whom, in accordance with the inflexible code of time, make a point of seeming not to be serious about anything, carry on a witty courtship action which always ends—sometimes to their surprise, for they have been scoffing at matrimony, but never to the surprise of the dramatist or the audience— in an agreement to marry.

. . . This was the state of affairs when Shadwell made his appearance upon the scene with his first play, *The sullen lovers* (May, 1668). In Lovell and Caroline he made certain concessions to the now established convention —their love passages are gay enough—but he did not permit them to jeer wittily at the eternal verities. And in his preface he attacked the reigning couple in comedy, describing the gay hero as "a Swearing, Drinking, Whoring, Ruffian" and the gay heroine as "an impudent ill-bred tomrig"; "and these are the fine people of the play." He returned to the attack in the preface and prologue to *The royal shepherdess* (1669), in both of which Collier's *Short view* is foreshadowed. . . .

John Harrington Smith
*MP* (January, 1948), pp. 24, 25


GENERAL

It is difficult to speak of his plays; they have almost every conceivable fault from the literary point of view; commonplace expression of a commonplace man. It was not fair to say that he was "in the realms of nonsense absolute," for his work bears the impress of the dullest sense. The humours are infinitely worried, driven home by blow after badly aimed blow. In *The Sullen Lovers,* a travesty of *Les Fâcheux*, a whole act is devoted to the excesses of Sir Positive At-all. . . . There is little art here; yet at the same time, if one expects no very high level, and is content to be mildly amused without any mental exertion, one may pass the time very pleasantly with Og. His plays have the sort of action that tells upon the stage in a farcical way. *Bury Fair* is a pleasant enough fancy, if the humours are rather obvious and often derivative. *The Squire of Alsatia* has a broad Middletonian bustle that quite submerges the moral that youth should be allowed to have his fling lest worse befall, and gives in its stead a certain sensation of life.

Bonamy Dobrée<br>
Restoration Comedy, 1660-1720 (Oxford Univ. Pr.,<br>
1924), pp. 117-18

Of the five dramatists whose works are included in the canon of Restoration comedy, but two, Etherege and Wycherley, wrote during the lifetime of Shadwell. The ceaseless brilliancy of the dialogue in *The Man of Mode* and the masterly innuendos of *The Country Wife* it was never Shadwell's lot to attain. If one must grant that his comedies lack the literary finish of the works of his two greater contemporaries, one should not therefore assume that his dialogue is inadequate. His "Men of Wit and Sense," who have been the subject of many sneering comments, are by no means dull. In their remarks on contemporary conditions and in their scenes of verbal fencing with the women characters, their lines have a frequent sparkle.

If Shadwell's plays do not possess the literary polish that is found in the comedies of Etherege and Wycherley, they do present a much larger gallery of characters. In addition to the lovers who are usually placed at the center of the action, such types appear as the cheat, the country gull, the cowardly hector, the hypocritical Puritan, the miser, the strumpet, the spendthrift, the beau, the foolish pet, the orator, the man of business, the sportsman, the veteran of the Civil Wars, the French surgeon, the Irish priest, the Church of England clergyman, the Jacobite alderman, the stock-jobber, the man or woman who affects French breeding, the pseudo-count, and the witch-finder. The older woman in pursuit of one of the younger men is a recurrent type.

Albert S. Borgman<br>
Thomas Shadwell (New York: New York Univ. Pr.,<br>
1928), pp. 253-54

None of Dryden's other controversies, excepting possibly the quarrel with Sir Robert Howard over the unities and rhyme in drama, brought such significant literary problems into question as did his controversy with Thomas Shadwell. With Shadwell Dryden argued over the merits of the comedy of repartee and the comedy of humours, the right of an author to borrow from ancient and modern authors, the proper estimate of Ben Jonson, the rationale of the heroic tragedy, and the relative importance of pleasing the public and instructing it. Shadwell thus stirred Dryden into thinking about important aspects of his craft and prodded him into writing significant criticism we might otherwise not have had. It may be only imperfectly understood that Dryden's position as a critic owes a great deal to his activities as a controversialist; it is even less well known that part of that position rests upon essays written in direct reply to Shadwell. . . . At the very least, Shadwell's influence for a time was such that it dictated the subjects of Dryden's prefaces, the connection of ideas, and sometimes the very choice of words.

R. Jack Smith
*RES* (January, 1944), pp. 30, 42

# RICHARD   SHERIDAN
1751-1816

> Son of an actor, Sheridan at 24 wrote *The Rivals,* which was presented at Covent Garden. He assumed Garrick's share in the Drury Lane Theatre in 1776, where *The School for Scandal* was produced in 1777. His new theater opened in 1794. From 1780 he was a political figure and orator as a member of parliament, governmental secretary and adviser, and treasurer of the navy. Arrested for debt in 1813, he died from brain disease a few years later.
>
> A. Glasgow, *Sheridan of Drury Lane* (1940)

Richard Sheridan had been before the public as a dramatist only two years, yet he had written the greatest comedy in the English language, and one of the greatest comedies in the repertory of the theater. Shakespeare had never tried his hand at the comedy of manners. Hence we can compare Sheridan in this field only to Congreve, and while Congreve's plays are more intense and possess a slight undercurrent of tragedy, the wit and brilliance of Sheridan's writing is ageless and untarnishable. The idea of a "scandalous college" was not a new one with Sheridan; he had himself known what it meant to be exposed to the pitiless tongues of the gossips. His experiences in Bath and the scandals connected with his marriage may have furnished him with the background of his play. Dick Sheridan was twenty-five now. He had matured since writing *The Rivals,* and since he had reached that maturity while living in the Great World he had sacrificed humor for wit; his writing had lost some of the warmth and humanity with which the earlier play abounded. *The School for Scandal* is a brilliant play. It is sharp and dazzling, like a diamond, and like a diamond the fires at its heart are cold.

Alice Glasgow
*Sheridan of Drury Lane* (New York:
Frederick A. Stokes, 1940), pp. 130-31

One could not expect any playwright's first play to be his best work, but "The Rivals" is a good deal better than most other dramatists' best plays, and highly characteristic of its author. It still lives, and will live, not only as a most amusing comedy with unaffected, spirited, and virile dialogue, but through its good-tempered satire of unchanging human foibles. Foote wrote witty farces, but his personages were crude caricatures of contemporary eccentrics, his humour vicious, rancid. In reading or seeing Sheridan's plays, all of them utterly British, as British as those of his predecessor, Shakespeare, and his contemporary, Goldsmith, we can indulge the national propensity to recognize and ridicule ourselves and all our racial limitations. Where Foote failed and Sheridan succeeds is through there being something lovable and human, though absurd, in nearly every type portrayed. Even the occasional bad hats, like Joseph Surface, are never stock theatrical lay-figures, but studies from the life, comprehensible and entertaining, although unprepossessing.

Kenelm Foss<br>
Here Lies Richard Brinsley Sheridan (New York:<br>
E. P. Dutton, 1940), p. 106

The *Critic* shows no sign of declining power, but it does contain a significant hint or two of want of fertility. To begin with, it is comparatively slight, and even so is made up of parts which have no necessary connection but appear to have been put together to suit the author's convenience. The best character in the play, Sir Fretful Plagiary, has very little concern with it and figures in one scene only. Then the idea of the burlesque as a satire on the exaggerations of tragedy is far from original, being well known in Sheridan's time from *The Rehearsal,* to say nothing of more recent examples.

The question is an important one, for if we conclude that Sheridan, so ready in wit, was, after all, by no means so ready in invention, it becomes much more easy to understand why he should have written no more plays. There are several other indications that this was at least partly the explanation: *The School for Scandal,* for instance, was constructed by a joining process, and neither *A Trip to Scarborough* nor *Pizarro* was original. A very early idea of Sheridan's was to dramatize *The Vicar of Wakefield*—another unoriginal subject. Among the papers he left were some notes for a comedy on the subject of *Affectation,* but though several of the characters were worked out there was no trace of a plot. . . . Altogether it seems reasonable to suppose that he had very little of that faculty for turning plots easily which is so often the enviable gift of otherwise undistinguished writers.

Lewis Gibbs (pseud. of Joseph W. Cove)<br>
Sheridan (New York: William Morrow, 1948), pp. 69-70

There are [a] few probable instances of specific parody in *The Critic*. But in the main the work is certainly a general burlesque of contemporary tragedy, with a special affection, one may guess, for *The Battle of Hastings* —for Sheridan's finest thrust was against the period's bogus Elizabethan verse, in which none was a greater proficient than Richard Cumberland. *The Battle of Hastings* is conducted in a spate of garrulity. Even a common command becomes "Herald, provoke the bugle: spread the joy," and Edwina indicates her feminine distaste for battle in a speech which gathers wind as it rolls towards its ultimate bathos. . . . Sheridan does not parody it: he burlesqued it. . . .

Sheridan inherited a great part of the burlesque tradition; but what he inherited he perfected, and like all the great burlesque writers he added his own contributions to the tradition—processions and the patriotic joke in particular. The critics of his own time remarked on his ridicule of commencements, stage situations, and processions. Looking back at *The Critic* from a distance of nearly a century and three-quarters, it appears chiefly remarkable for its admirable restraint. Here is the perfection of mock-serious writing—the poker face and the unwinking eye.

V. C. Clinton-Baddeley
*The Burlesque Tradition in the English Theatre after 1660*
(London: Methuen, 1952), pp. 74-75, 78-79

Original genius though he was, even Sheridan in *The School for Scandal* could not break entirely away from the eighteenth-century comedy tradition. . . . Charles Surface is the prodigal but warm-hearted libertine. Maria is the heiress who loves him and is won by him, but who has to defy the advances of suitors preferred by her guardian. Joseph Surface is the contemporary man of sentiment, with an admixture of the Restoration rake. Sir Oliver Surface is the wealthy relative who conceals his identity so that he may be a better judge of character. Rowley is the typical devoted family retainer.

It was Sheridan's triumph that on to this conventional framework he grafted novel developments and additions which resulted in a masterpiece of stage-craft. Comedy has always been a vehicle for slanderous tongues, but seldom in such concentrated fashion as in that "scandalous college" of which Lady Sneerwell is president, and which includes Mrs. Candour hiding her malice under an affectation of good nature; the scurrilous Mr. Crabtree with his poetaster nephew, Sir Benjamin Backbite, who specializes in satires and lampoons on particular people; and for a time Lady Teazle, till she hands back her diploma for killing characters.

Frederick S. Boas
*An Introduction to Eighteenth-Century Drama*
(Oxford Univ. Pr., 1953), p. 354

. . . The most general statement that can be made of *The School for Scandal* is that it is indeed a re-creation of Restoration comedy in its outward aspects, but that it differs vastly from its prototypes on the ideological level. The fabric of the play is woven from characters, situations and devices which are either in direct continuity from the Restoration or are throwbacks to it. In spite of this . . . Sheridan's play manages not to say a single one of the most significant things which the Restoration comedy of manners was designed to express.

Sheridan's obvious model was Congreve, but the quality (moral, not esthetic) of his play is closer to Molière. The reason is simple enough. The crucial problem of *The School for Scandal* arises out of the violation of Christian virtue rather than social mores. . . .

*The School for Scandal* . . . is more than a typical product of its Age. It reflects accurately the tastes of the very moment. For purposes of illustrating this conformity, however, it is better than most of its contemporaries, simply for the reason that it represents a most deliberate attempt to recapture the tone of the preceding Age. In this theoretical failure lay its bustle and brilliance of the high tide of English comedy. At the same time it satisfied in every particular the moral as well as the esthetic sensibilities of the dominant group who sat in judgment upon it. In short, Sheridan's *The School for Scandal* is one of the triumphant examples of the yoking together of opposed forces into a work of art.

Andrew Schiller<br>
PMLA (September, 1956), pp. 698, 704

The enigma of Sheridan's fame lies in these facts: that he never set out to become a dramatist; that his early and sudden fame later became a frequent source of embarrassment to him; that all his major dramatic works were composed and presented before he was twenty-eight; that most of his years were, by his choice, spent in political life instead of literary pursuits. In the arena of politics he was no mere spectator—rather he was one of the chief participants, friend and ally of the chief Whigs of his time and a power in party councils.

Arthur L. Woehl<br>
The Rhetorical Idiom, ed. Donald C. Bryant (Ithaca, N. Y.:<br>
Cornell Univ. Pr., 1958), p. 221

# CHRISTOPHER SMART
1722-1771

Smart was a precocious poet but improvident and given to drink. Married in 1751, he lost his fellowship at Cambridge. Moving to London, he hacked out pseudonymous verse and edited the weekly *Universal Visiter*.

Continued impoverishment caused his family to leave him for good. He was committed to Bedlam in 1763 (a second time) because of melancholia and religious mania; here he wrote *A Song to David*. Released, he was again put in prison for indebtedness, where he died.

Ned Callan, *Collected Poems* (1949), 2 vols.
Christopher Devlin, *Poor Kit Smart* (1961)

But these pages [of *Jubilate Agno*] yield a great deal more than the pathos of a romance. They show that be believed he had suffered a great and cruel injustice in being shut away in an asylum; yet, at the same time, they show that his heart was overflowing with kindliness and affection. He must have spent many solitary hours in musing over his grievances. On one page he writes of his jeopardy, of the slanderers, of the serpents that can speak. . . . Yet the spirit in which he writes is animated by a patient, often a joyful confidence, that all would be put right in God's good time.

. . . In this strange, chaotic composition, the better parts are of far greater value than the whole; the tribute to Jeoffry [his cat] in particular is a unique and delightful contribution to literature. But even there the writing is so unorganized, so lacking in unity, that the reader is continually joggled about between laughter, sympathy, and wonder. The value of the manuscript as a whole . . . is twofold; it throws a flood of light upon the sources of *A Song to David,* and it tells us a great deal about Smart which can be found nowhere else. . . . There were qualities in the man which more than balanced his faults; a child-like innocence, a bright celestial vision, a heart which was always affectionate, and a faith which survived years of misery and humiliation.

William Force Stead, ed.
*Rejoice in the Lamb* (New York: Henry Holt, 1939), pp. 44-45, 48-49

This preternatural excitement to prayer seems to have been poor Smart's only real mental aberration, unless his drunkenness be considered pathological. When his mind was removed entirely from the field of prayer, he was but little changed from his sane state. His powers of reason, though thus warped, were not taken from him, and he neither raved nor sank into mental lethargy. . . . But when the desire to pray struck him, Smart abandoned what the world chose to call rationality. Beginning with regular addresses to God at stated intervals, he later began to pray more irregularly and more protractedly; and finally he reached a stage in which he would call his friends from their dinner, out of their beds, away from entertainments, to come out into the streets and join in his vociferous orisons.

. . . This monomania eventually unfitted him for the ordinary activities of life; but just why or when he took so literally St. Paul's injunction to the Thessalonians—"Pray without ceasing"—is not known. . . .

One has but to read a few stanzas of *A Song to David* today to realize how much that glowing, apocalyptic chant was out of keeping with the reasonable eighteenth century, and to understand how it could come into its own in the nineteenth. It is a latter-day Psalm, conceived in the ecstatic spirit of those other Psalms Smart was then translating. In it, all of Smart's potentialities were at once realized—every nugget of beauty that existed in the ore of the *Jubilate Agno* is there fused and remoulded and shaped into a form all compact. The song is not the poem of a lunatic, but neither was its writer entirely sane. Rather he was rapt wholly away from the earth by the unearthly beauty he saw in terrestrial objects.

The general reader knows the legend of the *Song to David,* that Smart scratched it with a key on the wainscot of his madhouse cell during a fit of insanity, after his keepers had denied him pen and paper. The legend is an interesting one, and it deserves to be preserved as such. It seems to have had its origin in the *Monthly Review's* discussion of the poem. . . .

. . . It is true that the poem may have been written while Smart was confined as mad. As early as 1759 he spoke in the *Jubilate Agno* of "a psalm of my own composing," and this may have been *A Song to David.* On the other hand, it may have been the *Jubilate Agno* itself. Almost certainly the *Song to David* was not complete in January of 1763, when Smart presumably was released. . . . The ideas and many of the images of the *Song* were certainly in Smart's mind during the madhouse years, for they occur in the *Jubilate Agno.* But the order of the *Song* compared with the chaos of the *Jubilate* argues powerfully that the former was given its final form after Smart's confinement—probably between January and April, 1763.

Edward G. Ainsworth and Charles E. Noyes
*Christopher Smart* (Columbia, Mo.: Univ. Missouri Pr.,
1943), pp. 88-89, 108-9

With Smart's *Song to David* we have obviously passed on to something much closer to Mill's "natural" poetry, and in the songs of Blake we have it at its purest. The attitude of Smart's contemporaries to the *Song to David* is probably represented accurately by Mason's comment in a letter to Gray: "I have seen his *Song to David,* and from thence conclude him as mad as ever.". . . The difficulty in the *Song to David* (where it *is* difficult) is largely the sort of difficulty we encounter when we listen to an excited man speaking too fast: Smart gobbles his ideas, and his words have a hit-or-miss urgency to which the eighteenth century was unaccustomed in polite literature. It is true that the *Song* is far from being formless, but it is certainly much freer in its associations and much more abrupt in its transitions from one thought to another than was usual in this period. The contemporary reader looked in vain for a sustained argument, proceeding easily and logically from one point to another. Smart appears to be skimming his ideas as they come to the surface—in fact, faggoting his notions as they fall.

James Sutherland
*A Preface to Eighteenth Century Poetry*
(London: Oxford Univ. Pr., 1948), pp. 164-65

# TOBIAS SMOLLETT
1721-1771

A Scotsman, Smollett attended Glasgow University briefly, and then sailed as surgeon's mate to the West Indies, where he was married. Returning to London in 1744, he practiced medicine and began writing novels: *Roderick Ransom* (1748), *Peregrine Pickle* (1751), *Ferdinand Count Fathom* (1753), *and Humphry Clinker* (1771), among others. He edited the *Critical Review* from 1756, being fined and imprisoned in 1759 for a libel in the review. "Smelfungus," as Sterne called him for his *Travels in France and Italy* (1766), travelled in Europe because of poor health from 1763 to 1766 and from 1769 until his death near Leghorn, Italy.

L. M. Knapp, *Smollett: Doctor of Men and Manners* (1949)

## THE NOVELS

If any distinction between *Roderick Random, Peregrine Pickle,* and *Count Fathom* is to be observed in relation to . . . [Smollett's formula for the novel], it is to be noticed chiefly in the protagonists. In the first, Roderick, the Scottish adventuring traveler, represents "modest merit struggling with every difficulty to which a friendless orphan is exposed," and his hardships are designed to arouse in the reader sympathy rather than mirth. His intentions are generally commendable, but he is deficient in a sense of humor. In *Peregrine Pickle* the central figure stands at the opposite pole; favored by natural gifts and a wealthy uncle, he enjoys the fruit of the land and comes to grief through his pride and insolence. The reader is repelled, but not indignant, at his heartlessness and his overdeveloped love of horseplay.

Fathom . . . belongs to a long line of thorough-paced villains, of which Shakespeare's Richard III and Congreve's Maskwell in the *Double Dealer* are consummate examples. Unlike these noble or fashionable characters, he is but a scheming, vicious sharper, whose ambition is to live in luxury without labor and to escape the vengeance of his victims, which compels him to be forever on the move. His character is not redeemed by either a sense of humor or of morality. . . . The influence of the stage extends to the theatrical settings for Fathom's melodramatic adventure during the storm in the forest near Paris and Renaldo's reunion with Monimia in the English church.

George M. Kahrl
*Tobias Smollett, Traveler-Novelist* (Chicago:
Univ. Chicago Pr., 1945), pp. 52-53

It must now be evident that Smollett, in accordance with his theories of the novel, had planned a satire on high society and had drawn up before composition began an outline covering at least the major features of his story. By the terms of the definition in *Ferdinand Fathom* all the characters and incidents must be subservient to his plan. Despite his prodigality, few can be found that do not help to achieve his satiric intentions, and an analysis structure of the novel will show how he also sought to make them subordinate to his plot. A start can be made in this direction by recalling his almost naturalistic objection to the improbabilities he discerned in *Gil Blas,* particularly to the abrupt and frequent alternations in Gil Blas's circumstances. . . . Smollett wished to avoid such improbabilities. In his own work no situation must lose its savour or have its significance blurred by too rapid a transition to another. To prevent that *Roderick Random* is composed of a series of more or less prolonged and static episodes, each one of which is elaborated by experiences and adventures relevant to the situation in which they occur and calculated simultaneously to entertain and instruct the reader. When Smollett had extracted what meaning and amusement each affords, that episode rises to a climax out of which a new situation is created. In *Peregrine Pickle* the same method is employed. If Peregrine is to be an author, he must have the experiences of one. He must meet and deal with booksellers, know other writers, and attend the meetings of the author's club. By prolonging each stage of his hero's career, Smollett not only attained the scope his satire demanded, but also achieved a kind of realism that most picaresque fiction lacked. Between *Roderick Random* and *Peregrine Pickle,* however, there is an important difference. Whereas in the first novel the series of episodes adds up to nothing more than the history of Roderick's early life and a "representation of the sordid and vicious disposition of the world," the sum of the episodes in *Peregrine Pickle* is the plot which ends in Peregrine's renunciation of the world for the joys of a tranquil life with Emilia.

Rufus Putney
*PMLA* (December, 1945), pp. 1059-60

When we consider the modern period chronologically, we are struck by the vogue Smollett enjoyed during the 1920's. "The world is suddenly being flooded with Smollett," said one writer in 1926. Indeed, this decade was more productive of publications written by and relating to Smollet than any other ten years we have yet passed through. During this period five books about him appeared, his works were reprinted two or three times, *Humphry Clinker* was included in the Modern Library and World's Classics series, *Roderick Random* in Everyman's Library, and an unusually large number of articles were published in the literary periodicals, including two leading articles in the *Times Literary Supplement.* What was the cause of all this activity? Very little of it had any connection with the bicentennial of his birth. Did Smollett's hard realism accord with the disillusioned pessimism of the post-war years? Whatever the reason, the activity subsided in the succeeding decade, unaccountably and completely. Except for the continued contributions to the scholarly periodicals, signs of interest in Smollett have well-nigh vanished.

Fred W. Boege
*Smollett's Reputation as a Novelist* (Princeton, N. J.:
Princeton Univ. Pr., 1947), pp. 145-46

It is going too far to assert that Smollett lacked all sense of narrative form: he was obviously following the convention of the loose picaresque structure, and he knew what he was doing. Consequently he stressed the single episode rather than any unified whole. His method, however, is somewhat tedious to modern readers, who are predisposed to expect a more dramatic narrative pattern. Smollett's long series of episodes, similar in their general subject matter and satirical mood, except where they reveal his liveliest characters, become monotonous as narrative, despite the tireless vigor of the style. This is not always true: the initial portions of *Roderick Random* and of *Peregrine Pickle* are exceptions, as is *Humphry Clinker,* where the epistolary form and the material contribute variety. It is not in narrative power, but rather in his achievement of the ludicrous and the farcical in character and in action that we find one of Smollett's chief distinctions. After all, it is his power to provoke laughter that has, among other merits, kept Smollett alive. The quality and degree of laughter stimulated by his novels has always been a subjective matter, depending no doubt on subtle psychological factors within the reader.

Lewis M. Knapp
*Tobias Smollett* (Princeton, N. J.: Princeton Univ. Pr.,
1949), pp. 314-15

When the novelist abandons Fathom as major protagonist, the structure is considerably weakened. But with Smollett, as always, architectonics are not primary. His major concern is neither with the triumph of nature nor with the downfall of art. Clearly, he is more concerned with a common-sense *rapprochement* of the two opposing ideologies. Resultant is a conclusion in which excessive *art* is encouraged to put its talents to better use in civil society, and defective *nature* is taught to moderate its excessive sensibility.

This is certainly a conclusion for which there has been adequate preparation throughout, for Fathom's arts represent an extension of and development from nature. As a result, artifice becomes natural, and artificiality is to be distinguished only from the unnatural. Fathom's arts not only are natural, but are cultivated and developed by his genius and talents, with implications that are moral, as well as esthetic. In addition, both art and nature are held up as virtues in a state of moderation. Thus, Fathom's art is undeniably advantageous in dealing with the artful; with them, he is frequently deficient rather than excessive in his craft. In addition, his selfish passions, which are disguised by his arts, are condemned only for their excess, which Fathom must eventually learn to control. Renaldo too has natural appetites and passions, and although these are socially and not selfishly oriented, in their excessive state they are responsible for prejudices and false perspectives which distort the understanding. Renaldo's natural passions and feelings are undoubtedly both advantageous and virtuous in dealing with the natural. But in dealing with the artful they are excessive and impede fulfillment of his own goals.

M. A. Goldberg
*Smollett and the Scottish School* (Albuquerque, N. M.:
Univ. New Mexico Pr., 1959), pp. 105-6

## Roderick Random

This first novel [*Roderick Random*], like, indeed, the later and more mature works of the author, suffers from a lack of imagination in incident. Smollett was always content—he could not, in fact, be other—to be, as it were, the historian in fiction. He always fell back on his own experiences for a background—and then proceeded to embroider them; he drew on his friends and enemies for his characters—and then he caricatured them. In all his books there is at least an inch of fact to every ell of fiction. He could not invent: he could only exaggerate. As Thackeray put it: "He did not invent much, as I fancy, but had the keenest perceptive faculty, and described what he saw with wonderful relish and delightful broad humour." On the other hand, readers of Smollett's novels must disabuse themselves of the idea that these are in the main autobiographical. This is far from being the case. Smollett did not write his stories as a means for autobiography; even when there is the same incident in his life as in the career of one or other of his characters it is differently treated.

Lewis Melville (pseud. of Lewis S. Benjamin)
*The Life and Letters of Tobias Smollett* (London:
Faber and Gwyer, 1926), p. 39

First . . . we can conclude that Smollett's hero is not simply a projection of himself; he is extremely conventional. But he does represent Smollett's choice of a certain kind of satire which emphasizes a correspondence between the physical and the moral—a good whipping will strip off moral disguise; a blow on the head helps a fool to see his way; a chamber pot over the head reduces the victim's pride in his human reason. The *punishment* of vice is accordingly as important a way of exposing and exploring vice as the simple observation of vice in action; and punishment will usually take a physical (and brutal) form. It follows that Smollett's tone is very different from that of the Spanish picaresque writers, who tell everything in a matter-of-fact voice, with a cold realism in which the horrible is taken for granted as part of the world. In *Roderick Random* there is an obvious heightening; scenes and details are presented in a more lurid light and are piled one on top of the other until gradually they become symbolic rather than realistic, and such climactic sections as the narrative of Miss Williams take on a nightmare quality.

Second, Smollett may have felt that the conventionality of the observer would remove the reader's concern from that area and focus it on the thing observed, the vice. His error is in dropping a poetic convention into the realistic world of the novel. As Scott saw, a scene like the flogging of the schoolmaster seems wanton and cruel in its context; to see it in a true perspective it is necesary to remember the conventions of formal verse satire and imagine the scene in a discursive rather than a dramatic frame. The railing of a persona becomes something quite different when it is materialized in a concrete act of revenge. The characteristics we find in Roderick—his pride, vengefulness, envy—quite acceptable in formal verse satire where an author is always evident behind the convention and the strings of his manipulation, become character-traits that have to be accounted for in the novel form, which has conventions of its own stemming from a realism of presentation and a search for motives and subjective truth.

Ronald Paulson<br>
*JEGP* (July, 1960), pp. 391-92

## Peregrine Pickle

In Smollett's multifarious hack-work, abridgment and revision were the order of the day. Yet amongst his novels *Peregrine Pickle* is the only one which he ever thought it necessary to revise in any radical way. Quite special reasons obtained. . . . The particular charges of . . . book-sellers and others against *Peregrine Pickle,* according to Smollett's advertisement of the facts, have been: that it was immoral; that it was libellous; that it was libellous even against the author's benefactors; and that it was worthless.

. . . On the whole, the revision must be regarded as an improvement. It frees the book of many real blemishes; and if it does not directly enhance what was originally its glory, at least it never for a moment endangers that glory. So much cannot be said for many revisions.

It is true that in the revision haste and carelessness are written large. The manner of pinching together the torn edges of the narrative by a single sentence, or even a mere connecting clause, is eloquent of the author's hurry.

Howard S. Buck
*A Study in Smollett* (New Haven:
Yale Univ. Pr., 1925), pp. 6-7, 17

## Humphry Clinker

. . . Succinctness, precision, and ease . . . [are what] Smollett achieves throughout *Humphry Clinker* by increased frequency and length of enumerations. And this increase in enumerations . . . forms only the most striking manifestation of a change in style which pervades nearly every paragraph of the novel.

The superiority generally found in *Humphry Clinker*, over the novels of Smollett's earlier period, must therefore . . . be attributed in large part to a style so neat that the reader is carried along swiftly and easily, with none of the retardation which results from the frequently diffuse and turgid style of the earlier novels. Certainly Smollett's mood has also changed: he is mellower, more genial; and this change, too, is in part responsible for the superior enjoyment which so many readers have found in Smollett's last novel.

Louis L. Martz
*The Later Career of Tobias Smollett* (New Haven:
Yale Univ. Pr., 1942), p. 193

*The Expedition of Humphry Clinker*, Smollett's final work, and a masterpiece acclaimed alike by readers and critics since 1771, convinces all who read it that, had its author been given another decade of vigorous life, possibly he would have surpassed the highest levels achieved in the distinctive creations of Fielding or of Sterne. As it is, there is nothing finer, *sui generis*, in the eighteenth-century novel. This remarkable work is not, as some critics have stated, a rare, unexpected, and inexplicable literary miracle, but rather the logical culmination of the rich maturing of Smollett's art and personality. This conclusion is fairly obvious to one who reads with insight his life and antecedent works. This is not to imply, however, that there are no problems connected with this novel. More light is still needed concerning Smollett's purposes in writing it, and concerning the date of its composition, which seems to have been spread over a considerable period, perhaps from 1766 to 1770. Furthermore, there still remain in its text some unsolved allusions, and other editorial problems.

. . . A most winning quality of *Humphry Clinker* is that it conveys a lively sense of Smollett's farewell moods. Although the waves of his violent satire still run high in parts of the book, there is much calm water and serene sunshine. The variety of moods is humanly real and artistically pleasing. On the whole, Smollett is more mellow, more light-hearted, and more reconciled with humanity and with the social scene, and, like Bramble, he can laugh at his own explosive fits of peevishness and misanthropy as well as at the follies that infest the world, follies so ludicrous as to provoke universal laughter. And in generous measure, this final work expresses in artistic form not only laughter but that bitter-sweet quality, which is universal in nature and in the blood and spirit of mankind.

Lewis M. Knapp
*Tobias Smollett* (Princeton, N. J.: Princeton Univ. Pr., 1949), pp. 321-22, 323

## OTHER WORKS

. . . There is a recognizable similarity between the style of travel books and that of Smollett. Defoe and Swift reflect the voyagers in their use of simple, almost colloquial vocabulary and a plain, direct narrative style, adorned or expanded by circumstantially detailed descriptions. Richardson, wishing to explore the motives of the human heart and to inculcate a moral at each new revelation, chose as his medium the dialogue or monologue for which he created a discursive, dialectical, colorless style. The style of Fielding, because it ranges from the mock epic to the colloquial, is not readily epitomized. It is the polished, balanced, detached, thoughtful style of an essayist—an elaborate style, rich in rhetoric. Smollett, on the other hand, evolved a style not for narration, analysis, or reflection but for description. With an abundance of material at his disposal, he was confronted with the task of selection and emphasis—a task in the solution of which he employed an idiomatic vocabulary without conceits or archaisms and a style marked by rapid transitions and objective clarity. This style was admirably adapted to conveying information of all kinds; when employed as a medium of narration, however, it focused attention on physical perceptions and shifted the emphasis in a story from the idea to the action. . . . Again and again the appeal is addressed not to the intellect but directly to the senses and the emotions.

George M. Kahrl
*Tobias Smollett, Traveler-Novelist* (Chicago: Univ. Chicago Pr., 1945), pp. 152-53

# SIR RICHARD STEELE
1672-1729

> Born in Dublin, educated at the Charterhouse and Merton College, Oxford, Steele became a member of the Coldstream Guards, largely as a result of a poem on the funeral of Queen Mary. His moral prose treatise *The Christian Hero* (1701) was followed by his first sentimental comedy, *The Funeral.* The unsuccessful *The Lying Lover* (1703) and *The Tender Husband* (1705) were finally offset by *The Conscious Lovers* (1722). In the meantime he had started *The Tatler* in 1709, then *The Spectator* in 1711, next *The Guardian* and a series of other shortlived papers. Governmental work, including election to parliament, was capped upon the succession of George I when he was appointed supervisor of the Drury Lane Theatre and knighted in 1715.

> Rae Blanchard, ed., *The Tatler, The Spectator, and The Guardian* (1955)
> George A. Aiken, ed., *Dramatic Works* (1903)
> George A. Aiken, *Life of Sir Richard Steele* (1889), 2 vols.

## PERSONAL

Repeatedly in his periodicals—especially in the *Tatler*—Steele denounced stage abuses (those Collier had specified), but he did so with a novel moderation and tact, presenting his precepts forcefully but without arousing the antagonism of the playwrights, actors, and theater-goers of London. It was his particular gift, in Gay's famous phrase, to "make virtue fashionable." Where Jeremy Collier provoked resentment and indignation, Steele, without sacrificing essential principles, won a sympathetic hearing by virtue of being more temperate. He more shrewdly gauged his audience. Collier assailed plays that could be considered immoral only by puritanical standards; Steele attacked plays of a more extreme kind, such as *The Man of Mode*, avoiding the absurdities to which Collier's zeal extended. Steele's graceful humor was always a protection from the ridicule that other reformers suffered. Dramatists and stage managers were willing to accept reprimands from a sophisticated member of their own group.

John Loftis
*Steele at Drury Lane* (Berkeley, Calif.:
Univ. California Pr., 1952), p. 15

## PLAYS

Without question Addison improved no few scenes in this comedy [*The Tender Husband*], toned up lines, toned down phrases. From Dick's too generous estimate of the help which his friend contributed, the work of Addison amounted almost to collaboration by the time the play stood completed in March, 1705. . . . Late in March Christopher Rich, "the waspish ignorant pettifogger in law," accepted "The Tender Husband" in lieu of the unfinished "Election of Gotham." Steele with all speed urged the manager to rehearse his "chief actors" in the play, which on the face of it continued to draw upon the author's own career for its main action: the protagonist a young army captain, and the theme—more marked than hitherto—fortune-hunting.

Willard Connely
*Sir Richard Steele* (New York: Scribner's, 1934), p. 87

I would recognize three different, though related, aspects of Steele's comic theory as finally embodied in *The Conscious Lovers*: the employment of exemplary characters; the appeal to the emotion of sympathy; the self-conscious avoidance of licentious dialogue. (The third is, of course, a negative quality that was scarcely controversial.) These are the qualities that in combination represent the dramatic formula Steele evolved, and only one of them (the appeal to sympathy) was a uniform characteristic of earlier "sentimental" comedy. . . .

Consider, as a demonstration of the inadequacy of the term "sentimental comedy" to describe what was distinctive about *The Conscious Lovers*, the sharp differences between it and Cibber's *The Careless Husband*—the most conspicuous of the earlier sentimental plays. In Cibber's play the humanity of Lady Easy's concern for her husband's health is, of course, abundantly evident, and the strong appeal it makes to the sympathy of the audience is perhaps not different in kind from the emotion evoked by Indiana's distresses. But here alone—in the pathetic appeal—have the plays anything in common. *The Careless Husband* has in spirit much in common with the Restoration tradition. The play exhibits licentious characters (slightly subdued) preoccupied with adulterous sexual relations; it was censured for its lasciviousness—by among others, the author of the *Anti-Theatre*. Far from employing characters who provide models for conduct, Cibber supports explicitly in the dialogue of the play the satirical theory, to which Steele so strongly took exception, by which Restoration dramatists sought to defend their employment of depraved characters. . . . In short, to identify *The Conscious Lovers* as merely a preëminent exemplar of the type of comedy represented by *The Careless Husband* is to ignore differences that are quite as important in the evolution of drama as the similarities.

John Loftis
*Steele at Drury Lane* (Berkeley, Calif.:
Univ. California Pr., 1952), pp. 197-98

The comedy that more than any other epitomizes the arguments of the Whig controversialists is Steele's *The Conscious Lovers*, produced in 1722.

. . . It is in a special sense a comedy of ideas, of ideas that in dramatic form were in 1722 fresh and new. Whatever the ineptitudes and awkwardnesses of the play, it was in touch with lively political issues as few others were. Unfortunately, the ideas are not, for the most part, assimilated into dramatic action but are rather presented in conversation—with somewhat chilling results. Ponderous expository scenes, resembling *Spectator* papers put in dialogue, are interspersed with light and laughing scenes, but the juxtaposition never becomes a mixture. The plot, with its palpable absurdities, is too obviously a vehicle by which Steele can convey the opinions he formulated in the last years of Anne, when he was one of the chief Whig propagandists.

*The Conscious Lovers* attracted much contemporary comment from literary critics; for the play, the conspicuously successful work of a celebrity, embodies a theory of comedy evolved in protest against the comedy of the Restoration tradition. Most of the critical commentary, whether sympathetic or hostile to Steele, turned on principles of literary theory—on Steele's violation of the neoclassical doctrine of kinds by introducing into comedy pathetic incident and characters intended to arouse admiration. But the play also presents the distinctively Whig view of the merchant and of the merchant's relation to the gentry. By way of satire as well as by the direct statements of normative characters, Steele insists on the hollowness of the gentry's assumption of superiority.

John Loftis
*Comedy and Society from Congreve to Fielding* (Stanford, Calif.:
Stanford Univ. Pr., 1959), pp. 83-84

## GENERAL

His range was comparatively narrow. The best passages in the essays and the best scenes in the comedies are all, in a complimentary sense, "sentimental"; that is to say, the sentiment did not pass over into sentimentality. They have the freshness, the naïve charm, the delicacy and sincerity, which we associated with the "innocents" of literature, the Dekkers and Herricks and Clares. They perpetuate, in a heightened form, the lucid, untroubled, unsophisticated experiences of childhood. . . . It is not an accident, I fancy, that the most famous essay in *The Tatler*—that on his father's death—was a recollection of Steele's own childhood. The essay is entirely characteristic because, with all its pathos, it is not without the suggestion of humour, that flavour of the mock-heroic, which invariably accompanied him, whatever his theme might be, when he was most himself.

Unfortunately lapses of taste and lapses of power are not less characteristic of Steele's writings. I do not mean the occasional indecencies, which are never furtive and were probably altogether unconscious. (Steele was never "refined," instinctively chastened, like Addison.) I mean the insincerity and the stupidity which go with the sentimentality and the didacticism, and make the one nauseating and other tedious. Perhaps it would be possible to consider this sentimentality and this didacticism as respectively an excess and a defect of the "sentiment" which is peculiar to him. They are essentially the penalty exacted by an insufficient assimilation of experience. The humanistic and ethical view of the world, which is characteristic of the eighteenth century, had not *transformed* Steele as in different ways it transformed Addison and Swift. It was only half-digested, and its expression, in consequence, is only partially successful. It was not the arduously acquired philosophy of a lifetime, but a lesson learnt by rote and not by heart; or if by the heart, at least not by the head.

F. W. Bateson
*English Comic Drama, 1700-1750*
(Oxford Univ. Pr., 1929), pp. 43-44

The superiority of the *Tatler* and *Spectator* over all preceding English periodicals is beyond question. Although unoriginal in form and tone and in the nature of their contents, the periodicals of Steele and Addison revealed to English readers a better quality of literary journalism. It is now understood that they gradually developed the periodical essay out of the section of the *Tatler* entitled "From My Own Apartment." They thus produced in its highest form the essay serial, to be sure, but it is not wholly true that they created a new type of periodical—the single-essay type.

. . . Steele was a good journalist. He gave his readers what he knew they liked to read. It is reasonable to believe that before entering upon this new enterprise he made himself intimately acquainted with all the methods and devices of . . . his more successful predecessors. Moreover, there could have been no uncertainty in his mind as to the tone of his publication or the kind of matter that should fill his columns. . . . Manners and morals, matters of human conduct and social relations, had long been the subjects of discussion by writers of periodicals. . . . Steele not only produced the first periodical criticism of lasting value; he was the first journalist to reveal the possibilities of the periodical as a medium for literature.

Walter Graham
*English Literary Periodicals* (New York:
Thomas Nelson, 1930), pp. 68-70

# LAURENCE  STERNE
1713-1768

> Sterne was sent to Jesus College, Cambridge, by a relative, for his father, an army officer, died penniless. He became vicar of Sutton-in-the-Forest in 1738, married Elizabeth Lumley in 1741, who became insane in 1758, and left his pastorate a year later. At this time he began *Tristram Shandy*, the first parts being published in 1760, the same year that he published the first *Sermons of Mr. Yorick*. Four more volumes of *Tristram* appeared in 1761 amid denunciations of immorality; two more in 1765; and its final ninth volume in 1767. In the meantime he received the perpetual curacy of Coxwold in 1760, lived at Toulouse from 1762 to 1764 because of ill health, toured France and Italy in 1765 (his *Sentimental Journey*, 1768), was permanently separated from his wife in 1767, and published two further volumes of *Sermons*. He died of pleurisy in Old Bond Street; three more posthumous volumes of *Sermons* provided for his widow and daughter.
>
> Lodwick Hartley, *This Is Lorence* (1943)

## PERSONAL

Superficially considered, Sterne seems to have much in common with Swift and Johnson—his lifelong disease, his love of society, partly as an escape from melancholy, his devotion to la bagatelle, his dependence on women, his essential loneliness—without any of their power of personality, any of their hidden depths. His temperament seems too mercurial to win deep sympathy or to credit with real suffering. . . . There are elements of tragedy in Sterne. A consideration of these does much to discount all the charges of insincerity, of lack of seriousness and depth so frequently brought against him . . . and enables us to estimate better the quality of his humor, his irony, and in general his contribution to English literature.

Two things are of fundamental importance to an understanding of Sterne; he was acutely self-conscious, and he was all his life a sick man. Not only his beliefs and the substance of his novels, but their tone and their technical originality spring to a large extent from this self-awareness and ill health.

W. B. C. Watkins
*Perilous Balance* (Princeton, N. J.: Princeton Univ. Pr., 1939), pp. 100-1

## *Tristram Shandy*

The supernatural is absent from the Shandy menage, yet a thousand incidents suggest that it is not far off. It would not be really odd, would it, if the furniture in Mr. Shandy's bedroom, where he retired in despair after hearing the omitted details of his son's birth, should come alive like Belinda's toilette in *The Rape of the Lock,* or that Uncle Toby's draw-bridge should lead into Lilliput? There is a charmed stagnation about the whole epic—the more the characters do the less gets done, the less they have to say the more they talk, the harder they think the softer they get, facts have an unholy tendency to unwind and trip up the past instead of begetting the future, as in well-conducted books, and the obstinacy of inanimate objects, like Dr. Slop's bag, is most suspicious. Obviously a god is hidden in Tristram Shandy, his name is Muddle, and some readers cannot accept him. Muddle is almost incarnate—quite to reveal his awful features was not Sterne's intention; that is the deity that lurks behind his masterpiece—the army of unutterable muddle, the universe as a hot chestnut.

E. M. Forster
*Aspects of the Novel* (New York: Harcourt,
Brace, 1927), pp. 111-12

Sterne's contribution to the English novel, derived from Locke's remarks on duration, is his treatment of time. His characters, instead of living in a present which has reference to the past only as the plot requires it, live in a present which derives its character and manifestations entirely from the past. Hence in *Tristram Shandy* the past almost crowds out the present, and a reader is inevitably bewildered who expects to find in it the forward-moving time of the conventional English novel, which exists in the mind of the author and not at all in the consciousness of his characters. . . . In *Tristram Shandy* there are only two or three groups of scenes which are in any way comparable to the kind of time used in *Tom Jones.* . . . [Such] scenes do not occur in chronological order, and they are constantly inter-rupted as the past obtrudes itself upon the present. Without the past these scenes would be in themselves empty and trivial, instead of being as fine dramatic dialogue as may be found in the novel. The method is not unlike that of the experimental movie, in its use of the flash-back, in its device of representing concretely what is passing in a character's mind, in its piling up of apparently irrelevant details to create a single effect, and in its absence of a clearly controlled and easily perceived progression in time.

Sterne learned from Locke the secret of why time moves slowly or rapidly in the consciousness of an individual; namely, that its speed de-pends upon the rapidity of the succession of ideas. In analyzing and repre-senting through the medium of words the ideas as they pass through a character's mind, Sterne shows his greatest genius. Furthermore, he con-nects this subjective and personal time with calendar time. He took pains to make both kinds hold together, so that events in the private lives of his characters . . . can be dated as exactly as can a matter of historical record. . . . His references to historical events are made with care and with surprising accuracy; they extend in the experience of his characters from 1689 till the moment when he is writing seventy years later. These events are not lugged in to give a specious air of historicity, in the manner of the historical romance; they exist in the consciousness of his characters in the same way that a contemporary historic event exists in our minds today. They are related to a dozen trivial personal memories and they have the power of arousing emotions and of being recalled by emotions. This sense of the relation of time past and time present and of the merging of the two as they exist in the consciousness of the individual is Sterne's unique quality.

Theodore Baird
*PMLA* (September, 1936), pp. 803-4

Of the special experience which is *The Life and Opinions of Tristram Shandy* the constituents are diverse and present themselves in nonsensical phenomenal sequence, in indescribably modified inconsequence, no less than in terms of recognizable chronological cause and effect (as within the nearly drawn incident) and in understandable logic (as in the exploration of a brief state of mind). The great central matters of love and war are exhibited not in their glamorous phases, but in their tawdry aftermaths as demonstrations of that inevitable coming to earth of which Yorick and the jesters continuously warn; and in the last pages the "provision for continuing the race of so great, so exalted and godlike a Being as man" and "the act of killing and destroying a man" are brought in Tristram's mind into a juxtaposition which, seen in the light of these observations, must be heard as a profound and subtle laugh: one of the most breathtaking conclusions in literature. Into that experience called *Life and Opinions of Tristram Shandy* flow all things, from the borrowed matter that almost nonactively passes through the mind to the paper, from that inert stuff to episode and aphorism incomparably enriched in the suggestion they take on before they find place on paper. All of it is presented in a frame of reference of the completest relativity and the completest nonsense, the logical non sequiturs of the associational faculty. Of all, perhaps the most astounding and the most significant is the fact that Tristram is the son in the flesh of a woman who cannot understand an implication and a man who tortures all reality to fit a hypothesis—Tristram who is the genius of implication and had the intuition to find that reality was its own hypothesis, that if you kept expanding the hypothesis to fit the facts you presently had no hypothesis at all—moral or intellectual or scientific; you had only nature, but nature as perceived by a given mind, with qualities and habits of its own. In a book of truthtelling non sequiturs, this is the greatest non sequitur of all, the final expression in form of the reality of Sterne's world.

B. H. Lehman
*Studies in the Comic* (Berkeley, Calif.: Univ. California Pr., 1941), pp. 249-50

The increased richness and bawdiness of the comedy [in *Tristram Shandy*] are under the guidance of "dear Rabelais and dearer Cervantes." In the series of "misfortunes" upon Tristram's birth, in Mr. Shandy's desolation over his son's mashed nose, in the circumstances of the christening, Sterne's comic genius is at its height. In the *double-entendres* of Slawkenbergius's Tale it is frequently at its most obscene. The tale itself is an ironic answer to Warburton's advice about laughter in the company of priests and virgins. Even such a warm friend as Squire Croft of Stillington seemed scandalized by its ribaldry. Sterne's own explanation—that it was a satire on pedantry—is hardly sufficient to justify it.

The eccentricities continue. As we have seen, the "preface" is placed midway in Book III. The same book contains a marbled page. In Book IV a whole chapter is "torn out" and ten pages are dropped from the pagination. An entire chapter is needed to give an explanation. In Book IV there are also a Chapter on Chapters (aping Swift's Digression on Digressions) and a Chapter Of Things.

. . . These volumes [Books III and IV] were published not about Christmas time, as promised, but on January 29. There were several laudatory reviews, but there were also attacks. The *Monthly Review* made the charge not only of immorality but of dullness. . . . The very popular novelist Samuel Richardson—a knight *sans peur et sans reproche*—could not stomach the immorality. The Bishop of Sodor and Man concurred, admitting that he had read "accidentally" some of "Shameless Shandy" and had found the author "hardly capable of any sort of defense." Walpole found that the new volumes were "the dregs of nonsense" and reported that they had "universally met the contempt they deserved."

Lodwick Hartley
*This Is Lorence* (Chapel Hill, N. C.: Univ North Carolina Pr., 1943), pp. 118-19, 123

The problem of time in the novel, then, is to be handled in terms of the succession of ideas. This succession is determined by association, and Locke's principle of the association of ideas suggests a solution for the most troublesome technical difficulty in plotting—the order of events. If a novelist begins his narrative or an episode within the narrative in the midst of things, how and when shall he work in the omitted antecedent events?

And if he has more than one line of action, how shall he manage to get everything told? . . .

For antecedent events the standard technique is a narrative in retrospect, more or less obviously introduced. The method of *Tristram Shandy* does not subordinate antecedent events to an arbitrary rearrangement of calendar time; it integrates them with the portrayal of character, carefully leading the reader's train of ideas. The procedure is fully explained in the novel. The reader should . . . think as well as read: this thinking is largely the following up of implications, of suggested trains of ideas, that is, of digressions. . . . The method . . . is to choose for the digression a moment when some minor act is in progress . . . and to keep the act on the periphery of the reader's consciousness by occasional references to it. The digression which gives the antecedent events of uncle Toby's career and in part for the Shandy family is sustained in this manner for ten chapters.

H. K. Russell
*SP* (July, 1945), pp. 590-91

Sterne's uncertainty is not really uncertainty at all. His cry of authorial distress is one of the many false scents he lays down humoristically in order to give to his work the appearance of artlessness and primitive spontaneity. At the same time it points up the paradox of all novel writing, the paradox of which Sterne is very much aware: the antagonism between the time sequences which the novel imposes, and the instantaneous wholeness of the image of complex human experience which the novel attempts to present. Sterne has his guidepost in the philosopher John Locke, and it is according to Locke's theory of the human understanding that he finds his way down all the several roads that are continuously meeting in one point in *Tristram Shandy*, or, conversely, we might say that it is with the guidance of Locke that he contrives continually to get his roads crossed. To the French Academician, M. Suard, he said in conversation that "those who knew the philosopher (Locke) well enough to recognize his presence and his influence would find them or sense them on every page, in every line." Locke had attempted to explain the genesis of ideas from sensation. Simple sensations produce simple ideas of those sensations; associated sensations produce associated ideas of sensations, a process which becomes immensely complicated with the accretion of other associations of this kind. Besides the capacity of the mind to form ideas from sensations, it has the capacity of reflection. By reflection upon ideas acquired from sensation, it is able to juggle these into new positions and relationships, forming what we call "abstract ideas." Thus the whole body of logical and inferential "knowledge" is built up, through association, from the simple primary base

of sensation. There are two aspects of this theory which are of chief importance in Sterne. The one is the Sensational aspect, the other the Associative.
From the notion of sensation as the prime source of knowledge and as the
primitive character of experience, arises that doctrine of "sensibility" or
"sentimentality" which Sterne made famous: the doctrine that value lies
in *feeling* as such.

Dorothy Van Ghent
*The English Novel: Form and Function* (New York:
Harper, 1953), pp. 88-89

Yet *Tristram Shady* is a novel and nothing else but a novel for all that it
has never been found easy to pigeon-hole, a fact which should put us on
our guard against interpreting the novel as a literary form too narrowly.
To summarize the plot is to say even less about the book than such a
procedure usually does. We may borrow E. M. Forster's word and call it
a fantasy, which at least indicates that Sterne was not out to produce the
simulacrum of reality both Fielding and Richardson in their different ways
were after. Yet Sterne creates a world, and it is a solid world, a world that
extends the reader's knowledge of the world as he himself habitually knows
it. . . . Sterne's characters, like those of only the greatest writers, have the
enduring quality of figures in myth: more is suggested by them than they
actually state; they express ways of behavior, inclinations of temperament,
that are permanent from generation to generation.

Walter Allen
*The English Novel* (New York: E. P. Dutton, 1954), p. 73

This was Sterne's sort of dramatic rhetoric: a fantastically involved structure of association, every one *consciously* calculated to shift our bearings,
advance on new ground, and open the mind on an undiscovered prospect.
In his comic vision, love is neither ridiculous nor cynical; rather it is a
social occasion which elicits all the possible roles that human beings must
play in order to communicate. The sense of role in social play, the sense
that everyone is on-stage, in borrowed robes, surrounded by insubstantial
scenery, lies behind Sterne's dramatic rhetoric. He shows us that we create
our own cause and effect by the associations of ideas which allow us to
make sense of what Locke called our night of obscurity. He reminds us in
his shifts of focus, in his tenuous interpenetration of pathos and bathos,
in the sallies of one motive against another, that not actions, but opinions
concerning actions, disturb men. Yet . . . Sterne's perception is of the Augustan rather than the sentimental and romantic modes, for nothing is
further from his comic vision than the vague late-eighteenth-century cultural force of equalitarianism which at last refined the humor character

out of existence, loved him to death. Sterne never suggests that his humor characters are really just like us when you get to know their feeling hearts better. The sense of role is always maintained; his characters remain as roles, voices, in the dialectic of our mind. They are not whole, realistic figures; they are probable aspects of human motivation. . . . One cannot misunderstand the book in any more complete manner than to suppose that Sterne is admiring quaint private vagaries, or to suppose that the book is a texture of unconscious associations of a blithe spirit. Rhetoric must be conscious, studied, to catch men in probable public activity.

John Traugott
*Tristram Shandy's World* (Berkeley, Calif.:
Univ. California Pr., 1954), pp. 147-48

It is hard to say whether unity is imposed on *Tristram Shandy* by the function of the narrator, or discovered by the narrator in the great scheme of things. We are here confronted with the problem of knowledge: How much does the knower contribute to what is known? Sterne, as an artist and not a philosopher, is not obliged to answer this question. The narrator is coping with a great system, like Fielding's narrator, but he also enjoys what on the surface appears to be complete liberty. Theoretically he claims the right to start from anything that catches his attention and proceed in any direction. This right, like the convention by which the novelist may claim omniscience and take any point of view, cannot be fully exercised. No artist can use "unchartered freedom"; he must issue himself a charter, if no one else does. The basic assumption in Sterne is that immediate experience, subtle and elusive though it is, can be firmly placed in a general scheme. He would not accept Hume's denial of causal necessity and uniformity, though he is keenly conscious of the difficulty of attaining true knowledge; we have seen that he is close to Locke's position that man can have valid knowledge of a world which is after all much like Newton's. Tristram the narrator is not identical with young Tristram; as narrator he does not keep to the point of view of the child, or write straight "stream of consciousness"; he is the efficient agent of the far-reaching references in time and space; he is both inside and outside the moment; he is not only the knower of English empirical philosophy, but the philosopher who writes with confidence about that knower—a somewhat different matter. . . . At the same time Sterne undertakes to relate the individual to his world by the short cut of sympathy and love, the bonds by which society is held together, and here he is close to the ethics of Hume and Adam Smith.

Alan D. McKillop
*The Early Masters of English Fiction* (Lawrence, Kans.:
Univ. Kansas Pr., 1956), pp. 209-10

GENERAL

Since this work [*A Sentimental Journey*] represents the flowering of Sterne's "sentimentality," this would appear to be an opportune point at which to examine the elements of which his sentiment was composed. To Sterne the word "sentimental" had none of the derogatory connotations of the maudlin and bathetic that it generally has today. . . . Sterne saw his writing as a frame, a "show box," in which he could present a series of touchingly pathetic tableaux. He invited his readers to "take a peep" into his show box, to mingle their tears with his in a thrillingly delicious orgy of emotion —always on an intellectual level—that would leave the *feelings* shaken and the *soul* untouched. . . . In the midst of his most touching and pathetic creations, the artist is to be found, with his bag of tricks palpably open, his handkerchief ready, pointing out the emotional nuances, displaying his own reactions and feelings, inviting the reader to take part in a tripartite feast of sensations. Sterne the sentimentalist is actually Sterne the impressionist. His pathos is almost always couched in terms of personal reaction, and it is doubtful that even his saddest tableaux produced any real emotional shock among his readers.

Thomas Yoseloff
*A Fellow of Infinite Jest* (Englewood Cliffs, N. J.:
Prentice-Hall, 1945), p. 173

When Diderot and Sterne began writing their first important works of fiction, they were both concerned with the same problem: they wanted to procure the illusion of reality. The achievement of this goal did not depend on a photographic reproduction of life; they sought to go beyond this and to create a three-dimensional effect. As their writings increased, it became evident that the quality of depth was, perhaps, the most significant. Sterne stated unequivocally, by using a quotation from Epictetus to preface his book, that he was interested not so much in deeds or actions but in what men think of them. . . .

What was necessary for the successful illusion was possibly not merely Diderot's and Sterne's natural endowments of observation and perception but also some further stimulus from their readings. Sterne's "sagacious Locke" had pointed out that a dual action occurred in the process of man's acquiring knowledge: that each object perceived had in itself the ability to evoke certain characteristics to be discovered by each perceiver, and that the individual perceiver's reflections on his own sensations were at least as important as the sensations themselves. . . . Why limit oneself to repeating neoclassic generalities and reproducing the same "norm"? . . . Sterne had no intention, he said, of twisting and untwisting the same rope. The tantalizing aspect of reality was that everyone really saw it and reacted to it differently, and *that* . . . was the point to stress in building their illusion.

Alice G. Fredman
*Diderot and Sterne* (New York: Columbia Univ. Pr., 1955), pp. 90-91

# JONATHAN SWIFT
1667-1745

Born in Dublin and educated at Trinity College there, Swift became secretary to Sir William Temple in 1689, but not receiving political preferment, he returned to Ireland to be ordained in 1694. However, he returned to Temple at Moor Park in 1696; here he wrote *The Battle of the Books* (1704) and *A Tale of a Tub*. Here also he met Hester Johnson, who was to be the Stella to whom he addressed a series of letters in 1710-1713. Some believe her to have been Temple's daughter by a servant of his sister, though passed off as his ward; and some believe that Swift ultimately married her. She died in 1728. When Temple died in 1699, Swift went to St. Patrick's, Dublin, as prebend.

The following years found him frequently in England on governmental missions, often, however, falling out of favor with the Whigs who were in power. In 1710 he joined the Tories over the Whig alliance with the dissenters. His prose during this period included the Bickerstaff papers (1708-1709) and anti-Whig pamphlets. He became Dean of St. Patrick's, Dublin, in 1713. Around 1708 he met Esther Vanhomrigh, their love affair being the basis for *Cadenus and Vanessa* (1713). She died in 1723 after frequent disruptions in their relationship. Disagreement with Whig policy in Ireland called forth *Drapier's Letters* in 1724 and *A Modest Proposal* in 1729. He published *Gulliver's Travels* in 1726. Around 1738 the signs of his fatal sickness, a form of vertigo, were noticed; some have alleged that he was insane for a time before his death. He was buried in St. Patrick's alongside Hester Johnson.

Harold Williams, ed., *The Poems of Jonathan Swift* (1937, rev. 1958), 3 vols.

Herbert Davis, ed., *The Prose Works* (1937-1959), 14 vols.

Ricardo Quintana, *The Mind and Art of Jonathan Swift* (1936, repr. 1953)

## PERSONAL

Swift also had a neurological complaint which he failed to diagnose correctly. In fact, it was not understood until many years after his death. This is labyrinthine vertigo, or Ménière's Syndrome. The disease attacks the inner ear, causing either deafness or vertigo or both. Its origin is unknown; it can start at various ages, with no warning, and comes in recurrent spells which may grow more unpleasant and more extended as the victim ages. Today one finds sufferers reporting it as coming on suddenly. They may have violent fits of vomiting; often they feel too dizzy to stand up; and they sometimes lose their hearing. As a palliative, they take daily the pills prescribed against seasickness; and then they usually have no trouble. There isn't any cure. Cutting the aural nerve ends the symptoms but of course makes the patient permanently deaf. There is no connection between Ménière's disease and insanity.

Swift often complained of his poor memory, his deafness, and his nauseous seizures. These complaints, in his later years, are sometimes very little restrained.

. . . Shortly before Swift's seventy-fifth birthday, one of his eyes became badly swollen; he had a general outbreak of boils; he was delirious and in torment for a week; although he could eat, he hardly slept for a month. There is no mystery about this siege. It has been diagnosed . . . as orbital cellulitis—a feverish and most painful inflammation of the tissue lining the eye socket. The infection is purely physiological and has nothing to do with insanity.

. . . When nearly seventy-five, he went into the sort of decline that a brain lesion, associated with cerebral arteriosclerosis, can produce. He suddenly had great and quickly increasing difficulty expressing himself or understanding others. Swift had by this time been so long withdrawn from normal social life that the new turn remained generally unremarked until an unfortunate incident during the summer of 1742. An inquiry made in July led to a general investigation, the next month, which established that he had, since May, been unable to take care "either of his estate or person."

For the remaining years of his life, Swift was protected by a committee of guardians. To set up such a committee, it was legally necessary for there to be a declaration of his lunacy. But this form by no means equals a diagnosis. It was the most convenient way for a senile person, living alone, to be defended against various sorts of exploitation.

· Irvin Ehrenpreis
*The Personality of Jonathan Swift* (London:
Methuen, 1958), pp. 119-23


## Gulliver's Travels

I believe that the philosophy of *Lilliput* and *Brobdingnag* rests upon one clear axiom: the true values of the human drama are those which are wholly independent of the size of the actors; all others are purely relative and ultimately false.

If this be true, it is useless to argue whether Swift means the big men to be more admirable than the little ones. Nothing is admirable but what will endure the test of his practice by men of any size. But is there anything which will do this? . . .

Of all human values, those which we commonly call altruistic, would appear alone to equal advantage in both Lilliput and Brobdingnag; and the reason for this will become clear upon reflection. Self interests change their aspect as the importance of self varies. Altruism is a negation of self, as that is commonly conceived. Unfortunately, the Lilliputians do not exhibit any altruistic qualities by which I could illustrate my point. To have them perform noble and unselfish deeds would have interfered with Swift's plan of consistent ridicule which he employs in the first voyage. If a Lilliputian had rescued a child from the fire at the palace, at great personal risk, would the act have appeared ridiculous? I think not. It is certain at least that the devotion of Glumdalclitch for Grildrig is a sincere, touching affection, not at all grotesque; and that the benevolence of the King of Brobdingnag is wholly admirable.

William A. Eddy
*Gulliver's Travels: A Critical Study* (Princeton, N. J.:
Princeton Univ. Pr., 1923), pp. 154-55

But there is nothing of greater interest in these letters than the new and conclusive information which they supply about *Gulliver's Travels.* The date of composition was long a problem. . . . The view generally held was that *Gulliver's Travels* was completed by 1720, as if it was the product of the six years of depression when Swift was settling down for life in Ireland, and as if, for reasons which were never explained, it should then have been kept for six years unprinted. Swift had given no help in his correspondence. Though Bolingbroke and Vanessa might allude to *Gulliver's Travels,* he himself had never once mentioned it in any known letter.

He had mentioned it in his letters to Ford, to whom he also spoke about it when they met in Ireland. What he wrote about it—all that he is known to have written about it while he was engaged on it—is here set down together with the dates. . . . From these passages it is now clear that Swift was at work in earnest in 1721, that he had written the draft of the first two Voyages before the end of 1723, that he wrote the fourth Voyage next and had completed the draft by January 1724, and that he was then engaged on the third Voyage. At the beginning of April he expected to finish the book "very soon." But in February or March he had begun *The Drapier's Letters,* and he was occupied with them till the end of the year. The revision of the *Travels* and the incorporation of new material, suggested partly by the circumstances which had called forth the *Letters,* may be assigned to 1725. By August of that year he had finished his *Travels* and was transcribing them.

David Nichol Smith, ed.
*The Letters of Jonathan Swift to Charles Ford* (Oxford:
Clarendon Pr., 1935), pp. xxxviii-xxxix, xl

It is even easier to find in the *Memoirs* of Scriblerus passages which might have supplied Swift with "hints" for the projects of Laputa. The eighth, tenth, eleventh, and twelfth chapters abound with hare-brained schemes and experiments. It is generally agreed that these are the work of Arbuthnot. The external evidence, therefore, is against, rather than for, the orthodox theory that part of *Gulliver's Travels* consists of recast material originally written for the Scriblerus Club.

The internal evidence for the theory is the alleged inconsistency in tone of the first voyage and the incoherence of the third. The latter question can be taken up most profitably along with the discussion of the general structure of the *Travels*. The former argument depends on a presumption based on insufficient external evidence. For, examined without prejudice, the first two chapters of Gulliver appear to be a perfectly natural introduction to the story under cover of which Swift intends to shoot his wit: moreover, they contain events which are a necessary part of the political allegory. These introductory chapters are neither more or less imaginative, or more or less closely linked with the main purpose of the book, than are the corresponding chapters of the second voyage, which, if they show a slight deepening in tone, do so in accord with Swift's intention to deepen the character of his principal figure as an integral part of his main design.

What, then, is the main design of *Gulliver's Travels*? It is customary to call the book a satire: it would be more accurate and more illuminating to call it a politico-sociological treatise much of which is couched in the medium of satire. Only secondarily and accidentally is it a book of travels.

Arthur E. Case
*Four Essays on Gulliver's Travels* (Princeton, N. J.:
Princeton Univ. Pr., 1945), p. 105

The heroism of moderation is a way of dignifying the man who retains his rationality and resists the temptation to compete with animals in the desire for power. The animal myth is Swift's persistent device for portraying human irrationality in its horror: the young lady is warned against doing what monkeys can do better, Gulliver is made to see that much of human glory is a more complex version of Yahoo brutality. The animal myth brings disgust to our recognition of the failure of humanity; the passions which cloud reason are uncomfortably parodied in the appetites of animals. A stage behind the beast lies simple mechanism, the reduction of man to matter in motion which Hobbes needed for a kind of political Newtonianism and which the moralist could turn into a satiric reduction. The compulsive acts of passion become the mechanical force of gravity, without the intrinsic horror of beasts' antics but even more devoid of human qualities and all the more startling as a contrast to man's claim to rationality. The satiric use of mechanism can combine with the theodicy, as in Pope's *Essay on Man*, to show God's harmonious disposing in contrast to man's selfish proposing. The more man is led to greatness by irrational impulse the more readily he may fit into a cosmic order of which he is unaware. All this points to the constant emphasis, in Swift as well as Pope, on the need to remain human, to realize one's proper nature; in trying to become more than man, man inevitably becomes less. Extremes meet; high becomes low. The moment an impulse act escapes rational control it is on the way to becoming matter in motion, just as in the absence of taste a poet may turn either to automatic writing or to the mechanical use of rules.

Martin Price
*Swift's Rhetorical Art: A Study in Structure and Meaning*
(New Haven: Yale Univ. Pr., 1953), pp. 104-5

[There] is a rather blunt parallel to the irony that appears with such magnificent adroitness when Gulliver, as Swift's most life-like *persona*, reassures the reader of his honesty. When all four voyages are over, Gulliver complains that travel books disgust him and abuse the credulity of mankind. For this reason he will adhere strictly to the truth, inspired by the teachings of his noble Houyhnhnm master. Gulliver reinforces his statement with a quotation from the *Aeneid*. . . . As in his other misapplications of learning, Gulliver here believes he has shown that Fortune would not make him false as well as wretched. But his lines come from the speech in which Sinon convinces the Trojan leaders that the wooden horse, harmless, should be taken into the city. As Gulliver, believing he is presenting a convincing case for his honesty, parallels himself with greatest liar of antiquity, Swift subtly comments on the unsubstantiality of Gulliver's claim.

William B. Ewald, Jr.
*The Masks of Jonathan Swift* (Oxford:
Basil Blackwell, 1954), p. 138

When we consider the general drift and pattern of *Gulliver's Travels* as a whole in the light of Book IV, a sort of hierarchy of moral progression finally emerges. At the bottom are the Yahoos; then in ascending order come, first, the Lilliputians, to whom Gulliver (Brobdingnagian among them) is morally as well as physically superior; second, the Brobdingnagians, who are morally as well as physically superior to Gulliver (Lilliputian among them); and third and topmost comes Gulliver himself when he has been reconciled to death by the Struldbrugs, and finally humiliated by the Yahoos and regenerated by the Houyhnhnms. To go beyond that requires passing into another species altogether. Whether the Houyhnhnms are credible or plausible embodiments of the new moral dimension ... is a question of individual taste; but it can hardly be denied that they make a dramatically powerful contrast. For the contrast which Swift desires to drive home is not that between the Houyhnhnms and Gulliver (who is now regenerate), but between them and the Yahoos. The contrast between the Houyhnhnms and Gulliver, if indeed it amounts to one, is of small importance, because they are incommensurable; it is the difference between the goodness of Innocence, and the goodness of Innocence regained after painful experience, which must always carry the stains and scars of battle. But the contrast between the Yahoos and the Houyhnhnms symbolizes the dreadful one between the sophisticated brutishness of man and animal innocence. The Yahoos make visible the judgment of the King of Brobdingnag on the human race; but the judgment is now passed with an added intensity of moral aversion, so that we feel much the same shudder of revulsion which overcame the Houyhnhnm when Gulliver described to him a war among mankind.

John Middleton Murry
*Jonathan Swift* (London: Jonathan Cape, 1954), pp. 342-43

I am far from supposing that persons in *Gulliver's Travels* are portraits of men whom Swift knew. The King of Brobdingnag is not Sir William Temple; nor is Thomas Sheridan the King of Laputa. In all the characters there are elements inconsistent with the originals. . . . I suggest merely that the framework of the Houyhnhnms' character, for instance, goes back to Bolingbroke; that the giant king is derived from Swift's recollections of Temple, though with many additions and alterations; and so forth.

The most important question is how these observations alter one's reading of *Gulliver's Travels*. But to this the answers are so ramified that I shall no more than list a few implications. My analysis of the second voyage may go far to account for its *relative* placidity and its success, in comparison with the contemptuous tone of the first, the disjointedness of the third, and the harshness of the fourth; Swift had returned to the mood of his satisfying and fruitful years with Temple at Moor Park. The third voyage is one which has often been related to Scriblerian sketches; and an explanation for its inadequacy has been that here Swift was stitching up ill-connected fragments. My association of the Laputan king with Thomas Sheridan weakens that theory. Other scholars have shown that the political references and much of the satire on experimental science belong to the latter part of the reign of George I; so does the connection with Sheridan. My commentary on the fourth voyage helps to destroy the misconceptions of innumerable scholars and critics who identify the author, through Gulliver, with the values of the Houyhnhnms. Swift was himself saying, in the fourth voyage, that anyone who believes in the adequacy of reason without Christianity must see himself as a Houyhnhnm and the rest of mankind as Yahoos. By innuendo, he argues that the deists cannot, with any consistency, believe their own doctrines.

Irvin Ehrenpreis
*PMLA* (December, 1957), p. 898

In view of the evidence presented, the Houyhnhnms cannot be regarded as objects of satire. In view of phrases that Ehrenpreis wrongly interprets, they might be so regarded. Like others before him, Ehrenpreis mistakenly thinks Swift gives the Houyhnhnms only one quality of consciousness: reason. He speaks . . . of their "rule of nothing-but-reason" and of their "devotion to reason (i.e., to reason alone).". . . But this is neither Swift nor Gulliver. More than once Gulliver remarks, and Ehrenpreis quotes (and misinterprets) him as saying, "Reason alone is sufficient to govern a *rational* creature.". . . The proper word to emphasize here is *govern,* and, thus clarified (with reason the governor and the other aspects of consciousness subject to it), the idea is a commonplace accepted by Anglicans and deists and even by atheists from ancient times on down. Ehrenpreis errs grossly in saying that this maxim "runs contrary to the spirit of Christianity" and to that of sincere Anglicans. It simply places reason in a hierachy above the emotions or "inferior mind" and gives, by implication, reason something other than itself to govern. It is not "alone" in the mind. In *Gulliver* this governing function of reason is repeatedly emphasized. . . . The opposite principle, as Gulliver continues to say in Chapter viii, is to be governed ("discoloured") by passion and interest. At stake here are moral and psychological concepts; there is no hint of an interest in the Christian revelation, as Ehrenpreis seems to assume. . . .

The Houyhnhnms represent Swift's clearly imperfect concept of "perfection of nature." He did perhaps as well as could be expected. The Yahoos represent an opposite, and in between is poor fallible Gulliver, who at times speaks for Swift and at times only for himself. It is not strange that the portrayal of the Yahoos is far more powerful than is that of the "perfect" Houyhnhnms. Depictions of hell have been in all ages more vivid and more numerous than pictures of heaven. It is logically impossible, of course, to depict perfection.

George Sherburn
*MP* (January, 1958), pp. 94, 96

A close reading of Voyage Four makes clear that Gulliver is basically not Swift (although he may occasionally merge with Swift here and in the preceding voyages) but rather a dramatic foil deliberately created for ironic effect. He is the gull by means of whom Swift produces the very desirable esthetic effect of reader participation and indirectly communicates his message. If Gulliver is not Swift in the last part of the travels, then it follows that everything admired by Gulliver need not be also admired by Swift. As a matter of fact, Swift shows Gulliver as one who has been truly deceived by appearances, and at the end of the voyage Gulliver becomes the object of his satire. By ridiculing Gulliver, Swift indicates the inadequacy or the absurdity of a life of pure uncompromising reason like that of the Houyhnhnms. If Gulliver under the influence of a misapplied horse sense is shown to be a misanthropic fool rendered unfit for normal human society, it is only right to infer that because he doesn't adopt Gulliver's worshipful attitude Swift intimates at the close of Voyage Four that common-sense is not enough to live by and that the horses are not utopian models of virtue and piety. The horses, Swift thus concludes, are not only symbolic characters but also objects of a dramatic satire like the simple-minded Gulliver and the obviously nasty Yahoos. . . .

When placed in their proper historical and ideological context, then, the horses are in every important respect like the deists. Their ethical rationalism and naturalism approximate the deistic attitude. Their belief in the sufficiency of reason and common sense to solve all the problems of life and their distrust of the supernatural; their reliance on nature exclusive of doctrinal faith; their failure to organize their religious experiences within the ideological framework of a sacred book like the Bible; their failure to evolve a theology or ritual; their neglect of a religious establishment—all suggest an unorthodox way of life that Swift, a highly sensitive and aggressive clergyman of the established Anglican church, could scarcely extol, could scarcely recognize as religion in the first place. That Swift fought deism as a subversive force is well known. What is not so well known, however, is that he carried on the struggle against such religious heresy through the symbolic Houyhnhnms in his most famous work, *Gulliver's Travels,* and so again "reconciled divinity and wit.". . .

Martin Kallich<br>
Criticism (Spring, 1960), pp. 111-12, 122-23

Two main points have been suggested thus far in the analysis of the fourth book: (1) that the Houyhnhnm society does not represent Swift's idea of an utopian civilization, but is to be interpreted as ironical satire, and (2) that the satire is particularly, although probably not exclusively, directed against the extension of the political and social philosophy of John Locke, as implemented by the Whigs. These suggestions may be reinforced by a

consideration of Swift's attitude toward political change, and by an evaluation of the effect which the social life of reason has had on Gulliver by the
time his travels are concluded. . . .

The obvious comedy of Gulliver's return is mitigated by an overtone of
tragic misanthropy, as the reader witnesses the destruction of a mind striving beyond its depth for a rational formula in life. Herbert Davis has given
a penetrating analysis of Gulliver's position: . . . Gulliver has his last illusion taken from him, and the result is the misanthropic insanity of the
traveler. But it should be remembered that this is not Swift's misanthropy.
If it were, he could not have described it so acutely. Quite the contrary is
true. The satirist sees clearly the condition of his hero, and the source of
his troubles.

Richard J. Dircks
*Criticism* (Spring, 1960), pp. 145, 148-49

## A Tale of a Tub

For the real object of Swift's satire in the *Tale* is the corruption he saw in
English letters during the latter half of the seventeenth century, destroying
what he felt had been its finest achievements. This belief is repeatedly
stated, and never modified. He first stated it in the *Tatler,* dated September
28, 1710, satirizing current affectations of language, and clearly setting
forth what he regarded as the standards of good taste in English, namely
that simplicity which is unaffected by modish fashions. . . .

Herbert Davis
*The Satire of Jonathan Swift* (New York: Macmillan, 1947), p. 17

The apparent disorder of *A Tale of a Tub* is actually the most carefully
articulated order, disguised as disorder, for a purpose. The form of *A Tale
of a Tub* is a sweeping parody which determines the limits and sequence
of the individual sections of *A Tale of a Tub*, and which is itself determined
by the Grub Street formlessness that Swift intended to satirize through his
structure. *A Tale of a Tub* is neither erratic nor fortuitous in structure; its
carefully integrated pattern is arranged for the most thoroughgoing condemnation of the formlessness of Modern writing. Swift's structure, therefore, provides a natural setting for the development of his satirical themes,
the benighted state of Modern philosophy, science, and criticism, and, as
parody, is in itself a tacit satire on the forms in which the Modern writers
couched their Modern philosophy, science, and criticism. Together, matter
and method, they constituted the *status quo* in learning. Swift's virtuosity
in this two-fold attack on Modern learning is extraordinary. He becomes a
Modern, he writes like any Grub Street brother, he pleads the Moderns'
cause, he extols the Modern learning, all in the "Modern Kind" of writing.
. . . The pervasive symmetry and balance is handled with the greatest vir-

tuosity in the body of *A Tale of a Tub*, in the five units each consisting of a section of the allegory and a digression. To see only the unity of all the digressions, and the unity of all the allegory, to find only a vertical order in *A Tale of a Tub* is to break it in half, to miss the essential symmetry; for a vertical order explains only the sequence of the sections of allegory and offers no explanation for the sequence of the digressions except that they are fortuitous.

Miriam Kosh Starkman
*Swift's Satire on Learning in A Tale of a Tub* (Princeton, N. J.:
Princeton Univ. Pr., 1950), pp. 106-7, 144

Like [other] seventeenth-century works . . . , the *Tale* expresses a personal view of the universe; but it only *pretends* to be personal. It pretends to have "included and exhausted all that Human Imagination can *Rise* or *Fall* to." It pretends to demonstrate exhaustive learning. It pretends to be eccentric. It satirizes works like those we have noticed, and so itself offers an implicit analysis of eccentricity. In short, the *Tale* is *about* eccentricity rather than an example itself.

Swift's parody is built around the vehicle of his theme, his speaker. The queerness that is apparent in Swift's speaker has the same explanation as the other peculiarities we have noticed in the *Tale*: his mode of thought represents one aspect of the seventeenth-century sensibility. Having grasped the fact that the digressions and other eccentricities are manifestations of this sensibility, it is easier to see that one of the comic elements in the portrayal of the Grub Street Hack is his unabashed sacrifice of everything else for the effect of the moment—his willingness to collapse an argument for the sake of delicious details; or, in short, his casuistry. This aspect of the speaker is perhaps the key to the *Tale's* structure and to Swift's relationship to his material. . . .

Swift is saying in the *Tale of a Tub* that people like the Hack *are* dropped into this world, that this *is* the way things are—life *is* unstable, writings vanish, and we *are* in need of diversion—but that with the church and tradition we can make the best of them; by oneself, or with the pseudo-churches and diversions to which the moderns are addicted, reality is frustration and produces only frenzied activity like that of the Hack. . . . What Swift is presenting in the *Tale* (the "author's" *Tale*) is the general outline of an ideal—the concept of the rounded citizen, the versatile and encyclopedic individual, as well as the traditional compendium of knowledge, grammatical exegesis, saints, heresies, fools, of the Church Fathers. Thus the real form of the *Tale* is an encyclopedia of errors or fools; and its parody form is the encyclopedia of useless speculation, the modern's *summa*.

Ronald Paulson
*Theme and Structure in Swift's Tale of a Tub* (New Haven:
Yale Univ. Pr., 1960), pp. 28, 231-32, 234

## A Modest Proposal

But when in reading the *Modest Proposal* we are most engaged it is an effect directly upon ourselves that we are most disturbingly aware of. The dispassionate, matter-of-fact tone induces a feeling and a motion of assent, while the burden, at the same time, compels the feelings appropriate to rejection, and in the contrast—the tension—a remarkably disturbing energy is generated. A sense of an extraordinary energy is the general effect of Swift's irony. The intensive means just indicated are reinforced extensively in the continuous and unpredictable movement of the attack, which turns this way and that, comes now from one quarter and now from another, inexhaustibly surprising—making again an odd contrast with the sustained and level gravity of the tone. If Swift does for a moment appear to settle down to a formula it is only in order to betray; to induce a trust in the solid ground before opening the pitfall.

F. R. Leavis
*Scrutiny* (March, 1933), pp. 368-69

The *Modest Proposal* is a parody of countless pamphlets dealing with population and poverty. It burlesques the political arithmeticians. Its purpose, however, is not to cast ridicule upon these pamphlets and these writers as such, nor is the satiric energy generated by this kind of parody and burlesque being turned against mercantilism as such. The doctrines of mercantilism and the specific principle thereof which held that people are the riches of a nation were all accepted by Swift. What the *Modest Proposal* does is to drive home the thing he had elsewhere insisted upon in vigorous but perfectly straightforward terms: in Ireland, conditions being what they are, human beings—the riches of a nation—are an insupportable burden, with at least five children in six lying "a dead weight upon us, for want of employment." It is, of course, in the nature of comedy like this that far more should be involved than just the central themes and principles. Swift's humanity, his moral realism, and the intensity of his perceptions have all found expression in this short work which is so fully representative of his satiric genius.

Ricardo Quintana
*Swift: An Introduction* (London: Oxford Univ. Pr., 1955), p. 177

Thus, in his consideration of man in society Swift holds firmly to his conviction of the importance of the particular man, and is ready to abandon theoretical consistency if by so doing he can present a truer picture of the needs and duties of men. If the state can never function morally, at least it should not become so immersed in schemes of wealth and power as to forget those individual members who compose it. This is what Swift is saying, in a very different tone and with the indirection habitual to him as a satirist, in *A Modest Proposal for Preventing the Children of Ireland from Being a Burden to Their Parents or Country*, where private vices become public benefits in so singular a manner. Swift appears to have accepted the assumption of the mercantilist theory of the day that the natural strength of a nation consists in the number and increase of the inhabitants, and the *Modest Proposal* turns upon this conception. . . . But in his hands the idea that each person is "an economic unit whose annual value to the nation could be exactly computed" is changed indeed. To him the "people" are not only the riches of a country; they are moral entities towards whom their rulers have the responsibility of ensuring that they can live decently. In *A Modest Proposal* it is the purely economic attitude of their superiors towards the "labour and people" that is attacked. The English government and the Irish landlords regard the people merely as cattle to be exploited, and indeed one of the reasons for the misery of the people of Ireland, and for their wholesome emigration, is the rapacity of the landlords in turning over so much arable land to pasture. . . .

Kathleen Williams
*Jonathan Swift and the Age of Compromise* (Lawrence, Kans.:
Univ. Kansas Pr., 1958), pp. 111-12

GENERAL

. . . I doubt . . . whether we can find any particular mannerisms or tricks of phrase in his work so individual that they would give him away. His style is never mannered, and it is well to remember that even Stella and his friends in Dublin were never quite sure about his contributions to the *Tatler* and the *Examiner*, or even his separate political tracts written in London during the Queen's reign. Swift delighted to mislead them; but then, and much more emphatically later on, he seemed to expect that his friends ought to be able to recognize clearly that there were certain things which he could not have written, certain limits which they should know he could never be guilty of crossing. And likewise he would expect his editors and critics to-day to be sure that even in his most careless moments or in his lightest and most trivial mood he could never have written such sloppy, slovenly stuff as some of the papers still included among his works, or those paragraphs in *Gulliver's Travels* which were inserted in the earliest editions "contrary to the Author's manner and style and intention."

. . . [Rather] Swift is a master of conciseness, unequalled and unmistakable by reason of that quality alone, which gives a flavour as of salt to all his work, and preserves it from certain levels of dullness, banality, or mere impoverishment of style liable to appear in the writings of all his contemporaries.

Herbert Davis
*Essays on the Eighteenth Century*
(Oxford Univ. Pr., 1945), pp. 16-17

The poetry of Swift is not so irreconcilably different from the poetry of Donne and the sons of Ben as many literary historians have believed: both are poetry of wit. But wit for Swift was less a matter of style than a point of view. Donne's elegy called "Going to Bed" and Swift's "A Beautiful Young Nymph Going to Bed" are both poems that have been called indelicate and disgusting; they both describe the disrobing of a woman; and both are successful poems of wit. There could hardly be, however, two poems more patently unlike in their intention and effect. The audaciously physical metaphors, similes, and puns in the love-poem "Going to Bed" are centered in Donne's exultant cry of "Full nakedness!" Nakedness in "A Young Nymph Going to Bed" is made intentionally unattractive by enumeration of "artificial hair," "flabby dugs," and "running sores.". . . But even when they are most alike, the two poets do not share quite the same kind of wit. In many of Swift's poems wit is more than a matter of style. Its purpose is often one of scorn; and Swift's scorn, in his poetry and prose as well, can be magnificent. For Donne wit was generally an artistic tool. For Swift it was more often employed as a weapon.

Maurice Johnson
*The Sin of Wit* (Syracuse, N. Y.:
Syracuse Univ. Pr., 1950), pp. 72-73

As a satirist, then, Swift's work ranges from the most delightful comedy to a profoundly moving and even tragic despair. His techniques of writing, developed with remarkable virtuosity and effectiveness, cannot properly be separated from the ideas which defined his basic perception of life as both ridiculous and tragic. And if Swift's technical skill appears most brilliantly and abundantly on those occasions when his sense of the ridiculous overrides his sense of the tragic, still we are always conscious that our laughter may at any moment be converted into a deeper response. What, finally, gives Swift a just claim to high eminence as a literary artist, is that the disparity between the ideal and the actual has been a pressing and persistent problem to many men, and yet very few have equaled either the sustained intensity of Swift's purpose or the masterful artistic control with which he expressed this impassioned concern.

John M. Bullitt
*Jonathan Swift and the Anatomy of Satire* (Cambridge, Mass.:
Harvard Univ. Pr., 1953), pp. 15-16

# JAMES THOMSON

1700-1748

Born in Scotland, Thomson was educated at Edinburgh University, coming to London in 1725. His most influential poem, *The Seasons*, appeared in four parts during 1726-1730, and his plays followed, including *Sophonisba* in 1730 and *Tancred and Sigismunda* in 1745. *The Castle of Indolence*, in Spenserian stanzas, begun in 1733, was published the year of his death.

J. Logie Robertson, ed., *The Complete Poetical Works of James Thomson* (1908)

George C. Macauley, *James Thomson* (1908)

## The Seasons

The most interesting of all Thomson's philosophical speculations is a curious and, so far as I can discover, original theory of spirit-evolution, which is the combination of two familiar philosophic doctrines. Thomson almost certainly did not clearly conceive this theory until 1735 or thereabouts. Though it appears in both *Spring* and *Summer* in the final versions, the lines definitely expressing the idea were not added until 1744, in the case of *Summer* and 1746 in the case of *Spring*. The earliest appearances of the idea are in the third part of *Liberty,* published in 1735, and in a letter dated October 20, 1735. . . .

In spite of the fact that Thomson's theory is given only in . . . fragmentary allusions . . . , the essential point in it is plain enough. Thomson was simply applying the Pythagorean doctrine of the transmigration of souls to the idea of the vital scale; a spirit, instead of transmigrating from man to animals and back again, transmigrates, by Thomson's theory, to successively higher forms in the scale of being, rising toward infinite perfection.

The force which causes spirits thus to rise in the scale of being he identifies with love.

George R. Potter<br>
Englische Studien (1926), pp. 58, 62

The loose plan on which Thomson laid out *The Seasons* makes possible the coexistence of a number of patterns. There is the long ascent up the philosophic ladder that admits of an account of various levels of being. There is also the drama of the forces of nature within the extensive prospect: obscure impulses and instincts, vibrations and echoes in earth and air, the ceaseless, shifting play of light and color. All this has philosophical and religious implications, but it may at times be accepted without analysis. Sometimes it is not seen vividly and breaks down into lists and catalogues. Sometimes there is delicate notation of detail that is all the more striking because of its position in a larger scheme. Throughout there is likely to be a loose employment of the principle of contrast—the beautiful over against the ugly, the delightful against the terrible, the generative forces of nature over against violence and destruction.

The later additions do not restate at any great length the familiar doctrine of the rising scale of being. By the time Thomson had written the *Hymn* of 1730 he had said pretty much what he had to say on that subject.

Moreover, the later additions do not as a rule draw heavily on technical science; it was between 1727 and 1730 that Thomson was most ready to make use of new scientific ideas. The most important exception is the long description of the origin of springs in *Autumn,* and this passage is combined with descriptive geography. The theoretical basis of Thomson's geography . . . is the notion of a correlation between environment and human character and society that runs through much of his work. . . . The usual objection . . . is that the later geographical additions are of inferior value because they are not based on direct observation. At any rate they represent an attempt to extend the dramatic, picturesque, or sensational aspects of nature without primary regard to Thomson's own experiences or even to his favorite theories.

*Winter* and *Summer* were greatly expanded in this way because from the first they offered geographical leads that could easily be followed further. Here was an opportunity for a melodramatic treatment of nature and a presentation of extremes, the superlatives of the tropics and the polar regions. *Spring* and *Autumn* were primarily of the temperate zone and dealt mostly with English scenes; the characteristic topographical additions here are descriptions of famous English estates and views.

Alan D. McKillop
*The Background of Thomson's Seasons* (Minneapolis, Minn.:
Univ. Minnesota Pr., 1942), pp. 129-31

Evidently it is by that widely influential and for long immensely popular but chaotic poem *The Seasons* that Thomson must be judged. It is extremely uneven in performance because the impulse formative of the various parts springs from such different levels of awareness and response; and since it was so much a matter of patchwork and insertions no one can guess what incongruity is coming next. The purpose as it seems to have formulated itself gradually in Thomson's mind was to show the workings of Creative Nature: that, together with the framework of the progression of the year, is what holds the poem together at all, coherence being given by a certain inner rhythm of movement from, in each morsel, the material to the spiritual. To judge from the first 1726 version of *Winter,* Thomson seems to have begun as a landscape painter sensitive to light and "feel," by the very act of creating the harmony necessary for a picture led into a sense of the Deity, a sense that all was well, which in turn drew him on to the somewhat oddly emergent and totally unconvincing solution of the problem of evil which concludes the poem. The earliest version is a charming spontaneous thing, not too long, and there is just the right modicum of "philosophy" to give it substance. Then something disastrous happened, and the Scottish border poem became a didactic work, a kind of *Essay on Man.*

Bonamy Dobrée
*English Literature in the Early Eighteenth Century*
(Oxford Univ. Pr., 1959), p. 484

The moral and theological motivation of *The Seasons* obviously is of significance also in determining the quality of the poem's unity. In the final hymn,
Thomson emphasizes his purpose of communicating a vision of nature as
revelatory of God. To the extent that the concept of nature as a manifestation of the glories of God is dominant throughout the work as a whole, it
offers a powerful unifying force. . . . Implicit in such an outlook is a sublime
theme for poetry. . . . It is substantial basis and justification for such a
poem. All nature is a demonstration of God's power; here is sufficient
reason for writing about it, and here is the chief unifying element for whatever assortment of descriptions and episodes about nature the poet may
choose to assemble. The seasons represent a form of divine order; they are
thoroughly appropriate as a structure for glorifying God through His works
—and the glorification of God is perhaps the primary motive for *The
Seasons*.

Patricia M. Spacks
*The Varied God* (Berkeley, Calif.:
Univ. California Pr., 1959), p. 22

## GENERAL

It is easy to find fault with Thomson's work. His painting of nature is never
ennobled by intensity of spiritual feeling; he has many tedious passages and
more errors of taste both in subject-matter and in expression, and a hasty
reading brings these defects into prominence. The poem (or extracts from
it) is frequently studied for one purpose or another; but since large portions are seldom read for their own sake, and since those who judge it are
often more fastidious than robust in their taste and rarely are so familiar
with it that the faults no longer obscure the virtues, Thomson suffers much
from being damned with faint, patronizing praise. One may even be tolerably well acquainted with his work and yet remember little save its obvious
merits and defects, and consequently may think that the author always
paints with a broad brush and only the beauties which every one sees. But
let such a reader return to *The Seasons* with a fresh and open mind and he
will be struck with the closeness of observation it frequently exhibits, its
fine feeling for shy loveliness in nature and for the "beauty, which as
Milton sings, hath terror in it." He can hardly fail to admire the poet's
healthy manliness and human sympathy, the excellence of many of his
single lines, and the sonorous pomp, breadth, and Byronic power of his
larger pictures. He will have a far better understanding of the eighteenth
century after he has come to see these qualities in Thomson and to realize
that they are features of a piece which, from the days of Pope and Young,
through the dictatorship of Johnson and the increasingly romantic times
of Gray, Cowper, and Burns, and even to the stirring years of Wordsworth,

Shelley, Lamb, and Hazlitt, was the most popular and perhaps the most influential poem in English.

Raymond Dexter Havens
*The Influence of Milton on English Poetry* (Cambridge, Mass.: Harvard Univ. Pr., 1922), pp. 147-48

Thomson was the first modern poet to make Nature his theme. Earlier poets of course had not disregarded Nature; they had all delighted in its beauty; and the pastoral tradition can be exactly traced from Theocritus and Virgil down to Thomson. Chaucer, Spenser, Shakespeare, and Milton had observed and described its variety . . . and Thomson's contemporaries, Alexander Pope, Ambrose Philips, and John Gay, had happily used the countryside as a background for their pastorals. But earlier poets had made Nature subsidiary to humanity; it was the inferior support upon which the moral dramas with which they were concerned were played; and they only introduced it to give point and substance to imagery whose purpose it was to disclose human nature. . . . Thomson, however, described Nature for its own sake. He shifted the interest of poetry from mankind to it, and lightened his descriptions of any artificiality.

Douglas Grant
*James Thomson* (London: Cresset Pr., 1951), pp. 100-1

# JOHN VANBRUGH

1664-1726

> A well-known architect, who designed the old Haymarket Theatre and Blenheim Palace, Vanbrugh produced four important plays (one left unfinished): *The Relapse, or Virtue in Danger* (1696), *The Provok'd Wife* (1697), *The Confederacy* (1705), and *The Provok'd Husband*, completed by Colley Cibber and produced in 1728. He was a special target of Jeremy Collier in *Short View of the Immorality and Profaneness of the English Stage* (1698), which he answered in the same year with *A Short Vindication of the Relapse and the Provok'd Wife, from Immorality and Prophaneness*. Knighted, he was Clarenceux king-of-arms from 1704 until his death.
>
> Bonamy Dobrée and George Webb, eds., *The Complete Works* (1927), 4 vols.
>
> Laurence Whistler, *Sir John Vanbrugh* (1938)

The plays of Vanbrugh are a natural fruit of the temperament illustrated for us in these letters and episodes of his life. They are precisely the plays we should expect from a mischievous, tolerant and kind man of humour.

Vanbrugh accepted the convention of Restoration comedy, but leavened it with an element of feeling and the harmless pleasure of an old dog playing with hell-fire. His gallants are no longer of a world whose moral values are consistently those of Congreve or Wycherley. Promiscuous gallantry is no longer a matter of course—the proviso of a well-regulated career. In the plays of Vanbrugh it is a yielding to temptation. Adultery is no longer treated in the dry light of comedy. It is passionate; it takes to itself fine names. It is a comedy of heaving bosoms, and seductive phrase. Vanbrugh, in fact, killed the comedy of sex for the English theatre. In his own plays the disaster that arises so soon as art is divorced from life is not yet obtrusively palpable; but the comic treatment of adultery was doomed from the moment when in *The Relapse,* Berinthia was borne off by Loveless, faintly protesting, in a bed-chamber scene which persists to this day as the *scène-à-faire* of English comedy.

. . . Vanbrugh wrote but two complete original plays, and part of a third. The rest were closely adapted or translated from the French. Vanbrugh was the perfect translator. He was easily fired with the dramatic possibilities of a situation. In every case his adaptations from Dancourt, Boursault, even Molière, are better than their originals. Moreover, one of his two original and complete comedies was suggested by the conclusion of another play. These facts are a key to the quality of Vanbrugh's work. Vanbrugh drew his inspiration more from the theatre than from life. His best original creations . . . are cleverly sketched, effective stage figures; and one of his best-known characters, Lord Foppington of *The Relapse,* is Cibber's Sir Novelty Fashion theatrically improved precisely in the same way in which *The Confederacy* is improved from *Les Bourgeoises à la Mode.* Vanbrugh's spirit of authorship is hereby admirably illustrated. He accepted the material of his comedy with little care for its moral or social significance; his one aim was to amuse honest gentlemen of the town . . . a task for which his agreeable style, his gift of wise humour, his instinct for the theatre excellently qualified him.

John Palmer
*The Comedy of Manners* (London: G. Bell and Sons,
1913), pp. 224-26

Captain, afterwards Sir John Vanbrugh . . . was, as can be guessed from his multifarious life, above all things a man of the world, but a very simple and honest man of the world who did things as they came to his hand to do. As one might expect from his versatility, what he chiefly had to bring to the writing of plays was an abundant vigour, to which he added the common sense which earned him a nickname. As literary artist he is as unlike Congreve as can be imagined, but like him he was one of the three "most honest-hearted real good men, of the poetical members of the Kit-Cat Club.". . .

Vanbrugh had one valuable requisite of the writer of critical comedy, a contempt for all cant and humbug; but he failed to be anything of a poet because he had no peculiar vision, and thus his plays can add nothing either to our knowledge of life, or to our aesthetic experience. He presented life as he saw it, but he saw it no differently from the hundred and one other people with whom he daily mingled.

Bonamy Dobrée
*Restoration Comedy, 1660-1720* (Oxford Univ. Pr., 1924), pp. 151-52

The dramatic work of Sir John Vanbrugh is by no means so easy to treat *en masse* as is that of Etherege, Wycherley, or Congreve. Each of these earlier authors wrote three or four comedies definitely his own in conception and execution, relying little upon outside aid or inspiration; an analysis of their acknowledged plays furnishes a definite gauge by which to judge their aims and their accomplishment. It is otherwise with Vanbrugh. In exactly how many plays he had a hand is still a matter of dispute, but we are practically certain that we do not today possess all of his writing for the stage. Even some of the work which is admittedly his has strong affiliations with that of other men; several of his plays are no more than translations, and the most famous of them all [*The Relapse*] owes its genesis to another comedy of the day [Cibber's *Love's Last Shift*]. . . . It was . . . followed in the spring of 1697 by Vanbrugh's only other complete and original play, *The Provok'd Wife*. These two comedies, together with the fragmentary *A Journey to London*, left unfinished at his death, are the most important literary productions of their author.

Henry T. E. Perry
*The Comic Spirit in Restoration Drama* (New Haven: Yale Univ. Pr., 1925), p. 83

The completely impersonal aloofness of the typical Comedy of Manners school, which exploits every situation to the utmost solely for its comic possibilities, has been transmuted by a generous-hearted personality into a more rational and sympathetic treatment of certain aspects of the life which Vanbrugh knew. In particular, Vanbrugh's plays reveal a persistent interest in two social problems with which his intimate knowledge of upper-class society must have rendered him thoroughly familiar: the predicament of the younger brother, due to the operation of the law of primogeniture, and the problem of marital incompatibility, which seems to have had especial fascination for him. Vanbrugh's presentation is sympathetic, rational, and sustained, rather than indifferent, impersonal, and incidental, as is the case with the typical dramatists of the Comedy of Manners.

. . . His divergences from Restoration comedy embrace the spirit of his treatment, the substance of his material, and the nature of his dramatic devices. . . . First, returning to the method of Etherege, he tends to minimize the element of sheer plot intrigue. . . . He is content with simple situations, humanized by his interest in a new code of social values. Second, he discards the habitual contrast of true and false wits, and with it disappears also, unfortunately, much of the epigrammatic brilliance of Congreve and Etherege. . . . Third, his emphasis no longer falls on sex-antagonism between a rake and a witty woman of equal intelligence, indulging in sharp repartee for its own sake. . . .

Paul Mueschke and Jeannette Fleisher
*PMLA* (September, 1934), pp. 855, 886-87

The appearance of *The Provok'd Wife* at the new theatre in May, 1697, was in two ways more important than that of *The Relapse* at the old: it was a better play, performed by better players. The incentive to offer it to a company which included Betterton must anyway have been great. . . . As Sir John Brute, a part that was afterwards a favourite of Garrick's too, Betterton was superb. He was a small, stocky man, not good-looking nor elegant, but a very great artist. He seldom made any violent gesture, and preferred a rapt and silent audience to a vociferous one. . . . Opposite him, in the part of the provoked wife, was Mrs. Barry, who in the far-off days of the Restoration had borne Rochester one daughter, and Etherege another, and broken poor Otway's heart. Something of the fire had passed from her, but not the presence, the wonderful dignity in movement and repose. Lady Brute was probably her greatest part, and she set with Sir John an example of conjugal misery which the theatre strove to live up to for a hundred years; for they presented a picture very dear to the ribald heart of their creator: a gross and repellent husband bored with his wife— a wife debating with her niece whether or not to cuckold him. And the niece, Belinda, was of course Anne Bracegirdle. . . .

Among his papers, one MS was found of extraordinary interest: the fragment of an original comedy, so good, that had it been completed by him, *A Journey to London* might have stood beside his finest work. . . . Cibber had finished it, and so creditably, that *The Provok'd Husband*, as he called it, became the success of 1728, and ran for twenty-eight consecutive nights, thanks partly to a brilliant performance by Anne Oldfield. . . . Vanbrugh's plays continued to be universally popular for the next fifty years, but not so his houses. . . . In fact there is not one of his great works, not even Blenheim, that was made, or now remains, exactly as he intended it. Another ten years of life no doubt would have given the world more proof of his genius. . . .

Laurence Whistler
*Sir John Vanbrugh* (New York: Macmillan, 1939), pp. 37-38, 290-93

# HORACE WALPOLE

1717-1797

> Fourth Earl of Oxford, Walpole was a member of parliament from 1741 to 1767. He settled at Strawberry Hill, Twickenham, in 1747, where he wrote *The Castle of Otranto* (1764). He aided publication of various authors (including Gray), but Chatterton's appeal for help proved unhappy. He owes much of his literary fame to his letters written between 1732 and 1797.
>
> W. S. Lewis, gen. ed., *The Yale Edition of Walpole's Correspondence* (1937-    ); edition in progress, to total about 50 vols.
>
> R. W. Ketton-Cremer, *Walpole: a Biography* (1946)

It would be easier to underestimate than to exaggerate the importance of this "historical novel with the history left out" [*The Castle of Otranto*]; and to judge it fairly is impossible unless we realise that it was a bold and amazingly successful experiment in an absolutely untried medium. Other and far greater hands than Walpole's sowed the furrows he had driven; yet to his credit be it recorded that it was he who broke the first clod. If his castle, to our eyes, seems as insubstantial as any fastness of painted canvas wavering behind the stage of a village theatre, if his weapons and costumes suggest modern Wardour Street rather than mediæval Calabria, that is trick of perspective. Otranto is dwarfed by Torquilstone and the Château d'If, and by the Notre Dame of Victor Hugo. To the dazzled eyes of Walpole's contemporaries it was an abode of terror, and wonderment, and beauty.

Dorothy M. Stuart
*Horace Walpole* (New York: Macmillan, 1927), p. 163

In March, 1769, Walpole wrote a letter to Mr. Thomas Chatterton at Bristol thanking him for a communication of a copy from specimens of *Rowley's Poems*. It is courteous and even flattering; asks, without the least suggestion of doubt, where Rowley's poems are to be found: "I should not be sorry to print them; or at least a specimen of them if they have never been printed." It inquires after the period of Rowley's life and notes that the manuscript contains a reference to an oil painting. But Walpole's inference is to dispute the tradition that John van Eyck was the inventor of oil painting—not in the least to suggest that allusion to this art raises doubt as to the authenticity of the poems. In short, he was taken in by Chatterton's ingenious forgery.

Another letter from Bristol enclosed more extracts and suggested that Chatterton would like assistance to enter upon a literary career. Walpole wrote back, giving prudent advice against abandoning a definite livelihood.

At the same time, he wrote to Bristol for information about his correspondent; and he communicated the specimens of Rowley to Mason and to Gray. . . . Chatterton was indisputably trying to get help on false pretences; and Walpole now replied to his letters by a demand to see the originals. . . . [Then] he went off to Paris, and on his return found a very angry letter from Chatterton, to which he sat down and wrote a very arrogant reply; but thinking better of it, simply returned the manuscripts without a word. Two years later, he heard, at a literary dinner, from Goldsmith, the tale of Chatterton's suicide, and was naturally moved.

But, as legend grew up about the marvellous boy, Walpole found himself figuring in the mythology as "the fastidious and unfeeling being to whose insensibility we owe the extinction of the greatest poetic luminary, if one may judge by the brightness of its dawn, that ever rose in our or perhaps any other hemisphere."

Stephen Gwynn
*The Life of Horace Walpole* (Boston:
Houghton Mifflin, 1932), pp. 247-48

*The Castle of Otranto* (1764) was, like the mansion in which he wrote it, a dilettante's exploit in Gothicism, a pseudo-antique; in the one and in the other, Walpole let antiquarian taste and fantasy have free play, with less seriousness in the case of the story than he felt for his architectural hobby. Walpole relates that the tale originated in a dream, in which the hall and staircase at Strawberry Hill blended curiously with dim memories of an ancient college at Cambridge. "A gigantic hand in armour" was laid on the banister. The mighty hand suggested the gigantic helmet which crushes the son of the usurping Manfred. Dreaming in his own miniature castle, he conjured up the walls of the great fortress of Otranto, and saw them thrown down by the phantom of Alfanso, "dilated to an immense magnitude," when this monstrous apparition proclaimed the boy Theodore the rightful heir. The dream pictures were the basis; the story was a piece of machinery easily contrived; and Walpole kept true to the common sense of his century in not troubling himself in the least about probability in a story obviously untrue. But the mechanism is so nakedly exposed that he fails to be impressive; our emotions are untouched. And this was the more unfortunate in that Walpole remained a sentimentalist.

Ernest A. Baker
*The History of the English Novel* (London:
H. F. and G. Witherby, 1934), Vol. V, p. 178

It is a romance based on old materials, employing to some extent contemporary methods of characterization; it is constructed on dramatic principles of technique which few had used so far; the architectural and Gothic background gives a new colouring to the whole, providing a machinery, besides the supernatural, for terror and suspense and gloom. The desire to be true to medieval "costume" contributes its own share by giving the novel a more historical and scholarly turn—a factor which has led to *The Castle of Otranto* being called a historical novel without the history. From the above list of characteristics and contributions of the novel one would imagine it to be a triumph of art, a masterpiece of literature. That it most definitely is not. But the crudity of the attempt, the incongruity of its supernatural, the utter lack of suggestiveness do not in any way detract from the value of it in the history of the English novel. The story may lack artistic merit, but it contained in itself, in however unrefined and distorted a form, far-reaching ideas which were recognized as such and consciously developed by people in course of time. Walpole's words in the preface to the second edition were prophetic. The "new route" he struck out did pave "a road for men of brighter talents."

K. K. Mehrotra
*Horace Walpole and the English Novel* (Oxford:
Basil Blackwell, 1934), p. 21

As Walpole, worried and depressed, wandered about the little mock castle which he had constructed in brick and wood and plaster, Otranto began to rise, in all its gloom and horror, upon those slender foundations. The flamboyant gallery of Strawberry became grim and bare and enormous. The cloister echoed cavernously, and secret passages stretched beneath it. Elegant bedrooms turned into the forbidding chambers, hung with tapestry and carpeted with matting or rushes, of more ancient days. The picture of Lord Falkland, all in white, began to exercise its curious spell. Then one night early in June, . . . he "had a dream, of which, all I could recover was that I had thought myself in an ancient castle (a very natural dream for a head filled like mine with Gothic story), and that on the uppermost bannister of a great staircase I saw a gigantic hand in armour. In the evening I sat dawn, and began to write, without knowing in the least what I intended to say or relate." For the next two months he lived entirely in a world of Gothic fantasy. He put politics out of his mind; his correspondence dwindled almost to nothing; except for a very successful party for the French and Spanish ambassadors, entertaining ceased at Strawberry Hill. Night after night he immersed himself in the ambitions of Manfred, the woes of Hippolyta and Matilda. He wrote blindly on, often into the small hours of the morning, sometimes until he was so exhausted that he broke off the narrative in the middle of a sentence. On August 6 *The Castle of Otranto* was completed.

R. W. Ketton-Cremer
*Horace Walpole* (New York: Longmans, Green, 1940), pp. 211-12

# ISAAK   WALTON
1593-1683

> Born in Stafford, the son of an alehouse-keeper, Walton lived an uneventful life and seems to have had no formal education. He became a member of the Ironmongers' Company in 1618, but seems to have earned his living in London as a draper. He was married in 1626 and had seven children, all of whom died in infancy. His first wife dying in 1640, he remarried in 1647, but he was again a widower in 1663. He began writing late in life, publishing *The Complete Angler* in 1653. He wrote lives of Donne, Wotton, Hooker, Herbert, and Sanderson. After the Restoration he retired to his native Staffordshire. He spent his final years living near Winchester.

John Buchan, ed., *The Complete Angler* (1935)
S. B. Carter, ed., *Walton's Lives* (1951)
Geoffrey Keynes, ed., *The Complete Walton* (1929)

## The Complete Angler

. . . The historian falters in trying to say something of a book which has been second only to the Bible in popular fame. Against a rural background and in a partly holiday mood Walton fills in the portrait of the artist which the reader of the *Lives* can draw in outline. A love of angling is an outward and visible sign of an inward and spiritual grace, of a gentle, contemplative benignity of soul which abhors dissension and loves good old ways, whether in the choice of bait or ballads or barley-wine or the worship of the Creator. We may remember that this prose hymn of contentment in simple and external things appeared a few weeks after Cromwell expelled the Long Parliament. Walton's motto is "Study to be quiet," and in his mind the piety of primitive Christians is linked both with angling and with "the happy days of the Nations and the Churches peace." It would hardly have strained seventeenth-century etymology to identify "angler" with "Anglican." If at times the nature of his theme betrays him into unctuousness, we still feel . . . that doubtless God could have made a better man than Walton, but doubtless God never did. Of piscatory lore, practical and theoretical, he was of course a devoted if not always reliable master, and he proves the honourable estate and antiquity of angling with a brave show of frequently Brownesque learning and logic. Was it not the vocation of four of the Apostles and the avocation of Perkins, Whitaker, Nowell, and Wotton? Are not fish-hooks mentioned in Amos and Job? Walton's colloquial and poetic pastoral is the most homespun of idyllic day-dreams, the most substantial of poems of escape. He is as conscious, and as sincere, an artist as Theocritus or Virgil; only such an artist could have given the lyrics of Marlowe and Raleigh their perfect and foreordained setting. There was a mass of country literature before Walton and there has been a great mass since, yet he may be said to have had no predecessors and no successors. His mellow vision of field and stream, of lambs frisking and children gathering lilies and cow-slips, of anglers thanking God for the "Sweet day, so cool, so calm, so bright," or making good cheer in clean inns with lavendered sheets—the vision that is for ever England—is Walton's own creation.

Douglas Bush
*English Literature in the Earlier Seventeenth Century 1600-1660*
(Oxford: Clarendon Pr., 1945), pp. 224-25

## The *Lives*

Despite Walton's insistence on his truthfulness, he was of necessity en-gaged. He was more than engaged; he was wedded to his own time. In the seventeenth century, life-writing, in its diverse manifestations, groped to-ward a genre, but, though the need was felt shortly after the Restoration for the word "biography" and its variations, there was no code and no adherence to a code. Walton, to be sure, was more aware than most of his contemporaries of the differences between a character and a life, a picture and a narrative. But the character, in its own diverse manifestations, exerted a great pull on him. He praised Donne's satires because he thought of them as characters of sins. Among the topics of interest in *Reliquiae Wottonianae* which he specifically pointed out were Wotton's characters. The milkmaid in the *Compleat Angler* is Overburian, and the *Angler* in its entirety is worth consideration as a discursive character of the con-templative man. Walton's fondness for the character and his belief in its usefulness are evident in the *Lives*. He included in the *Life of Donne* what he himself called "a short, but true character" of Dr. Morton, and not only did he close this life in 1640 with a character of Donne, but he added substantially to the character in 1658. In 1670, he quoted part of Donne's "The Autumnall" in the *Life of Herbert*, and he called it "a Character of the Beauties" of Magdalen Herbert's body and mind. He included in the *Life of Sanderson* a long "Character of his person and temper." But the extent to which Walton relied on the character is best illustrated in the *Life of Hooker*. Here, Walton interrupted the narrative of the *Life* to give his reader "a Character of the Times, and Temper of the people of this Nation," and as part of this long account quoted Sir Henry Wotton's "true Character" of Archbishop Whitgift. Again, when he got Hooker to Bishops-borne, he gave a "true Character of his Person" and followed it by char-acterizing Hooker's disposition and behavior. Although Walton used the term "character" only this once in speaking of Hooker, his *Life* contains at least four other characters of the man. The second paragraph of the *Life* is a character of the grave and scholarly child; Hooker at Oxford is made the subject of two characters—one pictures the learning and behavior of the perfect student and the other the complete scholar; and Hooker is charactered, too, as the prototype of the good country priest, "a pattern as may invite posterity to imitate his vertues." When these characters of Hooker are viewed as a whole, Walton's picture "heightned by one shadowing" becomes immediately apparent. How deductive Walton's procedure is, he himself revealed in his character of Hooker as a youth. His picture is reconstructed "so far as Inquiry is able to look back at this distance of Time" and is based largely on an account of Hooker at the age of forty. Walton shaped the child in the image of the man. Complexity and development of personality are possible only when the biographer is aware that man is shaped by his past as well as his future. The deductive approach fostered by the character led to oversimplification and one-sidedness. The diminution of light and shade in favor of a heightening by one shadow tended to produce, in biography, a too even picture because it reduced the element of struggle in a life. It made for the emphasis of a dominant trait and the adjustment of details that were consistent at every point with that trait. . . .

Like every painstaking artist, Walton revealed, in the *Lives*, his own assumptions and predilections, his principles and his moral outlook. We have not read the *Lives* rightly because we have let the fanciful image of a naïvely honest and innocent man come between us and the image which the *Lives* themselves reveal. It is this other Walton—strenuously rectitudinous and dogmatically orthodox, at the same time that he was gentle and reserved; increasingly partisan as he became more personally involved in the day's chief issues, at the same time that he pleaded for moderation and objectivity; acutely conscious of tradition and historical parallels, at the same time that he deplored his lack of learning; unflinchingly dedicated to craftsmanship, at the same time that he belittled his artistry—it is this Walton we must picture in our minds to compensate for the angle of his vision.

David Novarr
*The Making of Walton's Lives* (Ithaca, N. Y.:
Cornell Univ. Pr., 1958), pp. 484-85, 496

# WILLIAM   WYCHERLEY

## 1641-1716

Though born near Shrewsbury, Wycherley lived in France for a few years, becoming a Roman Catholic, before briefly entering Oxford in 1660. He probably wrote his plays not long before their first performances, which seem to be as follows: *Love in a Wood*, early 1671; *The Gentleman*

*Dancing-Master,* late 1671 or early 1672; *The Country Wife,* 1672-1675; and *The Plain Dealer,* 1673-1676. The Duchess of Cleveland, Charles II's mistress, became his patroness and secured a commission in a foot regiment (in 1672) for him. He married the influential Countess of Drogheda around 1680; later he was imprisoned in the Fleet for debts, but stage successes altered his estate. He married a second time when close to death to prevent a nephew's inheritance.

Montague Summers, ed., *Complete Works* (1924), 4 vols.

Charles Perromat, *William Wycherley, sa vie—son oeuvre* (1921)

## THE PLAYS

His first three plays, counting *The Plain Dealer* as his third, reveal all his strange revulsions against the society in which he now lived as fully as any. Did he repent having ventured into this lurid light? . . . It is this gnawing doubt which makes it so difficult to see what he meant by his plays, what he was trying to do. A learner in the Spanish school, unrivalled in the management of plot . . . , he was master of the unities of time and place, but in the essential unity, that of atmosphere, he failed. Indeed, his plays, with the exception of *The Country Wife,* are the strangest hotchpotch. At one moment we are interested in the development of the story, then we are treated to an exhibition of virulent satire, now beguiled with the antics of a superbly ludicrous fop, entertained with the fencing of a coquettish tongue, or plunged into a bath of tepid romance.

It is his satire that is most interesting, and in it he differs from others who write in that vein, for his satire is never that of a prig, and it is characteristic of him that he always seems to include himself in his denunciations.

Bonamy Dobrée
*Restoration Comedy, 1660-1720* (Oxford Univ. Pr.,
1924), pp. 80-81

In fact, *The Plain Dealer* may be said to be made up of one diatribe after another upon the conditions under which we live, with special attention to the artificial ones evolved by mankind. A violent attack upon human vices and a searching revelation of human shortcomings, it is a depressing, almost an indecent, play. Yet this is not surprising, for Wycherley's last comedy is avowedly a piece of satire and it is the business of satire to degrade everything that it touches; it must emphasize all that is evil in man's nature and neglect those redeeming qualities which are to be found in even the most depraved of mortals. This pattern Wycherley follows consistently and wholeheartedly throughout all his work. . . . William Wycherley is at his best when he represses his universal bitterness and limits his range as in *The Country Wife*; when he lets himself be swept away to the violent extremes of *The Plain Dealer*, he loses that philosophical detachment so essential to any true expression of the Comic Spirit.

Henry T. E. Perry
*The Comic Spirit in Restoration Drama* (New Haven:
Yale Univ. Pr., 1925), pp. 53-55

*Love in a Wood*, a passable comedy, gives the impression that for years Wycherley had been noting carefully the sure-fire comic devices of the professionals. There are a few minor innovations—for example, the love-and-honor plot is in prose instead of verse—but in the main the play is built according to formula. There is the usual group of poeple at cross-purposes: Lady Flippant, a raffish widow who needs a rich husband; Sir Simon Addleplot, who wants a rich wife . . . ; Dapperwit, a fool who gets a rich wife . . . , and finds her "six months gone with child"; Ranger, a fine gentleman, who goes sniffing after a new love; Lydia, Ranger's betrothed, who pursues him and catches him in the net of matrimony; Christine, who wants . . . and gets the ultra-heroic and over-jealous lover, Valentine; and Alderman Gripe, who pursues, is cheated of, and finally marries a prostitute, thereby frustrating Dapperwit, his new son-in-law. Like all such gulling-intrigue comedies, the play is full of bustle and confusion; characters gallop on and off the stage in full cry; there are grossly vulgar and brightly witty scenes; there is no one dominant theme.

J. Harold Wilson
*The Court Wits of the Restoration* (Princeton, N. J.:
Princeton Univ. Pr., 1948), p. 157

*The Gentleman Dancing-Master* pictures two decent people surrounded by a world of folly. Decency means simply two things: the ability to see through to reality and the ability to make the forms one puts on reflect one's private life or "nature." Folly, on the other hand, means the substitution of appearance for one's nature, Spanish clothes for wisdom, a French accent for good breeding, or the form of marriage for the emotional basis of marriage. This kind of folly blinds its fools so they see into others no better than they see into themselves. To Etherege, folly was the confusion of private life with public front. Wycherley saw that much and more: folly represented a commitment to a life of pretense. The unconscious pretenders, Don Diego, Monsieur, and Mrs. Caution, are foolish, even to some extent evil, but without exception less happy than Hippolita and Gerrard, who pretend for a limited purpose, binding themselves temporarily to pretense to gain a permanent freedom from it. Such a contrast shapes a comic action based almost entirely on intrigue. Comedy becomes a chain

of results set off by an initial discrepancy between appearance and nature
or form and inner reality; for example, the loveless marriage a foolish
parent tries to impose. Wycherley's unique contribution to Restoration
comedy was a sense that folly, evil, and limitations to happiness were all
related, that there is a right way and a wrong way.

. . . [*The Country Wife*] does not deal simply with one right way *versus*
one wrong; it deals complexly with a gradation of "ways." The basic division is between Harcourt and Alithea on the one hand and all the rest of
the characters on the other. Harcourt and Alithea are the most successful
and the most right ethically; they seem foolish but turn out to be wiser
than all the rest. Among the other characters, there is another right way,
Horner's, more limited than Harcourt's and hardly ethical, but successful
in a narrow sense on its own terms. . . . Margery, and perhaps this is why
she is the title character, stands at the center: her country naïveté links
her to the sincerity of Harcourt and Alithea, but she lacks the social
acumen they have to make her sincere aims survive. The action of the play
brings Harcourt and Alithea out of the social whirl into a private world.
The happy ending, as so often in comedy, affirms the idea of poetic justice
. . . ; the good suceed, and the bad fail—unless they are Horner. For it is
he and the complexity associated with him that keep *The Country Wife*
from having simply a "happy ending."

Norman N. Holland
*The First Modern Comedies* (Cambridge, Mass.:
Harvard Univ. Pr., 1959), pp. 69-70, 83-84

## *The Plain-Dealer*

In "The Plain Dealer," a phrase from a popular game of cards called
"Plain Dealing," he decided to project a type he had known for twenty
years, a type he had observed in the circle of his friends both in France
and in England. The character of Manly, a misanthropist, Wycherley had
first noticed in Angoumois as a boy: it was the Marquis de Montausier.
And he had watched the behaviour of that man for nearly five years.
Returning to England, Wycherley had found again misanthropy rather
marked in the Earl of Dorset. . . .

Wycherley of course examined the play of Molière [*The Misanthropist*],
Anglicized some of its lesser characters and followed some of its structure,
but since he knew Montausier personally almost as well as Molière did he
had no need to make Manly a copy of Alceste. Memory came to aid his
imagination, and his own experience with English types supported his
inventive powers.

Willard Connely
*Brawny Wycherley* (New York:
Scribner's, 1930), pp. 114-16

The real character of Manly is, of course, neither serious, philosophic, nor misanthropic: Wycherley's contemporaries would have recognized him as a "humours" character and an object of satire. . . .

"Humours" were, of course, the main concern of the prose character, and the character types which it developed were also the familiar types exploited by the Restoration comedy; the age recognized a close relationship between the two genres. One of the types which emerges in the character of the seventeenth century and continues into the eighteenth is that of the "humourist." Like Manly, the "humourist" is a disgruntled and unsociable fellow, at war with the conventions of his society. He diverges from the norm and is therefore ridiculous. . . .

Far from being an instrument on which Wycherley plays his harsh misanthropic music, Manly is a recognizable comic type, a "humourist" whose plain dealing is a folly to be castigated, but whose incidental social criticism may often be valid even though it is too uncontrolled. Wycherley does not stand on the periphery of Restoration society, revolted by what he sees. In *The Plain Dealer* he typifies the attitude of his age toward the eccentric and the social malcontent.

Alexander H. Chorney
*Essays Critical and Historical Dedicated to Lily B. Campbell*
(Berkeley, Calif.: Univ. California Pr., 1950), pp. 162-69

Wycherley's last work, *The Plain Dealer* (1674), is ranked very high among his plays by virtue of his "satirical" vigor and forceful characterization. But it is inferior as a play and also as a comedy of wit. The large element of farce in the play and the contrived situations are hardly conducive to the best comic wit, and the dramatic action is often subordinated to the expression of Wycherley's wit. The high regard in which the play is held, despite these flaws, is due in large part to the identification of the author with the vituperative Manly and the belief that this play is a fierce satire on the corruptness of mankind. The belief that Wycherley expressed himself through Manly is . . . quite wrong; for though contemporaries referred to him as "Manly," it was principally in tribute to his masculinity and frankness rather than for any virulent hatred of mankind. This identification represents a complete misconception of Wycherley the Truewit and a total misunderstanding of the play.

Thomas H. Fujimura
*The Restoration Comedy of Wit* (Princeton, N. J.:
Princeton Univ. Pr., 1952), p. 146

[In contrast to Bonamy Dobrée's suggestion that Manly is not intended to escape censure] it must be urged, not only that Manly is loaded with rewards at the end of the play . . . but also that he has been represented throughout the play as an odd but essentially heroic character. . . .

The tastelessness of Manly's speech leads naturally to his revenge. Here the play's moral pretensions crumble, and intrigue and excitement get the upper hand. The revenge—to impersonate Fidelia and lie with Olivia— is obviously inconsistent with Manly's honesty, and must have made even Wycherley's contemporaries uneasy, yet Wycherley provides no explanatory commentary here, where it is wanted far more than in the exposure of Olivia. The reason seems, regrettably, that in Wycherley's eyes the revenge is morally insignificant and that he is indifferent to its effect on Manly's character as seen by the audience. Confidence in Wycherley as a moral satirist is severely undermined if he so casually sacrifices his hero's char- acter to exciting intrigue; and it is no less weakened if he does not recog- nize anything amiss with Manly's action except that it pains the disguised Fidelia. . . .

In short, though there are effective satirical thrusts in the play, its claims to moral seriousness cannot be upheld when the effect of its main plot is morally repugnant. The satire, furthermore, is rather a matter of ridiculing and exposing the stage's perpetual butts than one of forcing the spectators to search their own consciences.

T. W. Craik
*ES* (June, 1960), pp. 176-77

## GENERAL

Wycherley's "noble and useful satire" is not the product of an untroubled view of life—the view of a man who thinks in universal types of humanity. Wycherley's main business is still with manners, not with morals; and where his moral fury intrudes it spoils rather than uplifts his comedy. Ordinarily he accepted life. But suddenly he sees clean through the spec- tacle that has served his turn, and breaks into a furious, confused passion of disgust. Only in this way can we explain the alternating of scenes handled in a spirit purely laughter-loving with scenes of violent rage against humanity. It is precisely this moral fury of Wycherley which is accountable for passages that have persistently disgusted the critics. There are passages in any one of the four plays which, independently of any change of attitude or manners, are revolting. Laughter is extinguished; the jester bursts irrecognisable upon us, a ferocious prophet, dredging into the filth of human nature with precisely the sombre satisfaction with which certain devout people relish the possibilities of hell. The spirit of these scenes is as far from the easy nonchalance of Etherege as from the sunshine satire of Moliere. But it puts Wycherley quite definitely in touch with the French satirical school of comedy, despite the distance that is between them. More especially there are scenes where Wycherley's shrewd good humour and passing pleasure in the life of his time combine with his fundamental puritanism to produce scenes of a faintly subacid quality which agreeably suggest the manner of French comedy at its best.

John Palmer
*The Comedy of Manners* (London: G. Bell, 1913), pp. 120-21

[Let us] examine the basis of Wycherley's "satire." We must remember that he was always a Truewit, and that, consequently, his criterion was not a Christian system of ethics. As a Truewit, he wittily exposed the unnatural and the affected on the basis of his naturalistic philosophy; and when the conventional observance of Christian morality produced an artificial relationship, as in arranged marriages, he exposed conventional morality. . . . His "satire" was directed against "preciseness" (a punctilious insistence on honor), false wit, and coxcombry, rather than against violations of morality. At the same time, in accordance with his allegiance to the standards of true wit, Wycherley utilized the resources of wit and tempered the sharpness of his criticism with urbanity.

. . . An examination of his life and work reveals him as a Truewit —libertine, skeptical, naturalistic, and as much devoted to true wit as Etherege. The preponderant evidence . . . is against treating him as a fierce satirist and moralist, though one cannot deny that the satirical temper is strong in his works, especially in the form of ironic wit.

Thomas H. Fujimura
*The Restoration Comedy of Wit* (Princeton, N. J.:
Princeton Univ. Pr., 1952), pp. 118-19

# EDWARD  YOUNG

1683-1765

A graduate of Oxford, Young had hoped for a lasting career in parliament or in law, but he took orders when nearly fifty after disappointment in political life. He was made Royal Chaplain in 1728, and became Rector of Welwyn in 1730, where he remained without advancement until his death. He essayed plays with *Busiris*, a tragedy given in 1719; *The Revenge*, given in 1721; and *The Brothers*, given in 1753, though written ca. 1723. His poetry includes *The Universal Passion* (1725-1728), a series of satires; his well-known *Night Thoughts* (1742-1745); and *Resignation* (1762).

John Doran, ed., *The Complete Works* (1854), 2 vols.

Henry C. Shelley, *The Life and Letters of Edward Young* (1914)

One of the earliest and most important results of Thomson's popularizing blank verse was the appearance, in 1742, of the first part of *The Complaint, or Night Thoughts*, by Edward Young. There is, to be sure, no proof that it was Thomson's example which led his fellow-poet to use the measure; but since *The Seasons* was at the time in the flush of its first popularity, and since *The Complaint* is very different in character from anything its author had written before, there must have been some connection, and perhaps not a slight one, between the two works.

It is Young's good fortune that he is little read. Most lovers of poetry who know the eighteenth century only through anthologies think of *The Seasons*, the *Night Thoughts,* and *The Task* as esthetically on the same low plane, an estimate that does great injustice to Thomson and Cowper, who notwithstanding their defects, had genuine inspiration. Young lacked this and had little to offer in its place. The *Night Thoughts* is one of the dullest and falsest poems that ever achieved fame. It is rhetorical and declamatory in style, unpoetic in both conception and expression, commonplace in thought, sentimental, insincere, and lugubrious in its insistent religion. To the modern reader the hollow theatricality of its parade of gloom is particularly repellent because of the smug piety which is supposed to inspire it. The poem excites no admiration for its author, who, one is not surprised to learn, spent the best part of his life seeking those tinsel trappings which it belittles. The gross flattery contained in the dedications of his works and in his poetic references to persons of influence prepare us to hear that for years he danced attendance on two of the most profligate and unscrupulous noblemen of the time, and that he even stooped to beg aid of the king's mistress for advancement in the church! There can be no question that the gloom of his poetry is in part due to disappointed ambition, and that his scorn of worldly pleasures and honors rings hollow from a man who strove hard to obtain them.

Raymond Dexter Havens
*The Influence of Milton on English Poetry* (Cambridge, Mass.:
Harvard Univ. Pr., 1922), pp. 149-50

The search for sententiousness, the constant effort to be striking at whatever cost, is Young's besetting vice. In this respect, as in others, he may be called the English Seneca. He resembles Seneca, too, in his endless flux of words. He is never content to make his point and have done. Even where (as is often the case) he has hit the nail on the head, he goes on with a shower of rattling blows, which are quite ineffective, and only serve to fatigue the reader and to impair the force of the first stroke. The result in detail is a tendency to anti-climax so persistent that it might be called systematic; in the total large effect, it is an amount of repetition which in a sermon might be excused or even justified, but in a poem is insufferable. . . . In the *Night Thoughts* he is always raising his voice very much, but goes obstinately on; and the sense of fatigue grows. The later *Nights* contain many of his finest lines and passages; yet the effective value of the whole, as well as its changes of life, would have been greater had he stopped at the end of the fourth *Night,* or possibly even sooner. But he was without common sense.

J. W. Mackail
*Studies of English Poets* (New York: Longmans,
Green, 1926), pp. 125-26

One implication of Young's individualism, often unnoticed, is the trend toward subjectivity—a pronounced characteristic of later romanticism. By subjectivity here, I do not mean so much the habit of introspection as the habit of seeing the outer world in terms of his own mind; everything . . . is painted on the walls of his own consciousness and is derived from within. . . . In Young's satisfaction with the confines of his own mind we have something that approaches the solipsism of later romanticism. All outer reality came to be stained and colored by the romanticist's own temperament; he came to see in nature only what he himself put there.

Of course, in the fresh morning of romance Young does not go to this extreme; but the subjectivity of his literary method, deriving from his all-embracing conception of original genius, is a straw in the current. . . .

Harry H. Clark
*Transactions of the Wisconsin Academy of Sciences, Arts and Letters*
(1929), pp. 32-33

In his arguments against various shades of infidelity and immorality, Young adopts no very clearly formulated position. The various changes in Lorenzo show the opponents the poet has in mind from time to time. In *Nights I-III* Lorenzo is simply a libertine, enjoying life, its pleasures and follies, and thinking not at all of the necessity of preparing for death. In *Night IV* he becomes a deist for the most part, depending entirely on reason and not accepting Christian revelation. Yet here too his rejection of immortality is evidently to be regarded as atheistical. In *Night V* he becomes an advocate of Shaftesbury's theory of ridicule, at least as its enemies saw it. In *Night VI* and *Night VII* he is an atheist in rejecting immortality and in seeing everything as a flux of essences. In *Night VIII* he is still a libertine, devoted to the world, and a deist in his denial of the inspired nature of the Bible. In *Night IX* he is quite definitely an atheist, denying God, believing the world the result of chance and fate, and unlike the deists unaffected by the evidences of natural religion.

Isabel St. John Bliss
*PMLA* (March, 1934), p. 55

Reasons why Young's "fate," to use his own word in a different application, has been first a long period of popular success and then something approaching the oblivion he feared for his person may be sought in the passing of the taste for his brand of sentimentalism, in the selfishness and narrowness of his religious motives, in the shallow philosophy of pessimism he adopted, and in the literary defects of his work.

Two features of Young's work formed the basis of his appeal to the general reader: first, his idealized and extreme emotionalism, the ego let loose, the tearful trembling, all the excess of personal feeling; second, his moral and religious didacticism. The former accorded perfectly with the growing taste for sentimentalism and found ready acceptance. In France, for example, the *Night Thoughts* contended for favor with *Clarissa Harlowe* and *Ossian*, an indication that the emotional and sentimental quality was the chief attraction.

C. V. Wicker
*Edward Young and the Fear of Death* (Albuquerque, N. M.:
Univ. New Mexico Pr., 1952), pp. 89-90

# ROMANTIC LITERATURE

*Frances K. Barasch, editor*

# JANE AUSTEN
1775-1817

Jane Austen, the seventh of eight children of a back-country English clergyman, was born and raised at Steventon Rectory in Hampshire. She began writing for amusement before she was fourteen, and continued to write with varying degrees of application until her death. She never married, led a circumscribed social life, and spent much of her time with her sister Cassandra. Leaving Steventon in 1801 with her parents and her sister, she lived for a time at Bath and at Southampton, then returned to Hampshire and settled at Chawton in 1809 where she spent most of the remainder of her life. Although her contact with the outside world was sharply limited, her own life was rich in emotional experience. Sensitive, intelligent, witty, and perhaps embittered, Jane Austen recorded the human comedy, probing sham and subtly delineating a code of morality. Although four of her books were published during her lifetime, her fame as a novelist was not immediately widespread. Posterity accorded her greatness long after her death. Her six major novels are: *Sense and Sensibility* (1811); *Pride and Prejudice* (1813); *Mansfield Park* (1814); *Emma* (1816); *Northanger Abbey* (1818); and *Persuasion* (1818). Her earliest works and fragments were not published until the twentieth century. They are: *Love and Friendship* (1922, 1929); *Lady Susan* (1925); *Sanditon* (1925); *Plan of a Novel* (1926); *The Watsons* (1927); and *Volume the First* (1933).

R. W. Chapman, ed., *Novels* (1923), 5 vols.

Elizabeth Jenkins, *Jane Austen, a Biography* (1939)

## PERSONAL

. . . Our knowledge of Jane Austen is derived from a little gossip, a few letters, and her books. As for the gossip, gossip which has survived its day is never despicable; with a little rearrangement it suits our purpose admirably. For example, Jane "is not at all pretty and very prim, unlike a girl of twelve . . . Jane is whimsical and affected," says little Philadelphia Austen of her cousin. Then we have Mrs. Mitford, who knew the Austens as girls and thought Jane "the prettiest, silliest, most affected, husband-hunting butterfly she ever remembers." Next, there is Miss Mitford's anonymous friend "who visits her now [and] says that she has stiffened into the most perpendicular, precise, taciturn piece of 'single blessedness' that ever existed, and that, until *Pride and Prejudice* showed what a precious gem was hidden in that unbending case, she was no more regarded in society than a poker or fire-screen. . . . The case is very different now," the good lady goes on; "she is still a poker—but a poker of whom everybody is afraid. . . . A wit, a delineator of character, who does not talk is terrific indeed!" On the other side, of course, there are the Austens, a race little given to panegyric of themselves, but nevertheless, they say, her brothers "were very fond and very proud of her. They were attached to her by her talents, her virtues, and her engaging manners, and each loved afterwards to fancy a resemblance in some niece or daughter of his own to the dear sister Jane, whose perfect equal they yet never expected to see." Charming but perpendicular, loved at home but feared by strangers, biting of tongue but tender of heart—these contrasts are by no means incompatible, and when we turn to the novels we shall find ourselves stumbling there too over the same complexities in the writer. [1923; rev. 1925]

Virginia Woolf
*The Common Reader* (London: L. and V. Woolf,
1925), pp. 168-69

For Jane Austen, humankind was of first importance; and in her human world her own family stood foremost. . . .

Her father George Austen, was gentle and strongly attached to his family; he occupied himself with the cares of his parish, his farm, and his pupils, and left a reputation for scholarship and literary taste which was supported in his day by his having prepared two of his sons, with other pupils, for Oxford, and rests more firmly now on his quick perception of his daughter's gifts. Mrs. Austen was a countrywoman and busy gardener, with vital energy enough to carry her through long stretches of ill health. . . . In Jane's own generation, the eldest was James, whose career—at Oxford, in his first curacy, and, when he succeeded his father, at Steventon —never carried him far from his sisters. . . . Edward was adopted, while a boy by his distant cousins—Thomas and Catherine Knight of Godmersham in Kent. . . . Henry, next in age after Edward, was thought by the rest to have been closest of all the brothers to Jane herself in sympathy and understanding. . . . Cassandra, most important of them all in Jane's life, yet remains the most shadowy. A strong and subtle sympathy bound these two together. . . . Frank was next of the family, and nearest to Cassandra in steady good sense. Last of all came Charles; like Frank, his father's pupil until he became a sailor, and, like Frank, still tenacious when at sea of his share in family affections. . . .

Jane had always been, the rest of them recollected, a particular favourite in her own family; and there is independent evidence that she never wanted for appreciation and encouragement there. . . .

This group of people was the focus of Jane Austen's early life. . . .

Mary Lascelles<br>
Jane Austen and Her Art (Oxford Univ. Pr., 1939), pp. 1-5

One of the aspects of Jane Austen's character most frequently dwelt on with surprise and admiration by people who knew her as a woman in the height of her achievement, was her unpretending, exquisite simplicity; but though the simplicity was artless, it was a development, a quality that grew with the growth of her perfect taste. . . .

[Cassandra] told her niece that when she and Jane had been staying in Devonshire, they had met a young man. . . . He appeared to be greatly attracted by Jane; Cassandra's impression was that he had fallen in love with her and was "quite in earnest.". . . They parted in the full expectation of meeting again more happily. Shortly afterwards they heard that he was dead. . . .

The importance of what happened to her as it affected the development of her sensibilities and powers is great, but it lies in the fact that it acted as a pointer towards realms of undiscovered country; and the exquisite speech on woman's constancy written fifteen years afterwards is not uttered by Jane Austen in her own person, but by Anne Elliot, whom Jane Austen's experience enabled her to understand. . . .

It was the opinion of her descendants that she had no sooner settled down after the move to Chawton [in 1809] . . . than she began to write once more; and her writing took the form of reconsideration of *Sense and Sensibility*. . . . Eleven years had passed since the completion of the story, and those eleven years—her life since the age of twenty-three—comprised everything that could be accounted her development as a human being and as an artist. What she had learned from this apparently eventless existence is shown by the amazing rapidity with which she composed those three later novels, whose worlds of experience are so solid in their detachment, so infinite in the associations they bring about in the reader's mind with depths upon depths of human nature, that one would imagine they had been the slow growth of half a lifetime, instead of, as they are, that of little more than a twelvemonth each.

Elizabeth Jenkins<br>
Jane Austen (New York: Pellegrini and Cudahy,<br>
1949), pp. 27, 129-31, 211-12

## Pride and Prejudice

But in all its forms the dramatic novel need not be tragic, and the first novelist who practised it with consummate success in England—Jane Austen

—consistently avoided and probably was quite incapable of sounding the tragic note. The instance may seem strange, but it is only so in appearance. The art of Jane Austen has a more essential resemblance to that of Hardy than to Fielding's or Thackeray's. There is in her novel in the first place, a confinement to one circle, one complex of life, producing naturally an intensification of action; and this intensification is one of the essential attributes of the dramatic novel. In the second place, character is to her no longer a thing merely to delight in. . . . It has consequences. It influences events; it creates difficulties and later, in different circumstances, dissolves them. When Elizabeth Bennett and Darcy meet first, the complexion of their next encounter is immediately determined. The action is set by the changing tension between them and by a few acts of intervention on the part of the other figures; and the balance of all the forces within the novel creates and moulds the plot. There is no external framework, no merely mechanical plot; all is character, and all is at the same time action. One figure in the pure comedic sense there is in the book, Mr. Collins. Mr. Collins has no great effect on the action . . . he remains unchanged throughout the story. There are other pure comedic elements; for example, the permanent domestic tension between Mr. and Mrs. Bennett. But in most dramatic novels such figures and combinations are to be found. Hardy has his peasants to give relief and an additional emphasis of proportion to the action; they serve somewhat the same purpose as a sub-plot without being one. The real power of the Wessex Novels lies of course elsewhere, in the development of a changing tension making toward an end. If the chief power of *Pride and Prejudice* does not reside in that, at least half its power does.

Edwin Muir
*The Structure of the Novel* (London:
Hogarth Pr., 1928), pp. 42-43

Many pages of *Pride and Prejudice* can be read as sheer poetry of wit, as Pope without couplets. The antitheses are almost as frequent and almost as varied; the play of ambiguities is certainly as complex; the orchestration of tones is as precise and subtle. As in the best of Pope, the displays of ironic wit are not without imaginative connection; what looks most diverse is really most similar, and ironies are linked by vibrant reference to basic certainties. There are passages too in which the rhythmical pattern of the sentence approaches the formal balance of the heroic couplet. . . . The triumph of the novel—whatever its limitations may be—lies in combining such poetry of wit with the dramatic structure of fiction. In historical terms, to combine the traditions of poetic satire with those of the sentimental novel, that was Jane Austen's feat in *Pride and Prejudice*.

For the "bright and sparkling," seemingly centrifugal play of irony is dramatically functional. It makes sense as literary art, the sense with which a writer is most concerned. The repartee, while constantly amusing, delineates characters and their changing relations and points the way to a climactic moment in which the change is most clearly recognized. Strictly speaking, this union of wit and drama is achieved with complete success only in the central sequence of *Pride and Prejudice,* in the presentation of Elizabeth's and Darcy's gradual revaluation of each other. . . .

The triumph of *Pride and Prejudice* is a rare one, just because it is so difficult to balance a purely ironic vision with credible presentation of a man and woman undergoing a serious "change of sentiment. . . ." The problem for the writer who essays this difficult blend is one of creating dramatic speech which fulfils his complex intention. In solving this problem of expression, Jane Austen has her special triumph. [1945]

Reuben A. Brower<br>
The Fields of Light (New York: Oxford Univ. Pr.,<br>
1951), pp. 164-65, 181

In *Pride and Prejudice,* for the first time, Jane Austen allows her heroine to share her own characteristic response to the world. . . .

Elizabeth sets herself up as an ironic spectator, able and prepared to judge and classify . . . the simple ones . . . and the intricate ones. . . . Into one of these preliminary categories, Elizabeth fits everybody she observes.

Elizabeth shares her author's characteristic response of comic irony, defining incongruities without drawing them into a moral context; and still more specifically, Elizabeth's vision of the world as divided between the simple and the intricate is, in *Pride and Prejudice* at any rate, Jane Austen's vision also. This identification between the author and her heroine establishes, in fact, the whole ground pattern of judgment in the novel.

Marvin Mudrick<br>
Jane Austen, Irony as Defense and Discovery (Princeton, N. J.:<br>
Princeton Univ. Pr., 1952), pp. 94-95

To say that Darcy is proud and Elizabeth prejudiced is to tell but half the story. Pride and prejudice are faults; but they are also the necessary defects of desirable merits: self-respect and intelligence. Moreover, the novel makes clear the fact that Darcy's pride leads to prejudice and Elizabeth's prejudice stems from a pride in her own perceptions. So the ironic theme of the book might be said to centre on the dangers of intellectual complexity. Jane Bennett and Bingley are never exposed to these dangers; they are not sufficiently profound. But the hero and the heroine, because of their deep percipience, are, ironically, subject to failures of perception. Elizabeth has good reason to credit herself with the ability to discern people and situations extraordinarily well: she understands her family perfectly, knows William Collins from the first letter he writes, comprehends the merit and deficiencies of the Bingleys almost at once, appreciates Lady Catherine de Bourgh at first meeting. Her failures are with "intricate" people who moreover stand in a relationship of great intimacy to her: Charlotte Lucas, George Wickham, Fitzwilliam Darcy. And the book is given an added dimension because it shows that intimacy blurs perceptions: intelligence fails if there is insufficient distance between mind and object. [1953]

Andrew Wright
*Jane Austen's Novels* (New York:
Oxford Univ. Pr., 1954), p. 106

## Mansfield Park

. . . *Mansfield Park* is Jane Austen's *gran rifuto*, perhaps under the influence of the unhappiness through which she had been passing. None of her books is quite so brilliant in parts, none shows a greater technical mastery, a more audacious facing of realities, a more certain touch with character. Yet, alone of her books, *Mansfield Park is* vitiated throughout by a radical dishonesty, that was certainly not in its author's own nature. One can almost hear the clerical relations urging "dear Jane" to devote "her undoubted talent to the cause of righteousness"; indeed, if dates allowed, one could even believe that Mr. Clarke's unforgettable suggestion about the country clergyman had formed fruit in this biography of Edmund Bertram. In any case, her purpose of edification, being not her own, is always at cross-purposes with her unprompted joy in creation. She is always getting so interested in her subject, and so joyous in her management of it that when her official purpose comes to mind, the resulting high sentiment or edifying speech is a wrench alike to one's attention and credulity. And this dualism of motive destroys not only the unity of the book, but its sincerity. You cannot palter with truth; one false assumption puts all the drawing and colouring out of gear. . . .

On the whole, then, *Mansfield Park*, with its unparalleled flights counteracted by its unparalleled lapses, must count lower as an achievement than *Emma*, with its more equal movement, at a higher level of workmanship. Had it not been for its vitiating purpose, indeed, *Mansfield Park* would have taken highest rank. [1917]

Reginald Farrer
*Discussions of Jane Austen*, ed. William Heath (Boston:
D. C. Heath, 1961), pp. 85-86

. . . By way of transition to the round [character], let us go to *Mansfield Park*, and look at Lady Bertram, sitting on her sofa. . . . Lady Bertram's formula is, "I am kindly, but must not be fatigued," and she functions out of it. But at the end there is a catastrophe. Her two daughters come to grief. . . . Julia elopes; Maria, who is unhappily married runs off with a lover. What is Lady Bertram's reaction? The sentence describing it is significant: "Lady Bertram did not think deeply, but, guided by Sir Thomas, she thought justly on all important points, and she saw therefore in all its enormity, what had happened, and neither endeavoured herself, nor required Fanny to advise her, to think little of guilt and infamy." These are strong words, and they used to worry me because I thought Jane Austen's moral sense was getting out of hand. She may, and of course does, deprecate guilt and infamy herself, and she duly causes all possible distress in the minds of Edmund and Fanny, but has she any right to agitate calm, consistent Lady Bertram? . . . Ought not her ladyship to remain on the sofa saying, "This is a dreadful and sadly exhausting business about Julia and Maria, but where is Fanny gone? I have dropped another stitch"? . . .

[Jane Austen] is a miniaturist, but never two-dimensional. All her characters are round, or capable of rotundity. . . . Lady Bertram's moral fervour ceases to vex us when we realize this: the disk has suddenly extended and become a little globe. When the novel is closed, Lady Bertram goes back to the flat, it is true; the dominant impression she leaves can be summed up in a formula. But that is not how Jane Austen conceived her, and the freshness of her reappearances are due to this. . . . All Jane Austen's characters are ready for an extended life, for a life which the scheme of her books seldom requires them to lead, and that is why they lead their actual lives so satisfactorily. . . . In a few words she has extended Lady Bertram, and by so doing she has increased the probability of the elopements of Maria and Julia. . . .

All through her works we find these characters, apparently so simple and flat, never needing reintroduction and yet never out of their depth—Henry Tilney, Mr. Woodhouse, Charlotte Lucas. She may label her characters "Sense," "Pride," "Sensibility," "Prejudice," but they are not tethered to those qualities. [1927]

E. M. Forster<br>
Aspects of the Novel (New York: Harcourt,<br>
Brace, 1954), pp. 112-17

It must be admitted . . . that Henry Crawford is a good deal more interesting than his opposite number. He has something of Henry Tilney's turn for irony, and a certain glitter which Edmund certainly lacks. In conception and in execution, however, Henry Crawford is meant to be a villain— though, as Miss Austen quite appropriately shows us, even a villain may have some good qualities.

There is little cause, therefore, to suppose Henry Crawford anything like a heroic character. On the other hand, his love for Fanny—which develops only after he has decided to trifle with her affections—is genuinely moving, and at the same time consonant with one side of his personality. . . .

And for a while, spurred by his love for Fanny, Henry does try to change. At Portsmouth, he is unfailingly sweet and kind to her—but when he returns to London he also reverts to his old self. His elopement with Maria is an unsurprising finale to an unpromising beginning—though his author tells us that, had he married Fanny, "there would have been every probability of success and felicity for him. His affection had already done something." But this was not to be.

*Mansfield Park,* then, cannot be called an ironic novel. Like the fragmentary *Lady Susan* it is uncomplicatedly didactic. Want of breeding is responsible for the evils in Henry Crawford, as in all the other bad characters; good breeding supports and develops Fanny and Edmund. So this work can only be contrasted to the rest of the canon: it is much simpler than Jane Austen's novels; it is none the less delicate, honest, subtle. [1953]

Andrew Wright
*Jane Austen's Novels* (New York:
Oxford Univ. Pr., 1954), pp. 132-34

. . . There is one novel of Jane Austen's, *Mansfield Park,* in which the characteristic irony seems not to be at work. Indeed, one might say of this novel that it undertakes to discredit irony and to affirm literalness, that it demonstrates that there are no two ways about anything. And *Mansfield Park* is for this reason held by many to be the novel that is least representative of Jane Austen's peculiar attractiveness. For those who admire her it is likely to make an occasion for embarrassment. By the same token, it is the novel which the depreciators of Jane Austen may cite most tellingly in justification of their antagonism. . . .

And they can point to *Mansfield Park* to show what the social coercion is in all its literal truth, before irony has beglamoured us about it and induced us to be comfortable with it—here it is in all its negation, in all the force of its repressiveness. Perhaps no other work of genius has ever spoken, or seemed to speak, so insistently for cautiousness and constraint, even for dullness. No other great novel has so anxiously asserted the need to find security, to establish, in fixity and enclosure, a refuge from the dangers of openness and chance . . .

Yet *Mansfield Park* is a great novel, its greatness being commensurate with its power to offend. . . .

Its impulse is not to forgive but to condemn. Its praise is not for social freedom but for social stasis. It takes full notice of spiritedness, vivacity and happiness, as being, indeed, deterrents to the good life. [1954]

Lionel Trilling
*The Opposing Self* (New York:
Viking, 1955), pp. 208, 210-11

Anyone who agrees with Lord David Cecil that Jane Austen never wrote outside her artistic range should study *Mansfield Park*. With the exception of the amusing scenes in which Lady Bertram and Mrs. Norris appear, it is all written well outside her range. If one glances through the pages, the rancorous, censorious tone becomes apparent in the words with which the author tries to batter our moral sense. "Disapprove," "censure," "corrupted," "evil," "wrong," "misconduct," "sin," "crime," "guilt," "fault," "offence," "abhorrence" are only a few of the words that shriek at the reader with a sort of moral hysteria that stuns and bewilders him. And the morality itself is of a pretty low order. Fanny Price's attitude when she returns to her parents' wretched home in Portsmouth is not remarkable for decent feeling. [1955]

Frank O'Connor
*The Mirror in the Roadway* (New York:
A. A. Knopf, 1956), pp. 30-31

## Emma

... This is *the* novel of character, and of character alone, and of one dominating character in particular. And many a rash reader, and some who are not rash, have been shut out on the threshold of Emma's Comedy by a dislike of Emma herself. Well did Jane Austen know what she was about, when she said, "I am going to take a heroine whom nobody but myself will much like." And, insofar as she fails to make people like Emma, so far would her whole attempt have to be judged a failure, were it not that really the failure, like the loss, is theirs who have not taken the trouble to understand what is being attempted. Jane Austen loved tackling problems; her hardest of all, her most deliberate, and her most triumphantly solved, is Emma. [1917]

Reginald Farrer
*Discussions of Jane Austen*, ed. William Heath
(Boston: D. C. Heath, 1961), p. 102

When we say that a character in Jane Austen, Miss Bates for instance, is "so like life" we mean that each bit of her coincides with a bit of life, but that she as a whole only parallels the chatty spinster we met at tea. Miss Bates is bound by a hundred threads to Highbury. We cannot tear her away without bringing her mother too, and Jane Fairfax and Frank Churchill, and the whole of Box Hill; whereas we could tear Moll Flanders away, at least for the purposes of experiment. A Jane Austen novel is more complicated than a Defoe because the characters are interdependent, and there is the additional complication of a plot. The plot in *Emma* is not prominent and Miss Bates contributes little. Still it is there, she is connected with the principals, and the result is a closely woven fabric from which nothing can be removed. Miss Bates and Emma herself are like bushes in a shrubbery—not isolated trees like Moll. . . . [1927]

E. M. Forster
*Aspects of the Novel* (New York: Harcourt,
Brace, 1954), pp. 100-101

. . . There is an admirable concreteness about the prose of Jane Austen. There is a certain kind of economy too, but nothing so violent as speed. The characteristics, indeed, of her style are rather those of the essayist. The action is reduced to a minimum, and the mind turns instead to analysis, to decoration (scene-painting), to mildly ironic comment:

> It was hot; and after walking some time over the garden in a scattered, dispersed way, scarcely any three together, they insensibly followed one another to the delicious shade of a broad short avenue of limes, which, stretching beyond the garden at an equal distance from the river, seemed the finish of the pleasure grounds. It led to nothing; nothing but a view at the end over a low stone wall with high pillars, which seemed intended, in their erection, to give the appearance of an approach to the house, which had never been there. . . . *Emma*

Descriptive prose of this kind is not written in any mood of compulsion. A skilful writer may be able to disguise this lack of internal necessity by means of various "tricks of the trade," and the result is merely a "dead" perfection of phrase and rhythm. Jane Austen was not a skilled writer in this sense, and her lack of expertness betrays itself either in mere clumsiness, such as the repetition of the words "seemed" and "considerable" in the passage quoted here, or in a simplicity or naïvety of phrasing which is perhaps the secret of the attraction which her style undoubtedly has for a large number of people.

Herbert Read
*English Prose Style* (New York: Henry Holt, 1928), pp. 118-19

*Emma* is universal just because it is narrow; because it confines itself to the range of Jane Austen's profoundest vision.

For it is a profound vision. There are other views of life and more extensive; concerned as it is exclusively with personal relationships, it leaves out several important aspects of experience. But on her own ground Jane Austen gets to the heart of the matter; her graceful unpretentious philosophy, founded as it is on an unwavering recognition of fact, directed by an unerring perception of moral quality, is as impressive as those of the most majestic novelists. [1935]

Lord David Cecil
*Poets and Story-Tellers* (New York:
Barnes and Noble, n.d.), p. 121

It is the ambient air of Highbury which most charms us in this book. The little town and all its inhabitants are so real, so actual, that it is hard to believe we have never been there. The very cobbles, glistening after a sharp shower, are nearly solid enough to walk on. The sun burns our necks over Mr. Knightly's strawberry beds and the shade in Donwell Lane is refreshing. It is as if that stretching of the imagination, which enabled Miss Austen to like Emma, gave her a firmer grasp upon everything within reach.

Margaret Kennedy
*Jane Austen* (Denver, Colo.: Alan Swallow, 1950), p. 83

. . . My conviction [is] that *Emma* is a novel admired, even consecrated, for qualities which it in fact subverts or ignores.

Marvin Mudrick
*Jane Austen, Irony as Defense and Discovery* (Princeton, N. J.:
Princeton Univ. Pr., 1952), p. vii

*Emma* has nothing of the brilliance of *Pride and Prejudice*, but this difficulty was inherent in the material. The subject of *Emma* is a bad one, for it is a closed circuit; everything of importance takes place within the mind of the principal character, and this mind is a fantastic one, incapable not only of seeing events accurately, but also of judging itself and its own motives. Everything depends upon the reader's ability to perceive immediately when Emma starts to go wrong. The story has to be told with the minimum of externalization, and the technical devices by which the author manages to conceal the awkwardness of her subject make the book a delight and a flattery for the knowing type of reader. [1955]

Frank O'Connor
*The Mirror in the Roadway* (New York:
A. A. Knopf, 1956), p. 34

## Persuasion

There is a peculiar beauty and a peculiar dullness in *Persuasion*. The dullness is that which so often marks the transition stage between two different periods. The writer is a little bored. She has grown too familiar with the ways of her world; she no longer notes them freshly. There is an asperity in her comedy which suggests that she has almost ceased to be amused by the vanities of a Sir Walter or the snobbery of a Miss Elliot. The satire is harsh, and the comedy crude. She is no longer so freshly aware of the amusements of daily life. Her mind is not altogether on her object. But, while we feel that Jane Austen has done this before, and done it better, we also feel that she is trying to do something which she has never yet attempted. There is a new element in *Persuasion*, the quality, perhaps, that made Dr. Whewell fire up and insist that it was "the most beautiful of her works." She is beginning to discover that the world is larger, more mysterious, and more romantic than she had supposed. . . . She dwells frequently upon the beauty and the melancholy of nature, upon the autumn where she had been wont to dwell upon the spring. She talks of the "influence so sweet and so sad of autumnal months in the country." She marks "the tawny leaves and withered hedges.". . . Her attitude toward life itself is altered. She is seeing it, for the greater part of her book, through the eyes of a woman who, unhappy herself, has a special sympathy for the happiness and unhappiness of others, which, until the very end, she is forced to comment upon in silence. Therefore the observation is less of facts and more of feelings than is usual. [1923; rev. 1925]

Virginia Woolf
*The Common Reader* (London: L. and V. Woolf,
1925), pp. 180-81

*Persuasion* is about love. How far should love be restrained by prudential consideration? It is a different sort of subject from that of her other books; and the pensive sympathy, with which she discusses it, betrays a softening of her prevailing mood. Sad experience has taught her that the problems of the heart are too momentous to be decided with the unhesitating confidence of her high-spirited youth. [1935]

Lord David Cecil
*Poets and Story-Tellers* (New York:
Barnes and Noble, n.d.), p. 120

"There are those," Louis Kronenberger reminds us, "who think Jane Austen tea-tablish, as there are those who think that Mozart tinkles." "Those" have never read *Persuasion,* a sad love story with a happy ending. Here, more clearly and more sweetly than in any of the other novels, is exposed the conflict between two schemes of values: those of prudence, and those of love. Anne Elliot contains both and the result is a contradiction which causes nearly a decade of unhappiness to her; her reconciliation with Captain Wentworth stems not from the resolution of these opposites, but from a series of fortuitous circumstances which makes the match possible after all. Never, even at the end of the book, can she abandon her commitment to the prudential values, even when she is happily betrothed to Captain Wentworth, Yet she is complete, a fully human, heroine. John Baily writes: "There are few heroines in fiction whom we love so much, feel for so much, as we love and feel for Anne Elliot." [1953]

Andrew Wright
*Jane Austen's Novels* (New York:
Oxford Univ. Pr., 1954), pp. 160-61

*Persuasion* supplies us with the most convincing evidence, among Jane Austen's novels, of how basic the technique of metaphoric indirection is to her artistic method. For one thing, such dialogues turn up over and over here, as . . . suggested by the number of Captain Wentworth's speeches that refer obliquely to Anne, whether she is a member of his immediate audience or not. During the scene in which we have . . . heard him talk with the Musgroves of his naval career, for instance, he gets involved in a verbal tussle with the Crofts when he objects to the presence of women aboard ship; and it is perfectly plain to the reader that the Captain, though he apparently imagines himself taking a high naval line, actually reveals his resentment over losing Anne. . . . Not only does the technique appear frequently in the novel, but Jane Austen entrusts several highly significant scenes to it, including the one . . . in which Louisa professes her "firmness" of character and the Captain applauds the trait, speaking all the while from his sense of Anne's irresolution and not realizing that she overhears the conversation. . . .

Jane Austen dramatizes her characters through their linguistic habits. . . . Probably the sheer wit that sparkles in so many of the verbal exchanges is the most memorable feature of her conversations. But they are also distinguished by their lifelike flow. . . . There is a wonderfully easy movement within the single speech which combines with a natural progress from one speech to the next to give the dialogues an air of artlessness, of truth to life. . . . None of her contemporaries or immediate predecessors among the novelists commands a dialogue at once so fluent and so brilliant as hers. . . .

But the qualities . . . just mentioned are evident to any reader of Jane Austen. In fact they tempt us to overlook the actual depth of the characters that the dialogue reveals—and to ignore the more profound implications of the novels. For the underlying motif in Jane Austen's fiction is surely the disparity between appearance and reality, a problem that has haunted men's minds for centuries—all of which may suggest again that the works are less limited than is often imagined. . . . Indeed, Jane Austen's dialogue, taken as a whole, dramatizes the varieties of personality and explores the fundamental terms on which man lives with himself and with the world. . . .

And in the dialogues informed by the technique of metaphoric indirection, . . . the individual acknowledges the demands of propriety while voicing his deepest personal commitments.

Howard S. Babb
*Jane Austen's Novels* (Columbus, Ohio:
Ohio State Univ. Pr., 1962), pp. 227, 242-44

## GENERAL

She was a realist. She gave anew to the novel an art and a style, which it once had had. . . . Jane Austen's style is the language of everyday life—even with a tinge of its slang—to which she has added an element of beauty.

In the manipulation of characters and events, she left much less to chance than did Fielding. . . . Jane Austen brings together her village folk and their visitors, at the dinner-party and the ball, as naturally as they would meet in real life. . . . It is not to be supposed that there ever occurred a ball just like the one in *Mansfield Park*, or a strawberry party just like that one described in *Emma*. Jane Austen, like all country girls, was fond of dancing, and she not unlikely picked strawberries; but it would be to misinterpret her art to infer that in these scenes she is merely transcribing actual experience. What she is doing is building up scenes in her imagination, taking details from various occasions. . . . The matter of observation, in passing through Jane Austen's imagination, was never violently disturbed; the particular bias it received was from a delicate and delightful irony; there was precisely that selection and recombination and heightening of incident and character that distinguish the comedy of manners from real life. [1899]

Wilbur L. Cross
*The Development of the English Novel* (New York:
Macmillan, 1930), pp. 122-24

The key to Jane Austen's fortune with posterity has been in part the extraordinary grace of her facility, in fact of her unconsciousness: as if, at the most, for difficulty, for embarrassment, she sometimes, over her workbasket, her tapestry flowers, in the spare, cool drawing-room of other days, fell a-musing, lapsed too metaphorically, as one may say, into wool-gathering, and her dropped stitches, of these pardonable, of these precious moments, were afterwards picked up as little touches of human truth, little glimpses of steady vision, little master-strokes of imagination.

Henry James
*The Question of Our Speech, The Lesson of Balzac*
(Boston and New York: Houghton, Mifflin, 1905), p. 63

On the feelings of her men, of course, Jane Austen has nothing to say at first hand, is too honest an artist to invent, and too clean a woman to attempt the modern female trick of gratifying her own passions by inventing a lover, and then identifying herself with his desires, in so far as she can concoct them. Yet it would be quite a mistake to call her men pallid or shadowy. In point of fact, they are usually carried out with all her vivid certainty, yet considered only in relation to her women, and thus, by comparison, quieter in colour, deliberately subordinate in her scheme. Even the earlier heroes will be found perfectly adapted to their place in her books, when once that place is understood; as for the later ones, they stand most definitely on legs of their own, so far as their movements in the story require.

Perhaps the best of all is Knightley, not only in relation to Emma but also in himself. [1917]

Reginald Farrer
*Discussions of Jane Austen*, ed. William Heath
(Boston: D. C. Heath, 1961), p. 23

There are lives and memoirs of Miss Austen. But there needed none; for she was as incapable of having a story as of writing one—by a story I mean a sequence of happenings, either romantic or uncommon. Yet some of her synchronisms are notable. . . . Her first writings coincided with the last phases of the French Revolution, and the guns of Waterloo had scarce ceased to reverberate when she died. . . . But Miss Austen cared for none of these things, for she was essentially a comedian. . . .

Whether this supreme detachment makes her great, or only irritating, I will not here ask. I am concerned merely to note that she synchronizes with great affairs, and fits in only with small ones. . . .

Her primary concern in fiction was the manners of men, and not the human heart; and you may, I believe, search the later novels in vain for any indication that Miss Austen's nature, when she wrote them, was deeper or more expansive than twenty years earlier. . . . It would be difficult to name a writer of similar eminence who possessed so little knowledge of literature and history, whose experience of life was so narrowly and so contentedly confined, whose interests were at once so acute and so small, whose ideals were so irredeemably humdrum. . . . On the other hand, not indignation . . . but a just irritation, is constantly aroused in me by the monotonously subdued pitch of her ethical standards. . . . I refuse to call edifying in any intelligible sense works which accept as not only good, but natural, such worn and shabby institutions as simony, nepotism, and the marriage of convenience. The fact is that Miss Austen, beginning life with a temperament naturally cool and businesslike, took, not the world (which she never touches), but the parish, as she found it. There is a parochialism which is worse than worldliness. . . . When I call her writing truthful and apt, I have said all that should be said in praise of it. It is not good writing—it is frequently not even grammatical writing. . . .

Miss Austen is doing only the kind of work for which she is wholly competent. Undoubtedly she is entitled to that praise which belongs to a writer who limits her theme and her style to the exact measure of her interest, knowledge and powers. . . . The truth is that . . . her situation, character and knowledge were in almost every direction absurdly limited. She is only detached where she is in fact uninformed, and silent where uninterested. . . .

H. W. Garrod
*Essays by Divers Hands, Transactions of the
Royal Society of Literature* (Oxford Univ. Pr., 1928),
pp. 23-24, 29-31

All discriminating critics admire her books, most educated readers enjoy them; her fame, of all English novelists, is the most secure. . . .

Now Jane Austen's imaginative range was in some respects a very limited one. It was, in the first place, confined to human beings in their personal relations. Man in relation to God, to politics, to abstract ideas, passed her by: it was only when she saw him with his family and his neighbours that her creative impulse began to stir to activity. . . . Jane Austen was a comedian. Her first literary impulse was humorous; and to the end of her life humour was an integral part of her creative process. . . . It is the angle of her satiric vision, the light of her wit that gives its peculiar glitter and proportion to her picture of the world.

Nor does she give much space to the impressions of the senses. This was from no incapacity on her part. . . . She could paint for the eye with perfect certainty if she had wanted. But satire is an intellectual thing. . . . And the impressions of the senses are conveyed not by critical comment, but by direct record.

She avoided jarring characters too. Two-thirds of her *dramatis personae* are regular comic character-parts like Mr. Collins or Mrs. Allen. And even those figures with whom she is most in sympathy, even her heroines, are almost all touched with the comic spirit. . . .

Jane Austen's natural range was further bounded by the limitations imposed by circumstances. . . . The world of Jane Austen's experience was a very small one. . . . She excludes from her books all aspects of life that cannot pass through the crucible of her imagination. So that every inch of her book is vital. . . .

Mere technical accomplishment is not enough to explain the impression she makes on us. . . . Her books—it is the second reason for their enduring popularity—have a universal significance. [1935]

Lord David Cecil
*Poets and Story-Tellers* (New York:
Barnes and Noble, n.d.), p. 99

. . . Her books are, as she meant them to be, read and enjoyed by precisely the sort of people whom she disliked; she is a literary classic of the society which attitudes like hers, held widely enough, would undermine. . . .

To speak of this aspect of her work as "satire" is perhaps misleading. She has none of the underlying didactic intention ordinarily attributed to the satirist. Her object is not missionary; it is the more desperate one of merely finding some mode of existence for her critical attitudes. To her the first necessity was to keep on reasonably good terms with the associates of her everyday life; she had a deep need of their affection and a genuine respect for the ordered, decent civilisation that they upheld. And yet she was sensitive to their crudenesses and complacencies and knew that her real existence depended on resisting many of the values they implied. The novels gave her a way out of this dilemma. This, rather than the ambition of entertaining a posterity of urbane gentlemen, was her motive force in writing.

D. W. Harding
*Scrutiny* (March, 1940), pp. 347, 351

It was Fanny Burney who, by transposing . . . [Richardson] into educated life, made it possible for Jane Austen to absorb what he had to teach her. Here we have one of the important lines of English literary history—Richardson—Fanny Burney—Jane Austen. It is important because Jane Austen is one of the truly great writers. Not that Fanny Burney is the only other novelist who counts in her formation; she read all there was to read and took all that was useful to her—which wasn't only lessons. In fact, Jane Austen, in her indebtedness to others, provides an exceptionally illuminating study of the nature of originality, and she exemplifies beautifully the relations of "the individual talent" to tradition. If the influences bearing on her hadn't comprised something fairly to be called tradition she couldn't have found herself and her true direction; but her relation to tradition is a creative one. She not only makes tradition for those coming after, but her achievement has for us a retroactive effect: as we look back beyond her we see in what goes before, and see because of her, potentialities and significances brought out in such a way that, for us, she creates the tradition we see leading down to her. Her work, like the work of all great creative writers, gives a meaning to the past. [1948]

F. R. Leavis
*The Great Tradition* (New York: George Stewart, n.d.), pp. 4-5

. . . There is no longer . . . any excuse for thinking of Jane Austen as an untutored genius or even as a kind aunt with a flair for telling stories that have somehow or other continued to charm. She was a serious and conscious writer, absorbed in her art, wrestling with its problems. Casting and recasting her material, transferring whole novels from letter to narrative form, storing her subject-matter with meticulous economy, she had the great artist's concern with form and presentation. There is nothing soft about her.

Arnold Kettle
*An Introduction to the English Novel*, vol. I
(London: Hutchinson, 1951), p. 90

The fact is that parody has always been, for Jane Austen, the simplest reaction to feeling, the easiest irony. If she is older (*Sense and Sensibility* was revised for publication as late as her thirty-sixth year) and in general more seriously responsive to her medium, she still maintained her decisive remoteness from feeling. In her impulse to parody, Jane Austen hardly differs now from the precocious author of "Love and Friendship." In this she has not changed because she has had no reason to change. The first change and novelty is in her *handling* of parody; in her forced yielding to social convention, in the direct and unequivocal disapproval with which she circumscribes her amusement, and assures her readers that feeling— at least an excess of it—is not merely amusing, but morally wrong. Marianne, we are informed again and again, is, more than an object of irony, a very bad example.

Marvin Mudrick
*Jane Austen. Irony as Defense and Discovery* (Princeton, N. J.:
Princeton Univ. Pr., 1952), pp. 62-63

She knew exactly what she was doing. Perfection is not obtained by blundering, and even if it were, to blunder into perfection in six consecutive works would be inconceivable. Miss Austen was a highly sophisticated artist. That her life was retired is quite beside the point. Because her subject matter is in a sense trivial . . . it must not blind us to the fact that she is . . . the most forthright moralist in English. . . .

   In some respects, she was the last and finest flower of that century at its quintessential. She had escaped entirely the infection of sensibility and sentimentality; for her those qualities are material only for her satire. She is never for one moment soft in any way; indeed, there is no more intransigent, ruthless novelist in the world. She knew her limits, and the violence and crude high-spirited horseplay of the first novelists of the century are outside them.

Walter Allen
*The English Novel* (New York: E. P. Dutton, 1955), p. 115

# THOMAS LOVELL BEDDOES

## 1803-1849

Son of the celebrated Dr. Beddoes, experimental scientist, revolutionist, and physician to Southey, Coleridge, and other eminent contemporaries, Thomas Lovell Beddoes was born at Clifton, spent his childhood in Malvern and Bath, and vacationed in Ireland at the home of his novelist aunt Maria Edgeworth. His poetic genius, his grotesque humor, and his taste for the macabre were manifest in his behavior and in the early tales of terror he wrote at school, probably before he was fifteen. The publication of *The Bride's Tragedy* in 1823, while he was still at Oxford, made the promise of his genius the talk of the town. The less successful *Romance of the Lily* appeared the following year, but the public saw no more of his work for the remainder of his life. In 1825, he departed for Germany to study medicine, and although he returned to England from time to time, taking his M.A. at Oxford in 1828, he never settled in his homeland again. In Germany, he became interested in liberal politics, and when deported as a revolutionist, he took up residence in Zurich, where he continued his political activities and the practical jokes for which he had become notorious. He continued to write poems and plays which he could never bring to completion, and he attempted numerous revisions of *Death's Jest-Book*, which he failed to get published. Depressed and ill during his last years, he wandered about Germany and Switzerland until 1849. On January 26 of that year, he was found dead in his room. The medical report released forty years later pronounced his death suicide by poison. The products of his literary efforts—mainly fragments of projected plays—are *The Improvisatore* (1821); *The Bride's Tragedy* (1822); *The Romance of the Lily* (1823); *Torrismond* (1824); *The Second Brother* (1825?); *Pygmalion* (1825); *Death's Jest-Book* (1825-1837); *Dream Pedlary* (ca. 1829); and *The Ivory Gate* (1837).

H. W. Donner, ed., *The Works* (1935)

R. H. Snow, *Thomas Lovell Beddoes* (1928)

. . . It is precisely upon the stage that such faults of construction as those which disfigure Beddoes' tragedies matter least. An audience, whose attention is held and delighted by a succession of striking incidents clothed in splendid speech, neither cares nor knows whether the effect of the whole, as a whole, is worthy of the separate parts. It would be foolish, in the present melancholy condition of the art of dramatic declamation, to wish for the public performance of *Death's Jest-Book*; but it is impossible not to hope that the time may come when an adequate representation of that strange and great work may be something more than a possibility more thin than air. Then, and then only, shall we be able to take true measure of Beddoes' genius. . . . [1907]

Lytton Strachey
*Books and Characters* (New York: Harcourt,
Brace, 1922), pp. 257-58

Impregnated to the innermost core of his being with that form of moral disquietude which the weak and nervous creatures of all nations had experienced, he owed it to his temper, where the germs of disorder were deeper and more organic, to remain attuned to it, in an epoch during which the spirit no longer blew that way. His work, unequal in many respects, retains, however, a pathetic and touching interest. Several of his lyrical poems have an inspired flow, a poignant melancholy, which recall a Shelley. His best drama, *Death's Jest Book,* is perhaps the most astonishing miracle

of that intuitive divination which revived the spirit of the Elizabethan theatre among certain privileged writers of the nineteenth century. And if the
daring of the imagination, the spontaneously figurative quality of the language, the ease and strength of the rhythm, are made more intricate by a
restless intellectual research, this philosophical preoccupation is brought
into harmony with the passionate flight of an untrammelled genius, as in the
work of a contemporary of Shakespeare. [1927, rev. 1935]

Louis Cazamian
*A History of English Literature* (New York:
Macmillan, 1938), p. 1205

It is rather easy—and on the whole not fair—to condescend to *The Bride's
Tragedy*. There is mawkishness in it and over-emphasis, passages which
must be ignored if the flavour of what is good is to be appreciated. But
when Beddoes is at his best, he soars on broad, eagle wings. The scene of
Hesperus in the tapestried chamber need be apologetic to few. The business
of the moth is sheer inspiration, with the glimpse of tenderness amidst
anguish which it gives, and then the bursting out again of mental tumult in
the cry, "Choak her, moth, choak her"—the last thing he had in mind as
he put gentle hand between moth and flame! It is the tragedy of Beddoes
that his great things are inextricably tangled with his weak, that so often
one must use the phrase "fine things as there are" with the adder's tail of a
qualifying clause dragging after. . . .

It is of . . . lurid stuff that *Death's Jest Book* is made. And through it
all there is an incandescence of fierce language, and the daring metaphors
blaze with the sparkle of black stars before the bright glow of hell. In the
orderly sequence of the history of literature the play has no place; it belongs to no school and no period. Written in the nineteenth century its
language has, by right divine and not artifice, the fine unexpectedness of
the days of Elizabeth. Possessed of the verve of such robust and healthy
times, it is saturated with the grotesque and pessimistic diabolism of the
Germany of E. T. A. Hoffman. From its debris the disciples of Freud might
quarry unmentionable images. And, combining such elements, it was written by an Englishman who died in the reign of Victoria. It is unique.

But also, as a play, it has certain clearly marked limitations. Its brilliance
is akin to that of a diamond crushed under a pile-driver—scattered, chaotic,
begrimed, but still there and sparkling. Yet, despite all the diamond dust
that is in it, the play suffers from an excess of plain plaster. It is patched
and built, and the final edifice is a rickety one. Tediums encroach upon
intensities, a growth of rhetoric chokes the poetic, the plot often eddies
rather than flows; beside men firm of intent are others merely gesticulatory,
and women who do nothing but simper. So that in the last analysis, Bed-

does, who in individual scenes may take rank with Webster as a master of sombre intensities, has written a play which is chaotic and ineffectual.

R. H. Snow
*Thomas Lovell Beddoes. Eccentric and Poet* (New York:
Covici-Friede, 1928), pp. 44-45, 100-101

Sid Edmund Gosse points out as Beddoes's worst weakness "his inability to record conversation," and to distinguish his stage figures by the language allotted to them, nor would it be easy to discover in *Death's Jest Book* any weighty exceptions to this just remonstrance. But where is an explanation? Beddoes *could* record conversation—outside *Death's Jest Book*; we turn to his letters and we find one of the most spirited sketches of talk ever made:

> Capital was my first adventure in 1835 at Dover. London Coffee house, old gentleman in coffee room. Waiter, says I, I wish to smoke a cigar, have you a smoking room? *W.* No occasion, Sir, you can smoke here. *I* (*to O.G.*) Perhaps it may be disagreeable to you, Sir, in which case—— *O.G.* by no means. I'm myself a smoker (laying aside specs, and looking like Cosmogony Jenkins ——) *I.* I have good cigars, will you d.m.t.f. to accept one? *O.G.* Very kind. *I.* Come from Calais? *O.G.* Boulogne. Go to Bristol. *I.* Anche io sono Bristoliano. *O.G.* Know King? *I.* Wife my aunt. *O.G.* Are YOU? *I.* Son of well-known physician at Clifton. *O.G.* Not of D^r B.? *I.* Same, unworthily, *O.G.* That's curious. Your brother married my niece a fortnight ago. *I.* Happy man! Hear of it now for y^e first time. Tories will never be my heirs. *O.G.* O! G——! (reassumes specs and exit.) *I.* I! *exeo.*

That plainness, and artfulness, and quickness are the antipodes of the lugubrious and long speeches in *Death's Jest Book*—those prodigious passages which recall a description of Coleridge's conversation—"monopollylogues." Among these the painstaking reader discovers expressions of the Beddoes that might have been. Here are the enchanting songs . . . and here too are startling moments such as when the scientist in Beddoes speaks. Isbrand's soliloquy at the beginning of Act V is perhaps the best known and the most reverberant of these.

Edmund Blunden
*Votive Tablets* (London: Cobden Sanderson, 1931), pp. 294-95

Beddoes is no understudy of Shelley; he is often more like Edgar Allan Poe; often his words are parted, by that thinnest film which makes all the difference, from a pure series of beautiful sounds. *Dream-Pedlary,* and several of his lyrics, have this character. Many of them occur in his plays: the *Bride's Tragedy* (1822), the *Second Brother,* and *Torrismond*. Another tragedy, *Death's Jest-Book,* Beddoes kept on the stocks for years and never completed. None of these are really plays; the characters are fantastic, but the poetry is again and again magnificent.

Oliver Elton
*The English Muse* (London: G. Bell, 1933), p. 338

. . . On 24 August 1829, the Pro-Rector of Göttingen University had recommended to his colleagues on the University Court that the sentence of relegation, pronounced on Beddoes, should take the most lenient form and be communicated to him as gently as possible, because he had learned from several sources that Beddoes had lately shown a tendency to spleen and even tried to commit suicide. From about this time dates his beautiful philosophy, which teaches that there is one source of all spiritual existence, the soul of the universe itself, and that the thirst for knowledge (so ardently sought by Beddoes all his life) is nothing but the desire of the individual to return to the home of his birth. The search for truth is thus identical with the wish to die, and the greater is the spiritual part within us, the more intense must be our wish to be reunited with that spring of spiritual power from which our lives flow like sparkling rivulets.

Beddoes is above all others the poet of death. Nobody has arrayed her (for Death had been revealed to him as a warm and tender mother) in such alluring beauty, nobody has clad physical corruption in such unspeakable horror, nobody spoken with such nostalgic longing of the death he was himself to seek so persistently. . . .

Procter and Bourne decided against immediate publication [of *Death's Jestbook*], requesting the author in the meanwhile for substantial revision. Only Kelsall, with better knowledge of Beddoes' retiring pride, wanted to see the play published at once, although even he could not withhold his disappointment in the weakness of the character-drawing.

In a sense the critics were right also, from their point of view. *Death's Jest-Book* was not what [his friends] . . . had a right to expect from the literary progeny whose début more than six years before had been proclaimed superior to that of Chatterton and Keats. And Procter at any rate must have felt some responsibility for his protégé. The faults of Beddoes' performance were glaring enough. The plot was as complicated and confused as ever. The dialogue was impossible. All the characters seem to declaim into the void, and none answer the others. There is no individualization, and this was the reason why Beddoes had been able seemingly without effort to incorporate parts of older plays. It was all his own drama, his own wrestling with the problems of the spirit, problems unsolved. For Beddoes himself had not noticed that his idea remained at cross-purposes with the action of the play, his elaborate Elizabethan plot at war with the central theme. He had failed to find, in Mr. Eliot's phrase, "the objective correlative of his thought." . . . It is undeniable that Beddoes' sense of fun, too, fed on queer food sometimes and is not even yet always recognized by critics except under the name of the grotesque, for from his earliest infancy his mind had so familiarized itself with skulls and crossbones that he derived infinite amusement from tossing them about like custard pies in a slap-stick comedy.

H. W. Donner
*Plays and Poems of Thomas Lovell Beddoes* (Cambridge, Mass.:
Harvard Univ. Pr., 1950), pp. xi-xii, xl-xli

Now that scholarship has rent the veil which Victorian propriety laid over his eccentricities, his practical jokes, his foreign residence, his suicide, it becomes possible to see Beddoes not only as a very complicated, talented, and difficult man, as his contemporaries saw him (and as he certainly was), but as they could not see him—a man deeply troubled, pursued by guilt, yet at the same time a poet with a basic logic to his work which even today eludes many readers. Death and flowers remain [his chief imagery], but they are not incidental. Beddoes' flowers do not grow in haphazard profusion along the roadside of his poetry, to be gathered at random and pressed into anthologies and specimen booklets; they are the road itself, of his ideas. As with all good poets, his images are wedded to his conceptions, his themes—just how well wedded, has rarely been recognized. . . .

C. A. Hoyt
*SN* (1963), p. 85

# WILLIAM BLAKE

1757-1827

Born in London, William Blake was the son of an established hosier who could afford him a modest education. Blake studied at Parr's Drawing School, was apprenticed to an engraver, studied briefly at the Royal Academy, and conducted an engraving business of his own. At the age of four, he experienced the first of his mystic visions, which were to recur throughout his life and serve as inspiration for many of his poems. His brother Robert, who was born in 1762, became Blake's closest companion, his co-worker, his patient when he fell ill, and, after his death in 1787, the subject of several of Blake's visions. Against his father's objections, Blake was married in 1787 to Catherine Boucher, an illiterate but intelligent girl whom he taught to read, write, engrave, and color his plates. Only one volume of his verse, *Poetical Sketches* (1783), was published professionally; the rest were engraved and illustrated in his own shop. For a brief period he became the resident-guest at Felpham of his friend and patron Dr. Hayley. But after a frustrating experience there, he returned to London to live and work in poverty for the remainder of his life. He died August 12, 1827 and was buried at Bunhill Fields in an unmarked common grave. His reputation, which was slow in the making, is firmly based today on his remarkable prophetic compositions and on his inspired blending of the arts of painting and poetry in works such as *Songs of Innocence* (1787-1789); *The Book of Thel* (1789); *Tiriel* (ca. 1789); *The French Revolution* (1791); *The Marriage of Heaven and Hell* (1793); *Songs of Experience* (1789-1794); *Visions of the Daughters of Albion* (1793); *America* (1793); *Europe: A Prophecy* (1794); *The First Book of Urizen* (1794); *The Book of Los* (1795); *Vala*, or *The Four Zoas* (1795-1804); *The Mental Traveller* (ca. 1803); *Milton* (1804-1808); *Jerusalem* (1804-1820).

Geoffrey Keynes, ed., *The Complete Writings* (1925; 1957), 3 vols.
Mona Wilson, *Life of William Blake* (1927, rev. 1949)

## PERSONAL

Blake had a full passionate nature, which made vehement demands. Like us all he had his prematrimonial notions which were quickly upset by his matrimonial experiences. The final adjustments were made, but not without a good deal of pain on both sides. The vehement demands of Blake's nature worked in two directions, and besides a difficult matrimonial adjustment to effect, he was forced to consider sex in all its ramifications, and finally to enunciate a doctrine of sex, which has proved a great deliverance to the modern world.

Charles Gardner
*Vision and Vesture* (New York: E. P. Dutton, 1916), pp. 31-32

There is little independent record of Catherine Blake, nor is it neeeded. No one can understand Blake's life without being aware of the significance of her helpful and faithful figure, nor is it possible to think of him with a different type of wife without loss, even without the utter destruction of the fabric of his life. And what other test is there of a perfect marriage? If the early lyrics show that at first there had been dissensions the greater the victory for love and imagination. Blake's own words but prove that the doubts and mental distress, which had for a time clouded his life, had cast a shadow over hers also, and that they were both the freer and the happier for his renewed confidence in himself. His love for her was no selfish dependence, the love "that drinks another as a sponge drinks water," but that friendship of which he speaks so often as outlasting sexual love. The woman who had signed her name with a cross in the marriage register at Battersea Church had learnt from him, aided by her own love and belief in him, to share his work and to be his constant stay in spiritual as well as in material things. Even when he was away from her in a visionary Paradise, her bodily presence was necessary to him. Her life was one with his. [1927]

Mona Wilson<br>
The Life of William Blake (London: P. Davies, 1932), p. 297

Blake's mind was so sentitively strung as, in intercourse with others, to give immediate response to the right appeals. All speak of his conversation as most interesting, nay, enchanting to hear. Copious and varied, the fruit of great, but not morbid, intellectual activity, it was, in its ordinary course, full of mind, sagacity, and varied information. Above all, it was something quite different from that of other men: conversation which carried you "from earth to heaven and back again, before you knew where you were." Even a young girl would feel the fascination, though sometimes finding his words wild and hard to follow. To conventional minds, it often seemed a mixture of divinity, blasphemy, and licence; but a mixture, not even by them, to be quickly forgotten. In a walk with a sympathetic listener, it seldom flagged. He would have something pertinent to say about most objects they chanced to pass, were it but a bit of old wall. And such as had the privilege of accompanying him in a country walk felt their perception of natural beauty greatly enhanced. Nature herself seemed strangely more spiritual. Blake's mind warmed his listener's, kindled his imagination; almost creating in him a new sense. Nor was his enjoyment of all that is great in art, of whatever school or time, less genuine and vivid; notwithstanding an appearance to the contrary in some passages of his writings, where, in doing battle energetically for certain great principles, random blows not a few, on either side the mark, came down on unoffending heads; or where, in the consciousness that a foolish world had insisted on raising the less great above the greatest, he delighted to make matters even by thrusting them as much too far below. [1863; rev. 1942]

Alexander Gilchrist<br>
Life of William Blake, ed. Ruthven Todd (London:<br>
J. M. Dent, 1942), pp. 310-11

William Blake, of all poets perhaps the most single-minded, with the most stubborn integrity, remains also the poet of strangest mixtures, both grand transmutations and partial compounds. His attempt to achieve a poetic content that would, through an original mythology, synthesize the contraries of a visionary temperament and a social intelligence, and would not only relate but equate his two fundamental impulses—the evangelical and the humanitarian—is the root of his problem as a poet. He sought to dramatize the *singleness* of salvation—spiritual and social, inner and outer, the problem in which most modern thinkers still find only irredeemable polarities.

To trace the dialectic of innocence and experience, he tried to express (and to correct) the ideas of political thinkers like Paine and Godwin in the vocabulary of religious thinkers like Boehme and Swedenborg. The product of this effort is sometimes beautiful, sometimes merely grotesque, and often both grotesque and beautiful.

Mark Schorer
*William Blake. The Politics of Vision* (New York:
Henry Holt, 1946), p. 3

## Songs of Innocence

Blake was thirty years of age when he began to write the *Songs of Innocence*. This seems to be the astounding fact; for the *Songs of Innocence* express for the first time in English literature the spontaneous happiness of childhood. Now nothing in the whole world of emotion is of lighter texture than the happiness of a child. Like the dew, it vanishes with the first rays of the sun, and its essential quality, spontaneity, is a thing never to be recalled. . . .

The spontaneity of these songs is the spontaneity of art, not of nature, of imagination and not of experience. Nothing but the purest imagination could give so stainless an image. The spontaneity of a child is so elusive it escapes the faintest touch of self-consciousness and, but for Blake, might never have been brought into the realm of art. Its pure expression has never been made before or since. . . . Blake is universal; he expressed the natural delight in life of every happy child in the world. The cry of his "Little Boy Lost" is the cry of every child at the first discovery of loneliness.

Max Plowman
*An Introduction to the Study of Blake* (New York:
E. P. Dutton, 1927), pp. 34-35

## The Little Black Boy

This is one of the most beautiful and most characteristic of Blake's lyrics, and while the meaning is not quite on the surface, neither is it very deeply buried.

Blake is still far from the great myth developed in his prophetic books, where giants and genii thunder forth his mind, but he begins in these deeper songs to put his problems into the mouths of children. From the little black boy and the chimney sweeper those who have ears to hear may gather wisdom. . . . The poem begins with the Mother and ends with the Father, the earthly mother and the heavenly Father. It is an earlier and certainly much more poetic form of the doctrinal poem "To Tirzah" in "Experience," and here reflects Blake's phrase in "Jerusalem" . . . "O holy Generation" (in this case mother-love-and-care), "Image of regeneration." Again it represents the return to earth of the "Piper," for the Father in the last illustration is symbolically represented as being on earth. So that, simple and beautiful as is its surface meaning, it expresses much below the surface which is certainly not less beautiful.

Joseph Wicksteed
*Blake's Innocence and Experience* (New York:
E. P. Dutton, 1928), p. 111

Life growing up in this world forces nature to become younger, but any life or imagination which lingers in Beulah tends to become more helpless and infantile, and its imaginative environment grows in proportion more broodingly maternal. This is the world presented in the *Songs of Innocence*. There the divine imagination is an infant, symbolized in Christianity by the infant Jesus, the gentle and innocent Lamb of God. God from this perspective is a loving Father who sees the sparrow fall. Nature is a kindly old nurse, and a vigilant Providence appoints guardian angels to take care of the children. As is appropriate to the state of Beulah, it is especially in sleep and repose that these guardians are invoked. Here we find the harmonious society which the single organism represents in this world. All the forces of nature help to find lost children; glowworms are beacons to bewildered ants; and as in Isaiah, the lion lies down with the lamb and all animals are children's pets. The world of imagination in its pitying, tender, sympathetic and feminine aspect is in *The Book of Thel* as well as the *Songs of Innocence*; but the world of Mary and Susan and Emily is a world not of the unborn but of real children. Now real children are not symbols of innocence: the *Songs of Innocence* would be intolerably sentimental if they were.

Northrop Frye
*Fearful Symmetry* (Princton, N. J.: Princton Univ. Pr., 1947), p. 235

## The Book of Thel

Though *Thel* is essentially uncomplicated, it begins with the cryptic "Motto" from which most misinterpretations of the entire poem stem. . . . On the literal level the first two questions make fairly good sense; certainly one does not ask a denizen of the air about the characteristics of the nether world; one asks the mole. Blake's point, however, is that one does not ask about experiences at all; one must experience experience. "Understanding or Heaven . . . is acquired by means of Suffering & Distress & Experience," he wrote (*Annotations to Swedenborg*, 89). Thel's great tragedy is that she feels she can learn by merely asking, and then, satisfied in her new-found knowledge,

> . . . gentle sleep the sleep of death, and gentle hear the voice
> Of him that walketh in the garden in the evening time.

Blake thought this folly, not wisdom, and if *Thel* is read carefully, an embryonic hypocrite, like Tiriel, can be seen here succumbing to the curse that is the product of his own false wisdom. . . .

*The Book of Thel* is not another song of innocence, then, and Thel herself assumes a gloomier aspect than her many admirers have seen fit to allow. The fact is that Thel is proud, is indeed a prototypical Tiriel, or the early Heva (before her retreat to the vales of Har). . . .

R. F. Gleckner
*The Piper and the Bard* (Detroit: Wayne State Univ. Pr.,
1959), pp. 161-62

The great vehicle for symbolizing "the descent of the whole rational soul" is the Persephone myth. It is, of course, one of the archetypal nature myths of the world, but the Neoplatonists were not interested in its relation to the change of seasons. . . . Since the Neoplatonists' concern is primarily religious, Blake was probably interested immediately in their allegorical applications of the story, and he also saw in the myth an analogue to the Christian myth of the Fall. His interest probably stems from [Thomas] Taylor's *Eleusinian and Bacchic Mysteries*, approximately the first half of which is devoted to the Persephone myth. *Thel* and *Visions of the Daughters of Albion*, two of the early Prophetic Books, reinterpret carefully, though obscurely, the pagan myth. . . .

The silver rod [in *Thel*] is a symbol of the phallus, and the golden bowl represents the vulva. Does not intellectual strength come to man from the sex act? Blake asks. Does not love (i.e., the sex act) have, like intellect, a sacred origin and so belong in the same golden bowl? "Yes" is the answer to both questions; they are but variations on the same theme. Significantly, both the bowl and the phallus were important symbols in the Mystery rites. The bowl, one of the two vessels used by the initiate, was "sacred to the soul" and symbolic of intellect. The phallus, one of the four mystic objects last disclosed to the candidate, symbolized a recognition of the cathartic value of the fulfillment of sexual desire. Thel fled from this desire, but the less timid Oothoon (of the *Visions*), to whom passion appeared as a flower, plucked it. . . .

George Mills Harper
*The Neoplatonism of William Blake* (Chapel Hill, N. C.:
Univ. North Carolina Pr., 1961), pp. 246-47, 253

## The Marriage of Heaven and Hell

Take the case of Urizen. Blake had spent much time before he came to the writing of *The Marriage of Heaven and Hell* in trying to define that mental power which circumscribed the mind of man. He had conceived of a universal Poetic Genius as the source of being—a power which, while it permeated all life might yet be described as "the true Man." To balance this conception, he needed a contrary principle to express the obvious limitation which this power suffers; and at first he seems to have been content to call it "Reason." In *The Marriage of Heaven and Hell* Reason and Desire are the contrasted powers; but it appears to me that before he reached the conclusion of his great manifesto, the absence of precise correspondence with his thought which the word Reason conveyed, and the extraneous connotation it inevitably called up, had begun to impress him; so that when he leaves the pedestrian road of prose and finds his native freedom in *A Song of Liberty* (which is, without doubt, an integral part of *The Marriage of Heaven and Hell*), a personification appears, later identified as Urizen, simply to give more precise definition to the principle of life which is eternal limitation.

Max Plowman
*An Introduction to the Study of Blake* (New York:
E. P. Dutton, 1927), p. 32

. . . This prose-poem is one of the best first-hand introductions to Blake's ideas for him who wishes to pursue them farther, and wonderful fun at the very least for anyone who learns to read it. In *The Marriage* we see Blake at a crucial stage of his development, announcing, in the exultant mood of a man who has at last grasped a long-sought truth, the revolutionary philosophical bases of the apocalypse he saw augured in the American and French revolutions. Here is also the Blake we so admire in "The Tyger," building his ideas, their relationships, into the very structure of the work itself. And here he performs as well the almost impossible feat of writing a robustly humorous satire of his fallen idol Swedenborg from a point of view even more visionary than that of Swedenborg himself.

*The Marriage* has, to be sure, been quoted more often than almost any other work of the period, and it has been widely admired. But for all this, it has been misunderstood in varying degrees even by Blake scholars, and admired as something it is not, a brilliant fragment—a "scrapbook" one writer has called it—propounding the doctrine that man's salvation lies in the free play of energy. *The Marriage* . . . is a shapely masterpiece, fully realizing a well-defined intention; its quotable phrases are parts of a unified form which embodies a complex of ideas, of which the concept of energy is only one. . . .

*The Marriage* moves, like Blake's great epics—and indeed his prophetic lyric "The Tyger"—toward an apocalyptic conclusion, but in the last part there sounds a slightly less positive note, in the shift back to ironic point of view in which anyone who embraces energy becomes a "devil." It reminds one of Beethoven's tempering the positive resolution of his song cycle, *An die Ferne Geliebte,* by a brief snatch of its plaintive first theme. Perhaps even in the exultant mood in which Blake wrote *The Marriage,* he was not quite sure that the oppositions of this world could in fact become the contraries of the mental war.

And, indeed, the great synthesis of *The Marriage* was not to be a final one. Blake found that the dialectics of his initial formulation of the doctrine of contraries, in which he would simply transform into fruitful contraries all oppositions now splitting this world, could not bring about the Eden he envisaged for man. After his initial excitement at the possibilities suggested by such a synthesis had lessened somewhat, he no doubt saw that the intellectual battles of an Edenic mental war of art and science were not to be fought as long as corporeal wars were waged by "spectres" such as George III. Evidently something very like evil did after all have a real existence, though it was still not what the religious call evil. And accordingly we find Blake becoming more uncompromisingly apocalyptic, demanding a more radical revolution in the modes of thought and life.

Martin K. Nurmi
*Blake's Marriage of Heaven and Hell* (Kent, Ohio:
Kent State Univ., 1957), pp. iii, 61

*The Marriage of Heaven and Hell* assaults what Blake termed a "cloven fiction" between empirical and a priori procedure in argument. In content, the *Marriage* compounds ethical and theological "contraries"; in form it mocks the categorical techniques that seek to make the contraries appear as "negations." The unity of the *Marriage* is in itself dialectical, and cannot be grasped except by the mind in motion, moving between the Blakean contraries of discursive irony and mythical visualization. . . .

The specific difficulty in reading *The Marriage of Heaven and Hell* is to mark the limits of its irony: where does Blake speak straight? . . .

Not that Blake mocks himself; only that he mocks the Corporeal Understanding (including his own) and refuses unto death to cease setting traps for it. There is, in consequence, a true way of reading Blake, put forward by Blake himself, a first-class critic of his own works. But this is a true way which, as Kafka once remarked of true ways in general, is like a rope stretched several inches above the ground, put there not to be walked upon but to be tripped over. . . .

Blake states the law of his dialectic:

> Without Contraries is no progression. Attraction and Repulsion, Reason and Energy, Love and Hate, are necessary to Human existence.

The key here is *Human*, which is both descriptive and honorific. This is a dialectic without transcendence, in which heaven and hell are to be married but without becoming altogether one flesh or one family. By the "marriage" of contraries Blake means only that we are to cease valuing one contrary above the other in any way. . . .

The *Marriage* preaches the risen body breaking bounds, exploding upwards into psychic abundance. But here Blake is as earnest as Lawrence, and will not tolerate the vision of recurrence. . . . The altogether human escapes cycle, evades irony, cannot be categorized discursively. But Blake is unlike Lawrence, even where they touch. The Angel teaches light without heat, the vitalist—or Devil—heat without light; Blake wants both, hence the marriage of contraries.

Harold Bloom
*PMLA* (December, 1958), p. 501

## The Tyger; Songs of Experience

. . . We know that he had never seen a tiger in the forests, and one would almost say, if one judged by the illustration, that he had never seen one, where they were in those days kept, at the Tower. As one looks at the quaint creature in the design, one almost wishes that Blake had chosen to paint its purely spiritual form as he painted the ghost of a flea. But he had tried to portray the smile of the Deity on its lips, and to show the ultimate "humanity divine" of Nature's most terrific beast—unless it is best to regard the whole design as a mask, deriding those who expect upon a mortal page the picture of the Deity at work.

Joseph Wicksteed
*Blake's Innocence and Experience* (New York:
E. P. Dutton, 1928), p. 193

Blake's famous Song of Experience, *The Tyger* raises the cosmic question: How can the tiger of experience and the lamb of innocence be grasped as the contraries of a single "fearful symmetry"? The answer, suggested in the question form, is that the very process of the creation of the tiger brings about the condition of freedom in which his enemies (his prey) become his friends, as angels become devils in *The Marriage*. The tiger in Blake's illustration of this poem is notoriously lacking in ferocity, and critics have sometimes concluded that Blake was unable to "seize the fire" required to draw a fearful tiger. He could at least have tried, but he is showing us the final tiger, who has attained the state of organized innocence as have the adjacent lions and tigers of *The Little Girl Lost* and *The Little Girl Found* who demonstrated that "wolvish howl" and "lions' growl" and "tygers wild" are not to be feared. . . .

Blake had no difficulty drawing a fearful werewolf . . . or for that matter a fearful *flea*. But his tiger is not even baring its fangs.

David V. Erdman
*Blake: Prophet Against Empire* (Princeton, N. J.:
Princeton Univ. Pr., 1954), pp. 179-80, 180n

"The Tyger" is a poem of rather simple form, clearly and cleanly proportioned, all of its statements contributing to a single, sustained, dramatic gesture. . . . But Blake warns us that there is a great gulf between simplicity and insipidity. The total force of the poem comes not only from its immediate rhetorical power but also from its symbolical structure.

Blake's image of the tiger, at first sensuous, is to continued inspection symbolic. Things which burn brightly, even tigers, can be thought of as either purifying something or being purified. In the dark of night, in a forest, a tiger's eyes would seem to burn. The tiger's coat suggests this same conflagration. In any case, Blake is trying to establish a brilliance about his image which he elsewhere associates, not surprisingly, with the apocalyptic figure of his minor prophecies, Orc. . . . There are many examples of the same imagery throughout the prophecies. Another visual image which Blake may be suggesting here is consistent with what we shall see in the nature of the tiger itself. In many religious paintings (and in Blake's own work, the popularly mistitled "Glad Day," for example) the central figure seems to be emerging from or surrounded by a vast light: figuratively he "burns." Visually the fire image suggests immediate violence; traditionally it suggests some sort of purgatorial revelation. . . .

The tiger . . . is presented ambiguously. In spite of its natural viciousness, it also suggests clarity and energy. If the reader has had prolonged experience with poetry and mythology, other associations will sharpen these ideas. He will perhaps associate the "forests of the night" with the traditional dark night or dark journey of the soul through the dens of demons and beasts. The tiger's brightness may suggest the force which the sun so often symbolizes in mythology. If the reader has read Dante, he may associate the forests with Dante's descent from the dark wood into the underworld. . . . Finally, if he has read Blake's own body of work, he will know that since the fall of man was a fall into a material world, he may associate the night with matter. In forests in the darkness men are trapped in an enclosure similar to Plato's cave, hobbled by the growing rubbish of materialism, blocked off from light by material substance. Men stand in forests surrounded by webs of leaves, limbs, vines, and bracken (Blake's illustrations provide ample evidence for such a symbolic interpretation of fallen life). [1960]

Hazard Adams
*William Blake: A Reading of the Shorter Poems* (Seattle, Wash.:
Univ. Washington Pr., 1963), pp. 58-59

I consider an identification of the speaker in the poem to be the most crucial problem for interpretation because unless we understand his character we are unable to evaluate what he sees and says. It should be clear that he is not the omniscient Bard of the "Introduction" to *Songs of Experience* "Who Present, Past, and Future sees," because he has too many questions. Nowhere in the poem is he able to provide even such enigmatic answers to his questions as are possible for the speaker of "The Fly.". . . The speaker's questions sometimes express outrage comparable to that felt by Earth in "Earth's Answer." This awestruck voice in *Experience* is that of an average but also imaginative man who is almost overwhelmed by the mysterious prodigy he sees as a Tyger. In Blake's prophetic terminology, he belongs to the class of men called the "Redeemed.". . . What Blake's speaker sees and reacts to is a compound of truth and error which produces mystery. For the reader who achieves prophetic perspective, the primary focus of interest in the poem is on the speaker as *subject* and on the *Tyger* as *percept*, rather than as object. . . .

What Wicksteed and Erdman certainly establish is that the depicted Tyger is no accident and that it deliberately does not exist on the same level as the Tyger envisioned in the poem. Wicksteed's initial suggestions are not very convincing, however; the Tyger's mouth is not smiling, in fact its lined face suggests worry, and there is certainly nothing depicted which resembles the enigmatic smile the creator may have smiled, according to the poem. As for the Tyger's depicting the "humanity divine," strictly speaking, the Tyger would have to be even more heroic, as well as human, than the one suggested by the *poem* in order to reflect the Edenic state. . . .

John E. Grant
*Discussions of William Blake* (Boston:
D. C. Heath, 1961), pp. 65-66, 76-77

## The Four Zoas

*The Four Zoas* is a transitional poem in which Blake developed and expanded his earlier ideas through an elaboration and a deepening of that psychology of revolution with which he had been dealing almost from the first. Inevitably it was accompanied by a shift of emphasis from the earlier insistence on breaking the model of social convention to a more anarchistic insistence than ever on breaking the selfish human heart. If the world is to be free, men as individuals must free themselves. This was the revision, along lines already laid down, of a simple political attitude that had presumably come to seem too barren to account for the observable and infinite complexities of human nature. Yet as Blake's chosen epigraph from Ephesians testifies, he was perfectly aware that there as before he was concerned with what he believed were the sources of misery in the world, dominion and authority. "For our contention is not with the blood and the flesh, but with dominion, with authority, with the blind world-rulers of this life, with the spirit of evil in things heavenly." Things heavenly are comprised of the spirit of man, which Blake continually showed was capable of conditions both of degradation and of triumph. *The Four Zoas* is an elaborate poetic diagram that charts the course of these conditions. . . .

> Mark Schorer
> *William Blake. The Politics of Vision* (New York:
> Henry Holt, 1946), p. 312

The problem of presenting a unified vision of temporal periodicity had become clarified for Blake while writing what he finally called the *The Four Zoas*. It was probably during this part of his life that he read [Edward] Williams [translator of the "Welsh Triads"] or encountered the bardic triads in some form. Whatever he found in them to disagree with, they must have struck him as authentic in the same sense that he considered Macpherson and Chatterton authentic. He was not the least interested in documentary authenticity, but rather in the authentic original as it survived and was recreated continually in the human mind. The authentic original of Druidism which developed systematically from the central notion of cyclical recurrence was deeply involved with Blake's theme of creation, redemption, and judgment in *The Four Zoas*. The writing of this work made clear a distinction he later used in *Milton* and *Jerusalem*—a distinction between inspired, prophetic religion which united temporal process and eternal identity in one vision and its recurring distillate, "Natural Religion," which abstracted temporal process and the wheel of becoming into a false kind of absolute identity expressed in the form of theological dogma. In these later works, he called the first the "Everlasting Gospel," and the second "Druidism."

In *The Four Zoas*, he began with the conception of the cyclical pattern of natural necessity called the "Circle of Destiny"—in *Jerusalem,* "Divine Analogy"—and the problem of temporal recurrence dominated the work. Like the Druids, he recognized the larger cycle which contained man's historical destiny from Adam to Luther and included what he later called the "Twenty-Seven Heavens" and their "Churches." He also recognized the lesser lunar cycle which contained man's individual destiny from birth to rebirth and included the phases of life outlined in *The Mental Traveller*.

Most important, however, was the constant interplay of life and death, joy and sorrow, pleasure and pain, the one contrary living off the other, yet never completely absorbing it.

Peter F. Fisher
*JEGP* (October, 1959), pp. 597-98

. . . The beauty of *The Four Zoas* is finally a function of the radiant adequacy of its form, of Blake's skill and execution. Nothing infuriated Blake more than to be told that as painter or poet he could invent, but failed in execution. For him, "Execution is only the result of Invention," and "Ideas cannot be Given but in their minutely Appropriate Words." An unfortunate effect of much Blake criticism has been to name his major poems "the Prophetic Books" as if they were something other than poems, to be read as imperfect records of some fearful revelation. . . . Blake's poems are primarily poems, literary works that will yield their meaning and beauty to any reader who will go to them as he might go to Milton or Yeats. Blake does excel all other poets in the strength and originality of his conceptual powers, but he ought not to suffer for that uniqueness. There have been great poets whose conceptual powers were not extraordinary (Spenser and Tennyson among these) and poets greater than Blake who were content to derive much of the conceptual basis of their art from tradition (Dante and Milton are the supreme examples). Blake is, of course, not completely alone in thus combining intellectual inventiveness and individuality of vision. The generations of major poets directly after him—Wordsworth and Coleridge and then Keats and Shelley—exhibit something of this remarkable imaginative autonomy, a freedom from outworn conceptualizations of reality. Like Blake, they showed more enterprise in walking naked, in casting off eighteenth century ideas of order. The useful analogues to *The Four Zoas* are not in esoteric religious traditions, but in English Romantic Poetry. . . .

Harold Bloom
*Blake's Apocalypse* (New York: Doubleday, 1963), pp. 192-93

## *Milton*

*Milton* and *Jerusalem* . . . are inseparable, and constitute a double epic, a prelude and fugue on the same subject, for *Milton* is Blake's longest, greatest and most elaborate "Preludium." The lyric "And did those feet in ancient time," which opens *Milton,* is connected even more closely with the theme of *Jerusalem,* and our hymnbooks have rechristened it accordingly. *Milton* is an individual prologue to the omen of something universal coming on. The Last Judgment lies on the distant horizon, and is prophesied in the final line of the poem; and the "Western Gate," the power to realize what the visionary sees to be real, symbolized by the Atlantic Ocean which still blots out Atlantis west of England, remains closed all through it. *Jerusalem* deals with the complementary awakening in man and the full apocalypse. One is resurrection and the other Last Judgment, corresponding to the first and second coming of Jesus. . . .

The Epilogue to the great poem is exquisitely managed. With the four Zoas sounding the trumpets of the Last Judgment in his ears, Blake falls into a swoon, and revives in his garden with his wife bending anxiously over him, and before him a singing lark and a wild thyme, the early-rising bird and the early-flowering plant of the returning spring. One thinks of an earlier William and Catherine awakening on an Easter morning with church bells ringing as the poet's dream of the triumph of Christ gives place to its audible symbol. . . .

Northrop Frye
*Fearful Symmetry* (Princeton, N. J.: Princeton Univ. Pr.,
1947), pp. 323-24, 355

*Milton* is not an easy poem to understand. It is the product of an intense struggle in Blake's own mind, a struggle complicated by his relations with Hayley at Felpham, but concerned chiefly with the question that always haunted him: how had it come about that England, once the seat of inspiration and vision, was now the dispenser of rationalism to Europe— the land of Bacon, Newton and Locke? It is with this problem that Blake is going to grapple anew in *Milton* and he is going to use Milton himself, the poet of vision writing in the century of experiment, to exteriorise this problem. . . .

Milton was himself deeply tinged with the rationalism of his age, as Blake well perceived; and the interest for us . . . is the conflict between the rational and the prophetic elements in Milton, which Blake equated with the struggle between Jehovah and Satan. Milton did not work out this conflict while on earth, and the theme of Blake's symbolic book *Milton* is the account of his second visit to earth to find "self-annihilation." But, all the same, Milton stands, with the Cambridge Platonists in protest against the growing materialism of contemporary thought. . . .

". . . now no longer divided nor at war with myself . . . ," Blake had written to Hayley in 1804, at the time he was making a final revision of *Milton*. This inner unity becomes apparent in the poem. It is more controlled; it has structure; it is free from the "torments of jealousy" which gave rise to such wild and violent imagery in the earlier epic. The imagery of *Milton,* indeed, is drawn to a surprising degree from the world of nature; observed, it is true, not with but through the eye, yet observed in its minutest particulars. It might almost be called the epic of Nature, seen *sub specie æternitatis*. For it was Nature that Milton rejected, when he rejected his sixfold emanation, his three wives and three daughters, and the redemption of Nature is a corollary of Milton's self-annihilation. Hence the sheer joy in the life of flowers, birds and insects which runs through the poem. We see that Blake had used his three years in the country to good purpose, that his eyes and ears have been alert to every natural sight and sound.

Structurally, the poem consists of a redemption narrative interspersed with long passages of mystical teaching. The narrative is about Milton, who while on earth . . . had held wrong views of sex and nature, and was unkind to his womenfolk, but has repented of his error during the hundred years he has spent in heaven, and is anxious to atone for it. He is separated from his sixfold emanation, who wanders in the abyss in torment. Now at last he casts off his spectrous reason, the power which has dominated him hitherto—and descends again into the world of vegetation to redeem his emanation.

Bernard Blackstone
*English Blake* (Cambridge Univ. Pr., 1949), pp. 134, 136, 148

. . . Milton, whom he had known and loved from childhood, was always for Blake his primary master both for the Christian epic and for his understanding of the Bible. It was Blake's habit to record his differences rather than his agreements, but even when he is most critical of Milton he shows how closely he is following him. It seems almost incredible, for instance, that the incisive comment on Milton's view of the Trinity in *The Marriage of Heaven and Hell* could have been made by a reader who did not know the *Christian Doctrine*. Besides, in every age Milton has been a political symbol as well as a poet. . . . To anyone as far left of centre as Blake, Milton was not only the last of England's major poets, but England's one major prophet as well. Blake's poem, based on his conviction that Milton not only should be "living at this hour" but actually was, is a vision of Milton as the deliverer of his people, like Milton's own Samson, or, perhaps a closer analogy, as a guardian angel, like Michael in Israel (and, according to *Lycidas*, England as well). The notion that Blake was primarily concerned to "correct" Milton's theological and domestic difficulties rests on a story of Crabb Robinson's which is much better ignored.

Northrop Frye
in *The Divine Vision*, ed. Vivian de Sola Pinto
(London: Victor Gollancz, 1957), p. 101

. . . *Milton* [is] a majestic poem centering on the necessity for the poet's own clearing of his bodily eye, the purging from his own consciousness of everything that is not imaginative. In *Milton* we meet a greater Blake than we have encountered previously, a more profound poet, chastened in rhetoric, and thoroughly in control of his subject. . . .

I would make the claim that it is a poem worthy of a place beside the Book of Job and *Paradise Regained*. One question remains: is it a theodicy in as clear a sense as they are? Does it earn its Miltonic motto: "To Justify the Ways of God to Man?" It does, if one remembers exactly how the Bard's Song, that extraordinary transfiguration of a biographic incident, finds its place in the poem. Just as *Paradise Regained* afforded Milton the opportunity to explore the Jobean problem within himself, so Blake's *Milton* allows the later poet to advance his personal solution to the problem of evil as it confronted him in his own life.

Harold Bloom<br>
Blake's Apocalypse (New York: Doubleday, 1963), pp. 302, 363

## Jerusalem

At first sight, *Jerusalem* contains less poetry than any of Blake's other works. There are stretches of splendid lamentation; there are impressive philosophical choruses; but there is nothing resembling the lyrical quality found so often in *The Four Zoas* and at times in *Milton*. *Jerusalem* is pitched in a key at once darker and more sublime. The dignity of its profound thought and the spiritual fervour set the tone. The reader's imagination, however ignorant of the meaning behind the words, is stirred continually by such lines as—

> Then the Spectre drew Vala into his bosom, magnificent,
>     terrible. . . .

Between such passages and the elaborate choruses stand a great many epigrams, which in number and force surpass even those of *The Marriage of Heaven and Hell*. Obscure as Blake's plot may be, his teachings are never in doubt. . . .

And yet, on a second consideration of this "choral tempest" as pure poetry, the effect is whole and mighty. There is a completeness to the apparent chaos which can neither be escaped nor defined. One feels as though a new, great symphony had just been heard: there are definite statements of themes, there is the struggle of interweaving voices one cannot quite follow, there are involved development-passages of huge emotional sweep and change, which finally burst forth into the triumphant apotheosis. There is a new, dark splendour, a vast breadth, a sense of towering structure. The dimensions are threefold, solid, no longer mere frescoings. Such is the literary effect; the ideas are another matter.

*Jerusalem,* then, is the last and obscurest of Blake's epics. It should not be read until the reader has a considerable familiarity with Blake's technical vocabulary. Otherwise, all the subtler embroidery on his great themes will pass unnoticed, and *Jerusalem* will appear merely as an amazing chaos. But when the casual references to the mythology are immediately recognized, *Jerusalem* will be revealed as Blake's biggest storehouse (we dare not say "vehicle") of thought, decorated with splendid passages of poetry, austere, profound, and proudly beautiful.

S. Foster Damon
*William Blake. His Philosophy and Symbols*
(London: Constable, 1924), pp. 194-95

. . . *Jerusalem* makes on the reader the initial impression of a harsh, crabbed and strident poem. Blake first planned his idea of the beautiful book in the age of high rococo, the age of Watteau and Mozart, which in such genius came perhaps as near as any other in history to realizing Blake's ideal of art as the urbanity of the city of light, a clarity of vision beyond all faith from which everything that is not humane has disappeared, a spontaneous yet disciplined speech in language, outline and melody spoken only in a world of fully conscious innocence.

Northrop Frye
*Fearful Symmetry* (Princeton, N. J.:
Princeton Univ. Pr., 1947), p. 358

*Jerusalem* is Blake's final and in many ways most beautiful book, and is more interesting to examine than *Milton.*

Margaret Rudd
*Divided Image* (London: Routledge and Kegan Paul, 1953), p. 124

Though *Jerusalem* is generally considered to be one of the most enigmatic if not chaotic works produced by a major figure in English literature, actually William Blake explains its theme and structure within the work itself. The very nature of the structure, one of interfolded growth as described on plate 98, seems to have caused critics to shy away from a sufficient consideration of the basic form of the work. . . .

The thematic unity is that of "peace without vengeance" when set in the contemporary frame of reference of "the years of Napoleon's decline and fall and of the triumph of British and German arms." In view of Blake's richness, it is not surprising that most critics have chosen to treat other aspects of *Jerusalem* than the relations between theme and structure. Even the recent and long-awaited full-length commentary on *Jerusalem* by Joseph Wicksteed slights the structure by merely describing the poem as a "manysided and all-comprehensive Epic Drama" with a male "Time-Trinity" and a female "Space-Trinity" as "structurally necessary to the plot."

Karl Kiralis
in *The Divine Vision*, ed. V. de Sola Pinto
(London: Victor Gollancz, 1957), pp. 141-43

## GENERAL

It is the peculiar merit of his verse that it really gives the impression of childlikeness and a kind of dewy freshness. One feels this in a thousand places—in such lines as those to an infant, which Swinburne regards as the loveliest he ever wrote:

> Sleep, sleep: in thy sleep
> Little sorrows sit and weep . . .

and in such stanzas as these in which the poet's song and the wild flower's song blend together to make a single melody:

> As I wander'd the forest,
> The green leaves among. . . .

The true commentary on Blake is to read him side by side with Wordsworth's *Intimations of Immortality,* where the beauty of childhood is seen frankly through the medium of memory, and there is no attempt to deny or escape the burden of experience. The result of Blake's method is in one sense curiously paradoxical. He was himself the sincerest of poets; his faculty of immediate contact is perfectly genuine, and yet the mood induced in most readers is one perilously akin to affectation. We feel the aërial transparency and the frail loveliness of his inspiration, and for a moment and by a kind of ritualistic self-purgation we may identify ourselves with his mood—but only for a while and at rare intervals. For the most part a little investigation will detect a slight note of insincerity in our enjoyment, and, having discovered this, we fall back on the poets who accept fully the experience of the human heart. We find something closer to our understanding, something for that reason wholesome, in men like Wordsworth and Goethe—perhaps even in the more formal poets of Blake's own age. For after all it is not the office of the true poet to baffle the longing heart with charms of self-deception, and we are men in a world of men. The unmitigated admiration and the effective influence of Blake are to be found not among the greater romantic writers of the early nineteenth century, but among the lesser men—Rossetti, Swinburne, and their school—who in one way or another have shrunk from the higher as well as the lower realities of life.

Paul Elmer More
*Shelburne Essays. Fourth Series* (New York:
G. P. Putnam's Sons, 1906), pp. 236-38

. . . To pounce on Blake's poems and pictures, and to see in these only the works of a great creative artist is to miss half his value. For Blake's glory and Blake's significance to our age is just this, that religion and art were passionately fused in his own soul, and it is only by doing full justice to both, and by presenting him and his message whole and undivided that one can hope to write worthily of a genius at once the most creative and the most religious produced by the western world. . . .

How did Blake with his mystic vision regard Nature? Everywhere in his poetry one sees that he is passionately alive to her alluring beauty, and how the name of each object lingers on his ear with a loving cadence. . . .

But he also sees like St. Paul that the "whole creation groaneth and travaileth in pain"; everywhere he sees cruelty, and his heart pities not only the fly devoured by the spider, but also the spider snapped up by the bird. He sees an immense difference in her animals. Nothing is more perplexing to one's scheme of life and religion than a visit to the Zoological Gardens. One is glad to deny with Spinoza all final causes, and to believe that the Almighty created the grotesques in a humorous mood for His own sheer delight. Blake immediately relates each animal to God or to man. . . .

Charles Gardner<br>
Vision and Vesture (New York: E. P. Dutton, 1916), pp. ix-x, 22

And here lies the root of Blake's greatness. His feet stride from mountain to mountain; and if his head is lost among stars and clouds, it is only because he is a giant. His heaven is no abstract of metaphysics; it is a map which charts the soul of every living individual. His God is not some dim and awful Principle; he is a Friend who descends and raises Man till Man himself is a God. And by this dealing in universals Blake came to that point where such diverse temperaments as Milton, Fra Angelico, Nietzsche, El Greco, Paracelsus, Shelley, Michelangelo, and Walt Whitman may be invoked for fair comparisons. It is in a way not a bad sign of Blake's greatness that so many dissimilar sects claim him: the Revolutionaries, the Theosophists, the Vers Librists and their opponents, the Spiritists, and so on. We can treat of Blake as an Alchemist. There have been prominent Catholics who have welcomed many doctrines of this hater of priests! . . .

But at heart, Blake is one of the great Christians. The strangeness of his language has often repelled the orthodox; his attacks on priesthood have irritated many sects; and his generosity towards all Truth-seeking has seemed heretical. Yet behind all this, we find Blake becoming more and more passionate, even dogmatic, over the essentials of the Christian Faith. His tenderest lyrics, his most turbulent vortices of design, his inexplicable nadirs of thought, all resolve eventually into one thing: Man in the arms of God.

The world has long since done its worst towards Blake; and he has emerged triumphant, with the twin crowns of Poet and Painter. But this is not enough. The modern Trismegistus must receive his third crown, that of Philosopher, before his permanent place among the great of this earth can be determined.

S. Foster Damon
*William Blake. His Philosophy and Symbols*
(London: Constable, 1924), pp. x-xi

Blake cannot be classed. He was the most independent artist that ever lived. He had his own sources of inspiration (so peculiar and strange that no one else has dared to drink from them), his own strange technique, his own method of printing, his own method of illustrating, and his own secret way of reproducing his illustrations. He did everything for himself—including lighting his own fire and fetching his own beer. Little wonder, then, that his work is strange and seems to possess individuality in unique degree, and less wonder that it fails to conform with accepted ideas of what it could, would, might, or should have been.

Max Plowman
*An Introduction to the Study of Blake*
(New York: E. P. Dutton, 1927), pp. 3-4

Although Blake created his own myths and added symbols to those common to other mystics, he did not apart from these, attempt to create or even select any special phraseology for the expression of his mystical ideas. A bitter opponent of conventional Christianity, he yet often adopts the religious language of Bunyan and of the followers of Wesley and Whitefield, both in his letters and in his symbolic books. The explanation of this is undoubtedly that they stood for faith as opposed to rationalistic questionings. Faith for Blake implied in itself some measure of insight, and therefore the language of evangelical fervour spelt symbolic truth. [1927]

Mona Wilson
*The Life of William Blake* (London: P. Davies, 1932), p. 64

Like *America, The French Revolution* is rooted in history, and it is nearly as free in its treatment. Blake's interest was in the psychic value of events rather than in events themselves, and even in this relatively early poem, whose characters are the real figures of history rather than the giant motives he devised a year or two later, it is these values that he pressed. It is possible that Blake intended to end his series with some other poem on this subject. But for some reason, perhaps the obvious one that by 1795 the history of the Revolution had distorted the motives for which it had once been such a favorite symbol, this other poem does not exist, and in its absence we must use the early *French Revolution* as the end of the myth. The justification for this procedure is that the whole series is clearly directed to that conclusion in eighteenth-century history. Without these effects, the carefully developed causes of the series and the movement of the whole lose their meaning.

Mark Schorer
*William Blake. The Politics of Vision*
(New York: Henry Holt, 1946), pp. 297-98

In the earliest prophecies, *The Book of Thel* and *Visions of the Daughters of Albion,* text and design approach one another rather tentatively. In *Thel* the design is always at the bottom or the top of the page, but in the *Visions* the text is occasionally broken in the middle, and an important step has been taken toward the free interpenetration of the two which belongs to Blake's mature period. In the early prophecies there is often an unequal balance between the amount Blake has to say in each of the two arts. Thus *The Marriage of Heaven and Hell* is in literature one of Blake's best known and most explicit works, but for that very reason it is less successful pictorially. The text predominates too much, and what design there is follows the text closely and obviously. So much so, in fact, that some of the marginal decorations become a rather irritating form of punctuation. Thus on Plate II the words "whatever their enlarged & numerous senses could perceive" are followed by a little drawing of a bird; the words "thus began Priesthood" are followed by a black serpentine spiral, and the words "at length they pronounc'd that the Gods had order'd such things" are followed by tiny kneeling figures. On the other hand, *The Book of Urizen* is pictorially one of Blake's greatest works: here there is no plate without a major design on it, and there are ten plates without text. Blake here seems to be trying to forget about the poem, which with its short lines sits awkwardly on the plate in double columns. It is clear that there were pictorial as well as poetic reasons for the long seven-beat line of Blake's prophecies.

Northrop Frye
*JAAC* (September, 1951), p. 37

The important likeness between Blake and Yeats is that both are concerned with the dream of the inner life. To an extent this is true of all poets not limiting their subject-matter to externalities of description and narrative. But it is particularly true of those poets who consciously sort out their actors into these two main camps dealt with throughout the ages by theologians more than poets. "Poets and artists have begun again to carry the burdens that priests and theologians took from them angrily some few hundreds years ago," as Yeats said (*Essays, p.* 78). For Yeats was right in thinking that there are two conflicting selves in Blake, the artist half-drawn to the occult, and the mystic who fights against it. In fact, psychologically speaking, Blake, like the gnostics, stood with one foot on either side of a widening abyss: on one side, Christ and the angels of heaven; on the other side the gigantic evil figures and creeping things can be given power by that in our nature which is bestial rather than angelic. Two things kept the chasm from widening too much: the fact that Blake was an artist, and that even the minimum of creative labour is both a distancing and a unifying activity. And, more important, the fact that although Blake was aware of the conflict, he was not aware that his choice was reversible.

Margaret Rudd
*Divided Image* (London: Routledge and
Kegan Paul, 1953), pp. 189-90

. . . War and Peace is the pattern Blake saw as he watched "the New Age" with mingled delight and terror. For him the human question was framed not in terms of improved production but as a choice or an issue between the peaceful Looms of Jerusalem weaving clothing and a symbolically lucent atmosphere, and the Mills of Satan, casting steel cannonbarrel and filling the sky with the smoke of battles and burning towns. Factory smoke was not a major ingredient of the cloud over London. . . .

Blake thought of himself as a prophetic bard with a harp that could prostrate tyranny and overthrow armies—or, more simply, as an honest man uttering his opinion of public matters. And although he often veiled his opinion or elaborated it into a complex symbolic fabric having little to do with public matters on many of its levels of meaning, it has been possible to trace through nearly all of his work a more or less clearly discernible thread of historical reference.

David V. Erdman
*Blake: Prophet Against Empire* (Princeton, N. J.:
Princeton Univ. Pr., 1954), pp. vii-viii

The opening lines of *Tiriel*, though inept poetry, are an admirable introduction to the doctrinal complexities of the poem. Myratana is a queen, of course, but more important she is also a mother. And unlike the mothers in *Innocence* she is dying. By thus eliminating this great source of comfort and protection, Blake seems to suggest that once the end of innocence is reached the mother has no further hold over the child. In effect her function expires. On the other hand, the earthly father (Tiriel), who has no function in innocence, is here dominant. The tremendous difference in their treatment of the child is partly due to the nature of the change in the child himself. In innocence he is selfish (without knowing it), instinctive, uninhibited, and free; a mother's love and protection insures this freedom as long as possible. But when the child begins to think, to reason, to identify himself as an individual separate from others and from the divine, and with a will of his own (that is, when unconscious selfhood becomes conscious), protection and love are discarded and the father exerts his power to control the child, to bind him with the man-made laws, restrictions, duties, and morals of this world. And the state of experience is begun.

Robert F. Gleckner
*The Piper and the Bard* (Detroit, Mich.:
Wayne State Univ. Pr., 1959), p. 145

. . . Why did Blake establish his own set of symbols? Though . . . in a sense he was more conventional than some think, there is no doubt that he was also quite original with his symbols. Yet the fact remains that a careful study of his work often serves to explain even the most seemingly incomprehensible of them. Perhaps we have no right to quarrel with a poet who creates his own mythology unless we wish to contest the rights of any mythmaker. . . . Still there are those who would have Blake use the established mythology, seemingly unaware of the fact that even Samuel Johnson had complained that the classical mythology was simply worn out from use; and for Blake it was not simply shopworn but tainted with the connotations of the world of time and space, the centuries of light being shed from the wrong world. As he put it in his *Vision of the Last Judgment*: "Let it here be Noted that the Greek Fables originated in Spiritual Mystery & Real Visions, which are lost and clouded in Fable & Allegory" and "Allegory and Vision ought to be known as Two Distinct Things, and so call'd for the Sake of Eternal Life."

The use of the classic myth, then, is impossible to Blake because of its having been abstracted from vision or the eternal reality. Blake's recourse was to create his own system—"I must Create a System or be enslav'd by another Man's./I will not Reason & Compare: my business is to Create . . ." in order to communicate that eternal reality. . . .

Karl Kiralis
*Criticism* (Summer, 1959), p. 209

It is fairly obvious to the careful reader that Blake's was the foremost mythical imagination of his own time—if not of all time among English poets. Although he certainly had great creative originality, most of his myths, including their symbolic and allegorical significances, follow the broad outlines of the world's great myths which were readily available to him, in Thomas Taylor's work, in the didactic interpretations which Blake fitted to his own peculiar needs. He did alter both story line and symbolism to agree with his visionary understanding of the nature of man and the necessity of the creation of time and space to restrain man from falling into the absolute materiality of nonentity, and he did present the myths dramatically, but he surely did not "invent a private mythology." Blake's great originality lies rather in his unusual devices for adapting well-known myths and commonly accepted—though esoteric —symbolic values to his own interpretation of the history of thought of his time. In his violent reaction against the mechanistic cosmological concepts of the eighteenth century, Blake went back to the old revered myths of classical literature for enlightenment of his own imaginative world. It may be found, as further study of Blake is made against the background of philosophical movements of his day, that his originality lies in his arresting reinterpretations or adaptations in the light of his own times rather than in invention, though he would be a bold critic indeed who would deny Blake his fair share of that.

G. M. Harper
*The Neoplatonism of William Blake* (Chapel Hill, N. C.:
Univ. North Carolina Pr., 1961), pp. 262-63

Blake's composite form consists of language and design or, more particularly, of (1) *words* that appear as short-lined lyrics, sometimes rhymed; as long-lined prophetic poems, usually in septenary rhythm, never rhymed; and as prose mottoes or aphorisms; and (2) *designs* that have these constituent elements: (a) color, (b) border, and (c) picture or scene.

1. *Language*—Blake's sense of grammar and syntax is uncertain, his puctuation is eccentric, and his sentences lack logical connectives. These qualities appear in all the various styles Blake employs—in the highly terse and often obscure epigrams, in the song-like lyrics, and in the allegorical-pictorial prophecies. . . .

2a. *Color*— . . . Blake, by theoretical conviction and long practice, was a linear artist. Like the neoclassical aesthetician—to whom, in spite of himself, he now and then bears striking affinities—he rated color below line, Venetian painters below Romans and Florentines, harmony below melody, chiaroscuro below outline. . . . But Blake's originals are so incomparably superior to bad reproductions, however clear the line, and the rainbow splendors of the Stirling *Jerusalem* so surpass the black and white austerities, however fine, of the Linnell-Rinder copy that one simply cannot write off color as an irrelevant afterthought sometimes added by Catherine Blake. . . .

2b. *Border*— . . . Blake's [borders] stand in an ever changing, highly flexible relation to other elements of his form. As they invade and cross the text, grow out of the title, or support the main designs, they achieve the status of living members of a living body. That status they possess even when they represent the tiniest and humblest forms of natural life. . . .

2c. *Picture and Scene*—The pictures of Blake's illuminated books— frontispieces, separate pages without text, or designs, above, below, or in the middle of the text—bear many relations, both subtle and obvious, to the words they embellish. Occasionally they unambitiously redupli- cate the verbal scene. More often they are visual translations of Blake's metaphors. More frequently still they represent the personifications cre- ated in the poem or required by its meaning. . . .

For Blake was more than a poet who happened also to be a painter. He molded the sister arts, as they have never been before or since, into a single body and breathed into it the breath of life.

Jean H. Hagstrom
*William Blake. Poet and Painter* (Chicago and London:
Univ. Chicago Pr., 1964), pp. 13, 15, 16, 18, 140

# GEORGE NOEL GORDON, LORD BYRON
## 1788-1824

The son of "Mad Jack" Byron and his second wife Catherine Gordon, Byron was born in London in 1788. "Mad Jack," a notorious rake, had been married previously to the Marchioness of Carmathen, a divorcee, and was the father of her daughter Augusta, born in 1783. After her father's death in 1790, Augusta was sent off to relatives and saw her younger brother rarely until both were grown up. Suffering from a deformed leg, Byron was subjected to torturous and unsuccessful treatments, studied irregularly, moved frequently about Scotland and England, and suffered from the violence of his mother's temper. At ten, he inherited the title and Nottinghamshire estate of his great-uncle, Lord Byron. At thirteen, he was enrolled in Harrow, where for the first time, he made friends among boys his own age, the closest of whom died while still very young. At seventeen, he entered Trinity College, Cambridge, where he gambled excessively, read avidly, and wrote prolifically. *Hours of Idleness*, pub- lished and withdrawn when he was eighteen, and republished the following year, received some kindly reviews. At twenty-one, he published the controversial *English Bards and Scotch Reviewers* (1809), a work of satirical skill, though poor in literary judgment, and for which he made numerous literary enemies. After graduation, he returned to his estate, Newstead Abbey, and attempted some restorations, but his restless desire was to travel. In 1809, he and his friend John Cam Hobhouse set out on a Grand Tour. *Childe Harold*, I and II (1812), published at the conclusion of the journey, won Byron immediate fame, gave him entré into London's best society and into some of its better boudoirs. After a stormy affair with Lady Caroline Lamb, he left her for Lady Oxford, proposed to and was refused by Anna Isabella Milbanke, and took up with his own sister Augusta, who had come to London in flight from her husband Colonel George Leigh. Although Byron succeeded in winning Anna Isabella after all, the marriage ended in scandal after a year, when the Lady requested a legal separation from her brutal Lord. Both Augusta and Anna were left with Byron's daughters when he departed for the continent in despair and disgust, never to return to England. In Switzerland, he was maneuvered into a love affair by Claire Clairmont, the impetuous step-sister of Mary Shelley. Claire's child Allegra was born in 1817, only to die five years later in an Italian convent, where Byron had been boarding her. Moving on to Italy, he formed a liaison, his last one, with Teresa Guiccioli, the child-bride of an elderly nobleman. The years with Teresa were his most productive. He had completed *The Prisoner of Chillon* (1816), *Childe Harold*, III (1816) and IV (1818) and had begun *Don Juan* (I and II, 1819) before he had met her. Now he went on with *Don Juan* (VI-XVI, 1820-1823), wrote *Sardanapalus* (1821), *Cain* (1821), *The Vision of Judgment* (1822), and *Heaven and Earth* (1822). In 1822 also, he engaged Leigh Hunt to work on a new journal *The Liberal*, but tiring of the project, of Hunt, Hunt's wife and children, and of Shelley's widow and orphan, who had all been staying with him, he embarked on a new adventure—the Greek war for liberty. In July 1823, he sailed for Greece, but found the movement for independenc disorganized, disunited, and discouraging. Nevertheless, he persisted in his efforts to prepare his troops for battle, until catching cold one day in April, he developed a fever from which he died on April 19, 1824. Dead as well as alive, Byron the man and the poet has been hounded by moralists, partisan biographers, New Critics and old, but few have denied that he was a satirist *par excellence* who cracked the mold of English society and showed that it was made of clay. In addition to the works already mentioned, and almost equally well-read, are *Turkish Tales* (1813-1814); *Hebrew Melodies* (1815); *Manfred* (1817); *Mazeppa* (1819); and *The Island* (1823).

E. H. Coleridge, ed., *The Works of Lord Byron: Poetry* (1898-1903), 7 vols.; and R. E. Prothero, ed., *Letters and Journals* (1922), 6 vols.

Leslie A. Marchand, *Byron* (1957), 3 vols.

## PERSONAL

Dramatic and voluptuous pessimism seems to have been inborn in him —a sensuous and poetical leaning, which excited unbounded scorn for the unctuous optimism which flatters social democracy—the ragged sovereign who exceeds even oriental despots and gods in his taste for compliments. This and certain bitter personal recollections—unavowed wounded feelings—impelled him to burning words of acute hatred, thus exhausting revenge, for never was language of extreme violence more severed from vindictiveness in action. Ferocity there was in him. A display of moral baseness, of human infamy caught in the act, stirred him to fierce transport of delight. Such cruel rejoicing over the ignominy of man is said to be the resurrection of an ape or tiger ancestor. Unregenerate love of torture has been refined into sardonic exultation at men's vileness. . . .

Byron was so complex, contradictory, antithetical as the craniologists used to say, as to elude analysis. The more his conflicting words and perplexing actions are compiled into books, the more enigmatic, unknowable, he becomes. He finally remains a riddle in human nature; its solution is equally impracticable and unprofitable. Lady Byron once wrote of him (somewhere about 1817): "His character is a labyrinth; but no clue would ever find the way to his *heart*."

He has been described as having "two selves, one frantic, the other calm, and contemplating almost with wonder the frenzy," as existing "almost in the voice of mankind," and dwelling in cold and remote inaccessibility to all human sympathy—"natura remota ab nostris rebus seiunctaque longe." [1905; rev. 1921]

Ralph Milbanke, Earl of Lovelace
*Astarte,* rev. Mary, Countess of Lovelace
(London: Christophers, 1921), pp. 3, 10

Lord Byron's last journey . . . proved a failure: he had failed to reconcile the Greek factions; he had failed to capture Lepanto; he had failed even to attend the Conference of Salona; he had been personally responsible for the Souliots; he had imposed  no discipline upon his own brigade; the artillery experts had been a disappointment; the fleet had dispersed; the finances were as bad as ever; Trelawny and Stanhope had deserted him; there was no hope of Napier or Gordon coming to his assistance; the Committee in London were indifferent, if not disapproving. Even in Missolonghi, even within the walls of his own house, he was surrounded by treachery, spying, and intrigue. He had lost his health, his reputation, even his honour. What had he achieved in all those months since August? He had achieved nothing. And what, in the months that might still be accorded, did there remain for him to do?

There was only one thing that there remained for him to do. [1924]

Harold Nicolson
*Byron, The Last Journey* (London:
Archibald Constable, 1948), p. 245

Attempts have been freely made to cite Byron in evidence against himself by means of his poetry. We are told by Lord Lovelace and others with great elaboration that in *Manfred, The Bride of Abydos, The Corsair, The*

*Giaour*, and I know not what poems besides, Byron plainly convicts himself because incest is in some measure or another their thematic material. Great pains are taken to support this proposition by cross-references between the poems and Byron's letters. These devices will not be analysed here, because they are merely a corruption of all decent argument. A poet may very well tell us a great deal about himself in his poems, about his character, his emotional nature, his opinions, his habits, and even his comings and goings, and no poet has ever done this more freely than Byron. But to use his poetry as incriminating evidence against him in any specific circumstance in his life is utterly offensive to the propriety of criticism, and convicts the transgressor of entire ignorance as to the processes of which he speaks. There can be no compromise on this matter. Particular stress is laid by Byron's accusers on the song, "I speak not, I trace not, I breathe not, thy name." The personal occasion that seems to attach to this poem makes it not one whit more eligible for these improper purposes.

John Drinkwater
*The Pilgrim of Eternity* (New York:
George H. Doran, 1925), p. 65

He had once written that he liked women to treat him "as a favourite and somewhat forward sister." And he knew himself thoroughly. He was seeking in love a blend of gay friendship, sensuality, an almost maternal tenderness. . . . A somewhat forward sister. . . . Once the thought had struck him, incest was to haunt him. Was it not enough for him to imagine a dangerous passion, to believe himself fated for it? Was he not born of the Byrons and the Gordons, whose history was as terrible as that of the Borgias? From childhood he had felt himself marked down, like Zeluco, for some monstrous crime that would set him above and beyond the pale of human law. In this adventure he had to feel himself guilty, and to find pleasure in feeling more guilty than he really was. It could almost be said that it was Byron, and he alone, who, by giving to this quite natural love for an unknown half-sister the name of incest, transformed the lapse into a crime. Even that inability to escape from himself, which isolated him so dangerously from others, was here serving him; for in this woman who was so like him, it was still himself that he sought. In his desire for her there lurked a kind of strange narcissism. . . .

This love yielded him a pleasure all the more sharp and penetrating for his sense of sin. Beside this mingled draught of joy and remorse all his past adventures seemed savourless. Incest, by its violation of one of the most ancient of human laws, seemed to lend to the joys of the flesh the splendour of Revolt. Augusta, a far simpler soul, just yielded. . . . The strangest thing was that she still loved, in her way, that "impossible gentleman," her cousin and husband; but how could she refuse anything that her Baby Byron asked of her?

André Maurois
*Byron*, trans. Hamish Miles (New York:
D. Appleton, 1930), pp. 218-19

Since his arrival in Italy, Byron had been careful to keep clear of senti-ment; and it is the more surprising, then, that the adventures of a very few weeks or days—an assignation proposed at an evening party, followed next day by a secret rendezvous—should have been sufficient to revolution-ize his line of conduct. He was himself somewhat taken aback by this change of attitude. But the origins of any love-affair are hard to analyse; for, besides the immediate physical or sentimental sympathy that may be assumed to spring up between two human beings (an element that in the majority of love-affairs is often exaggerated), we must recognize the period of preparation that precedes acquaintanceship and the various factors that have produced a determination to fall in love. On Byron's side, the exist-ence of preparatory factors was fairly obvious. After two years of dissipa-tion he was sick of debauchery; mentally and physically he was a little tired; while to be out of love was a condition that had always irked him —it was as if his temperament were cut off from a drug it needed. Equally plain to distinguish were the motives of the other party. Teresa Guiccioli was between nineteen and twenty and had been married a year. The third wife of a rich Romagnol landowner, she had taken over a family of grown-up stepchildren, and the time had come when, by all the conventions, she might demand her liberty. Nor was Guiccioli the kind of husband to dispute her wishes—sixty years old, wealthy, and good-natured, absorbed in local politics, a cultivated man of the world, with his life behind him. He was prepared for infidelity though he would demur at scandal. Things might take their course according to the accepted usages of the Venetian moral code.

Peter Quennell
*Byron in Italy* (New York:
Viking Pr., 1941), p. 141

It would appear . . . that even Byron—accustomed as he was to easy con-quests—was slightly taken aback by the extreme facility and publicity of this one. . . . All the fans fluttered, and Teresa was delighted. She was far too pleased with the conquest of the most celebrated figure in Venice, to wish to keep it to herself. . . .

The winter months of 1820-21 were spent by Teresa in her father's house in Ravenna—and by Byron in the Palazzo Guiccioli, visiting her every day. It was a very different winter from the previous one. Then the love-affair was in its most stormy phase: although living in the same house, their meetings had been uncertain and perilous, their love-making frustrated by quarrels and mutual reproaches, and their future was still completely uncertain. In public they had maintained the semi-formal relationship of a lady and her "Cavalier Servente," driving together in Teresa's coach-and-six, and attending the theatre and the carnival balls. . . .

Iris Origo
*The Last Attachment* (New York:
Scribner's, 1949), pp. 41, 236

. . . Byron was a human being, shaped by the strange combination of his inherited traits and his unnatural upbringing, but essentially likable, disarmingly frank in his confessions of his own peccadilloes, with a delightfully fresh observation of human character and human frailties and a unique facility for lucid and concrete expression. I have come to feel that Byron is not, as he has been accused of being, more inconsistent than most men and women—only more honest in acknowledging his inconsistencies. That is what startles and delights the sympathetic reader aware of the human penchant for reticence and rationalization. . . .

One thing that seems to emerge more clearly than ever before, principally from hitherto unpublished letters to Byron, is that he had an extraordinary capacity for friendship, and that all his friends, men and women alike, were devoted to him. And finally, further study of biographical details strengthens the conviction of the essential honesty and self-honesty of Byron. He had a kind of "desperate integrity" (to borrow a phrase from a twentieth-century critic) in little things as well as big—in literature as well as in life—and all other things seem less important. As we become better acquainted with him, we are inclined to accept his idiosyncrasies and his deviations from approved conduct as we would those of a friend—in fact, as his own friends did. . . .

Byron's correspondence with Lady Melbourne hints very strongly that he had become involved in a liaison with his half-sister, Augusta. For Byron there would be a fatal fascination in such an intimacy because it was a "new sensation" and because it was forbidden. Augusta, goodhearted and amiable, was intent only upon giving pleasure to the brother of whom she was fond and whom she had grown to love still more for his generosity and kindly qualities during the weeks in London and in the days at her house in the country. Amoral as a rabbit and silly as a goose, she was scarcely aware of abstract moral questions, though she was full of pious phrases and gave Bibles to her family and friends. Byron was too reflective not to think of the dangers and the social consequences of his actions, and too self-torturing not to feel remorse. Like many of his contemporaries in the nineteenth century, he had escaped rationally but not emotionally from the fear-inspired religious training of his youth. The Calvinistic sense of sin haunted his subconscious mind, a ghost that could never be completely exorcised. But that fatalistic conception of human depravity blended with his own weakness to drive him on to further violation of the inhibitions of his own mind.

Leslie A. Marchand
*Byron: A Biography,* Vol. I (New York:
A. A. Knopf, 1957), pp. ix, xi, 403-4

## LADY BYRON

Secluded from all but him, "the intensity of his sufferings absorbed my feelings in his, almost to self-forgetfulness." The disclosure that she had been married without love, the frequent threats of suicide, the "vindictive exultation over my defenceless state"; his walks in the gallery at night with dagger drawn, his morbid dread of some mysterious deadly avenger, his hints at being a murderer, and then the speeches wild or cruel or charged with the incestuous significance he harped upon. . . .

These were her daily bread. Or there would be a set scene of fury, as on the night when he brought out her letters before and during the engagement, and read some passages, dwelling especially on one where she had said that she wished to be the means of reconciling him to himself. Again he reproached her bitterly for delaying to accept him; his rage was so extreme that she thought he would have struck her. Her first impulse was to disarm him by affection. . . . And then again a gleam of something like tenderness. One night, after he had been roaming the gallery as usual, armed with dagger and pistol, he came to her exhausted and piteously haggard. "Seeking to allay his misery," she moved her head until it rested on his breast. He said, more gently than usual but with piercing bitterness: "You should have a softer pillow than my heart."

Ethel C. Mayne
*The Life and Letters of Anne Isabella, Lady Noel Byron*
(London: Archibald Constable, 1929), pp. 164-65

She was seeking to match him with an abstract image of the man of genius, the man of virtue. He felt it, and was annoyed. Above all, she was too intelligent; she analysed every word he uttered, whereas he said whatever came into his head, anything at all, if only to prevent himself from yawning. From his rude outbursts, which a Lady Oxford laughed at and an Augusta never heeded, Annabella drew professorial deductions. The fair mathematician gauged every tiny variation in tone by a calculation of sentimental probabilities, and turned love into an equation. One moment their characters seemed too closely akin, the next they were not close enough. She overwhelmed him with waves of beautiful sentiments, described how she

was attacked by scruples, wanted to break off the engagement, and, over
and above all, was seized every other day with some incomprehensible illness. Byron's lucid, loveless scrutiny took her measure; "a perfectly good
person," he judged her, but over-solicitous, fated to self-torment without
end, and—his pet aversion in a woman—a weaver of romance. He had
always declared that in marriage he wanted "a companion—a friend rather
than a sentimentalist." But from morning to night in this household the
talk ran on nothing but sentiments.

André Maurois
*Byron*, trans. Hamish Miles (New York:
D. Appleton, 1930), p. 275

. . . Since the books of Ethel Colburn Mayne, du Bos [*Byron et le besoin
de la fatalité,* 1929], and Maurois, there is no more room for controversy
—by saying that Byron sought in incest a spice for love . . . and that he
required the feeling of guilt to arouse in him the phenomena of the moral
sense, and the feeling of fatality in order to appreciate the flow of life. . . .

His conduct towards his wife seems to have been of a moral cruelty so
exceptional as to make one for a moment doubt the reliability of the
historical evidence. But one quickly comes to see that no episode in Byron's
life is more true to type than this. . . .

The most subtle torture, the torture which was to wring the most exquisite cry of anguish from its victim, was this: Byron, by every kind of
allusion and insinuation, sought to instil into Annabella the suspicion of his
incest with Augusta, his "terrible" secret. . . .

He sought to measure the depth of his own guilt in Annabella's anguish,
in Augusta's remorse. [1933]

Mario Praz
*The Romantic Agony* (New York:
Meridian Books, 1956), pp. 70-72

Byron's accumulated observations of the farcical freedoms of Italian
manners and his own contacts with the frailties of Venetian women gave
him ample background for the rollicking bedroom comedy that is the climactic episode of the first canto, but what he wrote with the most exquisite
relish was the description of Don Juan's mother, Donna Inez, a transparent
portrait of Lady Byron.

Leslie A. Marchand
*Byron. A Biography,* Vol. II (New York:
A. A. Knopf, 1957), p. 750

In reading Annabella's various statements, it is important to note the dates
of their composition. Those of January and February 1816 were written

to provide lawyers with ammunition for forcing Byron to agree to a deed of separation; those of March 1816 were written at the request of her chief legal adviser, Lushington, for possible use if the case had to be taken to court; those of March 1817 were devised to assemble all possible evidence against both Byron and Augusta as improper persons to have the custody of Annabella's child; everything of later date was directed towards persecution of Augusta and justification of her own conduct in deserting her huband. The later statements must be regarded with caution as evidence of fact, not merely because her memory became dimmed by time— "I often am surprised when talking with you to find how much that was said and done in that 1815 you seem to have forgot," Mrs. Clermont wrote to her on 30th March 1830—but because the skeletons of fact became hidden under the constructions she built upon them.

Even the earliest and freshest recollections must be read with reservations. Not only were her statements devised as memoranda for her lawyers, as material for a prosecuting counsel; her impressions became distorted from the moment of their conception by the ponderous machinery of her analysis. As Byron remarked to Lady Melbourne during his first visit to Seaham, "the least word, or alteration of tone, has some inference drawn from it"—she was always "squaring her notions to the Devil knows what," and Byron's personality presented a problem in subtlety beyond her pedantic understanding.

Finally, she was devastatingly humourless. When he mocked her prudent determination to avoid a husband with insanity in his family, there was surely no more than a schoolboy's mischief in telling her that his grandfather committed suicide and he had a cousin who set fire to a house. The "mysterious & alarming manner" must have been almost certainly assumed in playful mockery when he told her, "Now I have you in my power, and I could make you feel it." His practice of acting a pose and his schoolboy sense of fun were alike encouraged by her literal and humourless understanding, so that he must have piled extravagance upon extravagance, marvelling at her limitless credulity. On the other hand, he must have been irritated by her smugness, as when she sought with wan endurance to "smile the clouds away" in a self-conscious effort "to call out his higher & more generous feelings."

Malcolm Elwin
*Lord Byron's Wife* (New York: Harcourt, Brace, 1962), p. 253

## Childe Harold

A whole revolution is implied in Byron's line:

*I love not man the less, but nature more.*

Any study of this topic must evidently turn on the question how far at different times and by different schools of thought the realm of man and the realm of nature (as Byron uses the word) have been separated and in what way. For there may be different ways of running together man and nature. . . .

Perhaps emotional misanthropy and the worship of wild nature are nowhere more fully combined than in Byron. He gives magnificent expression to the most untenable of paradoxes—that one escapes from solitude by eschewing human haunts in favor of some wilderness. [See especially *Childe Harold* II, xxv,ff.] In these haunts, he says, he became like a "falcon with clipped wing," but found in nature the kindest of mothers. . . . He not only finds companionship in nature but at the same time partakes of her infinitude—an infinitude, one should note, of feeling. . . . [1919]

Irving Babbitt<br>
*Rousseau and Romanticism* (New York:<br>
Noonday Pr., 1955), pp. 210, 217-18

. . . It is with a powerful requickening of our blood that we hear again the rolling guns and clattering squadrons of the stanzas on Waterloo, the storm and passion of the night by Lake Leman. The old thrill comes back when we read again of "the Niobe of nations,"

Childless and crownless in her voiceless woe,

her tombs and ruined Forum, the empty moonlit Coliseum, or hear the old moral, in accents of reverberating intensity, of the vanity of human life, the intoxicating sweetness of love, the sublimity and indifference of nature. . . .

Byron . . . was revealed for the first time in something of his true proportions when he emerged on the rostrum of the last two cantos of *Childe Harold* as the orator of the world's woes and his own. . . .

His use of the stanza is oratorical—it would be a poor measure that admitted of only one mode of fingering—and if his worst stanzas, those in which he endeavours to argue, are twisted and tormented, in the finest he achieves a richer language, a fuller compass of eloquence than the intolerable monotony of the rhetorical couplet permitted. . . . The third canto has the turbid flow of the stream of lava, choked at times with the *debris* and scoriae of imperfect phrasing and tortured rhythms, again flowing clear and strong but dark, and yet again growing incandescent in felicitous and magnificent lines and stanzas. The fourth has more of the movement of the Rhine as he describes it, an "exulting and abounding river," reflecting in its stream the blue of the heavens, the snows and storms of the Alps, the cities and the ruins and the passions of human history, till it loses itself in the "image of eternity," the sea. Nor is the passion unillumined by thought, though Byron's argumentative stanzas are his worst.

H. J. C. Grierson
*Proceedings of the British Academy, 1919-1920*
(Oxford Univ. Pr., 1920), pp 435, 444-46

One of the purposes which *Childe Harold* served was to furnish eager readers with an imaginary Grand Tour, and this at a time when Englishmen had been obliged for years to sit at home, through wars and rumors of wars on the Continent. Of course then, as now, the commonest tourist sites in Europe were ruins, tombs, and monuments of glories past. Childe Harold was therefore making a natural choice when he selected such sites as settings for his meditations, and they were given an especial poignancy for his readers by the fact that many of the conflicts commemorated were of recent wars, and wars in which Englishmen had taken a prominent part.

Yet the general elegiac tone of the first two cantos of the poem and the recurring themes of *ubi sunt* and *sic transit*, are very much in the tradition of the Gloomy Egoists of the preceding century. . . .

The Childe of the first two cantos, in many of his poses, is a Man of Feeling. He is suffering from unrequited love; in spite of his often-confessed preference for solitude and his dislike for mankind, he is a humanitarian —sternly against war and tyranny in all its forms; and in his meditations on the natural world he adopts many of the attitudes characteristic of Mackenzie's Harvey (*The Man of Feeling*) or of the sentimental heroes of Mrs. Radcliffe's Gothic novels. . . .

The Childe of Cantos III and IV is in some ways a different person. Like the verse of the later poems, he is less rhetorical, and more poetic; less traditional, and far more personal. The important transformation, as has been commonly noticed, is that the Childe becomes assimilated to Byron's own persona, although some colors of the original portrait remain, not only in the mind of the reader, but in sporadic passages of the later poems. The scandalous "past" of the Childe has become actual, and the "exile" of the Harold of Canto III has become real, not merely a literary device. . . .

What I am more interested to point out here is that the Childe becomes in these cantos one of the long line of Heroes of Sensibility, a line which begins in the Romantic movement and continues through the remainder of the nineteenth century. . . .

This agonized Hero of Sensibility was Byron's legacy to the literature of the age which succeeded him—not the healthy, ironic but life-affirming message of his great satire. Until almost the end of the century, both in England and on the Continent, Byron was remembered primarily as the author of *Childe Harold*, not of *Don Juan*. The agonized Hero of Sensibility appears again and again in the literature of the succeeding age: sometimes morbidly analytic of his own emotional and spiritual states, and in his *Weltschmerz* longing for some engagement to absolute truth which will rid him of his painful self-consciousness; longing to "mingle with the universe," but being continually frustrated in this desire by the reassertion of his skeptical, sometimes cynical, and sometimes remorseful ego.

Peter L. Thorslev, Jr.
*The Byronic Hero* (Minneapolis, Minn.:
Univ. Minnesota Pr., 1962), pp. 135-37, 139, 141, 144

## Manfred

Much has been said concerning the relation between *Manfred* and *Faust*, and Byron has more than once been accused of plagiarizing the idea of his poem from the great German. As a matter of fact certain ideas of a philosophical cast were probably inspired directly by a recollection of *Faust*. This talk of the "tree of Knowledge and the tree of Life," this pretension to profundities of ineffable science, have about them all the insincerity of borrowed inspiration. But the true theme of *Manfred* is not a philosophical question; the real poem, as Byron himself asserted, came not from reading, but was the immediate outcome of his own life, and Byron's life was the very impersonation of the revolutionary idea, the idea of reckless individual revolt which we have hardly yet outgrown. It is because *Manfred* more than almost any other English poem expresses the longings and ambitions, the revolt and the tragic failure of this idea, that its interest is still so great and must always remain great in any historical survey of literature. Where better can we read the desire of detachment, the longing of the individual to throw off the bonds of social law and make for himself a life apart from the world's life, than in Manfred's boastful words: "My pang shall find a voice. From my youth upwards/My spirit walk'd not with the souls of men"? Equally strong is the expression of self-centered pride. When Manfred rebukes the Spirit who claims dominion over his soul, he cries out scornfully:—

> Back to thy hell!
> Thou hast no power upon me, *that* I feel;
> Thou never shalt possess me, *that* I know:
> What I have done is done.

It is in such words as these that we recognize the vast difference between *Manfred* and *Faust*, not to mention Marlowe's *Dr. Faustus*. Of similar nature and growing directly from the revolutionary ideal of personal unrestraint is the longing for union with one kindred soul,—a longing which seems at once impossible and impious, yet inevitable: This is Manfred's

love for Astarte, the love of a soul that has violated common human attach-
ments in its loneliness and throws itself with guilty passionateness into one
sacrilegious desire of union. And the same loneliness, self-created and still
intolerable, speaks in the yearning cry after a more intimate absorption
into nature:—

> I said, with men, and with the thoughts of men,
> I held but slight communion; but instead,
> My joy was in the Wilderness, to breathe
> The difficult air of the iced mountain's top

And at the last comes the inevitable despair, the necessary failure, expressed in *Manfred* by the vain prayer of oblivion from self.

Paul Elmer More
Introd., in *The Complete Works of Lord Byron* (Boston:
Houghton Mifflin, 1905), p. xx

What Manfred said of Astarte ("I loved her, and destroy'd her"), what
Byron wished to be able to say of Augusta and Annabella (see the Incantation in *Manfred*), was to become the motto of the "fatal" heroes of
Romantic literature. They diffuse all round them the curse which weighs
upon their destiny, they blast, like the simoon, those who have the mis-
fortune to meet with them (the image is from *Manfred*,iii,1); they destroy
themselves, and destroy the unlucky women who come within their orbit.
Their relations with their mistresses are those of an incubus-devil with his
victim. Byron realizes the extreme type of Fatal Man described by Schiller in the *Räuber* and by Chateaubriand in *René*. [1933]

Mario Praz
*The Romantic Agony* (New York:
Meridian Books, 1956), pp. 74-75

*Manfred* . . . is a work of near perfection in the sense that it accomplishes
nearly perfectly what it sets out to do—embody the essence of the romantic
Byronic spirit, not omitting its theatrical or melodramatic aspects. The
blank verse is unusually firm, sure, and certain of itself and sets off to
advantage the intervening lyrics. The chief flaw I find is that the several
characters are sometimes insufficiently distinguished one from another in
the tone of their speeches. Their accents are too similar (reflecting Byron's
limited power to create characters other than Byronic), almost as if the
poem were an expressionistic debate between opposing aspects of the poet's
mind. From the succesive failures of the hero's quest, however, the structure of the poem derives both unity and balanced symmetry, qualities
present to a much less impressive degree in *Childe Harold*, which is improved by editorial selection. But the style of *Manfred* depends so

completely on the personality of the poet and our knowledge of him that it defies instructive formal analysis: the impassioned words derive their passion and power, as the best of Byron's romantic poetry normally does, from the strength of the poet's feelings.

Ernest J. Lovell, Jr.
in *The Major English Romantic Poets*, eds. Clarence D. Thorpe,
Carlos Baker, and Bennett Weaver (Carbondale, Ill.:
Southern Illinois Univ. Pr., 1957), p. 130

*Manfred* is not, as it has often been considered, a play that is essentially concerned with the relation between good and evil. The frame of the morality play is in itself misleading if we fail to realize that the play deals not with external verities that seem to strive for Manfred's spirit but with the reaction of his spirit itself to those apparent verities: they do not alter him, but rather in his own consciousness he creates and destroys them, or simply fails to do so. Many have recognized the fact that *Manfred* is a one-character drama, but few seem to have become fully aware of the implications therein. In the several scenes in which Manfred is not actually present, the image of his being dominates all other characters; only as psychological subordinates do these characters themselves achieve structural significance. The question of their origin, in other words, is not crucial and perhaps hardly meaningful—whether they are, within the play as an extended monologue, entirely figmental, or (the earthly beings at least) in part objectively real. Only in the impact upon the mind of Manfred of the forces or values which these characters represent are they significant. The play is certainly not about things; but only slightly more is it about ideas. Essentially concerned with the consciousness or the Self, it is, broadly, a psychological rather than a philosophic drama.

W. H. Marshall
*The Structure of Byron's Major Poems* (Philadelphia:
Univ. Pennsylvania Pr., 1962), p. 97

Manfred, after all, is not in any sense a representative or champion of Mankind. Byron was undoubtedly attracted by the notion of a hero who, though greater than his fellows in both rank and genius, none the less devotes himself to their cause, and Prometheus provided him with a prototype which was often in his mind that summer. Yet this conception does not affect Manfred—he shows pity and consideration for the human beings whom he despises, but he is not interested in bettering their lot. In his youth he had had "noble aspirations" of this kind: . . . but in reality he shrank from all contact with men, even as their leader and benefactor. . . .

Andrew Rutherford
*Byron. A Critical Study* (Stanford, Calif.:
Stanford Univ. Pr., 1962), pp. 88-89

## Don Juan

First of all, we shall make a sad mistake if we regard the poem as a mere work of satire. Occasionally Byron pretends to lash himself into a righteous fury over the vices of the age, but we know that this is all put on, and that the real savageness of his own nature comes out only when he thinks of his own personal wrongs. . . . There is in *Don Juan* something of the personal satire of Pope, and something of the whimsical mockery of Lucilius and his imitators. But it needs but a little discernment to see that Byron's poem has vastly greater scope and significance than the *Epistle to Dr. Arbuthnot*, or the spasmodic gaiety of the Menippean satire. It does in its own way present a view of life, as a whole, with the good and evil, and so passes beyond the category of the merely satirical. The very scope of its subject . . . classes it with the more universal epics of literature rather than with the poems that portray only a single aspect of life.

Paul Elmer More
*Shelburne Essays. Third Series* (New York:
G. P. Putnam's Sons, 1905), pp. 170-71

The two forces with which Byron was at war are the two great forces which dominated English life in the later eighteenth and early nineteenth centuries—aristocratic society—its ideals, privileges, policy; and that pietistic, Evangelical Christianity which, quickened by the Wesleys, had become the great shaping and inspiring religious influence in the life of serious English people within and without the Established Church. To both these influences Byron stood exposed in a peculiar way which made him at once deeply sensitive and passionately rebellious. . . .

If . . . Byron failed to convince his first readers and may still fail to convince us, of the serious satirical purpose of his poem, "the most moral of poems," it is because of the vein of irresponsible fun and flippancy which runs through it as through his conversation and letters, and secondly, because of the indulgence, or sympathy, with which he treats one element in the life he is satirising, the game of love. There is nothing in *Don Juan* resembling the morbid and revolting treatment of sexual life in Swift's poems and *Gulliver's Travels*. "There is no indelicacy," Byron writes to Murray, "if Hobhouse wants that let him read Swift, his great idol." Here Byron draws nearer to Fielding. Young men will love, and young love is probably the best thing life has to give. In the episode of Haidée, and again in *The Island*, Byron writes in a way to suggest that for his temperament a simpler, more primitive civilisation, less set around with inhibitions and reproving critics, would have cooled the fever of nerves that the complexities of civilisation excited to madness. [1922]

H. J. C. Grierson
in *Byron, the Poet,* ed. W. A. Briscoe (London:
G. Routledge, 1924), pp. 60, 82-83

It is unfortunate for the good name of *Don Juan* that Canto One is the first canto, for many people know the poem merely from the opening episode—witty, sprightly, entertaining, vulgar. Moreover, the reviewers of 1819 had not the advantage we possess of being able to set the incident of Donna Julia's bedroom and the seemingly heartless narrative of the shipwreck in the entire context, thus reducing these scenes to natural proportion in relation to the whole survey of life.

"You will certainly be damned for this," Hobhouse, to whom it was submitted, wrote on the manuscript. The process of damnation began betimes. In a famous passage comparing himself to Napoleon, Byron admits that "Juan was my Moscow." He did not retreat, but in 1819 he faced a strong coalition. As in the case of the domestic scandal of 1816, there is some evidence of division along the lines of political opinion, the more liberal journals venturing to support Byron; but at first the hostility was almost unanimous. *The Edinburgh Review* preserved a stony silence. Gifford, in the *Quarterly*, could not well condemn the poem, since his review was published by Murray; therefore he, too, was silent. The attack was led by *Blackwood's* in some lengthy "Remarks on *Don Juan*." "Maga" admits that Byron "has never written anything more . . . triumphantly expressive of the greatness of his genius"; "our indignation, in regard to the morality of the poem, has not blinded us to its manifold beauties." But the assertion is made that "a more thorough and intense infusion of genius and vice—power and profligacy" there has never been than *Don Juan*. . . .

*Don Juan* will never be forgotten; nor can it be ignored by the judicious. It has entered upon its second century of fame as that work which has more than anything else of Byron's achievement stood the test of disparagement and notoriety and imitation and time; which has grown in renown when his fame grew, and has kept its place when his fame suffered temporary but almost total eclipse; which has come to be regarded as his greatest contribution to literature; which is a wonderful memorial of a society "gone glimmering through the dream of things that were"; and which yet remains—and this is the final mark of its greatness—in all essentials still applicable to the life of to-day.

Samuel C. Chew
*Byron in England. His Fame and After-Fame*
(London: John Murray 1924), pp. 28-29, 75

With the possible exception of prose fiction (what a novel of manners *Don Juan* would have made!) there is no conceivable form of literature in which Byron could have found so good an outlet for his personality as that afforded by these stanzas, now hurrying onward in the full career of action, now caressing a beloved, now thrusting rapier-like through the heart of false dignities, and now pealing with laughter over the folly of mortals.

Byron achieved not only an unforgettable description of the fashionable society of his own time, but, since that kind of society changes only in external ways and not at all at heart, his *Don Juan* is applicable to the corresponding social group of our own day. [1930; rev. 1949]

Ernest Bernbaum
*Guide through the Romantic Movement* (New York:
Ronald Pr., 1956), pp. 206-7

Byron by making Don Juan a Spaniard achieves a brilliant appearance of objectivity. In the great cantos after his arrival in England, which to my mind make a profoundly moral poem, Byron is able to write about England as he has never written before—from an external position. He is able to attack the cult of sentimentality and romantic pessimism for which he was in part responsible. The thirty stanzas of exordium to Canto XIV and the twenty-six to Canto XII are sustained pieces of social criticism only surpassed in English verse by Pope's *Satires* and *Moral Essays*. . . .

Byron's greatness in the ottava rima poems is that he evolved a form perfectly adapted to his subject and his material, and so was able to use the whole range of the language with a virility and momentum such as is found nowhere else in nineteenth century poetry. The amazing variety of tone and the tremendous rhythmic energy of *Don Juan* come from Byron's complete understanding of the spoken language. . . .

The language of Byron was aristocratic, and though it had a great tradition behind it, this language is charged with a lower poetic potentiality than the Scots of Burns. There is thus far less explosive force in Byron's phrasing than in that of Burns, but there is an equally powerful use of the rhythms of colloquial speech. In *Don Juan* Byron is writing as he spoke to his friends and equals, and at the same time writng great verse.

Ronald Bottrall
*Criterion* (January, 1939), pp. 216-18

A second major consideration of this study is an evaluation of the significance of Byron's satire in *Don Juan*. The evidence already accumulated tends to correct the misconception that Byron's attitude toward the great problems of existence is wholly negative. Certainly Byron's vigorous and unequivocal denunciation of hypocrisy and insincerity in individuals, of essential unsoundness or flagrant abuses in social institutions, and of the worst features of modern civilization cannot be regarded as other than constructive in implication and effect. If Byron's mature satire is occasionally cynical, it concerns shameless human nature and human institutions. The gross and inhuman oppression of tyranny, the insatiable avarice, irrationality, and savagery of war, the pestilence, poverty, and polar inequalities of modern society—all these were evils so prevalent and so flagrant as readily to provoke cynicism. But certainly it is not reasonable to brand as "cynical" the satire which exposes and vigorously decries the evils of society. Byron's half-jocular claim to be regarded as a moral teacher is not to be dismissed at its face value. Byron fearlessly and uncompromisingly attacked the social evils of his day. The primary objects of his satire were insincerity and oppression. Stated positively, the major implications of his satire are sincerity and freedom. Assuredly the import of such satire is constructive.

The charge of cynicism is owing, at least in part, to Byron's habitual juxtaposition of the petty and the heroic, the base and the virtuous. As I have indicated in my study of the contemporary periodical criticism of *Don Juan*, Byron's sudden plunges from the sublime to the ridiculous and his astonishing juxtapositions of virtue and vice were deplored as evidence of a cynical want of faith in the reality of virtue. The same criticism has been expressed by a modern critic, Hugh Walker. . . .

But this criticism is not applicable to Byron. For Byron the admixture of the vicious does *not* make virtue unreal. Byron's representation of the startling proximity in human nature of virtues and vices clearly was intended not to disprove the reality of virtue but rather to emphasize Byron's profound conviction of the insensible but inevitable decline of virtue through overconfidence in its strength. Byron attacks not virtue but false virtue. The often reiterated accusation of the contemporary reviews that Byron's purpose in *Don Juan* was to bring contempt upon, to undermine by ridicule, all that ennobles or delights mankind it is impossible to support except by the violent wresting of certain passages from their context. Byron attacks not ideals but false idealism, false sentiment, false loyalty, false morality, false patriotism, and false freedom. With keen insight and utter fearlessness he analyzes and exposes the contrasts and contradictions in human life and relentlessly tears down insincerity, pretense, and sham.

P. G. Trueblood
*The Flowering of Byron's Genius* (Palo Alto, Calif.:
Stanford Univ. Pr. 1945), pp. 166-67

Though *Don Juan* stands almost alone among poems of the Romantic age, it belongs to it and is in its own way a true product of it. Though Byron rejected the Romantic belief in the imagination, he was true to the Romantic outlook in his devotion to an ideal of man which may have been no more than a dream, but none the less kept his devotion despite the ordeal of facts and his own corroding scepticism. He knew how difficult this ideal was to realize and what powerful obstacles it met in the corruption of society and the contradictions of human nature. He made many discoveries, seldom creditable, about himself and other men, and that is why at times he seems cynical and disillusioned. . . . He made a bold attempt to put the whole of himself in *Don Juan*, and the result is something quite outside the range of his great contemporaries. The alternations of his moods are matched by the extraordinary range of his subjects. There seems to be almost no topic on which he has not got something interesting or witty or penetrating to say. The story is only half the poem; the other half is a racy commentary on life and manners. *Don Juan* is the record of a remarkable personality, a poet and a man of action, a dreamer and a wit, a great lover and a great hater, a man with many airs of the eighteenth century and yet wholly of the nineteenth, a Whig noble and a revolutionary democrat. The paradoxes of his nature are fully reflected in *Don Juan*, which is itself both a romantic epic and a realistic satire, and it owes the wide range and abundant wealth of its poetry to the fact that Byron had in himself many Romantic longings, but tested them by truth and reality and remained faithful only to those which meant so much to him that he could not live without them. [1949]

C. M. Bowra
*The Romantic Imagination* (New York:
Oxford Univ. Pr., 1950), pp. 172-73

. . . *Don Juan,* a work of great originality and undeniable excellence, essentially unlike anything before it. . . . [It] has much to say to the mid-twentieth century, an age which, distrusting the grandiose, sentimental, and otherwise oversimplified quite as much as Byron did, has sought the poetic means of expressing its characteristic emotional complexity, as Byron also did, in the oblique, liberating forces of irony and ambiguity. *Don Juan* is, in fact, one of the most pertinent of all poems for us today, reminding us at a time when we are in particular need of reminder, that a poem is made for people other than its creator. . . .

*Don Juan* does . . . show a significant thematic unity. Its most significant structure is a considered organization of attitudes expressed by means of a rich variety of ironically qualified tones, and each of the chief narrative episodes bears an organic relation, clear but subtly varied, to the larger theme. . . .

Byron had not heard that a poem must be disjointed if it is adequately to express an age out of joint, but he can, nevertheless, ironically juxtapose images suggestive of both classical and nineteenth-century civilization and so give to the satire of the contemporary scene increased depth, order, and perspective. . . . Or he can use imagery drawn from his personal life and so leaven the "objective" narrative of Juan, the public myth of himself allowing him to use imagery which is personal but seldom private or cryptic.

Ernest J. Lovell, Jr.
in *The Major English Romantic Poets*, eds. Clarence D. Thorpe,
Carlos Baker, and Bennett Weaver, (Carbondale, Ill.:
Southern Illinois Univ. Pr., 1957), pp. 131, 140, 145

. . . Editors are justified in using Canto I as a sampling of Byron's two thousand octaves. If only one canto is to be publicized, the first is the best choice, for Byron has put into it the largest number of the many diverse properties of *Don Juan*. He shows here more of his epic estate than he does in any other canto. A double household of comic figures and a pleasant narrative afford him ample occasion for talk and commotion, for psychological, autobiographical, and incidental commentary, for two plaintive passages of sentimentality and two of social satire, a few spots of literary gloss and enough contemporary and historical allusions to keep the annotators busy.

These sundry components are arranged in a balanced proportion that Byron did not try to design elsewhere. He stops short of certain extremes, both in content and style, that are sometimes the chief merit and sometimes the chief flaw of other cantos. The action is the best farce in the poem, but it does not run into extravagant violence or extravagant fantasy. He does not let commentary drift and amble in his most casual or laziest manner and does not pile on decoration and sentiment. His disillusionment and pessimism spread wider and deeper elsewhere. The creative ardor that always excited Byron when he began a new kind of poem, coupled with a self-control and a care in verbal revision unusual for him, give many single lines and stanzas a maximum animation of wit and surprise. . . .

The first two cantos do not tell us all that Byron has to say in *Don Juan*, nor do they give us all the social types and institutions of his epic carnival, but taken together they pretty well comprehend all his manners and modes, all his tricks and methods in narrative, in characterization, in confession, and in commentary. The second is stronger and heavier in a sensational way, but in spite of its crude dichotomy of roughness and sentiment it is more limited than the high-spirited, farcical, and more lightly proportioned, more varied first canto. . . .

Although Byron took less care with the composition of the last six cantos, especially with revision, and paid a price for his haste, there is no decline or fluctuation of his witty or fanciful energies. One can find in them as many quotable couplets and epigrams as in the early cantos, and perhaps more stanzas that are memorable even out of their context. The pages of each English canto are alive with terse and mocking comment on the vanity and folly of human affairs, with clever verses, ingenious rhymes, odd conceits, and brazen incongruities. . . .

Byron's treatment of Juan, like that of some other matters in the English cantos, becomes fuller, more complex, more promising, just at the time when he stops writing.

Truman G. Steffan
*Byron's Don Juan*, vol. I (Austin, Tex.:
Univ. Texas Pr., 1957), pp. 186, 196, 258, 277

It was inevitable that the kaleidoscopic poem which reflected so clearly every passing mood and thought of the author should be limited by the preoccupations of that one heart and mind. And it is a tribute to Byron's understanding of the general human situation that he so seldom deviated into boredom, even though the major themes are few and frequently repeated: the vanity of ambition (already well-worn in *Childe Harold*), the pretentiousness of poets, his distaste for Tory tyrants and the Holy Alliance, the absurdity of "ladies intellectual," the hypocrisy of "Platonism" in love, cynical observations on love and marriage, the basic savagery of men faced with self-preservation (the shipwreck), the beauty of "natural love" (Haidée—"Half naked, loving, natural, and Greek"), the hollowness of glory and the brutality of war, the frailty of women and the inconstancy of men, the hypocrisies and boredom of English society, the exposure of cant in religion, in politics, in education, and a dozen excursions and digressions into speculative and personal prejudices. The intensity and vigor of the satire and the wit, the directness and the honesty of the exposure of sham feelings and conventional poses give life to many episodes and themes hackneyed enough in themselves.

Byron's choice of a hero was a fortunate one. He had less of the *alter ego* of the author than had Childe Harold. Byron took delight in creating a Don Juan who was not a heartless pursuer and despoiler of women like the legendary character, but a gentle innocent, first seduced by a self-deluding Donna Julia, then engulfed in the "natural love" of the sinless Haidée, repelled and revolted by the imperious commands of the Sultan's favorite, Gulbeyaz, who had bought him for her pleasure, passively accepting the caresses of the supple Dudu, essentially unchanged at being swept by circumstances into the position of favorite of Catherine the Great (though Byron allows us to assume that he was becoming more *gâté* and *blasé* as he grew in experience), and finally a detached observer of the intrigues and hypocrisies of the English society into which he was thrown in the last cantos, but ending on the solid breast of "her frolic Grace," the Duchess of Fitz-Fulke. . . .

Leslie A. Marchand
Introd., in *Don Juan* (Boston: Houghton Mifflin, 1958), pp. x-xi

The suggestion that *Don Juan* is constructed largely upon the use of dramatic irony, which the poet began to use early in his career and develop more or less consistently thereafter, runs counter to the dominant tendency in Byron criticism. Many of those who have written about the poem have regarded nearly all utterances in the first person as primarily and often exclusively, Byron's own. Such a viewpoint arises from excessive literalness in particular instances and from a basic failure to understand the structure of the poem; on occasion it has led critics toward the quest for such values as "sincerity" and perhaps even "consistency.". . .

In their dramatic function, in *how* they say rather than in *what* they say, the speakers in *Don Juan* achieve the irony that dominates the poem, thereby intensifying what is revealed in its panoramic view: the imperfection in Man's powers, the acute limitations upon what he can achieve for himself, and in fact the impossibility of his achieving an integrated and continuous view of the Self and therefore of the world upon which that Self must impose meaning. *Don Juan* should be regarded as a vast literary joke (some have called it a farce), which is humorous in its means but, beneath the clownish leer, serious in its implications. It is not satire, for it ultimately offers, in its description of the absurdities of the real, no suggestion of the ideal. Its irony is terminal rather than instrumental; this is achieved and sustained principally through a complex of individual monologues, in which the speakers, often unaware of the full situational context for their speeches, frequently reveal to us far more than they intend.

W. H. Marshall
*The Structure of Byron's Major Poems* (Philadelphia:
Univ. Pennsylvania Pr., 1962), pp. 174, 177

. . . He did not give to the planning of his satire the same close attention that he gave to individual lines and stanzas, and the way in which it was composed undoubtedly made for weaknesses of structure. . . . He kept having ideas for new episodes and for great extensions of the poem; and since a work of this expanding scope could not be seen as a whole even by the author himself, he soon abandoned any attempt at moulding it into a single meaningful design. And so Byron's comic epic became something of a large, loose, baggy monster, full of life, but lacking the concentrated power which comes only with organic unity such as we admire in *Paradise Lost,* or *The Rape of the Lock,* or *Tom Jones,* or for that matter in *Beppo* and *The Vision of Judgment.*

Andrew Rutherford
*Byron. A Critical Study* (Stanford, Calif.:
Stanford Univ. Pr., 1962), pp. 140-41

LETTERS AND JOURNALS

Byron himself in his letters never writes to produce a literary effect. He writes to give information, to express precise and definite sentiments; and he does it with a direct exactness which is at once the absence of all art and the perfection of art.

Between the prose of the letters and the tone of the poems we find profound similarities. The first is *vigour*. When Byron has formulated a judgment, experienced a desire, conceived a hate, these thoughts *must* spout up.

He cannot contain them, nor moderate them. Words underlined mark the force of the outburst. Everything is said, without reserve, without attenuation, savagely. His mother before him wrote like this. The second resemblance is *movement*. One of Byron's letters, like one of his poems, sweeps the reader along in an irresistible onrush. The identity of tone, and, above all, of rhythm between his prose and his verses, is such that sometimes, quite naturally, the letter becomes a poem without the reader being surprised by the change. A good example is the charming letter to Tom Moore on the Venetian carnival.

One could almost say that Byron's prose is more poetic than his poetry. The latter can sometimes incur the reproach of a little too much monotony in the rhythms, a little ingenuousness in the subjects. But his letters, like his journal, exhibit the rather mad poetry of the Elizabethan clowns. In prose, as in verse, he loves phrases with well-marked antitheses: "I am losing my relatives and you are adding to the number of yours, but which is best, God knows.". . . Sometimes he captures the very essential music of speech: "I have hopes, sir—hopes, but she wants me to come to Ravenna. Now this would be all very well for certainties; but for mere hope.". . . And so certain words recur like rhymes. An irresistible power runs through the phrases. When we see the originals of Byron's letters, difficult to read, imperious, never crossed out, we imagine the prodigious rapidity with which, never stopping, never hesitating, never retouching, this quick, firm pen etched a truthful portrait. It is in the letters, in the journals, in *Don Juan,* and in his delightful "short lyrics" that the greatest of the English romantics reveals himself, not far behind Voltaire and Swift, as one of the greatest classic writers. [1933]

André Maurois
Introd., in *The Letters of Lord Byron* (New York:
E. P. Dutton, 1948), p. xii


When there was no longer a disproportion between sentiment and object, when he could see things as they are, and could feel as a sane man feels, Byron began to cast about for a technique which should express adequately his new objectivity, his new cynical defences. The [colloquial] style had from his earliest years been ready to his hand in his *Letters and Journals,* but as long as he felt it necessary to impose himself on the world and salve his own hurt pride such a style could not seem to him appropriate. In the *Letters and Journals* there is an abundance of vigorous direct writing, magnificent examples of that aristocratic colloquial speech which had been the heritage of the English nobility from the Restoration down to Chesterfield and Sheridan. Byron is the last great writer to make use of it greatly.

Ronald Bottrall
*Criterion* (January, 1939), pp. 208-9

GENERAL

When all is said and done Byron remains a great poet because his poetry possesses certain great qualities in a fuller measure than his in many other ways more richly dowered contemporaries. They are not the purest, the highest gifts of the poet, but they are qualities which his poetry shares with that of some of our greatest older poets more fully than does the poetry of Wordsworth or Shelley or Coleridge or Keats. It is no intention of mine to endeavour to restore Byron's whilom reputation as the greatest of English poets after Shakespeare and Milton. . . . But poetry has many qualities and moves on more than one level. . . . And this is where Byron's poetry joins hands with that of Chaucer and Shakespeare and Milton and Dryden and Pope if it fails to ascend the highest heavens. It has force, passion, humour and wit, narrative and descriptive power, oratorical fire and conversational ease and flow. . . . Byron has been overestimated and underestimated—the fact remains that English poetry would be greatly the poorer without the passionate, humorous, essentially human voice that declaims in *Childe Harold* and flows like a torrent in *Don Juan*. [1920]

H. J. C. Grierson
*The Background of English Literature* (New York:
Barnes and Noble, 1960), pp. 112-14

That Byron never found the peace of transcendentalism must be evident to all who are acquainted with his work. . . . Although no one would undertake to prove that Byron was a profound thinker, he possessed a quality which many supposedly profound thinkers lack—a sense of the toughness of facts and an inability to dupe himself about them. It is useless to argue that he had either more or less intelligence than his great contemporaries, but surely he had quite enough intelligence to be a transcendentalist. Perhaps, indeed, he had *too much* intelligence of the realistic sort. Beneath all his protective histrionism, his mind possessed a certain desperate integrity which should command respect.

Hoxie Fairchild
*The Romantic Quest* (New York:
Columbia Univ. Pr., 1931), p. 362

Eliot's role as a literary critic has been very similar to Valéry's in France. . . . He has brought back to English criticism something of that trenchant rationalism which he admires in the eighteenth century, but with a more catholic appreciation of different styles and points of view than the eighteenth century allowed. The Romantics, of course, fare badly before this criticism. Vague sentiment vaguely expressed, rhetorical effusion disguising bad art—these Eliot's laconic scorn has nipped. For him, Byron is "a disorderly mind, and an uninteresting one.". . .

The real effect of Eliot's, as of Valéry's, literary criticism, is to impose upon us a conception of poetry as some sort of pure and rare aesthetic essence with no relation to any of the practical human uses for which, for some reason never explained, only the technique of prose is appropriate.

Now this point of view . . . seems to me absolutely unhistorical—an impossible attempt to make aesthetic values independent of all the other values. [1931]

Edmund Wilson
*Axel's Castle* (New York:
Scribner's, 1951), pp. 117, 119

Of Byron one can say, as of no other English poet of his eminence, that he added nothing to the language, that he discovered nothing in the sounds, and developed nothing in the meaning, of individual words. I cannot think of any other poet of his distinction who might so easily have been an accomplished foreigner writing English. [1937]

T. S. Eliot
*On Poetry and Poets* (New York:
Farrar, Straus, 1957), p. 232

Byron's work was a needed weapon in the armory of Romanticism because that reform of the standards and ways of living which the Romantics desired could not be effected as long as the sway of worldliness over human minds remained so strong. Wordsworth and Lamb and Landor might turn away from such worldliness and find delight in nature, in simplicity of life, or in noble traditions; but power and prestige and common sense still seemed to remain on the side of the worldlings. To ridicule their pretensions, show the selfishness of their politics, and unmask the hypocrisy of their religion and their moral codes, was the most valuable service of Byron to the romantic cause. [1930; rev. 1949]

Ernest Bernbaum
*Guide through the Romantic Movement* (New York:
Ronald Pr., 1949), p. 209

It is clear that much of Byron's poetry must be judged to be imperfect, for reasons well known and generally accepted. Much of his work is flawed because, for the achievement of many poetic effects, he lacked the necessary delicately tuned ear. . . . He lacked the indispensable gift necessary for writing consistently excellent lyric poetry, a heightened sensitivity to the subtleties of sound combination.

Ernest J. Lovell
in *The Major English Romantic Poets*, eds. Clarence D. Thorpe,
Carlos Baker, and Bennett Weaver (Carbondale, Ill.:
Southern Illinois Univ. Pr., 1957), p. 129

Reduce everything he ever wrote, and you will find an essential act of repulsion: either self-emptying into a *persona,* or a repudiation. He pushes away what he is; he repudiates even the *persona* of *Don Juan.* He has the insecure person's fierce need of elimination; he needs to feel unobliged to his subject-matter, his friends, his publisher, his mistresses, his house, his rôle, his reputation. And yet, by a method approaching "double-think," he seeks to eliminate this lust for elimination; and so he lands up with inappropriate impedimenta—the wrong woman, the wrong type of poem, the wrong reputation, the wrong stanza-form, and so on. His was a multiple nature, chameleonic and irresponsible. This is not to say that he cannot be found in a mood of single-mindedness, a denial of his changeability, a resolute act—all of which show now and then in his dealings over his daughters. Simply, his inconsistency amounted to a perpetual recombination of the same (or most of the same) elements.

There were limits to his unpredictability. He is never to be found propounding a philosophical scheme. He is never the thorough classicist or the thorough romantic. But there is, in the life and in the legend of Byronism, plenty enough; enough, in one person and one life, of other humans and their suppressed cravings to keep the rehashers busy for decades to come. What needs to be undertaken is a study of the literary implications of this much-quarried temperament. The personality, I suggest, pre-empts the style and the genre. Here was a sensitive man who for social and psychic reasons had to eliminate ties and sensibility. Only when he wrote farcically or confessionally was he a writer without reserve. And when he wrote confessionally he was eventually obliged to evoke *Childe Harold.* Even in *Don Juan* he can be sincerely himself only when writing from the viewpoint of farce. For in farce there is no considerateness, no sensitivity and no response. The personages are inhuman; they lack "presence"—in its religious sense, and are not *obliged* in any way. And, in Byron's writing, just as there is a farce of personages, there is—consummate in *Don Juan*—a farce of language. The serious poet at his dignified best or portentous worst is obliged to maintain a high seriousness, to ensure congruity and decorum. From all this, the *farceur* is exempt.

Paul West
*Byron and the Spoiler's Art* (New York:
St. Martin's Pr., 1960), pp. 12-13

His main achievement lies . . . in his satires in *ottava rima,* for his discovery of the *Beppo* style transformed him, almost overnight, into a major poet, and he retains this status only so long as he confines himself to that style —it was an essential condition of his greatness, the one medium that allowed his genius its full scope. Yet this discovery did not mean (as is frequently supposed) that Byron's difficulties were all over—that from now on masterpieces would flow easily or inevitably from his pen. Although he could now write superbly he was still faced with artistic and personal problems, his solutions to which vary in effectiveness from poem to poem; so that important discriminations must be made even within this group of satires which are superficially so much alike. . . . They [the *ottava rima* poems] were not the only works that Byron wrote in these years, but they were the best: apart from them the period 1817-24 was one of largely misguided experiment on his part, and the plays which were his other main concern are far inferior in quality.

Andrew Rutherford
*Byron. A Critical Study* (Stanford, Calif.:
Stanford Univ. Pr., 1962), p. xii

# THOMAS CAMPBELL
### 1777-1844

Born in Glasgow and educated at its University, Thomas Campbell, the son of a Scottish merchant, spent a good many of his mature years in London, where he contributed to the popular journals and became a member of its Whig literary circle. He ended his life as Rector of Glasgow University and was buried in Westminster Abbey, having achieved fame as a poet of martial lyrics and a defender of liberty wherever it was threatened. His best-known poems are *Ye Mariners of England* (1801); *Hohenlinden* (1802); *Lochiel's Warning* (1802); *The Battle of the Baltic* (1809); *Gertrude of Wyoming* (1809); and *The Last Man* (1823).

J. Logie Robertson, ed., *Complete Poetical Works* (1908)
J. Cuthbert Hadden, *Thomas Campbell* (1899)

I rise from a careful perusal of Campbell's poetry with a feeling of mingled surprise and indignation that he is at present so much neglected, and with the conviction that a later generation will do more honour to his memory than we have done. It is not enough to say that he had his fame in his lifetime, that he was well pensioned for what he did, and that he lived to disappoint the hopes which he excited at the beginning of his career. One might reply that the services he rendered his country by his patriotic songs have not ceased, or been superseded by any later master of the lyre; and, though he is by no means equal, and his inequalities are far from microscopic, yet the author little deserves neglect who has written such fine, bold, and varied poems. . . .

J. L. Robertson
Introd., in *Complete Poetical Works of Thomas Campbell*
(New York: Oxford Univ. Pr., 1907), p. iii

*The Pleasures of Hope,* in its frequent use of Abstraction and Personification, exhibits all the features of the didactic poetry of the eighteenth century; but in his later poems, notably *Ye Mariners of England, Hohenlinden,* and *The Battle of the Baltic,* Campbell discards these mannerisms and develops a style of his own that reflects the best and purest social idiom of the age. It would be hard to find any short poem in the English language that contains so many elements of the sublime as *Hohenlinden.* In eight stanzas the poet, by a series of master-strokes, has called up a living picture of conflict between two vast armies. . . .

Scarcely less skill in the selection and combination of metrical words is shown in *The Battle of the Baltic,* a composition in which patriotic emotion lifts the imagination of poet and reader into a still loftier atmosphere. . . .

Campbell's lyrics are much the best part of his poetry. . . . Campbell imposes form on his romantic matter with an easy freedom that suggests how much of his inspiration was derived from the exciting air of the revolutionary era. The swift movement of his rhythms, and his bold mixture of polysyllabic Latin words with picturesque monosyllables . . . are admirable. Other romantic features in his poetry are, doubtless, the product of a tendency in the public taste which had now for almost a generation favoured the revival of the ballad style originated by Percy's *Reliques.* But he may justly claim to have been the first to direct the new movement into popular channels. [1910]

W. J. Courthope
*A History of English Poetry,* Vol. VI (New York:
Russell and Russell, 1962), pp. 107-8, 110-11

No one, indeed, could in a fever of enthusiasm describe him as faultless. I do not refer to his scientific inaccuracies. In some of his longer poems—*The Pleasures of Hope* and *Gertrude of Wyoming*—he strews them lavishly. He introduces tigers to the shores of Lake Erie, hyaenas into South America, and panthers into Ohio. . . . They occur, however, in poems with which we need not occupy ourselves. Time has settled their account. He said all he had to say in them, but unfortunately had nothing to say. They are not without their felicities, their catching phrases, once much admired. Who has not heard of "angel's visits, few and far between," or quoted

'Tis distance lends enchantment to the view?

Fine things, you maintain. Yes, but these fine things cannot save them. As poems their day is gone. . . . What remains? A handful of lyrics, a few hundred lines of verse. . . .

It is, perhaps, his peculiar glory that he wrote the only martial lyrics in our language that have gained universal currency—*The Mariners of England* and *The Battle of the Baltic.* . . . It was left to a Scottish poet to write the poetry no Englishman had written, of the sea and English sailors; to celebrate Nelson, the best-beloved, almost worshipped hero of the navy and the nation. An achievement surely most surprising and most enviable.

That is not, however, Campbell's sole achievement. In that inimitable ballad *Lord Ullin's Daughter,* or, better still, in *Hohenlinden*—to take a single example of his lucid and admirable art—we have verses of which any poet, whatever his rank, might with pride have claimed the authorship. . . .

W. Macneile Dixon
*Glasgow Univ. Publication,* No. 12
(Glasgow: 1928), pp. 13-14, 17-18

Do you know "The Soldier's Dream"? It is European only in the sense that it describes a few things which are local rather than general—such as the bleating of goats on the mountain tops. Leave out the goats and one or two unimportant touches of the same thought, and you have a poem describing the heart of the soldier in all countries. . . . Like a good artist he makes no comment about the emotion—the poem abruptly breaks off with the awakening; and leaves the thrill of the dream and the pain of the awakening to haunt our minds. [1934]

Lafcadio Hearn
*On Poets,* eds. R. Tanabe, T. Ochiai, and I. Nishizaki
(Tokyo: Hokuseido Pr., 1941), pp. 644-45

The cause of Poland was a lifelong passion with him. When he penned his celebrated bad line Kosciusko was a fresh memory. In 1830 the Polish rising was crushed by a barbaric Tsardom. Campbell's fervour reawoke and took positive shape. He formed an association of the Friends of Poland and spent himself in their service for nine years. From first to last he was a poet who gave far more to Freedom than his songs.

There would seem to be little room for difference of opinion about the bulk of Campbell's poetry. Who among us can find pleasure in *The Pleasures of Hope,* although single lines will always be in the common speech? It is not a good reflective poem. It is derivative, poor in structure and not without passages of rhetorical nonsense. *Gertrude of Wyoming* (a lovely title, though the poet did not know how the accent fell in America) is stamped upon by George Saintsbury, who was a warm admirer of Campbell's best, as the clumsiest caricature of the Spenserian stanza. That judgement is mistaken. Uninspired the verse is, but not clumsy. Gertrude's story is a sentimental tragedy, too condensed to be clear. Welcomed with rapture in 1809, it can have very few responsive readers today. Jeffrey, by the way, was not wrong in telling Campbell that his excessive care for finish and polish was fatal. He was incapable of passing an untidy line, and yet he could allow absurd errors, such as the tigers on Lake Erie's shore, to stand uncorrected.

S. K. Ratcliffe
*Spec* (June 16, 1944), p. 545

. . . A word is due for Thomas Campbell, born July 27, 1777, died June 15, 1844, in whose once celebrated, now neglected and never-to-be-revived *Pleasures of Hope* he so early in life revealed a master of the Popean couplet—with complete absence, in the forlorn monotony of the form, of the Popean spirit and vigour of mind. . . .

Fine lines still keep vital . . . "Lord Ullin's Daughter" and the still famous warning,

> Lochiel! Lochiel, beware of the day
> When the Lowlands shall meet thee in battle array!

Thomas Campbell, with a few jewels, can never be kept out of the anthologies. And some of his inventions—"Coming events cast their shadows before" and " 'Tis distance lends enchantment to the view"—cannot be kept out of the English speech.

*TLS* (June 17, 1944), p. 295

# SAMUEL TAYLOR COLERIDGE
## 1772-1834

Born in Devonshire, Samuel Taylor Coleridge was the thirteenth child of an absent-minded, scholarly, and impoverished minister-schoolmaster. At ten, he entered Christ's Hospital, London, where he met Charles Lamb, who became his life-long friend. Distinguished for his scholarship in grammar school, he received even greater recognition for his learning at Cambridge University, which he entered in 1791. In 1794, he met Robert Southey, with whom he evolved the abortive socialist scheme called Pantisocracy. In 1795, he married Sarah Fricker, sister of Southey's wife, but he failed to carry out his responsibilities as a husband and eventually turned his affections toward Sarah Hutchinson, the sister of Wordsworth's wife Mary. His friendship with Wordsworth developed in 1797 when the two engaged in a literary project resulting in the revolutionary *Lyrical Ballads* of 1798. From this time until 1801, Coleridge wrote most of the poems which have made him immortal. Thereafter, his health and spirit began to decline. He had been taking drugs for some time, and as his addiction increased, he announced his farewell to poetry in "Dejection: an Ode" (1802). He came to depend for support on the generosity of friends and on occasional lectures, which he delivered brilliantly without notes. His ill health and despondency increasing, Coleridge in 1816 went to live with Dr. James Gilman, under whose care he recovered sufficiently to revise and publish several important poems and essays. He died in 1834, suffering in his last year from hostile criticism and befriended by few others than Charles Lamb. His literary output, much of it in fragments, was small but precious and is best represented by "The Conversation Poems" (1795?-1802); "France: an Ode" (1798); *The Ancient Mariner* (1798); "Love" (1799); "Christabel" (1816); "Kubla Khan" (1816); *The Friend* (1818-1819); *Biographia Literaria* (1817); *Lectures* (1810-1818); and *Aids to Reflection* (1825).

E. H. Coleridge, ed., *Complete Poetical Works* (1912), 2 vols.; John Shawcross, ed., *Biographia Literaria* (1907), 2 vols.

Lawrence Hanson, *Life of S. T. Coleridge: The Early Years* (1938); E. K. Chambers, *S. T. Coleridge: A Biographical Study* (1938)

## PERSONAL

In his ninth year Coleridge migrated to Christ's Hospital: and here the same habit of self-abstraction from his visible surroundings enforced itself. In the first impulse of homesickness, he was absorbed in memories of the scenes from which he was so early doomed to be parted for ever: then, as this yearning gradually abated, the passion for speculation took its place, and he made his first acquaintance with the philosophy of mysticism in the writings of the Neoplatonists. But almost at the same time the world of phenomena claimed his attention. The arrival of his brother Luke in London to study at the London Hospital gave a new direction to his thoughts, and soon he was deep in all the medical literature on which he could lay his hands. Such reading, as we can readily understand, seemed to reveal to him a new interpretation of things, an interpretation which it was so difficult to bring into line with his idealistic speculations that it practically remained unaffected by them. Hence the transition to Voltaire was easy. . . . Thus early was he awakened to consciousness of that inward discord which it was the task of his life to explain and to resolve—the discord engendered by the opposing claims of the senses and intellect on the one hand, and of what he here chooses to call *the heart* on the other. [1907]

John Shawcross
Introd., in Samuel T. Coleridge, *Biographia Literaria*
(Oxford Univ. Pr., 1954), pp. xii-xiii

Perhaps indeed the grand failure of Coleridge was the failure to be completely honest. He was completely honest neither with himself nor with his work. Where he was honest with his neighbours, it was not from principle, but by a flair which he had for grandiose behaviour. If his best work came from his connexion with Wordsworth, it was because here he made contact with an astonishingly matter-of-fact honesty; which he was able to recognize, let it be added, not as an ornament, or attribute, but as the essence, of Wordsworth's power as a poet. . . .

Inspired conversation. Here was an art in which not even his enemies denied to Coleredge an unchallengeable pre-eminence. It is valuable, in an age credulous of heroes but oddly sceptical of gods, to emphasize that character of the life of poetry which consists in inspiration. More fully and consistently than poets of great effectiveness, Coleridge hit this character. With the same ease with which other men are protractedly dull, Coleridge was without intermission inspired. Yet with an inspiration curiously self-indulgent. He yielded himself wholly to the momentary rapture, to the melting influences of his own temperament. It was not in him to save the transport for epic or Ode, for tragedy or for a sustained Lucretian flight. But in conversation, and in the Conversation Poem, he was for ever pouring out magnanimously, or with a grandly calculated carelessness spilling, the wine of a spirituality limitlessly fecund. [1925]

H. W. Garrod
Introd., in *Coleridge, Poetry and Prose*
(Oxford Univ. Pr., 1954), pp. ix, xiii

. . . His reverence [for Sara] was met by neither sympathy nor respect. Sara was heartless enough to make him get up on really freezing mornings in his nightshirt to light the fire, before she dressed herself and the children, and according to his own account broke out into outrageous passions, "like a wet candle spitting flame," he aply noted. The weather and his health were terrible and opium a ceaseless necessity. Once again he resolved at all costs formally to separate, but Sara's conventionality, which had helped to kill the marriage as a reality preserved it as a fact. Her one argument in opposing such a step was that "everybody will talk," although Coleridge's suggestion that he should take his two boys with him and superintend their education may have with reason alarmed her. Before Christmas, however, his patience was exhausted, and taking Hartley with him, he followed the Wordsworths to Coleorton. . . . [ca. 1926]

Hugh I. A. Fausset
*Coleridge* (New York: Harcourt, Brace, n.d.) p. 239

. . . Coleridge's failure to make good was primarily due to a fundamental instability of character. He had dreamed of the permanent, but had lived wholly in the present, talking brilliantly and incessantly, and snatching at every will-o'-the-wisp interest which a vivid imagination suggested to him. He could not integrate his life, and when troubles, for which he was not wholly responsible, came upon him, he had no reserve of endurance to make head against them. His gift of introspection sometimes gave him a whisper of this. "Sloth-jaundic'd all," he had once said of himself, and had bewailed his "chance-started friendships." It was not exactly sloth. His mind was always actively at work upon something, only it was generally the wrong thing. And "chance-started friendships" were to serve him well throughout life. So Coleridge drifted to disaster. . . . [1938]

E. K. Chambers
*Samuel Taylor Coleridge* (Oxford Univ. Pr., 1950), p. 133

On his arrival at Cambridge, Coleridge began writing letters in earnest. . . . He had been in his rooms no more than a month before dampness and draughts gave him a cold, which developed into a rheumatic attack. These ailments called forth the first of the detailed descriptions of his symptoms which were later to occupy an increasingly prominent place in his letters. They also provide the first existing reference which Coleridge made to opium. . . .

The meeting [between Wordsworth and Coleridge] confirmed the interest which each had felt in the other and his work; the recitation [of Wordsworth's poetry] went far to formulate in Coleridge's mind the famous distinction, made later, between fancy and imagination; and it encouraged views on poetic theory and practice already held by Coleridge, strengthening both his aversion to the existing poetic order and his determination to supplant it—and so, lending new force to the impulse which was to produce, only two years later, the epoch-making *Lyrical Ballads*.

Lawrence Hanson
*The Life of S. T. Coleridge* (New York:
Oxford Univ. Pr., 1939), pp. 29, 116-17

Contrary to a very general impression, Coleridge was not just the inspired talker, a financial burden and practical problem to friends who supported the man Coleridge for the sake of the poet. It is perfectly clear to any reader of the letters that he entered into the lives and concerns of his acquaintances with a zestful mind interested in all manner of things and able to forget itself in its own energy. For example, take his relation to Thomas Poole and Humphry Davy. When he talked to Poole, a tanner and agriculturalist, he asked him about the processes of tanning and the economics of agriculture. He stored up for him in his notebooks hints on how to plant trees and the sorts and uses of fertilizers. When Poole had a chemistry problem in his tanyard, it was Coleridge who asked questions of Davy, the solutions of which helped to further Davy's career. He also went to the Pneumatic Institution in Bristol. . . .

Kathleen Coburn
*Inquiring Spirit* (New York: Pantheon, 1951), p. 11

Opium more than any other cause has been held responsible for the failure of Coleridge both to fulfil all the promise of his genius and to win his everyday living by steady labors. During much of his life he depended upon gifts and loans from friends; his path was strewn with abortive plans and fragments. He himself attributed his "sloth" to opium, and that cause has not been much questioned. . . .

The relaxation of tension and conflict, accompanied by a sense of pleasant ease, occasionally helps to release for a time the neurotic person's natural powers of thought or imagination or (rarely) of action, though it does not give him powers that he did not have or change the character of his normal powers. Coleridge recognized this effect upon himself when he said . . . that opium by its narcotic effect made his body a fitter instrument for his soul. . . .

Coleridge's misdating of his poems—his habit of assigning them a date too early, attributing them sometimes to his youth or boyhood—arises not from sublime indifference to mundane dates but from the self-mistrust that finds them not the supreme poetic achievement that he requires them to be; the misdatings are, in fact, gestures of deprecation. . . . His "lies" were not usually of the well-ordered kind, calculated to succeed and establish him credit in the world. They were momentary even when they were repeated from time to time, and were almost always doomed to sink him into a deeper morass than before.

Elisabeth Schneider
*Coleridge, Opium, and Kubla Khan* (Chicago:
Univ. Chicago Pr., 1953), pp. 31, 40, 108

## CONVERSATION POEMS

The compositions which I denominate Poems of Friendship or Conversation Poems are "The Eolian Harp," "Reflections on having left a Place of Retirement," "This Lime-Tree Bower my Prison," "Frost at Midnight," "Fears in Solitude," "The Nightingale," "Dejection," and "To William Wordsworth" (sometimes printed "To a Gentleman"). The list is not complete; there are shorter pieces which might be added; but these are the most substantial and, I think, the best. The qualities common to all the eight are qualities of style no less than of subject. . . . Until he met Wordsworth, which was probably in 1795, Coleridge wrote in the manner which had been fashionable since the death of Milton, employing without hesitation all those poetic licences which constituted what he later termed "Gaudyverse," in contempt. . . . If one reads Coleridge's early poems in chronological order, one will perceive that Gaudyverse persists till about the middle of 1795, and then quickly yields to the natural style which Wordsworth was practising. . . .

"Reflections on having left a Place of Retirement" . . . begins with a quiet description of the surrounding scene and, after a superb flight of imagination, brings the mind back to the starting-point, a pleasing device which we may call the "return." The imagination, in the second poem, seeks not . . . a metaphysical, but an ethical height. The poet is tormented in the midst of his happiness by the thought of those who live in wretchedness or who die in war. . . .

["Dejection"] . . . is an ode in form only; in contents it is a conversation. It is not an address to Dejection, but to William Wordsworth. . . . In this sublime and heartrending poem Coleridge gives expression to an experience of double consciousness. His sense-perceptions are vivid and in part agreeable; his inner state is faint, blurred, and unhappy. He sees, but cannot feel. The power of feeling has been paralysed by chemically induced excitements of his brain. The seeing power, less dependent upon bodily health, stands aloof, individual, critical, and very mournful. By "seeing" he means perceiving and judging; by "feeling" he means that which impels to action. He suffers, but the pain is dull, and he wishes it were keen, for so he should awake from lethargy and recover unity at least. But nothing from outside can restore him. The sources of the soul's life are within.

George McLean Harper<br>
QR (April, 1925), pp. 287-89, 295

In "Dejection" he describes what for him must have seemed damnation, for he no longer is capable of the life that still seems so precious, paradoxically and tragically precious, since he no longer believes that there is any genuine objectivity in the communion with Nature. To the joyous man, Coleridge realizes, the world seems indeed a friendly place. . . . But Coleridge can advance no further: he does not describe Joy as a "consciousness of Whom we are." He has lost the mysticism of the conversation poems. [1945]

N. P. Stallknecht<br>
Strange Seas of Thought (Bloomington, Ind.:<br>
Indiana Univ. Pr., 1962), p. 164

The Wind Harp, though it is a far humbler responsive system, can "say" for him nearly as much as a plant can. It bursts into "The Nightingale" at line 80, quivers gently in "Fears in Solitude" at line 21, and supplies the return or resolution to "France: An Ode," to take three instances only. We will do well to linger a moment to try to realize its scope.

As the intellectual breeze plays on the organic harp, the music which arises orders all perception. It orders therefore the harp and the breeze as well; "all of animated nature" and unanimated nature too, if there be any. Whatever it is which responds—and, in responding, perceives—gives the perceived form, through its response, to whatever is perceived. This itself, of course, is Coleridge's response to Berkeley, a strong influence upon him at this time. He does not seem to have been willing, though, ever to suppose —for more than a moment—that the *being* of things was that they were perceived. The problem for him was rather: How much that we seem to find in things is put there by the mode in which we perceive them?

I. A. Richards
Introd., in *The Portable Coleridge* (New York:
Viking Pr., 1950), p. 39

The finest poem in this [Conversation] group is "Frost at Midnight"; and indeed it is one of the finest short poems in the language. I think it is much loved; it is certainly much praised; but even so I doubt whether it is adequately appreciated as the perfectly achieved work of art which it is. It has suffered even more than the other poems from piecemeal handling; it is so exceedingly quotable for extraneous reasons. [1951-52]

Humphry House
*Coleridge* (London: Rupert Hart-Davis, 1953), p. 78

The years . . . had enriched his perception of what constitutes the inner unity of a poem. The experience of writing the "diffuse" conversation poems had taught him how to organize his content around a key image or idea, in lieu of the external formalities of a genre, and thereby fuse form and content into a single entity. In "Dejection," the storm functions as a key image. With considerable viability, it concentrates into a unified statement Coleridge's complex and ambivalent feelings of listless dejection and aroused grief, and of hopeful anticipation and disappointing frustration. Vividly evocative of the tension resulting from these dual responses and fully integrated as a part of the storm imagery are the supplementary motifs of fertility-sterility and freedom-restriction. As a result, the poem, although outwardly formless, is inwardly a model of patterned statement.

M. F. Schulz
*The Poetic Voices of Coleridge* (Detroit:
Wayne State Univ. Pr., 1963), p. 33

## Kubla Khan

Nobody in his waking senses could have fabricated those amazing [last] eighteen lines. For if anything ever bore the infallible marks of authenticity it is that dissolving panorama in which fugitive hints of Aloadine's Paradise succeed each other with the vivid incoherence, and the illusion of natural and expected sequence, and the sense of an identity that yet is not identity, which are the distinctive attributes of dreams. Coleridge's statement of his experience has more than once been called in question. These lines alone, in their relation to the passage which suggested them, should banish doubt. [1927]

J. L. Lowes
*The Road to Xanadu* (Boston: Houghton Mifflin, 1964), p. 331

. . . Coleridge's verse caught up the evanescent images of an opium dream, and struck them into immobility for all time. The dream quality of "Kubla Khan" cannot be analyzed; like the rainbow tints of a butterfly's wing, it turns to dust on the fingers. But the swift shuttling of vistas is there to perfection. From "Alph, the sacred river" the scene shifts to brilliant gardens; then after a flash of "that deep romantic chasm," turns to the dome of pleasure; and suddenly, in that vision within a vision, emerge the glowing forms of the "Abyssinian maid" with a dulcimer, and the wild-haired youth who, like Coleridge, has "drunk the milk of Paradise."

No pain phenomena occur in the poem, for this is that rarity, a dream of pleasure purely, with all the intoxication and none of the tortures of opium. But Mr. Lowes's quick eye has caught, as most characteristic of "Kubla Khan," an effect which we know is the mark of opium; the extraordinary mutations of space. . . . And through all is maintained a restless ebb and flow of style, to match the eternal unrest of the dream scenery itself.

M. H. Abrams
*The Milk of Paradise* (Cambridge, Mass.:
Harvard Univ. Pr., 1934), pp. 46-47

We have noted in the poem of *Kubla Khan* an image-pattern of mountain-garden and caverned depths, of waters rising and falling, which we have seen also in *Paradise Lost*, and have followed back in Greek and Hebrew literature. When we examine the experience communicated by poetry and myth showing this image-pattern, we may, it is suggested, discern a corresponding pattern of emotion. Changeful and subtly interrelated as these patterns of emotion and imagery are found to be, yet the image of the watered garden and the mountain height show some persistent affinity with the desire and imaginative enjoyment of supreme well-being, or divine bliss, while the cavern depth appears as the objectification of an imaginative fear—an experience of fascination it may be, in which the pain of fear is lost in the relief of expression; in other instances the horror of loss and frustration symbolized by depth, darkness, and enclosing walls sounds its intrinsic note of pain even through the opposing gain and triumph that poetic expression achieves.

As in the preceding essay we traced a pattern of rising and sinking vitality, a forward urge and backward swing of life, reflected in an imagery deployed in time—an imagery in which winds and waters played their part—so now we find an emotional pattern of somewhat similar character presented statically, in imagery of fixed spatial relation—the mountain standing high in storm and sunlight, the cavern unchanging, dark, below, waters whose movement only emphasizes these steadfast relations of height and depth. [1934]

Maud Bodkin
*Archetypal Patterns in Poetry* (Oxford
Univ. Pr., 1951), pp. 114-15

. . . In this, the great and inimitable dream poem, the metrical beauty that stirred in the earlier poems, shone weirdly and variously in *The Ancient Mariner*, and lent *Christabel* no small part of its magical witchery, breaks into perfection. *Kubla Khan* is pure lyricism—sound, picture, sensation—clothed in the sensuous beauty of imagery that none knew so well as its author how to evoke. It is also the supreme example in English literature of the workings of the creative subconscious, unhelped—or unhindered—by conscious composition. That large and seemingly limitless pool of Coleridge's memory, into which was cast every conscious impression, is here allowed its one matchless expression, and returns its precious contents, refined, glorified, selected by the imagination, working secretly, undreamed of, but with great and abundant power. The taking of the opium, about which much has been said, may have provided the opportunity for this subconscious creation to take place, but that is the full extent of its power. Indeed, when all is said, this fragment of poem, together with the unfinished *Christabel* and the completed *The Ancient Mariner*, defy analysis. All three leave the reader, finally, wondering the more at such magic, such unearthly beauty, such miraculous hoverings between worlds, and above all, at the mortal brain that could have conceived such poems. The familiar plaint that Coleridge wrote so little great poetry turns, on reflection, into thankfulness and amazement that any man should have been enabled to break the bounds of mortality for so long.

Lawrence Hanson
*The Life of S. T. Coleridge* (New York:
Oxford Univ. Pr., 1939), pp. 260-61

*Kubla Khan* is a comprehensive creation, including and transcending not only the dualisms of *The Ancient Mariner* ("sun," "ice," and sexual suggestions recurring with changed significance) but also the more naturalistic, Wordsworthian, grandeurs. Though outwardly concentrating on an architectural synthesis, there is the other, mountainous, elevation suggested in Mount Abora; and indeed the dome itself is a kind of mountain with "caves," the transcendent and the natural being blended, as so often in

Wordsworth. It must be related to other similar statements of an ultimate intuition where the circular or architectural supervenes on the natural: in particular to the mystic dome of Yeats's *Byzantium*. The blend here of a circular symbolism with a human figure (the Abyssinian maid) and images of human conflict may be compared both to Dante's final vision and an important passage in Shelley's *Prometheus*. *Kubla Khan* is classed usually with *Christabel* and *The Ancient Mariner*, both profound poems with universal implications. The one presents a nightmare vision related to some obscene but nameless sex-horror; the other symbolizes a clear pilgrim's progress through sin to redemption. It would be strange if *Kubla Khan*, incorporating together the dark satanism and the water-purgatory of those, did not, like its sister poems, hold a comparable, or greater, profundity, its images clearly belonging to the same order of poetic reasoning. Its very names are so lettered as to suggest first and last things: Xanadu, Kubla Khan, Alph, Abyssinian, Abora. . . . The poem's supposed method of composition is well known. . . . It has a barbaric and oriental magnificence that asserts itself with the happy power and authenticity too often absent from visionary poems set within the Christian tradition.

G. Wilson Knight
*The Starlit Dome* (London: Methuen, 1941), pp. 96-97

If Coleridge had never published his Preface, who would have thought of "Kubla Khan" as a fragment? Who would have guessed at a dream? Who, without the confession, would have supposed that "in consequence of a slight indisposition, an anodyne had been prescribed"? Who would have thought it nothing but a "psychological curiosity"? Who later, would have dared to talk of its "patchwork brilliance"? Coleridge played, out of modesty, straight into the hands of critics.

Were is not for Livingston Lowes, it would hardly still be necessary to point out the poem's essential unity and the relation between its two parts. . . .

The unity of the poem focuses on just that transition from the first part to the second, and the pivot of all interpretation is in the lines:

> Could I revive within me
> Her symphony and song,
> To such a deep delight 'twould win me,
> That with music loud and long,
> I would build that dome in air. . . .

For "Kubla Khan" is a poem about the act of poetic creation, about the "ecstasy in imaginative fulfilment." [1951-1952]

Humphry House
*Coleridge* (London: Rupert Hart-Davis, 1953), pp. 114-15

*Kubla Khan,* to sum up, is a poem with two major themes: genius and the lost paradise. In the first stanza the man of commanding genius, the fallen but daemonic man, strives to rebuild the lost paradise in a world which is, like himself, fallen. In the second stanza, the other side of the daemonic re-asserts itself: the mighty fountain in the savage place, the wailing woman beneath the waning moon, the daemon-lover. The third stanza is a moment of miraculous harmony between the contending forces: the sunny dome and the caves of ice, the fountain and the caves, the dome and the waves all being counterpoised in one harmony. Finally, in the last stanza, there is a vision of paradise regained: of man re-visited by that absolute genius which corresponds to his original, unfallen state, of the honey-dew fountain of immortality re-established in the garden, of complete harmony between Apollo with his lyre and the damsel with the dulcimer, of the established dome, and of the multitude, reconciled by the terrible fascination of the genius into complete harmony.

In spite of the over-riding pattern of the poem, however, the imagery is so complicated and interwoven that a complete interpretation cannot be presented in one straightforward exposition. Instead, one is forced to establish the dialectic of thesis, antithesis, static harmony and desired consummation in the four stanzas, and then suggest how various images and ideas pass through it. . . .

The trouble is not that the poem has no meaning, but that it has too much. The reader can hardly be expected to bring to mind all the complicated involutions of sense which it contains in the time that it takes him to read fifty lines of poetry. On the contrary, his attention is far more likely to be caught throughout by the fascination of the sensuous imagery in its own right.

Nevertheless, if *Kubla Khan* is a petrified forest, it is also an enchanted forest. At every point it glows directly, and at every point, also, it reflects the intense subterranean energy of a mind which could not rest in its endeavour to apprehend all experience and reduce it to one harmony. It will always remain possible to enjoy it as a simple stream of images, and to ignore the opportunity which it affords of exploring the intricacies of Coleridge's visionary world. To be fascinated by these intricacies, one has first to share something of Coleridge's excitement at the potentialities of the basic images involved. Once we begin to sense this excitement, however, and its climax in the writing of a poem where, for a moment, his visionary world modelled itself into a single pattern, a paradigm that was also a focus of his major speculations in art and life, we may see that in this context more than any other the poem is what Coleridge himself was the first to call it: "a vision in a dream."

J. B. Beer
*Coleridge the Visionary* (London: Chatto and
Windus, 1959), pp. 266-67, 276

His distaste for the luxury and ambition of princes may help to explain *Kubla Khan*. He has clearly erected in that poem an antithesis between the measured and the measureless, the sunny and the sunless, the pleasure-dome and the deep romantic chasm, the pleasurable and the sacred, the decree of Kubla Khan and the prophecy amid tumult. Kubla said, Let there be a dome, and there was a dome. "But oh!" he heard from far "Ancestral voices prophesying war!" Setting aside the poles of drunken and sober Freudianism, critical analyses of the poem divide basically over attitudes toward the eastern potentate. Is the poem for Kubla or against him? Or, as possible but unlikely, does it lean neither for nor against? We need to resolve this point before we can declare Kubla the symbol of a poet decreeing the thing of beauty in his imagination, instead of a temporal lord creating in a mode less durable than the poet's mode opposed to it. Coleridge certainly in 1796, and almost certainly in 1798 or 1799, would have been against Kubla's presumption. If he associated the dome of his poem with wealth and pleasure, as well as with a potentate, he would condemn the dome rather than the supernatural forces that threaten it.

C. R. Woodring
*Politics in the Poetry of Coleridge* (Madison, Wisc.:
Univ. Wisconsin Pr., 1961), pp. 49-50

. . . It is a richly meaningful poem evidently full of mythopoeic and daemonic imagery, overtones, and conceptions, yet envisioned in a sequence ("as e'er was haunted . . .") in good part suggested by that of Wieland's visionary romance [*Oberon*]. Into this pattern were drawn any number of further reminiscences. . . .

W. W. Beyer
*The Enchanted Forest* (New York:
Barnes and Noble, 1963), pp. 141-42

As a self-contained poem, "Kubla Khan" develops thematically and metrically two points of view and reaches two climaxes: first, a description as seen partly through Kubla's eyes, and partly through those of an omniscient observer, of how Kubla combined discordant details of the landscape to produce Xanadu; and second, a narration by the poet of how he came to see Xanadu and why he has not told us more about it. Considered unfinished by readers from Coleridge's day to the present, especially if they thought that the description of the Khan's summer palace was meant as the introduction to a long narrative poem, "Kubla Khan" has considerable poetic unity and makes a satisfying statement capable of critical analysis. . . .

M. F. Schulz
*The Poetic Voices of Coleridge* (Detroit:
Wayne State Univ. Pr., 1963), pp. 114-15

## The Rime of the Ancient Mariner

The grand structural line of the voyage is the first determining factor of the poem. How has Coleridge plotted its course? . . .

Coleridge, with the scheme of the voyage charted as lucidly in his mind as on a map, bends his own imagination to the end of stirring ours to reconstruct it. And he first sets us framing the basic loop of the voyage through the agency of another trenchant interruption.

The ship is at the Equator twice. It crosses it in the Atlantic sailing south, and the equatorial calms of the Pacific are the stage for half the action of the story. To hold the ship in the tropics going south would be to blunt the keen edge of anticipation when the great stanzas are reached in which the imaginative splendour of the poem culminates. Yet the southward passage of the tropics is the first range of that vast arch on which the narrative is built. How is it to fulfil its structural office in the poem, and still be left to the imagination? Here are the stanzas in which the trick is done: [Part I, st. 7, 8]. . . .

And red as a rose, before the merry minstrelsy, the bride has paced into the hall, and when the tale is taken up again, the ship is driving before the storm-blast toward the pole. It is all as expeditious as a magic carpet. The vertical sun stands over the mast for an instant at noon, to mark the crossing of the Line. Then the dramatic incursion of the wedding revelry, like the knocking in *Macbeth,* snaps for a moment the spell of the tale, and, with the fine economy of practised art, blots the superfluous first passage of the tropics completely from the poem. And then the vertical sun itself, its temporary function as a seamark briefly served, is snuffed from the sky like a candle, to reappear at its appointed hour as a disastrous portent in the element above a rotting sea. That is the most superb *tour de force* in the poem—but it is not the only one. [1927]

J. L. Lowes<br>
The Road to Xanadu (Boston: Houghton Mifflin, 1964), pp. 115-16

. . . The fact is that it is impossible to extract any serious ethical purport from *The Ancient Mariner*—except perhaps a warning as to the fate of the innocent bystander. . . .

*The Ancient Mariner* actually has a moral ("He prayeth best, who loveth best," etc.). Moreover, this moral, unexceptionable in itself, turns out, when taken in its context, to be a sham moral. The mode in which the Mariner is relieved of the burden of his transgression, symbolised by the albatross hung about his neck—namely, by admiring the color of watersnakes—is an extreme example of a confusion to which I have already alluded: he obtains subrationally and unconsciously ("I blessed them unaware") the equivalent of Christian charity. Like many other works in the modern movement, the poem thus lays claim to a religious seriousness that at bottom it does not possess. To this extent at least it is an example of a hybrid and ambiguous art. [1929]

Irving Babbitt
*On Being Creative* (Boston: Houghton Mifflin, 1932), pp. 118-20

My thesis is, briefly . . . that the Ancient Mariner, who is at once Coleridge himself, Coleridge and all humanity—having sinned, both incurs punishment and seeks redemption; or, in other words, becomes anxiously aware of his relation to the God of Law (as symbolized by the Sun), and in his sub-consciousness earnestly entreats the forgiveness of the God of Love (represented by the Moon-symbol)—if haply such Love exists with power to succour the sinful soul.

G. H. Clarke
*QQ* (February, 1933), pp. 29-30

The thought of the storm image [as in *The Ancient Mariner*], and the place it has held in the mind, not of Europe only, but of a wider, older culture, takes us back to that order of conception, illustrated already in reference to wind and spirit, wherein the two aspects we now distinguish, or outer sense impression and inly felt process, appear undifferentiated. Dr. Jung cites from the Vedic Hymns lines where prayers, or ritual fire-boring, are said to lead forth, or release, the flowing streams of Rita; and shows that the ancient idea of Rita represented, in undifferentiated fashion, at once the cycle of nature of which rain and fire are off-spring, and also the ritually ordered processes of the inner life, in which pent-up energy can be discharged by fitting ceremonial. . . .

That poetry [such as *The Ancient Mariner*] in which we re-live, as such a supra-personal experience though in terms of our own emotional resources, the tidal ebb toward death followed by life renewal, affords us a means of increased awareness, and of fuller expression and control, of our own lives in their secret and momentous obedience to universal rhythms.

Maud Bodkin
*Archetypal Patterns in Poetry* (Oxford
Univ. Pr., 1934), pp. 47-48, 89

. . . What matters in *The Ancient Mariner* is not just that a man was becalmed and haunted but what sort of man he was. Naturally, he was Coleridge; for, as Mr. Bewley says, however detachedly he may have planned the poem he "could not help drawing in some measure from his full sensibility.". . .

The human experience around which Coleridge centres the poem is

surely the depression and the sense of isolation and unworthiness which
the Mariner describes in Part IV. The suffering he describes is of a kind
which is perhaps not found except in slightly pathological conditions, but
which, pathological or not, has been felt by a great many people.

D. W. Harding
*Scrutiny* (March, 1941), pp. 334-35

The poem is lively and colourful, as A. C. Bradley has well emphasized.
The movement and appearance of sun and moon are described in stanza
after stanza; and stars too. The sun peeps in and out as though uncertain
whether or not to give its blessing on the strange scene. The poem glitters:
the Mariner holds the Wedding Guest with a "glittering eye," which, if
remembered with his "skinny hand," preserves a neat balance. The light
is somewhat ghastly: as in the strange sheen of it on ice or tropic calm,
and the witches' oils burning "green and blue and white." Green light is
a favourite in Coleridge. . . . There is a very subtle interplay of light and
colour. The Life-in-Death figure is a garish whore with red lips, yellow
hair, white leprosy skin; the evil creatures are colourful; the supernatural
seraphs brilliant. The whole is dominated by a fearful intensity summed
in the image, rather dark for this poem, of a night-walker aware of a demon
following his steps. But the play of light and colour helps to give the somewhat stringy stanza succession and thinly narrative, undramatic sequence
of events a certain intangible poetic mass. I doubt if the rhyme-links, the
metrical rhythms, even the phrase-life, so to speak, would be considered
fine poetry without this and, what is equally important, the substance of
idea and meaning [in the poem]. . . .

G. Wilson Knight
*The Starlit Dome* (London: Methuen, 1941), pp. 89-90

If in the poem one follows the obvious theme of the "One Life" as presented by the Mariner's crime, punishment, and reconciliation, one is struck
by the fact that large areas of the poem seem to be irrelevant to this
business: for instance, the special atmosphere of the poem, and certain
images which, because of the insistence with which they are presented,
seem to be endowed with special import. Perhaps the best approach to the
problem of the secondary theme is to consider the importance of light or
rather, of the different kinds of light. . . .

This symbol [of the moon] functions in the poem, in connection with
the theme of imagination . . . in its value-creating capacity, what Coleridge
was later to call the secondary imagination. . . .

Now as a moment of great significance in the poem . . . the primary theme
of the sacramental vision is for the first time assimilated to the secondary

theme of the imagination. The Albatross, the sacramental bird, is also, as it were, a moon-bird. For here, with the bird, the moon first enters the poem, and the two are intimately associated. . . . The sun is kept entirely out of the matter. The lighting is always indirect, for even in the day we have only "mist or Cloud"—the luminous haze, the symbolic equivalent of moonlight. Not only is the moon associated with the bird, but the wind also. . . . And so we have the creative wind, the friendly bird, the moon-light of imagination, all together in one symbolic cluster.

As soon as the cluster is established, the crime, with shocking sudden-ness, is announced. . . . The crime as it were, brings the sun. . . .

It is the light which shows the familiar as familiar, it is the light of practical convenience, it is the light in which pride preens itself, it is, to adopt Coleridge's later terminology, the light of the "understanding," it is the light of that "mere reflective faculty" that "partook of Death.". . .

Life, order, universal communion and process, joy—all these things from which the Mariner is alienated are involved . . . in the description of the moon and stars. . . . The description of the water snakes picks up and extends the sense of the stars. The snakes become creatures of light to give us another symbolic cluster. . . . [1945-1946]

Robert Penn Warren
*Selected Essays* (New York: Random House,
1958), pp. 234, 236, 238-40, 243

. . . The haunting quality [of *The Rime of the Ancient Mariner*] grows from our intimate experience in the poem of the most intense personal suffering, perplexity, loneliness, longing, horror, fear. This experience brings us, with Coleridge, to the fringes of madness and death, and carries us to that night-mare land that Coleridge inhabited, the realm of Life-in-Death. There is no other single poem in which we come so close to the fullness of his innermost suffering. . . .

The central figure of "the albatross . . . binds inseparably together the three structural principles of the poem: the voyage, and the supernatural machinery, and the unfolding cycle of the deed's results." [Lowes, *Xanadu*, p. 221] Nothing less than an intensely personal symbolism would be ac-ceptable against the background of such intense suffering. . . . The albatross is a symbol of Coleridge's creative imagination, his eagle.

George Whalley
*UTQ* (July, 1947), pp. 382, 395

*The Ancient Mariner* is a structure, a perfectly ordered, a finely "complex, design wrought out through the exquisite adjustment of innumerable de-tails." It is not an opium dream like *Kubla Khan*; and that is the answer to the symbolists of psychoanalytic and biographical bent. Both poems are exquisite; but the latter is not even by the canons of poetry a severely logical design. . . .

It is the traditional ballad of the supernatural raised to its highest potency; but it is also, as Professor Elton says, "a great, a concerted and complex composition, playing at once on the simplest matters of the heart and conscience, and on the strangest visions of the senses, with the depth of colour and changing, recurrent rhythms that we know." Too simple for the symbolists; but neither that nor too complex for poetry, with which they are not content.

E. E. Stoll
*PMLA* (March, 1948), pp. 226-27

The *Ancient Mariner* speaks for its age in turning from social man to individual man and in caring for his inner motivation more than for his external activities. The two trends are not the same but they spring from such similar causes that it is hard to keep them apart. . . .

The diversity of the *Ancient Mariner*, of the multiple layers of meaning, of the different uses to which nature is put . . . is the true index of the vast complication of life that occurred in the Romantic period. It was as if the data for living had suddenly been multiplied. Not only were people learning more about the human mind but about human history and about the physical world. The industrial revolution was yet another complication. The situation was all the more difficult because on the whole the eighteenth century had pretended that their own rather simpler world was much simpler than it actually was. . . . The *Ancient Mariner* is modern in quite a special way through expressing, however subtly, this terrifying complexity. [1948]

E. M. W. Tillyard
*Poetry and Its Background* (London:
Chatto and Windus, 1961), pp. 81, 86

Though it will not tie to a table of dates or a map, the "Mariner" yet uses the keepings of European tradition and all the details of wind and weather which every map implies. Its imagery, both of religion and of the elements, goes deep below the surface of what we may happen to remember or happen to have seen.

But at the same time it uses to the full the vividness of visual description which was one of Coleridge's great poetic strengths. . . .

The poem's very richness at once tempts and defeats definiteness of interpretation; as we commit ourselves to the development of one strand of meaning we find that in the very act of doing so we are excluding something else of importance. . . . [1951-52]

Humphry House
*Coleridge* (London: Rupert Hart-Davis, 1953), pp. 86-87, 93

*The Ancient Mariner* illustrates . . . that a poem both makes something and says something. For it presents us with a pattern of events which is both self-contained and yet has a reference beyond itself. There is a certain kind of knowledge which can be conveyed only by symbols, that is by the life given to particulars in an art form. . . .

That the poet's philosophical presuppositions influence the mode of poetic meaning is also apparent in *The Ancient Mariner*. Coleridge's poetic theory was deduced from the observation of his own imagination and from reflection upon his friend Wordsworth's experience as a poet. His philosophy was built upon the felt need to fit this theory into an intellectual system embracing epistemology and metaphysics. At the centre of Coleridge's system is the conviction that we perceive and know by the operation of the imagination, which can mediate between the individual mind and external reality. The work of art is a product of the imagination, it is like real life, but . . . it is real life raised to a higher pitch, organized and shaped by the imagination into a pattern that will stimulate and provoke the understanding.

R. L. Brett
*Reason and Imagination* (Oxford Univ. Pr., 1960), pp. 106-7


[*The Ancient Mariner*] . . . is emblematic of the Romantic urge to explore the eternal soul and the temporal emotions. The voyage was Coleridge's, as it becomes the reader's: plunged like all men into the mist and gloom of life on this planet, he sought to comprehend the lifegiving source which called up that mist, to appreciate the luminosity which informed that gloom. *The Ancient Mariner* is the finest fruit of that labor.

E. B. Gose, Jr.
*PMLA* (March, 1960), p. 244


Despite its eighteenth-century orientation and obfuscated narrative, *The Ancient Mariner* remains vital and full-blooded and supremely expressive of Coleridge's naked voice. It balances balladic simplicity of narrative and diction with the Coleridgean voice of ratiocination and idealism (the fervid Coleridgean search for oneness underlying the "multeity" of experience) which we hear so clearly in the best of his other poetry and prose. But anemia in the form of Spenserian knights and ladies and Georgian sentiment and decorum soon weakens the ventriloquism voice. The ballad quickly becomes for Coleridge the mutated and imitable form that it was always for Scott.

M. F. Schulz
*The Poetic Voices of Coleridge* (Detroit:
Wayne State Univ. Pr., 1963), p. 64

*Christabel*

The figure of the fascinating villainess, Geraldine, betrays a clear affiliation with the behavior and motivation of the vampire, as this being had
been discussed and described down the ages. But, like Geraldine, the
vampire, though horrible, is also to be pitied, because it is not always
responsible for its condition. The lamia, a variety of vampire, is also to be
pitied, when its antecedents are known; moreover, the lamia, because of
the serpent characteristics which have been attached to it by legend, indicates an even closer relationship with Geraldine, a sort of serpent-woman.
Her amazingly contradictory aspects, with her strange vacillation between
sinister and kindly impulses, may well derive from the widely accepted
doctrines of metempsychosis, which posited sin and expiation as the basis
for its transformations; for the brand of some undivulged sin in her past
disfigures her body ineffaceably, to her shame and disgust. She seems,
likewise, to be under the control of some spirit power from the other world,
and has a mission to carry out, though she is apparently not completely
reconciled to it herself. She is demon, witch, snake, vampire, and appealing
woman by turns and sometimes at the same moment.

A. H. Nethercot<br>
*The Road to Tryermaine* (Chicago:<br>
Univ. Chicago Pr., 1939), p. 185

. . . The fact remains that *Christabel* is a fragment.

And it is a superb one, of considerable complexity, capable of interpretation on various levels of imaginative experience. It is the first vampire poem
in English. It is a masterpiece of incantation, of suspenseful narration, of
the supernatural. It is a provocative study of evil, its roots and fruits. But
especially it is a subtle psychological study, poignantly personal at last,
of alienation whether by chance or fault, and of consequent spiritual impotence and disintegration or Death-in-Life, the spectre with which, most
of the major poems show, Coleridge was all too tragically familiar.

W. W. Beyer<br>
*The Enchanted Forest* (New York:<br>
Barnes and Noble, 1963), pp. 181-82

Besides satisfying the eighteenth-century taste for scenery, the second part
of "Christabel" also appeases the appetite of the age for well-expressed
sentiments. The action dwells on Sir Leoline's sensitivity to a breach of
hospitality, accompanied ironically by his insensitivity to the needs of his
daughter. It also marks time while Coleridge reflects poignantly on the
sadness of sundered friends, in the lovely lines beginning, "They had been

friends in youth." Similarly, he contemplates in "The Conclusion to Part II" the paradoxical course that a father's love for his child takes when

> ... pleasures flow in so thick and fast
> Upon his heart, that he at last
> Must needs express his love's excess
> With words of unmeant bitterness.

With such sentiments we approach the hearth of domesticity and warm ourselves at the fire of friendship and family felicity celebrated in the conversation poems. Although the moral is not as obstrusive as in "The Ancient Mariner," obviously, such feelings are at variance with the unadorned action and impersonal point of view of the ballad. And most critics testify to the falling off in Part II of "Christabel" of the forceful effect of terseness, the narrative slowed down by description and exposition, its forward flow almost imperceptible, as feelings and thoughts are now tediously recounted, not vividly evoked through events.

M. F. Schulz
*The Poetic Voices of Coleridge* (Detroit:
Wayne State Univ. Pr., 1963), p. 66

## PHILOSOPHY, CRITICISM, POLITICS

The variety of motives which gave rise to the *Biographia Literaria* reveals itself in the miscellaneous character of the work. Intended in the first instance as a preface to the *Sibylline Leaves*, it grew into a literary autobiography which itself came to demand a preface. This preface itself outgrew its purposed limits, and was incorporated in the whole work, which was finally issued in two parts—the autobiography (two vols.) and the poems. Originally, no doubt, Coleridge's motive in writing the preface was to explain and justify his own style and practice in poetry. To this end it was necessary that he should state clearly the points on which he took exception to Wordsworth's theory. All this, however, seemed to involve an examination of the nature of poetry and the poetic faculty: and this in its turn suggested, if it did not demand, a radical inquiry into the preconditions of knowledge in general. To Coleridge . . . the distinction of fancy and imagination was a distinction of equal import for philosophy and for poetry. . . .

It is . . . evident in what sense, and what sense alone, Coleridge can consistently regard the imagination as the organ of philosophy. It is not the power of intellectual intuition (if by that we mean direct spiritual vision) but the faculty of the true apprehension of things sensible as the data and material of philosophical reflection: and herein lies the connecting link of poetry and philosophy. . . .

Enough has been said to show that Coleridge's failure to complete his deduction of the imagination is not merely another instance of his habitual lethargy of purpose. How he would have completed it in accordance with his more mature convictions is a question not admitting of solution, for the attempt was never resumed. We are left with his definition of the primary imagination as "an echo of the primary act of creation," and of the secondary as a more highly potentialized form of the primary: and the meaning of this figurative language we have to unravel as we may. [1907]

John Shawcross
Introd., in *Biographia Literaria*, Vol. I
(Oxford Univ. Pr., 1954), pp. lv, lxxiv-lxxv

. . . Of innumerable critical enterprises, he brought only one to completion —the *Biographia Literaria*: if indeed that odd medley of personal reminiscence, metaphysic, letters, political tirade, and criticism of poetry can be called complete. [1925]

H. W. Garrod
Introd., in *Coleridge, Poetry and Prose*
(Oxford Univ. Pr., 1954), p. xv

In general philosophy, in spite of the advance he sought to make on Kant, [Coleridge] . . . allowed himself to be too much dominated by the Kantian separation between the material and the spiritual, the causal nexus by which Nature seemed bound and the freedom of the will. In religion this meant that Christianity was made to appear to stand on a different basis, not only of spiritual appeal, but of miraculous revelation, from all other religions. In politics the same conservatism, united with the same philosophical dualism, was responsible for the distinction he drew between classes in respect to their capacity to enter into the full rights of citizenship. No more here than in religion did he seem completely to realize that if freedom is the soul of human life, it must have its spring in human nature itself, and must permeate the whole body. True, in Nature there are all degrees of freedom and individuality, corresponding to different natural orders. But the differentia of human life is just that in it first freedom has become a common possession, and none can be really free unless all are free. In science, finally it meant that while he was prepared to welcome the treatment of individual organisms from the point of view of a single principle dominating the life of the parts, he rejected the suggestion of applying the same idea to the evolution of the animal world, including man, as a whole.

In all these respects he seemed to be setting himself against the new currents of thought and feeling, into whose deeper spirit he otherwise penetrated further than any of his English contemporaries. That in the field of literary criticism these limitations had less opportunity of showing themselves, or that his own supreme genius in it enabled him to transcend them, is perhaps the reason why it is in this field that fullest recognition has been given by succeeding generations to his greatness as a thinker. . . .

To Coleridge belongs the credit of having been the first to realize, with the sharp pang of the most sensitive mind of his time, the inadequacy of . . . [eighteenth-century] ideas for the interpretation of the spiritual movements which were most characteristic of the age. [1930]

J. H. Muirhead
*Coleridge as Philosopher* (New York: Humanities Pr. 1954), pp. 260-61, 263

. . . Let me turn to consider the great importance, in the *Biographia Litteraria*, of the distinction between Fancy and Imagination . . . and of the definition of Imagination given in a later passage. . . .

My mind is too heavy and concrete for any flight of abstruse reasoning. If . . . the difference between imagination and fancy amounts in practice to no more than the difference between good and bad poetry, have we done more than take a turn round Robin Hood's barn? It is only if fancy can be an ingredient in good poetry, and if you can show some good poetry which is the better for it; it is only if the distinction illuminates our immediate preference of one poet over another, that it can be of use to a practical mind like mine. [1933]

T. S. Eliot
*The Use of Poetry and the Use of Criticism*
(London: Faber and Faber, 1955), pp. 76-77

Coleridge was not, I suppose, a good philosopher; he made too many mistakes *of the wrong kind*. He mixed with his philosophy too many things which did not belong to it, he let accidental and inessential prejudices too much interfere. In spite of them he took the psychology of the theory of poetry to a new level. . . .

Coleridge's best-known formulation of the difference between Imagination and Fancy comes at the end of the first volume of *Biographia* in those astonishing paragraphs . . . in which he contents himself for the present with stating the main result of a chapter that was never to be written. And although many readers have gathered from them that the distinction is in some way "metaphysical"; that the Primary Imagination is a finite repetition of creation; that the Secondary Imagination is an echo of the primary; that it dissolves to recreate or, at least, "to idealize and to unify"; and that it is vital, as opposed to Fancy which "has no other counters to play with but fixities and definites" and is "a mode of memory emancipated from the order of space and time"; neither Coleridge's grounds for the distinction nor his applications of it have as yet entered our general intellectual tradition. When they do, the order of our universes will have been changed. [1934]

I. A. Richards
*Coleridge on Imagination* (New York:
W. W. Norton, 1950), pp. 10, 72

The more one reads Coleridge the more impressed one becomes with what can only be called a psychological approach to all human problems. Whether it be punctuation, or political sovereignty, a criticism of *Richard II*, the position of the mediaeval Church, or the baby talk of children, the state of Ireland or the work of the alchemists, he sees it as a piece of human experience, understandable in relation to the whole human organism, individual or social, so far as that organism can be comprehended as a whole. Politics are not a matter of events, facts, theories, and the isolated external circumstances only. No more is what passes for logic. Nor chemistry. Emotion comes in, motives, unknown ones as well as those that are acknowledged. Unknown especially to the participants. . . .

It becomes clear to a reader of the many passages of self-searching and confession, especially in the notebooks, that his awareness of the existence of almost unrecognized psychological factors in all human activity, comes from his awareness of himself. . . .

What is farthest reaching and most creative in other fields, in his literary criticism, philosophy, social criticism, theology, is rooted multifariously in and rises out of his own experience. It surely does not invalidate his critical or systematic views at all to suggest that in this sense their great strength and piercing insight depends largely on the subjective element in them. Perhaps "personal" would be a less dangerous if less accurate word. . . .

The same acute personal realization . . . runs through the social criticism. When he wrote his strong plea—and one of his firmest pieces of prose—on behalf of Sir Robert Peel's bill to reduce the working hours of children in the cotton factories, he wrote from the conviction that the arguments of the opposition, based on the hue and cry of "free labour," were deceptive, and that the labour of the children was not free at all, that they were in fact slaves of an expanding commercial enterprise. This he knew and felt from his personal knowledge of what freedom is and what slavery is.

Kathleen Coburn
*Inquiring Spirit* (New York: Pantheon, 1951), pp. 14-19

To do Coleridge justice, he was capable of saturating his writing with thought, even with his own ever-recurring philosophical concepts, because it was natural for him to apprehend ideas poetically. He was a poet-philosopher. His criticism is neither a pure scientific treatise nor a poem about a poem, but something of both. He expressed his own acute and sensitive perceptions with a suggestive and infectious style, in which ideas are often rather implied than stated. Such, for instance, is his provocative metaphor for Dryden: "Dryden's genius was of the sort which catches fire by its own motion; his chariot wheels get hot by driving fast." Sometimes critical statements which have obviously germinated in his philosophical system nevertheless seem self-sufficient without commentary, and illuminate even for the unphilosophical reader both the ideas and their application to literature.

Louis I. Bredvold<br>in Coleridge on the Seventeenth Century, ed. R. F. Brinkley<br>(Durham, N. C.: Duke Univ. Pr., 1955), p. xxii

Since he believed that the truth might lie in a synthesis of what was true in all other philosophical systems, he undertook a stupendous amount of critical reading, not only in Latin and Greek but also in German, French, and English philosophical writing. During the long illness of 1800 and 1801 he read widely in the ancient philosophers and the Schoolmen, finding that much which had later been cried up as "new" was new only because it had been forgotten. He therefore grew to be "exceedingly suspicious of *supposed Discoveries* in metaphysics," and became increasingly aware of the necessity of knowing what had previously been said on a subject in order to establish the starting point for making an original contribution. . . .

R. F. Brinkley<br>in Coleridge on the Seventeenth Century, ed. R. F. Brinkley<br>(Durham, N. C.: Duke Univ. Pr., 1955), p. 39

It was inevitable, . . . Coleridge being Coleridge and his mental history being what is was, that when he came to define imagination, he would do so in a certain way, in keeping with certain deeply-held convictions. To IMAGINATION, which he liked to capitalize, he would give perhaps an exaggerated and transcendent importance, a mystic significance, linked with the forces of fertility, the powers of growth, and Godhead itself. To association, a rather sorry and secondary power, consisting in the automatic and mechanical linking of ideas embedded through the inlets of sensation in the passive memory, he would assign a subordinate place. . . .

One of Coleridge's chief claims to interest at the present day is that he was a pioneer psychologist with unequalled gifts of introspection. Not only was he aware that association is rather an emotional than an intellectual matter . . . but almost a hundred years before William James and James

Joyce, he was aware of the stream of consciousness, and expressed it, too, in the sovereign phrase: "the streamy nature of association which thinking curbs and rudders." Here is brilliant recognition of the collaboration of active and passive powers. . . .

Coleridge's awareness of what has nowadays come to be referred to as "the deep well" of the unconscious is not, then, in any doubt. He must have been intuitively aware of unconscious or semi-conscious processes in the composition of poetry from his own experience with the "Mariner," "Kubla Khan," and "Christabel," which antedated the reading of Schelling. "Kubla Khan" particularly, . . . presented with all the freshness of rain-washed April, seems to have welled up like a cold spring from inward depths. "The mighty fountain," with "ceaseless turmoil seething" and forcing itself from the earth in "fast thick pants" is an image, surely, of creative potency coming in continuous pulses. He did not, however, define his awareness till after he had made contact with the ever-present idea of an unconscious in German philosophy and literature. . . .

Coleridge, as usual, acted as the fruitful transplanter of German ideas into English criticism, and to Coleridge, as far as English criticism is concerned, with his full recognition of unconscious powers at work in poetry, belongs the chief credit for the rapid spread of the idea.

J. V. Baker
*The Sacred River* (Baton Rouge, La.:
Louisiana State Univ. Pr., 1957), pp. 114-15, 184-85, 191

*Aids to Reflection* was a challenge to an age which was tired of religious controversies. In its negative emphasis it is an attack upon the principle of latitudinarianism that passed as the dominant religious mode of the time. A close look at the book uncovers the pattern of early nineteenth-century religious thought, as it is reflected in the numerous allusions Coleridge made to his contemporaries and their religious ideas. . . .

His probing into rationalism and orthodoxy is not done systematically in *Aids*. Many people and many ideas, representing the most divergent points of view, are harshly treated. The only common denominator is his constant insistence that the errors were products of the understanding. It is also important to note that the method in this attack can be found in all Coleridge's other late works, such as the *Philosophical Lectures* and *Theological Notes*. In fact, the attacks on contemporary rationalism in these other late works can quite properly be considered with the negative message in *Aids* as related chapters in the case Coleridge was preparing against his age. Thus it is important to realize that the principle of organization in *Aids* is ideational rather than schematic. . . .

The strategy in many parts of *Aids to Reflection,* and in much of his criticism of contemporary divinity, whenever the subject was more congenial than Evidence-writing or teleology, was often merely to point out the inherent weakness in the logical and philosophical method of the author. For even more prevalent than benighted Evidence-writing and tracts on natural theology were books on theological subjects handled in an inept rationalistic way. The force and number of attacks Coleridge made upon inept rationalism is impressive. He was more interested in correcting the process of religious thinking in general than in changing the orthodox view of particular doctrines.

James D. Boulger
*Coleridge as a Religious Thinker* (New Haven: Yale Univ. Pr., 1961), pp. 5, 9, 15

Coleridge, of the English Romantic poets, gave most thought to politics. He had, no doubt, the most to give. Born with a fertile mind, he fertilized it interminably by reading. But his combination of turbulence and lethargy has kept the produce of this fertility sadly uncollected for more than a century. . . . With Wordsworth he broadcast . . . their new concept of nationalism as national self-determination. Every half-informed graduate, if not every schoolboy, knows of John Stuart Mill's tribute to Coleridge as one of the two seminal minds from which the most important ideas in Victorian England evolved. . . .

As a hired journalist, Coleridge produced verse explicitly political in forms related to conventional pasquinades, parodies, odes, and ballads. Even some of his nobler poems, like *France: An Ode*, were produced partly for pay and partly out of a conflict of political impulses. . . . Perhaps *France: An Ode* resulted ultimately from frustrations in the poet's marriage. It certainly resulted in part because Coleridge knew from his reading that palinodes could be written. But he had considerable interest in deciding which political views to retract. And the poem, too, has a biography. We must continue to ask, though the answer may never be forthcoming, what parts the editor Stuart played before and immediately after Coleridge gave *France: An Ode* its original shape. We can suspect that Stuart cared more about what the poem said, about the content that could be paraphrased, than Coleridge did.

C. R. Woodring
*Politics in the Poetry of Coleridge* (Madison, Wisc.: Univ. Wisconsin Pr., 1961), pp. 3, 5-6

As organicist and transcendentalist Coleridge is indeed a child of his time, with a particular affinity for the great Germans. It does not necessarily follow that he derives from them. As a philosopher he does not rival Kant or Schelling in sustained and systematic thought because it is not at bottom his purpose to do so; he is a poet-philosopher-critic, and his total contribution, though greatest in criticism, is not separable into its component parts. Coleridge is a genuinely organic thinker, whose mind is a totality and who aims always at synthesis. He appears incomplete if any of his gifts are isolated from the rest: indecisive as an aesthetician, shadowly oracular as a philosopher, fragmentary as poet and critic. . . .

The chief emphasis of Coleridge's criticism is psychological. Poetic creation is the fullest activity of the mind, and to understand a literary work one must look to the qualities of the mind behind it. But this is Coleridge's emphasis, not the whole of his search. The relationships of his position reach far. His psychology is organically one with his metaphysics, which assume an ultimate reality and an attempt to explain it. Mental faculties like reason, understanding, and imagination are not only components of mind, but organs of knowledge as well. Coleridge's aesthetics is psychological insofar as it is concerned with the effect, the mind's reaction to an aesthetic object; it describes by introspection the pleasure that the object can give. This pleasure, however, is the subjective counterpart of a beauty that objectively exists. The difference between Coleridge's psychological criticism and such contemporary psychological criticism as I. A. Richard's earlier work is almost antipodal.

R. H. Fogle
*The Idea of Coleridge's Criticism* (Berkeley and Los Angeles, Calif.:
Univ. California Pr., 1962), pp. xi, 1-2

# GEORGE  CRABBE

## 1754-1832

Born in Aldeburgh, Suffolk, George Crabbe received an informal education as apprentice to a village doctor, practiced medicine near Bury St. Edmund, and in 1780 left his unsuccessful practice and departed for London. His early poems were admired by Edmund Burke, who suggested that Crabbe take religious orders and later helped him obtain a curacy. In 1784, Crabbe married Sarah Elmy, whom he had courted for more than a decade. During an illness, he became addicted to opium, which did not prevent him from leading a normal life.

The son of a tax collector, Crabbe was, throughout his long life, interested in the problems of the poor. He portrayed their condition realistically and without sentimentality, but not without satirical comment. A man of the Enlightenment by birth and temperament, Crabbe is grouped with the nineteenth-century Romantics because the majority of his works was published simultaneously with theirs: *The Village* (1783); *Poems* (1807), including *The Parish Register*; *The Borough* (1810); *Tales in Verse* (1812), including *The Patron*; *Tales of the Hall* (1819); and *Posthumous Tales* (1834).

A. W. Ward, ed., *Poems* (1905-1907), 3 vols.; P. Henderson, ed., *George Crabbe: Poems* (1946)

René Huchon, *George Crabbe and His Times*, trans. Frederick Clarke (1907)

As for the faults of Crabbe, it is enough to say that he is an avowed imitator of Pope in all formal matters, and that the antithetic style of the master too often descends in him to a grotesque flaccidity. . . . But even where his style is wrought with nervous energy, it fails to attract an audience who have tasted the rapturous liberties of Shelley and Keats. . . . They are only offended by what seems to them the monotonous seesaw of the rhythm; and a style which opposes an effort of the judicial understanding at every pause in the flow of sentiment repels those who think wit . . . a poor substitute for celestial inspiration. . . .

To me personally there is no tedium, but only endless delight, in these mated rhymes which seem to pervade and harmonise the whole rhythm. And withal they help to create the artistic illusion, that wonderful atmosphere, I may call it, which envelops Crabbe's world.

Paul Elmer More
*Shelburne Essays, Second Series* (New York:
G. P. Putnam's Sons, 1905), pp. 128-29

Wherever he looked, he saw human beings taking the wrong turning, and he thus represents them in his poems. Sometimes his characters go wrong deliberately, like Peter Grimes in *The Borough,* who tortures and murders his boy apprentices. But the majority err through weakness, and the analysis and censure of weakness is a specialty of Crabbe's. . . .

Disapproval is common in the pulpit, but rare in poetry; and its presence gives his work a curious flavour, subtle yet tart, which will always attract connoisseurs. We take a bite from an unusual fruit, and come away neither nourished nor ravished, yet we are aware of a new experience which we can repeat at will. Were Crabbe insincere, we should not return; but disapproval is as natural in his hands as thunder in Carlyle's; and he never spares himself. An unusual atmosphere results; it is, so to speak, sub-Christian; there is an implication throughout of positive ideals, such as self-sacrifice and asceticism, but they are seldom pressed; only occasionally (as in the pathetic tale of the girl who mourns for her sailor-lover) does the narrator let himself go and testify. He prefers as a rule to shake his finger at men as they move by wrong paths from the cradle to the grave, and to remind himself with a sigh that he too is human. . . .

E. M. Forster
*Spec.* (February 20, 1932), p. 244

Indeed, these *Tales of the Hall,* as they are called, afford much more pleasure to read than the other lengthy compositions. They also have the distinguishing feature of forming rather a novel plan, happily devised by the author, in piecing them together. Indeed, so ingenious has he been in the process that many might be called the imaginary conversations between two brothers. Perhaps this belated discovery did, indeed, supply the needful tone lacking hitherto. Certainly, at last the most critical could hardly be dissatisfied on that score. For it is questionable whether anyone has produced quite the same effect in English verse, especially with such commonplace persons and themes.

J. H. Evans
*The Poems of George Crabbe*
(London: Sheldon Pr., 1933), p. 171

Had Crabbe died at fifty, he would be to-day as obscure a figure as Tickell or Parnell. *Inebriety, The Candidate, The Library, The Newspaper,* and even *The Village* would scarcely have kept his memory alive. But in 1807 this poet of a past age presented himself before the new generation with a volume of poems containing, besides his previous work, *The Parish Register* and *Sir Eustace Grey.* Success encouraged him, and *The Borough* followed in 1810, the *Tales* in 1812, *Tales of the Hall* in 1819. With surprising ease and swiftness this old man, who had been born under George II, established his position as a leading poet in the world of Napoleon and Wellington, Scott and Byron. He made the acquaintance of Scott, Campbell, Rogers, Bowles, Moore, and Wordsworth; he had become rector of comfortable Trowbridge, with his grandchildren growing up round him; and yet all was not well. He suffered from being too old, or else not old enough; the lover, long ago, of Sarah Elmy still felt woman's charm; he seemed terribly alone in the bustling streets of his properous parish. . . .

Crabbe wrote too much (*The Borough* alone contains ten thousand lines), and rewrote far too little; but he is in himself a typical representative —more typical than most of our poets—of that nation of shopkeepers which has yet produced the finest body of poetry in the world. . . .

F. L. Lucas
Introd., in *George Crabbe: An Anthology*
(Cambridge Univ. Pr., 1933), pp. xviii, xxxii

It seems strange that Saintsbury could describe [Crabbe] as an exponent of "the style of drab stucco" . . . , yet this statement is not unfair when applied to almost any of Crabbe's work except the two poems most critics neglect: "The World of Dreams" and "Sir Eustace Grey." Significantly, these same two poems and no others that I could discover describe the world of Crabbe's opium dreams. These poems offer, therefore, an unexampled opportunity to observe the effect of opium on that mysterious phenomenon, poetic inspiration. On two occasions something happened to Crabbe which "set the winds of inspiration blowing," tore him loose from the clutch of the heroic couplet, and caused the employment, in these two poems only, of an eight-line stanza with interlacing rhymes, almost as intricate as the Spenserian. This same force, in at least a score of stanzas of "Sir Eustace Grey," freed Crabbe's language from the restraint of eightheenth-century poetic diction, and gave it a simplicity and inevitability, which suggest Coleridge's *Ancient Mariner*. With the evidence presented, is there much doubt that this stimulus, which incited Crabbe to dash off "Sir Eustace Grey" in a single night, is the vivid recollection of an opium dream?

M. H. Abrams
*The Milk of Paradise*
(Cambridge, Mass.: Harvard Univ. Pr., 1934), pp. 20-21

If you want to read Crabbe—and it is well worth your while to read him—I advise you to begin with *The Tales*. These are later work, but if you like them, you will like the whole book in spite of its painful character. One of the reasons that you will like it is the remarkable observation of human nature everywhere shown. There are just twenty-one tales, not all equally good. I shall speak of those which seem to me the best.

Perhaps the prettiest in parts is "Jesse and Colin," but I should advise you rather to begin with "The Frank Courtship." This is the best study of character in the whole work, voluminous and varied as that work is. The scene is laid in a Puritan family, or at least in a family with Puritan tendencies. We have, first, a portrait of the stern father, Jonas, who in twenty years never smiles, cares only to be obeyed, keeps his wife continually trembling, yet is not consciously cruel or unloving, but strictly honourable, just so far as he knows how to be, and rigidly religious. . . .

There is not one word of comment or explanation, nothing but a plain narrative, yet from this narrative we become most intimately acquainted with four distinct characters, all of whom we find interesting, though perhaps only the girl is at all sympathetic, and even she not very much so. That is realistic art—to make you interested in things as they are, whether ugly or beautiful; and Crabbe was a great realist. If you will read that little romance in verse, it will give you, I think, a better idea of Crabbe than anything else which he has written. But there are twenty-one such stories, and a much larger number of realistic studies of country life, studies of personal observation. Crabbe painted all that he saw and painted it so perfectly that it is just as much alive to-day as it was in the time when he saw it. [1934]

Lafcadio Hearn
*On Poets*, eds. R. Tanabe, T. Ochiai, and I. Nishizaki
(Tokyo: Hokuseido Pr., 1941), pp. 447, 450

Crabbe must have possessed his share of the aesthetic response, or whence did he find reasons for introducing into his novels in verse those famous seascapes and landscapes and occasionally interiors which make him something of a counterpart to the Norwich School of painting? If they are inspected as it were with a magnifying glass, they show that their maker was capable of the finest touches. No "Ode to Autumn" was ever written with more of sensibility in the stresses and the sequence of sounds, as well as the sustaining movement, than the description of the doomed lover at his window in "Delay Has Danger.". . .

Crabbe's poem, "The Village,". . . was written in time to be admired and touched up by a man well fitted to understand the newcomer—Samuel Johnson. With that poem

I paint the Cot<br>
As Truth will paint it, and as Bards will not—

a striking chapter in English poetry and social criticism and controversy comes into sight.

Edmund Blunden<br>
Introd., in The Life of George Crabbe by His Son<br>
(London: Cresset Pr., 1947), pp. xvii, xxiv

There are not many today who would echo a critic's recent comment on Crabbe, "that he is (or ought to be—for who reads him?) a living classic." The decline of Crabbe's reputation in the nineteenth century is of course understandable. Far more genuinely than Byron, he defended the Augustan tradition by precept and practice at a time when Shelley and Keats were doing some of their best work. Yet the arch-romantic Scott was one of Crabbe's most enthusiastic admirers, and Charles Lamb dramatized one of his *Tales* ("The Confidant")! Unquestionably Crabbe had something to offer which transcended these labels. For us today that something lies both in the fact that he was the last of the Augustans and that, in his best work, he brilliantly adapted the heroic couplet to the art of narrative.

W. C. Brown<br>
The Triumph of Form (Chapel Hill, N. C.:<br>
Univ. North Carolina Pr., 1948), pp. 186-87

. . . In *The Parish Register,* for all his insistence on the material surroundings of his villagers, Crabbe has been showing us a human society. But the lady of the manor, an absentee landlord, has not been a character in village life at all: her empty house is all that has been seen of her, and this house has, so to speak, predeceased its owner. The poet first arrests our attention by describing a building instead of a person, and then arouses our misgivings by conveying it in terms of decay, darkness and emptiness. The only life-cycle to be observed in the decaying house is that of worms and bats. It is not until the end of the passage that we hear of human beings there, of the anger of the poor and the curses of surly beggars. But we have been prepared by the factual description of the Hall for the criticism of the Lady which the poet wishes to make.

L. Haddakin
*The Poetry of Crabbe* (London: Chatto and Windus, 1955), p. 77

Crabbe's descriptions of nature are wonderfully accurate. He had the trained eye of a botanist and in few poets do we get a more accurate picture of flowers and plants. . . . Even when Crabbe's subject-matter would repel us in real life, it may still please as poetry, for the ugly as well as the beautiful may provide aesthetic delight. . . .

By the time of *The Parish Register* Crabbe had turned towards a poetic form which would allow his gift for characterization greater scope. The whole poem is no more than a series of loosely connected stories about the people who make up the village of his day. It surveys the entire community; from the aristocracy down through the farmers, the small shopkeepers and their kind, to the poorest agricultural labourers and the poachers, smugglers and "failures" of the village. But it is not simply *The Village* on a larger scale and with greater detail. Some of the stories have little to do with what the nineteenth century called "the condition of the people question.". . .

We can call this social documentation if we will and we can regard the story as an attack upon the corruption of a society which allows such abuses of legal administration. But the poem is more than part of a humanitarian struggle to relieve the needs of the poor. To regard it as this and no more is to fail to appreciate the nature of Crabbe's artistic vision; is to fail to realize that Crabbe makes his own world out of this material. Nor should we mistake verisimilitude for lack of art. The truth to life of his scenes and characters is a tribute to his art.

R. Brett
*Crabbe* (London: BC/Longmans, 1956), pp. 20, 23-24

In studying the relationship of the sexes Crabbe is always aware of social and moral pressures, and of psychological reaction to such pressures. . . . It will be sufficient to illustrate from one of them probably the best, "Hester." Here the heroine is gradually conditioned, first to condone and then to practise, the lax morality of her environment. . . . As events and attitudes are described, the reader is all the time aware of the moral code which is being flouted, not by explicit reminder, but implicitly and, in a sense, dramatically, first, because a broken down old woman is recounting her former glories, but clearly hollow glories; and secondly, because Hester's father and her faithful shepherd-lover refuse to profit by her shame. . . . Crabbe's moral intention is never in doubt. Wrong-doing is always punished. In "Poems," "David Morris," "Joseph and Jesse"; indeed everywhere, the lesson is obvious. . . . "Hester" is an example—and any of the other longer tales in this collection might have been chosen—showing those qualities recognized as characteristic of Crabbe, his insight into the springs of human action, his vivid appreciation and his minute delineation of the complex intermingling of character and incident in human affairs.

Arthur Pollard
Introd., in *New Poems by George Crabbe* (Liverpool, Eng.:
Liverpool Univ. Pr., 1960), pp. 12-14

# THOMAS DE QUINCEY
1785-1859

Son of a prosperous Manchester merchant, Thomas De Quincey was educated at Bath, Wiltshire, and Manchester. An excellent student and hypersensitive youth, he ran away from the discipline of school, traveled through Wales, and lived in London hovels until his family found him again some time in 1802. He then attended Worcester College, Oxford, between 1803-1808, but never took a degree. By 1813, he was enslaved to opium, which he had begun to take for headaches while at Oxford. He mistakenly believed that opium rather than his own imagination was responsible for his inspired writings. One of the first to appreciate Coleridge and Wordsworth, De Quincey arranged to meet the great poets while he was still a student. After leaving Oxford, he took over Wordsworth's Grasmere Cottage between 1809 and 1817. His marriage to an uneducated country girl Margaret Simpson in 1816 after she gave birth to their child, caused a rift with the Wordsworths, who disapproved of the alliance. But the marriage was a happy one, despite De Quincey's illnesses and addiction. After his wife's death in 1837, De Quincey's mind suffered severely, and he became more and more withdrawn from society. He continued to write, however, until his death in Edinburgh, where he had lived since 1826.

As early as 1819, De Quincey had contributed to *Blackwood's Magazine,* then to the *London Magazine,* to *Tait's,* the *Instructor,* and the *Titan.* Most famous for his rhythmic prose style, he aimed at the same impassioned effects in his essays as other Romantics did in their poems. He is best remembered for *Confessions of an English Opium-Eater* (1821; 1856); *On the Knocking at the Gate in "Macbeth"* (1823); *Letters to a Young Man* (1823); *Essays on Kent* (1818-1823); *Murder as One of the Fine Arts* (1827-1839); *Autobiography* (1834-1853); *Suspiria de Profundis* (1848); *The Literature of Knowledge and the Literature of Power* (1848); and *The English Mail Coach* (1849).

David Masson ed., *The Collected Writings* (1889-1890), 14 vols.

H. A. Eaton, *Thomas De Quincey: A Biography* (1936)

Every now and then, as in the well-known *Note on the Knocking at the Gate in Macbeth,* De Quincey will display evidence . . . of almost daemonic subtlety. Very often, indeed, he will display evidence, if not of daemonic yet of impish and almost fiendish acuteness. . . .

Yet De Quincey is scarcely . . . to be ranked among the greatest critics. To begin with, his unconquerable habit of "rigmarole" is constantly leading him astray: and the taste for jaunty personality which he had most unluckily imbibed from Wilson leads him astray still further, and still more gravely and damagingly. In the volume on *The Lake Poets* I do not suppose that there are twenty pages of pure criticism. . . . On Keats, without any reason for hostility, he has almost the full inadequacy of his generation, with not much less on Shelley; and when he comes to talk even of Wordsworth's *poetry,* though there was no one living whom he honoured more, he is not very much less unsatisfactory. [1904]

George Saintsbury
*A History of Criticism,* Vol. III (New York:
Humanities Pr., 1961), pp. 478-79

The heaviest stone that can be thrown at De Quincey is his treatment of the men of letters and poets whose acquaintance he enjoyed. True, he was younger. True, also, he had been brought up in a kind of superstition which treats famous or notable people, especially writers, as meteors and monsters. Yet we cannot avoid the conclusion that he was not fit company for Wordsworth, Coleridge, Southey, Lamb, who, in spite of their differences, were fit and trustworthy company for one another. He forced himself on them. He took notes of their private life, and noticed the wrong things. He was an Interviewer, and worse, for he did not announce his intentions.

The things he tells are amusing, and obviously true; yet that does not acquit him. He was a man of genius, he was in their company, and might have associated with them on equal terms; but he chose to watch, and to tell. He was a newspaper man who got into good company by mistake. He seems not to have counted. Charles Lamb and Wordsworth simply do not mention him. [1926]

Sir Walter Raleigh
*On Writing and Writers,* ed. George Gordon
(London: Edward Arnold, 1927), pp. 146-47

*The English Mail-Coach* . . . has unique and wonderful qualities. . . . Its effectiveness as a virtuoso evocation of speed is sometimes objected to nowadays on the ground that De Quincey's ascription of terror and violence to even the maximum speed of a coach is rendered comic to us by our own experience of racing motors and aëroplanes. This seems to me a foolish objection and one which, moreover, De Quincey himself has been at pains to meet. It is the *sensation* of speed which counts, not the actual miles per hour. . . .

Although the second and third sections of the piece are those for which it in the main continues to be read, the introduction, which deals with the "Glory of Motion" in general, and connects the journey to be described with De Quincey's earlier coaching experience, does not detract from the effectiveness of the whole. Though rambling and jocular, in its author's high-spirited, reminiscent manner, it is neither arch nor tiresome; and its scherzando effect is admirably devised as a prelude to the far-flung, rhapsodic style of the succeeding movement.

Edward Sackville-West
*Thomas De Quincey, His Life and Work* (New Haven:
Yale Univ. Pr., 1936), pp. 252-53

De Quincey was thoroughly reactionary in his politics; he was an author of Gothic fiction that dealt almost exclusively with the feudal past; yet, strangely enough, he was a radical of a peculiarly intransigent nature in his approach to imaginative writing. He broke the conventional restrictions of British reserve in writing the *Confessions,* and he was one of the pioneers who brought to English prose the new element of subjectivity that was to be so important in the literature of the next century. . . .

It is in this field of personal writing that De Quincey did his finest work. The *Confessions,* together with the *Suspiria de Profundis,* the *Autobiographic Sketches,* and the *Reminiscences* of Wordsworth, Coleridge, Southey, and Lamb, constitute a body of literature which has permanent value. The hundreds of scattered essays on history, philology, politics, and theology have been superseded by more modern work. De Quincey originated the famous distinction between the literature of knowledge and the literature of power and his own works have demonstrated its validity.

As a writer of fiction he was a failure. He lacked the peculiar kind of inventive power needed to create character and devise original plots. He could put down on paper an amazingly accurate portrait of someone he had seen and known (he makes Wordsworth a living figure, and the description of his first meeting with Charles Lamb is vividly realistic), but he always had to have the living model in mind before he could make the portrait. He possessed a fine narrative power (see the "Revolt of the Tartars" and the magnificent last paper of "On Murder Considered as One of the Fine Arts"), but in these he had the advantage of being able to work with actual historical material. Even his taste in fiction was not good. He had an unfortunate predilection for German romantic tales. . . .

But if he lacked the faculty of being able to create seeming images of flesh and blood, it was certainly because of no inherent lack of imaginative power. This power in him was vast and terrible. He drew his material from that inexhaustible reservoir—the subconscious mind; he perceived the richness that lay concealed there; and at times his writing shuttles curiously between the levels of wakeful objectivity and the dark reaches of that hinterland which only the sleep-drugged brain can traverse. [1937]

Philip Van Doren Stern
Introd., in *Selected Writings of Thomas De Quincey*
(New York: Random House, 1949), pp. 15, 17-18

It was during those earlier years in Edinburgh as a regular writer for *Blackwood's* that De Quincey became an object of curious interest to students at the old University. Samuel Warren, later famous as the author of *Ten Thousand a Year,* was one of these. One night he called by appointment at Professor Wilson's to see the much-talked-of Opium-Eater. Standing near the drawing-room door was "a little slight man, dressed in black, pale, careworn, and with a very high forehead." The giant Wilson whispered to Warren: "It will be a queer kind of wine that you will see him drinking!" At dinner the student observed that the decanter by De Quincey's plate contained a beverage exactly resembling laudanum, of which the celebrity freely partook as he vivaciously discussed with Wilson the impossibility of "forgetfulness.". . .

J. C. Metcalf
*De Quincey. A Portrait* (Cambridge, Mass.:
Harvard Univ. Pr., 1940), pp. 97, 113-14

The unhappy boy, determining at last that he "had nothing to hope for" from his guardians in improving his frustrating situation at Manchester, took matters in his own hands and fled, in July, 1802. His first intention, he later admitted, was to head for the Lake District, drawn by the "deep, deep magnet" of William Wordsworth. But he could not present himself to his idol in the character of a runaway schoolboy—his "principle of 'veneration' " was too strong. He went, instead, by his family's home at Chester, and then to Wales, and finally to London, in pathetic pursuit of independence through futile, dragged-out applications to money-lenders. He nearly starved to death, found a "benefactress" in the "noble-minded" prostitute, Ann of Oxford Street, and at last—probably through the good offices of a family friend—returned ignominiously home to Chester in March, 1803. In that time of misery and misunderstanding, Wordsworth was the cynosure; and it is impossible to understand the whole pattern of the relationship between the two men without recognizing that a very important part of that relationship was the boy's "expectation, and desire, / And something evermore about to be" of those "romantic visions"— years before he knew Wordsworth, and even some time before he dared to begin a correspondence with the poet.

It *is* a bad thing for a boy to know himself beyond tutors placed over him by arbitrary authority, and to live in an atmosphere where there can be no praise he values; it is perhaps even worse for the man who as a boy chose his own tutor, enthroned his own idol, and finally came sadly away feeling that his worship was wronged and his just reward stinted. That is the larger pattern of the relationship between De Quincey and Wordsworth. As De Quincey sorrowfully wrote many years after the fact, there was an error on someone's part, "either on Wordsworth's in doing too little or on mine in expecting too much."

John E. Jordan
*De Quincey to Wordsworth* (Berkeley and Los Angeles, Calif.:
Univ. California Pr., 1962), p. 2

# MARIA EDGEWORTH
1767-1849

Although born in England, Maria Edgeworth was Anglo-Irish, the eldest daughter of Richard Lovell Edgeworth, inventor, traveler, agriculturist, magistrate, educational theorist, and moral reformer. In 1782, she settled with her family at their ancestral seat in Edgeworthstown, County Longford, Ireland, where she spent the remainder of her life, managing the family estate after her father's death in 1817. Encouraged by her father who made numerous contributions to her books, she collaborated with him on *Practical Education* (1798); *The Parent's Assistant* (1796-1800); and *Early Lessons* (1801-1815). Independently, she wrote novels and series of stories for children, such as *Castle Rackrent, an Hibernian Tale* (1800); *Moral Tales* (1801); *Belinda* (1801); *Popular Tales* (1804); *Leonora* (1806); *Tales of Fashionable Life* (1809-1812); *Patronage* (1814); *Harrington* (1817); *Ormond* (1817); *Helen* (1833); and *Orlandino* (1847).

Maria Edgeworth, *Tales and Novels* (1893), 12 vols.

Emily Lawless, *Maria Edgeworth* (1904); I. C. Clarke, *Maria Edgeworth* (1950); P. H. Newby, *Maria Edgeworth* (1950)

*Belinda* . . . is not a great novel; but, an acute and expert reviewer might have detected in its author something not unlike a great novelist, at a time when there was nothing in fiction save . . . various extravagances. . . .

The Absentee, to some extent, coalesces, has had better luck, and, perhaps, deserves it. This consists of the Irish stories from which Sir Walter Scott professed to have derived at least part of the suggestion of his own national kind; these began early in 1800, with the striking but rather too typical and chronicle-fashioned, *Castle Rackrent;* and which, later, produced its masterpieces in the . . . *Absentee* (1809) and in *Ormond* (1817). . . . There is one thing about them which deserves much study and which was probably what Scott honoured. . . . In her dealings with

Irish scenes and persons, she never misses it. She cannot touch her ancestral soil (it was not exactly her native, and one might draw fanciful consequences from the relation) without at once acquiring that strange creative or mimetic strength which produces in the reader of fiction—poetic, dramatic or prosaic alike—a sudden, but quiet, undoubting conviction that these things and persons were so and not otherwise. [1917]

George Saintsbury
*CHEL,* eds., A. F. Ward and A. R. Waller, Vol. XI
(New York: Macmillan, 1933), p. 329

. . . In her first novel, or story of any great length, for in other respects it is not much like a regular novel, Maria Edgeworth gave imagination full fling, and did not let any idea of a purpose interfere, although the favourite moral theme is implicit, the nemesis of self-indulgence, extravagance, and folly, as it must needs be in such a register of tragedy. In *Castle Rackrent, an Hibernian Tale. Taken from facts and from the manners of the Irish Squires, Before the year 1782,* which appeared in 1800, she wrote something intrinsically like history, the annals of an Irish family, who go, step by step, generation by generation, to the devil. . . .

*Castle Rackrent* is probably the first novel to give the history of a family through several generations, and the impression of a long lapse of time. Another innovation is the staging of the drama in the mind of simple Thady, whose character projects itself in his comments and emotions. . . . In *Castle Rackrent,* she had taken a holiday from her professional duties of educationist and moral reformer. . . . [1929]

E. A. Baker
*The History of the English Novel,* Vol. VI
(New York: Barnes and Noble, 1950), pp. 28-29, 32

Behind an ironist like Fielding is assurance, courage and complacency; behind Maria Edgeworth, and Irish irony, lie indignation, despair, the political conscience. The right and wrongs of Irish politics come into her works by implication. We see the absentees, the rackrenters, the bought politicians, the English, Jewish, Scottish heiresses brought in to save colonial insolvency. We see the buffoon priests and the double-minded retainers. We do not see the rebellion, the boys hiding in the potato fields, but we do catch the tension. The clever, wise daughter of an enlightened father, a woman always ready to moralize about cause and effect in the neat eighteenth-century way, Maria Edgeworth was Irish enough to enjoy without shame the unreasonable climate of human temper and self-will, Irish enough to be generous about the genius for self-destruction. She was a good woman, ardent but—as Sir Walter Scott said—formidably observant, probably cool, perhaps not strong in sensibility; but she was not sentimental. Her irony—and surely this is Irish from Swift to Shaw— turns a reckless gaiety upon human thick-headedness.

*Castle Rackrent* is the only novel of Maria Edgeworth's which can be read with sustained pleasure by the reader of today. Its verve and vivacity are as sharp as a fiddle's. It catches on like a jig; if it belongs to the art- less time of the English novel, it is not clogged up by old-fashioned usage. [1947]

V. S. Pritchett
*The Living Novel* (New York: Random House, 1964), pp. 40-41

In Maria's tales for children we meet the first living and breathing children in English literature since Shakespeare. What kind of stories were they? . . . They have more than the magic of rectitude. They have the charm of brightly painted pictures. The Bristol streets and shops glitter in the morn- ing sunshine and in the cathedral a robin hops and sings. Maria knew just the touch that will draw the child's attention, the green and white uniform, the coloured jars in a chemist's window (in *The Purple Jar*), all the bright, enticing joy of the simple objects of the material world. We are happy to think of the little girl who shared her bread and milk with a pig, or the "little breathless girl" who ran back to thank Simple Susan for her gift of flowers, crying, "Kiss me quick, for I shall be left behind.". . .

There is nothing to set beside the primrose freshness of Simple Susan. . . . But the best of the *Moral Tales* is undoubtedly *Forester*. Here, very thinly disguised, is none other than the great Mr. Thomas Day himself. . . . It is the story of civilisation triumphant.

P. H. Newby
*Maria Edgeworth* (London: Arthur Barker, 1950), pp. 24, 28, 35-36

. . . In *Castle Rackrent* the Irish novelist too can be seen to have gone beyond her brief, and in a way similar to Scott. For if we compare *Castle Rackrent* with *Waverley,* we see that Miss Edgeworth's pathetic hero, Sir Condy, is a historical as well as a national type; like the Baron Bradwar- dine in Scott's novel, he is the man who lives by the barbaric standard of honour in a commercial society where that standard can no longer apply. In the perspective of history, it could be argued, the Act of Union signified for Ireland what the failure of the Jacobites fifty years earlier had signified for Scotland, the final extinction of the code of honour as a standard of social conduct. Scott of course is fully aware of this historical perspective and establishes it with masterly precision without once stating it explicitly. It is implicit in *Castle Rackrent,* but in an altogether more shadowy way. That Miss Edgeworth was half-aware of the historical implications is revealed, I think, by her casting the whole into the mouth of Thady, the old retainer; for this gives to the story the elegiac tone of one who regrets or at any rate acknowledges the death of an old order, the irrelevance of much of his past.

Donald Davie
*The Heyday of Sir Walter Scott* (New York:
Barnes and Noble, 1961), pp. 65-66

# WILLIAM HAZLITT
## 1778-1830

The son of a dissenting minister and political radical, William Hazlitt grew up in a revolutionist atmosphere, attended a dissenting theological school, and became interested in philosophy and metaphysics. Pressed to earn a living he became a portrait painter, spent some time in Paris, and returned to England a lifelong devotee of Napoleon. In 1813, he began to write dramatic criticism for the *Morning Chronicle* and for Leigh Hunt's *Examiner*. He won public acclaim for his lectures on literature, delivered between 1818 and 1820. In 1819, he was separated from his wife Sarah Stoddart whom he had married in 1808. The following year he developed a passion for Sarah Walker, his landlady's daughter, which he indiscreetly recorded in *Liber Amoris*. Although he divorced his wife, his young *amie* would not have him, and he subsequently married Mrs. Isabella Bridgewater who left him in 1827 after three years of marriage. A querulous personality, Hazlitt denounced his old friends Wordsworth and Coleridge for their conservatism, attacked the aristocratic Scott and Lord Byron, and apparently remained on good terms only with the patient Charles Lamb, who was at his bedside when he died in 1830. He spent his greatest efforts on metaphysical, ethical, economic, linguistic, and psychological essays, and on his *Life of Napoleon*, but he is best remembered for the literary criticism which had attracted his contemporaries and especially had won the admiration of John Keats. His major works are *Principles of Human Action* (1805); *The Round Table* (1817); *Characters of Shakespeare's Plays* (1817); *Lectures on the English Poets* (1818); *Lectures on the English Comic Writers* (1819); *Lectures on the Dramatic Literature of the Age of Elizabeth* (1820); *Liber Amoris* (1823); *Spirit of the Age* (1825); *The Plain Speaker* (1826); and *Life of Napoleon* (1828-1830).

P. P. Howe, ed., *The Complete Works* (1930-1934), 21 vols.

P. P. Howe, *The Life of William Hazlitt* (1922); H. C. Baker, *William Hazlitt* (1962)

That he was a great critic there will probably now be little dispute. . . .

Hazlitt is not, like Coleridge, remarkable for the discovery and enunciation of any one great critical principle, or for the emission . . . of remarkable mediate *dicta,* or for *marginalia* on individual passages or lines, though sometimes he can do the last and sometimes also the second of these things. What he is remarkable for is his extraordinary fertility and felicity, as regards English Literature, in judgments, more or less "grasped," of individual authors, books, or pieces. . . . The fertility and the felicity of his criticism are things which strike one almost dumb with admiration; and this in spite of certain obvious and in their way extremely grave faults. [1904]

George Saintsbury
*A History of Criticism,* Vol. III
(New York: Humanities Pr., 1961), pp. 251-52

The virtue of his work lies not in his analytic criticism, which can be studied apart from his own language, but in the fusion of passion and insight; and in [his] . . . portrait of Coleridge, which has passed into the universal heritage of English letters, we may see blended together that perception of physical traits, which was heightened no doubt by Hazlitt's training as a painter, and that power of seizing the psychological peculiarities of a man and using them to explain the character of his writing.

Paul Elmer More
*Shelburne Essays. Second Series* (New York:
G. P. Putnam's Sons, 1905), pp. 79-80

Hazlitt's critical career really falls into two parts. . . . In the first he is the regular critic of either a daily or a weekly paper, who is bound to concentrate his thoughts on individual productions and performances, and to report as well as to judge the occurrences of a given evening. At this period, if "the players put him out," he was successful in dissembling the fact. Later, when his prime favourites were past their prime, and the rising talents were of the second order, when he was no longer a daily critic but a monthly essayist (if not a mere unattached playgoer), and when the drama in general, rather than this or that performance in particular, was the subject of his considerations—it may very well be that his early interest in acting declined, and that he resorted to the playhouse rather for its associations than for its realities. The theatre-habit is like the opium-habit: we cannot relinquish it even when its pristine raptures are things of the remote past. It is very likely that in his later years the theatre became to Hazlitt a place of memories and reflections rather than of present enjoyments; but it would be a mistake to suppose that the criticisms . . . were conceived and written in any such vague and reminiscent frame of mind. In the great majority of them, his perceptions are certainly acute enough, his interest vivid and unforced.

William Archer
Introd., in *Hazlitt on Theatre,* eds., William Archer and
Robert Lowe (New York: Hill and Wang, n.d.), pp. xxviii-xxvix

The [romantic] lover may . . . run together the ideal and the real. He may glorify some comparatively commonplace person, crown as queen of his heart some Dulcinea del Toboso. Hazlitt [in *Liber Amoris*] employs appropriately in describing his own passion for the vulgar daughter of a London boarding-house keeper the very words of Cervantes: "He had courted a statue, hunted the wind, cried aloud to the desert." Hazlitt like other lovers of this type is in love not with a particular person but with his own dream. He is as one may say in love with love. No subject indeed illustrates like this of love the nostalgia, the infinite indeterminate desire of the romantic imagination. . . .

[In *The Round Table*] Hazlitt converts criticism itself into an art of impassioned recollection. He loves to linger over the beautiful moments of his own literary life. The passing years have increased the richness of their temperamental refraction and bestowed upon them the "pathos of distance." A good example is his account of the two years of his youth he spent in reading the "Confessions" and the "Nouvelle Héloïse," and in shedding tears over them. [1919]

Irving Babbitt
*Rousseau and Romanticism* (New York:
Meridian Books, 1955), pp. 178, 185-86

His emergence, [as a writer] when it happened, was, as we should expect neither half-hearted nor mistakable. In the month of September some so-called "Common-places"—*On the Love of Life, On Classical Education* —begin to make their appearance; and simultaneously there is a note on the acceptance by Southey of the office of Poet Laureate. This is followed immediately by two letters under the heading *The Stage*. It was these last, we may imagine, which led Hazlitt's editor to conclude, however reluctantly, that he might be entertaining on his staff a dramatic critic unawares. Within a month of his appearance he is duly installed in that office; and from this moment he never looks back, but marches from department to department of Mr. Perry's paper, making each one of them his own. . . .

If Keats had been able to attend [Hazlitt's lectures of 1819] and if Crabb Robinson had been able to stay away, we should have had wiser and warmer words on the *Comic Writers*. Early in December Keats's brother Tom died, and soon after, having occasion to be in the neighbourhood of York Street, he "called on Hazlitt." He took away with him the Lectures, either in manuscript or in proof; for in his last journal-letter of the year for America we find him transcribing a long passage in illustration of their author's "fiery laconicism." The transcription comes between those of his own "Fancy" and "Bards of Passion and of Mirth," and not for the first or the last time Hazlitt's prose and Keats's verse go well in a letter together.

P. P. Howe
*The Life of William Hazlitt* (New York:
G. H. Doran, 1922), pp. 155, 274

Hazlitt's reaction against neo-classicism points really in two directions: through his polemical theorizing toward realism, through his appreciative criticism of pictures toward romanticism. He never succeeded in synthesizing his views, in evolving a consistent and well-rounded theory of the fine arts. The substance of his discussions is often wearisome, and the tone harsh, disputatious, strident. Yet his [art] criticism, with all the defects of impressionism upon it, has still the power at times to stir and to delight us. Some of the artist's rapture and fire, which remained a possession of Hazlitt long after he had given up his apprenticeship in the studio, is felt in these pages. Now and again he comments in phrases which we shall hardly forget when we look at the works that called them forth. For instance, this, descriptive of one of Raphael's cartoons:

> The Beggars are as fine as ever: they do not lose by the squalid condition of their garb or features, but remain patriarchs of poverty, and mighty in disease and infirmity as if they crawled and grovelled on the pavement of Heaven!

One virtue, not invariably found in works on aesthetics or in aesthetic criticism, may be freely accorded to Hazlitt—the virtue, namely, of being really inside his subject. However much he erred in logic, Hazlitt had experienced the aesthetic emotion.

S. P. Chase
*PMLA* (March, 1924), pp. 201-2

Almost everything that Hazlitt ever wrote—and being a journalist, he wrote a great deal—is coloured with politics. So active were his political prejudices that they pushed over into all his work, into descriptions of paintings and criticisms of the stage, into notes of travel and memories of youth. Yet it is not easy to describe them, largely because they are so widely dispersed through all his writings. Moreover, Hazlitt's reputation has always been that of a dog in the manger, and it is often assumed that his politics are mere snarling. He was simply against every one, we are told. . . . But it is impossible to study Hazlitt's writings without coming to the conclusion that he had a real desire for conformity, that he wished to work with other men, and that he was by no means lacking in common sense. . . .

In Hazlitt's opinion . . . a system of laws can be constructed "on the principle of the right of self-defence, or the security for person, liberty, and property." This means a very great diminution in the power of the state and in the amount of necessary legislation. But it does not imply anarchy. The individual rights on which the state is founded are clear enough in respect to their fundamentals, but there are many marginal rights that require interpretation; it is the function of the whole people, acting under universal suffrage, to decide on the ultimate boundaries of these rights.

Crane Brinton
*Political Ideas of the English Romanticists*
(Oxford Univ. Pr., 1926), pp. 122-23, 128-29

Hazlitt's training as a painter was valuable to him, though he gave up painting in despair. All his work is the work of an artist. He is never to be caught in a consumer's attitude.

> Contented if he might enjoy
> The things that others understand.

Such an attitude may be the best way of approaching the works of nature— it is one of the best ways. But to enjoy art without trying to understand it is to wallow in art, to be the rich man who cannot drive his motor-car, or cook an omelette, or write a readable letter. Hazlitt lived among the *makers.* [1926]

Sir Walter Raleigh
*On Writing and Writers,* ed. George Gordon
(London: Edward Arnold, 1927), pp. 127-28

Apart from his use of autobiography, his personal crotchets stick out like the quills of a porcupine from nearly every article, essay, or lecture that he wrote. He never ceased to be aware of himself, no matter of what subject he might be treating. It is clear from the written opinions of his contemporaries that he was universally regarded as "difficult." Scarcely any of his friendships remained unclouded for long periods—even Lamb suffered several eclipses—for none could brook the uncompromising directness with which Hazlitt looked upon life and upon the shortcomings of his friends. "He blowed us up," as poor Lamb said in 1814, his offence on that occasion being "political indifference"! It is easy for us to realize at this distance of time that Hazlitt's ruling passion was the search for truth and that no personal relationships were ever allowed to stand in its way. It was difficult for his friends to regard this quite so dispassionately as we can, though they loved him for his sensitiveness, generosity, and honesty of purpose. . . .

Hazlitt in his writings was first and foremost a student of human nature, but his eager pursuit of every hare that showed itself frequently led him into digressions upon special subjects, and similarly his more specialized essays were constantly breaking light upon questions of general conduct. [1930]

Geoffrey Keynes
Introd., in *Selected Essays*, by William Hazlitt
(London: Nonesuch Pr., 1948), pp. xix, xxi-xxii

I took up, a few days since, an essay of Mr. Arnold Bennett's; and I find him saying that English letters can show only one first-rate critic—Hazlitt. About the transcendent merit of Hazlitt I agree wholeheartedly. But I cannot dismiss quite as lightly as Mr. Bennett all the other great critical names. . . . Even so, I can forgive it to any one if he finds the touch of some of these critics a degree heavy. Not all of them have the obvious joy in poetry which makes Hazlitt so good a critic. . . .

Nor am I sure that one half of the merits of Hazlitt in criticism do not in fact proceed from a consuming zeal which he has for freedom and righteousness. . . . It would be hard, I suppose, to call Hazlitt a virtuous man. Yet this consuming zeal for freedom and righteousness Hazlitt has; and it makes a world of difference to his criticism. [1930]

H. W. Garrod
*The Study of Poetry* (Oxford Univ. Pr., 1936), pp. 39-40, 68

It is certain that the truth of Hazlitt's life, as indeed of most lives, lies at a deeper level than that of fact, that the essentials of his life thus far were not so much events, as the struggle towards thought, in his adolescence, towards expression, in his early manhood, then towards assimilation of the new regions of thought and feeling opened out to him by Coleridge, towards perfection in painting following upon the meeting with Coleridge, and towards re-creating himself both as a writer and as a painter in the humiliation that followed upon the first sexual episode in his life of which there is no record. But yet throughout all these years, no matter how his other preoccupations fluctuated, his development was closely and constantly related to his hope for the liberty and happiness and the progress of mankind; this hope reached its climax of intensity in the years in which he was making a beginning in political journalism; and his passings from one newspaper or periodical to another are therefore events of his "true life" in so far as they are symbols of the various crises through which he passed, and of the inveteracy of opinion which made it impossible for him to be in complete sympathy even with those who like himself were forward-looking in politics. . . .

In the first days of September [1818] the August number of *Black-*

*wood's* reached him. This, with its attack on "the calm, settled, imperturbable drivelling idiocy" of Keats, is often thought of as the "Keats" number, because the early death of Keats "set a seal upon his reputation," and made him the beloved of all. But it was Hazlitt whom this number had set out to slay. The attack on him was not, like the attack on Keats, confined to one section of the magazine. It sprawled like a fungus from cover to cover. . . .

Hazlitt recognized at once that *Blackwood's* attack was not a political or critical offensive directed against him but an attempt to cancel his existence as a writer. He seems also to have recognized the impossibility of dealing with such a campaign of lies by any of the ordinary means of exposure: insistence on truth, he knew, could bring no immediate victory in such a warfare. Yet in his first reaction to the attack, the writing of a *Reply,* truth was his only weapon. His manipulation of this weapon, in the immediate circumstances, is all-revealing as to the grain of his nature. He is faithful to it, even when his adherence to its puts him at a disadvantage.

Catherine M. Maclean
*Born Under Saturn* (London: Collins, 1943), pp. 311, 387-89

Despite his extraordinary production, Hazlitt's life between 1812 and 1820 was not entirely one of solitary scribbling. His bad manners, a scandal that became a legend, sometimes made him seem an Ishmael, but he had a few firm friends and a host of admiring, if somewhat fearful, acquaintances who tempered his misanthropy. However isolated his early and his later years, this middle period of his life was one of journalistic bustle, when the plays and art and politics that provided him with copy also thrust him out into the world. Coleridge and Wordsworth had washed their hands of him, and Crabb Robinson eventually decided that his friendship cost too much; but Lamb, of course, was loyal, and through him he met a flock of younger men—Hunt, Haydon, Reynolds, Keats, Barnes, Talfourd, Proctor, Clarke, and others—who filled, or helped to fill, his middle years. Sooner or later he quarreled with or lost sight of almost of all of them, and so relapsed into his solitude, but for half a dozen years or so he had a place in literary society. . . .

[The] . . . episode with Sarah Walker, which has always given pain to Hazlitt's admirers and satisfaction to the prurient, is, ironically, the most fully documented in his life. He himself recorded it with Rousseauistic frenzy in *Liber Amoris* (1823), an extraordinary compilation of the lovers' "conversations" and of his own correspondence. . . .

[The] . . . vision of ecstatic joy in his Table Talks is more appealing than the reality described in *Liber Amoris,* where we see Hazlitt hold his

"Infelice" on his lap and fumble with her clothing, but in his disordered state of mind the two were indistinct. He lived through most of 1821, it seems, in a state of suspended but erotic animation, hoping he might marry Sarah Walker and trying to forget that he already had a wife. . . .

What was mainly on his mind that fall, however, was the preparation of his magnum opus for the press. The publication, in January 1828, of the first two volumes of *The Life of Napoleon Buonaparte* by the firm of Hunt and Clarke was the chief event of Hazlitt's later years, and indeed, in his opinion, the chief event of his career. . . .

Perhaps the kindest thing to say about such a monumental failure as *The Life of Napoleon Buonaparte* is that it deserves its reputation. There are splendors here and there, of course: the preface is a vibrant presentation of Napoleon as the child and champion of the Revolution, which itself is shown to be the clear assertion of a people's right to self-respect and freedom; Chapter III . . . is a brilliant evocation of reformers' hopes and fears as they were caught in the convulsive test of their ideals; the lurid treatment of the Terror and of the horrors of the Russian winter are proof of Hazlitt's skill with words. But these are not enough to save the elephantine work. . . . In short, *The Life of Napoleon Buonaparte*, though partisan and ill-informed, is Hazlitt's most mature assertion of opinions that, as he believed, were "in the nature of realities." No reader can accept as fact, for instance, his bitter comment on the field of Waterloo—the sun that rose that day, he said, would set upon "the triumph of the despot and the slave throughout the world, and as long as it shall continue to roll around this orb of ours"—but it conveys his version of the truth, and truth, as he had wisely said, "is not one, but many."

Herschel C. Baker
*William Hazlitt* (Cambridge, Mass.: Harvard Univ. Pr.,
1962), pp. 218, 410-11, 459-62

# THOMAS  HOOD
1799-1845

Probably the greatest of English humorists of the nineteenth century, Thomas Hood, born in London, was the son of a Scottish bookseller and publisher. Like his father, he was a self-made man of independent spirit. He attended a school for young gentlemen until his father's death in 1811, and had already begun to dabble in verse when, at fourteen, he went to work, first in a counting-house, then in an engraver's shop. After a two-year visit with his Scottish relatives, he returned to London and the engraving business, continuing his literary interests while learning his trade. At twenty-two, he was appointed sub-editor of the *London Magazine* and contributed prose and poetry to it which made a hit with the public from the start. Through his affiliation with the *London*, he met John Hamilton Reynolds; Reynolds' sister Jane, whom he married in 1825; Charles Lamb, who became his dearest friend; and many another literary notable. With Reynolds, he published a financially successful volume of comic verse in 1825. Having become a disciple of Keats, who had been a personal friend of the Reynolds family, he imitated Keats' style and many of his themes in *The Plea of the Midsummer Fairies* (1827). The commercial failure of *The Plea* made Hood decide to concentrate on the more lucrative comic poetry. Financial setbacks, the loss of a child, an attack of rheumatic fever, and litigation over copyrights hounded Hood's mature years, five of which were spent in Germany where living costs were cheap. In his last two years, while desperately ill, he wrote the famous humanitarian poems for which he is best remembered now: "The Song of the Shirt" (1843); "The Bridge of Sighs" (1844); and "The Lay of the Labourer" (1844). His reputation among his contemporaries, however, was based on such comic and gothic poems as *Odes and Addresses to Great People* (1825); *Whims and Oddities* (1826-1827) *The Dream of Eugene Aram, a Murderer* (1829); *Comic Melodies* (1830); *Verses from Tylney Hall* (1834); "Ode to Rae Wilson" (1837); "Miss Kilmansegg and her Precious Leg" (1840); and "The Haunted House" (1844).

Thomas Hood, *The Works, Comic and Serious, in Prose and Verse* (1882-1884, repr. 1966) 11 vols.

Walter Jerrold, *Thomas Hood, His Life and Times* (1907); J. C. Reid, *Thomas Hood* (1963)

. . . His talents were early recognised on the *London Magazine*, . . . he had been honoured with the tribute of a dedication by Barry Cornwall, but to the wider public—the public on whose favour the penman is dependent for his bread and cheese—the name of Hood was but little known until after the publication in February, 1825, of the "Odes and Addresses to Great People.". . .

Though the little book was received with enthusiasm and achieved popularity there were not wanting critics who saw that there was a danger for the author in thus courting public applause by "light verse" when he had shown himself capable of higher things. Wainewright had implored, a couple of years earlier, "let not the shallow induce thee to conceal thy depth.". . .

"The Song of the Shirt" [1843] was one of those pieces that, touching the conscience and appealing to the sentiment of a people, took place at once as something of a folksong. It was sung about the streets by poor people "to a rude air of their own adaptation in a way that cannot fail to have touched the author." When Hood's name came to be mentioned as writer of the "Song" there were not wanting people to dispute it! Indeed it was definitely claimed for some unknown person, and a journal which referred to it as Hood's was asked to contradict that statement. Fortunately, however, there was incontestable proof, but over a year after its publication the author was compelled to reassert that he was the author. . . .

We have it on authority of the historian of *Punch* that the publication of "The Song of the Shirt" trebled the circulation of that journal. It may be said also to have trebled Hood's fame and popularity at the time. . . .

Walter Jerrold
*Thomas Hood: His Life and Times*
(London: Alston Rivers, 1907), pp. 163, 168, 367-68

Every reader of the "Song of the Shirt" will recall an illustration of the unexpected employment of a pun in the very agony of the woman's passion and despair:

> Work—work—work—
> In the dull December light! . . .
> The Brooding swallows cling,
> As if to show me their sunny backs,
> And *twit* me with the spring!

The last line is a daring experiment in contrast. On the face of it, a pun ought to be disastrous in such a context; yet no one, I think, can fail to feel that its effect is that, not of marring, but of heightening the tragedy of the poem, as Lady Macbeth's frenzied pun is felt to heighten the terror of the scene which follows the murder of Duncan. In *Eugene Aram*, again, the poet plays almost ferociously with a fantastic image when he makes the murderer tell us that grief was his grim chamberlain, and lighted him to bed. But—*pace* Edgar Allan Poe, who does not seem to have grasped the significance of this kind of art—what a fearful force such a touch adds to the narrator's remorse! What a white light it flashes into his mind! How true psychologically that maniacal outburst of morbid fancy!

In these cases, then, we have the grotesque element introduced incidentally. Well, when, instead of this method being occasional, the pun, the bizarre image, the extravagant fancy, the playful innuendo, are habitually employed in the treatment of a serious theme, we have what I have called the gruesome grotesques. . . .

Hood's greatest achievement in the line of the grotesque, however—many think, his greatest single achievement altogether—is the marvelous extravaganza entitled "Miss Kilmansegg and her Precious Leg." A long poem, running to some three thousand lines, yet maintaining its brilliancy and its vitality to the very end, this is perhaps open to criticism on the ground that it is really too clever and makes too great a demand upon the ordinary reader, who finds his own faculties at constant strain in the effort to keep pace with the author's subtlety and rapidity of thought, with the wit that flashes and sparkles on every page, with the extreme allusiveness which marks the poem throughout, and with its sudden turns from sportive fancy to poetic feeling . . . to sweeping invective, and . . . back to sportive fancy.

W. H. Hudson
*A Quiet Corner in a Library* (Chicago: Rand McNally, 1915), pp. 50-51, 54

Hood's *Literary Reminiscences,* fragmentary and rambling as they are, and touched with the habit of caricature, have long been recognised as one of our best aids to the reflection of Charles Lamb; he comes to life in them, as do others who were associated with the *London Magazine,* especially John Clare. Not without wisdom does Hood recall Elia and the Peasant seated side by side in cheerful debate, or walking through the strand arm in arm, Lamb in his black clothes, Clare in his special suit of green— "Look at Tom and Jerry—there goes Tom and Jerry." In Lamb's particular kindness for Clare, and Clare's immediate devotion to Lamb, there is a wealth of meaning—greatness on both sides. . . . They are a well-known treasury for biographers, the entire *Reminiscences.* . . .

Edmund Blunden
*Votive Tablets* (London: Cobden Sanderson, 1931), p. 290

. . . I can think of no better and quicker way of learning familiar idioms than by reading the comic poems of Hood—especially the comic ballads, which are in themselves a veritable museum of idioms. . . . [See *Faithless Nelly Gray*]

This man had a double gift. One day he would make all England laugh, and the next day he would make them weep. The tears remain; the hearts are still touched by these verses of pathos and simple beauty. But the laughter has ceased; and the funny poems, as I tell you, are chiefly valuable for the study of puns, household phrases, idioms, and mere tricks with words. [1934]

Lafcadio Hearn
*On Poets,* eds., R. Tanabe, T. Ochiai, and I. Nishizaki (Tokyo: Hokuseido Pr., 1941), pp. 634, 636

Hood's special idiosyncrasy is to turn the screw of verbal conceit upon his subject. In *Eugene Aram* alone he cut out these tricks, even forbearing in the last verse when his temptation was always strongest. . . . But if Hood's puns are often disastrous, they do frequently show . . . a kind of second sight. They are like the cackle out of the grave in *Hamlet.* They add malice to the knife and give the macabre its own morbid whimsicalities.

Take that terrible poem, *The Last Man*. The earth has been desolated by plague and only two men are left alive. They meet at a gallows and one, out of jealousy, decides to hang the other. He does so and is left, wracked by conscience, to lament that he cannot now hang himself:

> For there is not another man alive,
> In the world to pull my legs.          [1947, rev. 1964]

V. S. Pritchett<br>
The Living Novel (New York: Random House, 1964), p. 71

While the majority of Hood's work is humorous, he had in him the capacity for real poetry. This is shown in the little volume *The Plea of the Midsummer Fairies* (1827). The book opens with the "Plea," which is dedicated to Lamb, and which is real fairy verse on the theme of Shakespeare intervening between Time and the followers of Titania. . . .

The poem is of some length, running to over one hundred twenty stanzas, but there are few lines which do not bear the grace and charm of imagination. "Hero and Leander," which follows this fanciful creation, suffers from the reader's instinctive comparison with the greater vigour and passion of Marlowe's poem; but it has stanzas of effective description, as when the sea-maid having dragged the body of Leander down with her to the ocean bed, finds him dead in her arms. . . .

This volume does not exhaust the fertility of Hood's imagination. In the *Dream of Eugene Aram* he shows real power of handling the macabre, and although this forms an unpleasant series of stanzas, it is well-wrought and not over-emphasized. The poet has the skill of ending on a quiet but dramatic note. . . .

We have done but little more than touch on the various aspects of the work of a very courageous and prolific writer, but the work of Thomas Hood has been too much neglected and he well repays the reader who studies his productions as a whole. Not only has his poetry variety, technical dexterity and frequently imagination, but his prose is no less flexible and flowing, having similar qualities to his verse.

N. Hardy Wallis<br>
in Essays by Divers Hands, Transactions of the<br>
Royal Society of Literature<br>
(Oxford Univ. Pr., 1947), pp. 109-10, 113-14

Hood wrote a "Lamia" in dramatic form, and "Ode to Melancholy" and several other pieces which are no more than dilute Keats, and an "Ode to Autumn," which, though its lines abound in Keatsian echoes, has a certain cloying beauty that is its own. But only the sonnet "To Silence" suggests that had he persisted in writing Romantic poems Hood might have attained real independence of speech. . . .

The elaborate experimentalism of Hood's style on some occasions is as remarkable as its apparent simplicty on others. Whereas "The China Mender" recalls Swift, "She is far from the Land" belongs rather in the tradition of Skelton. But these two conventions by no means exhaust those of which Thomas Hood was master. There is the punning poem in ballad metre, deriving from Goldsmith's "Elegy on the Death of a Mad Dog"; there is the complicated discursive and allusive narrative style of "Love and Lunacy," which develops features of Byron's "Don Juan"; and there is a device closely akin to the metaphysical quibble turned to comic effect, a trick which Hood employed with success even in his first *London Magazine* "Ode to Doctor Kitchener," with its sustained culinary metaphor that is worthy of Cleveland or Cowley. . . .

It is curious that with so much of the equipment of a first-class satirist, with dislikes, enthusiasms, a strong social sense, endless inventiveness, and shrewd powers of ridicule, Hood should have written no poems that can truly be described as satires. . . . Yet those poems that are closest to satire, pieces for which the fifteenth-century term *flyting* is the most suitable description, are on the whole his most successful. . . .

*TLS* (September 19, 1952), pp. 1-2

For all the charm and talent of his early serious poems, I cannot feel that they represent the character of his authentic gifts and individuality, which was for the grotesque, as in "The Last Man" and "Miss Kilmansegg and her Precious Leg," the exuberantly comic and pun-crammed piece, the sombre and macabre, as in *The Dream of Eugene Aram* and "The Haunted House," the poem of gentle domestic sentiment, as in "The Death-Bed," and "Farewell Life," and such humanitarian verses as "The Song of the Shirt" and "The Bridge of Sighs." In these poems is to be found the real Hood the poet, not in the clever but overly bookish productions that make up the bulk of *The Plea of the Midsummer Fairies*. It was not, however, until Hood had rid himself of his ambition to become another Keats and came to draw his subjects and his emotions more directly from life that he wrote poetry that is remembered. The critics of his first serious book may not have been wholly wrong, then, nor may it have been altogether a bad thing that Hood was diverted into other fields by its failure and so avoided becoming, as well he might, a poet as unreadable and as sterile as Leigh Hunt.

J. C. Reid
*Thomas Hood* (London: Routledge and Kegan Paul;
New York: Hillary, 1963), pp. 94-95

# [JAMES HENRY] LEIGH HUNT
1784-1859

Born in London of an American loyalist father who returned to England to escape the Revolution, Leigh Hunt received his only formal education at Christ's Hospital from 1791-1799. After some years as a free-lance drama critic and clerk in the War Office, he became, in 1808, editor of his brother's newly established journal, *The Examiner*. In 1813, he was imprisoned for two years for defaming the Prince Regent. The sentence made him a public figure, and he was visited in his cell by such leading liberals as Byron, Shelley, Hazlitt, Moore, and the Lambs; his release in 1815 inspired a sonnet by a nineteen-year-old student named Keats, whom Hunt subsequently befriended and encouraged. In 1816, he published *The Story of Rimini*, which (although it had some influence on younger poets) is our best example of Hunt's failure as a poet. In 1822, Hunt was invited by Shelley and Byron to Italy to edit *The Liberal*. He arrived just before Shelley's death and was stranded along with his large family when Byron lost interest in the journal and departed for Greece. Returning to England in 1825 on borrowed funds, Hunt was still in need of money two years later when he agreed to write the first life of Byron. An embittered account, the *Life* made enemies for Hunt among the critics as well as the friends of Byron. For the next twenty years, Hunt eked out a living as a dramatic critic (the first of his kind), editor, and essayist, but could never keep clear of debt. Finally, in 1847, he was given a government pension in recognition of his contribution to ethical journalism. His last considerable work was the readable and honest account of his own life, which he wrote in 1850. During his later years, he was befriended by Dickens, Carlyle, Browning, and Thackeray. His major publications were *The Examiner* (1808-1822); *The Story of Rimini* (1816); *The Indicator* (1819-1821); *Lord Byron* (1828); *Imagination and Fancy* (1844); *Autobiography* (1850); and *Selections from the English Poets* (1859).

H. S. Milford, ed., *Poetical Works* (1923); C. W. and L. H. Houtchens, eds., *Dramatic Criticism, 1808-31* (1949); *Literary Criticism* (1956); *Political and Occasional Essays*, with Lawrence Huston, ed. (1962)

Edmund Blunden, *Leigh Hunt and His Circle* (1930)

. . . He has the immense and surprising credit of having first discovered the greatness of the tragic part of Middleton's *Changeling*, as an individual exploit, and in more general ways he has that, which Macaulay duly recognised in a well-known passage, of being perhaps more *catholic* in his tastes as regards English Literature than any critic up to his time. He has left a very large range of critical performance, which is very rarely without taste, acuteness, and felicity of expression; and he has . . . the very great advantage of possessing a competent knowledge of at least one modern literature besides his own, and some glimmerings of others. [1904]

George Saintsbury
*A History of Criticism*, Vol. III (New York:
Humanities Pr., 1961), p. 246

*The Story of Rimini* as it was published in 1816 is a very different thing from the revised version of 1832, with its "rejection of superfluities," its correction of "mistakes of all kinds." It may be quite true, as the author protested, that the first edition contained weak lines, together with "certain conventionalities of structure, originating in his having had his studies too early directed towards the artificial instead of the natural poets." Yet, in fact, the second version is much more artificial than the first, and what was young, spontaneous, really new at the time, has given way to a firmer but less felicitous style. . . .

Arthur Symons
*The Romantic Movement in English Poetry* (London:
Achibald Constable, 1909), p. 219

We must forget Dante, if we can, when we open *The Story of Rimini* (1816), and it is best to forget Chaucer also, if justice is to be done to Hunt. Hardly a page but is stained by vulgarity, or by something that no artist should print. . . . It is a tale in verse, and, with whatever stumbles and disgraces, as a tale it moves; it has the spirit of beauty, intermittent but undeniable; it is full of natural imagery, luxuriously felt and rendered; it has no purpose except the story, and the imagery, and the expression of beauty; and, amidst the most desperate lapses, it has style. [1912]

Oliver Elton
*A Survey of English Literature, 1780-1830,* Vol. II
(London: Edward Arnold, 1961), pp. 225-26

To no single man is the praise of having transformed the eighteenth century magazine, or collection of light miscellaneous essays, into its subsequent form due so much as to Hunt. Allowing for the undeniable truth that if a certain thing has to be done, evolutionary fate always finds some one to do it, it may still be said that, without Hunt, *Sketches by Boz* would have been a kind of Melchisedec, and *Household Words* improbable. . . .

His influence on pure criticism and on poetry was not very great, but in neither was it negligible. In verse, he had, beyond doubt, the credit of being the first deliberately to desert the stopped decasyllabic couplet which had reigned over the whole eighteenth century and the latter part of the seventeenth, reviving the overrun of the Jacobeans and first Carolines. Keats may not have learnt the change from Hunt only, but from the originals as well; yet this does not lessen Hunt's importance. [1914]

George Saintsbury
*CHEL*, eds., A. W. Ward and A. R. Waller, Vol. XII
(Cambridge Univ. Pr., 1953), p. 221

It has been the fashion of recent years to belittle Hunt, to patronize him as a man of small account. . . . But this is a myopic view. . . . Hunt was not a great creator certainly, but he was a great introducer. His peculiar quality was that he considered poetry as an art, not as a rag-bag for inconsequential erudition. Would that a score of Hunts could be dotted round among our colleges; it would do us a world of good. I can never forget that it was his *Imagination and Fancy* which first taught me what poetry was. There is no better text-book for the appreciation of poetry than that volume. He had what I may call a touch-stone mind; he knew instinctively what was good and never feared to proclaim it. His limitations are plain enough, and became only too plain to Keats later on. But that he stimulated Keats to increasing effort, no one can fail to see. [1925]

Amy Lowell
*John Keats,* Vol. I (Boston: Houghton Mifflin, 1929), p. 136

Letters exist to give an unfaded impression of the friendship during 1817. It appears that Hunt looked up to Shelley as a sure guide in the wilderness of this world. . . . Shelley regarded Hunt as the sure guide to a good piano, at all events, and Marianne as equally competent to scrape Apollo and Venus into a whiteness suitable to his library. Mary Shelley (Marina) was a little inclined to think Hunt "contrary," and Marianne uneconomical, but these were minor matters. . . .

Two numbers of *The Indicator* . . . [in August 1820] were devoted to Hunt's early and late task of making England read Keats. . . . Too soon the poet [Keats], with this mountain-height of artistic tranquillity at his feet, had to bid farewell to the unavailing loyalty and foredoomed expectancy of his friends; the "Maria Crowther" dropped down the Thames with Keats aboard, "the rains began to fall heavily," and Hunt deserted an attempt to write a jocular *Indicator*, ending instead with a troubled farewell to the voyager. . . .

It may be discerned through Hunt's long recriminations and contentions [in *Lord Byron*] that he would have gloried in Byron, had not certain characteristics on both sides clashed, and obscured the view. . . . In spite of these handicaps, he was fascinated by Byron, his memory recorded impressions of Byron when everything else drifted hazily by, and such moments of unblemished kindness as Byron happened to offer him were to him almost the finest thing in the world.

Edmund Blunden
*Leigh Hunt and His Circle* (New York:
Harper, 1930), pp. 121, 154, 235

"Feel the passion," says Hunt of actors, "and the action will follow." Of dramatic critics we might say "feel the passion and the words will come." While reading Leigh Hunt we feel something of that anticipatory excitement usual in the theatre before the curtain goes up. His is an excellent complementary performance as well as good criticism, sound and penetrating, apt in phrase and figure, pulsating with the intimacy and warmth of friendly talk. For the first time in English dramatic criticism the life of the stage gave life to a professional critic's prose, and there is an abundant sense of communication across the footlights. . . . For the life of the theatre he looked to the actors rather than to the authors, and the 19th century actors justified him by keeping the theatre alive during the generations when playwriting was moribund. William Hazlitt was doubtless a better writer than Hunt, but doubtless also he was less good as a theatre critic. [1945]

A. C. Ward
Introd., in *Specimens of English Dramatic Criticism, XVII-XX Centuries* (Oxford Univ. Pr., n.d.), pp. 6-7

In a day when much dramatic criticism was mere foggy generalization, Hunt was specific. Actors, authors, and stage managers alike found in his criticism something tangibly useful that might be adopted in the next day's rehearsal. If a play were based on ancient tradition, Hunt's knowledge of the classics, usually detailed and thorough, enabled him to express a sound opinion; or, if the play were an adaptation or translation from the French or Italian, again his judgment was based on a firsthand knowledge of the language and a familiarity with the author's other writings, as well as with the historical period in which the plot was laid.

L. H. and C. W. Houtchens, eds.
Introd., in *Leigh Hunt's Dramatic Criticism, 1808-1834*
(New York: Columbia Univ. Pr., 1949), pp. vii-viii

Had there been no Elia, Leigh Hunt might have won the affection of a century for his personal essays. Had there been no Hazlitt he might have figured as the critic of his day; as an editor he showed immaculate taste and immense strength.

He "discovered" Shelley and Keats; encouraged Byron (until Byron offended him, and he grew distasteful to Byron); gave Lamb his first major opportunities in criticism; won recognition for Morley and befriended Carlyle. He launched new periodicals with the same enthusiasm that he showed in launching new poets—though his choice of poets was, as a rule, shrewder than his editorial policy. But in considering his achievements it is essential to weigh him as a journalist—not as a man of letters, and as journalist he has had few rivals. [1948]

J. E. Morpurgo
Introd., in *The Autobiography of Leigh Hunt*
(London: Cresset Pr., 1949), pp. xiii-xiv

Critics who are looking for critical evaluation of a piece of literature in which appreciation is clearly rooted in sound principles should find no little satisfaction in Hunt's injunction to readers of "The Eve of St. Agnes." Keats's greatest poetry, Hunt has just said, is doubtless to be found in "his last noble fragment, *Hyperion* . . . not faultless—but . . . nearly so." But for "the most delightful and complete specimen of his genius," we must go to "The Eve of St. Agnes.". . . The man who wrote this had ideas about good writing that are sound for any time and any place, ideas, too, that are singularly free not only from Cockneyism but from unhealthy literary traits which characterize the bad or negative half of Romanticism by which the whole is frequently stigmatized. Hunt was no classicist, yet the basic principles he proposed and constantly applied belong as often as not to better non-Romantic as to better Romantic literature. His tendencies to modernity, as distinguished from singularity, of the kind we have learned to look for in good writers of all time, are but an evidence of perceptivity and universality of view: the older writer simply sees earlier what later may be regarded as a fresh discovery of something that always has been and always will be true.

C. D. Thorpe
Introd., in *Leigh Hunt's Literary Criticism,* eds., C. W. and
L. H. Houtchens (New York: Columbia Univ. Pr., 1956),
pp. 72-73

Hunt has been praised for the languid grace of his writings; he has been correlatively, criticized for a certain lack of vigor. And, so far as his later writings are concerned, there is some truth to the criticism. But Hunt has been judged too much by his later writings. *The Examiner* has tended to be forgotten. There is no lack of vigor in *The Examiner,* but power and indignation and scorn linked with controlled skill of sentence and sharp turn of phrase. . . .

The main "weak point" of Hunt's verse is that in breaking with the aristocratic formalism of the heroic couplet he fell into a sometimes slipshod informality. But this weakness has too often been ridiculed without recognition of the important service Hunt rendered to English poetry by his innovations even though he went too far. With *The Story of Rimini,* for all its faults, a new fluid quality entered English poetic narrative, and stylistic foundations were laid not for *Endymion* alone but for *Julian and Maddalo* and even, on a new plane, *Epipsychidion.* This fluidity is apparent also in the short dramatic narratives, in *Mahmoud,* or . . . in "Abou Ben Adhem." Hunt was attempting to create a new poetry for the new middle class.

K. N. Cameron
*Shelley and His Circle,* Vol. II (Cambridge, Mass.:
Harvard Univ. Pr., 1961), pp. 271, 273-74

The Political Examiners were works of passion, weekly intelligence, and education. Hunt began with political emotions and prejudices, the desire to instruct, a stock of ideas, imagination, and a motto from Pope—not, as Hunt at first believed, from Swift: "Party is the madness of many for the gain of a few." Events and the printer's messenger came so fast that ideas were often not in stock; it took imprisonment to give Hunt one hour a day with books of politics, law, and history. Meanwhile, current events and exuberance kept readers thoroughly involved.

The Examiner frequently declared the importance of restoring to political writing a "philosophical spirit." By this spirit he did not mean political theory or a fixed platform. Rather, he meant that he intended to apply traditional Ciceronian morality to political questions. . . .

Often the Political Examiners took the form first suggested by the editorial, the speech, or the debate in Parliament that excited their creation. Rarely did Hunt organize them as expanded syllogisms or other structures of logic. Both the imaginative and the conventional methods of organization, referred to in earlier paragraphs, may be regarded to some extent as escapes from the difficulty Hunt had in arranging ideological argument. On the other hand, mischance frequently prevented him from rounding out a strong discussion of topics on which he had something worth while to say. In consequence, many lopsided Political Examiners contain neat or vital passages. Like most of the familiar essays of the Romantic period, Lamb's and Hazlitt's as well as his own, Hunt's political pieces best achieve organic unity when they center in a single emotion—indignation, the rare joy of a victory, or the anger of disappointment.

Carl R. Woodring
Introd., in *Leigh Hunt: Political and Occasional Essays*,
eds. L. H. Houtchens, Lawrence Huston, and
Carolyn Washburn [Houtchens] (New York:
Columbia Univ. Pr., 1962), pp. 31, 69

# FRANCIS, LORD JEFFREY

1773-1850

Lawyer, editor, literary critic, and essayist, Francis Jeffrey (Lord Jeffrey after 1834) was educated at Glasgow and Edinburgh Universities. He was one of the founders in 1802 of the influential *Edinburgh Review and Critical Journal*, a Whig organ for political reform and literary conservatism. The lifelong friend of Sir Walter Scott despite the latter's defection from the *ER* to the rival Tory *Quarterly Review*, he also became the friend of Thomas Moore after attacking Moore's character and accepting his challenge to a duel, which never came off. At first a severe critic of the Romantic poets, he later reversed his opinion and befriended Wordsworth, who had been his chief victim. After 1821, he became active in British politics as an M.P. and judge. Despite his shortcomings as a critic, he had a talent for recognizing genius in others: William Hazlitt, Thomas Carlyle, and Charles Dickens, for example. His essays on law, politics, biography, history, travel, as well as literature are rarely read, but may be found in *Contributions to the Edinburgh Review* (1844), 4 vols.

D. Nichol Smith, ed., *Literary Criticism* (1910)
H. T. Cockburn, *Life of Lord Jeffrey* (1852)

There may have been something political in the attitude which the *Edinburgh* assumed towards the great new school of poetry which arose between 1798 and 1820. But politics cannot have had everything to do with the matter, and it cannot be an accident that Crabbe is about the only contemporary poet of mark, except Byron, Campbell, and Rogers, whom Jeffrey cordially praises. Above all, the reasons of his depreciation of poets so different as Scott and Wordsworth, and the things of theirs that he specially blames, are fatal. . . . A man who pronounced the *Daffodils* "stuff" puts himself down once for all, irrevocably, without hope of pardon or of atonement, a person insensible to poetry as such. . . . [1904]

George Saintsbury
*A History of Criticism*, Vol. III
(New York: Humanities Pr., 1961), p. 290

. . . Jeffrey (to speak in his own manner) though not a great, is not a bad, writer. His style is eighteenth century to the backbone. He was wont to decry the writers of the age of Anne, and loved the Elizabethans much more . . . ; and herein he belongs to his time; but there is no doubt as to his own pedigree. [1912]

Oliver Elton
*A Survey of English Literature. 1780-1830*, Vol. I
(London: Edward Arnold, 1955), p. 393

Francis Jeffrey was a shrewd, affectionate, kindly, sensible man. He did not bother his head with poetry. When he read a poem, he felt that he had seen this kind of thing before. He had a loyal heart, and he liked best those poems which exactly resembled those he already knew. He is never tired of appealing to common sense and old usage. A departure from old usage he calls "mannerism." Take his quarrel with Wordsworth's characters. It amounts to this, that they are not common. . . . Wordsworth's treatment of these characters and themes is not identical, Jeffrey complains, with their treatment by others. . . . [1926]

Sir Walter Raleigh
*On Writing and Writers* (London: Edward Arnold, 1927), p. 155

Although he had much to say about original genius, he did not use the term in the romantic sense; to Jeffrey it meant not expansiveness, lawlessness, the Titanic pose, but artistic individuality untrammeled by subservient imitation of models—or spontaneity moderately conforming to the generally accepted, or traditional, standards. Romantic ennui, self-contemplation, aestheticism, the new ethics, he ruled out with an angry flourish. He genuinely enjoyed the landscape, first, for its beauty of line and color, and second, for the pleasurable associations that it recalled, but without any sense of mysterious significance. Indeed, he sought to exclude all truth that transcends reason, applying the term "mysticism" undiscriminatingly to everything that he found unintelligible. The pose of infallibility—in anyone other than himself—bored and irritated him. What appeared to him the limitless conceit, the aggravated self-consciousness, the sense of uniqueness, the illusion of originality, and the uncompromising perversity of the Lake School, with attendant vulgarity and affectation, excited him almost to violence. He rejected the idea of progress as "a splendid illusion," yet believed that taste progresses. He excoriated emotional excess in others, yet in his private life—particularly in his later years—was himself given to emotional orgies, and in his reviews often expressed his likes and dislikes in superlatives. . . . But his reviews were characteristically dominated by common sense and reason.

J. R. Derby
*MLQ* (December, 1946), p. 500

Now it is certainly true that, while none of the Reviewers could be described as a "retired and lonely student of nature," the one among them who came nearest to it was Wilson, who wrote of Wordsworth in terms of high praise; and the furthest removed from it was Jeffrey, who was, on the whole, contemptuous of Wordsworth's aims and achievements. . . . From time to time he used Burns or Crabbe as a stick to beat Wordsworth with; let him follow these models if he wished for simplicity and naturalness! . . . (*Edinburgh Review*, January 1809).

This is good criticism, for, although wrong-headed, it is trenchant enough to make us pause and search our minds for the answer. Jeffrey's practical common-sense has suggested a typically rough-and-ready course of action. You want simplicity?—very well! read Burns and Crabbe: they are simple; and they are universally admired; and they will teach you not to overdo it. In fact, of course, both the earthly knowingness and humorous extravagance of Burns's familiar style, and the harsh creaking of Crabbe's grim narratives, would have failed dismally to cope with Wordsworth's subject matter; but Jeffrey was not of a sufficiently literary turn of mind to appreciate such points.

John Wain
Introd., in *Contemporary Reviews of Romantic Poetry*,
ed. John Wain (London: George G. Harrap, 1953), pp. 52-53

Jeffrey's repudiation of the "eccentric" element in Wordsworth's work is of especial significance; for it is linked directly with Jeffrey's general presuppositions about poetry. These emerge fairly clearly from his "Essay on Beauty" [*Edinburgh Review*, XVIII, May, 1811], which was originally written as a review of Alison's *Essay on the Nature and Principles of Taste* (1790), but was republished in the *Encyclopædia Britannica*, and continued to appear in it till 1875. . . . Wordsworth had evidently, in Jeffrey's eyes, been guilty of "bad or false taste.". . .

Jeffrey is probably at his best on Crabbe, who he calls in one place the most original writer who had come before him. All Jeffrey's reviews of Crabbe are excellent. He had very much admired *The Village* when it first appeared (1783), and when Crabbe's 1807 volume was published Jeffrey gave it a warm welcome, holding that it was sufficient warrant for Crabbe to be considered "one of the most original, nervous, and pathetic poets of the present century.". . .

Even when he is unjust Jeffrey is always worth reading. His reviews are clear and lively, and he had a genuine eye for weaknesses and strengths, when they fell within the range of his vision. His mind was also sensitive to many different kinds of features of poems, and took account of them in forming critical judgments. He was, however, an extrovert and a humanist, with apparently little religious sense, and this deficiency must have made it very hard for him to understand Wordsworth.

Theodore Redpath
*Romantic Perspectives*, eds., Patricia Hodgart and Theodore
Redpath (New York: Barnes and Noble, 1964), pp. 28-29, 31

# JOHN KEATS
## 1795-1821

A Londoner by birth, John Keats was sent at eight to a private school in Enfield where he was befriended and tutored in literature and the classics by Charles Cowden Clarke, son of the headmaster. Orphaned at fourteen he became the ward of Richard Abbey, an insensitive merchant. Keats was taken out of school in 1811 and apprenticed to a surgeon. However, he continued to read with Clarke, and at nineteen made his first attempt at writing poetry. In 1816, Keats was introduced by Clarke to Leigh Hunt and his circle. Encouraged by his new friends, he published his first volume of verse in March, 1817. The following month he began a more ambitious project—a long, digressive romance *Endymion*, which, although it had many beauties to commend it, was harshly treated by the critics when it was published in April, 1818. During his next and last two years, despite the death of his brother Tom and his own failing health, he devoted himself entirely to poetry, achieving in record time the remarkable power of expression and skill in composition which characterize the *Poems* of 1820.

Meanwhile, he had fallen deeply in love with Fanny Brawne early in 1819. Within a few months, however, he had become aware that he was consumptive and that his marriage to Fanny would never take place. His condition aggravated by grief and frustration and complicated by a heart attack, Keats agreed to seek health in Italy. In Rome during the winter of 1820-1821, he was attended only by his friend Severn. He died in February, 1821 before his pen had gleaned his teeming brain. His letters and fragments were collected after his death, but all his great poems were published during his brief life in *Poems* (1817); *Endymion* (1818); *Lamia, Isabella, The Eve of St. Agnes and Other Poems* (1820).

H. W. Garrod, ed., *The Poetical Works of John Keats* (2nd ed., 1958) Sidney Colvin, *John Keats: His Life and Poetry, His Friends, Critics, and After-Fame* (1917); W. J. Bate, *John Keats* (1963)

## PERSONAL

Since [Keats'] . . . firm expressions of indifference to critical attack have been before the world, it has been too confidently assumed that Shelley and Byron were totally misled and wide of the mark when they believed that *Blackwood* and the *Quarterly* had killed Keats or even much hurt him. But the truth is that not they, but their consequences, did in their degree help to kill him. . . . What actually happened was that when a year or so later Keats began to realise the harm which the reviews had done and were doing to his material prospects, these consequences in his darker hours preyed on him severely and conspired with the forces of disease and passion to his undoing. . . .

Blow on blow had in truth begun to fall on Keats, as though in fulfilment of the constitutional misgivings to which he was so often secretly a prey. First the departure of his brother George had deprived him of his closest friend, to whom alone he had from boyhood been accustomed to confide those obsessions of his darker hours and in confiding to find relief from them. Next the exertions of his Scottish tour had proved too much for his strength, and laid him open to the attacks of his hereditary enemy, consumption. Coming back, he had found his brother Tom almost at his last gasp in the clutch of that enemy, and in nursing him had both lived in spirit through all his pains and breathed for many weeks a close atmosphere of infection. At the same time the gibes of the reviewers, little as they might touch his inner self, came to teach him the harshness and carelessness of the world's judgments, and the precariousness of his practical hopes from literature. Now were to be added the pangs of love, love requited indeed, but having no near or sure prospect of fruition: and even love disdained might have made him suffer less. The passion took him, as it often takes consumptives, in its fiercest form. . . .

His own account of the matter to Fanny Brawne was that he had written himself her vassal within a week of their first meeting: which took place, we know, some time during the period of watching by Tom's sick-bed.

Sidney Colvin
*John Keats* (London: Macmillan, 1917), pp. 315-16, 332

Keats's senses were, as we know, infinitely more acute than most poeple's; when to his normal abnormality in this respect was added the sting of sexual desire, goaded to a pathological degree by his disease, he could no more master himself than he could fly. No wonder the world was dust in his mouth and contact with his kind a burning nausea. These were all symptoms, a fact which we must never lose sight of in thinking of the last few months of Keats's life. [1925]

Amy Lowell
*John Keats*, Vol. II (Boston: Houghton Mifflin, 1929), pp. 419-20

[His last] . . . days were dark and long. Keats lay in his bed in painful longing for kindly death. Anxious letters came from friends, but he had no wish to see them. He was too far now from life. His sister and his beloved wrote. Their letters remained unopened. Fanny Brawne's letters were only to be given to him if he expressed a wish to hear from her. He never did. . . .

Severn was . . . kept by the bedside. As Keats neared the grave he became calmer. He would talk a good deal, but so peacefully that Severn could not even now entirely suppress a tiny flame of hope. One night when he had been in tranquil converse with his friend, Keats asked that on his gravestone there should be written: "Here lies one whose name was writ in water." [1937]

Dorothy Hewlett
*Adonais* (New York: Bobbs-Merrill, 1938), pp. 382-83

There were many things to draw Keats and Hazlitt together. They were alike in a certain perceptivity: to beauty in nature and poetry, to people, to life itself. Both possessed to a high degree an inimitable quality of mental vivacity. Keats was infinitely the more sensitive, but Hazlitt's delicately attuned intuitions in men and literature struck him with admiration: Hazlitt's depth of taste was one of the three things to rejoice at in all this modern world. Keats found in Hazlitt's theories of poetry and of the relation of poetry to life much that struck in him either immediate or ultimate response. It is perhaps safe to suggest that, altogether, Hazlitt, as much as any other man, including Wordsworth, helped Keats to the aesthetic philosophy he had partially formulated and was still evolving at the time of his death.

C. D. Thorpe
*PMLA* (June, 1947), p. 488

. . . Intense feelings, both on love and on poetry, had been brought to the surface by his meeting with Isabella Jones. . . .

That *Bright Star* in its first form was inspired by her seems inescapable. How much it can also be regarded as addressed *to* her is another matter. It may be simply the poetic expression of the tumultuous feelings on Love, Fame, and Poetry, a theme to which Keats returns frequently in the next few months, and which this chance yet apparently destined meeting had so strangely released. . . . [1954]

Robert Gittings
*The Living Year* (Toronto: William Heineman, 1960), p. 36

All that Mr. Gittings has found out about [Mrs. Isabella Jones] . . . is interesting but for reasons of his own he tries to exaggerate her importance in Keats's life. His major effort to that end is to try to prove that the *Bright Star* sonnet was originally written about her. We have examined in detail Mr. Gittings's process of proof that the *Bright Star* sonnet was originally written before October 31st, 1818 and find it worthless.

J. M. Murry
*Keats* (New York: Noonday Pr., 1955), p. 123

[In 1829, Fanny] . . . thought his character should be rescued from the misrepresentations of his friends as well as of his enemies. For that reason in the end she approved Brown's intentions of telling the full truth of Keats's life. . . .

Unknown to her and to most of Keats's friends, a new generation was already springing up to whom his work spoke with the authentic voice of poetry. In the very month Fanny Brawne wrote her troubled letter to Brown [,] the Cambridge Union maintained in debate against Oxford that Shelley was a greater poet than Byron—sign of an undergraduate cult in which every ardent reader of *Adonais* was also a champion of Keats.

Aileen Ward
*John Keats. The Making of a Poet*
(New York: Viking, 1963), p. 412

## FANNY BRAWNE

Fanny Brawne was beautiful and young and small. She liked Keats; perhaps she liked him chiefly for liking her. She liked to be liked, and to be liked by someone whom their mutual friends were inclined to think a poet of genius was very pleasant to her. She wanted to be admired by everybody. . . .

Keats did not shine in society; the life which Fanny Brawne most enjoyed was not a life that he could share. And there could be no thought of her giving up her delights for his sake. He would have given up everything for

her, it is true. But unfortunately one thing was obvious, and Keats knew
it well: Fanny Brawne did not love him as he loved her. [1925]

J. M. Murry
*Keats and Shakespeare* (Oxford Univ. Pr., 1951), p. 112

Fanny Brawne first met Keats at the Dilkes'. . . .

She thought enough about him to lose her assurance when they met
again: she pretended not to like him. Occasionally she had "a chat and a
tiff" with him, sometimes she forgot her poise and said outrageous things,
once he gave her a reprimand for her language; but she listened to him
with a heartfelt admiration, and his conversation, serious, gentle, punning,
or discursive, she found interesting in the highest degree. . . .

[During his last illness in February, 1820] . . . her mental companionship was a continual solace. Yet the careful optimism in his notes suggested
the uncertainty of his health, and at times the very thought of her threatened to make him fevered. . . .

Fanny treasured his letters, and his comment on his restless mind and
powerless small body sank into her mind, for when in middle age she
told Medwin of Keats's illness, she sent him two lines of *Absalom and
Achitophel*:

> The fiery soul, that working out its way,
> Fretted the pigmy body to decay.

Joanna Richardson
*Fanny Brawne* (New York: Vanguard, 1952), pp. 23-24, 57, 59

Much must depend upon something which still, because of her own reserve, remains uncertain, the character of Fanny Brawne. For many years
after Keats's death, she was thought to have been trivial, shallow, thought-
less; in recent times, particularly since the publication of her letters to
Fanny Keats, opinion has swung the other way. She is now often represented as a true mate for Keats, understanding, stimulating, thoughtful,
patient. In the light of what actually happended, there must be some
unreality in either view. What does fit the facts is that both are partly true,
but of different times in her life. [1954]

Robert Gittings
*The Living Year* (Toronto: William Heineman, 1960), p. 195

Whatever else may be said about Fanny Brawne, two things stand firm.
First, she was the woman, or the girl, to be with whom was life for Keats,
and to be parted from whom was death. Medical science might give a
different report of the matter; but that is how Keats as a man experienced
Fanny Brawne. Secondly, with due allowance for the difference between

imagination and experience, that is how he experienced her as a poet. The brief period during which he was coming nearer and nearer to her, and she to him—I speak of simple physical proximity—was the period in which his poetry touched its greatest splendour. . . .

I am, belatedly but entirely, convinced that Fanny Brawne shared her mother's warmth of heart. She was forthright, quick, witty, graceful, and strange: I almost believe a bit of a tomboy. And she was very young.

J. M. Murry
*Keats* (New York: Noonday Pr., 1955), pp. 24, 33

## *Endymion*

. . . With all its faults, obscurities, and digressions, *Endymion* is the spirit of youth rampant. Its adolescence is irresistible; to read it is to touch the dayspring of life.

First and foremost, let us brush away the dusty cloud of extraneous meanings with which the Victorian critics have well-nigh smothered its brightness. *Endymion* is no allegory. Keat's mind was not of the kind which works in parables. He was as clear as daylight in thought and expression, with his feet planted firmly on the good round earth, and his eyes busy beholding the beauties of a material universe which includes friendship, love, and all sorts of human intercourse as well as clouds, trees, sea flowers, and moonlight. . . .

Keats was right in saying that *Endymion* was as good as he could make it; it was. But as a long poem, with a beginning, a middle and an end, all working together for a total effect, it was a failure. . . . Yet as a heap of fragments of marvellous beauty, it is an abiding solace and an enduring work of art; and as an illustration of poetic psychology, its value is incalculable. [1925]

Amy Lowell
*John Keats*, Vol. I
(Boston: Houghton Mifflin, 1929), pp. 455-56, 460

Keats himself wrote with regard to *Paradise Lost*, "There is always a great charm in the openings of great poems." *Endymion* opens with a line that is a household word and continues in the next twenty-three lines in a vein of rich, quiet beauty which sets the tone of the whole poem. In this opening section there is the germ of all the beauty that is *Endymion*: "sweet dream," and "quiet breathing," "the sun, the moon, Trees old and young," "daffodils with the green world they live in," "clear rills," "the mid forest brake," "fair musk-rose blooms," and "the mighty dead, All lovely tales that we have heard and read."

The story of Endymion has a dew upon it. It has not the actuality of the later work; the beings in it are not strongly coloured, bold and definite but shadowed forth in "dim dreams" and only occasionally emerge clear and bright from the shifting many-hued cloud of youthful imaginings. [1937]

Dorothy Hewlett
*Adonais* (New York: Bobbs-Merrill, 1938), p. 170

Probably no verses in Keats's poetry come nearer—or appear to come nearer—to describing a mystic fusion with absolute Being, than the well known passage in the first book of *Endymion*:

> Wherein lies happiness? In that which becks
> Our ready minds to fellowship divine,
> A fellowship with essence. . . . [I,777,ff.]

Commentators have been attracted repeatedly to this passage, which has usually been accepted as a kind of prospectus of Keats's subject and key to the meaning of his poem. . . .

. . . [The] prevailing interpretations of *Endymion* have linked its theme with the neo-Platonic tradition or some variant thereof, usually finding the key to this theme (and the main authority for allegorization) in the passage on "fellowship with essence." If now this obscure phrase, and the passage which surrounds it, is stripped of all transcendental connotation and is accepted as a young poet's description, albeit not very precise, of imaginative "empathy," the transcendental interpretations evaporate. Detached from the one cardinal passage, so long their mainstay, these interpretations cannot easily be re-attached elsewhere, for scarcely another passage in the entire poem can be shown to have a positive transcendental content.

N. F. Ford
*PMLA* (December, 1947), pp. 1061, 1076

It was the sheer beauty of the story of Endymion, its association with the moon, and its theme of endless youth and love that first appealed to him —both to his worship of nature and to the idealism which still regarded a fair woman as a pure goddess. His head was filled with "lovely tales" from his winter's reading of Elizabethan poetry, which had set him an example for retelling the Greek myths with a wealth of description and adventure and amorous encounter and an admixture of allegorical significance. Some idea of a spiritual development to be undergone by his hero in winning immortal love was also taking shape in his mind, an expression of the "religion of joy" he had found given tangible form in the Elgin Marbles. All the varied experiences of the last year, hope and discovery

and discouragement, all the arguments on poetry and art and religion he
had heard at Hunt's and Haydon's, all his own aspirations toward some
dimly sensed goal, were stirring in his mind and gathering around the
center of Endymion's quest.

Aileen Ward
*John Keats. The Making of a Poet*
(New York: Viking, 1963), pp. 115-16

## Isabella

The poem is uneven in execution, and it would be easy to point out faults
both in the taste and in the workmanship, which are all the more noticeable in comparison with their surroundings. Moreover the studied emphasis
which he lays upon the avarice and pride of the wicked brothers and upon
the limp ecstasy of Lorenzo's passion, serves in reality to weaken that
very effect which he desired to intensify. But these flaws are easily out-
weighed by the vivid poetic feeling and essential truth with which he has
grasped the fundamental emotion of the story. [1905]

Ernest De Selincourt
Introd. in *The Poems. John Keats*
(London: Methuen, 1954), p. liv

The more I read it [*Isabella and Other Poems*, 1819], the more disposed
am I to think this book to be, of all the world's books, upon the whole,
the most marvellous. I do not say the greatest, but the most marvellous.
It was finished before Keats had completed his twenty-fifth year; and there
is nothing in it which is not, in its kind, a masterpiece. *Isabella*, which
Lamb thought the "finest thing" in the volume, was writen when Keats
was not yet twenty-three; he had just turned twenty-three when he made
the first draft of *Hyperion*. Of the longer pieces, the most perfect is, I
think, *The Eve of St. Agnes*—more fully there than elsewhere we feel what
Matthew Arnold means when he speaks of Keats' "perfection of loveliness."
Yet even *St. Agnes Eve* must yield to the Odes. The Odes stand apart,
if for no other reason, yet because in them, for the first time, Keats finds
his own manner. [1926]

H. W. Garrod
*Keats* (Oxford Univ. Pr., 1950), p. 62

[*In Isabella*] . . . Keats made an infelicitous choice of a metrical crucible.
. . . He chose *ottava rima*. The instinct was undoubtedly right which led
him to prefer, for a story so short as that which he projected, a stanzaic
form rather than the loose heroic couplet of *Endymion*; and he was probably also right in feeling . . . he needed a stanzaic form less elaborate than
the Spenserian stanza.

But there are certain difficulties inherent in the metre which Keats was as yet hardly craftsman enough continuously to overcome. . . .

It is a poem of transition. In many ways it is, in its brief compass, oddly like *Endymion*. Both are unequal, the beauties of both, exquisite though they are, are of parts rather than of the whole. In neither are the horses of the sun under full control; but at least in *Isabella* there are fewer of those dizzying plunges almost to destruction, fewer of those erratic wheelings and divagations that make the reader of *Endymion* sometimes feel that the poet is not only incapable of holding his team on their course, but almost care-less of what the course should be. In *Isabella* the course is known, the con-trol is being learned, and from now onwards Apollo can hand the reins to Phaethon with no apprehension of disaster.

M. R. Ridley
*Keats' Craftsmanship*
(Oxford: Clarendon Pr., 1933), pp. 18, 19, 56

In *Isabella,* which was written in 1818, the occasional mawkish sentimen-tality of diction betrays the continued and even heightened influence of Hunt; yet in the main the poem stylistically reveals this effort towards emancipation. . . .

*Isabella* . . . illustrates the nature of Keats's stylistic advance between the composition of *Endymion* and that of *Hyperion*. It reveals a careful employment however diverse and disunited their character of prosodic and rhetorical devices of discipline and restraint. . . . After the completion of *Endymion* . . . he attempted to rid his verse of [its] . . . negligent slackness. His diction became less polysyllabic, more native in origin, a bit stronger in consonantal and phonetic body; he cut the adverb and adjective and drew more upon the verb; he employed patterns of pause and stress more closely conventional; he made use, however crudely, of devices of repetition and parallelism upon which his former mentor, Hunt, had frowned, but which Keats himself believed would add emphasis and structural tightness to his lines; and he attempted, finally, to write his verse-narrative in a close-ly-knit stanza rather than in the loose and flowing couplet of Browne and of Hunt. [1945]

W. J. Bate
*The Stylistic Development of Keats*
(New York: Humanities Pr., 1958), pp. 30, 41-42

Much of Keats's immature sentimentality lingers on in the opening picture of the young lovers; yet as the poem moves ahead, it begins to show a striking new sense of the dramatic at work. Already Keats was learning to submerge himself in the character and feelings of his hero and heroine and to tell his story in flashes of visualized action—the jealous brothers biting their lips in silence, the murderers dipping their swords in the stream,

Isabella tossing back her hair as she digs in Lorenzo's grave. Boccaccio set him a good example of concise, straightforward narrative; but even more significant are Keats's additions, where a new note begins to sound in his poetry. In Boccaccio's tale the brothers murder Lorenzo merely because of his illicit passion for their sister; Keats added an economic motive with the brothers' greedy ambition to marry *Isabella* to a wealthy noble.

Aileen Ward
*John Keats. The Making of a Poet*
(New York: Viking Pr., 1963), p. 173

## Hyperion; The Fall of Hyperion

I realize that to students of Keats I make a strange statement in speaking of a version of *Hyperion* begun and abandoned, another begun and left off, and the first taken up again. I am quite aware that recent criticism believes the published *Hyperion* to have been the poem which Keats started during Tom's illness [Winter, 1818]; and the (so-called) *Fall* or *Vision* of *Hyperion* to be a recast. The authority for this opinion is Brown, who has stated that in the evenings during November and December, 1819, Keats was "remodelling the fragment of 'Hyperion' into the form of a 'Vision.'" I think it very likely that Keats was working on the *Vision* during these months, more likely still that he told Brown he was going to do so, and tried only to be once more baffled; but I most surely believe that he had begun it much earlier, probably before the other. [1925]

Amy Lowell
*John Keats*, vol. II
(Boston: Houghton Mifflin, 1929), pp. 339-40

Miss Lowell . . . makes the extraordinary statement that the second *Hyperion* was written before the first. I call the statement extraordinary because it is Miss Lowell herself who possesses and first published the letter to Woodhouse on 22nd September 1819, which, I had thought, finally settled the problem of the two Hyperions. Miss Lowell speaks of her "startling discovery": but it is not easy to see wherein the discovery consists. That the second *Hyperion* was written before the first is scarcely a discovery; it is a theory, and a demonstrably mistaken one. In arguing a matter so vital, however, one cannot appeal to internal evidence, though it is quite conclusive to me. [1925]

J. M. Murry
*Keats and Shakespeare* (Oxford Univ. Pr., 1951), p. 242

On September 21 [1818, Keats] . . . writes to Dilke. . . . The next day, as it seems, he writes to Reynolds: "This morning, poetry has conquered. I have relapsed into those abstractions which are my only life.". . .

.

The new-conquering poetry, . . . the "abstractions which are my only life," announce the beginnings of *Hyperion*. . . . Keats speaks of himself to Woodhouse as "cogitating on the characters of Ops and Saturn." I do not think it worth while to stay to refute the view of Miss Lowell that this Hyperion is *Hyperion: A Vision*. I will content myself with noticing that *Hyperion: A Vision* contains no word of Ops—Ops belongs to the greater [the first] *Hyperion*. [1926]

H. W. Garrod
*Keats* (Oxford Univ. Pr., 1950), p. 49

. . . In Keats's own works his theory of what great poetry should be is best exemplified in his *Hyperion* and *The Fall of Hyperion*. The scene is better portrayed in *Hyperion*; the poetic theory is the more apparent in the Revision. But for the present purpose it is unnecessary to differentiate between the two poems. The Hyperion story is a story of evolutionary progress. . . . But it is also something more: it is tragedy, supreme, irrevocable tragedy— the tragedy of downfall and defeat. Ancient Saturn and all his compeers of the old order, save Hyperion, have been ruthlessly deposed and cast out of heaven. Beings of pristine splendor, born to power and uncontested rule, now suddenly overthrown and supplanted by a younger more brilliant dynasty before whose might resistance is folly, their sufferings are tremendous. Hyperion alone, in proud, regal magnificence, still reigns on; but knowing full well that he, too, is to fall, he lives in weak, ungodlike dread. All this is laid bare to the soul-penetrating vision of the poet, who, having qualified himself through knowledge of the misery of the world, has been permitted to ascend the high altar of poetic truth, where, under the guidance of his monitress Moneta, in one supreme imaginative leap, he finds himself in a position from which he may see and understand everything.

C. D. Thorpe
*The Mind of John Keats* (Oxford Univ. Pr., 1926), p. 202

A determination of dates is here of more importance than questions of chronology often are, since if the bulk of the new *Hyperion* was completed before the end of September [1819] it belongs to the end of Keats' great creative period which culminated with *To Autumn,* and we are automatically saved from a prejudice which has, I think, vitiated a good deal of criticism of *The Fall of Hyperion*. If we attribute it to the winter of 1819, then we expect to find in it evidence of flagging powers, the work of a man physically debilitated by disease, and spiritually exhausted by hopeless passion; and we naturally find what we expect to find. But if it is to be dated earlier, then we have to start with no such presupposition, and with clearer eyes; and we may find ourselves . . . being drawn towards a different critical conclusion. . . .

For all its greatness it was no more than an experiment; in a sense it was even a failure; Keats' reach had exceeded his grasp and he knew it. But he learnt more from the failure than any facile success could have taught him; he learnt power and control, and just because so much of *Hyperion* was "mere" craftsmanship, work that had to be done in "an artist's humour," and partly against the grain, he learnt more about the use of his tools than in any other way he could have acquired.

M. R. Ridley
*Keats' Craftsmanship*
(Oxford: Clarendon Pr., 1933), pp. 59, 95

*Hyperion* represents the climax of Keats's progressive efforts to re-create and to reanimate the life of Ancient Greece, the Greece of the gods, the demi-gods, and the heroes. . . .

*Hyperion* represents the extreme points in Keats's reaction against the prettiness, the triviality, the colloquial idiom, and the sentimentality—in brief, the cockney qualities—of the poetry which he wrote under the influence of Leigh Hunt in 1815 and 1816. . . .

*Hyperion* is a conscious and direct imitation of Milton's *Paradise Lost,* which is a classical epic in genre and which has many classical and un-English characteristics in diction, imagery, figures of speech, and sentence structure. Keats had too much creative imagination, however, to make a literal and mechanical imitation. He employed the devices of Milton's style as creatively as Virgil had employed those of Homer's style. . . .

C. L. Finney
*The Evolution of Keats's Poetry,* Vol. II
(Cambridge, Mass.: Harvard Univ. Pr., 1936), pp. 494, 506

The entire stylistic tendency throughout *Hyperion* is at once in the direction of intensity and restraint. Such rhetorical and prosodic devices as Keats had already drawn upon in *Isabella,* in order to gain the discipline and structural coherence so completely lacking in his earlier verse, were again employed in *Hyperion*. But the hand which manipulated them was surer and more skillful in its touch. Much, in addition, was gained from Milton; but often in those instances where Milton had notoriously deserted disciplinary measures which had been common in English verse, Keats carefully avoided his methods and abided by stricter orthodoxy than almost any of his own contemporaries. . . . Keats simultaneously began to employ whatever stylistic means would burden even further the connotative intensity and richness of imagery with which his lines are fraught. [1945]

W. J. Bate
*The Stylistic Development of Keats*
(New York: Humanities Pr., 1958), p. 91

The second *Hyperion* is more allegorical than the first, and yet it is obviously more courageous and more direct in the way it faces life. What Keats had to say could not have been more directly expressed than in the vision of Moneta. It is even arguable that the expression is too direct for the highest poetry. Spenser constructed a complicated system of belief, which he converted into allegory; Keats, on the other hand, expressed his own experience as directly as possible. *The Fall of Hyperion* is an attempt to express an intuition about the ultimate nature of reality in the only way possible, the parabolic.

The contrast between the poet and the dreamer, which is the real theme of the poem, is a final expression of a conflict which had agitated Keats as early as *Sleep and Poetry*. "The strife and agonies of human hearts," of which he speaks in that poem, may indeed refer to his ambition to write tragedies; but this ambition was closely connected with his desire to write poetry which would not be merely the opium of the middle classes or the expression of personal emotions. [1958]

Kenneth Muir
in *John Keats. A Reassessment,* ed. Kenneth Muir
(Liverpool, Eng.: Liverpool Univ. Pr., 1959), pp. 113-14

It has frequently been assumed that Keats, in revising the earlier version of *Hyperion* into *The Fall of Hyperion: A Dream,* was liberating himself from the influence of Milton and, especially, of *Paradise Lost.* In the new induction to *The Fall* he abandoned the epic structure of the first *Hyperion* for a form that is both more personal and allegoric—that of a vision or dream. The change is sweeping, involving not only structure but style, and apparently reflects the poet's dissatisfaction with the epic nature of the earlier version. . . . Both in its method and effects, *The Fall* is clearly closer to allegory than to epic. Such changes have led many to conclude that in *The Fall* Keats to a large degree rejected Milton for a new master, Dante, whom he had been studying both in Cary's translation and, quite probably, in the original Italian. Throughout the *Purgatorio* Dante is required to make repeated ascents by means of steps; in her role as guide and admonisher, Moneta resembles Virgil and, later, Beatrice; and in the thirty-first canto of the *Purgatorio,* Beatrice, like Moneta, parts her veils. These and other resemblances were sufficient to persuade Lowes that "The structural background of the 'Vision,' to state it summarily, is the 'Purgatorio,' " a judgment that has stood unchallenged.

Few critics would disagree with Kenneth Muir that *The Fall of Hyperion* is "very much a purgatorial poem" or that the new conception embodied in its induction owes an important debt to Dante's quest for higher vision. Yet it would be wrong to assume that Keats had thereby rejected Milton.

. . . In *The Fall* Keats divested himself of many of the rhetorical peculiarities of Milton's style and of the unimaginative reliance on the structure and
method of Milton's epic. But on a far more profound level, the fabric of
his vision was the result of a highly selective and original interweaving of
Miltonic themes—possible only through a comprehensive reinterpretation
of *Paradise Lost* in the light of his own thinking and experience.

S. M. Sperry, Jr.
*PMLA* (March, 1962), pp. 77-78

Though Keats borrowed several details from the *Divine Comedy,* the first
canto of *The Fall of Hyperion* is not an imitation of, but an answer to,
Dante. The reading of Dante was a challenge to Keats which he accepted.
I think that no one has as yet fully accounted for the strangeness of Keats's
introductory lines:

> Fanatics have their dreams, wherewith they weave
> A paradise for a sect.

These lines become wholly intelligible only if we realize that Keats here
was replying to Dante. He had read Dante's *Inferno* of eternal torments,
he had been to the earthly paradise where the pageant of the Church appeared under the trees, and he had even cast a glance into Dante's heaven,
wherefrom the greater part of mankind was forever excluded. And when
he sat down to rewrite *Hyperion,* he felt he had to match Dante's vision
with a vision of his own. . . .

Even though you clothed your dream in words that were "shadows of
melodious utterance"—Bridges thought the phrase peculiarly Dantesque—
you are still a fanatic and your paradise is a dream, Keats seems to say to
Dante in his introductory lines. I too have dreams, and no one can forbid
me to tell them. . . .

And the dream Keats begins to relate is also an answer. He will do what
Dante does in the last cantos of *Purgatorio* and the first canto of the
*Paradiso,* he will speak about transhumanization. Not for a sect, however,
but for all humanity. . . .

Moneta and Beatrice are related not only in externals, but in their very
function: they show to Keats and to Dante the way of salvation. . . . The
overcoming of the self by suffering is part of *Hyperion* as it is part of the
*Comedy.* And in the sublimation of instincts into the higher powers of art
and music he would perhaps have pointed the way toward the paradise
for all mankind and not for a "sect" only.

John Saly
*K-SJ* (Winter, 1965), pp. 76-78

*Eve of St. Agnes*

*The Eve of St. Agnes* expresses, as perfectly as Keats could express it, the romance and the delight of a love satisfying and victorious. But side by side with it he gave the picture of a love which is at once a fascination and a doom, delineated in the same mediaeval atmosphere, with the same passionate conviction, and with even deeper significance in its reflection upon actual life. Whilst he was still at work on the *Eve of St. Agnes* the companion picture was in his mind. For he tells how Porphyro took Madeline's lute

> Tumultuous, and, in chords that tenderest be,
> He play'd an ancient ditty, long since mute,
> In Provence call'd "La belle dame sans mercy." [1905]

> Ernest De Selincourt
> Introd. in *The Poems. John Keats*
> (London: Methuen, 1965), p. lvii

. . . Fresh from treading in his *Hyperion* attempt, in the path of Milton. Keats in *The Eve of St. Agnes* went back, so far as his manner is derivative at all, to the example of his first master, Spenser. He shows as perfect a command of the Spenserian stanza with its "sweet-slipping movement," as Spenser himself, and as subtle a sense as his of the leisurely meditative pace imposed upon the metre by the lingering Alexandrine at the close. . . .

The poetry throbs in every line with the life of imagination and beauty. . . .

When Madeline unclasps her jewels, a weaker poet would have dwelt on their lustre or other visible qualities: Keats puts those aside, and speaks straight to our spirits in an epithet breathing with the very life of the wearer —"Her warmed jewels."

> Sidney Colvin
> *John Keats*
> (London: Macmillan, 1917), pp. 339, 401

*The Eve of St. Agnes* has its origins in the same "exquisite sense of the luxurious" as that from which *Isabella* was born. It takes us back to the Keats whom we know; the true Keats, as I think; the effective poet; yet a poet effective, it may be, only in a certain ineffectiveness. Both poems represent, as it were, a kind of relapse into sense and luxury: the relapse of a temperament laboriously aspiring towards harder and sharper effects, the realities of thinking and suffering, aspiring towards those unsustainable heights, but for ever falling back upon "the shadows of the mind," "the abstractions which are my only life." [1926]

> H. W. Garrod
> *Keats*
> (Oxford Univ. Pr., 1950), pp. 51-52

... Keats has at last entered triumphantly into his kingdom. There is none of the fumbling and the sense of insecurity which marred the beauties of *Isabella*. The control of the metre is complete; the narrative moves straight forward with neither halt nor hurry; the pictures have strength and clarity of line; and the outstanding beauties, of which there are many, are not irrelevant adornments but parts of a harmonious whole. Whatever else *The Eve of St. Agnes* may be, it is the deliberate work of a trained craftsman; and as such it richly repays examination.

M. R. Ridley
*Keats' Craftsmanship* (Oxford: Clarendon Pr., 1933), pp. 96-97

*The Eve of St. Agnes* was the first poem in which Keats was inspired by his love for Fanny Brawne. . . .

*The Eve of St. Agnes* is the only complete and perfect long poem which Keats composed in the course of his life. . . . [It] seems to us, when we first begin to consider it, to be a spontaneous expression of genius, springing like Pallas Athena full grown from the forehead of the poet. In the case of the other long poems, such as *Endymion* and *Hyperion,* we can trace the slow process of conception and growth. In the minute records of Keats's life, however, there is no mention of *The Eve of St. Agnes* before it was composed. The intuition and the composition of the romance were sudden, spontaneous, and rapid. The matter of it, however, had germinated for years in the fallow soil of the poet's mind.

C. L. Finney
*The Evolution of Keat's Poetry*, vol. II
(Cambridge, Mass.: Harvard Univ. Pr., 1936), 538, 540-41

[In the *Eve of St. Agnes,*] . . . Keats exemplifies even further than in *Hyperion* a striving for a heightened intensity of expression—an intensity at once impassioned and weightily rich in sound and image and, at the same time, strengthened and constrained by disciplinary bonds even firmer and stricter than formerly. [1945]

W. J. Bate
*The Stylistic Development of Keats*
(New York: Humanities Pr., 1958), p. 117

*The Eve of St. Agnes* is Keats's "Epithalamion" in narrative form, celebrating the joys of a first love fulfilled in a runaway marriage. . . . [It] . . . is Keats's first great achievement in what he later called "the knowledge of contrast, feeling for light and shade" which he thought essential to a poem: the stillness of Madeline's room, "silken, hush'd, and chaste," balanced against the noisy celebrations in the hall below; the warmth of her bed contrasted with the chilly night; the pallid moon outside the triple-arched window casting soft amethyst and rose on Madeline's breast as she knelt in prayer. . . . . This is a "song made in lieu of many ornaments" in honour of his love.

Aileen Ward
*John Keats. The Making of a Poet*
(New York: Viking, 1963), pp. 244-46

## *Ode on a Grecian Urn*

The epigram [ending *The Grecian Urn*] indeed will not bear intellectual examination. A proposition of Euclid is true but it is not beautiful; nor, if it were, could the mere knowledge of what is ideally beautiful satisfy the wants of the soul; but as an example of the power of Poetry at once to illustrate and to supplement the functions of a sister Art, the Ode itself is a marvellous performance.

W. J. Courthope
*A History of English Poetry*, vol. VI
(New York and London: Macmillan, 1910), pp. 353-54

From the drowsed intoxication of the senses, he rises to a glorious clear-eyed apprehension of the spiritual eternity which art, with its "unheard melodies," affords. The three consummate central stanzas have themselves the impassioned serenity of great sculpture. Only less noble are the daring and splendid imagery of the opening and the immortal paradox of the close.

C. H. Herford
*CHEL*, eds. A. W. Ward and A. R. Waller, vol. XII
(Cambridge University Pr., 1914), p. 90

For myself, let me say frankly that I have never so much admired as I should, that is to say, as other persons do, those famous lines from the *Ode on a Grecian Urn* in which Keats, more formally, perhaps indeed more flatly, than there was need, instructs us that

Beauty is truth, truth beauty,

and that we neither have, nor can want, any other knowledge. Whether this is to have a theory of truth, and not rather neither to have one nor to want one, I am not sure. [1926]

H. W. Garrod
*Keats*
(Oxford Univ. Pr., 1950), p. 33

Beauty is truth, truth beauty.

. . . This line strikes me as a serious blemish on a beautiful poem; and the reason must be either that I fail to understand it, or that it is a statement, which is untrue. And I suppose that Keats meant something by it, however remote his truth and his beauty may have been from these words in ordinary use. And I am sure that he would have repudiated any explanation of the line which called it a pseudo-statement. On the other hand the line I have often quoted of Shakespeare,

*Ripeness is all . . .*

strikes very differently on my ear. The statement of Keats seems to me meaningless: or perhaps, the fact that it is grammatically meaningless conceals another meaning from me. The statement of Shakespeare seems to me to have profound emotional meaning, with, at least, no literal fallacy. [1929]

T. S. Eliot<br>
Selected Essays: 1917-1932<br>
(New York: Harcourt, Brace, 1932, repr. 1950), p. 231

As in the *Ode to a Nightingale* Keats contrasted the mortal world of pain, decay, and death with the immortal world of beauty and joy in which the nightingale sang, so in the *Ode on a Grecian Urn* he contrasted mortal life with the immortal life of art. The persons carved on the urn have advantages as well as limitations. They are held immovable and immortal in a moment of ecstatic endeavor. They cannot achieve the objects for which they strive, but they will not suffer the decay and death of mortal life.

C. L. Finney<br>
The Evolution of Keats's Poetry, Vol. II<br>
(Cambridge, Mass.: Harvard Univ. Pr., 1936), p. 638

The truth that Keats embraces is not that of his large humanitarian aspirations, nor the smaller measure of truth granted to the philosophic intellect, it is the truth, that is, the reality, apprehended through the senses. . . . Neither beauty nor truth is for Keats a real abstraction, a Platonic Idea; beauty is something beautiful, the "material sublime." When he tries to generalize from a melancholy ecstasy, he remains at odds with himself. The urn is a joy for ever, but the marble figures are cold.

Douglas Bush<br>
Mythology and the Romantic Tradition in English Poetry<br>
(Cambridge, Mass.: Harvard Univ. Pr., 1937), pp. 107-8

The silence of the urn is stressed—it is a "bride of quietness"; it is a "foster-child of silence," but the urn is a "historian" too. Historians tell the truth, or are at least expected to tell the truth. . . .

The "truth" which the sylvan historian gives is the only kind of truth which we are likely to get on this earth, and, furthermore, it is the only kind that we *have* to have. . . . The sylvan historian does better than that:

it takes a few details and so orders them that we have not only beauty but insight into essential truth. Its "history," in short, is a history without footnotes. It has the validity of myth—not myth as a pretty but irrelevant make-belief, an idle fancy, but myth as a valid perception into reality. . . .

"Beauty is truth, truth beauty" has precisely the same status, and the same justification as Shakespeare's "Ripeness is all." It is a speech "in character" and supported by a dramatic context. [1943]

Cleanth Brooks<br>
The Well-Wrought Urn<br>
(New York: Reynal and Hitchcock, 1947), pp. 142-43, 150-51

The transcendent act is concretized, or "materialized," in the vision of the "immortal" scene, the reference in Stanza IV to the original scene of the Urn, the "heavenly" scene of a dead, or immortal, Greece. . . .

This transcendent scene is the level at which the earthly laws of contradiction no longer prevail. Hence, in the terms of this scene, he can proclaim the unity of truth and beauty (of science and art), a proclamation which he needs to make precisely because here was the basic split responsible for the romantic agitation (in both poetic and philosophic idealism). That is, it was gratifying to have the oracle proclaim the unity of poetry and science because the values of technology and business were causing them to be at odds. And from the perspective of a "higher level" (the perspective of a dead or immortal scene transcending the world of temporal contradictions) the split could be proclaimed once more a unity. [1943]

Kenneth Burke<br>
A Grammar of Motives<br>
(Englewood Cliffs, N. J.: Prentice-Hall, 1945), p. 462

Mr. Burke's elucidation of the Truth-Beauty proposition in the last stanza is the most convincing dialectically that I have seen; but Keats did not write Mr. Burke's elucidation; and I feel that the entire last stanza, except the phrase "Cold Pastoral" (which probably ought to be somewhere else in the poem) is an illicit commentary added by the poet to a "meaning" which was symbolically complete at the end of the preceding stanza, number four. Or perhaps it may be said that Keats did to some extent write Mr. Burke's elucidation; that is why I feel that the final stanza (though magnificently written) is redundant and out of form. [1945]

Allen Tate<br>
On the Limits of Poetry<br>
(New York: Swallow Pr. and William Morrow, 1948), pp. 178-79

. . . I found myself blaming Mr. Cleanth Brooks for not making the poem as emotional as it ought to be. He treats ["Ode on a Grecian Urn"] . . . as an entirely coherent philosophical position expressed by irony and paradox. . . . But it seems to me to make rather bad philosophy, and rather a dull poem, which the thing need not be . . . .

One might feel, as Robert Bridges [?] clearly did, that the last lines with their brash attempt to end with a smart bit of philosophy have not got enough knowledge behind them, and are flashy. . . . I do not feel this myself, only that the effort of seeing the thing as Keats did is too great to be undertaken with pleasure. [1947]

William Empson
*The Structure of Complex Words*
(Norfolk, Conn.: New Directions, 1951), pp. 368, 374

. . . It is surely clear that in these words ["Beauty is truth," etc.] it is not Keats but the Urn who speaks. . . .

The meaning of this message is beyond dispute. Mr. Garrod rightly paraphrases it, "there is nothing real but the beautiful and nothing beautiful but the real." Keats uses "truth," as others do, to mean "reality." He then adds, through the Urn, that this is the only knowledge that we possess and that we need no other. It is the Urn that speaks, and it speaks for a unique kind of experience, of which it states the central essence. . . .

Truth is another name for ultimate reality, and is discovered not by the reasoning mind but by the imagination. . . . Keats calls this reality "beauty" because of its overpowering and all-absorbing effect on him. In fact, he substitutes the discovery of beauty through the imagination for the discovery of facts through the reason, and asserts that it is a more satisfactory and more certain way of piercing to the heart of things, since inspired insight sees more than abstract ratiocination ever can. [1949]

C. M. Bowra
*The Romantic Imagination*
(Oxford Univ. Pr., 1950), pp. 146-47

The *Ode on a Grecian Urn* is Keats's consummate expression of emphatic feeling and thought. In it empathy arises from prolonged and passionate contemplation of a beautiful object and is refined into aesthetic emotion, which in turn is expanded and uplifted into more comprehensive perceptions culminating in the Platonic merging of Beauty and Truth at the end of the poem. [1949]

R. H. Fogle
*The Imagery of Keats and Shelley*
(Hamden, Conn.: Archon Books, 1962), p. 172

Even if we seem to be able to carry away some general proposition such as Keats' "Beauty is Truth, Truth Beauty," we are left to make what we can of these conversible propositions, unless we see them as the conclusion of a poem which has to do with illustrating the permanence of art and the impermanence of human emotions and natural beauty. The reduction of a work of art to a doctrinal statement—or, even worse, the isolation of passages—is disastrous to understanding the uniqueness of a work: it disintegrates its structure and imposes alien criteria of value. [1949]

René Wellek and Austin Warren
*Theory of Literature* (New York: Harcourt, Brace, 1956), p. 99

The much-debated "Beauty is truth, truth beauty" must be interpreted in this context. The Urn is a "Cold Pastoral"; that is to say, like pastoral poetry (the only sense the noun *pastoral* had in the nineteenth century), it is allegorical. Behind the particular unions of opposites depicted on the Urn (motion and immobility, growth and permanence, time and timelessness, etc.) a general synthetic principle is implied. This is the necessity for uniting Romanticism ("beauty") and realism ("truth"), the subconscious with the conscious mind, the feeling with the concept, poetry and philosophy. It is Keats's protest against the Romantic "split man." And the point of particular interest is Keats's *social* motive in propounding this generalization. The Urn is "a friend to man." The lesson that it teaches will be consolatory to the next generation as well as to Keats's.

F. W. Bateson
*English Poetry. A Critical Introduction*
(New York: Longmans, Green, 1950), p. 219

The intention of the poem . . . must be to hold up art as the source of the highest form of wisdom. It is in the more embracing sense . . . that the urn has become in the final stanza a silent form which, although silent, paradoxically speaks to man. . . .

It is the poet . . . who speaks the words, "that is all/Ye know on earth, and all ye need to know," and he is addressing himself to man, the reader. . . .

The great end of poetry, Keats wrote, is "that it should be friend/To soothe the cares, and lift the thoughts of man," for art (unlike man, who cannot return to tell us of his postmortal existence) allows a glimpse into that region which shows the full meaning of those experiences which now produce only mortal suffering, divulges the end for which they are destined, and so eases the burden of the mystery. And art eases this burden of holding out to man the promise that somewhere—at heaven's bourne, where the woes of this world will be resolved—songs are forever new, love is forever young, human passion is "human passion far above," beauty is truth; that, although beauty is not truth in this world, what the imagination seizes as beauty must be truth—whether it existed before or not.

E. R. Wasserman
*The Finer Tone*
(Baltimore: Johns Hopkins Pr., 1953), pp. 49, 59, 61

Whether the final words of the poem are supposed to be spoken by the Urn or whether they are intended to be the poet's own comment does not greatly affect the meaning. The words—

> That is all
> Ye know on earth, and all ye need to know—

are dramatically appropriate. Momentarily, and in response to the beauty of the Urn, the poet can accept the proposition—a natural development of his own earlier aphorisms—that beauty is an image of truth, and that therefore, if we see life steadily and see it whole, the disagreeables will evaporate as they do in a great work of art. Keats seems to protect himself from the criticism of common-sense by leaving it doubtful whether his own views are to be identified with those of the Urn. Art claims that life could be as meaningful as art. When we are experiencing a work of art we are prepared to give our assent, though at other times we may be sceptical. [1958]

Kenneth Muir
in *John Keats. A Reassessment,* ed. Kenneth Muir
(Liverpool, Eng.: Liverpool Univ. Pr., 1959), p. 70

## Ode to Autumn

The vein in which he composed [*To Autumn*] is one of simple objectivity, very different from the passionate and complex phases of introspective thought and feeling which inspired the spring odes. The result is the most Greek thing, except the fragment *To Maia,* which Keats ever wrote. . . .

Sidney Colvin
*John Keats* (London: Macmillan, 1917), p. 422

. . . [He] composed the *Ode to Autumn*—pure Keats, uncontaminated and calm, if ever a poem was. . . . It need not be pointed out with the finger how deeply Shakespearean that perfect poem is—Shakespearean in its rich and opulent serenity of mood. Shakespearean in its lovely and large periodic movement, like the drawing of a deep, full breath. This is not that majestic marshalling of design which marks the constructed period of Milton; this is natural and spontaneous poetic power. [1925]

J. M. Murry
*Keats and Shakespeare* (Oxford Univ. Pr., 1951), pp. 188-89

The *Ode to Autumn* represents the final stage in Keats's development of the form of the ode. . . .

[It] . . . is the most purely sensuous and imaginative of Keats's odes. Unlike his earlier odes, such as the *Ode to a Nightingale*, it is not an interpretation of a problem of his experience. It is, as he wrote Reynolds, an expression of the sensation, or sensuous impression, which he received from the warm, golden stubble fields during his walk into the country around Winchester on Sunday, September 19 [1819]. . . .

The sensations of autumnal beauty, which inspired him to compose the *Ode to Autumn* . . . caused him to react suddenly from the artificial style of Milton to the natural style of Chatterton.

C. L. Finney
*The Evolution of Keats's Poetry*, Vol. II
(Cambridge, Mass.: Harvard Univ. Pr., 1936), pp. 707, 709

The last great poem . . . which Keats was to write after concluding his revision of *Hyperion* constituted a complete return in both emotional and prosodic conception to the great odes of the preceding May [1819]. The diction, like that of the other odes, is almost monosyllabic, strong in consonantal body, and English in origin. . . .

And thus Keats returned—if to deliver only the briefest yet most serene and flawless of swan-songs—to that instinctive delight in the things of the earth. . . . For poetry, to Keats, despite the almost chaotic transition of mind which he had undergone since concluding the odes, still consisted above all else in the restrained but highly impassioned exercise of the five senses. [1945]

W. J. Bate
*The Stylistic Development of Keats*
(New York: Humanities Pr., 1958), pp. 182, 184

In the *Ode to Autumn* he again employs the seasons through which to convey what is in his mind; and he does so, as everyone has agreed, with flawless beauty. The *Nightingale* looks beyond the passage of time to an eternal summer; the *Urn* to a world which never bids the spring adieu. Time is transcended in them; their origin is the desire to deny time. But *Autumn* is saturated with the sense of acquiescence in the passing. The *Nightingale* and the *Urn* look to eternal joy; *Autumn* rests in a poignant fusion of joy and sorrow. [1948]

D. G. James
*The Romantic Comedy* (Oxford Univ. Pr., 1963), p. 114

. . . The whole movement and vocabulary of the Odes suggest a rich, slow brooding over beauty and joy, with a full realization both of beauty and the pain that its disappearance will bring, but with an enjoyment of such intensity and depth that it makes the moment eternal, in quality if not in duration.

The *Ode to Autumn* is pre-eminently the record of such an experience. It is in a sense a return to the mood of the *Ode on Indolence*—making the moment sufficient to itself. It is the most perfect in form and detail of the Odes, and also the most difficult to penetrate below the surface, for it is apparently the most purely objective and descriptive. The emotion has become completely fused with the object, and expresses itself completely through it. There are no questions and no conflict in the poem: the season of ripeness and fulfilment is seen as though it is quite final. Autumn as a poetical symbol is commonly the prelude to winter. Keats sees it as a still pause in time, when everything has reached fruition and ripeness is all. [ca. 1951]

Graham Hough
*The Romantic Poets* (New York: W. W. Norton, 1964), p. 178

I would argue . . . that Herford was wrong in saying that *To Autumn*, unlike the *Nightingale* and the *Grecian Urn*, does not include the "sense that beauty, though not without some glorious compensation, perishes." On the contrary, central to the poem is the sense that a new good is purchased only at the price of the loss of a former good. Far from being an objective, self-sufficient evocation of the "beauty of the present moment" it is, as Mr. J. M. Murry once suggested, a projection in image and symbol of the calm Shakespearian vision: "Man must abide his going hence, even as his coming hither. Ripeness is all." It is in *To Autumn* rather than in the sonnet *On Sitting Down to Read King Lear Once Again* that Keats realizes "The bitter Sweet of this Shakespearian fruit."

Arnold Davenport
*John Keats. A Reassessment*, ed. Kenneth Muir
(Liverpool, Eng.: Liverpool Univ. Pr., 1959), p. 101

## LETTERS

[If] . . . to be true, interesting, attractive, witty, humorous, idealistic, realistic, speculative, discursive, and gossipy in turns is the note of a good letter-writer, then indeed Keats was one. If to tell one's friends just what they want to know about one's doings and thoughts, and about the doings and thoughts of mutual friends, is to be a good letter-writer—that is where Keats, of all men of genius in the last century, excelled. If consideration for the feelings of others in the manner and degree of communicating misfortunes or disagreeables be an epistolary virtue, Keats was largely dowered with that virtue. If to present a true picture of the essential qualities of one's personality is a valuable art, Keats manifested that art in a high form in his letters. And if, when wrung by disease and misery, it is better to leave some record for a pitying posterity than to carry a ghastly secret into the oblivion of the grave, then in this also Keats exceeded others who have made the world richer with their letters. Lastly, the man is not dissociated from the poet in them. Not only is the poetic mode of thought frequently the ruling mode in the prose fabric of these letters; but they are set with gems of verse of all waters, dashed in just as they were composed, a part of the man's life enacting and reflected throughout, and ranging in quality from the merest doggerel calculated to fatten by laughter ("Laugh and grow fat!") to the very masterpieces of poetic craft by which Keats has most blessed his race. [1895]

Harry Buxton-Forman
Introd. in *The Letters of John Keats*, ed. Maurice Buxton-Forman
(Oxford Univ. Pr., 1952), p. vi

The best of Keats's poems, of course, can be fully appreciated without extraneous help; but the letters throw light on all, and they are almost necessary to the understanding of *Endymion* and of some of the earlier or contemporaneous pieces. They clearly reveal those changes in his mind and temper which appear in his poetry. They dispose for ever of the fictions once current of a puny Keats who was "snuffed out by an article," a sensual Keats who found his ideal in claret and "slippery blisses," and a mere artist Keats who cared nothing for his country and his fellow-creatures. Written in his last four years by a man who died at twenty-five, they contain abundant evidence of his immaturity and his faults, but they disclose a nature and character which command on the whole not less respect than affection, and they show not a little of that general intellectual power which rarely fails to accompany poetic genius. . . .

In spite of occasional despondency, and of feelings of awe at the magnitude of his ambition, Keats, it is tolerably plain from these letters, had a clear and habitual consciousness of his genius. He never dreamed of being a minor poet. He knew that he was a poet; sometimes he hoped to be a great one. [1909]

A. C. Bradley
*Oxford Lectures on Poetry*
(New York: St. Martin's Pr., 1955), p. 210

Keats seems to me also a great poet. I am not happy about *Hyperion*: it contains great lines, but I do not know whether it is a great poem. The Odes—especially perhaps the *Ode to Psyche*—are enough for his reputation. But I am not so much concerned with the degree of his greatness as with its kind; and its kind is manifested more clearly in his Letters than in his poems. . . . The Letters are certainly the most notable and the most important ever written by any English poet. Keats's egotism, such as it is, is that of youth which time would have redeemed. His letters are what letters ought to be; the fine things come in unexpectedly, neither introduced nor shown out, but between trifle and trifle. [1933]

T. S. Eliot
*The Use of Poetry and the Use of Criticism*
(London: Faber and Faber, 1955), p. 100

## GENERAL

Because he did this wonderful student work [*Ode to Maia*] we are apt to think of him as one whose career was determined. He means to us the Ode to the Nightingale and odes unwritten of the same kind. His furthest point of progress is La belle dame sans merci or the fragment of The Eve of St. Mark; and who could go further than that? Yet these are not his furthest point of progress, and it is not they that hold the promise of incredible things. He could not have done better that way; but he was starting on a different way foreshadowed in The Fall of Hyperion. . . .

There is a fullness of experience in those Lines to Fanny as in no earlier poem of his yet it is all poetized. He can make phrases about it as rich as any he made about the nightingale—

> And great unerring nature once seems wrong.

Perhaps that is the finest line he ever wrote; more than any other, at least, it promises the incredible things that he would have written. [1920]

A. Clutton-Brock
*Essays on Books* (London: Methuen, 1921), pp. 118-19, 127-28

The basis of the likeness between Shakespeare and Keats lies in a similar completeness of humanity confronted with the same world of experience. They are as it were seeds of the same species growing in the same environment, except that one is forced into maturity by an excess of heat years before the other. But their similarity is really that of the same germ reacting to the same conditions. Shakespeare followed a predestined path; so did Keats: and those paths are alike. . . .

He followed the greatest, not as a disciple, but as one compelled by his own nature to tread the same path. Probably he had learned to know his own nature more fully by following it out in Shakespeare, by understanding Shakespeare to his depths; but life itself conspired to urge him on to reach at twenty-three a point which Shakespeare did not reach till many years later. Life prodigally heaped upon him the miseries of the world, for he was her beloved son. [1925]

J. M. Murry
*Keats and Shakespeare* (Oxford Univ. Pr., 1951), pp. 6, 210

. . . Keats had written the great 1819 odes, subjecting himself to the severe discipline of established form, yet allowing himself the freedom and independence necessary to achieve distinct individual effects. The odes are quietly chaste in tone, yet richly luxuriant in thought and imagery; they are sober, yet magnificent; restrained, but gloriously free. Here, I think, and in *Lamia*, Keats had most nearly found himself. Had he gone on writing, it would probably have been in a verse similar to that of these poems in the middle manner, the excrescences of *Endymion* pruned away, the austerity of *Hyperion* relaxed into forms of rich, abundant beauty. Only this we cannot know. Sad that this most gifted singer should never have been given opportunity to go beyond the experimental stage. Yet how marvellous those experiments!

C. D. Thorpe
*The Mind of John Keats* (Oxford Univ. Pr., 1926), p. 177

The . . . facts [of Keats' life] and extracts [from his papers] seem to show unmistakably that Keats was keenly alive to the social and political movements of the day, that he took an active interest in history, and studied past events in the light of their probable effect upon the present and the future. That he did not to any extent lug into his poetry echoes of the turmoil and bickering of his day proves nothing, unless it be his good taste. There is no great proof for an attitude of detachment from this world and its affairs in the fact that Keats went to medieval romance, Greek mythology, and to nightingales and autumn for his poetic themes. For him these seemed the most congenial frames for his pictures of human life and nature. He wrote as he did largely because that was his idea of poetry. When he does break from his rule, stepping into the realm of the practical in his verse, as in *Isabella*, he strikes with two-fisted energy in hot denunciation of greed, oppression, and inequality. Such outbursts reveal the intensity with which Keats thought and felt on such subjects; the instinct and the fire were there, as the letters show, but sublimated, the poet habitually suppressing the reformer.

C. D. Thorpe
*PMLA* (December, 1931), p. 1244

. . . Keats' capacity for ignorance and powers of scepticism gave him, paradoxically as we might think at first sight, great balance of mind and ability to suffer disillusion without strain. So far as doctrine went he quickly saw through the hocus-pocus of perfectibility; and in practice he could achieve a certain stability and "capability of submission" to what he thought were inevitable aspects of human experience. He could rest, as Shelley could not, in acceptance of and belief in suffering; so that whether he saw the world in the light of what is eternal or naturalistically, he did not see it as a world from which suffering could be removed. [1948]

D. G. James
*The Romantic Comedy* (Oxford Univ. Pr., 1963), p. 110

. . . The most living thing in Keats's poetry has been the re-creation of sensuous beauty, first as a source of delight for its own sake, then as a symbol of the life of the mind and the emotions. . . . The academic education which he never had tends to foster abstract thought; but Keats would never have lived by it whatever his training. He not only cared little for, but positively resented intellectual truths, which make demands upon the mind without being verifiable in immediate experience. . . .

For Keats, the necessary precondition of poetry is submission to things as they are, without trying to intellectualize them into something else, submission to people as they are, without trying to indoctrinate or improve them. . . . Keats found this quality [of "negative capability"] at its fullest in Shakespeare. [ca. 1951]

Graham Hough
*The Romantic Poets*
(New York: W. W. Norton, 1964), pp. 169-70

# CHARLES LAMB

1775-1834

Best known as the "familiar essayist" and companion to the chief Romantic poets, Charles Lamb was a Londoner by birth, education, and inclination. He was born in 1775 at the Inner Temple, London, where his father worked as a law clerk, attended Christ's Hospital School in London, and after a brief employment in the South Sea House, spent the remainder of his career as a clerk in the East India House, London. At the age of forty-five, adopting the pseudonym Elia, he began to write a series of essays for the *London Magazine*, which immediately caught favor, were collected and published in 1823 and 1833, and are still read with great pleasure today. Prior to that he had had moderate success rewriting, with his sister, *Tales from Shakespeare* for children and editing Elizabethan plays. His earlier attempts at poetry and drama, however, were futile. His private life was beset by madness and frustration on the one hand, friendship and affection on the other. A victim of hereditary insanity, Lamb spent six weeks in an asylum at the age of twenty; his sister Mary, who had murdered their mother in a fit of violence, was remanded to Lamb's care, but her frequent relapses were his constant concern. His love for three women was never fulfilled, and he remained a bachelor all his life, directing his paternal instincts toward his sister Mary and Emma Isola, an orphan he adopted in 1823. His friends were numerous and devoted: Coleridge, Wordsworth, Southey, Hazlitt, and Hood, to name a few. He died in London of a disease contracted after a fall and was buried at Edmonton in 1834. His chief works are *Tales from Shakespeare* (1807); *Specimens from the Dramatic Poets* (1808); *Essays of Elia* (1823); *Last Essays of Elia* (1833).

Thomas Hutchinson, ed., *Works in Prose and Verse of Charles and Mary Lamb* (1924), 2 vols. in 1

E. V. Lucas, *Life of Charles Lamb* (rev. 5th ed., 1921), 2 vols.

That Lamb is one of the most exquisite and delightful of critics, as of writers, is a proposition for which I will go to the stake; but I am not prepared to confess him as one of the very greatest in his critical capacity. . . .

Take the most famous instances of his criticism—the defence of Congreve and Wycherley, the exaltation of Ford, the saying . . . that Heywood is "a prose Shakespeare," the enthusiasm shown towards that rather dull-fantastic play *A Fair Quarrel*, while the magnificence of the same author's *Changeling* was left to Leigh Hunt to find out—these and other things distinctly show the *capriccio*. Lamb, not Hunt is really the "Ariel of Criticism," and he sometimes pushes tricksiness to a point which would, we fear, have made his testy Highness of Milan rather angry. [1904]

George Saintsbury
*A History of Criticism*, Vol. III
(New York: Humanities Pr., 1961), pp. 238-39

He was indeed a soul set apart, but it was to man, not to God. He alone found the secret of sacrificing his heart to stern and unrelenting duty and of dwelling the while resolutely on the surface of life, a patron of puns and a devotee of the genial vices. And this is the quality of his writings as well as of his character, although some, I know misled by their devotion, would discover graver traits in his work.

Paul Elmer More
*Shelburne Essays. Second Series*
(New York: G. P. Putnam's Sons, 1905), p. 93

Lamb's puns may seem to need an apology. The pun is almost dead. It was the fashion of Lamb's age; to make the best pun of the evening was fame. Punsters of repute were hunted in society. Perhaps the best puns have all been made; we have to get on as best we can with the inverted commonplace, the paradox, and the transferred initial consonant.

Lamb almost raised the pun to a higher power. His puns very often *mean* something. A pun is like one of those scientific toys that rotate in a vacuum: he almost made it do work. [1926]

Sir Walter Raleigh
*On Writing and Writers*, ed. George Gordon
(London: Edward Arnold, 1927), p. 123

The success of the [Mary Lamb's] *Tales* was immediate and lasting. From the day of their first publication, they have never lacked readers. Within the first ten years five editions were required to meet the demand, an output that approached best-selling in those days. Since 1807 the stories have never been out of print. Their popularity has not been due solely to the art of the original. Shakespeare's plays have continued to flourish and the

*Tales* have continued to flourish alongside of them, not by any means as commentaries, but as independent works of art and imagination. Their author's personality makes its own appeal. . . .

If Charles [Lamb] had done no more than produce his critical *Specimens of Dramatic Poets* and Mary her delightful *Tales*, they would have atoned sufficiently with the public for a crime in which the public was so little interested. Posterity has never wasted sympathy on poor murdered Elizabeth Lamb. But her own children were prevented by an unalterable law of nature from weighing matters with the same objectivity. The daughter, who had committed the crime, and the son who had condoned it, were doomed to go on endlessly expiating a guilt they had never accepted. . . .

When Charles Lamb was forty-five, he ranked among a host of minor literary lights in England. All that he had done up to this time would have earned him small fame with posterity. His assembled *Works* had been published in 1818, chiefly through the influence of Leigh Hunt. . . . Editors like Leigh Hunt and John Scott saw the developing humanist in Charles Lamb and took long chances on his future. Though his *Works* had no success to boast of, the personality behind them seemed a factor to deal with. . . . Charles Lamb was a rich discovery. It required Scott's influence to set Lamb's feet upon a fresh literary path, to show him that in this field he was already an accomplished author, and to wean him away from his hopeless affair with the theatre. The slight transition from "Lamb" to "Elia" was all that was needed to enrich the flow of wit, anecdote, and wisdom from the same pen. Only a slight shift and enlargement of the imagined audience of one of Lamb's letters resulted in an essay of rare beauty and charm. The change was first exemplified in "Recollections of Christ's Hospital Five and Thirty Years Ago," which appeared in the *London Magazine* for August 1820. It marked the beginning of Charles Lamb's fame as an English essayist.

Katharine Anthony
*The Lambs* (London: Hammond, Hammond and Co., 1948),
pp. 96, 105, 123-24

*The Essays of Elia* are Lamb's most popular writings. They are forced upon school-children with an insistence that is almost justifiable, for he who does not discover *Roast Pig* could well have been spared the pains of learning to read. But it was as "the first to draw the public attention to the old English dramatists" that he wished to be remembered. The echoing voice of Elia is heard in Leigh Hunt, in Thackeray (who took upon himself the canonization of Saint Charles), in Stevenson, Chesterton, Montague, Lynd and, grossly distorted, in the gossip-writers of the daily press. Elia influenced the writers; and, through their printed homage, won pedagogues and the love or passionate hatred of schoolboys; but Charles Lamb reinstated readers in their own domain, resurrecting for them the beauties of the English Renaissance, saving and salving Webster, Ben Jonson, Beaumont and Fletcher, Marlowe, Middleton—even Shakespeare himself—after the neglect and ill-usage that they had received from the hooks of the pretentious Augustan iconoclasts. . . .

His very scholarship has dulled many editions of his works, for whereas Lamb could use his knowledge without emphasizing the ignorance of his readers, his editors have insisted on a supply of explanatory footnotes, dragging the eye joltingly from the body of the text to the bottom of the page, wrenching the mind from Lamb's familiarity that is above incidental knowledge, adding unimportant information on details, but diverting from the deliberate casualness with which Lamb proceeds to his real conclusions.

To attempt to assess Lamb as a stylist is to defy critical tenets, for his English rambles, stammers as his speech, runs and falters. He knows not concision though he is a master of precision. He chases an insignificant idea into significance and makes of an interloping inspiration a literary occasion. He is archaic and yet never "precious." His writing is often amorphous, for his prose style is rebellion against the formalism of his immediate predecessors, as is the habit of verse adopted by his friends Coleridge and Wordsworth.

J. E. Morpurgo
*Charles Lamb and Elia*
(Harmondsworth, Eng.: Penguin Books, 1948), pp. 16-17

Lamb's mind was the antithesis of neat and office-like. It resembled an antique shop or an old bookstore where, in spite of the clutter, the dust, and the overlay of accumulation, the proprietor can at a moment's notice bring to light whatever treasure is desired. It never judged "system-wise" but always by "fastening on particulars." It was proudly unmethodized, desultory, tangential. If it worked obliquely in ways beyond prediction, it was because it fed upon the tantalizing obliquities of life no less than of literature. Its knowledge was a matter of informed tastes rather than of pursued facts. . . .

The highly, at moments even dangerously, self-conscious artist we cherish as Elia emerged late in Lamb's life as the flowering of his varied career as a professional writer. By that time Lamb had long since mislaid, except for album purposes, the poet of slight endowment he had started out by being. Years before, too, he had discarded the novelist whose all but non-existent talent for narrative stamped *Rosamund Gray* and his contributions to *Mrs. Leicester's School* as no more than apprentice work. He had also buried the dramatist with "no head for playwriting" whose blank-verse tragedy, *John Woodvil*, was but the feeblest of Elizabethan echoes, and whose little farce, *Mr. H.*, was so disastrous a failure that its author had joined in the hissing. . . .

Lamb was the possessor of an epistolary style quite at odds with the style we know as Elia's.

In addition to being the best introduction to Lamb, Lamb's are among the world's best letters. In them we almost hear him talk. To be sure, his stutter is gone, and an incredible fluency has replaced it. But, as in all good letters, the illusion of direct communication is maintained. . . .

If Charles Lamb does not belong in the company of the greatest critics, neither do they belong in his. It is not so much that they stride ahead of him as that he elects to amble to one side of them, well off the main thoroughfares. Even in criticism, he is a lonely figure who goes his own way. That the paths of his choice happen to be bypaths is part of the enticement and originality of his approach. He is one of the most satisfying and least pretentious of critics; major in a minor way, though major nonetheless.

John Mason Brown
Introd., in *The Portable Charles Lamb*
(New York: Viking, 1949), pp. 20, 24-25, 30

Two long critical essays contributed by Lamb to a quarterly edited by Leigh Hunt in 1810-11, *The Reflector*: namely, "On the Genius and Character of Hogarth" and "On the Tragedies of Shakespeare, Considered with reference to their Fitness for Stage Representation" . . . were paradoxical, or aggressively unorthodox. Lamb set out to demonstrate that the common view of Hogarth "as a mere comic painter, as one whose chief ambition was to *raise* a laugh," was wrong, and that instead Hogarth's works were a grand school of life. In the other paper he maintained that Shakespeare was reduced by the details of the material stage from that infinite scale on which he addresses the imagination of his reader. In both instances, whether we concede his argument or not, the vitality of the critic's mind and the abundance of his armoury brought into action with rapid freshness, and be it added the noble construction of the whole, are something beyond the ordinary. The two essays served at once as classics often quoted by Lamb's contemporaries. . . .

The manner and tune of the Essays [of Elia] is as changeful as their occasion and topic, for Lamb saw English prose as an instrument with stops enough for every use and grace. If he is moved to speak direct thoughts, he lets Elia go and is as laconic as can be. "When I am not walking, I am reading; I cannot sit and think. Books think for me." "I called upon you this morning, and found that you were gone to visit a dying friend. I had been upon a like errand." But the comic spirit in Lamb may come in upon his realities of feeling with instant change of note. "There is no home for me here. There is no sense of home at Hastings. It is a place of fugitive resort, an heterogeneous assemblage of sea-mews and stock-brokers, Amphitrites of the town, and misses that coquet with the Ocean." Such allusions as occur there, of course, make *Elia* difficult to catch in all his meaning and picturing at first glance.

Edmund Blunden
*Charles Lamb* (London: BC/Longmans, 1954), pp. 24, 30

The value of the [Elia] essays does not lie only in their reflection of an interesting and appealing personality, in their charm of style, or in their pleasant and erudite eccentricities. Lamb was doing in prose something akin to what others, especially Wordsworth and Coleridge, were doing in poetry, and his essays at their best exhibit an equally careful and artful poetic structure. . . .

One of the distinguishing features of much "romantic" poetry as compared with the poetry of the preceding century is the replacement of an external "public" principle of structure by one that is internal and "private." The poet, that is, neither defines his private, unique, experience in terms of the general, the abstract, nor does he use the particular experience merely as a point of departure for a public discourse. He rather invites the reader to share a unique experience, and it is this which determines the form of his poem. We are presented not with a rationally ordered sequence, but with a psychologically ordered movement of consciousness. . . .

All this, of course, is part of what Coleridge meant by "organic" form and is a common characteristic of many of his poems and of many of Wordsworth's. What has not been sufficiently noticed is the extent to which it is also characteristic of Lamb.

Even at first glance, "Old China" bears some resemblance to Coleridge's poem ["Frost at Midnight"]. The major part of the essay consists not quite of reverie, but of two monologues, both of which are nostalgic recollections of the past. . . .

As is the case with Coleridge's poem, what belongs to the public world and provides a meeting place for reader and author is not a set of ideas but a specific situation, a set of physical objects. But again, as in the poem, this situation is more than a simple frame, more than an occasion for the monologues. . . .

The description of the china . . . serves to create a tension between internal and external, between real and ideal. It also serves to control that tension. Like Coleridge's still and frosty weather, the china provides the point of stasis from which the essay begins and to which it returns. . . .

The intensity of feeling is also controlled by the tone in which the china is described. In the monologues, Lamb approaches sentimentality. But as he so often does, he avoids sentimentality through ironic humor. . . .

Finally, the china, the work of art *in* the essay, becomes a symbol for the work of art, the essay, which contains it. . . . For the aging human beings with their changing thoughts and feelings are also fixed in words like the figures fixed in glaze. *In the* essay, Bridget and Elia are also quaint and changeless, "grotesques . . . that under the notion of men and women, float about, uncircumscribed by any element," free from the "angles of our world." And the work of art, unreal in this, is like the tea cup also real as the thing which exists and continues to exist.

Richard Haven
*ELH* (June, 1963), pp. 137-42

Lamb's comparative failures in literary types other than the essay directed him gradually but inexorably toward that medium. His earliest emotional expressions, like those of most youthful writers, took the form of verse. He was known as a poet when a young man and even after he began writing prose. Although one critic has observed that "His poetry is the least poetical thing he has written," he has left in the midst of his generally mediocre verse two or three poems of a high order of excellence. But Lamb came to realize the limitations of his Muse, and in a manuscript passage not printed in "Witches, and Other Night-Fears" he wrote of the end of a dream: "When I awoke I came to a determination to write prose all the rest of my life." The transition between his poetry and prose was not, however, so sharp as that. Indeed, he wrote poetry at periods throughout his life, but the trend was always towards prose. . . .

To see the difficulties under which he worked and over which he triumphed, and to see the toil and thought that went into the creation of his prose lyrics is to see the greatness that was Elia. His steady growth in excellence—his progressive evolution—makes appropriate to him the words of his lifelong friend, Samuel Taylor Coleridge: "You will find this a good gage or criterion of genius—whether it progresses and evolves, or only spins upon itself."

Sir George Leonard Barnett
*Charles Lamb. The Evolution of Elia*
(Bloomington, Ind.: Indiana Univ. Pr., 1964), pp. 11, 232

# WALTER SAVAGE LANDOR
1775-1864

The last of the Romantics, Walter Savage Landor was born in Warwick and matured at a time when revolutionary and Romantic movements were at their heights. But although he was infected by the former spirit, he never succumbed to the latter, and remained always an ardent Republican and a loyal and austere classicist. Educated at Rugby and Oxford, his impetuous and quarrelsome nature and his enthusiastic Republicanism got him into difficulties and caused him to withdraw from both schools. At twenty, he published a volume of poems, retired to and continued his writing in Wales and Bath. In 1808, he raised an army to fight Napoleon in Spain, and although the adventure was a failure, he returned to England a hero, nevertheless. At thirty-six, he married Julia Thuillier, with whom he toured Italy from 1815-1821 and settled in Florence from 1831-1835. A quarrel in 1835 ended in their final separation, and Landor returned to Bath where he remained until 1858. Then, to avoid action for libel, he returned to Florence where he spent the remaining years of his life. The *Imaginary Conversations* were begun in Italy where he also wrote a good deal of literary criticism. In 1847, he published a series of poems in Latin and a volume of Hellenic narratives in English. Many of his best poems—the short lyrics and epigrams—were written in his declining years. Most notable of his works are *Gebir* (1798); *Count Julian* (1812); *Imaginary Conversations* (1824, 1828, 1829, 1846, 1853); *The Citation and Examination of William Shakespeare* (1834); *Pericles and Aspasia* (1836); *Pentameron* (1837); *Hellenics* (1847); *Last Fruit Off an Old Tree* (1853); *Antony and Octavius* (1856); *Dry Sticks Fagoted* (1858); and *Heroic Idyls* (1863).

T. E. Welby and Stephen Wheeler, eds., *The Complete Works* (1927-1936), 16 vols.

R. H. Super, *Walter Savage Landor: A Biography* (1954).

Landor is monumental by the excess of his virtues, which are apt to seem, at times, a little too large for the stage and scenery of his life. He desired to live with grandeur; and there is grandeur in the outlines of his character and actions. But some gust of the will, some flurry of the nerves, was always at hand, to trouble or overturn this comely order.

Arthur Symons
*The Romantic Movement in English Poetry*
(London: Archibald Constable, 1909), p. 173

The fact remains that the bulk of Landor's longer poems too much resembles in form—and it is in that respect alone that we are speaking of them—a very perfect school exercise, a collection of glorified Newdigates.

It is not so with his shorter pieces. Even the blank verse introductory lines to the Collection of 1846 contain verse with more idiosyncrasy in it than the "pale and noble" staple of their larger forerunners; and the mote-like myriads of epigrams, in the wide sense, that follow, derive sometimes the greater part, and almost always something, of their admitted charm from the fingering of the measure. Certainly this is the case with the two peaks of his poetry, "Rose Aylmer" and "Dirce."

George Saintsbury
*The History of English Prosody*, vol. III
(London: Macmillan, 1910), p. 87

Such influences [as Pindar, Virgil, Milton] do not impair, but rather explain, the poetical independence of *Gebir,* a work as wonderful in its way, . . as Blake's oracular books or the *Lyrical Ballads.* It does not mark a date like *The Ancient Mariner* or *Tintern Abbey,* for Landor founded no school or tradition: and none but he could carry forward, or purify, or perfect the manner that he invented. And it is a manner imperfect enough, with the imperfections and splendour of youthful strength and pride; the language often half-hewn, rigid, hieratic, like some early monument in that "land of Nile" where the story is laid. [1912]

Oliver Elton
*A Survey of English Literature. 1780-1830,* vol. II
(London: Edward Arnold, 1961), p. 16

In the *Imaginary Conversations,* scenes as it were chosen from unwritten dramas, Landor's artistic instinct guides him to follow this principle. The moment that he delights in depicting is that one preceding the climax of the action, when some great resolution has been taken, but has yet to be fulfilled, as in the *Leofric and Godiva,* or when, as with Catharine of Russia, some great action long planned has at last been executed, and now that the climax is over, the character, as it were, recoils upon itself, and is revealed in all its complexity. He is at his greatest when some heroic soul is faced with death, and, freed at last from the trivialities that tended to obscure its true proportions, it stands out in clear outline, the light of eternity behind it. [1915]

Ernest De Selincourt
Introd., in *Walter Savage Landor, Poetry and Prose,*
ed. E. K. Chambers (Oxford Univ. Pr., 1955), p. xxviii

The most important fruit of this period was the poem *Gebir,* which appeared in that *annus mirabilis* 1798. . . . None of the morning stars of that new day attracted less attention than did *Gebir,* but among its few readers was a reviewer who accused the author of "the common error of those who aspire to the composition of blank-verse, by borrowing too many phrases and epithets from our incomparable Milton." "I challenge him to produce them," Landor fulminated in an unpublished rejoinder. . . . Landor's enthusiasm for *Paradise Lost* began shortly before he wrote *Gebir,* and because his earlier pieces were composed in heroic couplets of the pronouncedly neo-classic type. But the fact is that, as Southey's blank verse ought not to be Miltonic but is, so Landor's ought to be but is not.

R. D. Havens
*The Influence of Milton on English Poetry*
(Cambridge, Mass.: Harvard Univ. Pr., 1922), pp. 294-95

Landor could not throw himself wholly or for long into the interests, passions, and minds of others. His *Imaginary Conversations* are not in the least dramatic. How many people have been excited by the names, and disappointed by the talk! It ends by being like a bad dream; we are always back in Landor's library, and someone is always *prosing*. [1926]

Sir Walter Raleigh
*On Writing and Writers*, ed. George Gordon
(London: Edward Arnold, 1927), p. 139

No English poet, not even Milton, really *reproduces* the antique; if he tries, the result is a *pastiche*. He can appropriate something of its form and temper to express his own vision and his own sentiment; and this is the achievement of Walter Savage Landor, in his *Hellenics*, epigrams, and lyrics. His peculiar cleanness and distinctness of outline are learned in this school. He aims at a Greek severity, or a Greek delicacy; giving himself, as he says, "the toil of smoothing under hardened hand, with Attic emery and oil." But his debts to Greek cannot be disentangled from his debts to Latin, which he used as a second mother-tongue. . . . Landor's own voice, a proud and resonant voice, is heard everywhere behind that of Agamemnon, or Silenus, or the numberless personages of his prose *Imaginary Conversations*. Idylls in verse like the beautiful *Hamadryad* and its sequel *Acon and Rhodope*, whatever they may owe to the Sicilian poets, are essentially Landorian, as well as modern and "romantic," and a product of the age of Keats or Tennyson. [1933]

Oliver Elton
Introd., in *Walter Savage Landor. Poetry and Prose*,
ed. E. K. Chambers (Oxford Univ. Pr., 1955), pp. xxiv-xxv

I may now . . . offer a paraphrase exposition of my own for the Landor passage, [*Gebir*, III, 4-18]. . . .

Young, eager, idle, active, irresponsible (*panting*, further, has a very large number of metaphoric implications—it is a typical "wheel" metaphor, the spokes being different relations to a more or less connected rim), made thirsty, heated, needing rest, refreshment (with some others of the symbolic senses of water); I read Shakespeare and underwent the influences which lead a man to write and read poetry. *Too* can here couple almost any of the sense items: I, like Shakespeare; I, like others; Avon as well as other influences; Shakespeare as well . . . *Drank of Avon* is a "wheel within wheel" metaphor, revolving, in one set of motions, together with *panting* and, in another set of emotions, together with *dangerous draught* and *feverish thirst*. The influence is thirst-arousing, perhaps salt, intoxicant, alternative. (These motions bring in a very mixed and fleeting throng of feelings.)

Yet it is impossible, not allowed (feeling of injustice suffered, or of regret alone, as the emphasis is moved from *I* back to *never*) to me—whatever my merits (in a matter where "even a little seems a lot" and "the greatest is unworthy")—to

1. Perform the "Orphic" functions of the Poet.
2. Write in the spirit or purpose or manner, and on the subjects, of Homer, Virgil, Dante, Shakespeare.

The specific form of the metaphor here loads the statement with feelings of loss and inevitability—the vanishing of a possibility of the mind.

An act in human history is over, it comes to an end like a day. What was known in it—the distances and heights, the symbols of man's strength and security, his hope and religion—cannot be recaptured (as symbols, *hills, turrets,* and *spires,* like the suggested water of line two, have powers upon feeling independent of any specific interpretations that may be stressed by individual readers, they carry a general feeling for which any detailed exposition would be chiefly a rationalization). Can any poet now restore *those* powers of poetry (Apollo, Animism, Belief) that are themselves now closing a cycle? [1933]

I. A. Richards
*Speculative Instruments*
(Chicago: Univ. Chicago Pr., 1955), pp. 193-94

. . . Landor's [prose] style seems to be not so much Attic as a mixture of the Laconic and the Asiatic. It is obviously highly mannered prose. When Landor ceases to be regal he frequently becomes deplorable. He irritates us by constantly wrapping a plain idea in an elaborate and studied metaphor. . . .

Pericles is the ideal aristocratic republican, Landor in Greek attire taking a series of graceful attitudes. Aspasia is the ideal of intelligent, cultivated, emancipated womanhood—decidedly not Mrs. Landor in Greek dress. If only, among these charming and dignified murals of a sort of Greek Versailles, we could have an Aristophanic whiff of a fried-fish shop! It must be said, though Landor's critics do not say it, that *Pericles and Aspasia* is very hard to get through. . . .

*Crysaor* with its rugged approaches to sublimity is major poetry; nearly all the *Hellenics* are definitely minor. The imperfect performer on the organ was content to become a consummate master of the flute. . . .

In conception and execution the *Hellenics* are unique in English, and they have no parallel in classical literature unless in the late Greek mythological idylls and the individual tales of Ovid. Landor's narrative pieces are indeed very Hellenistic and Ovidian not merely in their objective, pictorial, and general "literary" qualities, but in their preoccupation with romantic love and the fate of young lovers. If these poems were serious studies of human passion, one would hesitate to say that the author of *Crysaor* had immensely narrowed his range, but since they are in the main only decorative reproductions of the antique, one does say so. [1937]

Douglas Bush
*Mythology and the Romantic Tradition*
(New York: Pageant Book Co., 1957), pp. 230, 232-33, 239, 243

In sheer bulk of production Walter Savage Landor . . . far outdid any of the Anglo-Latin poets since the seventeenth century. Besides the 254 closely printed pages of his *Poemata et inscriptiones* (1847), he published many more Latin poems in *Dry Sticks Fagoted* (1858), *Heroic Idylls* (1863), and the second edition of *Hellenics* (1859). In addition to these we must remember the thirty-one Latin poems in his *Poems* of 1795, only one of which was ever reprinted. During the early part of his literary career he was known principally as a Latin poet, since, with the exception of *Gebir* and *Count Julian*, all of his important work before the appearance of *Imaginary Conversations* (1824) had been in that language. Indeed four of these early volumes were entirely in Latin: *Iambi*, 1800; *Ode ad Gustavum regem*, 1810; *Idyllia nova quinque*, 1815; and *Idyllia heroica*, 1820. The last two of these represented the first appearance of some of his best narrative poems, better known now in the English translations which Landor later published. Yet in spite of this demonstration of his power in narrative, his genius for lyrical and epigrammatic Latin verse matured slowly. The best of his shorter *poemata* were not published until 1847 or even later. . . .

The *Idyllia heroica* vary greatly in length, theme, and quality. The earliest, "Pudoris ara" (1806), is a rambling conversation between Helen and her mother concerning the former's abduction by Theseus, with an interpolated story about the marriage of Ulysses and Penelope. It lacks both structural unity and artistic purpose. . . .

However significant Landor's Latin idylls may be for the historian of literature, it must be admitted that most of Bush's strictures upon them are well sustained. In general the style is characterized by a grandiose attempt at simplicity rather than by simplicity itself, and the subjects are not usually worthy of the care bestowed upon them. . . . It is probable that "Pan and Pitys" was Landor's own favorite, for he later wrote two poems in which it is referred to in a complimentary fashion. It is a pleasant piece of pastoral atmosphere, which ends rather surprisingly with the brutal murder of Pitys by Pan's rival, Boreas. In the English translation made for *Hellenics* Landor removed some of the bloody details. In other ways, too, the English version is slightly to be preferred, but in the case of "Corythus" the Latin is undoubtedly better. "Corythus" is the most completely satis-factory of the Latin idylls. Its subject matter, the murder by Paris of his own son, whom he does not recognize, followed by his own death and reunion with Oenone, is the most worthy of heroic treatment of any of them, and Landor handles it well. . . .

There are many poems on public affairs, but very few of them are really excellent. The most striking exception in this group is the fine ode to Garibaldi printed in *Heroic Idylls* (1863).

Only in the field of the epigram did Landor achieve real distinction in Latin verse. In the satirical epigram, it is true, he rarely rises above mere invective, but in the short poem of personal feeling, be it on love, old age, or death, his work challenges comparison with the best. The poems in this group all represent mature work, since few of the good ones appeared before 1847 and some of the best are found in *Dry Sticks* (1858) and *Heroic Idylls* (1863).

Leicester Bradner
*Musae Anglicanae* (New York:
Modern Language Assn., 1940), pp. 315-18, 320

The sculpture of the Greeks was not only the favorite art of Landor but it was also a major source of his inspiration. When the Aspasia of his novelette *Pericles and Aspasia* remarked (Letter XLVIII) that "coldness is experienced in the highest beauty," that brilliant lady expressed a senti-ment which her creator largely derived from the cold and regular perfection of Grecian statuary. . . .

Landor felt also that in the poetry of his maturity, he had achieved a beauty akin to that of the Grecian artists; for this reason he confidently appropriated the Horatian boast of the immortality of his own poetry. . . .

To represent the "sculpturesque faculty" of Landor the . . . character-istically neat and polished account of the dwelling in *Corythos* [sic] may be chosen, because it shows a happy blending of classical subject and sculp-tural style in the story of the son of Paris and Oenone [See Part I, 11. 193-99]. . . .

In *Pericles and Aspasia,* besides discoursing upon love and statecraft and literature, Landor did not neglect the opportunity to set forth his ideas con-cerning the arts of the Greeks. In the novelette he gave long and serious consideration to ancient art, particularly sculpture; for the "mighty power" of the sculptors excited him as much as anything in Greece—Aspasia alone excepted! . . . [1943]

S. A. Larrabee
*English Bards and Grecian Marbles*
(Port Washington, N.Y.: Kennikat Pr., 1964), pp. 235-37, 241-42

Unfortunately, Landor had no conception of the construction of a plot or of a dramatic scene. The dialogue of the play [*Count Julian*] is frequently forceful and the scenes are moving, but the situation is too often the same at the end of the scene as it was at the beginning: or, if not, the change has been brought about by sheer violence. "I have not the constructive faculty," Landor told the actor Macready quite truthfully a quarter of a century later. "I can only set persons talking; all the rest is chance." There are also the usual blind spots in Landor's understanding of people. . . . Yet in the final evaluation the tragedy is worthy of the admiration Southey expressed for it and the pleasure Landor himself felt. . . .

*Pericles and Aspasia* was published about the end of March and was immediately hailed by the reviewer in the *Examiner* as the finest of Landor's writings, "and we know of no higher praise to offer it." It is a book that comes closer to our preconceptions of Landor as a writer about classical times than most of the *Imaginary Conversations*. . . . The best known of all, and the longest, is the dramatic scene in blank verse, with the choral odes, written (it is pretended) by Aspasia herself—"The Shades of Agamemnon and of Iphigeneia.". . . The dramatic situation is excellent, and Landor loses none of its value. . . . The poetry in *Pericles and Aspasia* is a return to Landor's re-creation of the classical spirit in modern verse, and with the Latin Idyllia of earlier years forms the core of his "Hellenic" poems. The entire book is lively and varied evidence of the impact of classical literature on an imaginative, very intelligent, slightly sentimental nineteenth-century Englishman who loved that literature and for whom books were a better world than what he saw around him.

R. H. Super
*Walter Savage Landor* (New York:
New York Univ. Pr., 1954), pp. 104-5, 263-64

# MATTHEW GREGORY LEWIS
1775-1818

Born in London of a prominent family, son of the Deputy-Secretary at War, grandson of Thomas Sewall, "Monk" Lewis was educated at the Westminster School, where he was known as a precocious child, and at Oxford. He prepared for a diplomatic career by studying in Germany, met Goethe at Weimar, and fell under the influence of the German writers of sensational literature. At twenty, he published *The Monk*, which won him instant fame. Translations of German tales, other novels, and plays followed, but none ever fulfilled the promise of his first book. He died at sea on a return voyage from Jamaica, where he owned property. Some of his better known works are *Ambrosio, or The Monk* (1795); *Castle Spectre* (1797); *Tales of Terror* (1799); *Tales of Wonder* (1801); *The Bravo of Venice* (1805); *Rugantino, a Melodrama* (1805); *Venoni* (1808); and *Romantic Tales* (1808).

L. F. Peck, ed., *The Monk* (1952)
L. F. Peck, *The Life of Matthew Gregory Lewis* (1961)

You may laugh as much as you like at "Alonzo the Brave and the Fair Imogene," but it is quite certain that the pair showed the way to something like a new use of the anapæst; that Lewis was a perfect master of easy metre years before Moore and decades before Praed and Barham; and that, in his time and place, he was really important prosodically.

George Saintsbury
A History of English Prosody, vol. III
(London: Macmillan, 1910), p. 92

[The year 1795] . . . saw the publication of his first book *Ambrosio, or The Monk,* which brought him immediate fame.

The fate of this novel shows how a book with few merits from an artistic point of view can yet, by reason of its other qualities, achieve fame, and even inspire ideas that in the hands of more skilful artists may form the foundation for admitted works of art. The secret lies in the capacity possessed by literary phenomena of this description for hiding in a poor and distorted form far-reaching ideas, which are instinctively recognized as such and which exert their own influence. At the same time there may be connected with them something akin to the literary strivings of their day, making them of its essence, and thus lending them certain significance as historical documents. By such reasoning can the vitality of Lewis's romance be explained. . . .

To say the least, it must be admitted that as the work of so young and inexperienced a writer, *The Monk* is a singularly ripe achievement. Doubts concerning its originality have been increased by the fact that Lewis never again attempted anything original in the larger prose forms, but contented himself with poems, plays or adaptations. Nevertheless, the truth of the matter is that on the whole Lewis was right in his statement: he had found the themes for his work chiefly in French and German romanticism, but in fields that we are right in regarding as common property and fair game for any writer. [1927]

Eino Railo
The Haunted Castle
(New York: Humanities Pr., 1964), pp. 89-92

No rationalistic scruples inhibited Matthew Gregory Lewis. . . . His reading of Tieck, Spiess, Musäus, and other prolific spawners of the macabre filled his head with fantasies of the grotesque, the horrible, and the criminal. But in his notorious romance, *The Monk* (1797) [sic], a nightmare of fiendish wickedness, ghastly supernaturalism and sadistic sensuality, there is almost indubitably something else than mere literary sensationalism; it gives evidence of a psychopathic conditon perhaps inherent in the extremes of the romantic temperament. The crude purposes to which Lewis adapted the great themes of Faust and Ahasueras suggest deliberate parody; but he was intensely serious, though capable only of such coarse, broad strokes in characterization and setting as make his scenes of lust and torture and rotting corpses repellent beyond description. They are even more revolting in the original version which, in fear of legal action, Lewis afterwards modified.

Samuel Chew
*A Literary History of England*, ed. A. C. Baugh
(New York: Appleton-Century-Crofts, 1948), p. 1195

*The Monk* is one of the authentic prodigies of English fiction, a book in spite of various crudenesses so good that even after a century and a half it is possible to consider it unhistorically; and yet it has never quite become a standard novel. Several reasons for this must be its intermittent unavailability, its reputation for eroticism, its not being reinforced by excellence in Lewis's other imaginative work, so that it has had to stand alone. But the chief reason must be that it has long suffered from a prejudice against the "Gothic" novel in general, which I am anxious not to combat except as it affects our experience of *The Monk*. Deservedly forgotten—all but two or three exemplars—save by enthusiasts and specialists, this grotesque school helped usher in the English Romantic movement and debauched taste without ever really participating in the glories of the movement unless in the book before us. Here we might take refuge in the notion that *The Monk* is only incidentally a Gothic novel, and owes its excellence to other qualities; that it is good in spite of being to some extent a Gothic novel. But I don't think this is true. *The Monk* seems to me exactly a Gothic novel. . . .

John Berryman
Introd., in *The Monk,* ed. L. F. Peck
(New York: Grove Pr., 1952), p. ii

Now let us shift our focus towards the fantastic and sombre genius of Matthew Gregory Lewis, who painted his grim and ghastly themes in dark and lurid colours. His inflamed imagination and violent exaggeration of emotion suggest adolescence, yet he thrills his readers and makes their flesh creep. This author of remarkable talent makes horrors come crowding thick upon us, and often crudely resorts to the physically horrible, through images and descriptions of loathsome corruption, mouldering cerements, and fes-

tering relics of death and the grave. Yet, so great is the interest of his unadorned narrative, with its quick succession of events, that such bold exaggeration seems only fitting.

Of all the tales of horror, *The Monk* (1796) [sic] is probably the most
extravagant. "Lewis had enlivened his sensational story of rape, incest, murder, magic, and diablerie, with an obvious sensuality." "These puerile effusions dashed down within the space of ten weeks," are not altogether contemptible: *The Monk* remains a romance of extraordinary fascination and
power.

Devendra P. Varma
*The Gothic Flame* (London: Arthur Baker, 1957), pp. 139-40

... *Tales of Wonder,* a title which, together with *The Monk* and *The Castle
Spectre,* was during his life and still is most frequently associated with his
name. Some of the material for this work he probably had in hand as
early as 1793, when he wrote to his mother from Weimar of a volume of
original and translated poems he hoped to publish. . . .

When *Tales of Wonder* finally appeared late in 1800 or early the following year, the public was disappointed. [Sir Walter] Scott gives as reasons
for this the false hopes raised by the delay, the fact that the popularity of
ballads and ballad-mongers was already waning, Lewis' misguided sense of
humor, and that, by the inclusion of many well-known poems, the work was
expanded to two substantial and expensive volumes. . . . Of the sixty pieces
in the collection, about two thirds had been published before. . . . Lewis'
book was soon known as *Tales of Plunder,* many people feeling, as Anna
Seward did, that the editor had dishonestly imposed on the public. . . .

Louis F. Peck
*A Life of Matthew Gregory Lewis*
(Cambridge, Mass.: Harvard Univ. Pr., 1961), pp. 116, 124-25

# THOMAS MOORE
1779-1852

Poet, composer, singer, satirist, and socialite, Thomas Moore, the son of
a prosperous Dublin grocer, was educated at Trinity College, where he
developed his earlier interest in poetry and translated the erotic *Odes of
Anacreon.* Although an Irish patriot, Moore was a man of easy conscience
and chose poetry over politics. In 1798, he took his odes to London and,
within two years, published them under the patronage of the Prince Regent.
In 1802, he published a volume of prurient verse, which was also well-
received in high society. Appointed to an official post in Bermuda, he
served a few boring months, then leaving it in charge of a deputy, toured
the United States and Canada, and returned to England. His disenchanted
verse impression of this tour was published in 1806. In 1807, he published

the first of a profitable series of *Irish Melodies*, which continued to appear intermittently until 1834. In 1811, at thirty-two, he married the sixteen-year-old actress Elizabeth Dyke. The marriage was a happy one, and five children were born to Moore and his "darling Bessie." Meanwhile, his personal charm and sweet singing in the drawing rooms of London made him the toast of the town, second only to Byron as most popular poet in society. His contemporaries over-rated two of his narrative poems based on oriental themes then in vogue, and they chuckled at the political satires and familiar lampoons he contributed to *The Morning Chronicle*. Between 1818 and 1822, however, he had to forsake London for the continent to avoid prosecution for his deputy's embezzlement back in Bermuda. His best prose may be found in the official biography of his friend Byron, which he handled discreetly if not honestly. Senile in his last years, he died in 1852 at the age of seventy-three. Although his poetry and prose pleased his contemporaries, only a few of his melodies are remembered today: "Believe me, if all those endearing young charms"; "The young May moon is beaming"; and "Oft in the stilly night." Representative of his best work are *Poetical Works of the Late Thomas Little, Esq.* (1802); *Epistles, Odes and Other Poems* (1806); *Irish Melodies* (1807-1834); *Odes of Anacreon* (1810); *Lalla Rookh* (1817); *The Fudge Family in Paris* (1818); and *Letters and Journals of Lord Byron* (1830).

A. D. Godley, ed., *Poetical Works* (1910)
H. M. Jones, *The Harp That Once* (1937)

Of all modern English poets [Moore] . . . has written the most and the best songs directly to and for music; and of all English poets he was—unless I mistake—the most thoroughly practical musician.

> George Saintsbury
> *A History of English Prosody*, Vol. III
> (London: Macmillan, 1910), p. 83

There is not a trace of true passion, sensual or otherwise in the "Poems of Mr. Little," and the love scenes where Moore tries to be serious in *Lalla Rookh* or the *Loves of the Angels* resemble vital love as much as the sugar wreaths on a wedding-cake resemble living flowers. There are tender passages in his songs, of a sweet and natural emotion, but they belong to the friends and the wife he loved, and have nothing to do with the rest of his shallow, brilliant, and sometimes tinsel poetry. The man was thin, and fortunately for his success, he did not know it. On the contrary, he believed himself, even though he was modest about it, to be a poet of substantial power. Such a faith enabled him to go on writing thousands of verses, with loose fertility, on every kind of subject. . . .

The graver satires, such as "Corruption" and "Intolerance," written in imitation of Pope, have neither weight, humour, felicity of phrase, nor savage bitterness. He had no more capacity for grave or cruel poetry than a butterfly has for making honey or using a sting. But the lighter satirical poetry, the *Twopenny Post-Bag,* the *Satirical and Humourous Poems,* could not be bettered. They stand alone in their excellence. . . .

*Lalla Rookh* is the representation in words of the florid, fanciful music which pleased his time. When in the Irish music he touched a sadder, wilder, tenderer, and more imaginative music—which in its mirth was broken into plaintiveness, and in its plaintiveness turned on itself with laughter, which mingled with its note of joyous defiance the passionate pain of the exile for the home where so many brave men had died under oppression—he was lifted by the music into a higher region of poetry.

Stopford Brooke and T. W. H. Rolleston
Introd., in *A Treasury of Irish Poetry in the English Tongue*
(New York: Macmillan, 1900), pp. 35, 37-39

*The Fudge Family* is a deft and pleasing variety of the epistolary tale or sketch, used by Smollett in *Humphry Clinker,* and by Richardson before him, and by Mr. Henry James long afterwards in *The Point of View.* The father, Mr. Phil Fudge, the correspondent and creature of Castlereagh; the son and daughter; the young Irish patriot, the tutor, Phelim Connor, who half embodies and half burlesques Moore's liberal and shamrock sentiment, are all alive, and expose themselves naturally and without effort. Moore, in fact, is the best satirical improvisatore that we have, for ease, sharpness, and fertility combined. [1912]

Oliver Elton
*A Survey of English Literature. 1780-1830,* Vol. II
(London: Edward Arnold, 1961), p. 273

*Lalla Rookh* was the delight of a whole generation; and without experiencing this spell to the same degree, one can still realise it. . . . The whole is suavely romantic, somewhat over-sweet, but relieved by a sprightly vivacity and the intensity of a coloured vision. By combining tenderness with a veiled ardour, humour with the soberly sensual grace of Eastern imagery, Moore complies with the needs and curiosity of English taste, without exceeding the treasure enforced by a clearly felt desire for idealisation. In no other work does the talent of the writer more clearly show its affinity with properly feminine aesthetics. This vast fairy tale, of thin substance, but overflowing with inexhaustible lyricism, displays an art already Victorian, which would seem in some respects to announce the touch of Tennyson. The magic of the style, and the easy, varied happiness of an astonishing prosodic virtuosity, would make it a kind of masterpiece, were it not for a certain lavishness which overburdens the delicacy of its arabesques, and for the too fragile structure of this palace of the "Arabian Nights." [1927; rev. 1935]

Louis Cazamian
*A History of English Literature*
(New York: Macmillan, 1938), pp. 1100-1101

["To Nea"] is porcelain, if you like, but it is well wrought and there is a place for it. . . .

"Paradise and the Peri" is as empty of character and passion as an improvisation might be—indeed, with its indeliberate structure and its surface presentation it might be an improvisation. It is nothing but description; we should read it as we look at tapestry—in which all the figures are brightly colored. . . . The peri and the angel, the man and the child, are there so that the scene and each may be described. The character or the passion that makes a narrative poem is not in "Paradise and the Peri.". . .

"The Kiss" [is] a piece which has not the overtone that would make it poetry, nor the wit that would make it an epigram. "Sail on, sail on, thou fearless bark" is merely a Byronic echo. . . .

"Oft in the Stilly Night," which we remember for the striking image of the banquet hall deserted, . . . carries contradiction between the thing that is being said and the measure it is being said in; it is in the tone of a man talking to companions, not in the tone of a man who realizes that he has become lonely. "The Last Rose of Summer" has two charming lines:

> Since the lovely are sleeping,
> Go, sleep thou with them.

Whatever is in the verses is in these two lines; the rest is only these lines diluted.

Padraic Colum
*Commonweal* (February 5, 1930), p. 389

Judged by the standards of our day, Thomas Moore was not a great poet. But there is no sane reason why he should be so judged; for literary standards are as changeable as feminine fashions. And since the fancies of art and literature are further comparable to feminine fashions in that they move in cycles, it may well be that the exuberant style, the vigorous colouring, the disciplined form, and the musical lyric, of which Moore was the master will again return to favour, and that Moore himself will be restored to the high place he once held in the estimation of the literary world.

Moore, however, was not merely a poet. He was a classical scholar, a historian, a political thinker, a biographer, a novelist, a composer of music, a singer, a satirist, a wit, an artist, and an actor. He had an extraordinarily likeable personality; he was generous, quite incapable of a mean action, and had none of the vices for which genius is so often made the excuse. In addition he was a patriot; and though a choice of one of the more spectacular forms of patriotism would have won for him an easier and less vulnerable fame, his countrymen have good reason to be grateful that his physical disabilities and his temperament made it imperative that he should choose the pen in preference to the sword. For it was due entirely to Moore's pen that Irish national sentiment was kept alive during Ireland's darkest and most disastrous years. . . .

Seamus MacCall
*Thomas Moore* (London: Gerald Duckworth, 1935), pp. 7-8

. . . In July, 1806, Francis Jeffrey himself undertook an Olympian examination of *Epistles, Odes, and Other Poems*. Jeffrey, who had already goaded John Thelwall in an abusive pamphlet, and drawn from the irritated Southey the statement that in taste he was a mere child, proposed to correct both Moore and the aristocratic reading of the age. The fact that the poems had sweetness, melody, smoothness of diction, brilliant fancy, and some show of classical erudition but added to the offense of their existence. the author's celebrity "rests on licentiousness"; he is the "most poetical of those who, in our time, have devoted their talents to the propagation of immorality." . . .

Moore did not have money enough to traverse the kingdom from end to end and challenge him to mortal combat. He went up to London only to discover from Rogers, who had just dined with Jeffrey, that the reviewer was at hand. . . .

Monday morning, at the canonical hour for bloodshed, the two embattled Irishmen drove to the stately woods of Chalk Farm, where Regency gentlemen were accustomed to settle their little differences. . . .

The subsequent proceedings were rapid and confused. . . . According to Moore's recollection, just as the pistols were raised on both sides, an officer rushed out from behind a hedge, struck Jeffrey's pistol with his staff, knocked it some distance into the field, and arrested the editor, while a second officer took possession of Moore. . . .

At the end [of *Irish Melodies*] is that song which has gone round the English-speaking world, that song, the beautiful falsity of which ridicule cannot kill nor parody quench, because it has caught the sweet nostalgia of romanticized love as no other English lyric of sentiment has ever done:

Believe me, if all those endearing young charms. . . .

It is useless for criticism to protest that Shakespeare and Shelley can better this writing, useless to point out the laughable ineptitude of "dear ruin," useless to speak of sentimentality and hollow compliment. The world has taken Tommy to its bosom for this song, as it has for " 'Tis the last Rose of Summer" and certain others, because these triumphs are in their own genre absolutely and flawlessly *right*.

H. M. Jones
*The Harp that Once*
(New York: Henry Holt, 1937), pp. 93-97, 108

. . . It would be well if interest were revived in a curious volume of his [Moore's] which he called, rather clumsily, *The Travels of an Irish Gentleman in Search of a Religion*. Those who are disposed to see Moore as "apologetic," the sychophant of London society, will find him here decidedly apologetic in the more authentic sense of the word, an outspoken defender of the Faith of his fathers and a stern opponent of the "arrogant, anti-Pope upstarts" who constituted the greater part of the Protestant Church in Ireland in his day. . . .

If Tom sometimes lost touch with the Faith he did not lose his reason in spite of the blandishments of the noble lords and the prizes held out to him if he would renounce his religion. Knowing how highly he valued social position, we can admire his negative loyalty all the more. His poem, *The Irish Peasant to his Mistress,* is not only one of his finest melodies, but a camouflaged piece of confession and a beautiful tribute to the Bride of Christ at the same time.

Beda Herbert<br>
Irish Monthly (February, 1952), p. 49


How songs [in *Irish Melodies*] were an immediate success and how they found their way at once into the hearts of peers and plowmen has become a familiar tale. Perhaps the greatest single reason for this appeal to the world of non-professional singers was that Moore shaped the songs to suit his own voice. Blessed with more than an amateurish interest in music throughout his life and thoroughly familiar with the works of the great English and continental composers, none the less he never pretended to be a professional musician. . . . He was inclined to trust his own innate musical sense rather than the sometimes elaborate eighteenth-century rules of composition and above all to meet the demands of his own singing, for he had a delightful voice and performed often with his own piano accompaniment. His singing apparently was less that of a trained concert vocalist than that of an itinerant harper. He refused the metronomic beat of strict tempo in favor of musical recitative, intended to bring out the full mood of the song. . . .

Critically, what can be said of . . . ["Tis the Last Rose of Summer"]? The lyrical weaknesses are evident enough. The "pathetic fallacy" is indulged to the point of sentimentality—the roses blush, give sighs, pine on the stem. Trite, stock phraseology, such as "Love's shining circle," "friendships decay," and "the gems drop away," are too patly taken from eighteenth-century verse to have freshness or force. . . . Furthermore, stanza two may seem an excessively prolonged amplification of stanza one and sentimentally weak in depicting the speaker in the poem as extending kindness by scattering leaves over the garden.

Granted all this, which seems obvious enough, why has the song survived? . . .

Marred by excessive sentimentality and triteness of wording, the song boasts a fine blending of syllable with note and a simple, clear emotion that suits well the melancholic fall of the melodic line of the music. For the critic offended by the sentimentality the song is a failure; for others it is a minor triumph. The only cardinal sin critically is to judge the poem apart from the music.

H. H. Jordan
*SEL* (Winter, 1962), pp. 405, 432, 436

# THOMAS LOVE PEACOCK
1785-1866

Born into a seafaring family, Thomas Love Peacock had little formal education. He began work as a merchant's clerk at fourteen, served in the Navy when he was twenty-three, and at thirty-four went to work at the East India House where he remained for thirty-five years. The want of schooling did not prevent Peacock from publishing a prize poem in *The Monthly Preceptor*, from studying the classics, collecting art, reading in the "Oriental Repository" at the East India House, or studying Spanish in his later years. At nineteen he published the pamphlet poem *The Monks of St. Mark*, at twenty his first full-length book, at twenty-five, *The Genius of the Thames*, one of his major poems. In 1810, he took a walking tour to Wales where he met Jane Gryffydh whom he married ten years later. One of their four children became the wife of George Meredith the novelist, but the marriage was an unsuccessful one.

In 1812, their mutual publisher Hookham introduced Peacock to Shelley, and a life-long friendship was established. Peacock tutored Shelley in Greek, hid him from the bailiff when Shelley was in debt, became sole executor of his estate after the death of Shelley's father, and wrote the memoir of his famous friend. His poetry had far less worth than Shelley's, but he excelled in the burlesque novel; satire was his forte. His romance-parodies helped end the vogue of the Gothic novel in England, and his witty attacks on Tories, authors, aesthetes, and fanatics of all sorts were entertaining as well as effective; best among them are the sharply-drawn caricatures of Southey, Wordsworth, Coleridge, and Shelley. Among his chief works are the poems *Palmyra* (1806); *The Genius of the Thames* (1810); *Rhododaphne* (1818); *The Four Ages of Poetry* (1820); and the novels *Headlong Hall* (1816); *Melincourt* (1817); *Nightmare Abbey* (1818); *Maid Marian* (1822); *The Misfortunes of Elphin* (1829); *Crotchet Castle* (1831); *Memoirs of Shelley* (1859; 1860); and *Gryll Grange* (1860).

H. F. B. Brett-Smith and C. E. Jones, eds., *Works* (1924-1934), 10 vols.

Carl Van Doren, *The Life of Thomas Love Peacock* (1911)

Peacock's novels are unique in English, and are among the most scholarly, original, and entertaining prose writing of the century. . . . His learned wit, his satire upon the vulgarity of progress, are more continuously present in his prose than in his verse; but the novels are filled with cheerful scraps of rhyming, wine-songs, love-songs, songs of mockery, and nonsense jingles, some of which are no more than the scholar's idle diversions, but others of a singular excellence. They are like no other verse; they are startling, grotesque, full of hearty extravagances, at times thrilling with unexpected beauty. The masterpiece, perhaps, of the comically heroic section of these poems is "The War-Song of Dinas Vawr," which is, as the author says in due commendation of it, "the quintessence of all war-songs that ever were written, and the sum and substance of all the appetencies, tendencies, and consequences of military."

Arthur Symons
*The Romantic Movement in English Poetry*
(London: Archibald Constable, 1909), pp. 230-31

Too full of experience to be sanguine, too uncompromising to apply any criticism but that of ideal morality, too vigorous to be wholly apathetic, incapable of changing with the times, Peacock's old age was bound to alternate between vituperative moments and the hours of happiness spent in the seclusion of his garden or study and in converse with his intimates. The remarkable lack of bitterness in *Gryll Grange* is attributable to the fact that he was growing more and more fond of the latter way of passing time, and tending less and less to hope, and therefore to care very much about public affairs. . . .

Within the frame of the actual novel, discussion has taken the place of argument—there is not a single dispute in *Gryll Grange*—tolerance of intolerance; satire is still present, but satire of a kind that springs more from love than from hate; Peacock has not even the heart to ridicule Lord Curry-fin without more than compensating for it by making him interesting and socially popular, accomplished and courageous. . . . So far *Gryll Grange* is merely an old man's edition of *Headlong Hall*. Were it not for a few outbursts, saving the book from being unduly soft, it would read almost like a general recantation. . . .

In comparison with the early novels *Gryll Grange* is as the Comedy of Manners compared with the Old Comedy. Its comment, even when topical, is generalised; the characters are shadows not of public life but of the imagination; their conversation has little allusive or extraneous interest. Yet in Peacock's creative work there is always a considerable intermixture of what is easily recognisable as his own experience and observation of his friends. How far these have entered into the characterisation and speeches of many of the persons in *Gryll Grange* it is impossible to say, although one feels perfectly sure, for instance, that he had known Miss Ilex and Miss Niphet. Yet, feeling himself to be a survival of the old days, largely out of his place and happy only in retirement, he has put himself into the book; and he has likewise introduced Shelley.

A. M. Freeman
*Thomas Love Peacock, A Critical Study*
(New York: Mitchell Kennerley, 1911), pp. 325, 329-31

Type in Peacock hardly ever passes into character. His work continually borders on character drawing, but he values the play of wit and theory too well. The whole world is a *salon* to him.

If there are any of Peacock's persons who are felt to be living human characters, they are to be found among his young ladies and his drunkards. The first are real, perhaps because they are pleasant and sensible (which few of the men are), perhaps because the author takes fewer freedoms in the portraiture. It is difficult to say exactly how they make so pleasant an impression—probably by their freedom from censoriousness, and by the good will of the other characters towards them. [1926]

Sir Walter Raleigh
*On Writing and Writers*, ed. George Gordon
(London: Edward Arnold, 1927), pp. 152-53

[In *Memoirs of Shelley*] Peacock tells a straightforward tale in a straightforward way, all the more convincing for its modesty of statement and for the plain love that inspires its impartial course. Harriet, says Peacock, was beautiful, pleasant-spoken, frank, cheerful, "and she was fond of her husband and accommodated herself in every way to his tastes.". . . The plain and tragic truth is that Shelley simply and decisively fell in love with Mary Godwin, who, in Peacock's view, was intellectually better suited to Shelley. . . .

Peacock spared nothing, and tempered nothing. Without fuss or partisanship he sets down the truth for all to see.

Humbert Wolfe
Introd., in *The Life of Percy Bysshe Shelley*
by T. J. Hogg, E. Trelawny, and T. L. Peacock, Vol. I
(London and Toronto: J. M. Dent and Sons, 1933),
pp. xxviii-xxvix

It is true, of course, that what Peacock has to offer is not everyone's dish, and he is not so great that anyone need feel under obligation to pretend to enjoy him. If you demand the grand manner or the heroic tone, he is not for you. If you must have an ingenious plot, or psychological subtlety in the study of character, or a broad social panorama, do not look to the author of *Crotchet Castle*. If you go to books for sober-sided instruction, do not go to him. But if you like good talk, you will hear in his pages some of the best that English literature affords. If you have a relish for genial satire, you will find that he is one of its masters; a marksman whose shafts speed straight to folly on the wing. If you would meet a writer whose words are always nimbly at the service of his wit, and whose wit is nearly unfailing, you should not delay meeting him. If you would sit in the best of jovial company, hour after hour, enjoying the lively play of language and ideas, with prejudice striking sparks from prejudice, and crotchet meeting crotchet in eloquent collision, then Thomas Love Peacock is your man.

B. R. Redman
*The Pleasures of Peacock*
(New York: Farrar, Straus, 1947), pp. ix-x

Many lovers of Peacock prefer *The Misfortunes of Elphin* to any of the other novels. Their reason is one—the irresisitible and unforgettable figure of the drunkard Seithenyn. He is a creation on a Shakespearean scale which Peacock never approached again.

But there are some lovers of Peacock who when they have met Seithenyn find themselves thinking—if he could do this, why did he not do it oftener? There is nothing of the mere comic silhouette or ventriloquist's dummy about Seithenyn; drink is the whole of his philosophy, but he has infinite variety in his approach to the subject. Everything that he says seems unexpected because it is so much his own. He is one of those rare characters in fiction who stand out with a glorious solidity from the first moment, making the other persons in the scene fade by comparison into mere types or shadows. . . .

*Crotchet Castle,* published two years later, in 1831, was the last novel he was to write for many years. Here we have his whole whimsical imaginative outfit most effectively and merrily assembled; and though the plot meanders as casually as ever, it inevitably gains strength and coherence from the fact that a greater number of the characters are carefully drawn than in any of the earlier books. In *Crotchet Castle* we find the immortal Dr. Folliott, and also the piquante Lady Clarinda, the romantic Captain Fitzchrome and the gentle and fearless little Miss Susannah Touchandgo—a portrait, it is thought, of Jane Gryffydh. Mr. Crotchet himself is a new and more intelligent example of the retired business man pursuing culture. . . .

Some of the conversations in *Crotchet Castle* are superb in their zest and speed of acceleration towards a climax: as when Dr. Folliott concludes his vehement protests against the alabaster Venus by upsetting himself out of his chair. This whole chapter—"The Sleeping Venus"—exemplifies the dramatic nature of Peacock's dialogue—its opening so quiet, yet so obviously charged with inflammable material. . . .

That Peacock is constantly thinking in theatrical terms may easily be overlooked by a careless reader, for he gives little indication in his text of how he is visualising a certain situation. There is no underlining of the comic intention behind the drunken Seithenyn's use of words like honourable and elasticity and his obstinate and defiant repetition of them. So too in *Crochet Castle,* the state of the love-sick Captain Fitzchrome is delicately indicated by his absent-minded efforts to contribute to a discussion to which he has not been listening.

O. W. Campbell
*Thomas Love Peacock*
(New York: Roy Publishers, 1953), pp. 63, 69-71


Thomas Love Peacock . . . stands alone and apart not only from the novelists who were his contemporaries . . . but also from the whole sequence of English novelists. He has been imitated but he has never been seriously rivaled. His work exists in a purity his disciples have not been able to match; his limits were narrow and strict, and to attempt to broaden them is merely to destroy the delicately poised world they contain. In his way Peacock achieved perfection, and more than once. . . .

For Peacock was always a poet, and he is never more a poet than in his satirical novels. . . .

Peacock's art was perfect from *Nightmare Abbey* onwards. Variation was possible, but not progression. After *Headlong Hall* his main characters are always more than the opinions they express; they have, however slightly sketched, that kind of life which makes them imaginable as living beings outside the contexts in which they exist.

Walter Allen
*The English Novel*
(New York: E. P. Dutton, 1955), pp. 145, 150-51


Thomas Love Peacock is remembered today chiefly for his witty, ironic novels of talk; he began, however, as a poet. As a young man he wrote some light, satiric verse, but during his first period (that is, before his meeting with Percy Bysshe Shelley late in 1812) he expended his major energies on poetry of more serious intent: *Palmyra and Other Poems, The Genius of the Thames*, and *The Philosophy of Melancholy*. . . .

Despite his skill, and his obvious delight, in humourous verse, the prevailing tone of Peacock's early poetry is romantic, and there is evidence in his letters to Edward Hookham, who was to be his publisher for *The*

*Genius of the Thames,* that this choice of attitude toward his material was deliberate. . . .

It was not until he turned to the novel, however, that Peacock found a literary genre to which his gifts were truly suited. With the first of these, *Headlong Hall,* it was clear that he had perfected his tone and widened the range of his subject matter to take in a great "array of false pretensions, moral, political, and literary." He had, moreover, worked out his form— the virtually plotless novel of talk, in which characters who are addicted to some single viewpoint or "crotchet" are brought together at a country house party, or in an isolated neighborhood given to visits, or sent on a journey. It was to serve, with but minor modifications, for his seven works of prose fiction and was to be, indeed, Peacock's original contribution to the form of the English novel.

K. N. Cameron and Eleanor L. Nicholes
*Shelley and His Circle, 1773-1822,* Vol. I
(Cambridge, Mass.: Harvard Univ. Pr., 1961), pp. 105-8

# MRS. ANN WARD RADCLIFFE
1764-1823

Born in London at her father's haberdashery, Ann Ward led a sheltered and quiet childhood, enlivened at times by visits to her uncle Thomas Bentley in Chelsea, where she met his partner Josiah Wedgwood and other stimulating men of the time. In 1772, she joined her parents at Bath, where her father had opened a branch for Bentley and Wedgwood. She occupied her time learning the domestic arts and reading romances. At twenty-two, she married William Radcliffe, a young journalist and Oxford graduate, whom she had known for two years. They settled in London, where William earned a meager living as a translator and reporter. To occupy her free time, she wrote *The Castles of Athlyn and Dunbayne* (1789), which her husband encouraged her to publish. Three more successful novels followed and then fame. To save her from the press of the crowd, William took her to Holland and Germany, then urged her to publish her journal of their tour. Her next novel *The Italian* appeared in 1797, and, in the same year, William purchased the *English Chronicle.* The death of her father in 1798 and her mother in 1799 left her independently wealthy, and she resolved to publish no more, for she wished now to dis- associate herself from the cheap imitations and parodies her novels had inspired. *Gaston de Blondeville,* begun in 1802, was written for her own pleasure, not for publication. Although she avoided society, she enjoyed travel within Britain, often making several trips in a single year; she liked the theater, the opera, and especially the Royal Academy, and entertained modestly at home. Shy by nature, the lady novelist who influenced so many great writers—Lewis, Scott, Coleridge, Byron, Keats, and the Brontës—was small, dark, and pretty, an incongruous figure for one so gifted in creating horror and suspense. During her life, her reputation as "magician of thrills" was based on *The Castles of Athlyn and Dunbayne* (1789); *A Sicilian Romance* (1790); *The Romance of the Forest* (1791); *The Mysteries of Udolpho* (1794); and *The Italian* (1797). *Gaston de Blondeville* (1826) and *Poems* (1834) were published posthumously.

*The Novels of Mrs. Ann Radcliffe* (1821-24); *Gaston de Blondeville* (1826), 4 vols.

M. F. McIntyre, *Ann Radcliffe in Relation to Her Time* (1920); Aline Grant, *Ann Radcliffe* (1951)

In . . . *The Romance of the Forest* (1791), *The Mysteries of Udolpho* (1794) and *The Italian* (1797), . . . motives, methods, or machineries are fully developed; and, among Mrs. Radcliffe's admirers, each has its partisans. The first is the freshest, and its heroine Adeline, perhaps, is more attractive than her successors, Emily and Ellena. The far-renowned *Mysteries* supply the fullest, the most popular and, perhaps, the most thoroughly characteristic example of the style. *The Italian* is the most varied, the least mechanical, and, in the personage of the villain Schedoni (whose almost legitimate descendant the ordinary Byronic hero undoubtedly is), has, by far, the most important and, almost, powerful character—a character not, perhaps, wholly impossible in itself, and, even if so, made not wholly improbable by the presentation in the book. [1917]

George Saintsbury
*CHEL* eds. A. W. Ward and A. R. Waller, Vol. XI
(New York: Macmillan, 1933), pp. 333-34

In *The Mysteries of Udolpho,* long tours in quest of the picturesque alternate with exciting melodrama, and the two are skilfully harmonized by her sense of atmosphere. . . . Smugglers were now available to provide a change for the tedious banditti, and there were all the rest of the novels of sensibility and romances of adventure to draw upon. Mrs. Radcliffe almost trespasses into the novel of personal relations, and almost achieves lifelikeness in the vulgar Madam Cheron, whose ambitions land her in such fearful disillusionment when she is married to the unscrupulous lord of Udolpho. But her genius is for something entirely different. The vast and gloomy and impossible castle frowning along the edge of a precipice in the Appennines is a magnificent stage for blood-curdling events; it reeks with terror, it thrills with suspense. Emily—that is the name of the heroine in the present novel . . . is filled with dark foreboding when she first sets eyes on its menacing battlements; once inside, she is prey to the ever-intensified suspense. Mrs. Radcliffe has as good a talent for grim interiors as for broad landscapes. . . . [1929]

E. A. Baker
*The History of the English Novel,* Vol. V
(New York: Barnes and Noble, 1950), pp. 197-98

Rebels in the grand manner, grandsons of Milton's Satan and brothers of Schiller's Robber, begin to inhabit the picturesque, Gothicized backgrounds of the English "tales of terror" towards the end of the eighteenth century. The little figures of banditti, which formed the pleasing decorative details in the landscapes of the Salvator Rosa school then in fashion, came to life in the writings of Mrs. Ann Radcliffe, "the Shakespeare of romance writers," and took on gigantic and Satanic proportions, becowled and sinister as Goya's bogeys. Montoni, the scoundrel and adventurer of the *Mysteries of Udolpho* (1794), takes pleasure in the violent exercise of his passions; the difficulties and storms of life which ruin the happiness of others stimulate and strengthen all the energies of his mind.

Mrs. Radcliffe's masterpiece is the character of Schedoni in *The Italian, or the Confessional of the Black Penitents* (1797). At that time the chief source of mysterious crimes . . . was to be found in the Spanish and Italian Inquisition. . . . Schedoni, therefore, is a monk; when he comes on the scene he appears as a man of unknown origin, but suspected to be of exalted birth and decayed fortunes. Severe reserve, unconquerable silence, love of solitude, and frequent penances, were interpreted by some as the effect of misfortunes preying upon a haughty and disordered spirit, by others as the consequence of some hideous crime which filled his troubled conscience with remorse. [1933]

Mario Praz
*The Romantic Agony*
(New York: Meridian Books, 1956), pp. 58-59

Her first novel had little of the melancholy, the descriptive beauty, or the power of her later works but her husband recognized in it something different from the regular run of novels of the day and a story that he felt would be popular. He had evidently had no idea how she was spending her solitary hours until that evening when Ann laughingly but half hesitantly showed him what she had been amusing herself with in his absence. William had been immediately and intensely enthusiastic.

In 1789 *The Castle of Athlyn and Dunbane* was published. The romantic scene which served as a background for this tale of death-traps, dangers, and marvelous rescues was the Highlands of Scotland. . . .

[Her last book *Gaston de Blondeville*] . . . is quite different in tone from Mrs. Radcliffe's other works and the difference is not all in the archaic words and turns of expression. Reading it is like watching a gorgeous pageant in eight scenes with a thread of drama running through the brilliant spectacle. The sentences are long and rhythmical and the detailed descriptions of costume, of the order of the feast at the King's table, the entertainment following it, of the ordered procession of the hunt and the rigid etiquette of the tournament are like so many tapestries unrolled before us. Yet there is suspense in the story of the merchant that begins so obscurely, almost hidden in the pageantry, and mounts to a climax that coincides with the great tournament that is the magnificent final gesture of the King's entertainment.

Aline Grant
*Ann Radcliffe, A Biography*
(Denver, Colo.: Alan Swallow, 1951), pp. 50, 117

Judged conventionally, Mrs. Radcliffe's Emily is a dim enough character, but she is adequate to her creator's purposes, she is incarnate sensibility, and her function in the novel is simply to feel, to feel the appropriate emotions of wonder, awe, and terror. From this point of view, *The Mysteries of Udolpho* may be considered as a machine for making the reader feel similar emotions. The *Alpes Maritimes* and castles in the Appenines, then, are just as important . . . as the characters who haunt them. It is this that is new—new because it is successful for the first time—in the fiction of Mrs. Radcliffe. In her work the characters are wholly subordinate to environment; it plays upon them, invades them, almost takes them over altogether. . . .

She placed her story, a thriller, in a situation in time where it could appear to be not improbable. And her handling of the story is brilliant. She communicates a real sense of mystery, and her management of suspense is admirable. She cheats once or twice, by modern standards, and she has been criticized for producing at the end rational explanations of what had appeared to be supernatural happenings. Here she had merely anticipated the basic logic without which the thriller cannot exist.

Walter Allen
*The English Novel*
(New York: E. P. Dutton, 1955), pp. 101-2

*The Mysteries of Udolpho* (1794), the most popular of Mrs. Radcliffe's works, exhibits all the potent charms of this "mighty enchantress.". . . It is a book which it is impossible to read and forget. Its noble outline, its majestic and beautiful images harmonizing with the scenes exert an irresistible fascination. It gradually rises from the gentlest beauty towards the terrific and the sublime.

In *Udolpho* Mrs. Radcliffe works on a broader canvas, on a larger and more sublime scale, enriches the characteristic traits of her genius, and perfects all her peculiar machinery. She has now conquered the enchanted land of romance and appears quite familiar with its massive towers and solemn glooms . . .

There is a mystic vagueness about the lovely landscape setting of Udolpho seen for the first time. Its gloom at nightfall, the ominous picture of its sombre exterior and shadow-haunted halls prepare us for the worst when we enter its portals. Our anticipation is a queer mixture of pleasure and fear, as we shudder at the impending events within its walls. Mrs. Radcliffe prepares each tragic denouement by sketches and panoramic views, which provide a backcloth for the enactment of the awe-inspiring horrors that follow in quick succession at Udolpho. . . .

*The Italian* (1707), is probably her finest work, the high-water mark of her achievement. The story is more skilfully constructed, has a greater unity of plan and concentration than *The Mysteries of Udolpho*, while her pictures are more individual and distinct, her figures more terrible, and her situations more thrilling and vivid. Although the Inquisition scenes during the later chapters are unduly prolonged, the story is coherent and free from digressions. . . .

In Mrs. Radcliffe's work there is the finest flowering of the novels of Terror. She eclipsed for a while the geniuses of Richardson, Fielding, and Smollett, but her own star dimmed at the ascendancy of Walter Scott, the Ariosto of the North.

Devendra P. Varma
*The Gothic Flame*
(London: Arthur Barker, 1957), pp. 88-89, 94-95, 98, 128

# SAMUEL ROGERS
1763-1855

A wealthy man who could be a friend of the arts without being an artist, Samuel Rogers is mainly remembered as a man of taste who entertained and aided the leading literary figures of his day in his elegant establishment at 22 St. James' Place. Born in Stoke Newington in 1763, he inherited his position in a City bank from his father, a former warehouse manager and banker. Educated at nonconformist schools, he began to write poetry at an early age. His travels took him to Scotland and France, where he met society, dined with Lafayette, and was introduced to Condorcet and de la Rochefoucauld. He acquired many of the art treasures which Napoleon had taken out of Italy and sold in Paris and was a benevolent guide to all who came to see his collection. A good friend of Sheridan and of Charles Fox, he corresponded with Wordsworth, visited with Byron in Italy, and intervened in the Moore-Byron and Moore-Jeffrey quarrels. Little of his poetry is now read, although the 1830 edition of *Italy* and *Poems* (1834) are worth seeing because of the illustrations supplied for them by James Turner and Thomas Stothard. Offered the Poet Laureateship, Rogers judged his own worth when he declined in favor of Alfred Lord Tennyson. Representative poems are *Ode to Superstition* (1786); *The Pleasures of Memory* (1792); *Epistle to a Friend* (1798);

*The Voyage of Columbus* (1812); *Jacqueline* (1813); *Human Life* (1819); and *Italy* (1822).

*Poetical Works* (1875); G. H. Powell, ed., *Reminiscences and Table-Talk of Samuel Rogers* (1903)

R. E. Roberts, *Samuel Rogers and His Circle* (1910)

We can read worse things now, but we cannot read "The Pleasures of Memory." It is not poetry, and there is nothing in its smooth commonplaces to make up for its not being poetry as, to some extent there certainly is in the later never quite so popular, *Italy.* But, before *Italy,* there had been *An Epistle to a Friend,* which begins to be more personal and thus more interesting; *The Voyage of Columbus* . . . ; and *Jacqueline,* which Byron found "all grace, and softness, and poetry". . . was actually published under the same covers with "Lara." We can read none of these now, but we can read the *Italy,* almost as if it were prose, but with no distaste at its being in verse.

Arthur Symons
*The Romantic Movement in English Poetry*
(London: Archibald Constable, 1909), p. 70

The once famous *Pleasures of Memory* are inferior Goldsmith; *Italy* and the rest are of that mediocre blank verse which is not so much "crippled" as "watered" prose; and the octosyllabics which he wrote after the popu-larity of Scott and Byron, are not very different from the least good ex-amples of Scott.

George Saintsbury
*A History of English Prosody,* vol. III
(London: Macmillan, 1910), p. 90

. . . Byron says that he continued Roger's friend "until the black drop of his liver oozed too palpably to be overlooked." The visit paid to Byron and Shelley at Pisa does not appear to have improved matters, and indeed it is clear that Byron never really wanted him to come. . . .

With the Lake Poets, on the other hand, Rogers's relations were uni-formly happy. He recognized from the beginning the genius of Wordsworth and Coleridge and Southey and he remained their constant friend, supporter and business adviser. Southey's recantation of his earlier political opinions involved some coolness between him and Rogers later on, but with Words-worth, and especially with his sister Dorothy, the friendship became increas-ingly intimate, though . . . Rogers characteristically became more critical as Wordsworth's eminence became more widely recognized. . . .

Already, before Rogers died, the public estimate of his poetry was very much what it is to-day. It was, in a sentence, damned by Byron's praise of the *Pleasures of Memory*: "There is not a vulgar line in the poem." Poetry cannot live by elegance alone. It is unfair, and indeed, except as regards metre, incorrect, to represent Rogers as of the school of Dryden and Pope. His impeccable taste and . . . "laborious artistry" were, on the contrary, essentially of his time. During Roger's later years, the wind was blowing in another direction, and it shows the soundness of his judgment that he made no attempt to catch the breeze.

Edward Boyle
*National Review* (August, 1925), pp. 89-91

In the memoirs, diaries, journals, and reviews of the first half of the nine-teenth century, Samuel Rogers . . . has an importance which is in sharp contrast to his present obscurity. It is no fault of the modern reader that he cannot remember one of Rogers' poems. Even before Rogers' death, his contemporaries had judged his work as essentially worthless, but they continued to speak with admiration of the "bard, beau, and banker" of St. James' Place. They remembered always the little house which he had made one of the great sights in London, of cultured society in the western world. Here above all was revealed Rogers the man of taste, arbiter elegantiarum, a role which he played with a curious combination of modesty, pleasure, and pride. . . .

To every visitor it was amazingly tasteful, or to use an even more favorite word, *recherché*. It was a *bijou*. It was furnished with works of art and *vertû*, not just excellence, but a pure and chaste excellence, virtue in its moral sense. These protestations of exquisiteness fall flat before the catalogued contents of the house. . . .

Rogers was not greedy of his collection; it was made to be enjoyed. His house was open to almost any person who came with a proper recommendation, and he was kind in himself showing people around. Though he received them with "cold, quiet, indiscriminate politeness," he delighted in their appreciation of his collection, which Emerson called "the chief private show of London."

Donald Weeks
*PMLA* (June, 1947), pp. 472, 483

. . . Samuel Rogers [is] the only English writer, so far as I am aware, who combined in one lifetime the somewhat disparate arts of banking and poetry. It would be idle to pretend that Rogers is a figure of importance, or one whose works literary fashion will some day rediscover. His poetry— and I have read most of it before considering myself entitled to make such a statement—is dead beyond much hope of resurrection. There was never a great deal of it, and it is one of the lasting miracles of literary history that upon so scanty a foundation he should have been able to rear so lofty a reputation.

Nevertheless, *The Pleasures of Memory* gauged the taste of the time to a nicety; it said nothing much, but it said it very smoothly, with the result that, by 1816, nineteen editions of it had been sold. As for *Columbus*, the last word may safely be left with Wordsworth: on being asked for his opinion of it, he replied, with crushing ambiguity: "*Columbus* is what you meant it to be." *Human Life* is perhaps the most readable of the longer flights, though even this Miss Mitford described as "one of those sort of poems which are very short and seem very long"; and *Italy* is certainly the most sustained and ambitious of them all. . . . There are, indeed, some good things in *Italy*, if one is prepared to dig for them, though most of them, oddly enough, are in prose. There is, pre-eminently, the famous note on Raphael's *Transfiguration*, upon which Rogers is reputed to have worked ceaselessly for a fortnight. . . .

But when all is said and done, these poems have had their day and have achieved the purpose for which they were written. . . .

Is it quite impossible to find in all his collected works any lines that serve a little to justify his pretensions? I think we may do so in at least two cases. There are, first, the touching verses that he wrote as an epitaph on the robin-redbreast of Miss Johnes of Hafod. . . . Really, well-known as it is, it is charming; and then, far less well-known are the brief lines called *Captivity*. . . .

M. Bishop
Introd., in *Recollections of the Table-Talk of Samuel Rogers*
(London: Richards Press, 1952), pp xi, xv-xvii

Justice cannot be done to the *Italy* in a few short quotations. It must be read through, not hurriedly, and be savoured as the very personal work of a man of acute and cultivated mind, simple and kindly feelings, and a highly developed talent for elegance of expression. It never falls below the level of good conversation, and in many passages rises to true poetry —not least, oddly enough in the passage where he abandons metre and writes, for a page or two, prose of an incomparable ease and lucidity. *Foreign Travel* is a faultless essay, *Marcolini* a jewel of story-telling. If only Rogers had written more! . . .

Roger Ellis
*Studi in Onore Di Riccardo Filangieri*, Vol. III
(Naples: L'Arte Tipografica, 1959), p. 183

# SIR WALTER SCOTT
1771-1832

Born in the Highlands of an old Border family, Walter Scott, later Sir Walter, was raised and educated in Scotland, served in the Scottish dragoons, studied Scottish lore, and wrote his best novels in the Scottish idiom. After a successful career as law student, sheriff, clerk of the session, editor, translator, scholar, and especially poet, he turned novelist at the age of 43 in order to increase the diminishing returns from sales of his poems. A Tory and would-be aristocrat, Scott invested heavily in an estate called Abbotsford, which he furnished elegantly and where he entertained lavishly. A business failure in 1820 and the financial crash of 1826 left him heavily indebted, and for the rest of his life he wrote rapidly, often carelessly, to repay these debts. His entire output is too numerous to list here, but among his major works are *Minstrelsy of the Scottish Border* (1802-1803); *The Lay of the Last Minstrel* (1805); *Marmion* (1808); *The Lady of the Lake* (1810); *Rokeby* (1813); *The Lord of the Isles* (1815); *Waverley* (1814); *The Antiquary* (1816); *Life of Napoleon* (1817); *Rob Roy* (1818); *The Heart of Midlothian* (1818); *Ivanhoe* (1819); *Peveril of the Peak* (1823); *Quentin Durward* (1823); *Woodstock* (1826); and *Anne of Geierstein* (1829).

H. E. Scudder, ed., *Complete Poetical Works* (1900); Andrew Lang, ed., *The Waverley Novels* (1902-1904), 25 vols.

Sir Herbert Grierson, *Sir Walter Scott, Bart.* (1938); Hesketh Pearson, *Walter Scott* (1954)

## PERSONAL

In Scott life and books interpenetrate; their call to him is a harmonious one; and together they make for him a third thing, which may be described as experience. Ballads and tales of the border he learned when young, and often by ear, not from print. He rode, and kept lively company, and read human nature, including that of lawyers, in undress. He was crossed in love, saying little; he spun a wide and a tough web of friendship with persons of all ranks; he founded a family, and, full of the romance of the soil, planted himself upon it; he became a master of humours, chronicle, anecdote, legend, dialect, costume, law, and genealogy. He read enormously, not in order to be learned, but to lengthen backwards his vivid perception of the present; seemingly at random, but unconsciously in the service of his future craft; so that when the time came, his pen went with a mysterious ease and speed, and his memory, not verbally very exact, but of the strongest kind, gave him back for use all its appropriations.
[1912]

Oliver Elton
*A Survey of English Literature. 1780-1830*
Vol. I (London: Edward Arnold, 1955), p. 298

## POEMS

Much has been claimed for Scott's poetry because of its appeal to un-poetical persons, who, in the nature of things, would be likely to take an interest in its subject-matter; and it has been thought remarkable that poetry composed, like much of *Marmion*, in the saddle, by one "through whose head a regiment of horse has been exercising since he was five years old," should have seemed genuine to sportsmen and to soldiers. . . . Scott's appeal is the appeal of prose, the thing and the feeling each for its own sake, with only that "pleasurable excitement," which Coleridge saw in the mere fact of metre, to give the illusion that one is listening to poetry.

Arthur Symons
*The Romantic Movement in English Poetry*
(London: Archibald Constable, 1909), pp. 112-13

. . . Scott had less of *musical* music in him than any recorded poet, except perhaps Shelley. . . . Yet in prosodic music there have been few apter scholars; and not many greater masters when variety and excellence are taken into joint consideration. . . .

If the man who could make this apparently loose and lounging measure suit such things . . . as the martyrdom of Constance and nearly the whole of Flodden, as the picture of the Tees and the final vengeance of Bertram in *Rokeby*, as a dozen descriptive passages in *The Lady of the Lake* and the *Lord of the Isles*, was not an artist—why, then, the Devil has at least one person's leave to fly away with this poor fine art. . . . The chief charge that can be brought against the later poems is that Scott allowed himself to slip too much into the unbroken octosyllable, on which . . . the danger of a slipshod and monotonous fluency wars and watches with ceaseless malignity.

George Saintsbury
*A History of English Prosody*, Vol. III
(London: Macmillan, 1910), pp. 77, 79

In *The Lady of the Lake* (1810), which was inspired by Scott's enthusiasm for the wild country of Loch Katrine, the plot, though better managed than the plots of the earlier poems, is subordinate to the descriptive pas-sages, to such episodes as the stag-hunt and the gathering of the clans, and to the beautiful songs, *Rest, Warrior, Rest* and the plangent *Coronach*. . . . To its lack of interest may be in part attributed the blame for the falling off in Scott's popularity which he later ascribed wholly to the emergence of Byron. The sales of *Rokeby* (1813) were alarmingly small. Scott had no intimate knowledge of the Yorkshire setting and consequently the "thunderous, cumulative topography" which is a feature of the Scot-

tish poems is diminished. The heroine is the first of various tenderly remi-
niscential portraits of Scott's first love. Of more significance is the figure
of Bertram, in whom we observe the characteristics of the Byronic hero-
type—the somber personage compounded of crime, remorse, and magna-
nimity—in all its features, antedating *Lara* by a year. . . .

He could manage mysteries fairly well (as that of the disguised King
James in *Marmion*), but he did not know the value of reticence. . . . Only
in the lyric did he curb his redundancy and often achieve a condensed
poignancy. The most memorable passage in the *Lay* is the version of the
*Dies Irae*. More stirringly than in any passage of narrative is the martial
spirit conveyed to the reader in the *Pibroch of Donald Dhu* and in *Mac-
gregor's Gathering*; and in *Proud Maisie* (the song in *The Heart of Midlothian*) romantic pathos is quintessentialized as it is in none of the long
poems or novels.

Samuel Chew
*A Literary History of England*, ed. A. C. Baugh
(New York: Appleton-Century-Crofts, 1948), pp. 1209-10

As a poet Scott did not attempt the mystical, the profound, the subtle, or
the ornate. He commanded a wider range, however, than is sometimes
recognized. In some of his lyrics, such as *The Sun Upon the Weirdlaw
Hill* and *Rebecca's Hymn*, he was successful in the noble, reflective style
of the eighteenth century. In others, like *Proud Maisie* and *County Guy*,
he could evoke an atmosphere of remoteness and wonder. His epic poetry
was a trumpet call. Much of it was composed in the saddle and avowedly
addressed to "soldiers, sailors, and young people of bold and active dis-
positions." Its spontaneity, its impetuous stride, the swift strokes of its
descriptions of nature, the animation and clarity of its battle scenes, and
its appeals to patriotic sentiment, reminded readers, more than any other
English narratives in verse, of *The Iliad*. It was a comparison which Scott
himself would have deprecated; but despite the obvious differences, the
resemblances were too many to be denied.

Ernest Bernbaum
*Guide Through the Romantic Movement*
(New York: Ronald Pr., 1949), pp. 141-42

As a poet Scott's range was very narrow; he interpreted poetry almost
entirely as balladry, and this was the kind of poetry he sought to imitate
himself. He did produce one very beautiful poem in this vein:

> Proud Maisie is in the wood
>     Walking so early;
> Sweet Robin sits on the bush,
>     Singing so rarely.

Yet within his limits he was a highly original poet in that what he achieved had never been done before in English. *The Lay of the Last Minstrel, Marmion* and *The Lady of the Lake* represented something new: they were neither ballad nor epic but written in a form and style in between. They were written, as he said of *The Lay of the Last Minstrel,* "to illustrate the customs and manners" of the periods and places he chose to describe. The stories were "romantic," high adventures of a kind as implausible almost as those found in Mrs. Radcliffe's novels. But they were very exciting stories; and the circumstances in which the actions took place were rendered with all the accuracy of Scott's antiquarian scholarship.

Walter Allen
*Six Great Novelists*
(London: Hamish Hamilton, 1955), p. 72

Scott's narratives cannot be dismissed as mere best-selling potboilers that appealed to the antiquarian taste of his day. . . . For all his antiquarianism, he was an historian, and to him history was a process. He was the first artist to conceive of history as the organic evolution of competing styles of life. His antiquarianism he could express in ballad-collecting and ballad imitating. But his instinctive apprehension of life as historical process demanded a more comprehensive form, specifically the long poetic narrative. . . .

The first of Scott's story-poems is *The Lay of the Last Minstrel,* which is narratively the weakest. . . .

But it bears the promise of Scott's peculiar development of the genre, particularly in its untiring raciness of execution, which makes one forgive him much that would be unpardonable in a more careful poet.

*Marmion* in part fulfills that promise. Here the minstrel framework is discarded, and in the long canto introductions addressed to several of his friends Scott assumes the role of minstrel himself. . . . Scott's view seems to be that past history is interesting because it bears the same relation to modern civilization that an individual's previous experience bears to his present conduct. But our general knowledge of history is confused and fragmented. The artist's task when dealing with history . . . is to give form and meaning to the incoherence of our cultural memory, so to speak. . . .

All in all, *Marmion* marks Scott's first success (though only a partial one) at the kind of narrative which blends "real" history with imaginative romance.

In *The Lady of the Lake,* Scott's best narrative poem, the mingling of these elements is handled in masterly fashion. . . . The narrative movement is fluent and coherent, though marked by several separate scenes of independent brilliance. The stag-chase opening, for example, is as skillful a beginning as one can find in narrative literature. . . .

The over-intricacy of the story of *Rokeby* as a whole springs from Scott's emphasis on character and his effort to pivot changes in the developing action upon characterization instead of situation. . . .

Oddly, *Rokeby* is weakened by Scott's effort to bring history out of the background into the foreground of his presentation. . . . In *Rokeby* the public event affects private experience, whereas in *The Lady of the Lake* the public event is affected by private experience. The importance of this reversal would be difficult to exaggerate. The earlier method encourages distortion of the historical forces involved in a particular story, the later does not. In fine, with *Rokeby* Scott makes his most decisive advance toward the form of the historical novel.

Karl Kroeber
*Romantic Narrative Art*
(Madison, Wisc.: Univ. Wisconsin Pr., 1960), pp. 169-72, 176

## THE NOVELS

*The Antiquary* is a book in which the life in time is celebrated instinctively by the novelist, and this must lead to slackening of emotion and shallowness of judgment, and in particular to that idiotic use of marriage as a finale. [1927]

E. M. Forster
*Aspects of the Novel* (New York: Harcourt, Brace, 1954), p. 62

*Old Mortality* is a novel of a very different kind. At first sight we might feel inclined to put it among the novels of action and have done with it. But it is a novel of character as well. Apart from the main action, in a different world, there are few characters, Cuddie Headrigg and his mother among them, who are not bound by the plot, and act as independently as if they were in a different novel of their own. The hero, Henry Morton, is a typical novel-of-action figure. The story could quite well be carried forward by the chief roughly characterised figures, Morton, Claverhouse, Evandale, Burley. The real children of Scott's genius, here as in the other Waverley Novels, are supernumerary. . . . Once, in Jeanie Deans, this type of character becomes the chief actor, and Scott writes the greatest of his novels. But mostly they are such as might appear in any picaresque novel, alongside Partridge, Parson Adams, or Lismahago, greater than they, but of the same family.

Scott was best, then, as a novelist of character. His heroes and heroines are wooden and unreal. The action has almost always an artificial origin. It does not arise from the passions of the hero, for the hero has generally a most gentlemanly incapacity for passion. . . . His dangers are romantic, and quite apart from the "real world"; and he returns to mediocrity and himself very little changed by them. . . . Scott's novels are the result of an unsatisfactory compromise. He is a fine novelist of action, and a great portrayer of character; and his right hand is always at war with his left. [1928]

Edwin Muir
*The Structure of the Novel*
(London: Hogarth Pr., 1960), pp. 33-36

*Ivanhoe* would live by its episodes alone, and the suspense that links one incident to the next. But there is a plot, and a better one than in most of Scott's romances, linking Ivanhoe's fortunes with those of Richard and the disordered realm to which he returns. The hero had to be rewarded with the hand and wealth of Rowena; he was "too good a Catholic to retain the same class of feelings towards a Jewess." But Thackeray was not the first to object that it would have been happier for Ivanhoe and fairer to Rebecca had she become his wife. Scott defended himself by reminding his readers that such a union would have been impossible in those days. And at the same time he stated his views on the doctrine of poetic justice. A lofty character "is degraded rather than exalted by an attempt to reward virtue with temporal prosperity." It is not well to teach the young that "Verily, Virtue has its reward. . . ." Scott would have saved himself much ingenuity and kept closer to the tenor of real life had he always observed this doctrine, and not so often twisted history and probability to make prosperous conclusions for his romantic plots. [1929]

E. A. Baker
*The History of the English Novel*, Vol. VI
(New York: Barnes and Noble, 1950), p. 180

The lasting worth of *Ivanhoe* is that, unlike its predecessors, it is a first-rate book for children, of the kind that love stories of adventure. I testify of what I know, for my introduction to the Waverleys was hearing some chapters of *Ivanhoe*—probably the siege of Front de Bœuf's castle, and the tournament—read aloud to me during an illness. I must have been too young even to question about the name of the book; for, some time after, having the free run of many book-shelves, I came—it seems to me now, by chance—on *Ivanhoe* and realised with a gasp that the whole of this marvellous book was available at my pleasure. . . . But most assuredly no one ever ordered or advised me to read this or any Waverley Novel; and from the time I first read one, my delight has lasted and increased. There should be a copy of *Ivanhoe* in reach of every child that can read. . . .

No one would particularly care for *The Abbot* were it not for the study of Mary, Queen of Scots. The immortal beauty is slightly drawn; but I

may quote an opinion about this presentment of her. After Maurice Hewlett had written his *Queen's Quair,* I asked him if he had read *The Abbot*
before writing it?" "No," he said, "but since." "And what did you think?"
"I thought," he said, "that Scott was a great swell." Hewlett knew more
of the Rennaissance world than perhaps even Scott; but I think he realised
that Scott gave a better picture of Scotland in the sixteenth century—and
of Scotland's queen—than he, for all his talent and his labour, had attained to. . . .

*Kenilworth* followed *The Abbot* in 1821. Queen Elizabeth also is approached with gloves on; but I do not know any other study of her that
makes one so ready to believe that she could charm, subjugate, and ter-
rify. Amy Robsart, too, is a moving presentment; and the whole of the
feasting at Kenilworth may rank among Scott's finest *tours de force.* Indeed, the book ranks among his best, or, if one is to discriminate further,
among those which, though excellent, are still inferior in reality and depth
to the first creations of his lusty invention. The whole intricate structure
is admirably contrived: for instance, it seems at first a straining of coinci-
dence that Tressilian, Amy Robsart's rejected lover, should find Amy in
his room at Leicester's mansion; yet the explanation when it comes is
perfectly natural. [1930]

Stephen Gwynn
*The Life of Sir Walter Scott*
(London: Thornton Butterworth, 1932), pp. 286, 299

The five novels conceived and written during the broken years [1817-1819],
represent the peak of Scott's creative power. They were the work of something less than thirty months, a fecundity for which in literary history there is scarcely a parallel. They were produced during, and in the
intervals of, deadly sickness; but, with one exception, the shadow of pain
does not fall on them, for they present the normal world of his imagination
in all its sunlit spaciousness.

In *Rob Roy* especially there is no hint of the shadows, for the quality
of delightfulness which was conspicuous in *Guy Mannering* has made it
for many good judges—Lord Rosebery was one and Stevenson another—
the favourite among the novels. . . .

In construction the novel is one of his worst. The plot is in essence
picaresque, the main interest being movement in space, but the purpose of
such movement is casually conceived. The preliminaries are out of all
decent proportion, and many a reader has stuck fast in them and never
crossed the Border. The hero is only a name, Edward Waverley many
degrees further removed from reality. . . .

Critics as diverse as Lady Louisa Stuart, Walter Savage Landor and
Edward Fitzgerald have given . . . [*The Heart of Midlothian*] first place
among his works; and, though in Scott's case the scale of precedence is

hard to fix, I think the judgment is right, for every merit which the others possess is shown here in a high degree. The first five-sixths of the book are almost perfect narrative. The start, after his fashion, is a little laboured, while he is sketching in the historical background; but when the action once begins there is no slackening, and the public and private dramas are deftly interwoven. The last chapters have been generally condemned as weak and careless, a picking up of loose ends and tying them into a clumsy knot; and indeed there is no defence to be made for the death of Sir George Staunton at the hands of his own son. There was a story there of the Greek tragedy type, but it demanded a different kind of telling; as it stands, the reader is not awed by dramatic justice but staggered by inconsequent melodrama. Yet, apart from this blemish, I feel that the conception of the Roseneath chapters is right. Scott was always social historian as well as novelist, and he wanted to show Scottish life passing into a mellower phase in which old unhappy things were forgotten. Artistically, too, the instinct was sound.

John Buchan<br>
Sir Walter Scott<br>
(New York: Coward-McCann, 1932), pp. 181-82, 188

*Rob Roy* is less of a purely historical novel than *Old Mortality*. Once again Scott turns back on his early and even recent experiences. Francis Osbaldistone is the young Scott, impatient of confinement in his father's office, a poet, a dreamer, and a lover. Not that Di Vernon is a picture of Miss Belsches. She is rather, I suspect, a reflection of the most courageous and unconventional and loyal of his early young women friends, Jane Cranstoun. The differences between Francis and his father recall probably some of Scott's own early family jars; but in the picture he has drawn of the older Osbaldistone's financial adventures and perils he cannot but be thinking of his own recent experiences "at a crisis so tremendous that" it shook John Ballantyne's soul to recall it: "Accustomed to see his whole future trembling in the scales of chance, and dexterous at adopting expedients for casting the balance in his favour, his health and spirits and activity seemed even to increase with the animating hazards on which he staked his wealth; and he resembled a sailor, accustomed to brave the billows and the foe, whose confidence rises on the eve of tempest or of battle." That is Scott as the Ballantyne's saw him in the crisis of 1813, when it seemed not unlikely that he would leave Scotland, "for I will not live where I must be necessarily lookd down upon by those who once lookd up to me." (*Letters*, IV, p. 332). . . .

The third facet of Scott's life is that vivid life of the imagination, which shines for us in the works, and that most genially and spontaneously in these early stories, "the Scotch Novels"—*Waverley, The Antiquary, Old*

*Mortality, Rob Roy,* and those which were just about to follow when Lockhart first dined with Scott—*The Heart of Midlothian, The Bride of Lammermoor, A Legend of Montrose.* How were all these composed amid so many other tasks and distractions?—There were articles for *The Edinburgh* "this for the love of Jeffrey the Editor—the first time this ten years," for *Blackwood's Magazine,* "this for love of the cause I espoused," for *The Edinburgh Encyclopaedia* on "Drama," "this for the sake of Mr. Constable the publisher," for *The Quarterly Review,* "this for the love of myself . . . or which is the same thing for the love of £100 which I wanted for some odd purpose"—so he describes some of his activities to the Duke of Buccleuch to whom, in his final illness, he is writing long letters. . . .

When that year [1818] closed Scott had actually published, or in the press, or clearly in his mind, all the great "Scotch Novels," as they were called. He had received the offer of a baronetcy, negotiated the sale of his copyrights, learned of the death of Charles Carpenter with the prospect it brought of securing his children's future and "permitting me to do something for my poor brother Tom's family besides pleasing myself in plantings and policies of biggings with a safe conscience." In November he concluded through John Ballantyne a bargain with Constable for a set of New Travels on the Continent which, however, was never written, no further visit being made to the Continent till 1831. [1938]

Sir Herbert J. C. Grierson
*Sir Walter Scott, Bart.*
(New York: Columbia Univ. Pr., 1940), pp. 158-59, 172, 177-78

The much more serious charge against Scott [in *The Antiquary*] is that he used the wrong pen, the genteel pen, not merely to fill in the background and dash off a cloud piece, but to describe the intricacies and passions of the human heart. But what language to use of the Lovels and Isabellas, the Darsies, Ediths, and Mortons! . . .

One is tempted, indeed, to suppose that he did it, half-consciously, on purpose—he showed up the languor of the fine gentlemen who bored him by the immense vivacity of the common people whom he loved. Images, anecdotes, illustrations drawn from sea, sky, and earth, race and bubble from their lips. They shoot every thought as it flies, and bring it tumbling to the ground in metaphor. Sometimes it is a phrase—"at the back of a dyke, in wreath o' snaw, or in the wame o' a wave"; sometimes a proverb —"he'll no can haud down his head to sneeze, for fear o' seeing his shoon"; always the dialogue is sharpened and pointed by the use of that Scottish dialect which is at once so homely and so pungent, so colloquial and so passionate, so shrewd and so melancholy. . . .

Scott's characters, like Shakespeare's and Jane Austen's, have the seed of life in them. They change as we change. But though this gift is an essential element in what we call immortality, it does not by any means prove that the character lives as profoundly, as fully, as Falstaff lives or Hamlet. Scott's characters, indeed, suffer from a serious disability; it is only when they speak that they are alive; they never think; as for prying into their minds himself, or drawing inferences from their behaviour, Scott never attempted it.

Virginia Woolf
*The Moment and Other Essays*
(New York: Harcourt, Brace, 1948), pp. 64-66

The dullest of the mature novels is *Peveril of the Peak*. In his prefatory letter to the book Scott admits to having fetched the Countess of Derby out of the cold grave in which she had lain for twenty years, and to making her a Catholic instead of a Huguenot. Though written in the authentic idiom it shows signs of fatigue and much of it is mere verbiage. The author knew it was not good and apologised for other defects than mere anachronisms.

Una Pope-Hennessy
*Sir Walter Scott* (Denver, Colo.: Alan Swallow, 1949), p. 90

Scott liked *The Antiquary* better than his other stories because it recalled the early scenes of his life, and he put a great deal of himself into the chief character, "Jonathan Oldbuck," who also displayed many peculiarities of his youthful acquaintance, George Constable, the man who had taught him to appreciate Shakespeare. Though Scott was steeped in Shakespeare, and could scarcely write a page without quoting or paraphrasing passages from the plays, none of the novels contains so many conscious or unconscious Shakespearean echoes as *The Antiquary,* which was due to the author's memories of George Constable. Because of its humorous revelation of Scott's personality the novel will always be popular with his admirers, and as it contains his first great character "Edie Ochiltree" it will always be ranked among his best works; but it is clear that half-way through the book he suddenly realised that he had forgotten the plot, and promptly changed the entire atmosphere of the story by dragging in the theme of the lost heir, already used in *Guy Mannering.* "Oldbuck" is the most entertaining bore in literature; his humour redeems him; and Scott himself must have tended to bore people on antiquarian matters, being saved from dullness by his sense of fun.

Hesketh Pearson
*Sir Walter Scott, His Life and Personality*
(New York: Harper, 1954), pp. 129-30

. . . *Ivanhoe,* which I cannot bring myself to believe represents Scott at his best, is commonly our introduction to Scott in childhood for another reason which now limits his circle of readers. It contains no Scots dialect. It is therefore immediately accessible to us as the greater novels are not. . . .

It is [his] . . . feeling for the historic past behind the individual that is the clue to Scott's genius. History is the fourth dimension through which his characters move. And he sees them naturally in indissoluble connection with the great historic events of their times, with those movements of feeling and ideas from the conflict of which the future will be born. The clearest instance of this is probably the beginning of *Rob Roy,* when Frank Osbaldistone goes to visit his uncle in Northumberland. The year is 1715, the year of the accession of George I to the throne. Frank's father is a merchant in London, a Whig and a dissenter, the representative, it might be said, of the new power of finance. Frank's uncle, with whom he stays at Osbaldistone Hall, belongs to an older generation, with a very different way of looking at the world. He is a Jacobite and a Catholic. And it would be possible to go through all the characters as they appear and docket them in a similar way. . . .

Walter Allen<br>
*Six Great Novelists*<br>
(London: Hamish Hamilton, 1955), pp. 83, 92

The *Waverley* novels are an extended dramatization of the valuable diversities and complexities of mankind asserting themselves against laws too abstract, too rigid, too impersonal . . . There is, also, the assertion by the vanquished of the rights that remain to them as individual human beings.

The peculiar heroism of Jeanie Deans's actions in *The Heart of Midlothian* springs from this kind of assertion. She succeeds in modifying the traditions of her people to accommodate them to the new conditions of present society without sacrificing any of their enduring virtues. . . .

Jeanie's success symbolizes the unification of individual righteousness and social lawfulness, which unification is the theme not only of *The Heart of Midlothian* but of all the *Waverley* novels. That theme, which first found expression in Romantic verse narratives, was to become—largely through the influence of Scott—one of the central and characterizing preoccupations of Victorian prose fiction.

Karl Kroeber<br>
*Romantic Narrative Art*<br>
(Madison, Wisc.: Univ. Wisconsin Pr., 1960), pp. 186-87

*The Heart of Midlothian* is nowadays in better repute than any other of Scott's novels, and Robin Mayhead voices influential opinion when he is prepared to salvage this book alone from the body of Scott's *oeuvre*. Even at that, he can really respect only the first half of the book, and in fact his case for a "deeply pondered and carefully worked-out theme"—the nature of human justice—can't be endorsed even so. (The case could be better argued, surely, with *Redgauntlet*.) Joan Pittock, rejecting Mr. Mayhead's case, reveals how low Scott's reputation has sunk when she decides that nevertheless *"The Heart of Midlothian* emerges as Scott's best novel," simply because "Scott's own national antiquarian and legal interests were called more constantly, more powerfully (but not, on the whole, more coherently and significantly) into play than elsewhere.". . .

As for *Waverley,* one important and unexpected feature of this novel is the way it profits from the seven years' gap in Scott's writing of it. For although the difference between the writing of 1805 and the rest stands out very plainly when we know to look for it, it does not jar on the reader who knows nothing about it. On the contrary it has a powerful effect on him without his noticing it. For as it happens Scott broke off the first writing at just the point where Waverley moves out of English into Scottish society; and the change in attitude and style thus corresponds with the change of social milieu, contributing at once something to the different atmosphere that Scott at this point needs to create. . . .

For my own part I am moved continually and powerfully, and it is because I am so moved that I consider *Waverley* one of the greatest novels in the language.

Donald Davie
*The Heyday of Sir Walter Scott*
(New York: Barnes and Noble, 1961), pp. 12-13, 16, 27, 38

The hero of the Waverley Novels is seldom a leader of men. He is always a potential leader, because of his rank as a gentleman. He represents, however, a social ideal, and acts or refrains from acting according to the accepted morality of his public. Law and authority are the sine qua non of his being. Nigel is emotionally justified in drawing his sword in the park, but by doing so he has broken the law. Because he represents the individual acceptance of law and authority, he can only surrender himself. The hero of the Waverley Novels stands at the beginning of a tradition of which Sean O'Faolain celebrates the close in a book called *The Vanishing Hero.* Instead of a commander, this hero is an ideal *member* of society. By Mr. O'Faolain's account, the hero vanishes when society no longer defines him: "the Hero is a purely social creation. He represents, that is to say, a socially approved norm, for representing which to the satisfaction of society he is decorated with a title." On the other hand, Mario Praz' study of Victorian fiction, commencing with Scott, is entitled *The Hero in Eclipse.* We are always in danger of a confusion of terms: it goes without saying that Mr. Praz' title refers to another person altogether, the romantic hero who is pitted *against* society. Such romantic characters figure large in the Waverley Novels, but the proper hero of Scott implicitly accepts his society. His nearly complete passivity is a function of his morality—the public and accepted morality of rational self-restraint. . . .

The passive hero is beset by a number of worries and concerns that are in no sense rational. His inactivity may be accounted for by the constraining force of his morality and by the passive ideal of civil society; but he is also prey to serious anxieties. Emotions, we have assumed, are the property of dark heroes; but the proper hero has a distinct emotion of his own. Again *The Heart of Mid-Lothian* is helpful, since Reuben Butler is an extreme case. His anxiety is exaggerated because his role is so subordinate to that of the heroine—even more so than that of Arthur Philipson in *Anne of Geierstein*.

In *The Heart of Mid-Lothian* the hero's mental state grows so intense that he becomes literally sick. Interestingly enough, the dark hero, George Staunton, also falls prey to a malady of the mind. In both cases Scott magnifies the strength of mind of his remarkably active heroine, Jeanie Deans, by contrast with the sick heroes.

Alexander Welsh
*The Hero of the Waverley Novels*
(New Haven: Yale Univ. Pr., 1963), pp. 35-36, 142

## General

Scott is a novelist over whom we shall violently divide. For my own part I do not care for him, and find it difficult to understand his continued reputation. His reputation in his day—that is easy to understand. There are important historical reasons for it, which we should discuss if our scheme was chronological. But when we fish him out of the river of time and set him to write in that circular room with the other novelists, he presents a less impressive figure. He is seen to have a trivial mind and a heavy style. He cannot construct. He has neither artistic detachment nor passion, and how can a writer who is devoid of both, create characters who will move us deeply? Artistic detachment—perhaps it is priggish to ask for that. But passion—surely passion is low brow enough, and think how all Scott's laborious mountains and scooped-out glens and carefully ruined abbeys call out for passion, passion and how it is never there! If he had passion he would be a great writer—no amount of clumsiness or artificiality would matter then. But he only has a temperate heart and gentlemanly feelings, and an intelligent affection for the country-side: and this is not basis enough for great novels. And his integrity—that is worse than nothing, for it was a purely moral and commercial integrity. It satisfied his highest needs and he never dreamt that another sort of loyalty exists.

His fame is due to two causes. In the first place, many of the elder generation had him read aloud to them when they were young; he is entangled with happy sentimental memories, with holidays in or residence in Scotland. They love him indeed for the same reason that I loved and still love *The Swiss Family Robinson.* . . .

In the second place, Scott's fame rests upon one genuine basis. He could tell a story. He had the primitive power of keeping the reader in suspense and playing on his curiosity. . . . [1927]

E. M. Forster
*Aspects of the Novel*
(New York: Harcourt, Brace, 1954), pp. 51-53

The charge against Scott's character-drawing made by hasty critics may be due to his avoidance of two habits, which have given certain novelists a specious appearance of profundity. One is the trick of dissecting a character before the reader's eyes and filling pages with laboured analysis. No doubt a certain amount of analysis is required from the writer, but Scott held it his main business to make men and women reveal themselves by speech and action, to play the showman as little as possible, to present a finished product and not to print the jottings of his laboratory. . . .

The other trick which he shuns is the spurious drama which is achieved by a frequent recourse to the pathological. Scott is honourably averse to getting effects by the use of mere ugliness and abnormality. He was perfectly aware of the half-world of the soul and glances at it now and then to indicate its presence, but he held that there were better things to do than to wallow in its bogs.

John Buchan
*Sir Walter Scott*
(New York: Coward-McCann, 1932), pp. 346-47

. . . Through his knowledge of the past and his imaginative insight, Scott developed very striking and fruitful ideas about the nature of a nation. The history of Scotland and England was not to be envisaged as that of one national type, but as that of many, some of them delightfully and humorously different from the norm. One of the reasons why his novels were superior to his poems as expressions of his full personality was that they enabled him to delineate the rich variety of those types which made their contributions to British life. Like Burke, Scott conceived of a nation not as a constitutional and legal system but as a living organism, and of its present as therefore only most superficially intelligible without a knowledge of its past. What we were today could only be appreciated through sympathetically apprehending what our forebears had been. Toward those forebears, though he never concealed the faults and limitations that commingled with their merits, Scott felt the deepest sympathy and gratitude —in which sentiments, rather than in a sense of superiority to other nations, he considered true patriotism to consist. And thus the historical novel, in the hands of its creator, became a means of national self-consciousness, self-knowledge, and patriotism.

Ernest Bernbaum
*Guide through the Romantic Movement*
(New York: Ronald Pr., 1949), p. 145

It was from his own Border country and its traditions that Scott found his way into the past. As he says himself, "He that traverses these peaceful glens and hills *must* refer his researches to antiquity." Without antiquity, ruin and battlefield, the very line of demarcation

Far in the distant Cheviot blue

are meaningless to the eye and say nothing to the imagination. With many minds this compulsion to make the place speak and tell its story seems to be a thing given by Nature, and so it was with Scott. . . .

I am building up by instance and example my conception of Scott as the founder of a new and historic school, and here let me interpose one word of caution. We are so accustomed to regard Scott as the central figure in the Romantic Movement (if you think of it as a European movement I believe the word "central" is justified), and we are so accustomed to think of the Middle Ages as the Ages of Romance, that when you go over the list of Scott's writings you are surprised to notice how rarely he goes behind the Reformation, and one must add, with how little profit. Our positive knowledge, our popular knowledge, of the Middle Ages would have been no less if Scott had laid down his pen at the last page of *The Heart of Midlothian* and resumed it only to write *Redgauntlet*. *Ivanhoe* is one of the best stories ever written, but for all it has to tell us of England in the reign of Richard I it might be inscribed "Scene —a forest. Time—as you like it": with a Saxon virago calling on Prussian deities in the idiom of Macpherson. Indeed, I am not sure that Scott did not give a lasting distortion to our conception of mediaeval history, by his fancy that Norman and Saxon persisted as consciously hostile races. . . .

To show Scott's originality and mastery in this field, take a passage from one of his poorest works, *The Monastery*, where he is describing the state of the church tenants on the eve of the Reformation. He dwells on the superior skill of those protected holders of monastic land, and, though doubtless in humble measure, their greater wealth. They are better informed, better fed, more independent, than their neighbours. From the kindly monks the boy of talent might get some learning, while the fathers of the hamlet, having more time for reflection as well as stronger motives for improving their properties, bore amongst their neighbours the character of shrewd, intelligent men who dreaded nothing more than to be involved in the feuds of secular landlords.

Now here you have, it seems to me, a new type coming into existence, the result of certain peculiar circumstances which could only exist in a border country remote from the control of the Crown. . . . They are not a yeomanry, open-handed and careless; they are a true peasantry, and one which, we all know, has exercised a profound influence on our civilization throughout the world. . . .

I must not linger even on the outskirts of this illimitable theme. But I should like to point out that romance, being in its origin a local sentiment, gave a new significance to place, to the scene of action; and it was Scott who first applied the incoming craft of local description to the composition of history. [1948]

G. M. Young
*Essays by Divers Hands, Transactions of the Royal Society
of Literature* (Oxford Univ. Pr., 1950), pp. 72-77

Scott's characters are embedded in a context of tradition. Historic and social processes crystallize out in his dramatis personae. It is in that sense that he made history live, but the history lives because of the characters. This may be seen in any one of his novels. . . .

Scott grasped, as no other English novelist has done, the organic relationships between man and man, man and place, man and society, and man and his past, the impersonal past of history.

Walter Allen
*The English Novel*
(New York: E. P. Dutton, 1955), pp. 127, 129

While there are few writers whose achievement is more difficult to assess, it is clear that Scott's importance is very great. The popularity of his books was prodigious: their circulation exceeded that of the work of any earlier novelist and revolutionized the status of the novel as a vendible commodity. That it has now been the dominant literary form for more than a century is in a considerable measure due to him. Richardson and Fielding had established the novel: Scott made it irresistible. He also confirmed its respectability, which had remained in some doubt throughout the previous century. . . . He gave the historical romance a new popularity and a new prestige. He also did something more important. If the nineteenth century was to prove (among other things) the Age of History, the period in which mankind became more conscious of historical perspectives than it had ever been before, it was due to no one more than to Scott.

Ian Jack
*Sir Walter Scott*
(London and New York: BC/Longmans, 1958), pp. 30-31

What we have in Scott's *Dryden* is a masterful picture of the period, with literature in the foreground and the great figure of the most important man of letters of the age as the highlighted center of interest. It is true that in one major respect the picture is only partially successful: Scott was forced to fill out the portrait of his central figure with assumption and conjecture, for he had only a few known personality traits to work with. Since the research for the past hundred and fifty years has failed to turn up the kind of material which would help scholars to develop a full account of Dryden's personality and character. . . . It can safely be said that no one yet has given us a clearer view of Dryden's personality than Scott. And as compensation for his imperfect delineation of the poet, we have the magnificent panorama of Restoration social, cultural, and literary history—surely reward enough and to spare for any reader.

Bernard Kreissman
Introd., in *The Life of Dryden* by Sir Walter Scott
(Lincoln, Nebr.: Univ. Nebraska Pr., 1963), pp. viii-ix

# PERCY   BYSSHE   SHELLEY

1792-1822

The son of a Sussex knight, Percy Bysshe Shelley was born at Field Place the family estate, and like many a squire's heir was educated at Syon House Academy and Eton. He was sent to Oxford, too, but was sent down for authoring a pamphlet called *The Necessity of Atheism*. Soon after his expulsion, he married Harriet Westbrook, a sixteen-year-old friend of his sister. During the next three years, he made political tours of Britain, wrote pamphlets, and delivered inflammatory speeches to working-class audiences. He became the father of two children, met William Godwin whose philosophy he admired, fell in love with Godwin's daughter Mary, and eloped with her to Europe in 1814. After Harriet Westbrook's suicide in 1816, Shelley married Mary and in 1818 returned to Europe where he spent the remainder of his short life. Two of his and Mary's children died in Italy, and Shelley himself drowned during a storm in the Gulf of Spezia on July 8, 1822.

Radical in politics, abstruse in philosophy, abstract in poetry, and immoral by conventional standards of behavior, Shelley achieved little recognition as a poet during his life and was frequently misunderstood even by his close friends Lord Byron and Leigh Hunt. A controversial figure in literary circles since his own day, his works continue to be read, nevertheless, by both admirers and detractors, who generally agree, however, that his most important poems are *Queen Mab* (1813); *Alastor* (1816); *Laon and Cythna* (*The Revolt of Islam*) (1817); *The Cenci* (1819); *Ode to the West Wind* (1819); *Prometheus Unbound* (1820); *To a Skylark* (1820); *Adonais* (1821); *Epipsychidion* (1821); *Hellas* (1822); and *The Triumph of Life* (1822).

Roger Ingpen and Walter E. Peck, eds., *The Complete Works of Shelley* (1926-30), 10 vols.

Newman I. White, *Shelley* (1940), 2 vols.

## PERSONAL

Shelley's development, as a thinker, a poet, and a responsible member of society, [grew] from the attitude of revolt, through conflict and suffering, to the attitude of compromise in his relation with the world and with his own soul. . . . Several interests . . . occupied his thought—politics, religion, benevolence, poetry, love—and [he was] . . . not merely . . . a dreamer and a romantic poet of idealism, but . . . an earnest and perplexed citizen of the actual world, struggling to adjust himself to his environment, to secure his own happiness, and to achieve success in the work that he conceived to be his particular contribution to human welfare.

Floyd Stovall
*Desire and Restraint in Shelley*
(Durham, N.C.: Duke University Pr., 1931), p. vii

From descriptions of Shelley during the previous year, it is possible to get a fairly adequate notion of his physical appearance as he left England for ever [in 1818]. He was a young man midway between twenty-five and twenty-six years of age, round-shouldered, narrow-chested, slender, and of somewhat better than average height when he abandoned his habitual stoop and stood erect. . . .

His manners were gentle and sympathetic, with a simple native dignity born of his sincerity. Intimates like Hogg, Peacock, and Hunt soon learned that occasional unconventionalities were merely the unconscious expression either of abstraction or of sudden impulse. He had learned by bitter personal experience that intense conviction and utter sincerity of purpose, even when reinforced by extensive reading and study, are no guarantees against misunderstanding and partial frustration. The shock of this surprising discovery—the knowledge that even his particular idol, the author of *Political Justice*, could not do him personal justice—depressed and sobered him. [1940]

Newman Ivey White
*Shelley*, Vol. II (New York: A. A. Knopf, 1947), pp. 556-57

The Shelley who departed from England in March, 1818, was beginning to be a public character. He had been recognized as a poet of original tone, style and subject, fertile in mighty visions such as the age was expecting from its artists, abounding in expressions sublime and beautiful. He was known and feared for his reputed views, even for his real ones —absurd, abominable, yet some morning (God forbid) they might become part of the presaged uprising of "the mob." Of his personal habits and acts many a wicked whisper was going round. It was certainly an exaggeration that he had murdered his first wife, but epicures of crime were most unwilling to hear that he had not. Occasionally someone would speak up in public for Shelley, but then it could hardly be in any quarter except where his associates were supposed to be of the same hell-fire club. The Lord Chancellor . . . had obviously been horrified by Shelley or he could not have made the resounding decision that he must not have his own children with him. Nevertheless Shelley's last days in London were not disturbed by any incident arising from these causes; he was not expelled thence in any sense but one: his own sense that however delightful the face of England's capital was, behind it lay terrible chaos. [1946]

Edmund C. Blunden
*Shelley. A Life Story* (New York: Viking Pr., 1947), pp. 203-4

In Shelley's professions—and they are many—of what he was or wished to be he is often the soldier of freedom, dauntless in suffering or defeat, or the lover of men whom, for the truth he told them, they branded and cast out. At other times he is a youth of noble nature and lofty aims consumed by a fever of the soul and bound for early death. The portrait is in the main just, and the two sorrows, from without and from within, are history. "A man," wrote Carlyle, "infinitely too weak for that solitary climbing of the Alps which he undertook in spite of all the world. A haggard existence, that of his." But it was the trouble at the heart's core, and not the trouble in the world that made him the supreme lyrist of our tongue, for poetry begins at home.

A. M. D. Hughes
*The Nascent Mind of Shelley* (Oxford Univ. Pr., 1947), p. 245

Shelley could not tolerate frustration or suppression. Not that he was habitually irascible; on the contrary, he was easygoing, humorous, and agreeable in his daily living. But any powerful frustration produced an emotional crisis, a reaction doubtless having its base in some early "spoiling" of a first son in a family of girls. Fundamentally, as all his friends agree, he was unusually warm-hearted, loving, and generous. But along with this capacity to love went an equally strong capacity to hate. And

Shelley turned on those whom he considered to have injured him, with cold fury—e.g. the Lord Chancellor, Southey, the Westbrooks; others he seems to have deliberately blotted out of his life. The lack of any kindly mention of his parents in his later letters, for instance, is remarkable, and it is hard to forget or to forgive the comment on the "foolish dedication [of *Queen Mab*] to my late wife." We seem to be confronting a rejection pattern with deep roots.

K. N. Cameron
*The Young Shelley. Genesis of a Radical*
(New York: Macmillan, 1950), p. 9

Shelley's voice of 1822 is, in every sense, the voice of a seer, *non mortale sonans*. Ariel in a sense he had become—not the ballet-fairy Ariel of M. Maurois's popular fantasy but an Ariel endowed with peculiarly Shelleyan attributes: a man half disembodied, half of him a far-flying Platonic daemon, half of him a mortal still having "no fears and some hopes" about what lay beyond the Veil and ready, like Prospero's servant, to be released from the world of shifting semblances, conscious enough of "some fault of his" which had made his mortal life so difficult—chiefly, it may be, the fault of letting some of his dreams aspire too absurdly far.

Neville Rogers
*Shelley at Work* (Oxford Univ. Pr., 1961), p. 194

## MARY SHELLEY

Mary was from the beginning a very cautious diarist, fully realizing the possibility that her journal might be read by others. One has merely to inspect the journal through certain critical periods in the life of the Shelleys to find out how cautious Mary was. For one thing, there is almost a complete absence of direct information about Claire, and absolutely nothing explicit about Claire and Byron. Mary does not even mention the birth of Allegra at Bath on January 12, 1817. In fact, she even uses a little camouflage by recording several days after the event, "Four days of idleness." The death of Harriet is merely, "A letter from Hookham with the news of the death of Harriet Shelley." The death of Mary's first child is only, "Find my baby dead. . . . A Miserable day." The birth of Clara is simply, "I am confined Tuesday 2nd." The death of her darling William is not recorded at all.

F. L. Jones
*Mary Shelley's Journal*
(Norman, Okla.: Univ. Oklahoma Pr., 1947), p. viii

While Shelley was alive she reflected some of his radiance. His friends accepted her as Shelley's attractive mistress and later, as his wife, if they would rather have been spared her company as the intelligent, reflective, detached daughter of William Godwin and Mary Wollstonecraft. But at Shelley's death the magic circle dispersed; and Mary lived to feel the disenchanted gaze of Shelley's friends upon her. . . .

The reasons for this reside partly in Mary's own nature. She was well aware that she was considered a cold, unemotional woman. She was one in whom passion was very strongly restrained, due largely to the inhibiting effect of her early life in an "enlightened' and bleakly rationalistic atmosphere. She was never, like most of her female contemporaries, taught the arts of womanliness, and in an age when men expected women to studiously reveal a desire to please them, the increasing substantial seriousness of Mary Shelley's bearing appalled and scared the life out of these friends of earlier, flimsier days. There was also in her a strain of the Wollstonecraft melancholy which had driven her mother to attempt suicide on two occasions and her sister, Fanny Imlay, to commit it. . . .

On the whole, Mary has never been properly credited with the integrating influence she exerted over Shelley, to which he himself admitted. The wonderful spirit of understanding which existed at the outset of their life together had a most unifying effect on Shelley's later work; and students of the creative mind might do well to consider Shelley in this light. For in Mary, Shelley found for the first time combined erotic and intellectual elements. . . .

Muriel Spark
*Child of Light. A Reassessment of Mary Wollstonecraft Shelley*
(Hadleigh, Essex: Tower Bridge Publications, 1951), pp. 3, 32

She won the love of Shelley and at least a part of the fickle affections of Trelawny; she was courted by John Howard Payne and Prosper Mérimée; she was liked and respected by the Hunts, the Lambs, the Novellos, the Gisbornes, Bryan Procter, Sir John Bowring, Robert Dale Owen, and— at certain moments—Lord Byron. She proved herself a woman not only of charm but also of a liberal and independent mind. After Shelley's death, it is true, she slipped more easily into the ways of polite society. . . .

At the age of eighteen Mary Shelley wrote *Frankenstein*, a horror story which is at the same time a surprisingly mature study of loneliness and of the effect of environment. Stimulated by its success and encouraged by Shelley she continued to write during his life; after his death she wrote and published for twenty years more. . . .

In spite of a little turn for irony, sporadically directed at her characters or her friends or herself, Mary Shelley was a romantic. In her actions, in her enthusiasms, and especially in her choice and treatment of subject and character in her writings, she showed her preference for those exotic and emotional elements that marked the literary movement of her time.

Elizabeth Nitchie
*Mary Shelley* (New Brunswick, N.J.:
Rutgers University Pr., 1953), pp. xii-xiii, 107

## Queen Mab

The poem was written by Shelley when he was eighteen, and, whatever promise it may show, is a crude and juvenile production. [1932]

Sir Paul Harvey
*The Oxford Companion to English Literature*
(Oxford Univ. Pr., 1946), p. 648

*Queen Mab* . . . was not, contrary to the widely circulated belief, a post-adolescent product, either in whole or in part. Shelley, when he wrote it, had considerable political and literary experience behind him. . . .

And, in the deepest sense, *Queen Mab* is original. In spite of the wide reading behind it, it is not a bookish poem but a poem arising from life, the reaction of a mind sharpened by shattering experience to the social realities of the world around it, and transmitting material in the crucible of this experience. It is the bitter and angry cry of a young revolutionary, its visionary penetration that of a man rising on the wave of titanic historical struggle to see deep and far, farther and deeper in essentials than many later and more particularized thinkers. . . .

That the style of the poem has some weaknesses of immaturity is undeniable and inevitable. Shelley is, at times, unable to sustain a passage when sustained power is needed, and the emotion, starting with vigor, sometimes thins to brittleness. Other passages lose the effect of suggestion through prosaic directness and over-elaboration. But the degree of one's sensitivity to these faults depends largely on one's reaction to the content.

K. N. Cameron
*The Young Shelley. Genesis of a Radical*
(New York: Macmillan, 1950), pp. 240-42

When *Queen Mab* is studied in relation to Shelley's whole development as a poet, it is possible to see his mature vision adumbrated in it. The view of the transforming power of the imagination is there. The Orphic myth underlying his apocalyptic vision is present. The doctrine of Eros derived from Plato's *Symposium* is suggested. However crudely and diffidently, Shelley in *Queen Mab* is moving into that psychic domain which he was destined to accept as his "proper post." Nor can it be said that he left the rationalism of such men as Godwin behind; rather, he transformed it into an imaginative vision. Shelley's quest was, in part, a search for the imaginative form of his early radical ideas.

R. G. Woodman
*The Apocalytic Vision in the Poetry of Shelley*
(Toronto: Univ. Toronto Pr., 1964), p. 86

## Alastor

With the composition of *Alastor* Shelley commenced his work as a true poet, conscious for the first time of the power of the creative spirit within him. . . .

Floyd Stovall
*Desire and Restraint in Shelley*
(Durham, N. C.: Duke Univ. Pr., 1931), p. 141

*Alastor* takes up the theme of isolation. The word in Greek means an avenging demon; it is not, it would appear, the name of the hero of the poem. Its subtitle is "The Spirit of Solitude," and this is the Alastor that pursues the young poet-hero—at least if we are to believe Shelley's preface: "The poet's self-centred seclusion was avenged by the furies of an irresistible passion pursuing him to speedy ruin." It must be confessed that the moral is less evident in the poem itself, where the hero's loneliness on earth is viewed with complacency, if not approval. The poem is a dreamlike allegory of the fate of the poet in the world. [ca. 1951]

Graham Hough
*The Romantic Poets* (New York: W. W. Norton, 1964), p. 129

It should be observed that images and symbols of light and harmony have the same dominant roles in Shelley's presentation of vision motifs in *Alastor* that they have in the *Hymn to Intellectual Beauty* and in comparable parts of other ideal poems. In *Alastor*, too, rainbow coloring and Aeolian music are employed as special aspects of visionary light and harmony in ways that are characteristically Shelleyan. . . . Just as this poem gives the first of Shelley's imaginatively detailed and intricate treatments of the vision narrative, so also it is his first attempt to develop an elaborate synesthetic pattern as an essential element of that narrative. The central device of this synesthetic pattern is the air-prism, designed especially to express a height of visionary awareness in the nameless hero. . . . The symbolic relationships and fusions of the air-prism enhance the organic integrity of the poem. . . . In short, the air-prism device uses intersense harmony to illustrate profound reaches of insight within a theme that deals fundamentally with the apprehension of a single, all-pervasive harmony. Such a theme demands a vehicle which will support its organic complexity, and in *Alastor* it is the synesthetic concept of the air-prism which most notably implies and realizes the fusion of superficially disparate descriptive, figurative, and symbolic strains.

Glenn O'Malley
*Shelly and Synesthesia*
(Evanston, Ill.: Northwestern Univ. Pr., 1964), pp. 56-57

## Ode to the West Wind

The sweeping movement of the verse, with the accompanying plangency, is so potent that, as many can testify, it is possible to have been for years familiar with the Ode—to know it by heart—without asking the obvious questions. In what respects are the "loose clouds" like "decaying leaves"? The correspondence is certainly not in shape, colour or way of moving. It is only the vague general sense of windy tumult that associates the clouds and the leaves; and, accordingly, the appropriateness of the metaphor "stream" in the first line [of Stanza II] is not that it suggests a surface on which, like leaves, the clouds might be "shed," but that it contributes to the general "streaming" effect in which the inappropriateness of "shed" passes unnoticed. . . .

Here, clearly, in these peculiarities of imagery and sense, peculiarities analysable locally in the mode of expression, we have the manisfestation of essential characteristics—the Shelleyan characteristics as envisaged by the criticism that works on a philosophical plane and makes judgments of a moral order. In the growth of those "tangled boughs" out of the leaves, exemplifying as it does a general tendency of the images to forget the status of the metaphor or simile that introduced them and to assume an autonomy and a right to propagate, so that we lose in confused generations and perspectives the perception or thought that was the ostensible *raison d'etre* of imagery, we have a recognized essential trait of Shelley's: his weak grasp on the actual. [1936]

F. R. Leavis
*Revaluation* (London: Chatto and Windus, 1956), pp. 204-6

To Mr. Leavis's objections to the comparison of "loose clouds" with "decaying leaves" one can only assert that there are quite adequate resemblances between them. The clouds and the leaves are carried in precisely the same fashion by the power of the wind. Furthermore, the resemblance holds for shape and color as well as movement. Swift-flying clouds may present the same angularities as leaves, and leaves flying horizontally through a gray sky will take the hue of their surroundings. But to attempt to defend in turn the visual particularity of each image is to miss the true point: that the controller, organizer, and unifier of the scene is the power of the west wind, which is also the point of the poem. Mr. Leavis appears to be isolating some archetypal cloud and leaf from their relationships with the wind and with the composition of the scene. "The kind of reading" which he would evidently apply is inappropriate to the poem, obscures its true design, and if employed in this spirit would demolish any poetry whatsoever. [1949]

R. H. Fogle
*The Imagery of Keats and Shelley*
(Hamden, Conn.: Archon Books, 1962), pp. 265-66


. . . In *Promotheus Unbound* Shelley's imagination seizes only upon the sudden moment of conversion. For social revolution and the utopian order will result from the descent of numinous forces into human life, and, in this context as in others, man is passive to the sudden visitations of transcendence. This, indeed, is the theme of the *Ode to the West Wind.*

For the West Wind symbolizes something more than a spirit of social revolution. As Fogle remarks, "The West Wind is an absolute and hidden power which informs all things." It is akin to the unseen Power which occasionally visits the mortal world. . . .

Being both "destroyer and preserver," the wind symbolizes the destruction and regeneration which are twin aspects of any sudden revolution.

Having thus implicitly converted the wind to a symbol of a numinous force making for change in the social order, the poet can pray to be identified with the wind. In so doing, he finds a symbolic ground for optimism. His principles must triumph because they are urged by its irresistible violence.

David Perkins
*The Quest for Permanence* (Cambridge, Mass:
Harvard Univ. Pr., 1959), pp. 163, 165


## Prometheus Unbound

He stands in the lap of patient Nature and twines her loosened tresses after a hundred wilful fashions, to see how she will look nicest in his song.

This it was which, in spite of his essentially modern character as a singer, qualified Shelley to be the poet of *Prometheus Unbound,* for it made him, in the truest sense of the word, a mythological poet. This childlike quality assimilated him to the childlike peoples among whom mythologies have their rise. Those Nature myths which, according to many, are the basis of all mythology, are likewise the very basis of Shelley's poetry. [1899; 1908]

Francis Thompson
*Shelley* (London: Burns and Oates, 1909), pp. 46-47

I have re-read *Prometheus Unbound*, which I had hoped my fellow-students would have studied as a sacred book, and it seems to me to have an even more certain place than I had thought among the sacred books of the world. [1900]

W. B. Yeats
*Essays and Introductions* (New York: Macmillan, 1961), p. 65

The poem appeals at once to our yearning for universal sympathy and to our yearning for human perfection. These two sentiments, when stimulated, tend to diverge and to develop themselves in competition with each other. But Shelley will not have them do so. From the first, he keeps winding and fusing them together in a single stream of undifferentiated emotion. . . . Prometheus and Asia . . . are not married, but merged. The poem as a whole frustrates and repels our poetic sense by attempting the music of the spheres on a single string.

G. R. Elliott
*The Cycle of Modern Poetry*
(Princeton, N.J.: Princeton Univ. Pr., 1929), pp. 17-18

The Promethean Age of Shelley's vision is one in which mankind has cast out hate and fear, has destroyed the evil deity of its own creation, and through its mastery of science controls the forces of nature. . . .

Shelley's belief that man's physical perfection was to be coincident with his moral regeneration and that all nature, animate and inanimate, would share in his liberation from pain and sin was expressed in *Queen Mab*. Therein an evolutionary process in the attainment of this goal was clearly stated. In *Prometheus* the evolutionary emphasis is not so explicit. . . . For dramatic effectiveness, in *Prometheus* the conflict of man with his own evil nature and with his environment is externalized. Jupiter is the adversary in the struggle whose climactic moments are the theme of the drama. The change, therefore, in the Titan's soul and the resultant change in all nature is catastrophic, dramatically much more effective than the story of a slow evolution but false to fact. Shelley, in short, is speaking in the form of a parable.

To the theme of man's moral regeneration and the consequent transformation of the physical universe common to *Queen Mab* and *Prometheus*, Shelley in the latter poem adds the thought of man's mastery through science of the forces of nature. . . .

The Prometheus myth itself allegorizes man's conflict with the forces of nature and predicts his mastery of them. Shelley's greatness lies in his power to discern relationships among diverse ideas, to synthesize them, and to express them in memorable and beautiful form. . . .

The importance that attaches to *Prometheus Unbound* is, in my belief, as much philosophic as poetic. That Shelley's scientific conception of the universe was very much like our own has this significance chiefly; the problem which he sought to solve is, in its terms, the problem which we have set ourselves: to reconcile materialistic with mystical thought or, as we inadequately phrase it, "science and religion.". . . Once understood his statement of it is, indeed, very much like ours. Whether his solution will generally commend itself remains to be seen. My own belief is that *Prometheus Unbound* is not only a beautiful poem but necessarily, if beautiful, filled with stimulating and profound ideas. I think it one of the few great philosophical poems in English.

C. H. Grabo
*A Newton Among Poets* (Chapel Hill, N. C.:
Univ. North Carolina Pr., 1930), pp. 195-98

The drama of the tangible stage has laid upon it the duty of being the critic, interpreter and reflector of human life. The drama of the human spirit, composed by the creative impulse of humanity, not merely by its generative fever, enacted in the light of the sun, not in the shadows cast by the moon or the limelight, demands that life shall reflect and ultimately embody it.

Shelley's *Prometheus Unbound* is a drama of this order. We do not go to it for facts concerning early Greece or the Europe of 1820, but for fundamental verities that are clamped to no age and are therefore current in and applicable to all ages and places; ideas and thoughts that "look before and after" towards a golden age of "what is not" but was and will be; an age which, because humanity has set out a circumnavigation that will bring it back to its native harbour in the realm of the spirit, is at once in the romantic past and still more romantic future.

James H. Cousins
*The Work Promethean: Interpretations and Applications of
Shelley's Poetry* (Madras, India: Ganesh and Co., 1933), pp. 22-23

Benevolence is the true character of man. To this Godwinian teaching, [Shelley] . . . adds, in the first Act, the lesson of his own adventuring: that benevolence is unchained by suffering, by repentance of scorn and hatred, by pity for the wicked, by unfailing fidelity to the higher vision, and by love. In the second Act, he adds the Platonic dream that this innate beauty is redeemed from decay by visitations of the Idea, or Reality, of Beauty; and imagines an outer world brought into conformity with this innate beauty by the destruction of the horrors of injustice, intemperance, and hatred. Then, in the third Act, he avers that Life, which is a veil of this spirit, had better be called Death, for death has long since become his symbol of all imperfection, ugliness; but what he and other men have called death, is the true life, the greatest visitation of the divine. . . . Thus, at last, in the triumph of benevolence and beauty over the ugliness that is falsely called life, a perfect moral character is achieved. The emotional harmony of that character, and a sympathetic harmony, or peace, in all natural things, overflows into the lyrics of the fourth Act. . . .

The unbinding of Prometheus is in fact a story of what has actually happened, in some degree short of the ideal perfection, to each of countless individual men. But the perfecting of society is a story of what has never happened, or what perhaps never can happen until there is a biological change in the fundamental nature of man.

May one not be warranted, then, in detecting . . . a movement, unrealized by the poet himself, away from the preoccupation with the perfection of society toward the perfecting of the individual?

Benjamin Kurtz
*Pursuit of Death: A Study of Shelley's Poetry*
(New York: Oxford Univ. Pr., 1933), pp. 187-89

What we really have in *Prometheus Unbound*, above all else, is a drama of the individual human soul, and its effort to free itself from the evil within and without. Prometheus' punishment and suffering is that which every person must pass through who would gain self-mastery. He is tempted first to surrender his individuality, his own sense of right and wrong, in order to escape from pain; he is tempted to sell his soul by conforming to the way of the world—"the world" in exactly the Christian sense. He is then tempted from within—as a man, rejecting the dull stagnation of common life, should become embittered, and either retire from the world or prey upon it, instead of trying to make it better.

Ellsworth Barnard
*Shelley's Religion* (Minneapolis, Minn:
Univ. Minnesota Pr., 1936), pp. 122-23

As a drama, even for the study, it is nothing. As a contribution to political science it is worthless. As a work of moral philosophy it is as vain as Shelley's own principles. Yet what magnificent blank verse! And what swift and beautiful songs! The imagery of the poem is a rainbow. In fact, the poem itself is a mirage; and a mirage is beyond condemnation. It may be unsubstantial, even illusion, but it is radiant, beautiful and iridescent.

George Cowling
*Shelley and Other Essays*
(Melbourne, Australia: Melbourne Univ. Pr., 1936), p. 64

The fourth act . . . is an intoxication, a riot, a complicated and uncontrollable splendour, long, and yet not too long, sustained on the note of ecstasy such as no other English poet, perhaps no other poet, has given us. It can be achieved by more than one artist in music: to do it in words has been, I think, beyond the reach of nearly all. It has not, and cannot have, the solemnity and overwhelming realism of the *Paradiso*, but it has all its fire and light. It has not the "sober certainty of waking bliss" which makes Milton's paradise so inhabitable—but it sings from regions in our consciousness that Milton never entered. [1939]

C. S. Lewis
in *English Romantic Poets,* ed. M. H. Abrams
(New York: Oxford Univ. Pr., 1960), p. 266

*Prometheus* has a mass and weight, a majestic and slow glacier-like movement, quite different from the earlier poem [*The Revolt of Islam*]: it is truly dramatic rather than narrative. . . .

We might point in *Prometheus* to (i) profound myth and (ii) profound thought. But there is a passage in Act IV . . . devoted to the Child-Spirit, where a perfect *fusion* of the mythopoeic and philosophical faculties is both the subject of the passage and in strong technical evidence while we read. The metaphysical symbolism matches in quality Coleridge's highly condensed *Kubla Khan* and Yeats's two *Byzantium* poems. To call it a statement of "ultimate reality" reduces it to triteness, but it is certainly no less. [1941]

G. Wilson Knight
*The Starlit Dome* (New York:
Barnes and Noble, 1960), pp. 204, 219

[In *Prometheus*, Act IV] the astronomer in Shelley joins with the bright lyrist in the imagined interplay of moon and earth, which even for him is a remarkable episode—for nobody else could have dreamed so of the love between those two, and he writes as though it was an easy thing to present. It is the utmost assertion in all his writings of his creed of love, one and the same whether felt by man and woman or by whatever is, and while we hear with wonder the voices of his "lamps of heaven," and confess that they are the imaginary voices of nature, we know that human wooing has never been more beautifully remembered. [1946]

Edmund Blunden
*Shelley. A Life Story* (New York: Viking, 1947), pp. 257-58

. . . *Prometheus Unbound* [is] . . . the first great poem in the canon as well as Shelley's first successful attempt to synthesize the ideas which he had handled (separately or confusedly) in the works of his apprentice period.

Like *Alastor*, the *Prometheus* is a poem about a situation in the human mind. It is presented in a non-historical context because, although it has a bearing on every moment of man's existence, the situation has no history. Like *Alastor*, too, and like *The Revolt* (though much more subtly and satisfactorily), the *Prometheus* utilizes the psyche-epipsyche concept. Like *The Revolt* it places the responsibility for ridding the cosmos of evil squarely in the hands of virtuous and thoughtful leaders. The real philosophical advance here is the development of the idea that evil is largely, though not by any means entirely, the result of spiritual blindness, and that if man were able, by an act of willed spiritual self-reform, to overcome at some great hour his inheritance of hate and superstition, there would be almost no limits to what he could think and do.

Carlos Baker
*Shelley's Major Poetry* (Princeton, N.J.:
Princeton Univ. Pr., 1948), pp. 6-7

It is well at the beginning . . . to observe a certain weakness in Shelley's mind which it is impossible to overlook. This weakness was a willingness to obtain emotional satisfaction at the expense of a certain honesty, and along lines which his imagination and thought in strictness forbade him. He was too often the victim of high emotions for their own sake; and to enjoy them he was unwilling to acknowledge that they were incoherent with the general pattern of his sensibility. He was, that is to say, excessively given to "enthusiasm," and too little critical of the conditions under which alone such enthusiasm may be properly permitted. Of all the great Romantic poets, Shelley most justifies the suspicion felt by a colder age for strong feeling; and in this bad sense Shelley is the most typically Romantic poet. This weakness in Shelley can be illustrated . . . from *Prometheus*. . . .

We are aware that . . . rhetorical imprecision is being exercised to obscure a state of affairs not likely to satisfy all emotional demands. [See, for example, *Prometheus*, III.iv.] Shelley is trying to obtain an emotional satisfaction through the mere cloudy use of words. . . . And the language only too readily lends itself to veiling this fact instead of stating it. It is the language of enthusiasm where we might have expected the language of dismay. This is the kind of disingenuousness which frequently mars Shelley's work. [1948]

D. G. James
*The Romantic Comedy* (Oxford Univ. Pr., 1963), pp. 65-66

*Prometheus Unbound* is not a prophecy but a challenge. It is concerned not with events in time but with the eternal situation of man and the universe. Shelley was always seeking for a single abiding reality behind the multiplicity of transient things, and his mind turned naturally to the universal and the permanent whose faint reflections he saw in the phenomenal world. For him poetry was the only way in which to grasp this ultimate reality, because it must be understood not through the intellect but through the imagination. It follows that in nearly all his poetry, but above all in *Prometheus Unbound,* we are brought into close touch with what Shelley means by the imagination, the inspired insight into "the very image of life expressed in its eternal truth" and "those forms which are common to universal nature and existence." Because he believed this, Shelley wrote as he did, not merely refusing to polish his texts, because they represented for him the uncontaminated messages of inspiration, but placing his main emphasis on that eternal sphere in which his spirit was at home. Few men share to the full the philosophy which Shelley made part of his being. For most of us the world of abstractions is duller and dimmer than the visible world, and what is true of most men is true also of poets. Mystics have indeed the gift of making their transcendental experience real to us through the intensity of their vision. But Shelley was not a mystic. He was a metaphysician, and that is the secret both of his strength and of his limitations. [1949]

C. M. Bowra
*The Romantic Imagination* (New York:
Oxford Univ. Pr., 1950), pp. 124-25

Shelley's sensitivity to harsh, sharp touch-images is perhaps most definitively realized in the soliloquy of Prometheus, *Prometheus Unbound,* Act I . . . (ll.31-43) [.] The Titan's agony is the pain of cutting, of tearing, of splitting, reinforced by the sensations of cold which merge with the ungentle touch of the knife. He is pierced by the spears of the glaciers, whether only by the intense cold of the glacial air or actually by the sharp edges of their "moon-freezing crystals" as well. The "bright chains" which eat into his bones do so in physical fact, as well as figuratively by their burning cold. And in like manner the "keen hail" afflicts him, piercing his flesh with knife-like edges as well as knife-like chill.

In treatment of sensations of heat and cold Shelley is generally, as in the Prometheus soliloquy, harsh, keen-edged, and painful. Cold to him is piercing and agonizing; it is an enemy to man. [1949]

R. H. Fogle
*The Imagery of Keats and Shelley*
(Hamden, Conn.: Archon Books, 1962), pp. 70-71

The fourth act was an afterthought, a lyrical rhapsody in which the powers of Nature, the Earth and the Moon, hours and spirits rejoice at their liberation. It is not, however, unrelated to Shelley's deepest thought. The moral regeneration of the world through love is in his system also accompanied by a physical regeneration; nature takes part equally in the redemption. Shelley was not indeed inclined to separate natural and spiritual forces. Professor Grabo has shown that Shelley echoes or seems to echo Newton's identification of electrical energy with a quasi-immaterial "Spirit of the Universe," which is also the physical expression of that which in the moral sphere is love. . . .

To the shoemaker there is nothing like leather: but the literary critic, to give that unscientific observer his due, is perhaps more likely than the scientist in a literary moment to notice how fragmentary and capricious were Shelley's dealings with science. The important substratum of truth in this way of thinking about Shelley is that he does not see a dualism between material and spiritual life; each is one aspect of the same reality; and the rejuvenation of the one can only be accomplished (though not by any process expressible in scientific terms) by the parallel regeneration of the other. Thus the cosmic and natural imagery of *Prometheus* is not inessential to it, an additional lyrical rhapsodizing, as is sometimes said: it is a vital part of the whole imaginative concept. [ca. 1951]

Graham Hough
*The Romantic Poets* (New York: W. W. Norton, 1964), p. 138

The drama in Shelley, in so far as there is any, is essentially an internal one and takes place within the mind of Prometheus; it is a clash of ideas rather than of persons. The personifications are Shelley's means of making clear to the reader the progress of this internal drama. The bringing in of the whole material universe by means of the Fauns, Spirits of Earth and Moon, etc., is original and goes beyond Aeschylus—though we find in him indications of the same feeling of all things being alive, as when his Prometheus calls upon the divine sky, the breezes, rivers, ocean, all-mother earth and the all-seeing sun to "see what I suffer from the gods, a god" (*Prometheus Bound,* 88-92). . . .

*Prometheus Unbound* may be defective as a drama, but it is not formless. The movement of the whole poem is from the mind of Prometheus outwards. The effects of the change in him are seen spreading in ever-widening circles—over men, over the earth, the moon and out into the "the void's loose field" (IV,154). This provides loose, but sufficient, structure for the poem.

Peter Butter
*Shelley's Idols of the Cave* (Edinburgh:
Edinburgh Univ. Pr., 1954), pp. 169, 171

Prometheus is what man becomes through death, and death itself is the awakening from the dream of life. In this sense, Prometheus is the psychic potential of the dreaming divinity in man. Ultimately to awaken is to die. . . .

Concerned as he is with man's earthly redemption, Shelley in *Prometheus Unbound* must stop short of this ultimate form of apocalypse. Here on earth man can become no more than "the mirrors of /The fire for which all thirst" (*Adonais,* 484-5); he must accept a "heaven-reflecting sea" pavilioned as it is on chaos. The recreated universe of the Promethean imagination is a world which mediates between man's mortality and man's divinity. . . .

The image of eternity is the vision of the last act. It takes place before the cave of Prometheus and Asia where the "echoes of the human world," mingling with the diviner nature of Prometheus and Asia, receive "the gathered rays which are reality.". . .

Shelley's apocalyptic fourth act celebrates the perfection of man's sensibility. Such perfection means "that he is conscious of an infinite number of ideas in a minute" with the result that the minute of perfected consciousness is eternity. Even if this eternal minute is a "perishing ephemeron . . ." the man who has experienced it has enjoyed "a longer life than a tortoise."

R. G. Woodman
*The Apocalyptic Vision in the Poetry of Shelley*
(Toronto: Univ. Toronto Pr., 1964), pp. 149-51

## The Cenci

As his own moral universe replaces that of Godwin, as *Prometheus* supersedes *Queen Mab*, the ideal world itself is quickened with human experience and he "speaks a language which human beings understand." . . .

This change in Shelley rendered possible his immense achievement in delineating human beings in *The Cenci*. This work is spoken to men: it is imagined dramatically. Shelley uses the opportunities for great dramatic situations, and he constructs without wavering; not only is there the tender inspiration of the ending, but the perhaps rarer inspiration which makes him break the pathos of the last scenes by putting between them the different, less pressing, emotion of Bernardo's pleading with Camillo: thus giving two separate experiences of those last hours, in place of one long-drawn-out emotion. It is here too that we realize the marvellous subtlety of Shelley's psychological observation, for which he had nowhere else in his work full scope. . . .

A. E. Powell
*The Romantic Theory of Poetry*
(New York: Longmans, Green, 1926), p. 204

From the Preface to *The Cenci* and from the letters of that time, we are now able to formulate the following definition: Poetry is an unmoral, free emotional expression or presentation of the images and ideas which throng the mind of the poet. But fundamentally neither the absence of moral reference nor the apparently increased grasp on mundane reality which we see in this drama wholly accord with the poet's metaphysic. He was an idealist of the Platonic cast, and accordingly believed that poets as seers participated in the eternal, the infinite, the one. . . .

To be moral . . . to Shelley meant to be true to an ideal truth which also produced pleasure. This was the doctrine which he advocated. But while he expressed his abhorrence of the didactic manner, his zeal for reform and his rather violent prejudices often led him into it, both in his poems and in his critical opinions on the works of others.

Melvin T. Solve
*Shelley. His Theory of Poetry*
(Chicago: Univ. Chicago Pr., 1927), pp. 27, 197

Byron called it "sad work," and if not for the same reason ("the subject renders it so") I agree with this judgment of a friend and contemporary of the poet. For Shelley it was an experiment—an attempt to be objective, *sachlich*. But he was writing against the grain of his personality, and knew it. . . . It is a pastiche of Elizabethan drama, of Webster in particular, and as a form has no originality and lacks the "something wholly new and relative to the age" which Shelley recognized in *Don Juan* and longed to possess. Even at its most forceful the verse is wooden, unnatural. [1935]

Herbert Read
*The True Voice of Feeling*
(New York: Pantheon, 1953), pp. 233-34

Although it cannot be claimed that *The Cenci* has yet established itself as part of the main body of popular literary drama along with, for instance, *Phèdre* or *Antigone*, nevertheless, . . . there is sufficient evidence to show that it is a genuine acting drama. Why, one may well ask, has the misconception that it is a closet drama so long persisted? There are, in our opinion, several reasons for this. In the first place, *The Cenci* was refused production in its own day because of the incest theme, and a play which begins without a stage history is likely to continue without one. In the second place, the popular concept of Shelley as an "ineffectual angel" doubtless influenced producers and others in the notion that he could not produce anything so "practical" as a genuine stage play. And, in the third place, . . . the adverse comments of the 1886 critics—dictated largely by moral prejudice—influenced later scholars and critics. In the present century, however, as audiences are becoming more liberal in their acceptance of challenging themes, there seems no reason why *The Cenci* should not take its recognized place as one of the classics of the stage.

As a result of this new approach to *The Cenci* Shelley is seen to be an even more versatile writer than we had realized. Not only can he produce realistic political tracts, such as *A Philosophical View of Reform,* and complex metaphysical-social lyrical drama such as *Prometheus Unbound* but he can also produce a great acting play.

K. N. Cameron and Horst Frenz<br>
PMLA (December, 1945), p. 1105

In language, as in form, *The Cenci* is more of a *tour de force* than a logical step forward. Those digressions on natural beauty, which had adorned all his poems since *Alastor,* are missing. Nor does the play conform to any party line, political or metaphysical. . . . He took pains, too, with the narrative and pruned his style, avoiding ornate images and exploiting the technique of understatement so dear to the English. . . .

He had a genuinely tragic story to tell, and he was ready to submit his poetic talents both to the discipline and to the needs of the story. The result is that *The Cenci* stands head and shoulders above all the other plays of its time. It is perhaps the best serious English play written between 1790 and 1890.

Desmond King-Hele<br>
Shelley: The Man and the Poet<br>
(New York: Thomas Yoseloff, 1960), pp. 120, 127

## Adonais

Shelley thought well of his *Adonais* (1821), and it has more weight and substance than any other of his poems. All is concentration, and clear structure, and sustained passion. The only fault is the tirade against the wicked journalist who, as Shelley erroneously thought, had been the death of Keats. There is a strain of high oratory throughout *Adonais,* which suggests the influence of *Childe Harold;* an impression strengthened by the peculiar swing of the Spenserian stanza. It is not in the least like Spenser's movement; and it is much more compact, and less fluid, than in the *Revolt of Islam.* Shelley uses the old scheme of a lament followed by a consolation; but the traditional shepherds become the desires and dreams that hover by the bier. The mourners are Sidney and Chatterton and other poets cut off too early. The consolation, with a true instinct, is not too precisely defined. It is only certain that Adonais lives on—by his work and in the memories of men—as "made one with Nature"—and yet as in some sense keeping his personality, in "the abode where the Eternal are." In the poem itself, indeed, Keats (as has often been said) has no clear identity; but it is no fault, in a work with such a purpose, that it is not a portrait. In these passages Shelley, like Wordsworth in his great ode, is a master of high speculative verse; and, like Wordsworth, he does one of the hardest things in the world—he makes that kind of verse lyrical.

Oliver Elton
*The English Muse* (London: G. Bell and Sons, 1933), pp. 335-36

It is from the thirty-ninth stanza onwards . . . that [*Adonais*] . . . gathers strength; and the theme is just that of *Alastor*, the mystery of death. But the poet's treatment is now boldly pantheistic or transcendental. Indeed Shelley seems to glimpse at last the ultimate source of his own and mankind's suffering. It is not just kings and priests that are the source of evil (one might add to-day capitalists and communists and fascists). It is individual existence with all which that involves of inevitable conflict, the fierce competition for power: "Thou shalt starve ere I starve." Only in some mystical unity in which individual existence is transcended can all the ills which Prometheus was to have cured find their true end. . . . [1944]

H. J. C. Grierson and J. C. Smith
*A Critical History of English Poetry*
(London: Chatto and Windus, 1956), p. 364

The whole broad structure [of Shelley's theism] rests on the faith that there is available to the perceptive and imaginative man an inexhaustible reservoir of spiritual energy, not unlike what Blake apotheosized in his Los symbol. In two impassioned stanzas of *Adonais*, the elegy for Keats, Shelley attempts to define his meaning. First, it is the "plastic stress" of the one supreme Spirit which sweeps through the dull, dense world and tortures the unwilling dross toward its own magnificent likeness. Second, it is that "sustaining Love" which bursts bright or dim through the realm of being according to the imaginative capabilities of its various recipients. All creatures and things are as mirrors reflecting "the fire for which all thirst." The state of grace in Shelleyan theology is the near approach to the Supreme Likeness; the state of sin is a turning away from the Supreme Good. But the Supreme Love is always available to those who earnestly seek it. This is all that "gives grace and truth to life's unquiet dream." It is more than enough.

Carlos Baker
Introd., in *Selected Poetry and Prose*
(New York: Random House, 1951), pp. xv-xvi

The poetic techniques . . . throughout the poem are essentially those of satiric and dramatic irony. In accordance with the satiric method, the relationships of the proper symbols, or else the interpretations of the properly distributed symbols, are inverted. This for example, is the technique behind the interpretation of the white Death: the images are the proper ones, sun, atmosphere, and their interaction; but the values assigned each image, although appropriate to the immediate occasion, are the inverse of those eventually discovered in the images. The procedures of dramatic irony, on the other hand, result from statements that are figuratively true in their thematic context, but that will later prove to be true literally in the symbolic rendering. A greater truth has been stated than is realized at the moment—as, for example, in the cry of one of the Splendors, "Our love, our hope, our sorrow, is not dead."

But although these are the *methods* of the elegy, its central *mode* is, of course, neither of these. Rather, beneath the level of the elegiac conventions, the Adonis myth, Keats's biography, and the philosophic commentary; beneath the complex framework of interrelated images; beneath the distribution into three connected movements—the poem gains its energy from a system of ironies whose function is to compel a progressive revelation. . . . The evolution of the poem gains its inevitability from ambivalences and inversions of such a nature that, while the materials nearly tolerate a coherent interpretation from false perspectives, they are weighed to compel their true ordering and interpretation. The ultimate revelation of the elegy, therefore, has been present from the beginning, and the forward drive through the three acts of the drama resides in the urgency with which the elements of the poem need to press upon their observer the full and proper meaning they contain.

E. R. Wasserman
*The Subtler Language* (Baltimore:
Johns Hopkins Pr., 1959), pp. 359-61

Shelley was right in calling *Adonais* "the least imperfect of my compositions." It is structurally the most coherent and technically the most polished of his longer poems . . . *Adonais* is one of the few poems in which he achieves all his aims. Keats's death gives him a fine chance to utilize his religion-philosophy of Platonism-pantheism. His picture of Adonais being absorbed into the One Spirit . . . is acceptable to people of most religions, because it can be read as a generalized version of their own faith. This handy background philosophy is defined clearly yet without undue emphasis. There is none of the esoteric sludge which clogs the channels of communication in *Epipsychidion*, and only once or twice do we feel we are being asked to grieve too loud and too long.

Desmond King-Hele
*Shelley: The Man and the Poet*
(New York: Thomas Yoseloff, 1960), p. 311

## Epipsychidion

The romantic lover often feigns in explanation of his nostalgia that in some previous existence he had been enamored of a nymph—an Egeria—or a woman transcending the ordinary mould. . . . In the somewhat unclassical sense that the term came to have in the romantic movement, Shelley is himself the perfect example of the nympholept. . . .

At the time of writing *Epipsychidion* the magic vision happened to have coalesced for the moment with Emilia Viviani, though destined soon to flit elsewhere. Shelley invites his "soul's sister," the idyllic "she," who is at bottom only a projection of his own imagination, to set sail with him for Arcady. *Epipsychidion,* indeed, might be used as a manual to illustrate the difference between mere Arcadian dreaming and a true Platonism. [1919]

Irving Babbitt
*Rousseau and Romanticism* (New York:
Meridian Books, 1955), pp. 180-81

. . . There is nothing vulgar about the philosophy expounded in *Epipsychidion*. The only comparable work, by which it was much influenced, is Plato's *Symposium*, and the one is as sure and noble in conception as the other. Shelley himself compared his poem to the *Vita Nuova* of Dante, and he suggested that both poems were "sufficiently intelligible to a certain class of readers without a matter-of-fact history of the circumstances to which (they) relate"; and to a certain other class both poems must, he said, "ever remain incomprehensible, from a defect of a common organ of perception for the ideas which (they) treat." What Shelley meant by love in this poem is not in doubt—in his own words it is "the bond and the sanction which connects, not only man with man, but with everything which exists." But like Plato and Dante, Shelley was ready to insist that such love is not necessarily ethereal, but should be embodied in our human relationships. [1935, rev. 1953]

Herbert Read
*The True Voice of Feeling* (New York: Pantheon, 1953), p. 225

*Epipsychidion* was avowedly written with Dante's work in mind, and it is inconceivable, however faulty may be the artistry, that the poem was intended to celebrate the pleasures of sexual love.

Ellsworth Barnard
*Shelley's Religion* (Minneapolis, Minn.:
Univ. Minnesota Pr., 1936), p. 282

All his life Shelley was seeking this lost Antigone, and thinking he had found her in a living, breathing woman—Harriet Grove, Mary Godwin, Emilia Viviani, perhaps Jane Williams. In the ecstatic *Epipsychidion* (inscribed to Emilia V——) he dreams that he has escaped with his Antigone to a lone and lovely isle in the Aegean. The gem of the poem is the description of this ideal island, into which are woven reminiscences of pastoral poetry and aspects of the Italian scenery with which Shelley had become familiar, all blended in the poet's liquid and undulating verse. But now he knows that the lady and the isle alike are dreams. [1944]

H. J. C. Grierson and J.C. Smith
*A Critical History of English Poetry*
(London: Chatto and Windus, 1956), p. 364

One discovers . . . in this complex poem, the odyssey of a creative soul, which in the beginning dimly conceived the possibility of its fullest development through the establishment of contact with divine power. This power was the Being whom the ascendant spirit first "met on its visioned wanderings." Presently (though such adverbs as *presently* have no real significance in the timeless sequence of the poem) this vision passed "into the dreary cone of our life's shade." Like "a man with mighty loss dismayed," the spirit set out upon its great quest, seeking among the "untaught foresters" for

> One form resembling hers
> In which she might have masked herself from me. . . .

The climactic moment [of the central section of the poem] is the advent of the long-lost Vision, the immortal soul, the epipsyche, the reawakened imagination, the sun-symbol, the vernal dawn after the winter's night of the soul. Then the spirit rises free and clear to merge for the first time with light. . . .

The third part of the poem is largely descriptive of the wonderful island to which, now that the great reunion has been effected, the soul will retire with its "bride."

Carlos Baker
*Shelley's Major Poetry* (Princeton, N.J.:
Princeton Univ. Pr., 1948), pp. 232-33, 235, 237

For all its nobility and beauty many may still feel that the poem finally remains chain-weighted from an excess of symbolism for, link by link, tangled at times in knots, there hangs upon it the whole system of symbols through which Shelley was wont to express his poetico-philosophical apprehensions. He himself was never happy about it. His final revulsion . . . had to do with his revulsion against Emilia and was emotional in origin. But he may have had artistic misgivings. . . . And quite possibly he was aware of the basic difficulty of trying to think more Platonically . . . than he was able to feel.

Neville Rogers
*Shelley at Work* (Oxford Univ. Pr., 1961) p. 247

In *Epipysychidion,* composed early in 1821, Shelley's personal or "confessional" expression of his vision theme reaches its greatest development. The poem is frankly, though somewhat riddlingly, autobiographical—"an idealized history of my life and feelings," as Shelley told a correspondent. As history, it has a distinct air of finality, and in writing it Shelley seems to have been thoroughly conscious of his opportunity to give one portion of his work its definitive handling. The spiritual union with Emily (Emilia Viviani), which it chiefly celebrates and which represents the limit of his personal aspiration toward the ideal, is described with extraordinary assurance. Not least remarkable about its style, peculiarly rich even for Shelley, are the frequency and variety of intersense analogies. . . .

The special achievement of *Epipsychidion* is the detailed, sustained, extremely refined fashion in which Venus symbolism and synesthesia cooperate within the comprehensive scheme of the embodied ray. Together, as well as in ways proper to each, they insist subtly and repeatedly that all rays, though refracted in every sort of human, natural, and celestial prism, converge in one unbroken light.

Glenn O'Malley
*Shelley and Synesthesia* (Evanston, Ill.: Northwestern
Univ. Pr., 1964), pp. 89, 111

### The Triumph of Life

According to Trelawny, [Shelley] . . . once said, "It is difficult to see why or for what purpose we are here, a perpetual torment to ourselves and to every living thing;" and again, "Wise men of all ages have declared everything that is, is wrong." *The Triumph of Life* is his final and most convincing illustration of this sad text. Through the vast mass of humanity the car of Life takes its remorseless way, maddening, deforming, destroying all. Ahead of it rushes a lust-intoxicated mob of human beings, and in the midst of their "fierce and obscene" dance "One falls and then another in the path Senseless." [1937]

Ellsworth Barnard
*Shelley's Religion* (New York: Russell and Russell,
1964), pp. 106-7

Certainly it is an unavoidable conclusion that when Shelley wrote *The Triumph of Life* he had a profound and almost morbid conviction of the pains and penalties of living. But it is a misconception of Shelley's character and writings to assume either that this was something new or that it negates his fundamental optimism. He held these same beliefs, and expressed them with equal poignance, in *Prometheus Unbound,* which asserts the perfectibility of the human spirit. Only a few months before *The Tri-*

umph of Life he had written *Hellas*, which is anything but despondent. All of his associates regarded him as one whose view of human life was fundamentally optimistic. [1940]

Newman Ivey White
*Shelley*, vol. II (New York: A. A. Knopf, 1947), p. 371

At the time of his death he was working on the best poem he ever did, but *The Triumph of Life* is also one of his most difficult works, embracing what is best in all seven Shelleys. If it is now possible to understand what he meant his poetry to be and to do, something like poetic justice has begun to operate in Shelley's posthumous career. . . .

The voluntary (or involuntary) surrender of personal integrity in exchange for non-spiritual values is the theme of Shelley's last poem, *The Triumph of Life*. Using the stanza form of the *Divine Comedy,* with Rousseau as substitute for Dante's Virgil, Shelley pictures the life of this world as a cold inferno set in the midst of unapprehended paradise. Nearly all the great personages in history pass down the dusty roadway, following the triumphal chariot of the Worldly Life. Like barbarian prisoners in a Roman triumphus, they are in chains. "In the battle Life and they did wage," Rousseau explains, "She remained conqueror." The notable exceptions, absentees from the procession, are the sacred few who could not tame their spirits to the Worldly Life's omnipotence. These are of Athens and Jerusalem—Socrates and Jesus Christ. It is a measure, the final one, of Shelley's tragic view of life that his sacred few, though sacred, should be so few.

Carlos Baker
Introd., in *Shelley, Selected Poetry and Prose*
(New York: Random House, 1951), pp. xii, xiv

### PHILOSOPHY AND CRITICISM

. . . With Shelley revolution meant the fluttering of an opaque and dizzying flag between the poet's inner eye and the truth of human nature. He was peculiarly the child of his age, betrayed by his own feminine fineness of nature, and lacking that toughness of fibre, or residue of resistant prose, which made Byron and Wordsworth followers but not altogether the victims of the ever-despotic Hour. With a child-like credulity almost inconceivable he accepted the current doctrine that mankind is naturally and inherently virtuous, needing only the deliverance from some outwardly applied oppression to spring back to its essential perfection.

Paul Elmer More
*Shelburne Essays. Seventh Series*
(New York. G. P. Putnam's Sons, 1910), pp. 6-7

The acuteness of the opposition between the ideal and the real in Hölderin recalls Shelley, who was also a romantic Hellenist, and at the same time perhaps the most purely Rousseauistic of the English romantic poets. But Shelley was also a political dreamer, and here one should note two distinct phases in his dream: a first phase that is filled with the hope of transforming the real world into an Arcadia through revolutionary reform; and then a phase of elegiac disillusion when the gap between reality and his ideal refuses to be bridged. [1919]

Irving Babbitt
*Rousseau and Romanticism* (New York:
Meridian Books, 1955), p. 76

The philosophy of Plato helped to give Shelley's thought its final shape. . . . Gradually features definitely Platonic begin to show themselves in his published writings: a few hints in *Prometheus Unbound* (1820); marks of a stronger influence in *Adonais* and especially in *A Defence of Poetry*, of the following year. . . .

When we turn to *A Defence of Poetry* it becomes clear that the metaphysical basis of Shelley's thought has been deeply modified by new elements. The doctrine that all things exist as they are perceived is reaffirmed, but with the significant qualification "at least in relation to the percipient." . . . The poet is no longer a mere manipulator of sense impressions; he paints his vision of the immutable Forms which are seen with other eyes than those of sense. . . . Shelley's Forms, in accordance with an interpretation of Plato current in his day though now generally abandoned, exist in the mind of the Creator, "which is itself the image of all other minds.". . . [1926]

A. E. Powell
*The Romantic Theory of Poetry* (New York: Russell
and Russell, 1962), pp. 206, 214-15

A more precise formulation of [Shelley's] . . . ideas is to be found in a series of moral and philosophical essays which belong to the same period as *Alastor*. These are important because they show that most of the ideas that were to be embodied in his later and greater poems, and in *A Defence of Poetry,* were already taking shape in Shelley's mind.

The critical slander which accuses Shelley of intellectual adolescence, muddled thinking and obscure writing can hardly be based on a reading of these essays. Although they suffer from their incompleteness, they are remarkable by-products of a few weeks' poetic activity in a man's twenty-fourth year. In so far as they are complete, they are acutely and logically reasoned; and even as fragments they must strike any unprejudiced reader as the expression of a curious and vital intelligence. [1935, rev. 1953]

Herbert Read
*The True Voice of Feeling* (New York: Pantheon, 1953), p. 222

. . . The central religious idea of Shelley's mature thought is the conception of an active Spirit of Good, unchanging and all-pervading, which works in a passive, chaotic flux of the unorganized elements of mind, and from this flux creates a world of harmonious and beautiful forms; but the efforts of this Spirit are opposed and partially frustrated by a recalcitrant Spirit of Evil, and hence arise the discord, the ugliness, the suffering that are ever present in human life. Now, somewhere in this process there are created self-conscious beings, which partake of the nature of the Spirit of Good to which they owe their existence, and are capable of recognizing their community with it; knowing, from its operations in themselves and in the external world, that it is intelligent (although essentially other than mind), benevolent, and even "possessed of a will respecting their actions." This Spirit, I have contended, may legitimately be called a personal God. Finally, Shelley assumes (as does every religious thinker) that above and beyond the contradictions that are everywhere present in the manifested world, there stands a unifying principle, "a supra-rational Absolute," which the human mind cannot comprehend, but the existence of which man's whole nature demands that he assume.

Ellsworth Barnard
*Shelley's Religion* (Minneapolis, Minn.:
Univ. Minnesota Pr., 1936), p. 96

An overstress of emotion has been the curse of Shelleyan criticism. Shelley the thinker is distorted and obscured in the haze of emotional speculation. He is thereby wholly falsified, for if ever a man lived the intellectual life and was less the victim of unreason and blind emotion it was Shelley. . . . Shelley was not chiefly preoccupied with clouds, skylarks, and beautiful dream maidens; . . . he spent vastly more time and thought upon questions of practical politics, and upon the problems of good and evil, and of free will and determinism. Shelley's was a poetic mind but also a philosophic mind, realizing that ideal of poet-philosopher which he most admired in the great minds of the past. . . .

A great mind and a rare nature are not to be put into a sentence or a book. Minds grow. The boy who wrote *Queen Mab* is not the mature man who wrote *Prometheus,* nor is the youth who eloped with Mary Godwin, the husband who bore with her coldness and lack of understanding. . . . His beliefs on most questions altered profoundly in the course of twelve years, and also, if not his character . . . his temperament and his emotional responses to experience. . . . To understand Shelley it is best to believe that in his thirty years, he lived longer, both emotionally and intellectually, than most men live in eighty. . . .

He was poet-philosopher to a degree not yet generally recognized, for his philosophy is not easy and is veiled by the beauty of the symbolism and imagery which he employs. Had he been natural scientist, philosopher, or political scientist, the powers of his mind would be more widely perceived. Hard thinking is not credited to poets who are mistakenly supposed to be wholly emotional. The understanding of Shelley depends upon the perception that he wrestled with ideas to the formulation of a philosophy. It is necessary to trace these ideas, some of them at first irreconcilable, to their ultimate synthesis. Shelley then is seen to be more than an exquisite lyric poet. He is also a thinker who is able to express his subtle philosophy in verse.

C. H. Grabo
*The Magic Plant* (Chapel Hill, N. C.: Univ.
North Carolina Pr., 1936), pp. vii, 412, 421-22

Shelley was a keen and a constant reasoner, but intuition or, as he sometimes called it, feeling was his greater light. He would assail with mettlesome logic propositions that had no hold on either his understanding or his heart; but the heart, in a conflict between them, would drive the discursive reason from the field, or keep it at any rate at bay. And more and more he discounted it and the writers who excelled in it, and in whom he had himself at times rejoiced. . . . His philosophy ministered to his longings, twining and conforming with them, but he never achieves nor even desiderates a formal consistency. Accordingly, the metaphysical speculations are in intimate touch with the poetry; they go before and come after it; they are its fruit and its food. It behoves us, therefore, taking the letters of 1811 and 1812 and the verse and prose of *Queen Mab* as the outcrop of one intellectual period, to follow him in his exploration and make out the tangle or conflict, for nothing less it is, of ideas thrown out and thrown together in his divinations and desires.

A. M. D. Hughes
*The Nascent Mind of Shelley*
(Oxford Univ. Pr., 1947), pp. 191-92

As we look over . . . the growth of Shelley's mind, the thing that strikes us most forcefully is the remarkable consistency of his ideas from his youthful to his mature thought. There was development, but there was no significant change. What development there was lay in the gradual and careful pruning and logical modification. Shelley was often tentative in expressing his ideas, and when convinced of his error, he was courageous in admitting mistakes and in changing his point of view. His was the mind of a scientist in search for truth. . . .

Shelley's mind grew, but it grew in breadth and in depth, and not by radical change from one position to another. . . . In other aspects of his thought—in morals, in politics, and in metaphysics—Shelley modified his ideas, but only imperceptibly. Perhaps the most radical change was in his ethical principles. Here he gradually moved from the prevailing eighteenth century conception of the absolute, fixed, and discoverable principles of morals to the nineteenth, or even the twentieth century, conception of morals as purely relative in value and as based in utility. Love, or sympathy for one's fellows, was for him the basis of the moral life, and the imagination was the civilizing force in society. Given knowledge of the facts of nature and good will toward all men, Shelley believed that love, made active by a sympathetic imagination, would usher in the Good Life. Shelley has frequently been referred to as a modern Prometheus or a latter-day prophet. . . . Certainly, the dominant theme in his prose as in his poetry is the prophetic assurance that mankind can achieve the Good Life only by the wedding of knowledge and love or human sympathy.

David Lee Clark
*Shelley's Prose. The Trumpet of Prophecy*
(Alberquerque, N. M.: Univ. New Mexico Pr., 1954), p. 33

Both Shelley's range as a "poet-philosopher" and the "modern" applicability of his thought are greater than is commonly supposed. This underestimation is due partly to that "overstress of emotion" which characterizes the textbook and anthology accounts and partly to a neglect of Shelley's prose works.

Central to his thinking, as to that of Hunt and Godwin, is the humanitarianism of the period, a humanitarianism the spirit of which is concentrated in the two famous lines in *Julian and Maddalo*—

Me — who am as a nerve o'er which do creep
The else unfelt oppressions of this earth —

and which found expression in his philosophy of love. This philosophy anticipates in some respects such modern psychological theories as Freud's on the libido; for Shelley conceives of love as a unifying force with widely variant manifestations, biological, psychological, and social—sexual love, romantic love, friendship, love of humanity, love of nature. . . .

In reading Shelley's prose, even more than in reading his poetry, one feels that of all the great English poets of the past (not excluding Blake or Byron) he was the most modern in his social thinking. It has been said that he was neglected by his age; but as Newman White pointed out, it was not so much that his age neglected him as that it was afraid of him. In Shelley's day as in ours there were those who wished to have certain problems regarded as settled and others as taboo; but Shelley regarded little as settled and nothing as taboo. He questioned everything: political and parental authority, marriage and divorce laws, Christian theology, the relation of sex to love, the nature of the self.

K. N. Cameron<br>
Shelley and His Circle, Vol. II (Cambridge, Mass.:<br>
Harvard Univ. Pr., 1961), pp. 612, 620

Till his last moment he continued in his "wanderings of careful thought," and the problems of semblance and reality, life and dreaming, were the subject of his last, unfinished poem. Their answer—the answer to the question formulated in its last lines "Then, what is life?" I cried—is one at which we were left guessing by his death.

The universal system of which Lionel is a disciple

is, in fact, Platonic philosophy: it was out of this that he, Shelley-Lionel, sought to gain an apprehension of Reality. Yet Shelley, though gifted for philosophy, was not a philosopher but a poet and what he took from philosophy he took for his own poetical purposes, gifting it with his own "originality of form and colouring." To attempt to formulate a reasoned exposition of his derived notions, which, even at the end, had hardly achieved the status of a system of his own, would indeed be to "scale the inaccessible with a ladder which is immediately withdrawn."

Neville Rogers<br>
Shelley at Work (Oxford Univ. Pr., 1961), p. 22

## GENERAL

The ideas of Shelley seem to me always to be ideas of adolescence—as there is every reason why they should be. And an enthusiasm for Shelley seems to me also to be an affair of adolescence: for most of us, Shelley has marked an intense period before maturity, but for how many does Shelley remain the companion of age? I confess that I never open the volume of his poems simply because I want to read poetry, but only with some special reason for reference. I find his ideas repellent; and the difficulty of separating Shelley from his ideas and beliefs is still greater than with Wordsworth. And the biographical interest which Shelley has always excited makes it difficult to read the poetry without remembering the man; and the man was humorless, pedantic, self-centered, and sometimes almost a blackguard. Except for an occasional flash of shrewd sense, when he is speaking of someone else and not concerned with his own affairs or with fine writing, his letters are insufferably dull. He makes an astonishing contrast with the attractive Keats. [1933]

T. S. Eliot
*The Use of Poetry and the Use of Criticism*
(London: Faber and Faber, 1955), pp. 88-89

. . . My first concern must be to vindicate the high value of Shelley's poetry. It is curious that all these detractors of the poetry make vague but generous gestures of acceptance which are at variance with their detailed statements. . . . As for Mr. Eliot, though he confesses that he never opens the volume of his poems "simply because I want to read poetry, but only with some special reason for reference," yet, as we have seen, Shelley's poetic gifts "were certainly of the first order." Not a critical judgment, but some moral asceticism, would seem to be the basis of Mr. Eliot's disdain. He does, it is true, accuse Shelley of "a good deal which is just bad jingling," but he admits that *The Triumph of Life,* though unfinished, is a great poem. [1935, rev. 1953]

Herbert Read
*The True Voice of Feeling* (New York: Pantheon, 1953), pp. 217-18

Few poets have suffered more than Shelley from the modern dislike of the Romantics. It is natural that this should be so. His poetry is, to an unusual degree, entangled in political thought, and in a kind of political thought now generally unpopular. His belief in the natural perfectibility of man justly strikes the Christian reader as foolishness, while, on the other hand, the sort of perfection he has in view is too ideal for dialectical materialists. His writings are too generous for our cynics; his life is too loose for our "humanist" censors. Almost every recent movement of thought in one way or another serves to discredit him. . . . But reaction must not be allowed to carry us too far; and when Mr. Eliot offers up Shelley as a sacrifice to the fame of Dryden it is time to call a halt. . . . [1939]

C. S. Lewis
in *English Romantic Poets,* ed. M. H. Abrams
(New York: Oxford Univ. Pr., 1960), p. 247

[Shelley was] . . . one of the deepest scholars among English poets. Because of his amazing facility among the tongues, his quick conception, his strong retentiveness, and his ability to imagine that which he knew, he held many ideas of many men in an assimilation which made them his own. Consequently we have found in him that for which we sought, and Shelley scholarship has tended to become a record of overemphasis.

Bennett Weaver
in *The English Romantic Poets: A Review of Research,*
ed. T. M. Raysor (New York: Modern Language
Assn., 1950), p. 171

Though I agree with Mr. T. S. Eliot that his letters are not very good reading, I find them after 1814 on the whole manly and not without qualities of shrewdness and humor. Some of his short lyric poems are personal, really do give utterance to a private sense of weakness and unhappiness, but they are fewer than is commonly supposed, and, so far as I can remember, he never published any of them. . . .

It must be sufficiently apparent that I consider Shelley a great poet. I do not, however, share the confident belief of many of my colleagues that the anti-Shelleyanism of the New Critics is a mere fad or fashion that will soon pass away. . . . It is clear to me that within fifty years practically everybody will be saying about Shelley what the New Critics are saying now. The disesteem of Shelley is going to become general, and it may continue for a century or more. . . .

F. A. Pottle
*PMLA* (September, 1952), pp. 595, 601

# ROBERT SOUTHEY
## 1774-1843

Poet, biographer, historian, and social reformer, Robert Southey was raised along Rousseauist lines by an eccentric aunt and was a rebel and idealist in his youth. Expelled from Westminster School for writing a protest against flogging, he went to Oxford where, with his new friend Coleridge, he formulated a scheme called Pantisocracy, an ideal society to be founded in America. In 1795, he married Edith Fricker, the sister of Coleridge's wife Sarah. Two years later, he accepted an annuity from his schoolmate Charles Wynn, which put an end to the dream of a new socialist society. By 1803, Southey had completely abandoned his early liberal leanings and had become a Tory, but not without retaining his humanitarian views and his Godwinian belief in man's perfectibility. He settled in Keswick, in the Lake District of England, where he maintained a life-long friendship with Wordsworth, and later with Walter Savage Landor. He quarreled, however, with his brother-in-law Coleridge, whose abandoned family he supported at times, and also made enemies with the young Lord Byron. Poet Laureate from 1813-1843, he wrote poems for state occasions, which were often ridiculed, contributed to the Tory *Quarterly*, and produced his major prose works during this period. His later years were troubled by the deaths of a son and daughter, and the insanity of his wife, which ended in her death in 1837. Soon after his marriage in 1839 to an old friend Caroline Bowles, Southey's mind began to fail, and after a period of senility, he died in 1843. Although appreciated by the older Romantics, his poetry was severely attacked by the younger ones. His histories and lives have been superseded, and only a few of his shorter poems are still read. Among his more interesting works are *The Battle of Blenheim* (1798); *Thalaba* (1801); *The Inchcape Rock* (1802); *Madoc* (1805); *The Curse of Kehama* (1810); *Life of Nelson*

(1813); *Ode during Negotiations with Napoleon* (1814); *Roderick* (1814); *Life of Wesley* (1820); *A Vision of Judgment* (1821); *History of the Peninsular War* (1822-1832); *Colloquies on Society* (1829); and *The Doctor,* including *"The Three Bears"* (1834-1847).

M. H. Fitzgerald, ed., *Poems of Robert Southey* (1909); Jacob Zeitlin, ed., *Select Prose of Robert Southey* (1916)

Jack Simmons, *Southey* (1945)


Humanitarianism . . . was the parent, if socialism was the offspring of the factory movement, and that movement from the first came under the guidance of Tories.

With this movement will be for ever identified the names of Southey, Oastler, Sadler, and above all of Lord Shaftesbury.

The character and the career of these leaders is the best illustration of the intimate connection between the attack on the iniquities of the factory system and toryism.

Southey (1774-1843) was in 1830 a Tory of the Tories. His whole career is paradoxical. He had once been a Jabobin, he had never been a Whig. He understood revolutionary enthusiasm; he had no desire for moderate reform or appreciation of its benefits. The foundation of his political creed was belief in the advantages to be derived from the free employment of the influence of the Church and the resources of the State for the benefit of the poor. This creed made it easy for the philanthropic Jacobin of 1794 to develop into the humanitarian Tory of 1830. It was natural for Whigs to see in Southey a weather-cock which, having turned rusty had set up for a sign-post; it was equally natural that in Southey's own mind the essential identity of his sentiment in youth and in old age should conceal from him the apparent transformation of his political principles. His fame in his own day rested on his position as a man of letters. Even his friends could not have thought him a powerful reasoner; they must have expected that though his writings might be long remembered for their literary merits, he would never exert any memorable influence as a social reformer. But it is now manifest that while Southey's literary reputation has declined, his ideas on social questions exerted a permanent influence. He was a Carlyle without Carlyle's rhetorical genius and rough humour, but also without Carlyle's cynical contempt for humanitarianism. He was essentially a philanthropist. He is to us the prophetic precursor of modern collectivism. To his own generation he was the preacher of Tory philanthropy. The text on which he preached with the utmost vehemence was the duty of abolishing the cruelties of factory life. [1905]

A. V. Dicey
*Lectures on the Relation between Law and Public Opinion*
(London: Macmillan, 1952), pp. 224-25

[In the *Life of Nelson*] Southey shows his usual incapacity for appreciating Napoleon and the French, and he was not conversant with the science of naval warfare. Yet he achieved a classic memoir, which is not merely a romance. He has an intuition of Nelson's genius and greatness as a man, he writes with a noble measure and reserve, and the skill of his narrative, interweaving as it does history and biography without confusion, and unfolding the character of his hero from point to point through his actions, is memorable enough. [1912]

Oliver Elton
*A Survey of English Literature. 1780-1830,*
Vol. II (London: Edward Arnold, 1961), p. 11

Now, should respect for Byron or Shelley involve our thinking of Coleridge and Southey, under the Castlereagh administration, as an "opium-eater" and a "renegade," under the administration of a "jackal . . ."?

Byron and Shelley misunderstood both Castlereagh and Southey. We owe the *Vision of Judgment* to Byron's misunderstanding of Southey, and therefore must say with the tolerant Kent, "I cannot wish the fault undone, the issue of it being so proper." But more profit is to be got out of thinking of Byron's friendship with Scott, based as it was upon mutual knowledge, than by giving historic value to his libels upon Castlereagh or Southey. Some of these libels are great literature, and some are not, but they are none of them a sound basis for history. Yet they have been repeated for a century, and are often repeated to-day by historians of literature; who, indeed, go farther. Byron had a deep admiration for the courage of Castlereagh, albeit, as in an Icelandic blood-feud, this genuine admiration was combined with relentless hatred. Defenders of Byron to-day think it necessary to call Castlereagh a "jackal.". . .

And strangely enough, those who most bitterly attack the period of the "Georgian Stables" lavish their abuse upon Southey "the renegade"—Southey "betraying his old faith"—Southey who abandoned all the causes which he had "once enthusiastically supported." Yet Southey was the first of a little group of Tory humanitarians, who raised a constant protest against the evils of the Industrial Revolution. . . .

A very real humanity marks all the great writers, and many at least of the great statesmen of the time. . . . We see it in Charles Lamb, defending his friend Leigh Hunt to his friend Southey, and we see it in the correspondence which followed between Lamb and Southey, a model for all time to those who become involved in controversy with their friends. [1925]

R. W. Chambers
*Man's Unconquerable Mind* (Philadelphia:
Albert Saifer, 1953), pp. 318, 324, 326, 339-40

Every one is agreed that his lyrics fail in depth, intensity, and dignity, that his histories are not only dull, but unscientific, that his controversial writings have no life-giving connexion with eternal truths to raise them above their subjects. He was not a great poet, because his easy facility in verse led him to circumvent, rather than surmount, obstacles in the conquest of which the poet is proved. He was not a great philosopher, because his powers of ratiocination were but the feeble servants of his lusty prejudices. . . . Now, although the *Life of Nelson* is still more popular than any other prose work of the Lake School, no one would be so rash as to quarrel with the critical verdict of a century upon Southey's work. It is just these facts about him, his freedom from the qualities of genius, his nearness to ordinary human beings, his respectability, that make his political thought valuable to us. He is not that abstraction, an "average man"; but he is very much of a man. . . .

If Southey seems an inconsistent politician he is always a consistent humanitarian. It is a shame to use so dull a word for the rare feeling that touches his absurdities with life, and even with wisdom. Southey felt in himself the sufferings of others. The sight of cruelty always impelled him to be cruel to the doer of the cruel thing—an impulse which the bad man would not have and the reasonable man would not indulge. [1926]

Crane Brinton
*Political Ideas of the English Romanticists*
(New York: Russell and Russell, 1962), pp. 84-85, 92

At Oxford [Coleridge's] . . . primary object was to see Robert Allen, now a sizar at University College. . . . The visit, however, was another turning point in his life, for Allen introduced him to Robert Southey of Balliol, whom he found "a nightingale among owls.". . . It may have been in Southey's mind, rather than in Coleridge's, that the germ of the scheme which came to be known as Pantisocracy originated. In 1793 he had written to friends of the attraction he found in the poet Cowley's dream of retiring with books to a cottage in America, and there seeking the happiness in solitude which he could not find in society. . . . In similar vein he must have spoken to Coleridge, and Coleridge, who never knew the difference between a dream and a way of life, jumped at the hint.

E. K. Chambers
*Samuel Taylor Coleridge* (Oxford Univ. Pr., 1938), pp. 25-26

Shelley's opinions at first were considerably . . . favourable. . . . In spite of different opinions about the Irish, Catholic Emancipation, and Parliamentary reform, he discovered that Southey was "great and worthy," "an advocate of liberty and equality" (but in the future), a professing Christian